Marriage
Personalities

DAVID FIELD

HARVEST HOUSE PUBLISHERS
Eugene, Oregon 97402

Names of persons and details of situations have been changed to protect the privacy of the individuals involved.

Except where otherwise indicated, all Scripture quotations in this book are taken from the New American Standard Bible, © The Lockman Foundation 1960, 1962, 1963, 1968, 1971, 1972, 1973, 1975, 1977. Used by permission.

MARRIAGE PERSONALITIES

Copyright © 1986 by David Field
Published by Harvest House Publishers
Eugene, Oregon 97402

Library of Congress Catalog Card Number 85-60127
Trade edition ISBN 0-89081-476-7
Cloth edition ISBN 0-89081-546-1

Printed in the United States of America.

ACKNOWLEDGMENTS

Writing a book is a team effort. My parents, Gene and Jo Ann Field, are wonderful—hardworking and supportive of their children. Thanks, Mom and Dad! Debby, my sister, displays great loyalty. What I took for granted—a secure, loving family —still works in me today as I "rub shoulders" with my wife, Lonna, and the three fine children that God has given in my life: Tory, Jonathan, and Dana. Lonna's parents, Lon and Ruth Setser, have always been people who have believed in us enthusiastically. My family and all my patients have given me cause to write this book on marriage.

I want to thank the publishers for their confidence in my materials. This project was in the hands of a few very special people who worked behind the scenes. Carol Manley and Carl Heuss typed and retyped. Diane Wilson read chapters and edited. Betty Allbee, my secretary, served as head of the "encouragement bureau." Thank you, team!

To Lonna—
My God-provided special partner

CONTENTS

1. Marriage Opportunities 9
2. Characteristics of a Healthy Marriage 15
3. Marriage Personalities 25
4. The Active-Passive Marriage.................... 31
5. The Active-Resistant Marriage 45
6. The Helper-Helpee Marriage 59
7. The Macho Marriage 69
8. The Pretense Marriage 81
9. The Kids' Marriage 87
10. The Active-Active Marriage 95
11. Common Marital Detours 105
12. Overcoming Dependency 117
13. Healthy Self-Orientation 127
14. Resolving Family-of-Origin Issues 135
15. Understanding and Preventing Affairs 149
16. When Separation May Be Appropriate 159
17. Negotiation Skills 163
18. Marital Goal-Setting 171
    Appendix: Marital Assessment Questionnaire 179
    Helpful Source Materials......................189

CHAPTER 1

Marriage Opportunities

It had been a full but satisfying day. As my last two patients left the office, I loosened my tie, unbuttoned my collar, and leaned back at my desk to catch my breath before heading home. Eight solid hours of counseling was draining work, yet I wasn't quite ready to call it a day. I wanted to review the cases I had handled.

I thought about my first appointment with a young woman who had been married only two years. Joan complained about the loss of love and affection for her husband. She was infatuated with a fellow employee and wanted to know if God could lead her out of her present marriage and into another one. As I probed, I learned how she was deeply hurt by her husband's inability to attend to her emotional needs. As a result she had built a wall around herself, and gradually the warm, loving feelings for him had deteriorated. She hadn't gone looking for an affair, but the fellow employee had tried to help her, and in the process they had fallen in love.

It didn't take long for me to realize that Joan was in an Active-Passive marriage relationship, with elements of a Kid's marriage also present. She was frustrated that her husband would not take an active role in the relationship, and her immaturity had led her to look elsewhere for fulfillment. As I reviewed with her the dynamics of a third-party relationship, I explained that—based on my years of experience as a counselor—the likelihood of it succeeding was remote. Also, she would miss out on a significant opportunity for personal development if she escaped from her marriage relationship. When our hour was up, she agreed to bring her husband with her to the next appointment.

My second hour was spent with both Jim and Lori. For the first 15 minutes Jim harangued about how their kids were out of control and his wife was responsible for the lack of discipline. The longer he talked, the more visibly deflated Lori became, until she seemed almost like molded Jello in the chair next to him. When Jim finished his tirade, I asked Lori to respond, and she sadly said that it was impossible to talk to her husband. "When I don't agree with him, he just says I don't know what I'm talking about. So we don't talk."

This was a classic Macho marriage. Jim had so dominated his wife that she no longer believed she was a significant person. Lori needed to be encouraged by our session, to realize that she could assert herself for her own well-being and the good of their marriage. And Jim had to realize he was destroying the marriage. He needed to support his wife's attempts to parent. "Of course, you don't have to follow my advice," I told him. "But if you do, it will make a big difference."

Right before lunch, Steve and Joyce had come for their fourth appointment. They were in their midthirties, both talented individuals, active in the community. There was no doubt about their love and commitment to each other. Their problem was stress. They were involved in too many good activities to the detriment of their children and marriage. "We've done the assignment," Steve reported. "Here's what we've cut out of our schedule. And this is our plan for spending more quality time with our children." I couldn't help but be pleased. Here was an Active-Active marriage—two people taking full responsibility for their lives, and learning some new skills to make themselves a better couple.

My first appointment after lunch was with a woman who had left her husband, though I sensed that she really still loved him. Carla had been very dependent upon her family, especially her father, as a child. When she married, she transferred that dependence to her spouse. After three years of marriage, she woke up one day to realize that she felt more like a child than an adult. And that made her furious. She realized that no one had ever let her make a decision. She was determined to begin deciding what she was going to do with her own life.

Carla was the victim of a Helper-Helpee relationship. Actually, she had the right idea for solving her dependency problem, but was going about it in the wrong manner. We reviewed some ways that she could assert herself without cutting herself off from those she loved.

Then there was Tony and Gwenn. This sharp-looking couple entered my office and sat on opposite sides of the room, like two gladiators ready for battle. They admitted they argued most of the time, yet neither had filed for a divorce. Obviously, neither was about to surrender an inch to the other. I couldn't resist a chuckle as I recalled how I turned to Tony about ten minutes into our session and asked, "Is it possible that you're so stubborn that you won't admit any mistakes because you don't want to give your wife the upper hand?" He quickly answered, "I'm sure it is." Then I turned to Gwenn and said, "And I bet you're just as stubborn as your husband." She agreed.

Here was yet another marriage personality—the Active-Resistant couple. Tony and Gwenn were a difficult case because their greatest strength—their strong individual personalities—was also their greatest weakness. It would be a challenge to help them learn to become vulnerable to each another.

The final session of the day was with a middle-aged couple who had drifted off the beaten path in their marriage. This was their final session after six months of counseling, and in many respects it was a victory celebration. When Darrall and Bonnie first came to me, she felt neglected by her husband, and he felt smothered by her constant badgering. Now that tension was gone. They related some of their successes in the past few weeks, how they had worked through disagreements, and the fact that today she was able to be open with her husband, and he felt close to her without being crowded.

When Darrall and Bonnie had first come to my office, I had sensed that theirs was another Active-Passive relationship. They still have an Active-Passive marriage, but it is working much better. Before they left, we prayed together and thanked God that He had enabled this marriage to function well again, and asked Him to use them to encourage other couples.

This was not an unusual day. Each of these people had a unique marriage personality. A few years ago I might have tried to counsel these couples in similar ways. But none of them could be placed into a singular package called marriage, given some universal pat answers, and sent home with all their problems solved. Success with these patients came by recognizing them as people with different marriage personalities, and adjusting the treatment to fit those personalities.

Perhaps you've never considered the fact that your marriage has a personality. Sure, your marriage is different from every other marriage. But there are certain characteristics—how you relate to each other, your family backgrounds, the way you handle pressure—that give it a certain personality. Realizing the dynamics of that personality can help you understand your relationship and how to better relate to your spouse.

Many couples I meet with have what I call an "average" marriage. They aren't great, but they aren't ready to call it quits either. Unfortunately in our society, we find it hard to accept being "average." I want to assure you that average is okay. It means that there are good times and bad times. There are strengths and there are weaknesses. There are marriages in worse shape than yours, and marriages in better shape. In any case, your marriage has room to grow.

My goal in writing this book is to help you face your marriage the way it really is. Perhaps you've read other marriage books or attended seminars that "preached" an ideal for marriage. You may think that every marriage should be a heavenly experience, and that if yours isn't, there's something drastically wrong. The truth is that every marriage has struggles, and few are photogenic. So let's deal with the reality of your marriage instead of trying to make it fit the perfect model.

At times you may find this book a little like surgery. When we go to the hospital for an operation, the purpose is to improve our physical health. I've had four operations in my life, and each time when I woke up in the recovery room, I felt worse than before the surgery. But in each case, as I allowed time for healing, I experienced significant improvement, and the end result was that I functioned better.

You may find that minor or major surgery is necessary in your marriage. It is admittedly painful when the scalpel digs into your relationship. What you read in this book may not always be pleasant. But my prayer is that God will use what I say to cut away some of the nagging discomfort and help you enjoy a healthier marriage.

Even if your spouse doesn't cooperate, you will not find it a futile effort. I believe it is the responsibility of every person to do as good a job as possible in the marriage relationship, whether the spouse cooperates or not. When we become Christians, surrendering our lives to the control and authority of Jesus Christ, we assume the responsibility for developing and maintaining our own spiritual lives.

That responsibility continues even though we're married. Some people forget that they are still to take care of themselves as a person, spiritually and in other ways. When they shift that responsibility to their spouse, and expect their fulfillment in life from that relationship, they are disappointed. I can never legitimately place the responsibility for my Christian life on anyone else's shoulders. It is mine and mine alone. I will be the first to recognize and accept the fact that my environment, including my spouse, will influence my attitudes and my motivation about growing in my relationship with Christ. But it's not the partner's responsibility; my spiritual dignity is maintained and developed only as I take responsibility for my spiritual walk with God.

Most of us would like to believe that marriage should be a haven of rest, a place of retreat, and a source of energy. Somehow it seems unfair that marriage can produce rumblings, difficulties, disagreements, and disappointments. Perhaps the biggest challenge you'll face in this book is the idea that your marriage difficulties are significant opportunities. No, I don't have a persecution complex. I'm simply stating a fact based on years of counseling couples who have marital problems. I've concluded that problems in marriage—things that seem beyond our ability to cope—make us eligible to experience God's power through His Holy Spirit. If you're willing, marital struggles can strengthen you as you work through them, thereby producing growth.

I'm not suggesting that just because you allow Christ to work in you, there will be immediate improvement in your marriage. God promises to bless us if we follow Him and obey Him, but we do that not for the changes, but because He is worthy. God will use the problems in our marriages to develop our individual walk with Him. That's why I can say with confidence when people come into my office: "I realize that this is extremely painful. You would rather have almost anything happen to you besides marriage problems. But I want to remind you that in the midst of your problems, the two of you are on the verge of the greatest opportunity you've had yet in your marriage, for this will force you to become more dependent upon Jesus Christ and His power to work in and through you.''

So don't run away from your marital problems. I'm hoping that this book will help you see that you are not alone in your struggles, and that God provides the resources to help you enjoy a happy, healthy marriage. It begins by realizing that all marriages are *not* alike. We're going to examine seven common marriage personalities, and in the process, you will no doubt find that you fit one of those seven styles. You'll see where you have strengths and weaknesses, and receive some suggestions for making your marriage stronger.

We will also look at some common marital detours that are reflected to some degree in most or all of the personalities. And then we'll talk about some basic skills that can help you better relate to your mate.

In the back of the book I've enclosed a Marital Assessment Questionnaire. I encourage you and your mate to take this test in order to help you see the strengths and weaknesses of your marriage. I've used this questionnaire with a wide cross-section of people, so when you've tabulated your score, you'll see how your marriage compares with other marriages. It's not a hard and fast assessment, and it's certainly not perfect. Its primary purpose is to give you a feel for where you fit on a continuum between a healthy-optimal relationship and one that may be struggling.

By now you're probably curious to launch into the marriage personalities. But first we need to have a framework for our discussion. So we're going to take a look at what constitutes a healthy marriage. Then, as we look at each personality, we'll be able to see where it tends to be stronger or weaker in terms of our model. So let's get started!

CHAPTER 2

Characteristics of a Healthy Marriage

When a mother retains a piano teacher for her child, she expects the instructor to teach the child the keyboard, use of the pedals, how to read music, and a general understanding of music theory. The teacher would be remiss if he or she told all the things not to do on the piano but never taught the student the right way to use the instrument. Obviously, the only way to effectively teach piano is for the teacher to show the student how to do the things that he or she expects. Once the student knows the standard, it's much easier to recognize when he's doing it wrong.

The same is true in marriage. It's easy to examine the problems in marriage without knowing the guidelines for a healthy relationship. What do I mean by a healthy marriage? I define a healthy marriage as:

> TWO PEOPLE WHO HAVE COMMITTED THEM-
> SELVES TO TAKE INDIVIDUAL RESPONSIBILITY
> TO WORK TOGETHER FOR THE FULFILLMENT
> OF EACH OTHER.

In other words, a healthy relationship requires two people, each vitally interested in and committed to the betterment of the other.

Many couples have firsthand experience with what doesn't work. But what are the criteria by which they evaluate what they are doing? Several studies, plus the experience of marriage counselors around the country, have led to a general consensus as to what contributes to a healthy marriage. These seven characteristics will serve as reference points as you evaluate your marriage and the various marriage personalities.

It is my belief that the healthier the marriage, the more the relationship will demonstrate these seven qualities. There is no particular reason for the order in which these characteristics are listed; they are simply integral parts of a fully functioning, rich relationship. When one or more of these elements are missing, the marriage suffers.

Characteristic Number 1: Time Together

It is imperative that a couple have unhindered time together. This needs to be both structured and casual. Structured time falls into the category of planned vacations, weekends, or "dates." This time has the advantage of allowing the couple to have the relationship regularly nurtured.

Casual exchange can occur in the kitchen after dinner, perhaps when both are helping clean the dishes, or when a person returns home from work or a shopping excursion. It's a time for expressing appreciation to each other and keeping each other informed about the details of your lives.

A relationship cannot maintain its health unless the husband and wife continue to have meaningful contact. This contact exercises the marital muscles. When a cast has been placed on a broken limb, the muscles tend to atrophy because they are not used. In the same way, the relationship muscles shrivel up without the exercise of time together.

Because of the pace of our society, time together does not just happen automatically. When couples spend time together, it is usually because they fought through the jungle of time commitments to set aside that special weekend or "date." In addition, when they do find a few casual moments together, they take advantage of that precious time.

It is one thing to arrange time together; it is quite another to *want* to be together. Couples can go through the motions of establishing time together, but this doesn't always mean that they enjoy it. Couples with a healthy relationship honestly enjoy being together. They are like giant electromagnets, drawing each other into their own magnetic field.

No one, not even the best marriage therapist, understands what causes that magnetism. But we do know that it happens.

The couples who enjoy being together and schedule time to do so are happier and healthier in their relationship.

Characteristic Number 2: Spiritual Emphasis

Couples who recognize that there is a God and that He is actively involved in their lives tend to have healthier marriages. They not only recognize God as a viable agent in their lives, but also attempt to live in a way that is pleasing to Him. Often this means having to adapt themselves to change and personal development. In attempting to please God, moral behavior is influenced daily by His direction, with an emphasis on being kind, selfless, and cooperative with family as well as with all people in our society. This spiritual emphasis provides a common reference point for moral and ethical behavior that goes beyond each individual. In other words, both of them look to their spiritual principles as guidelines for behavior. Hopefully this influences their motivation to adapt to the other person without always having their own way.

When two people do not have a similar spiritual value system and are not involved together in some sort of spiritual activity, they are more vulnerable to difficulties. Very simply, a spiritual emphasis plays a significant part in a person's values with regard to marriage. Self-sacrifice and forgiveness are integral parts of most spiritual value systems, and are applicable to married life. That's not to say that a couple which does not have a spiritual emphasis cannot have a fairly successful marriage. Many do. However, those who subscribe to a spiritual emphasis tend to function better because it serves as a significant common ground.

As two individuals are submissive to Christ and desire to please Him, there is a positive spillover onto the marriage. This does not mean that one person must believe exactly like the other in regard to all spiritual matters. But if they try to be Christlike, they will think the best of the other, not need to defend themselves, and consider each other as equally important in God's sight. Acting that way endows them with more potential for marital harmony than those who are not striving to be Christlike.

Of course, we all occasionally offend our spouses. Sometimes they are hurt by what we do even though it was unintentional.

The Bible says clearly that we are to forgive other people as we have been forgiven by Christ. The Bible also clearly instructs an individual to seek forgiveness from the person he has offended. If a person is serious about being Christlike, then he must be serious about seeking forgiveness from his spouse whom he has offended. This very act of Christlikeness maintains harmony in any marriage relationship. Forgiveness is like the shortening that keeps bread or cake from sticking to a pan and burning in the oven.

Scripture provides guidelines for the basic foundational structure of a marriage relationship. These foundational principles include marriage permanence, partnership, roles, and responsibilities, and serve as a model to all couples. This structure protects the couple and helps them stay on track.

However, within these guidelines every marriage will exhibit unique expression. When I say the word "chair," you may picture a solid-oak, straight backed kitchen chair. Or you may picture the most comfortable family room easy chair. Another person might visualize a slow-moving rocking chair. No one can debate that all three mental pictures are valid, yet they are quite different.

The same is true of spiritual guidelines for marriage: The principles apply to all, but they are implemented differently in each marriage. Two men who desire to show love to their wives—a biblical principle—may do so in different ways. One may express it with flowers and a special night out, while another may take care of the kids so she can have a night free to go shopping. Both are valid expressions of love.

Characteristic Number 3: Negotiating Ability

The ability to listen and respond without defensiveness is imperative to the success of any marriage. Responsive listening is not just hearing words, but observing body language. Communication can happen with a hug, a held hand, a pat on the back, or a walk in the park together. Though marital communication is not exclusively dependent upon words, there are times when it is necessary for individuals to confront the issues at hand.

Good communication requires two individuals—one who is expressing his thoughts and feelings while the other listens without responding prematurely. The listener's job is to attempt to understand what his spouse is saying. To turn away, reduce eye contact, pout, or in any way ignore the speaker is nonproductive. Effective listening respects a partner's point of view, whether you agree with it or not.

Just because one person thinks something is true does not necessarily mean that it is. In any marriage relationship, two people can have an identical experience and yet describe it differently. One view of what happened is not necessarily complete. Therefore, we need to understand how our partner sees things. Whether we agree with what one sees is not as important as trying to understand his vantage point, while demonstrating respect by listening to him. Healthy negotiation takes two people who are committed to the process. This is a learned skill for most people, and we will devote a full chapter to it later.

Characteristic Number 4: Maturity

A marriage that functions successfully usually involves individuals who are somewhat mature. This maturity allows them to be submissive and responsive to each other. Because they feel good about themselves, they do not need to be defensive but can honestly learn and respond to the frustrations, joys, and victories of their partner. Unfortunately, maturity doesn't automatically happen at any prearranged, postadolescent life phase.

A mature individual is humble rather than self-willed, resistant, negative, and uncooperative. He is willing to admit error and learn from other people. While he loves himself, he also admits his weakness and humbles himself before God and others. Maturity also speaks of loyalty, that special respect for another individual which leads to confidentiality. Loyalty means that one partner does not emotionally "undress" his mate in front of other people. To constantly gossip and complain about our spouses erodes the marriage commitment.

Maturity also involves persevering in the midst of disappointment and hurt. No marriage goes the way we want it to all the time. Just as a farmer adjusts when bad weather hurts his crop, so couples must learn how to persevere through the difficult, frustrating, and disappointing times of marriage.

Finally, maturity is the willingness to seek help from others. Occasionally problems in a relationship seem overwhelming. The willingness to seek help is not a sign of weakness but a sign of wisdom. It is impossible for me to know everything about computers without instruction. Similarly, wise couples realize they don't know everything about marriage. We can love our spouse and want the best in our relationship without fully understanding how to produce that result. The wise couple studies strong marriages, attends seminars, seeks counsel, or reads books in order to strengthen their relationship.

Characteristic Number 5: Play and Humor

It may seem ironic to suggest play and humor as part of a healthy marriage relationship, especially after talking about maturity. However, people who are mature have the capacity for fun. We all know that life occasionally throws curves at us. Sometimes the best way to deal with hurts and disappointments is to laugh. Laughter is healthy because it relieves tension and helps us accept reality.

Also, it is simply fun to have a good time! A couple that exercises together or plays a sport or game or goes out to mutually enjoyable activities can often prevent relationship paralysis.

Humor is similar to play and involves warmhearted and nonsarcastic teasing. Practical jokes and laughing at ourselves and others is humor in action.

A lady who lived near the outskirts of a city recognized the value of humor. One day she found a donkey in her front yard. She called the humane society and asked them to come and pick it up. When the two men arrived, she changed her mind and asked instead if they would rope the donkey and take it to her upstairs bathroom. At first they refused, but she was persistent and persuasive. After the donkey was placed in the bathroom, they couldn't resist asking her why she was doing this. She answered, "My husband always comes home, plops down in his overstuffed chair, takes off his shoes, grabs the paper, and asks, 'What's new?' Tonight I'm going to tell him!"

Characteristic Number 6: Intimacy

My mother used to make the best chocolate cake in the neighborhood—at least in my opinion. Chocolate cake just wasn't chocolate cake without Mom's special peanut butter chocolate frosting on it. To me, intimacy in marriage is like the peanut butter frosting on that chocolate cake. It's knowing and being vulnerable to another individual. The very nature of intimacy implies that it is private. Throughout our lives we are intimate with only a very few people. There may be one, two, or ten people with whom we develop a close relationship. Unfortunately, some people never develop a close relationship with anyone.

Intimacy involves appreciation, attraction, physical encounter, and prayer. It means being known on the inside as well as the outside. It is allowing yourself to be appreciated by your lover and to thoroughly and honestly enjoy her appreciation of you. Intimacy requires sharing inner thoughts and feelings with each other. It happens when two people are able to pray together about their own frailties, insufficiencies, hopes, and dreams.

Intimacy also involves sexually pleasing each other. Just because two people have a sexual encounter does not mean that they have been intimate. Intimacy in the bedroom happens when each partner not only receives physical pleasure but also gives physical pleasure. The focus is not on getting sex but on giving sex. It is true that many spouses, instead of enjoying sex, fake it because they are unable or unwilling to talk about what feels good to them. That very resistance prevents sexual intimacy.

It is vital not only to be sexually educated but to also become a student of what pleases your spouse. And there is no way to do this without adequate time for foreplay—not only in the bedroom but also prior to going into the bedroom. In our fast-paced society, it has become increasingly difficult to shift gears from parenting pressure and vocational concerns to have an electric sexual encounter.

Every marriage has its own built-in cues to signal each other when they want to get together. Some raise their eyebrows or have a certain kind of smile. Others even have a schedule. There is really no right or wrong way to let each other know that you want to have sex as long as it is clearly understood and adaptable to your situation.

Finally, sexual intimacy does not mean perfect sex. It means two people who willfully and playfully work to please each other. The goal is not perfect sex but mutual pleasure.

Characteristic Number 7: Commitment

Commitment serves as the cornerstone of marriage. Without an intentional, persevering, and complete commitment to the relationship, it can become vulnerable to emotional and/or legal divorce. There is nothing so solid as two people who have individually and intentionally committed themselves to a marriage relationship "for better or worse, for richer or poorer, in sickness and in health, till death do them part." This commitment goes beyond circumstances because it is completely unconditional.

Genuine commitment is an individual choice. Any commitment oriented around self-satisfaction tends to be unstable simply because people tend to stay in the relationship only as long as it feels good or meets their personal needs. Healthy and permanent love is characterized by my choosing to love someone. That choice is dependent upon my integrity rather than my partner's performance. Does this mean I always have warm, mushy feelings? Hardly! It means that as my feelings fluctuate, my commitment overrides my feelings.

Commitment involves exclusiveness. It says that no one else will be a part of our intimate relationship. It places the other partner in a "numero uno" position. Not only is the partner important, but also the relationship itself. The two individuals and their relationship are equally honored.

Trust is that part of the commitment in which two people entrust their lives to the relationship without any reserve or hesitation. Trust is built not so much on the trustworthiness of a spouse as on trust in ourselves to live consistently with our own values and commitment. It is not possible to make another person trustworthy, so we must work on being trustworthy ourselves.

In cases where trust is an issue, the problem usually resides within the person struggling to trust, not the object of trust. This does not apply to all cases, nor does it excuse the behavior of the one who is the object of trust. If she does not feel she can trust him because he has failed her in the past, then he needs to "clean up his act" and become a faithful partner. But her struggle with trust will not be resolved automatically because he acts responsibly.

Commitment also has to do with the power balance of a relationship. It is easy for the balance in a relationship to be upended when either party is overly self-consumed. A marriage made up of individuals who are self-oriented usually gravitates to one of two extremes—married singles with either too much overt individuality or else fusion, with loss of individuality.

Married Single   Merging Marriage

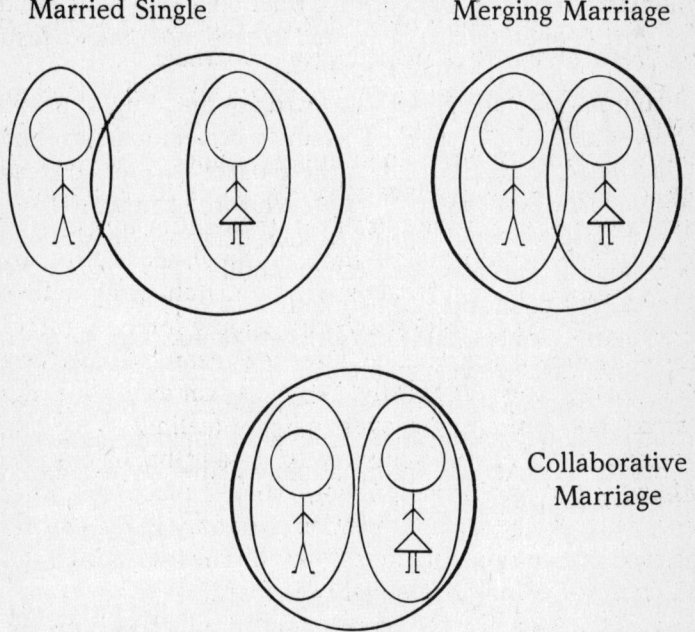

Collaborative Marriage

The diagram shows the extremes of over-self-commitment. Married singles are mutually self-oriented. They demonstrate their lack of commitment to the relationship by being first concerned and committed to themselves, then secondarily committed to their spouse and the relationship. Consequently, they are not inside the marriage circle but on the very edge. Often one partner is a married single while the other is inside the marriage circle.

The other extreme, that of being self-involved, is called fusion or merging. Although the two parties of a merging couple are inside the marriage circle, they are overinvolved with each another. They are depending too much on the other person to fulfill their needs, which is also an expression of selfishness.

The healthy relationship is the collaborative marriage relationship. Here two people have individually committed themselves to the marriage relationship and have stepped inside the marriage circle. They remain within the marriage boundaries because they continue to choose to do so. They maintain their own individuality, yet work together as a team. They are not overly dependent upon each other, nor are they trying to escape from each other. The optimal marital commitment is demonstrated by the collaborative relationship in which both people are cooperatively committed to each other and to Jesus Christ.

In summary, healthy marriages are not made up of people who live under the illusion of having a perfect marriage, nor do they need to be married to the perfect partner. Instead, healthy marriages consist of people who are committed to the process of growing and living together. They are dedicated to understanding and adjusting to each other. They accept the complex task of mutual adjustment.

Within that context, there are a variety of marriage personalities. Now that we've established the criteria for healthy marriages, let's examine these personalities. In the process, we will see how these characteristics are upheld or weakened. My prayer is that this information will help you enjoy a healthier marriage.

CHAPTER 3

Marriage Personalities

I am awed by the fact that every marriage is a unique relationship. There has never been and never will be a relationship exactly the same as that between you and your spouse.

If every marriage is unique, then where does the concept of marriage personalities come in? We can note that every individual is unique, yet mental health professionals have identified several personality and behavioral categories. In the same way, marriage and family therapists have observed that marriages can be grouped into categories. Those categories are determined by the similar behavior styles that exist in marriage relationships.

Instead of seeing marriage as a large, undefined mass of relationships, it helps us position couples into categories for better understanding. There is enough observable evidence to classify marriages, and I do not believe that it offends the uniqueness of a marriage to say that couples are similar to other married couples. In fact, sometimes it helps couples to know that they are not alone, that they are not the only ones who struggle with a certain set of problems.

Recently more and more people I know have had a color analysis. There are skin tones, hair colors, eye colors, and other factors that affect how the colors of clothing look on different individuals. After a person has her colors analyzed, she receives a color chart which helps her pick out clothes that compliment her.

But dividing people into four different color groupings doesn't mean they lose their unique identity. My wife is a "Winter." She has her chart and buys her clothes according to that chart. As I understand it, my wife is not like every other

"Winter." Her basic (primary) colors are the same, but her accent (secondary) colors are different, which allows her to develop a unique wardrobe.

Marriage personalities work in much the same way. The following are seven marriage personality types I have uncovered from research and my clinical experience.

> ACTIVE-PASSIVE: This is the most common personality (approximately 28 percent of all marriages). It consists of an aggressive partner (usually the wife), who diligently strives to make the marriage work, and a passive partner, who is led or directed.
>
> ACTIVE-RESISTANT (24 percent): Consists of two talented, strong-willed individuals, one who is aggressively seeking closeness in the relationship and the one who is actively resisting the effort.
>
> HELPER-HELPEE (8 percent): This relationship is sustained by the fact that one person (the helpee) needs the other (the helper).
>
> MACHO (12 percent): One partner (almost always the husband) totally dominates this marriage.
>
> KIDS (5 percent): This is a marriage between two immature "kids" who are not ready to cope with the pressures of life. They need outside help, often from their parents, in order to survive.
>
> PRETENSE (3 percent): This is the rarest category. It is a "make-believe" marriage between two people who have no romantic attraction to each other. They have totally different backgrounds, interests, goals, and values.
>
> ACTIVE-ACTIVE (20 percent): This marriage is founded on a firm commitment to each other, and both partners are equipped and motivated to make the marriage work.

The above percentages are not based on clinical research but on my own observation as a counselor. (Other counselors have encountered similar results.) Each marriage personality category has its own set of characteristics that differentiates it from others. In the chapters devoted to each specific marriage personality, I point out those unique characteristics as well as the outward style, inward experience, strengths, weaknesses, and ways to improve the marriage.

You probably have a few questions about marriage personalities. First of all, what are the ingredients that go into shaping a marriage personality? One major ingredient is the personality of the two individuals involved in the marriage. If one partner is highly assertive, capable, and directed while the other is somewhat passive, indecisive, and searching, that will affect the chemistry of their marriage.

Another factor is the condition of the two people when they meet. This includes their maturity, ages, and current life circumstances—whether good or not so good. A person's history—life events, both positive and traumatic—also affects how he or she approaches a marriage relationship. The family experience (I frequently refer to it as "the family of origin") also affects each individual. A person's perception of his parents' marriage will influence what he expects from his own marriage relationship. If the parents constantly argued and fought, a person may do the same, or possibly overreact and refuse to confront any conflicts.

Also of utmost importance are our values and beliefs. For example, if the husband believes in settling disagreements immediately and his wife doesn't, that is a conflict of values which affects the resolution style of the marriage.

Education and intelligence also play a part in the development of a marriage personality. They influence values, negotiating style, and whether or not the relationship is competitive (struggle for control), unilateral (one person in control), or bilateral (shared control).

A couple's social and religious environment affects their marriage personality. If a newly married couple from a strong ethnic background continues to live in that ethnic community, they are expected to be like other marriages in that community. Social status—whether yuppie, religious fanantic, blue collar, or socially elite—also influences a marriage.

Does a marriage personality ever change? Not usually. Just as the personality of a child is developed between six months and six years of age, the basic marriage personality is formed during the mutual accommodation stage (premarital through two years postmarital). After that there are refinements, but most changes have to do with adjusting to life demands rather than with changing the basic marriage-behavior style.

Exceptions are the Kids' marriage and occasionally the Pretense marriage. A couple in a Kids' marriage, if they survive, usually grow up and shift gears to another marriage personality. On less frequent occasions, couples in Pretense marriages shift gears to another personality slot. The basic personality of the other five kinds of marriage will usually not change dramatically, but the degree of marital health may fluctuate.

Does every marriage fit into one of the seven marriage personality categories? Definitely not. Some marriages defy all definition and understanding. The concept of marriage personalities is only one way (and I believe a very good way) to promote a better understanding of marriage itself. It would be presumptuous for anyone to say that we fully understand marriages and that every marriage fits into one of these marriage personalities. Yet most marriages clearly reflect one specific marriage personality or a combination of two of them.

Are there degrees of marital strengths and weaknesses within marriage personalities? Yes. We might compare it to a blue house. There are many shades of blue. One home might be painted pastel blue and another a rich lake blue.

As you read the description of your marriage personality, you will get a feeling for whether your marriage typifies all the strengths and/or weaknesses of that personality. You will also get feedback on the health of your marriage from the previous chapter and the common marital detours in Chapter 11.

You may ask, "Can my marriage fit into more than one category?" Certainly. If someone asked you the color of your home, instead of saying "light blue" or "dark blue," you might answer "blue-green." Just as a home can be a mixture of two basic colors, so a couple's marriage can be a combination, such as Active-Passive and Helper-Helpee. Generally, however, I do not find that couples mirror more than two of the distinct marriage personalities.

Note that I have not said anything about men and women fitting into particular roles in marriage. The issue we are addressing is how each partner behaves in relationship to the other, regardless of the sex. Certainly there are identifiable differences between the sexes due to biological and cultural influence. However, in marriage personalities the emphasis is upon the role itself, not the sex of the person who fills that role. One Active-Passive marriage could have the husband in the active role while another marriage could have the wife as the active spouse. The only exception is the Macho marriage, where the man almost always fills the macho role.

As you read each of the chapters on the seven marriage personalities, it is important that you keep an open mind. It does not work to read about each personality and then decide which one you *want* to be. You need to decide which one you *are*. It is important to accept ownership of your marriage personality, with both its pleasant and unpleasant aspects, for that is the starting point for improving the relationship.

In order to adequately paint a picture of each marriage personality, I tell a story about a couple who typifies that marriage personality. I describe their beginning, outward style (the way they look to other people), inward experience (thoughts and feelings), some of their strengths and weaknesses, and some suggestions for improving the marriage.

In limited space we cannot describe each personality to the degree that it fits every marriage. However, in reading each "model," there should be enough information to give you a strong indication as to which personality best describes your marriage. To help you make an accurate decision, I have pointed out almost all the negative aspects of each personality. Not every marriage has all of these, nor are they all severe. But left unchecked, they can and probably will get worse.

Finally, I've tried to give a few suggestions for each personality. But you'll also note that some problem areas, common to several personalities, require more detailed discussion. I hope you'll take advantage of the latter chapters to work on one or more of these areas.

Now let's proceed with our examination of the marriage personalities, beginning with the most common.

CHAPTER 4

The Active-Passive Marriage

If you watch reruns of the old "Honeymooners" TV show or read the "Dagwood" comic strip, you're aware of the Active-Passive marriage. Art Carney and Dagwood play the classic role of passive husbands. Such men have borne the brunt of jokes for centuries, like the one about Joe, who attended a marriage seminar. There were two registration lines, one for henpecked husbands and the other for nonhenpecked husbands. When Joe bypassed the longer henpecked line, one of his friends yelled, "Hey, Joe, what are you doing in that line?" Joe answered, "My wife told me this is where I belong."

Active-Passive marriages are the most common of the seven marriage personality types. Most people, when asked to describe a typical American marriage, identify one or more characteristics of this relationship. The active partner pushes or prods the passive partner to make the marriage and family work; the passive partner feels corralled, directed, or even henpecked. Sometimes the husband is the active partner, but usually the man is the passive one who constantly feels nagged. Let's examine a typical case.

Tom and Susan have been married for 20 years. Both are frustrated with the marriage, yet they trudge forward, sometimes despairing, sometimes comfortable. Tom is tired of being unfavorably compared to Susan's father and brother. It seems that every attempt to please her is either too little, too much, too late, or too soon. While Tom still loves Susan, he is disheartened by her nagging and complaining and has stopped reaching out to her. Instead, he retreats from the "combat zone" and loses himself in a hobby or television.

They met in high school when Tom was a senior and Susan

a sophomore. He had a slight, five-foot-nine-inch frame, a pleasing smile, and short, brown, oiled hair. He said little in or out of class and never caused problems for any of his teachers. Susan was friendly, responsible, conforming, and energetic. She was neither a party girl nor a prude. Teachers liked her because she participated in class and was genuinely interested in learning.

When they began to date, it was Susan's openness and attentiveness that helped the relationship take root. At times he waited for her after school while she finished a project for the yearbook or the debate team. Tom was not pushy and always treated Susan with respect. After awhile their dates became ritualistic—movie, drag Main Street, and a snack at the local hamburger stand.

After graduation, Tom spent a year at a technical school, then returned home to a job at a local business. In the meantime Susan discovered "life" beyond their commuity and decided she wanted more than the mundane routine of a small town.

Their engagement was unusual. Tom couldn't find the words to ask her to marry him, so he didn't. Instead, he said things like "How many children would you like to have?" and "If we get married, spring would be a nice time for the wedding." One Saturday afternoon Tom and Susan examined a display of rings at a jewelry store. When Susan mentioned that one was particularly appealing, Tom returned later and purchased it. He let her discover the ring in the glove compartment of his car by saying, "Honey, would you get a Kleenex for me, please?" She found the ring, smiled, and gave him a big hug.

Unfortunately, the manner in which they decided to marry became a pattern for dealing with all important interpersonal issues. Tom found it difficult to express his feelings because he was easily embarrassed. It was easier for him when Susan made the first move and he responded. They had a small wedding because he was uncomfortable among crowds. Though Susan wanted a large wedding, she thought to herself, "I'll respect his wishes. After all, a small wedding will be easier on my parents too."

After one year of marriage, it was obvious to Susan that Tom's job was not going anywhere and that her own opportunities were limited. Tom liked his work, but it was not paying the bills. When he failed to look for better employment, Susan took matters into her own hands, found him a job in the city, and insisted that they move. Tom hated his new job but would not do anything about it except secretly blame his wife. As he retreated from her, Susan took on more domestic duties—home chores, finances, responsibility for "baby-prevention," and maintaining relationships with in-laws and friends. She constantly found herself taking the initiative in their marriage. When they needed more money, she went to work. When they needed a larger home for children, she found it and arranged for a loan at the bank. When the kids needed a church, she found one with a good Sunday school program.

They were not that unhappy for the first 12 years of their marriage. However, Susan began to run out of energy as she rehearsed her disappointments: "I get so tired of trying to keep this family together by myself. I wish he'd show more interest." Tom's mental tape deck projected scenes of her disapproval and nagging, and of always surrendering to what she wanted. As a result, resentment mounted and distance increased.

After years of little direct communication, Tom and Susan lack confidence in their ability to deal with each other. Not that Susan hasn't tried a few things. She has read several books and articles and even attended a marriage workshop. Occasionally she "lets him have it." Other times she shares her problems with friends or family while seeking advice or consolation. When they do talk, Tom and Susan concentrate on subjects like the kids, dinner menus, news items, church programs, or work.

Sex is sporadic and tense. Tom "wants it" but is not confident enough to pursue it unless she gives him some cue. Sex is also frustrating for Susan. Her conscience says that it is her duty but her feelings are confused. She does not want him to touch her while at the same time she desperately wants to be touched and loved. When they do have sex they perform with little or no foreplay and Susan climaxes infrequently, which further intimidates Tom's sense of masculinity.

Susan's emotions are mixed—disillusionment, disappointment, anger, guilt, loneliness—yet she remains hopeful and determined. In fact, underneath it all, Tom and Susan still care for each other. But they seem unable to break through the crust of hurt and disappointment.

● ● ●

Active-Passive marriages vary in marital fulfillment. However, I rarely find them exceptionally good or bad. They make up the middle road—typical relationships with their share of ups and downs. These marriages consist of good, conscientious, down-to-earth people. Most of the time their relationship has a casual flow. When there is a major disappointment for the active partner, he or she is likely to get on the passive partner's case in a big way. Otherwise this relationship is characterized by the active partner pushing and/or pulling and the passive partner being led or directed.

When this couple comes to my office for counseling, it's because she (the active partner) has initiated contact with me and has talked him (the passive partner) into coming "at least once to try it." In extreme cases, she issues an ultimatum. She is bursting at the seams with a well-rehearsed agenda for our time.

In marked contrast, the husband looks like the hunted, not the hunter. He figures that his wife has brought him to be "fixed up," and that it will be two (counselor and wife) against one. While he settles into a half-reclined position, she sits forward and immediately begins her laundry list of grievances.

Fifteen minutes into the interview, the husband still hasn't said anything. When he finally does speak she interrupts and/or corrects him, and when he doesn't talk she complains. Verbally, she is a skilled technician and he is a neophyte. When she takes him to task, he hangs his head, shaking it with a defeated look. I know he is thinking, "What's the use?"

Perhaps you're already taking sides. As you read the case of Tom and Susan, my educated guess is that you sided with Susan. How do I know? Because active partners are the ones who will read this book! You know what it feels like to live day to day with a nice, compliant, undependable, and unassertive person. You probably approach household chores thinking, "If I don't do this, it won't get done." For those chores he must do, you find yourself having to continually remind him. It's frustrating because he's undependable. At times you may catch yourself thinking, "He wasn't this way before we got married, and if I'd known he was going to be this way I would not have married him." Ironically, as I probe I usually find that in the beginning the husband's "go-along-for-the-ride" behavior was perceived as a "quiet strength" and a "likable, easygoing nature."

If you are an active partner, your feelings are very real and understandable. But be careful not to focus all the blame on him. I too am tempted to take your side, but I know from experience that both partners have contributed to the marital struggles. Taking sides in the "blame game" only reduces the chances for reconciliation. Instead, it's important to understand the characteristics of an Active-Passive marriage—how it begins, its inward and outward style, its strengths and weaknesses, and how to live with and adjust to your partner. You can learn to compensate for your weaknesses, build on your strengths, and move toward a more enjoyable and healthy marriage.

Beginnings

Most Active-Passive relationships start out complementary—filling each other's empty spaces. Tom and Susan were like that. When they met she was talkative and he was quiet, which meant he did not have to work as hard at the relationship. He was attentive because he had a physical drive and her energy and enthusiasm were attractive to him. She interpreted this attention as true involvement and concluded that he would and could be attentive in all areas. What she interpreted as quiet strength was actually his lack of confidence.

When there is anxiety in a relationship, men tend to become quiet and women tend to talk. Unchecked, it can get carried away. Susan had a natural concern to organize and establish the relationship. There was nothing unnatural about her drive; however, she overdid it. Over the years she became more and more active, making most of the decisions, while Tom conceded more and more of his vote to her. Now Susan interprets Tom's quietness, which used to be a strength, as desertion, while he thinks Susan wants to run him and maybe even the world.

Outward Style

In an Active-Passive marriage, outward behavior is dissimilar.

She appears to be her own person. If not formally employed, she usually works as a volunteer in activities such as church organist, Girl Scout leader, blood drive coordinator, Little League committee person, political worker, or Band Boosters fund drive chairperson. While she's on stage, the husband is part of the audience. Amazed and somewhat overwhelmed, he would like to ask her, "Why do you do all of this?" She would probably answer, "Someone has to do it, and you're sure not by sitting around or being gone."

The wife's competence extends into the home, and she usually handles the money, social arrangements, and church activities. She is the more active parent in listening, discipline, and support of the children. Through her drive, the children take advantage of such opportunities as music lessons, children's clubs, and athletic programs.

She does her best to keep her man on course as well, keeping his chore list full. He works steadily but, according to her, he could always improve. He shows up for meals but participates little in family talk. After supper he watches TV, retires to another room to read, or leaves to play ball. He believes he is not competent, capable, and adequate, like his wife. His impression is that she will never be satisfied. He remembers when he cleaned out the garage and how she pointed out all the things he missed. He thinks to himself, "So I missed something. Can't she appreciate what I did do?"

Friends and acquaintances may take sides. Some feel sorry for him because he has to put up with her overbearing manner. They would like to see him stand up and politely put her in her place. Others sympathize with her. "She has to do all the work," they think. "Why doesn't he try harder? I don't know how she puts up with him." If you do find yourself siding with one or the other, that may reflect your own relationship. Often it is easier for us to see our own situation in other marriages than to see it in ourselves.

Rarely does the couple sit and visit just for the fun of it. When they do talk, conversation is usually topical and safe. They are uncomfortable with discussion about their marriage, individual hopes and dreams, or personal victories or concerns. The children rarely see displays of affection between Mom and Dad, and are shocked or giggle with embarrassment if and when they do embrace. This couple has forgotten how to be lovers. Now they are doers—doers for their kids, families, friends, church, and employers. Love pats, winks, and mushy kisses are desired but also tension-producing.

Their physical relationship is only partially fulfilling. The wife's complaints about the sexual relationship are usually one or more of the following: He wants sex but doesn't do anything else in the marriage; he ignores sex altogether; she wants closeness, but her complaining drives him away. She may try to get results in the bedroom by initiating sex, or, if that does not work, she may turn off to sex herself, thinking, "If he is not going to take care of me, then I don't need to take care of him." In some cases her respect for him as a person may deteriorate to the point that sex becomes nauseating.

Meanwhile he finds it difficult to be sexually turned on by a person who is "on his case" all the time. He wants sex as much or more than his wife, but his feeling of being looked down upon throttles his natural drive to please her. Consequently, he shys away, waiting for cues from her as to when it is okay. Intercourse can be mechanical because they feel little freedom to "play" with or enjoy each another physically.

Inward Experience

Sometimes an Active-Passive couple feels helpless, as if the marriage is beyond both of them. But each suffers in his or her own private world, wanting it to be different but having no idea that the other person feels the same way. Attempts at improving the relationship are scary because neither wants to be hurt again. They resemble the military standoff of World War I with the Germans entrenched along one battle line and the Allies in trenches on the other side. Between them was "no-man's-land," and neither side dared advance toward the other. It is easy for this couple to stay in their own trenches because their fear of being hurt is more powerful than their confidence to deal honestly and openly with each other.

In highly developed, problem-plagued Active-Passive marriages, the wife will become angry. She has tried hard to make this marriage work but has received little cooperation. Expectations of what her man was going to do have floated away like helium-filled balloons. She feels he misled her and is upset that she fell for this guy.

Both parties feel they were gypped. He has to put up with a parental woman. She has to put up with a childish man. "If onlys" are a part of their mental dialogue: "If only she would quit putting me down"; "if only he would listen to me." They are imprisoned by their feelings, convinced that there is little they can do to change the situation.

Notice, despite the outward differences, their inward similarity. Underneath the surface the man and woman are very much alike in how they approach life. The diagram shows this inward similarity.

Active Partner	Passive Partner
Angry	Defeated
Victimized	Victimized
Dependent	Dependent

Each partner depends on the other for fulfillment and each is disappointed. They married to *get* rather than give. Their expectations are selfish: Her happiness depends upon his being capable and adequate; his happiness depends upon her being tolerant of his shortcomings.

This couple does not recognize how dependent they are on each other because the dependence is deeply rooted within them. Therefore they focus on outward differences. The more they look at each other's shortcomings, the more the symptoms increase. His quietness is not only a cause of her anger, but also an effect. Her demands cause his disinterest and his inattentiveness causes her needs.

I do not want to suggest that all Active-Passive marriages are tense. Many get along fairly well, and the reason they do is because the partners have come to the place in their personal growth where they are not so heavily dependent on each other. However, marital tension tends to fluctuate as one or both partners feels insecure and attempts to gain security in the spouse.

Strengths and Weaknesses

Most of us like to drink liquids either cold or hot—not lukewarm. Room-temperature Coke and lukewarm coffee leave a lot to be desired. In a sense the Active-Passive marriage personality is lukewarm. Like a pastel color, it doesn't shine brightly, nor is it totally dark and dull. This marriage doesn't attract much attention because so many of them exist.

The strengths and weaknesses of Active-Passive marriages are not extreme in most cases. These are average individuals in average marriages, living in average neighborhoods with average lifestyles. The important strengths are their persevering and stable nature. They are caring parents with a concern for their community. These couples tend to be loyal. They hang in there in marriage, job, and community. Sometimes their daily slice of life is not too exciting, but they come back the next day. They are proficient at living with the status quo.

As parents, they are not highly directive. They do not say, "You can do it, and here is how," or, "Watch me!" Instead, they say, "If you want to do something, we'll try to help." They are not neglectful, but neither are they out in front of their children showing them the way. They try their best to parent effectively with the personal resources available.

Their style of community cooperation is as willing participants rather than initiators or leaders. They respond to good causes, whether helping a sick neighbor, volunteering at the church, or giving to a special need.

Finally, these couples are dependable. They show up for work, band concerts, family get-togethers, and church activities. They are "Steady Toms" and "Stable Susans" who live according to predictable routines which include set meal times, paying all the bills each month, and always showing up at scheduled meetings.

While family structure is a strength, the family process is a significant weakness. Family process is the ability to effectively communicate and assertively deliver thoughts, feelings, and wants to others in the family. Their nemesis is fumbled communication rather than lack of communication. Abbreviated sentences, little or no eye contact, a raised or lowered voice, and avoidance of saying what one is really thinking describe the passive partner. He is in retreat, and the active partner is constantly frustrated with her passive husband. She cannot motivate him to tell her what he thinks, feels, or wants.

A common interaction might look something like this. Jane tells Dick that her parents have invited them for Sunday dinner in two weeks. Her question is simple: "Do you want to go?"

What Dick really wants to do is watch football on Sunday afternoon. Besides, he is uncomfortable at her parents' place because he feels like an outsider with dissimilar interests. But he thinks, "If I don't go, I'll never hear the end of it." So Dick answers, "Well, I guess that's okay if that's what you want to do." Not "yes" or "no" but "I guess so." Dick is indirectly telling Jane that he does not want to go and is at the same time shifting responsibility for the decision back to her. That way, if anything goes wrong, she is to blame.

In addition to an ineffective communication process, a second weakness in this couple is a subtle but ongoing feeling of inadequacy caused by comparing themselves to other couples. Among their acquaintances they can always see a better husband or a more understanding wife. When a person does not feel good about himself, it affects his confidence. And personal self-doubt undercuts confidence in dealing with a spouse. In the example of Dick and Jane, they maintain contact, but self-doubts limit their communication. Rather than learning to share their thoughts and feelings in a constructive and nondefensive way, they continue to tolerate fumbled communication.

When couples struggle with ineffective communication and feel inadequate, the natural result is a third weakness—evasive behavior. They avoid each other because they do not believe they are capable of pleasing each other. Look at Dick and Jane again. Dick is cleaning the garage, but thinking, "No matter how well I do this, Jane still complains. So the heck with it." Dick rushes the job, then goes inside disgusted. As he enters the house, Jane asks, "Do you want to have the Butlers over tonight?" "You decide," he snaps as he walks by her. "At least you could act interested!" she retorts. He ignores her comment and Jane is trapped. Does she go ahead and invite the Butlers, knowing that Dick will cooperate in a passive, sabotaging manner? Or does she confront him and give attention to his brush-off? She decides it's easier to make her plans and avoid the confrontation. Both are evasive. He avoids her because of previous put-downs and she ignores his intimidating silence.

Finally, from a clinical perspective, the major problem that exists to varying degrees in all Active-Passive marriages is dependency. Dependency is when one partner leans too much on the other to meet his or her individual needs. Usually this leaning occurs because when they married, they subconsciously expected their spouse to be all they needed them to be. Common sense suggests that this kind of unrealistic hope leads to trouble. Each partner, to a different extent, expects the other to meet his needs. Neither has accepted responsibility for his own life.

Improving the Marriage

It's important to remember each individual in the Active-Passive marriage entered the relationship with the best of intentions. The bottom line is that he or she cares for his mate and does not want to hurt him. He desires fulfillment in the marriage and wants the same for his spouse. There are many positive elements still at work between them, though they may be enduring significant disappointments, as the symptoms described in this chapter demonstrate. However, not all the symptoms described apply to all Active-Passive marriages.

Let's address the active partner first. Rather than complaining about what the passive partner has or has not done, she needs to give her spouse more compliments. She should also ask for his advice. This can open the door for the passive partner to feel like a competent person who is needed in the relationship. This may feel risky for the active partner who has lost confidence in her spouse. But it is important to give her partner room to develop and express his feelings in the decision-making process.

The active partner also assumes the risk of living in a relationship that will never be exactly what she would like. For example, a woman may believe that her husband should be the spiritual leader in the home. However, if he tends to be uninvolved and lacks initiative, she might work for months or years trying to get him to fulfill his "appropriate" role. But the more pressure she exerts, the more inadequate and passive he feels. It is my suggestion that she accept the reality of who he is, as an individual created by God. Go ahead and initiate some of the spiritual activity yourself, or just leave it alone for awhile. That is not to excuse his biblical responsibilities, but it does recognize his personality, and it allows God to change him as he realizes what God requires from him.

It is also important for the active partner to look at herself in the mirror and see how she presents herself to the family. She needs to realize that the general tone of attack or self-pity is not productive. It is important for the active partner to reduce her habit of blaming and complaining, regardless of the partner's behavior, because it will never motivate him to change.

Finally, I suggest that the active partner make a list of the positive elements of her marriage relationship. When she is disillusioned with the marriage, she tends to mentally rehearse what she doesn't like. She needs to change that pattern, following the instructions in Philippians 4:6-9, where Paul tells us to think about things that are good and righteous and pure. Paul goes on to say in verse 11 that he has learned to be content. I believe his contentness was at least partly the result of reminding himself of what was good and right instead of reviewing what was wrong.

The passive partner also faces a significant challenge. He needs to break through his natural tendency to avoid confrontation and learn to be more direct with his spouse. If this seems impossible, then he needs to take a course in assertiveness or obtain counsel and support from a close friend.

Let's take, for example, the husband whose wife criticizes the way he cleans the garage. In confronting his wife, Dick might say something like this: "Honey, I don't mind cleaning out the garage, but I don't want to hear complaints about how I clean it. If you choose to complain about it, you need to know that I will not clean out the garage. So either let me clean it my way, which I'll be glad to do, or if you want to complain, then you can clean it yourself or have it done by someone else."

It's important that this be said in an objective, caring way, without any hostility. Such directness will provide more strength to the passive partner and the marriage. This doesn't come naturally for him, so he must depend upon Christ for his strength.

What if the attempts by the active or passive partner are ignored? Remember that each person has a responsibility to act responsibly in a marriage relationship. This responsibility does not change whether a spouse responds to our attempts or not. Regardless of the response, a person often benefits in spiritual and personal growth as he or she attempts to act out his personal beliefs.

Attempts at improving and enriching this marriage by one or both parties will usually achieve positive results. The key is that both husband and wife learn to be less dependent on each other and more dependent on Christ. Jesus has made every provision for us to feel accepted, loved, and fulfilled in our relationships. As we learn to allow Him to be the source of our happiness and peace, we will be freed from overdependence on the behavior of our spouse.

The Active-Passive Marriage

	Behavior	Feelings
Active	Pushing/pulling the other	Victimized, taken advantage of
Passive	Avoiding and withdrawing	Victimized, taken advantage of

Theme—Leaning
Major Problem—Dependency
Secondary Problem—Family of Origin
Major Strength—Stability

CHAPTER 5

The Active-Resistant Marriage

I first met Jan and Ken at our city's annual charity ball. She was dressed in a full-length gown, he in a black tuxedo. Instantly I was drawn to Jan because of her vivacious, outgoing personality. She seemed to radiate self-confidence and drew my wife and me into easy conversation. She seemed particularly proud to tell us that she was a homemaker with two small children. On this night she was to receive an honorary award for her many hours of volunteer work.

Ken was not quite so outgoing. He was a successful businessman, and it was obvious that he had many friends and acquaintances. It didn't take long to realize that he had a keen wit which was often directed at his smiling wife. Everyone in the group enjoyed this couple and they were the center of much attention. Both were socially poised individuals who seemed to have it all together.

That's why it was a shock when, one week later, Jan was in my office asking for help. In the public eye, this couple looked great. Their struggle for intimacy was a private one, unnoticed by all except perhaps their closest friends. All of their social charm did not extend behind closed doors. They are a classic example of an Active-Resistant couple.

Ken and Jan met in college and were college sweethearts. In her eyes, he was a "great big senior" and to him, she was a "cute little sophomore cheerleader." Jan was flattered that an older guy would choose her and liked the fact that he was from a good family and seemed somewhat religious. And he enjoyed the fact that she was fun, attractive, and very popular.

Jan was a hard worker and goal-oriented. Her parents had sacrificed in order to equip her as an individual, and she had taken full advantage of this to win several honors and become socially graceful and in tune with many areas of life. However, she lacked self-assurance and constantly felt the need to accomplish more in order to gain approval. She couldn't stand the thought of rejection for her actions or skills. Of course, no one knew that she had these feelings of self-doubt because on the surface she remained polished and confident.

Ken's dad was a blue-collar worker and his mother a warm person who was very involved in her church. His mother and older sisters spoiled him, and in school his natural talent made him a leader, even though he was not a highly directed individual.

As soon as Jan and Ken married they moved to another city, where Ken enrolled in law school. He enjoyed his chosen career and quickly developed close friends with whom he spent a great deal of time. Jan agreed to work because money was scarce but soon began to resent the time Ken was spending with his friends studying and seemingly taking life easy. In addition to her job, she had to cook and clean while he took no initiative to help around the apartment. That seemed unfair to her, and she did not hesitate to tell him so. Being intimidated by Jan's faultfinding, Ken tried to ignore it at first, then chose to laugh it off with sarcastic humor. Over the next few months, however, she became more and more critical of Ken's attitude. Hoping to avoid further conflict, Ken began to lie to Jan about what he was doing. He didn't really want to lie, but neither did he want to hurt Jan. He simply decided that what she didn't know wouldn't hurt her.

After Ken's graduation, they moved to a small town and Ken set up his law practice. It wasn't long before Ken realized that the town was too small and that perhaps the city would provide more opportunity for developing a large practice. Jan backed him and even helped out by doing his accounting and decorating his new office. She also enjoyed the larger city, finding it a great place to expand her opportunities and abilities.

At first, setting up a new practice caused some monetary strain. During this tight-money time, Jan not only felt anxious but also frustrated with Ken. Often he chose to go to the men's club instead of making business calls. Jan was again quick to tell him how she felt, and was dismayed when Ken tartly informed her that she was his wife and only his wife, and that he could take care of "his" business. Ken also felt that he should not talk to Jan about business situations because they only caused her to worry and yell at him.

Soon after their move, their first daughter was born. Jan enjoyed this new little life and began to invest most of her time with their firstborn. This was very satisfying to Jan, but unfortunately it began to separate her from Ken. Because she was continually tired, she quit her job, but that strapped them financially. Jan noticed that when they went out together, they would still talk, but there was no sense of connection. They would discuss general topics, such as business, friends, or their children, but when they tried to talk freely with each other, Jan felt an emptiness.

Ken continued to monitor comments about his business or his work, having learned that Jan was always ready to give him unsolicited advice. If he disagreed, an argument followed. Unfortunately, Ken never experienced arguments in his home, so they made him extremely uncomfortable. He felt overwhelmed while arguing with Jan and inept at defending his own viewpoint.

As the children grew, Jan became more and more oriented around her kids and their activities. Ken, on the other hand, spent his free time at the golf club, playing cards, or in local politics. He spent very little time at home and didn't care to hear what was going on, preferring instead to retreat in silence or simply walk away from his angry, frustrated wife. To him, his reward for trying to do his best was a wife who was always on his case.

For Jan, though, her reward for trying to be the best mother she could was rejection. She felt she had received a raw deal in this marriage. Although she was angry, she was also lonely and sad. The more she experienced feelings of hurt and pain, the more her self-doubt increased. She tried to compensate for those feelings by busying herself in community volunteer work.

In many ways it seems ironic that Ken and Jan chose each other. Jan did not feel she deserved to be accepted for who she was. So she married someone who did not do a good job of demonstrating affection or approval. Ken did not feel adequate in handling interpersonal contact, so he married someone who could. Unfortunately, Jan reminded him continually of his inadequacy. Instead of dealing with his feelings of failure, he retreated while flinging verbal barbs at his wife. Ironically, both chose someone who could compensate for their felt internal weakness, though they didn't realize it.

The Active-Resistant couple present themselves as sharp, capable individuals, able to carry on easy conversations and handle themselves well socially. Others see them as fun-loving and enjoyable to be around. Often they are the life of a party. However, it is not uncommon for them to part in social situations—each going his own way. When they are together, they tend to keep their distance with "fun-loving" jokes or some mild form of sarcasm. They, as well as others around them, laugh off the "jabs," but underneath the laughter the hurt can be devastating.

The Active-Resistant roles are populated by both sexes. However, the man is more often the resistant partner and the woman the active partner. Many times these marriages are made up of talented professional individuals with strong opinions and values, and the marriage is characterized by competition. With the increasing number of professional women in the work force, the number of Active-Resistant marriages has also increased. For purposes of illustration, I am identifying the woman as the active spouse and the man as the resistant partner.

As we examine this marriage, you'll notice many similarities with the Active-Passive personality. But it is important to note the differences also. The Active-Passive marriage tends to be more socially cautious while the Active-Resistant one is socially involved and works as a team while "on stage." You'll find that the Active-Passives tend to be more compliant, easygoing, and cooperative while the Active-Resistants are assertive and individual thinkers. Active-Passives want to know the rules while the Active-Resistants question the rules. When struggling, the Active-Passive is like a "cold war," with silence, unfinished discussions, and lingering issues. The Active-Resistants usually have a "hot" war, with stubborn, verbal bouts and each partner wanting the last word.

Beginnings

This couple is attracted to each other by their strengths and apparent confidence. Each is an individual who seems to have it all together. Each likes being around people who are somewhat assertive, aggressive, and forward-moving. Their friends know what they want to do in life, and they have opinions about everything from politics to religion. While each is comfortable in groups, the active one is usually more socially adept and skilled than the resistant partner. Often it is the active partner's social electricity that initially attracts the resistant partner.

This couple has a history of accomplishing their short-term goals. In fact, when they decide to become engaged, they often don't marry right away because each wants to finish his own personal projects, such as school or special training or saving a certain amount of money. Often they're in their midtwenties when they do marry, having dated from one to three years or even longer.

Feelings of love and physical attraction for each other usually serve as a temporary cover for a serious problem. If you were to interview their parents and friends, you would probably discover that both the man and the woman could be accused of being stubborn and self-willed. They have developed a lifelong habit of wanting things their own way and believing that their way is always best. But in the excitement of their high-profile relationship, friends ignore that tendency and are excited about this couple's future.

Outward Style

The theme of the Active-Resistant marriage is temperature. Usually the active partner is accused of being overly emotional and sensitive. She continually wants the relationship heated up. She wants to be noticed and complimented and to have her husband act like he enjoys her company. On the other hand, the resistant one is charged with being emotionally distant and cold. She doesn't want to turn down the thermostat. He thinks, "It's warm enough already, and if it gets any hotter, I'll melt."

Over and over the active partner attempts to promote closeness in the relationship, only to get little or no response from the resistant partner. He projects a noninvolved, disinterested, almost placid stance. In effect he keeps the active one on edge because she never quite knows where she stands with her uncommunicative husband. His standard reply to her "How do I look?" question is met with a mumbled "Okay." If she asks, "Honey, do you love me?" he nonchalantly answers, "Of course."

His basic personality is marked by a logical, cognitive approach to life. Because he is often professional, he is used to making decisions that affect other people's lives or that involve large amounts of money. He considers himself good at just about anything he chooses to undertake and could be classified as a perfectionist. That's one reason it's hard for him to accept the failure he feels in his marriage. It is difficult, if not impossible, to tell a perfectionist that he is not perfect.

The goal for the active person in this relationship is to experience some heartfelt communication. She continually seeks to put life into the relationship and desperately wants him to pay attention to her. Unfortunately, she often chooses complaining and "pity parties" as an avenue to secure his affection. He chooses to resist her subtle attempts for closeness. In fact, the more she complains, the more he moves in the opposite direction. He immerses himself in his work, hobby, volunteer activities, or even an affair.

Sometimes the only way he knows how to show he cares is by buying things for his wife. In fact, he prides himself on this ability. Unfortunately, these attempts do not satisfy her need for closeness.

When Jan and I discussed this particular aspect of the Active-Resistant relationship, she recalled her anger when Ken bought her a new car for her birthday. She thought it ironic that he would give her anything at all, since they had not even spoken to each other for two weeks. Needless to say, she was as confused by his attempt to please her as he was at her anger over the surprise gift.

Many times the resistant husband sees his wife's demands as an avalanche—the snow careening down the mountainside, overwhelming everything in its pathway. Just as most people would do anything to avoid an avalanche, he does whatever he can to stay out of her way. He unconsciously fears that he'll be lost in the flood of her demands, so he resists at all costs. He firmly believes that if he cooperates with her just a little, she will only want more and he will never be able to satisfy all her demands. He doesn't retreat like a whipped puppy; he just resists.

The wife has a legitimate need for attention, recognition, and closeness. Unfortunately, the more she wants to be close, the more he tends to resist. The more he resists, the more attention she craves, and the cycle continues unbroken.

At this point it is not uncommon for the active wife to be hurt and confused by her husband. Often she blames herself for being inadequate, unattractive, or unappealing. She may attempt to lure him into closeness with sexual advances, a new hairdo, community accomplishments, or anything she believes is important to him. In Jan's case, she found herself ignoring her own personal preference and dressing exactly the way Ken wanted her to dress. But he rarely cooperated with the compliments she desired, which made her angry for stooping so low.

Through all of this, the woman's emotions are playing volleyball, bouncing back and forth between hurt feelings and anger because of his insensitivity—an insensitivity that only seems apparent in their relationship. Over the years she can become hostile toward her husband, but she often covers it up with layers of denial. Sometimes she will try to distance herself from him, either by not speaking to him or by complete avoidance for a day, a week, or perhaps even a month. Then, when she can no longer stand the loneliness, she returns to try again. It is extremely difficult for her to accept the fact that she is unloved.

The outward style of the Active-Resistant relationship covers a wide range from healthy to unhealthy. As you can see, the behavior of either party affects the relationship.

	Active Partner	**Resistant Partner**
Healthy	Assertive	Controlled
Healthy	Correcting, Complaining	Reserved
Healthy	Accusing	Cool
Unhealthy	Demanding	Hardened

Inward Experience

Internally both partners are trapped in feelings of loneliness, caution, and confusion. Each can handle most things in life, but neither has figured out how to deal with the spouse. Because they are determined individuals, they bury their confusion and pretend that nothing is bothering them. The morning after a disheartening encounter, they may sit at the breakfast table carrying on a polite conversation. Both know they are bothered, and they know their partner knows they are bothered, but both are too stubborn to talk it through. They are lonely people who need to bridge the gap, but their pride won't allow them to.

When I visit with these people on an individual basis, each will tell me of the partner's lack of appreciation. Each has persuaded himself that he is a good person, thinking, "I get applause and credit from work, my friends, and my church peers—I must not be all bad." When the couple does try to affirm each other and share their feelings, it often ends in misunderstanding.

The active partner, usually the woman, came into the relationship wanting love, affirmation, and affection, yet felt undeserving of it. She believes she has to earn love and doesn't believe she can be loved just for who she is. Over and over she tries to prove herself to him, hoping and praying that somehow he'll respond.

Afraid of being engulfed and trapped, the resistant partner backs away, believing that by loving her he will not be able to fulfill his own needs. He never doubts that she wants everything he has to give, and thinking that this still won't please her, he decides to not even try.

When an Active-Resistant marriage starts having problems, both partners often feel some anger and guilt. They are angry not only at each other but also at themselves for participating in a futile endeavor. They realize that their problems are not unilateral; each has some responsibility for the success and failure of their relationship, so each has a sense of self-blame. This guilt often becomes so painful that they angrily blame the other partner.

As this guilt, anger, and even depression builds, behavior begins to be conditioned by the partner. The marital cesspool stagnates their ability to be responsible for self. In addition, they begin to believe that the behavior of the spouse is intentional and premeditated rather than a reflection of individual personality. For example, the resistant partner resists for self-protection, but she perceives his resistance as rejection.

The more the active partner feels rejected and unloved, the more she becomes aware of her need for intimacy and closeness. Intimacy, or the desire for it, becomes the focus of her life. Often this craving moves into fantasy as she begins to expect more than is found in most marriages. The halfhearted or minimal attempts by her husband to promote closeness are rejected because they fall far short of what she has convinced herself she needs and deserves.

The resistant partner believes that love means taking care of his wife by giving, providing, and accomplishing. She rejects his way of showing love, and he rejects what she says she needs, knowing that it is extreme. So both feel rejected.

Strengths and Weaknesses

There is no question that this couple has many fine attributes. They know how to have fun. They're active, involved, and proficient workers. They usually do well earning, budgeting, and giving money. The church, the community, and their children profit from their expertise and competence. Leadership and initiative are natural to them. They make decisions and follow through with those decisions. You can see why these people are sought by others.

This couple is usually fairly direct with each other. They might not like what they hear from their partner, but at least they don't wonder what the other person thinks about a particular issue. That directness is limited, however, because each finds it difficult to talk about inner feelings.

Their children soak up the competence, individuality, decisiveness, and responsibility displayed by Mom and Dad. These kids receive attention and expert guidance, and as a result they believe in themselves. However, they find themselves sandwiched between Mom and Dad when the parents do not get along. The kids admire their parents' skills but are hurt and offended by their parents' conflict.

The strengths of the Active-Resistant are centered around the strengths of each individual. Ironically, those individual strengths contribute to their most glaring weakness. How do you get two strong and often stubborn-independent people to work together in caring harmony? It's like trying to mix oil with water. Consequently, this couple tends to compete, which leads to tension and sets up their struggle with closeness and intimacy.

Fear of disapproval and/or failure motivates these two individuals to work hard. However, this same fear creates havoc in their marriage relationship. Trust is one of their major weaknesses. They simply do not believe that their spouse will love and accept them if their personal weaknesses are known. They are extremely cautious about displaying or discussing any weakness or need for fear that the other partner may take advantage of them. They believe they must somehow prove themselves while protecting themselves from each other.

Unfortunately, this creates an unending cycle. The active partner works harder and harder, hoping somehow to get recognized by her husband. Her pushing forces him to resist, causing her to feel abandoned and rejected, which is her greatest fear. She doesn't realize that she is actually sabotaging the closeness she so desperately craves by reminding her husband of his shortcomings. He then sabotages any closeness he needs by pointing out her faults or defending his behavior.

Both partners have a deep need to feel worthwhile. She feels a sense of accomplishment when she is appreciated, recognized, and supported on an interpersonal level. He feels self-respect when he accomplishes on a professional, vocational level. Each, in the drive to feel worthwhile, roadblocks the other person. He does not cooperate in fulfilling her need for closeness because he thinks that will hinder his need for professional growth. She in turn rejects his form of love (gift-giving, material provisions) because she feels bought off while her deepest needs continue unmet.

This couple tends to always remain the same distance apart. When she moves toward him, he takes one step back. If she takes one step back, he feels the freedom to come a little closer. It's like they are holding hands, but at arms' length. They are connected, but they are afraid of losing their own identity to the other person. Somehow they never learned how to be close to another person. To them, closeness means they must lose part of who they are, and that causes too much anxiety. So instead they back away.

Why Do They Struggle with Closeness?

The family-of-origin experience is likely the major contributing factor to the closeness/intimacy problem. Although they are probably not aware of it, this man and woman are working out unresolved difficulties they had as children. Some marriage therapists have suggested that marriage is the process of putting closure on the unfinished business of our family of origin. In other words, our parents and siblings so affect us that we often choose marriage partners in an attempt to compensate for what we did not receive in childhood.

Active-Resistant partners approach family life differently. The active partner questions her worth. As a child she was involved in many activities and developed the idea that her parents loved her more if she performed well and loved her less if she was bad. Sometimes, at a young age, one or both parents may have minimally supported her. This experience intensified her need to feel secure and appreciated. She developed an unconscious attitude that she cannot be accepted by anyone because Mom or Dad, or both, did not accept her. This feeling of rejection by a parent runs so deeply that the active partner, while desiring closeness, does not expect it and in fact may sabotage it. She will nag her husband about closeness, but by nagging will guarantee distance. She lives in chronic fear of rejection but doesn't know how to prevent it.

The resistant partner has a family heritage that emphasized rightness above closeness. One or both parents were often overprotective or overinvasive, and he feels that his boundaries as a person have been offended. He resents any "hovering" or crowding because his family smothered him.

Improving the Marriage

Considerable stability can be established when the active partner modifies her striving for closeness. If she will redirect her energies in some other activities, it may remove the pressure felt by the resistant partner. This will allow him to reenter the relationship. When the resistant partner feels room to breathe, closeness becomes more appealing.

It may seem unfair to suggest that adjustments start with the active partner. In reality, though, that is the best place to begin. It is simply a fact that the active partner is more motivated and aware of the relationship and therefore more capable of initiating adjustments.

The active partner can help the resistant partner by doing such things as curtailing phone calls, suggesting that he stay at work or go back to work if he needs to, or being gone (at a meeting or shopping) when he gets home. The gap she creates gives him room to enter the relationship.

Also, it is imperative that she retrain her mind to accept that his providing behavior is his way of showing love. She must let him love her in that way instead of allowing herself to think she is being bought off.

Finally, she must confront her fear that if she does back off on her demand for attention and accepts his "payoffs," he will never do anything more than just provide for her. She's afraid he'll *never* want to get close to her, that he'll think that what he is doing is sufficient. That's a risk she takes, but obviously her attempts to persuade him haven't worked. Usually, given enough time, the resistant partner's need for closeness draws him back to her.

Likewise, the resistant partner needs to confront a fear that his wife will demand marathon feeling-oriented discussions, and be offended if he does anything on his own. His fear is unfounded. Yes, she would like attention, but she doesn't need large doses. As far as having him around all the time, he would get in her way. But she would feel good if he displayed interest in being with her.

A major challenge for both partners is to risk telling each other how they feel. A few simple changes can close that gap. Instead of accusations and sarcasm, the resistant one could walk up to his spouse and compliment her. When giving the compliment he should maintain eye contact, smile, and give her a hug. Initially the active partner may be suspicious. She may ask, "Why are you telling me that?" "What do you want?" "What do you have up your sleeve?" But if he listens without reacting, she will soon begin to realize that he is genuinely interested in her.

The active partner also needs to be brave and make a statement like, "You know, sometimes I pick on you because I want so much from you. I do care for you, but I realize that part of what I want is only for me, not for you. That's unfair, and I want you to know that I'm beginning to realize that, in your own way, you're doing the best you can to show me that you care." When the active partner tells her husband that she has expected too much from him, it often frees him up to be closer to her.

This couple needs to realize that their most significant strength—individuality—can easily become their biggest weakness. Their greatest help will come when each chooses to place himself as raw clay on the turning spindle of the Master Craftsman. The apostle Paul expressed it best in Philippians 2:3-8:

> Do nothing from selfishness or empty conceit, but with humility of mind let each of you regard one another as more important than himself; do not merely look out for your own personal interests, but also for the interests of others. Have this attitude in yourselves which was also in Christ Jesus, who, although He existed in the form of God, did not regard equality with God a thing to be grasped, but emptied Himself, taking the form of a bond-servant, and being made in the likeness of men. And being found in appearance as a man, He humbled Himself by becoming obedient to the point of death, even death on a cross.

When these two capable people choose to submit to God, significant progress can be made in the relationship. This does not mean that they lose their will, but rather that they are choosing to put themselves under the direction of the Lord Himself. This passage declares that true selfhood is realized when an individual allows Christ to give him the power to be a servant to someone else.

This same concept appears in Matthew 20:26-28. In the preceding verses James and John had desired a prominent position in Jesus' kingdom. Christ's response was: "Whoever wishes to become great among you shall be your servant, and whoever wishes to be first among you shall be your slave; just as the Son of Man did not come to be served, but to serve, and to give His life a ransom for many." Jesus declared His strength by becoming a great servant. Likewise, the invitation to this couple is to be the best at what Jesus prescribed—being a servant.

The Active-Resistant Marriage

	Behavior	**Feelings**
Active	Manipulating closeness	Unloved/wants love
	Independent	Optimistic
Resistant	Keeping partner at arms' length; independent	Smothered, crowded, afraid of love, confident

Theme—Lack of Intimacy
Major Problem—Self-Orientation
Secondary Problem—Family of Origin
Major Strength—Individual Competence

CHAPTER 6

The Helper-Helpee Marriage

The Helper-Helpee marriage is a relationship of contrasts. It began because one person had a problem and the other was available to help, and it is sustained by one or the other having to meet a major ongoing need in the partner's life. Bob and Karen are perfect examples.

Karen was a junior at the university when she met Bob, who had transferred there as a second-semester freshman. She was 20; he was 21. Three years before, lack of money, problems at home, a few misdemeanors, and poor grades had caused Bob to join the Army. Military life helped him get a handle on things, and now getting an education was Bob's goal. Karen was an excellent student, but she struggled with feelings of social inadequacy. A dating relationship with another student had recently gone sour and she was crushed—so much so that she stopped taking care of herself. Her hair was a mess and her clothing unkempt.

Five weeks into the semester their respective dorms had an exchange party. Bob and Karen each went alone and ended up sitting at the same table. Bob was not timid, so he introduced himself to Karen and the others. Karen was immediately attracted to him. His black hair and dark brown eyes accompanied a kind and strong countenance. Later, when Karen asked him about his classes, Bob admitted his struggles in English. His writing skills left much to be desired. Karen offered to help and he gladly accepted.

Karen could hardly contain herself as she prepared for the first "tutoring" session. She put on her favorite outfit and set her hair perfectly. They met at the library, and as they talked Karen discovered that Bob had some learning disabilities that had gone undetected until the latter part of high school. He was intelligent but still needed special help.

Afterward they went out for a Coke, and Karen told Bob about her recent break-up. Bob listened and encouraged her, pointing out her strengths. He didn't seem like so many other guys, looking out for themselves. He was genuine and directed, and Karen was impressed. Bob liked her too. He respected her intelligence, sensitivity, and good looks.

The rest of the year, they helped each another and their friendship led to a more serious relationship. However, there were problems. He felt like she had to have him around, and occasionally it was more of an obligation to be with her than a desire. She became nervous when he was with other women from his classes. She knew she should not be jealous, but she was. When she admitted her fears to him, he felt sorry for her. After all, she had done a lot for him; he might not have done so well in school without her help.

Karen was very thankful to Bob. He not only helped her get out of a rut, but he believed in her. Karen felt dependent upon Bob and did not want anything to disrupt the relationship, so she covered reactions that she thought might upset him. But she was not totally at ease in the relationship. Sometimes she felt like his project rather than his equal. She was secure, like a peasant with the king, but how do a peasant and a king have an intimate relationship?

Bob and Karen were married after she graduated. Bob still had two years of school, so she worked while he completed his education. She helped him complete school assignments and he listened to her frustrations about work. Gradually Bob began to feel like he had a child on his hands. Karen needed constant reassurance, and it seemed like she dealt with very few things on her own. He started losing respect for her but wouldn't tell her so because he didn't want to hurt her. Since he could not be truthful about his feelings, he tried to put them aside, hoping that someday the relationship would improve.

Karen confided to a close friend that Bob was like a father. She liked his caring and take-charge spirit. However, she did not take kindly to being treated like a child, though she had to admit that she felt better when he was around. She expected Bob to respond to her needs—after all, she was always ready to help him out—and felt some anger when he acted as if he didn't care. There were many times that she believed he got his way by ignoring her, not even asking for her opinion. It was as if she was the one doing all the adjusting. She felt trapped between needing him and resenting him.

Over the years, with two children and three moves, Bob lost his energy and motivation to help Karen. He was tired of "pumping her up." He felt guilty for failing to help her and angry at her for failing to improve. One weekend he finally told her how he really felt, and she crumbled. She was upset, hurt, and frantic. Karen assured him that she would get better. Over the weeks she did make strides, but Bob did not acknowledge them. Then Karen began to think about all the times she had given in to him and tried to cooperate: "This is the thanks I get for all my work, the moves, and the children."

Karen's anger began to come out. As she laid into Bob, he thought to himself, "If I tell her how I feel, she gets upset and can't handle it, but if I keep it to myself I get frustrated. It would be easier to get out of this whole mess." But Bob didn't really want to terminate the marriage, since he didn't believe in divorce. She had done her part, and he felt sorry for her, but he knew they needed help.

• • •

There are many Bob-and-Karen-type marriages, in which one or both of the partners has an ongoing problem that nips at their heels like an overzealous neighborhood hound. The malady comes in many forms. He is 43; she is 25. He is black; she is white. She has an MBA; he runs a garage. She attended prep schools; he doesn't know what purpose is served by the smaller fork in a dinner setting.

About 8 to 10 percent of American marriages fall into this personality. In addition, this personality is often a secondary trait to another marriage personality, such as Active-Passive or Active-Resistant. When you get together with a Helper-Helpee couple, you often feel this is a mismatch. Debbie is from the city and appreciates classical music. Dudley grew up in a less sophisticated environment and has never attended a symphony concert. What are some of the challenges they might encounter? She wants a Florentine lamp; he would be satisfied with the $8.99 special. She wants to attend the opera;

he prefers a country-western concert. She follows *Dress for Success*; Levi's are fine for him. She orders chicken cordon bleu at a formal restaurant; he prefers a hamburger at McDonald's.

Just what does Debbie see in Dudley? She probably sees a project—someone who needs "fixing up." They're getting along depends upon Dudley improving. Remember the story of Cinderella? When the prince discovered that Cinderella's foot fit the slipper, he was elated. When they married, did they move into his castle or to her humble dwelling with her wicked sisters? The castle, of course. Cinderella was the one who had to adapt to new surroundings. She had to change, not the prince; he was already royalty. That sounds simple enough in a fairy tale, but in real life it's not quite so easy.

Back to Debbie and Dudley. When they are in a social setting, each is very aware of the other's presence. Debbie is thinking, "I wonder how he's doing? He seemed pretty nervous about this reception. I get so tired of being concerned about him; I'm going to have a good time regardless." He is thinking, "She's probably wondering how I'm doing," and/or, "She is ignoring me and it doesn't seem to bother her."

The difference between Debbie and Dudley suggests that one of them is a caretaker (Debbie) and the other one is taken care of (Dudley). Their friends tend to ask Debbie how Dudley is doing. Those friends also believe that Dudley is the one who needs to get his act together, which reinforces her "togetherness" and his limitations. It is difficult for the couple and their friends to abandon the idea that the marriage problem is the helpee's and that if the helpee changed, the relationship would improve.

I'm a little nervous when I work with a Debbie and Dudley in marital therapy. They are often so unequal that to accomplish some form of compatibility is a tall order. Not all Helper-Helpee marriages end up in counseling, but when they do, I buckle up for a rough ride. But compatibility is possible if both partners are willing to work. First they need to understand the dynamics of their relationship. So we'll examine that, then look at some ways to improve the marriage.

Beginnings

Books and movies abound with stories that have a rescue

theme. Someone in need is rescued by the "good guy." The knight in shining armor comes to the rescue of the maiden in distress. In my youth, Roy Rogers and Dale Evans always came through in the nick of time. More recently, Luke Skywalker saves his people from oppression. Helper-Helpee marriages exude the theme of rescue. The helper (savior) rescues someone (helpee) in distress. The saving begins in the premarital relationship and continues as a pattern throughout the marriage.

Take, for example, Sandra, who was having a tough time with her parents. She moved to a large suburban area to find work. No matter what she did for them, her parents barely responded. Cookies, trips home, and calls went begging for appreciation. Naturally, Sandra felt rejected and despondent.

In addition, she was having some health problems. Ray, an older, single coworker, noticed that Sandra was not her normal, cheerful self. At a lunch break he asked her, "Say, what's going on—something bugging you?"

Sandra was caught off-guard, and her emotions took over. Two tears trickled down her cheeks. "I'm sorry for crying. It's nothing."

"Come on, tell me about it," Ray said as he leaned forward, his elbow on the table and cheek resting in his hand.

He looks like he really cares, she thought to herself. So she told him what was bothering her. In the following weeks, Ray helped her see things from a different vantage point, insisted that she see a doctor, and even put a few "bucks in the till" to pull her through financially. They became closer and closer friends, and finally decided to marry.

If Sandra had not had a problem and Ray had not pitied her, the relationship would probably never have started. Now that it has, a style also has begun. Ray, the savior, is to take care of Sandra. He expects to give, she expects to take. But too much of that will not be good for their marriage.

It's a similar story for most Helper-Helpee marriages. The couple begins their relationship by dealing with their parents or difficulties like depression, anxiety, failing school, poor vocational performance, social inadequacies, poor self-concept, or poor financial management. Their relationship is centered around one person helping the other who is in need. Often the couple misinterprets this helping relationship as romance.

While this couple feels good about each other, they are also somewhat indebted for the help, and that feeling of indebtedness binds them. They do not feel particularly romantic because part of their attraction is due to feeling sorry for the other person. However, they continue the relationship because neither wants to hurt the other.

Outward Style

This may seem harsh, but generally speaking, participants in the Helper-Helpee marriage are givers and takers. Both are using the other person to meet their own needs. The helper gains fulfillment by taking a helping role and the helpee meets his personal needs by being a receiver from his partner. I believe these thoughts and beliefs are mostly subconscious, so before this couple can change, they must realize that they have an exaggerated focus on themselves. They are more interested in pleasing themselves than in meeting the needs of others.

The external contracts can take a variety of forms. One may be a "doctor," the other a "patient." One is a "counselor," the other a "counselee." One is a "socialite," the other a "social trainee." No matter what the particular arrangement, the characteristic of the marriage is that one partner is in charge of the other.

The problem-theme orientation is kept alive when the helper says things like "How are you feeling today?" or "Be sure and take your pills" or "I filled out that job application for you." The helpee feels trapped between "Who does he think he is? I can do it myself" and "I don't know what I would do without him."

Another wrinkle in some of these marriages is the reciprocal arrangement, in which partners take turns being the helper. The roles may reverse every few months or may last several years. Even though they shift roles—each taking turns as the helper—the basic dynamic of the marriage stays the same: orientation around a problem and someone coming to the rescue.

Jim and Renee are a perfect example. Jim was a salesman but had a serious kidney problem. His wife struggled with depression and anxiety that occasionally required hospitalization. Jim had his best months in sales when Renee was emotionally slumped. However, when his kidneys acted up, she immediately improved. Her depression and anxiety vanished as she took charge of the family.

Inward Experience

It is wearing to have to deal with the same problem over a long period of time. Helpers and helpees know what that feels like. They get tired of dealing with the same issue or issues over and over again. At times they feel exasperated, not necessarily about the whole marriage, but with regard to their "difficult" area. The helper is tired of helping and the helpee is tired of being helped. It is like a leg chain for prisoners: They are not immobilized, but they definitely are slowed down, and they always know it's there.

Two common emotions for this couple are anger and guilt—anger because they are frustrated and guilt because they think they should do a better job. In our example of Bob and Karen, she was angry because she subconsciously thought Bob should have done a better job of assisting her. She may even have wondered why Bob could not generate some new, creative ways to come to her aid. Bob was angry too. He was upset with himself for not doing a better job and upset with Karen for not trying harder and standing on her own without needing him so much.

The anger leads to guilt feelings. For example, Bob felt guilty because Karen still had a problem; he felt it was his fault for not being a better helper. Karen felt guilty for not doing better. She reasoned that Bob's help was more than sufficient, and therefore it was her fault for not improving. Note that neither Bob nor Karen felt true guilt, since they had not done anything wrong. Rather, they were uncomfortable with themselves because their efforts were not successful.

By feeling angry and guilty, the partners avoid self-examination. If each were to examine his own motivation, he would discover selfishness. The helper's self-worth is measured by his successes in the lives of other people. This "savior" works very hard at picking up people who are in need. Often he is threatened by people who are of equal stature, so he takes on individuals whom he considers of less ability and adequacy. His desire to be a caretaker is often motivated by the desire to feel good about himself rather than by helping others.

The helpee is also selfish. She spends a large portion of her life focusing on self-improvement. In some ways she likes nothing better than to have a helper available as a constant companion and counselor. At other times she is offended by the helper because she knows that, in order to really be healthy, she needs to solve her own problem.

As ridiculous as it may sound, both partners subconsciously recognize that in order for the marriage to survive, there must be a problem. In extreme cases they will even cooperate in maintaining a problem or creating a new problem.

For example, the helper can actually sabotage the helpee's improvement by continually focusing on the helpee's shortcomings. The helpee, on the other hand, keeps the cycle going by being resistant or noncompliant.

In the midst of this melee, each partner ends up blaming the other for the difficulty of the marriage relationship. Neither of them likes the role, but they don't know what to do about it. The relationship does not result in growth for either person. In fact, growth is a threat.

Strengths and Weaknesses

One significant strength of the Helper-Helpee marriage is empathy. Even though neither partner likes the problem focus of the marriage, each does display an ability to understand. Obviously, this empathy is taken to the extreme. But that ability is important to the health of any marriage relationship.

Another good thing about this marriage is that each partner wants to improve as a person. Each wants to make personal and spiritual progress, but can't figure out how to do it.

Continual focus on problems is the major weakness of the Helper-Helpee marriage. Part of what contributes to their difficulty is inability to equalize the relationship. For example, how does a person who is 15 years older than his spouse ever become the same age? Obviously that's not possible. Those built-in differences tend to keep a couple separated more than they want to be.

Improving the Marriage

Significant improvement will begin to take place in this marriage when the two people move away from the focus on their problems. To make that shift, it is essential that they start relating to each other in an upbeat, progressive, and goal-oriented way.

Also, the helper must stop helping the helpee little by little. In order to facilitate this, he may need to channel his helping energies in another direction, such as his local church or Boy Scout club. The more he stops being his wife's "caretaker" or "counselor," the more she is able to take responsibility for her own personal improvement. It's the same idea as a parent helping a child learn to function independently.

It is important for the helpee to not overreact when this happens. She may be angry because she feels he is abandoning her, but she needs to recognize this as an opportunity to develop as an individual. The helpee, to bring significant improvement in the relationship, must take some risks. It is a risk to live without the security of her helper in that problem area.

To make the transition, she might consider having a spiritually mature person disciple her. This will help her learn how to go to God for strength to overcome her weakness. She will gain an increased sense of personal identity as she places her security in God. And she will realize that God can help her develop strength in any area where she lacks confidence.

As the relationship matures, this couple has the potential to help other couples work through their differences. One of the strongest relationships is one that has struggled because the two partners are so different. Their new and healthier focus can involve taking what they've learned and sharing it with other people who are struggling. There are tremendous opportunities in a Helper-Helpee relationship to discover areas where individual growth can take place, resulting in a more mature, loving, and giving relationship for both husband and wife.

Many couples are tempted to maintain the status quo even though they do not like it. Change is an unknown quantity, and there is no guarantee that it will succeed. They need to realize that by equalizing the relationship, they will enjoy each other more. Instead of a "parent-child" relationship, they can treat each other as equal adults. The results will be rewarding.

The Helper-Helpee Marriage

	Behavior	Feelings
Helper	Parenting, counselor	Sensitive, needs to be needed
Helpee	Childish, counselee	Overwhelmed, vulnerable

Theme—Helping/Problems
Major Problem—Dependency
Secondary Problems—Family of Origin and Low Self-Esteem
Major Strength—Empathy/Sensitivity

CHAPTER 7

The Macho Marriage

When I hear the word "macho," my mind is flooded with images of John Wayne, the leather reins of his horse clenched in his teeth, charging single-handedly toward three desperadoes, a rifle in one hand and his Colt 45 blazing in the other.

This image accurately reflects the Macho marriage personality. It's dominated by a husband (in almost every case) who is powerful and competitive and who believes that a real man has to be tough, never showing weakness or sensitivity. In this relationship, his word is law. All is fine as long as the wife cooperates.

Wayne and Wanda have this kind of marriage. She was 19 years old when they met in the singles' group of her church. He was 20, a transfer to the local university, and a new Christian, having asked Christ to be his Savior less than a year before. He actively participated in the discussion and shocked her because he was so opinionated. He insisted that his view was right and would not back down. Wanda was attracted to his undaunted behavior, yet also felt that he was insensitive to other people.

Wayne had noticed Wanda's long brown hair and pretty features earlier in the evening. It happened that their cars were parked next to each other, so he introduced himself. He also noticed that her zippy little sports car was a far cry from his clunker. The next Sunday he teasingly asked if he could drive her car, and promised her a Coke as a reward. They had a great time laughing and telling stories.

After a few months of dating, Wanda's initial uneasiness slipped away except for one area. Usually Wayne was charming and considerate, but sometimes he would compliment her with an accompanying barb such as "You're fun to be with, and by the way I like your car and then you. Ha!" She didn't know if he was serious or just trying to get a rise out of her. Most of the time she took it with a forced smile, hoping the conversation would move on to some other topic.

There were several times when she tried to confront him: "Wayne, that hurts. Please don't say that anymore." Wayne would react, "I didn't mean to hurt you. If that hurt, you must be a big baby. That's ridiculous!" That made her feel put down, and often those dates ended with her in tears.

Wanda's parents liked Wayne and he really liked them. Her family was almost as appealing to him as she was: They were great people, full of warmth, commitment, and understanding. Wayne's childhood home was laced with problems—alcoholism, abuse, siblings in foster homes, truancy, and trouble with the law. Wayne had learned how to survive fights with his dad, siblings, and peers. Even though Wanda's family wasn't perfect, it was far better than his rough heritage.

Wanda was a sensitive girl when they started dating. She wanted to please her parents, friends, and especially Wayne. She hated conflict, and in order to keep peace she would not say anything if she thought it would cause hurt feelings. The parenting she received was well-intended, but Mom and Dad had a habit of finding fault with her shortcomings. She was average in school and took little initiative with anything. This upset Wanda's parents, and in their exasperation they criticized her: "You only got a 'C' in that course?" "If you'd work a little you could do much better." "Are you going to lie around the rest of your life?" "I told you to get the house dusted by 4:30, and now it's 5:00—can't you do what you're told?" The steady diet of put-downs contributed to her skinny self-esteem. At times she would yell back, but usually she stood in a silent stupor, secreting signpost tears.

Wayne's newfound faith made Wanda nervous at times. He would talk to the waitress and gas station attendant, and wanted her to help pass out tracts on the street corner. She had attended church all her life and had become a Christian as a seven-year-old through her mother's direction. Church was okay, but it did not thrill her. Wayne insisted that she become more spiritual, but her personality and inoculated Christian experience curtailed her progress. She wanted to please him, but she could not make herself do some of the things he demanded.

Rather than patiently allowing Wanda to grow at her own pace, Wayne pushed. One day he said, "You must not love me if you don't do the things that are important to me." She tried to explain: "Wayne, you don't understand. I do love you, but I can't do some of this stuff." "Yes, you can," he responded with a glare and slightly flushed cheeks. He stormed off, she felt terrible, and nothing was resolved. After an awkward cooling-off period, they reconnected. Unfortunately, that was typical of how they dealt with conflict—Wayne attacked and Wanda crumbled.

Wayne had clear convictions about how their marriage should work. He wanted to do everything by the book—his book. But a bigger problem was how he enforced compliance. He was abrasive, like sandpaper rubbing against a baby's skin. Wayne coerced, pushed, threatened, accused, and issued ultimatums. It was important for him to be in charge of his marriage and to appear like he was successful.

Wanda was unsure whether Wayne did these things for her or to look good in the eyes of other people. He was picky and demanding: "How come you didn't get the house picked up—do you expect me to live like a slob?" or "Make dinner—I'm hungry!" She felt used: "All I am is a cheap slave that has sex with him on the side." Sometimes it helped for her to remember that he came from a rough background, but she still felt she deserved better treatment.

One day, in the midst of a disagreement, he lifted his fist to hit her. Fortunately, he caught himself. Shocked and dismayed, he walked out of the house. "What's happening to me?" he asked as he wandered the street. He had sworn never to treat his wife like his dad treated his mother. But it was happening anyway. After he apologized, Wanda wanted to draw close to him, yet she was afraid. It was like being next to a ticking time-bomb, not knowing when it is going to explode.

Wayne and Wanda have accumulated many good memories—vocational development, the birth of two children, good friends, and a lay ministry outreach. However, Wayne is frustrated by his wife's inability to deal with issues and she is overwhelmed by his harshness. Wanda is always on guard, and Wayne vacillates between being demanding and avoiding her when he is upset. Occasionally the situation explodes with Wayne's angry demands and Wanda's nervous tears.

• • •

Macho marriages cover a broad range from fairly healthy to very unhealthy relationships. This is a male-dominated relationship, with Mrs. Macho standing in the wings as a combination wife and servant. My experience suggests that about 12 percent of marriages fit this category. With the shift in attitudes about men and women and their roles, this marriage personality is not as prevalent today as it once was.

Some Macho couples are very happy with their relationship because it meets their need for structure, direction, and security. Others are devastated because of the ever-escalating abrasiveness of the relationship. Many ask me if this marriage can ever change. To be honest, it can change only with effort and affirmation by both parties. Let's examine the background and characteristics of this personality, and find some ways to improve it.

Beginnings

The source of the Macho marriage can be traced to the families of origin. The family experience for both partners has a significant impact on how they view themselves and what they expect in a marriage relationship. Usually the macho man comes from a family where relationships were not at a premium. As an adult, he may not know or care where his siblings live. He has taken care of himself since age 12 or so. He has learned that it's a "dog-eat-dog" world and that you're a fool if you trust anybody.

Dad and Mom had a poor marriage. He never saw his parents hug and would be shocked if his dad ever expressed any affection for him. As a boy, he heard more about what he did wrong than what he did right. Our macho man learned from his dad and peers that a "real man" never shows weakness or talks about his fears. He learned to ignore his feelings and, worse yet, to deny that he even had feelings of fear, regret, loneliness, or sadness. His muscles have covered an emotional vacuum. He is a tough guy who will get the job done, but in the process he rapes relationships.

Mrs. Macho's family experience left her with limited self-confidence. Somehow, she never learned that she was an okay person. She feels bad about herself and guilty for not being better. Either Mom and Dad did not reassure her, or else they were "on her case" all the time. Her feelings were ignored or put down. As a teenager she was shy or hostile, but in either case it was an overreaction to her poor self-view. She left home questioning her worthiness and feeling unloved—and that somehow it was her fault.

When they start dating, his outward, positive, controlling manner provides an immediate sense of security for her. Even though he can be pushy at times, she likes his strength. His muscles or social prowess look so comforting that she doesn't consider the fact that his strength can also be used against her. For example, he may push a physical relationship in dating. If she says no, he may issue an ultimatum: "Either we make out or I'll go with someone else." It's not unusual for her to succumb to his threats and afterward feel sorrow. Yet there are enough rewarding experiences in the premarital relationship to convince her that things will be okay in the marriage.

Outward Style

Occasionally we still see "caveman" jokes in the comics. Typically, the "caveman" appears rough and gruff. He has a club in one hand and with the other is dragging his fair maiden by her hair. Mrs. Caveman looks bewildered and overwhelmed. He is the conqueror and she is the conquered, leaving no doubt about who is in charge.

Some Macho marriages are very much like the caveman relationship: He barks and she jumps. He gives the impression that he owns her. She is both afraid of him and dependent upon him. Her behavior may be submissive, quiet, shy, and nervous, or she can be defiant, argumentative, and challenging. He may not be outwardly gruff, but rather subdued, stern, persistent, and sarcastic. In some cases the Macho marriage is not overtly male oppressive. He may be laid back and somewhat sensitive and she may be outwardly adequate. However, when push comes to shove, he makes sure that he wins what he wants to win. He maintains control and she backs down because he is more forceful physically, verbally, or intellectually.

The macho man comes in many forms—truck driver, construction worker, drill sergeant, sales manager, or corporate hatchet man. He is black-and-white in his thinking and has a reputation that "you don't cross him or he'll get you." He really wants people to like him, but the only method he knows is to literally *make* them. He's afraid that his wife, if given the choice, would reject him, so he keeps her in line. Often he demands, "Get me a cup of coffee!" without any "please" or "thank you."

Mrs. Macho is usually friendly, sensitive, and cooperative. She likes things to go smoothly, so she spends her energy avoiding conflict. This usually means giving in to her husband's wishes. Because she has doubts about her ability to handle life, she tries to please other people so that her immediate environment will feel secure and stable.

This marriage looks like a traditional one, with the man as head of the house and the woman as homemaker and caretaker for the children. The relationship is often interwoven with traditional male/female sex role stereotyping. Men are strong, brave, and rational; women are weak, naive, and emotional. Men bring home the money and women do the housework. She takes the role of being servant, as if she deserved nothing better. While he goes to the races or golfing, or to a pro game with the guys, she stays home with the kids.

It is not uncommon for two Christians in a Macho marriage to misuse the Bible. He uses the Bible as a weapon to prove that he is the head of the house. His wife must be submissive and cooperate with his decisions. Obviously, the intent of Scripture has been misappropriated. The husband uses the Bible to maximize his position while she thinks, "If God is on his side, then He's against me." Sadly, some women think they're disobeying God anytime they do not go along with their husband's wishes.

Their sexual relationship is usually a physical release for him and an ordeal for her. There is little romance or foreplay. He wants sex and it is her job to give it. She seldom reaches a climax, adding to her list of life's disappointments. Where once she felt lovingly conquered, now she feels manhandled.

You might be getting the impression that Macho marriages

are always volatile. Actually some are very pleasant, and the couples involved feel secure in them. However, those who do need help often don't get it because the husband is resistant to counseling. Sometimes the wife will come alone, without her husband knowing it. These marriages can be traumatic, characterized by violence and alcohol abuse. Often she enhances his drinking problem by cooperating rather than confronting. I have encountered situations where she will not have him committed for treatment because he has threatened to leave her, beat her, or "make her pay." She goes along because she doesn't know of any alternatives. As she becomes more burdened and defeated, he becomes angrier.

Man	Woman
Macho (controlling)	Respect (sometimes out of fear)
Upset	Bewildered
Attacking/Mean	Broken

Inward Experience

What is this couple's internal condition? Do these people like themselves? Actually both partners have a low sense of personal worth. Below his gruff exterior there is fear—fear of losing control, or being embarrassed, or having his internal weakness exposed. He focuses on weaknesses in other people in order to avoid facing his own. Noncompliance from others is met with swift reprisal because of his personal insecurity. In addition to Mr. Macho's fear and self-doubt, he may also suffer from low self-esteem, which is expressed in his tendency to be sarcastic, critical, or jealous.

The wife also doubts her worth and thus questions whether she deserves to be treated in a respectable manner. She constantly second-guesses her attempts to please him. Because she is on edge, it is not uncommon for her to repeat "mistakes" for which he has previously reprimanded her. While outwardly submissive, she rehearses her inadequacy or fantasizes about "telling him a thing or two."

What she doesn't realize is that she is very much in control of the marriage. That probably sounds illogical. But she often sets up her husband's undesirable behavior with her struggling self-worth and insecurity. This gives her an excuse not to grow and saves her from the risk of attempting to be a more complete person. She can even "use" her husband to punish her for being inadequate. When she serves supper late and he criticizes her, her "mistake" and his "discipline" reinforce her subconscious belief that she should be punished for worthlessness.

Strengths and Weaknesses

A major strength of the Macho marriage is structure. Because of Mr. Macho's role-orientation and need for control, the marriage and family tend to have a predictable, weekly schedule. Also, everyone knows what is expected regarding rules, household chores, manners, and beliefs. There is a clear line of authority, so most family members feel some security. The parents do as much for their children as possible. Because Dad has high expectations and will not tolerate many mistakes, the children are survivors. They may not have close feelings for Dad, but they do know what it takes to make it in the world.

The Macho marriage usually has two main areas of weakness: lack of warmth and excessive role-orientation. Both are signs of insecurity. By lack of warmth I mean that they are not comfortably loving each another. Because they feel insecure, they are more sensitive to how they are being loved than to how they can love each other. He may think, "She is not very affectionate" instead of, "How can I show her that I really love her?"

I believe this couple is too secretive. They desperately want to be loved but try to get love in unproductive ways. He "asks" for love when he complains about her lack of affection. She "asks" for love when she is nice to him. Neither of them can figure out what is happening. Somehow she is supposed to know that his complaint is really a request: "Will you show me that you love me?" He is supposed to know that a fresh-baked pie is a request: "Will you show me that you care?"

The second area of difficulty is excessive role-orientation. Mr. Macho is embarrassed if anyone in his family does something that, in his mind, does not fit what is appropriate for men, women, boys, and girls. He objects to his daughter playing Little League baseball. His son must never cry, for that is a sign of weakness. Such control may work until the children move into adolescence and peer-group involvement. Then they are quite capable of sabotaging Dad's control.

Problems occur when Mrs. Macho breaks rules. If Mrs. Macho goes back to work outside the home, she finds that other people do not live the way she lives. She may conclude that she has been mistreated for too long. Unfortunately, she may overreact when others encourage her not to put up with it anymore. If she starts throwing ultimatums at her husband, there will be fireworks, but little progress. She soon learns that it does not pay dividends to "fight fire with fire."

Fortunately, there are some things that she can do to help her situation.

Improving the Marriage

Mrs. Macho can influence her husband by responding to him with confidence, and by calling his bluffs. Suppose her husband demands, "Get me a cup of coffee." She could respond, "Get the cup of coffee yourself." However, he will take that as defiance, and the results won't be pleasant. A better option is to calmly say, "Honey, I'll be glad to get it for you in a minute, when I get done with my project." Or she could say, "You know, dear, I don't mind getting your coffee, but it works better and I'm more cheerful when someone says 'please' to me."

Now the wife is confronting, but with a touch of humor. She is not attacking, but neither is she retreating. The results are even better if she says it with a smile. She could even gently tease him with, "I'm sure you can say 'please.' I know it's in you. Why don't you try it sometime? You never know what kind of a good response you might get from me."

Of course, Mr. Macho may not be humored and may respond with a louder ultimatum: "I said, I want my coffee now!" This is when she can't back down. Maintaining the same calm, loving tone of voice, she can say, "I'm sorry if you *must* be upset, but I'm busy right now, and it will be a few minutes before I will bring you some coffee."

What she is doing is establishing her own identity without putting down her mate. In fact, she'll probably feel closer to him because she is not so afraid. She does not have to wear a "Tread on me" sweatshirt. She needs to take care of herself and get beyond the belief of "This is all I deserve." She'll discover that she can still cooperate with other people while being her own person.

When Mrs. Macho confronts her husband, it's important that she also reassure him. He might take personal offense if she wants to join a bowling league on her own. She could say something like, "Honey, I really want to join this league so I can spend time with some of my friends. I don't want you to take it personally. I enjoy being with you, but I can be a better wife if I take a break once a week and am involved with this group." Note that as she confronts him she also reassures him that she loves him and that this will ultimately help both of them. It's another way of gently sidestepping his tendency to issue ultimatums.

Some readers may object that this wife is not being submissive. We need to realize that biblical submission does not mean acting like a doormat and allowing the husband to crush the wife emotionally. Submission is taking the responsibility for our spiritual and marital life. If a man is hurting his wife, she does both of them a disservice if she doesn't confront him. She doesn't have to do it in a hostile or demeaning manner. However, she may need some coaching from a caring friend in order to do it in a direct but positive way.

A good biblical example for the wife of a macho man is Moses. He felt powerless and gave God many reasons why he could not do what God told him to do. Moses needed to look beyond his feelings of weakness to God Himself. God promised to supply all of the power Moses needed. In the same way, Mrs. Macho can deal with her need for love and security by being more assertive, direct, and honest, relying on God's strength to go beyond her natural tendency to accept things as they are.

There's also a biblical model for the husband. He is somewhat like the apostle Paul—confident, assertive, and goal-oriented. Paul wanted to maintain his strength and power, but God showed him (in 2 Corinthians 12:7-10) that he needed to learn how to be strong in his weakness. Our macho man needs to discover that he can channel his strength by listening to his wife. Unfortunately, it may take a major disappointment to motivate him to do so. He needs to see how he hurts her;

then maybe he will work on improving his interpersonal skills.

The most important thing a husband can do for this marriage is to support his wife as an individual. Compliments and encouragement will do a lot for her self-image. He might try saying things like "You had a lot of good things to say tonight at the meeting" or "Honey, if you get time, will you call Sears about the special?" or "You know, Dear, if that is something you want to do, there's no doubt in my mind that you can do it. I'm for you 100 percent." The more Mr. Macho honors his wife, the more she will blossom.

It is extremely important that Mr. Macho learn how to make requests of his wife rather than present demands. His normal habit pattern is to tell people what he wants, when he wants it, and how he wants it done. It would help if he prayed and asked God to give him an awareness and sensitivity to his wife's feelings.

Mr. Macho is usually a very proud person, and therefore it is difficult and unappealing to him to appear humble or weak. He must realize that Jesus demonstrated His greatest strength when it appeared He was weak. First Peter 2:23 says, "While being reviled, He did not revile in return; while suffering, He uttered no threats, but kept entrusting Himself to Him who judges righteously." Jesus demonstrated that He was strong enough to leave His case in God's hands, even though He was being treated unfairly. He did not defend Himself because He knew that God would defend Him.

The macho husband can grow in his relationship with Christ by learning through his marriage to submit himself. For example, in the sexual arena, he might concentrate on giving his wife pleasure. By not always having his own way, he demonstrates true strength. That will make an impact on his spouse, for she will feel truly loved and will begin to experience freedom to be who she is. She will become a better wife, and that will benefit him too!

The Macho Marriage

	Behavior	Feelings
Mr. Macho	Challenging, controlling	Inadequate, untrusting
Mrs. Macho	Cautious, unassertive	Undeserving, bewildered

Theme—Dominant, Submissive
Major Problem—Self-Orientation
Secondary Problem—Family of Origin
Major Strength—Structure (Roles defined)

CHAPTER 8

The Pretense Marriage

Hal and Holly met in an unusual way: They happened to be at the same hotel attending different conferences. One morning while having breakfast in the coffee shop, Hal asked for some sugar from Holly's table. Later that day they ran into each other again and exchanged information about their respective conferences. He was attending a meeting for Vietnam veterans. She was representing her university music department at a seminar about teaching music theory to children.

Neither remembers why, but they decided to meet that evening for dinner. There they were, two total strangers, sitting in the restaurant exchanging life stories. Hal had coal-black hair, a mustache and beard, and wire-rimmed glasses. His was a rough background. He had had problems with his stepfather and he hated school. He finally joined the Army to get out on his own. The effects of the war on his fellow vets, both psychologically and physically, concerned him, and he was very vocal about his belief that the military should do more than they were presently doing.

Holly was slightly overweight, dressed in a tan outfit with pleated skirt and matching top. Her hands were empty of rings and her face was accented by little makeup. The second of two girls, she had grown up in a musical family. She had devoted most of her life to music at the expense of her social life. To Holly, Hal's life looked intriguing. And Hal couldn't believe that Holly was so naive.

The remainder of the week became a blur as Hal and Holly spent every available minute together. By the time their conferences were over, they did not want to separate. Holly's parents resisted their attempts to get together, but the more they resisted, the more Holly wanted to see Hal. The attraction she felt for Hal was a mystery to her. She only knew that it was exciting to be with him. Family and friends tried to reason with her, but the warnings only pushed her closer to Hal. Finally she left home, university, and music, and they were married.

Not long after the marriage, Hal and Holly both wished that their chance meeting had never taken place. Holly finally saw what her parents and others had warned her about. Hal was so different that she could not relate to him. Now that she had to live with him, she was no longer intrigued by his differences. What she thought was love had been infatuation. Hal got tired of her being naive and straight. He decided he didn't want to be "reformed" after all. They even had trouble being in the same car because he wanted to listen to country-western or pop rock and she wanted to hear the university station that played classical music.

When it came to truly caring for each other, everything seemed forced. He still had his ways; she still had hers. There was little common ground, and their attempts to work together seemed fruitless. It was not that Hal didn't like Holly, but just that he couldn't relate to her because she was so different. Holly felt sorry for Hal and his hard life experiences, but that was not the same as loving him.

Hal and Holly settled into a roommate relationship. Her activities and interests were in no way similar to his. He worked at the local garage and she found a job with the symphony. He picked up a few friends from the garage; she spent most of her time with other music buffs. They had separate bedrooms, checking accounts, work schedules, and TV sets. Hal would say to himself, "She is a respectable and capable person, but she just doesn't turn me on." Holly thought, "I can't understand what he sees in his rough friends and why he lives the way he does. What was I thinking when I married him?"

Both Hal and Holly feel bad about what has happened, but they can't figure out any significant solutions. Still, they maintain the relationship, not wanting to hurt each other and still hoping that things might change.

Occasionally I run into a Hal and Holly in my office. I

immediately sense that they need a "respirator" to help them maintain marital life. Usually they aren't looking for a marital counselor but a marital *coroner*—someone to pronounce the relationship dead. It is easy for me to end up working harder on their marriage than they do, but I quickly explain that their marital limbo will not change without effort. They have to decide to work at it, and if they do, I'm willing to help.

The Pretense marriage is a "make-believe" relationship. Just as synthetic diamonds look like the real thing, the Pretense marriage is a synthetic imitation. Sure, there is a legal agreement between the two parties, but there is little in the way of a real marriage. They have different interests, backgrounds, goals, and values. They seem unable to connect in love and intimacy. Their relationship is neither passionate nor hostile; at best it's lukewarm. Marital magnetism, infatuation, romance, and enthusiasm are foreign feelings.

Pretense marriages make up only 3 percent of all marriages. In the past more Pretense marriages were consummated because of social and moral patterns. For example, many premarital-pregnancy marriages and arranged relationships were imitation marriages. Also, in the past it was more difficult to be single than it is today, so marriage often happened for survival rather than for commitment. There are fewer arranged and "for-survival" marriages today, and certainly premarital pregnancy no longer automatically prompts marriage. Also, couples are more likely to terminate a Pretense marriage, chalking it up to "bad judgment" or "a mistake."

Beginnings

In most Pretense marriages there is more outward pressure for the couple to marry than inward desire. There are several situations that seem to feed Pretense marriages, such as when one or both partners are rebounding from a bad relationship. Occasionally a Pretense marriage is arranged by family and friends. The family believes it is a perfect match, and the children are obedient, hoping that it will work out. Wealthy families have been known to do the picking for their sons and daughters. During the Vietnam War some marriages took place to avoid the draft. Occasionally a widower marries only because he needs a "mother" for his children. Unmarried pastors looking for a church have married because they believed they would improve their chances for a pastoral position. All in all, when I see a Pretense marriage relationship I usually find external pressure for the marriage rather than any strong romantic striving for each other.

Outward Style

This couple is usually friendly and cordial. They are not out to "get" the other party, nor are they attracted to the other party. They seem like good friends rather than lovers. In contrast, most married people act like they are connected to one another by showing affection or even conflict. But the pretense couple does not deeply experience love or hate in the hurts or joys of each other because they are not emotionally connected.

Their physical relationship is more mechanical than romantic. Sex takes place on rare occasions, and one or both may fantasize about other partners during their sexual encounter. They tend to be silent not only in public but also at home. He may have a favorite chair in the family room, she a special hobby to keep her busy. Sitting at the dinner table is like being a guest at a friend's home rather than being with your family. Both tend to get involved in third-party activities such as their children's hobbies, pets, jobs, and friends. They are very much like married singles—to the extreme. Unfortunately, affairs are not unusual among one or both partners.

Socially, this couple shows no red flags. Actually you don't see them together much socially because they travel in separate circles. Sometimes this is a marriage where both partners are more interested in their professions, and marriage is a secondary concern, held onto for conscience sake but not holding a high priority in their lives.

Inward Experience

For individuals in the Pretense marriage, the biggest challenge is dealing with their lack of feelings. Their inner struggle is "How do I force myself to care for someone to whom I do not feel attracted?" This is by and large a secret that neither discusses with the other, for they realize that such a discussion would not be productive.

In addition, this couple has never fully committed themselves to the relationship. And because the numbness and sense of entrapment is so overpowering, they begin to live for other purposes than the marriage. There is a sense of hopelessness that there is no reasonable solution to their dilemma.

Strengths and Weaknesses

There is some strength to the Pretense marriage, and it revolves around structure. Even though there is little emotional exchange between Mr. and Mrs. Pretense, they do maintain a structure for themselves and their children. This provides security for the children and a sense of order to the family. It is difficult to suggest any other strengths in the relationship because the very essence of the Pretense marriage is the lack of relationship.

Absense of emotional attraction is the primary weakness of the Pretense marriage. Certainly, marriage is not exclusively dependent upon romance, but in this case the lack of emotional attachment and romantic feeling undercuts their ability to have a "real" rather than a synthetic marriage.

Improving the Marriage

The Old Testament describes marriage as a process of leaving, cleaving, and becoming one flesh. We are told in Genesis 2:24 that God's plan is, "A man shall leave his father and his mother, and shall cleave to his wife; and they shall become one flesh." In this particular marriage relationship, the couple has left their parents but have trouble cleaving or bonding to each other to become one flesh (emotional and physical attraction).

The solution is not so much whether or not they should divorce, but whether they want to get married. Though this couple is legally married, they need to become emotionally married. I realize that it is impossible to force someone to love another person, but it is possible to *learn* to love another person. That may be a limited possibility, but it is better than living emotionally separated lives.

This couple is in a position where they need to seek Christ to provide the power and energy to love each other beyond their own capabilities. They must realize that they can't manufacture love without help from the Lord. The very fact that they are in need of a deeper level of love for their spouse makes them eligible to receive from God as only He can provide.

I must also present a caution: Take it slow and easy. It is important to keep regular contact, but it is also important not to expect an immediate rejuvenation of strong positive feelings. I also recommend that the couple in the Pretense marriage make themselves available to a trained marriage counselor. If either individual begins to feel guilty or angry because he is not attracted to his spouse, that will only serve to further separate them. Possibly through counseling, the individual can admit to the lack of feelings in a healthier way, opening the door for the growth of warm feelings.

Finally, energy needs to be spent getting into the relationship, not out of it. It will take commitment, but some couples in this position have discovered that concerted effort by both sides has resulted in enlivened and enriched relationships. It takes work and desire, but it can be accomplished.

The Pretense Marriage

	Behavior	Feelings
Husband	Individual activity	Numb, lonely
Wife	Individual activity	Numb, lonely

Theme—Lack of Romantic Attraction
Major Problem—Commitment
Major Strength—Structure

CHAPTER 9

The Kids' Marriage

This chapter is about premature marriages. The Kids' marriage is a union between two children who are not ready to face the difficulties of life on their own. Like a premature child who needs neonatal intensive care, this couple needs "intensive care" until they grow up. Their lives are filled with one marital crisis after another. The following event is typical of a Kids' marriage.

Jake's boss told him he had earned a raise of 30 cents an hour. His job at the car dealership as the cleanup man was paying off. He and his wife, Jackie, could sure use the extra money, too. When he arrived home, he proudly announced his good news to Jackie and said he was going out to celebrate with his friend, Sonny. "Just the two of you?" she asked. "Yeah, we're going to the Airliners' game!" he said, not thinking that his wife might want to go too. Jackie didn't mind Jake spending time with Sonny, but she did not trust Sonny's girlfriend, Ann.

Jackie waited up for Jake, but he didn't show. Taking matters into her own hands, she went looking for him at a favorite restaurant. He was there, all right, and so was Sonny, Ann, and another girl. The four of them looked like they were having a great time. Jackie fumed all the way home: "That dirty, rotten creep. If he thinks he can get away with this, he'd better think again."

An hour later, Sonny let Jake off and went on home. Jake tried to open the door, but it was locked. He tried his key and turned the knob, but something was barricaded against the door. "What's going on here?" he yelled.

Then he heard Jackie yelling at him. "Going out with Sonny

alone, huh? I saw you, all four of you, up at the restaurant. You creep, I'll never trust you again! Your clothes are outside in the corner."

Without thinking, Jake started ramming his body into the door. It made him mad that he was accused without even a question. Nobody was going to keep him out of his own apartment! Meanwhile Jackie called her parents and the police.

The door was broken by the time the police arrived, and Jake and Jackie were yelling at the top of their lungs and throwing things at each other. The police tried to settle things down until her parents arrived. Jackie went home with them while Jake took his clothes back inside and sacked out on the couch to guard the entrance to the apartment.

For the next few days, Jake and Jackie were like two siblings in their respective corners, pointing fingers at each other and shouting, "He did it!" Gradually, however, their blame turned to remorse and a little curiosity. "I wonder what she's doing," Jake thought. Jackie wondered, "Maybe I did assume something about Jake and the others at the restaurant."

Jake called Jackie's mom to see how she was. Jackie called Sonny to see how Jake was doing. After a few more days, when things had calmed down, they made up and that night they made love like never before. They were back together as if nothing had ever happened.

Jackie's parents took a deep breath, crossed their fingers, and fervently prayed. They knew that Jake and Jackie could easily go through another "hot war" with just the slightest spark. They didn't know whether to stay out of it or try to help. One thing was certain: Jake and Jackie's feelings for each other changed like the wind. One minute they were madly in love, the next minute they couldn't stand each other.

• • •

The Kids' marriage is a little like my early driving experience. I was a 16-year-old kid who thought he knew what he was doing. I considered myself as good as any adult driver until a few minor fender-benders proved me wrong. The Kids' marriage is made up of partially trained "drivers" who experience numerous marital "fender-benders."

Beginnings

They meet in high school, "fall in love," and have a great time together. Their love is actually "puppy love" or infatuation and is rarely more than skin deep. Their relationship develops because both of them have a base of security without the responsibility of providing for themselves. When they have a spat they can go home and cool off, so a relationship problem is not overwhelming.

What they have feels good, but it is also unrealistic. It is one thing to pull off a relationship when all your basic needs are taken care of by your parents; it's quite another to fashion a relationship when you're also responsible for a job, apartment, and daily chores. Once they marry, this couple can't go home and cool off after a spat. Now they must confront each other in difficult circumstances, whereas before they dealt with each other only when it was convenient.

People in Kids' marriages are almost always teenagers. Most of us still have a significant need for development between the ages of 16 and 20. We are still getting our act together with regard to values, goals, spiritual convictions, and vocation. People who marry during this time hinder their personal development. They move into marriage before being successfully weaned from their family of origin.

It is my belief that if each partner in these marriages had continued personal development without marrying, most of them would have chosen a different partner at age 22 than at age 18. If they did choose the same person later on, at least both of them would be better equipped to negotiate the multiple demands of marriage.

Only about 5 percent of all marriages fit the Kids' personality type. And after they have been married two to five years they usually move into one of the other marriage personalities. It is very unusual to find a Kids' marriage in couples that have been married longer than 12 years. They either grow up in their marriage or give up on it.

Outward Style

This marriage is as unpredictable as a typical American teenager. It's energetic, impulsive, independent yet dependent, fun-loving, broke, and absentminded. If it were not so serious at times, it could almost be comical. Years later they will laugh about it, but not now. They fight over who should dry the dishes and clean the bathroom. He becomes jealous when she tells him about some guy who made a pass at her at work, and he might give her a spanking for being "bad." They tend to spend as much time with their single friends as with each other.

The Kids' marriage is usually very active. It is normal for these two people to fight, then make up, then fight again, then make up, and so on. Usually their parents are very much involved, trying to bail the kids out of financial disaster or help them find an apartment. It's not uncommon for other people to become involved as well, such as the court system, a social worker, a family abuse center, or the neighborhood church trying to help with food or clothing. This couple rarely operates on their own because of their childish, immature behavior.

Inward Experience

What this couple think and feel inside is related to how they behave. When they are outwardly impulsive they are also thinking and feeling impulsively. When something happens to them, they don't think about the impact of their reactions. They just react! For example, if Jake's friend Sonny gets a new stereo and Jake decides he wants one too, he buys it. So what if the rent is due next week and they need grocery money? It is an impulsive act, based upon current emotions, without thought for the future.

Their emotions are felt to the fullest. When they are angry they are really angry, and when they are jealous they are really jealous, and when they are loving they are really loving. They can be intimidated by mature adults. It is difficult for these kids to admit that they have needs or to take advice from others. They experience an unsettling fear that they are not as "together" as others, but behave defiantly when confronted with their inadequacies. For example, if a parent confronts Jake about using rent money to buy the stereo, Jake's response may be "Look, Mom, if you're going to give me a lecture, forget it. I'll get the rent money somewhere else."

Strengths and Weaknesses

The major strength and weakness of this marriage relationship is the same—its youth. Because they are young and energetic, this couple can adjust to difficult and trying circumstances and forget bad experiences without falling prey to bitterness. After they fight and make up they move on instead of being resentful.

But youth is also a weakness. These two people are immature and not ready to carry on the responsibilities of a marriage. That is not to say they do not love and care for each other, for frequently they do. However, they enter into this tremendous responsibility ill-equipped to fulfill the task of relating to and being responsible for each other.

Another weakness is their high degree of self-focus. They are not objective, and frequently they are overly sensitive and reactive. It is difficult for them to see life from someone else's perspective. When two people are focused upon themselves, the task of working together as a team becomes far more challenging.

Hopefully a Kids' marriage has another source of strength: Most young couples can benefit from the wisdom of their parents or other concerned adults. A Kids' relationship is like a canoe tossed about on the ocean. Parents, like a large ship, can come alongside to protect the canoe. This gives a couple time to mature until they can handle the "ocean" on their own. Advice on housing, finances, jobs, and education (and at times even financial assistance) can make the difference in this couple surviving their premature marriage.

Improving the Marriage

Not only does this couple need contact with their parents and other interested couples, but they need to be in a situation where they have to answer to someone. This is best accomplished by answering to a couple or a pastor who is not family-related. They should meet with this mature couple at least once a month to review their marital, financial, spiritual, and vocational lives. This will give them a chance for regular feedback and will provide a systematic approach toward reaching maturity.

When I have a couple like this in counseling, I am very direct and confrontive. Because they act like children, I treat them like children. I do not ask them to do an assignment—I tell them. I do not ask them to be nice to each other—I tell them. But it is important to verbalize confidence at the same time you are guiding them. I tell them that they will grow up and start acting more mature one of these days. However, until they do, they are going to have to put up with other people guiding their lives.

Another thing they should do is attend a couple's seminar or retreat at least once every six months. This will give them helpful training as well as contact with other young couples. It also helps if they get involved in some type of couples' Bible study or fellowship group where they can have regular, ongoing interaction with other couples.

When they get into problems, it is extremely important that they not try to resolve these problems alone. Their immaturity will probably sabotage most of their well-intentioned efforts. They need some objective, outside advice and help in order to maintain marital stability.

I am not suggesting that you do everything for a Kids' couple or shield them from the consequences of their impulsive, immature behavior. If she wants a divorce because they had a fight and he spanked her, then sit down with her. Let her talk about her feelings, but help her see that a divorce is overreacting to the fight.

Studies have concluded that as many as nine out of ten teenage marriages end in divorce, most within the first two years of marriage. The most important thing we can tell a teenage couple is to wait it out. If they can follow the direction of mature family and friends, and survive the tough growing-up years, there is definitely hope for this marriage.

The Kids' Marriage

	Behavior	Feelings
Husband	Impulsive, boastful,	Questioning, oppositional
	Mistake-prone	Mood swings
Wife	Impulsive, mistake-prone	Unsure, afraid, mood swings

Theme—Immaturity
Major Problem—Self-Orientation
Secondary Problem—Family of Origin
Major Strength—Energy of Youth

CHAPTER 10

The Active-Active Marriage

So far we've examined six marriage personalities. Though all six have their relative strengths, we have observed that, left unattended, each personality has built-in weaknesses that can destroy the marriage. This last personality fits about 20 percent of all marriages, and tends to be the most stable.

The Active-Active marriage personality is one in which both partners have individually decided to "put their best foot forward" in the relationship. They also are well-equipped with the abilities and talent to pull off a good marriage. Just what do we mean by "well-equipped"? A well-prepared marriage partner is one who is mature and directed, has resolved the past, has a good family model, is content with self, is giving and approachable, and values God, other people, and himself. If this sounds like a "Super Spouse," that is not my intention. It is simply a fact that some people are better equipped to succeed in marriage.

An example from a fifth-grade teaching situation illustrates my point. The teacher may tell one set of parents, "Your son tries hard and does as well as he can, given his capabilities. But he is not an 'A' student." To another couple the teacher may say, "Your son has a great deal of potential, but he is not working; he's only doing the minimum." Note that one student has the potential, but is not committed, while the other student has the commitment, but not as much potential. An Active-Active marriage is made up of people who have the potential for an excellent relationship *and* the commitment to make it happen. Let's look at one such marriage.

Jerry was 24 and Barb 22 when they met through a mutual friend in a large Southern city. Jerry was a successful computer programmer, thanks to the training and experience he received while in the Navy. She was preparing to graduate from college.

While Jerry appeared settled, his youth had been turbulent. Much of his life he had acted like a bowling ball, deliberately knocking over everything that got in his way. As a teenager he rebelled against his parents' discipline and spiritual leadership. Consequently he tried just about everything which could lead to trouble. Eventually he was arrested. The choice was simple: Join the military or go to jail. He chose the military, and while there his drill sergeant, new friends, and being away from home made him examine his life. Soon he stopped fighting his parents, society, and God, and started living responsibly. Now the rebellious years were past, and the valuable lessons learned, plus his programming expertise, personal drive, and individual character, gave him promise of a bright future.

Barb was the second of three girls and had always been reasonably responsible, compliant, and active. Her parents were easygoing, responsible people. Her dad worked at a local factory and her mom had a part-time job to help her daughters through college. Because half the school expenses were hers, Barb also worked part-time, yet she still had time for several extracurricular activities.

Things seemed to "connect" for Jerry and Barb. They had some mutual friends, similar values, and spiritual sensitivity. Jerry was impressed by her aerobic conditioning, her hard work in school, and her spunk. Barb was amazed that Jerry could be aggressive yet also approachable and sensitive to her as a person. They were soon making plans for a big wedding.

It was evident early in the marriage that Jerry and Barb cared deeply for each another and were highly committed to their relationship. Still, their different backgrounds meant considerable adjustment. Jerry's family was strong-willed, assertive, aggressive, and directed. Barb's family was relaxed, easygoing, and fairly nonconfrontive. Different bedtimes, eating habits, forms of entertainment, and conflict-resolving styles produced many challenges for Jerry and Barb to work through.

Barb worked for several years to build up a cash reserve before they had children. Jerry's job continued to improve as his reputation spread in the computer industry. After nearly nine years of marriage, they had two children, ages three and one-and-a-half. They were established in their church and the community and had many friends. But Barb, because she was busy changing diapers and communicating in "toddler language," had lost some of her confidence. She loved the kids, yet they were draining on her. She struggled to remain mentally alert now that she no longer had her job.

One evening when Jerry came home he announced with great excitement that they were moving to the West Coast. Barb tried to go through the motions of affirming and complimenting Jerry on his great challenge and opportunity. She wanted to be excited too, but he had caught her off-guard. In the past they had always talked through major decisions together. She was hurt that instead of talking through this decision, he had simply announced it. Barb was also overwhelmed by the thought of a move.

Later that evening Barb told Jerry that, although she was excited, she was also hurt and wasn't sure if she could handle a move. Jerry was hurt by her words. "Barb, you're not backing me. I'm very disappointed in your lack of support for me, especially when this is such a great opportunity."

"Jerry, I love you," Barb responded, "but I don't think you understand how disoriented I feel. You're asking me to leave close contact with my family, my friends, and my church to move to the West Coast where I know practically no one."

For the next few days, silence reigned in their relationship. Finally, one night after the kids were in bed, they broke through and started talking. Jerry admitted that he was hurt, and that he also knew he had hurt her. "Honey, I'm sorry. I want you to know that even though I really want to take this job, I'm willing not to. The bottom line is that you're more important to me than any job."

Barb broke down and cried when she realized again how much Jerry loved her. They embraced as Barb told Jerry that she was not opposed to moving. "I feel low on energy and confidence. I want to make sure that I can hold up my part of the relationship when we move." As they resolved their conflict and hurt, they talked the rest of the evening about their options. That opened up a whole new arena of creativity as they critiqued the jobs, their future, their goals, and their current situation. Finally they agreed on the decision to move.

Jerry and Barb turned a potentially bad situation into something that was not only better for them individually, but also for their marriage. Throughout their marriage relationship, Jerry and Barb have worked to maintain a balance between their individual endeavors and their joint acitivities. For a few years they jogged together. Later they started playing tennis with friends. That was not only fun for both of them but allowed interaction with other people.

Most of the time Jerry and Barb function well in their marriage. Both choose not to let difficulties and disagreements go unattended. Occasionally they do hurt each other, but soon after the hurt comes forgiveness, resolution, and a continuing, forthright, loving commitment to each other.

Notice in this story how much Jerry and Barb work at having a successful relationship. Many people think a strong commitment only means that there will never be a divorce. There are many nondivorced couples who stay together because of their commitment to marriage, but they are not necessarily fulfilled in their marriage. The Active-Active couple venture beyond that level. They have decided not just to survive their marriage, but to develop and fashion it for individual, mutual, and societal good. Let's look at the elements that make up this personality, and also at ways to understand, maintain, and improve the relationship.

Beginnings

This couple starts their relationship from a position of strength. Often they're in their early or midtwenties when they marry. Because they are older, they've usually finished their education, are established vocationally, and have developed their beliefs and values based upon their own persuasions, not just the persuasions of their parents or society.

Several studies have shown that age 24 for men and 23 for women is the best time to marry. Before that they are like a loaf of half-baked bread: It looks done—browned—on the outside, but it's only thickened batter on the inside. Between the ages of 18 and 22, most individuals need to take a hard look at themselves apart from their family. That's when they can clearly define their own individuality, strengths, abilities, and spiritual drive, and can deal with past hurts they may have experienced. When people have successfully laid the past to rest, accepting the good as well as the bad, they are much more eligible for moving into a positive marriage relationship.

In addition, there are practical reasons for being apart from the family before marriage. People learn to take responsibility for cleaning their laundry, cooking their meals, balancing their checkbooks, and using their time wisely. There is no one else to blame for bad decisions. Between 18 and 22, most of us figure ourselves out and get a healthy start on life, making for significantly less pressure on a marriage.

Outward Style

The general theme of the Active-Active marriage is "intentional commitment." Each partner is a distinct individual with gifts and talents. Each takes responsibility for his own behavior. And each has chosen to be forever attached to the other, working to make their marriage better year after year. This commitment does not come from a feeling of obligation but from a sense of preferring one another.

This couple is not intimidated by difficulties and disaster but takes advantage of them. They are mature enough to recognize the need for cooperation, sacrificing to make the relationship workable and fulfilling. Their relationship is described in Ecclesiastes 4:9-11: "Two are better than one because they have a good return for their labor. For if either of them falls, the one will lift up his companion. But woe to the one who falls when there is not another to lift him up. Furthermore, if two lie down together they keep warm, but how can one be warm alone?"

As I have interviewed Active-Active couples, I have concluded that they truly enjoy each other when they are alone and when they are with other people. Their strength lies in each contributing to the marriage rather than in depending on the marriage. They are givers, not takers; and in giving, each receives.

They attempt to solve their problems quickly. Though they know what they want, there is greater desire to consider what is best for the other person and to accommodate accordingly. Once a problem is solved, it becomes another confirmation of the strength of their marriage relationship, and serves to encourage them in subsequent conflict.

Every marriage has times when one or both partners struggle

with life issues. The Active-Active couple has the knack for supporting each other when there is need. If they are both employed, they take turns encouraging each other's vocational endeavors. They approach parenting as a team. They collaborate on their financial planning, home repair, and vacations.

Mutual support includes listening, objective feedback, and constructive criticism. For example, if the husband is thinking about starting a new business, the wife might say, "I have no doubt you can do it, Honey. But how does this fit in with our other business? And have you considered the number of hours it will take to get it off the ground and keep it going?" Constructive criticism is usually well-received because it comes from someone who believes in him. This same person who confronts him also takes pleasure in his successes. Jealousy is rare. They are even willing to allow each other time off from the relationship for individual growth. This might mean attending a conference for professional purposes or spiritual growth, or just a brief vacation from the "family battle."

Sex is not an ordeal but a good deal. It is truly enjoyed by both partners. Each takes initiative, and there is a fair degree of sexual experimentation. In the midst of foreplay, they inform as well as consult with each other on what is pleasing. Consequently, their sexual encounters are enjoyed and often orgasmic. They have "fun" in the bedroom.

In social situations, this couple is comfortable together. When people visit with them, it is pleasant because this marriage is made up of two people who treat each other with respect. They do not tear each other down with sarcasm but humor and tease each other in a fun-loving and caring way. They believe in each other and they aren't ashamed to hold hands and praise each other publicly. Ironically, even with all this openness, they do not stop being individuals. They are like a figure-skating duo displaying separate moves that are beautifully choreographed into a unified performance.

The predominant feature of an Active-Active marriage is the value this couple places on their relationship. Almost without exception, both partners consider success in marriage more important than any job or social activity. If a job change would weaken the family, they turn down the job offer, despite the potential professional and financial rewards. This doesn't mean that the couple won't get sidetracked at times, but their sensitivity to the marriage relationship usually guides them back to focus on what's best for the marriage.

Time is a pressure point for this couple. If they aren't careful, they can give away all their time to children, jobs, friends, church, hobbies, and shopping and not have any time left for each other. Lack of attention to each other can leave their marriage shipwrecked on the rocky shores of less important things. This doesn't mean that a person who highly values his marriage must have an insignificant job and stay home all the time checking off his "honey-do" list. What I am saying is that the Active-Active couple needs to remember what is most important in life. They must remain disciplined enough to maintain the marriage as the priority. It's not that other activities are eliminated—though some may need to be—but that they are put in their proper place.

Inward Experience

This husband and wife are free to be themselves. Their minds are not crowded with thoughts of protecting themselves from their partner. Confessing their hurts, dreams, frailties, vulnerabilities, and daily successes keeps the relationship fresh and alive.

They rarely, if ever, feel like the other is "out to get them." In fact, they usually feel that the other person is looking out for them. They are also confident that their spouse will be honest with them even when it means a disagreement. This builds tremendous trust. Inwardly, they not only expect loyalty from each other, they also rest in it.

The Active-Active personality has a marathon flavor to it. I am amazed at the stamina of marathon runners. Twenty-six miles of steady plodding is a world apart from a 100-yard dash. Long-distance runners know that they are in for the long haul, not the short puff, and that the best way to finish is to keep a steady pace through the predictable, critical phases of the race. Active-Active couples persevere through the tough stages of adult life. When she has a bad day and feels like her husband is not in tune with her, she does not fall apart. She knows that marital life has its problems, and that things will be better soon because the overall relationship is sound. She has enough common sense to realize that no mate she might have chosen could perform to all expectations or needs all the time.

This couple is objective about married life, allowing for mistakes without becoming pessimistic about the relationship. They may be disheartened, but they soon realize that a mistake is only a temporary setback in the marriage marathon.

Strengths and Weaknesses

The Active-Active marriage personality has many more strengths than weaknesses. One of the major strengths is the maturity level of the partners. They demonstrate maturity by being reponsible to the relationship and by their willingness to attend to their spouse's needs with the same energy that they give to their own needs. Mature people realize that life doesn't always go their way, so they bend and work as team players.

Along with their maturity, they display ability to negotiate. They work through problems rather than around them. When they discuss an issue, both of them are clear about the next step and what to expect from each other.

No doubt another strength is their commitment to the relationship. Their primary focus is on their marriage, and they do not allow other people or situations to infringe on that focus. In addition, they are secure in their respect for each other. They believe in their spouse, hope for his or her best, and genuinely love their partner.

Interpersonal affection is another strength. Children profit from this aspect of the marriage. Mom and Dad love each other and are proud to say it and show it. Hugs, love pats, and kisses are a regular part of this marriage. Children may be embarrassed or amazed at how Mom and Dad continue to find each other interesting.

Because Mom and Dad focus on their relationship, children not only see an example, but at times may feel excluded from their parents. "Marriage first, children second" is this family's motto. This is not to say that the children are not loved: They are. But marital love and affection serve as a primary foundation for parental love and guidance of the children.

There are a few weaknesses in this marriage, and one of them is the distinct identity of the individuals. Sometimes two strong individuals experience conflict because their individual needs seem contradictory. But outsiders are usually more uncomfortable with their intensive conflict than are the couple themselves, who know how to deal with it.

Another weakness is that of exclusiveness. Because these two folks get along so well, they may not feel a need to be involved with many other couples. Their relationship can develop into an "island syndrome," in which they operate independently of others around them. Though this is comfortable for the couple, it is not necessarily healthy in the long run. They can learn from others and also be an example of a productive relationship.

One important area to watch for in the Active-Active marriage is the influence of major life events. Rarely do problems develop from within their relationship. However, external events, such as the birth of children, job changes, layoffs, responsibilities with extended family, or individual traumas, can cause marital struggles. There is never a doubt that they care for each other, but at times they can find themselves being irritable with each other because of outside pressures.

Improving the Marriage

The Active-Active Marriage is not a perfect marriage. Like any other relationship, it is vulnerable to the continued stress and strain of life. This couple needs to rely not only on themselves but also on God. Their greatest danger is in taking the relationship for granted. That is why they need to focus daily on their relationship with Christ. This gives them a solid base from which to reach out to other people. Because they have so much to give, this couple needs to give to others. They also need to continue to monitor their progress and further develop their skills so that they always grow in their relationship.

The Active-Active Marriage

	Behavior	Feelings
Active	Inform, respect, and support individuality	Empathetic, self-accepting

| Active | Inform, respect, and support individuality | Empathetic, self-accepting |

Theme—Intentional Commitment
Major Problem—Family of Origin
Secondary Problem—Life Stages
Major Strength—Mutual Collaboration

CHAPTER 11

Common Marital Detours

Of the hundreds of people who have come to me for marital therapy, I have never found one who wanted to create an unhappy marriage. Though most couples start their marriage with high expectations and the best of intentions, some get caught in difficult situations and don't know what to do. Sometimes I say they're victims of marital detours.

When driving a car, it is not uncommon to run into a detour, especially in the summertime. I don't like them, but they are a fact of life. But detours actually serve a useful function: Because of road construction, they provide an alternate route. We don't go looking for detours, but if we ignore them, we find it much harder to reach our destination.

Detours serve a similar function in marriage. We may not like them, but they are real. We can complain, feel bad, feel guilty, and blame our spouse, or we can adjust to the detour and continue along the marriage journey. The secret to healthy married life is not removing the detours, but adjusting to them.

One or two detours should not ruin a marriage. However, when those problems are not resolved, additional detours can be crippling. We have examined the characteristics of healthy marriages, and marriage personalities with their strengths and weaknesses. With that as a foundation, let's look at the most common marital detours. I have classified them into three main areas:

Category One: Relationship Issues

1) Communication breakdown
2) Sexual dissatisfaction

3) Loss of hope for a good relationship
4) Values conflict
5) Vacuum of spiritual exchange

Category Two: Personal Issues

1) Negative emotions
2) Numbness—no feelings
3) Fantasizing

Category Three: External Factors

1) Excessive involvement of friends
   or family in the marriage
2) Murphy's Law syndrome
3) Financial stress

Let me clarify that we are not necessarily discussing unstable
marriage relationships here. If a couple decides not to divorce
because of their Christian beliefs, those beliefs provide protection (stability) around their marriage. Unfortunately, the
internal workings of that relationship may be seriously hurting.

When a couple has an unstable marriage, I do not suggest
that they escape. Rather, they need to take the initiative toward
improvement. Either partner can get the ball rolling by saying
something like this: "Look, you're bothered by this relationship, and I am too. What can we do to get out of this rut?"
The following issues are potential areas of improvement.

Relationship Issues

1. *Communication breakdown.* One of the most obvious
detours to a healthy marriage is dysfunctional communication.
This can be reflected in hot wars (shouting) or cold wars (silent
grumbling). But this is not just a reflection of the tone of voice;
even when there is conversation, many couples cannot resolve
their past or present conflicts.

The most common cause of communication breakdown is
that individuals dig in their heels and insist on their rights
rather than trying to negotiate and compromise. We see
this in most marriage personalities. For example, in the

Active-Resistant marriage, the partners go their independent ways. In a Macho marriage, the husband is more interested in winning and exhibiting his power and influence than in doing what is best for the relationship. Hot wars are common in Active-Resistant, Macho, and Kids' personalities; cold wars are more prevalent in Active-Passive, Helper-Helpee, and Pretense relationships.

Because of consistent frustration, silence sometimes becomes the pattern of the communication in a relationship. One or both partners may say very little in order to avoid overt conflict but be hiding frustration and hostility. Other examples of dysfunctional communication in marriage are:

a) Negative behavior—tone of voice which is biting and sarcastic, or negative facial expressions such as sneering, boredom, disgust, or anger.

b) Blaming—consistent attacking in which one or both partners are reminded of their failure and inadequacies.

c) Cross-complaining—a situation in which one partner brings up a topic to discuss, then the other partner adds another topic before the first one is worked through.

d) Multiple focus—an inability to focus on one problem at a time because of the multiple issues that face them.

e) "You" statements—one or both parties use "you" statements such as "You always..." or "You never..." rather than "I" statements, like "I am responsible for..." or "It was my idea and I would like to..."

f) Caustic comments—sarcasm, cynicism, or hitting below the belt. This includes making fun of personal frailties, vulnerabilities, and past hurts.

g) Dredging up the past—bringing up past problems and failures in the midst of conflict as weapons to attack the other person and reinforce one's own position.

Even the best of marriages are not immune from these dysfunctional communication patterns. However, they become a serious problem when a couple consistently uses these methods.

I should point out that communication difficulty may reflect a lack of skill. Some couples want to communicate but struggle at it because they simply do not know how. I've heard many people say, "We just can't communicate." Whenever I hear that, my immediate response is, "That is absolutely not true. You cannot *not* communicate." Everything we do in a marriage relationship is communicating something to our spouse. What they really mean is that they do not like the communication that goes on between them.

There is help available for those who desire to improve their communication skills. They might consult a counselor, or participate in a small group, or read some of the excellent books that are helpful to couples and individuals. Some of these are listed at the back of this book. I have also given additional pointers on effective communication in the chapter titled "Negotiation Skills."

2. *Sexual dissatisfaction.* The frequency and/or quality of sex can often be a frustration. I realize I take a risk in suggesting any normal frequency of sexual intercourse. From my own counseling practice, couples have spanned the range from seven times a day to total abstinence (or one or two times per year). However, one to three sexual encounters per week, or four to twelve times per month, is the usual range.

This is not to suggest that if you do not have sex within that range you are abnormal and wrong, since frequency may be influenced by factors such as the amount of stress related to parenting young children, job responsibilities, physical drive, or how well two people are getting along. Most couples report that frequency varies at different stages in their marital life. Frequency does not necessarily decrease with age. Many couples become sexually rejuvenated when their children are older and they have more time for each other.

Generally, men tend to complain about the lack of frequency in their sexual encounters while women tend to complain about the quality of the sexual encounter. This doesn't necessarily mean that she must have an orgasm every time. Some men measure satisfaction by their wife's orgasm: If she is not orgasmic, they feel emasculated. But women are generally more concerned about whether there was expression of love, caring, tenderness, and responsiveness.

Unhealthy marriages exhibit reduced frequency of physical contact and a lack of compassion in the midst of sexual contact. It is not unusual for a woman in an unhealthy Active-Resistant or Macho marriage to lie in bed at night praying to herself, "Please don't touch me. I can't stand it, and I don't know what I'll do if you try." She lies there in fear that he will want to engage in sexual intercourse when she can't even bear the tension of him being in the same bed. At times she may even feel prostituted in the midst of her own marriage, and may reject any of her husband's advances. On the other hand, a husband can also be the rejecter, denying his wife's sexual desires. Occasionally bitterness is so intense that there is no sexual contact whatever.

3. *Loss of hope.* Some marriages are characterized by loss of confidence and hope. The partners don't know where they are going and have no confidence that things will ever improve. We see this especially in Active-Resistant, Helper-Helpee, and Pretense marriages when long-standing problems are never resolved and a status quo relationship develops. The couple is treading water in the "ocean of marriage." Such a situation often spawns feelings of numbness, bitterness, or depression.

4. *Values conflict.* A serious marital detour is an extreme difference in values. Couples with conflicting ideas in too many areas (such as recreation, hobbies, political parties, food preferences, and spiritual beliefs) will usually experience disharmony. No matter where this couple turns, they find disagreement. It's not that they are intentionally looking to disagree—it's just that they have little in common. They deal with each other only about their disagreements, which seriously upsets marital harmony and balance.

5. *Vacuum of spiritual exchange.* Common spiritual values can cement a marriage. It is hard to destroy a relationship that is built by two people who love God and are committed to obeying His command to love each other. This couple can pray together and for each other. They can confess their needs and exchange ideas, thoughts, or feelings regarding their own personal spiritual walks. When one or both partners don't have such spiritual resources, there is less reserve to deal with the challenges which marriage presents.

This and the other detours we've examined are problems that a couple have in relating to each other. There are also problems that one partner can face that will adversely affect a marriage.

Personal Issues

1. *Negative emotions.* Individuals who are caught in an unhappy marriage frequently experience several negative emotions regarding their relationship. Their "laundry list" includes bitterness, anger, resentment, and fear. These emotions are usually the result of unresolved hurt in the relationship. After years of daily depositing negative feelings, people become so hardened that attempts at melting the negative emotions are like taking on an iceberg with a match.

Marriages where one or both partners have chronic bouts with depression, anxiety, and other personality disturbances find it hard to enjoy their relationship because so much time and effort is extended toward the psychological trauma and struggle. At this point it doesn't matter which came first—psychological problems and then marital problems, or vice versa. If someone has severe psychological deterioration, those individual problems must be addressed before healing can come to the marriage.

2. *Numbness.* The lack of empathy for a mate is very common in unhealthy marriages; numbness exists. It is as if someone has given such people a shot of relationship anesthetic, and they are numbed as a result. They feel neither love nor hate; instead, they feel nothing. This is a very deteriorated position in marriage. Many times I have heard, "I think he is a nice person and I really don't want to hurt him. However, I don't love him and I need to go on with my life." As a counselor it is much easier to deal with negative emotions than it is with someone who is numb.

3. *Victimized.* People in unhealthy marriages often feel victimized. It's easy to believe that the other partner is getting the best part of the deal, particularly in Active-Passive and Helper-Helpee relationships. These people rehearse all the occasions when they feel they were taken advantage of by their partner. They're convinced that if only the partner would change a few behavior patterns, the marriage would be better.

The focus of their mental agenda is on the other party rather than on themselves.

Along with that victimized feeling is an exaggerated level of sensitivity, which we often see in Active-Resistant and Macho marriages. Individuals take the behavior and words of their partner far too seriously. Every word, facial expression, and experience makes them feel threatened, abused, or perhaps abandoned by their partner. This exaggerated sensitivity can lead to a complete lack of trust (paranoia). Some people suspect that their partner is literally out to destroy them. A man might see his wife at the bank and think, "She never goes to the bank. After our fights over money, I bet she's cleaning out our joint savings account."

4. *Fantasizing.* Another serious detour in a marriage is when one or both partners privately fantasize about being single and/or being attached to someone other than their mate. When fantasizers hear about somone getting a divorce, they become jealous and think even more about what it would be like to be free from the constraints of marriage. They spend more time thinking about how to get out of the marriage than how to live successfully in it.

In addition, they may fantasize about a relationship with another person, whether it be a friend or casual acquaintance. This kind of mental unfaithfulness is often disastrous. Not only is it dishoneset, but it is not reality. When one imagines another person, he usually focuses on her strengths and then compares them to his partner's weaknesses. This can further discourage him from being actively involved in the marriage relationship. The fantasizer has lost hope that his partner will change in a specific area (weight, sexual prowess, vocational ability) which he feels is absolutely necessary for a happy, fulfilling relationship.

Fantasizers make a serious mistake by expecting fulfillment from their mates or another person. True and lasting fulfillment comes only through a relationship with Christ. Knowing and acting on this allows the couple to face reality and work constructively on their marriage.

Besides relationship and personal issues, there are at least three external factors that can detour a marriage.

External Factors

1. *Excessive involvement of friends and family in the marriage.* Chronic problem-filled marriages often lure other people to take sides. Friends, neighbors, or church members get recruited by each partner in order to reinforce his or her position, and so the couple is further divided. He has convinced his friends and acquaintances that she is at fault, and she has convinced her friends and acquaintances that he is at fault. The "friends," through their gossip and personal opinions, fan the flames between the couple, so that even if the husband and wife want to reconcile, it may be difficult.

Unfortunately, some communities and neighborhoods are vultures when it comes to the pain of a married couple. Unhealthy marriages serve as local soap operas for the public, providing them with entertainment and gossip material. This may sound bizarre, but many people get a kick out of another person's pain. If a wife decides to try to resolve the difficulties in her marriage, she can be ridiculed by her friends for attempting such an "absurd" move.

The only way to avoid this problem is to talk with only one or two close friends who will support you as a couple. When large numbers of people know, it is disruptive to marital reconciliation.

2. *Murphy's Law syndrome.* It seems that for some couples what can go wrong will go wrong. Upheaval may come from lack of job stability, financial insecurity, or difficulties with kids or extended family. One child may be sick in the hospital while another is having troubles in school. Dad cannot keep a steady job, and unemployment checks do not cover the family budget needs, so Mom has to work.

It is not that a couple invites life problems—they just seem to happen. Unfortunately, these put pressure on the marriage. There are well-established correlations between extended unemployment and divorce. The death of a child often causes marital upheaval and divorce. This should remind us that what "Murphy's Law" couples need is not our advice, but help in getting through their crises. This is not to say that these folks haven't contributed to their problems. However, they deal with a reality of life that others never know, and they need support, not criticism.

3. *Financial stress.* Sometimes too much money is just as damaging to a marriage as too little. The materialistic lure of fame or fortune can grab one or both partners. Their priorities center on what they can achieve or possess, and that becomes more important than the marriage. Other couples are just trying to survive. They wonder where the next meal is coming from or how to recover from bankruptcy.

Some marriages face a never-ending tension between a compulsive spender and a paranoid saver. One says, "You have to enjoy life" while the other says, "That's why I want to save now so I can enjoy it later." All of these produce financial stress, and can be destructive to a relationship unless a couple has a solid commitment to each other and the skills to work through their problems. While no marriage is immune from this pressure, Active-Resistant and Active-Active couples usually have better control of this area than other personalities.

Summary

A few detours are common in every marriage, and the three broad categories we've examined are certainly not a complete listing. But when eight or ten or more symptoms are present, you have serious marital difficulties.

So the question becomes "Can unhealthy marriages be cured?" Certainly! Just as healthy marriages can deteriorate because partners stop doing the things that keep a marriage healthy, so unhealthy marriages can improve when partners determine to work together to resolve their differences. It begins by realizing that God uses problems to help us mature.

While the apostle Paul was not writing about marriage when he confronted his "thorn in the flesh," we can use his insights to show how to deal with marital problems. In 2 Corinthians 12:7-10 Paul acknowledged that he had a problem that buffeted him. It was his human reasoning that informed God that he would be a better servant if he didn't have this "thorn." In the same way, we can honestly tell God that we feel we would be better servants for Christ if we didn't have some of our marital problems.

However, Paul discovered that eliminating his problems was not the answer. Paul made a significant statement when he said that he had learned to be content with his weakness, because "When I am weak, then I am strong." Paul learned that his very weakness introduced him to the strength of Christ. Likewise, I believe that when an individual or couple have difficulties in their marriage, that very weakness can introduce them to Christ's strength, which will ultimately strengthen their marriage relationship. Unfortunately, many individuals short-circuit that power by complaining about their problems rather than receiving God's help.

Where do you begin? First, jointly identify your marriage personality. (Remember—you're not choosing what personality you want, but recognizing what your personality already is.) Second, review this chapter and Chapter 2 to pick out healthy and unhealthy behaviors that are true of your marriage. Third, take the Marital Assessment Questionnaire found in the Appendix. This will help you evaluate your marriage.

Once you've identified the strengths of your marriage, make a conscious effort to continue them. Then pick out one or two weaknesses that are easier to work on, and design a plan for improving them. If you work on a couple of problem areas and then experience success, this is far more productive than rehearsing all your problems at the same time.

Major Problems in Marriage

As you evaluate your marriage through the first 11 chapters and the Marital Assessment Questionnaire, you will probably identify one or more root problems. We're not talking about the fruit on the marital tree, but the roots that produce the fruit. We're going to look at such things as dependency, self-orientation, family of origin, and communication (where most marital problems originate). It is my desire that you can find positive solutions in these basic root issues so that, no matter what your marriage personality, you can experience a healthier marriage.

It is impossible for me to escape the comment of James 1:2-4: "Consider it all joy, my brethren, when you encounter various trials; knowing that the testing of your faith produces endurance. And let endurance have its perfect result, that you may be perfect and complete, lacking in nothing." As you read the rest of this book, remember that problems are opportunities for personal growth. Don't be afraid to confront your problems. God can and will use them for your benefit.

CHAPTER 12

Overcoming Dependency

One of the most traumatic events in the life of a baby is when his pacifier is taken away from him. Screaming, yelling, pleading, begging, tears, and pathetic facial expressions are all part of his guilt-producing routine that says, "How could you be so cruel, so unsympathetic, so uncaring?" Eventually, after a few rough nights, the child discovers that he can live without that pacifier. There's no hard rule about when it is appropriate for a child to stop using a pacifier, but it must happen someday. A six-year-old sucking on his pacifier in first grade would seem out of place.

While weaning a child from dependency on a pacifier is an obvious responsibility of parents, we are often not so diligent in other areas. Too many permissive parents don't allow their children the privilege of developing a sense of identity and personal confidence. Others are so protective that their children grow up without learning how to deal with life issues. This makes them dependent on their parents, society, or other individuals. Often that person is their mate.

By dependency, I mean a condition of leaning on other people because of a lack of personal self-sufficiency. Dependency is transferring responsibility for our own lives to other people. It's blaming others for our own unhappiness. It's feeling intimidated by other people. It's obstinately declaring that we don't need others, though underneath we really do. It's constantly deferring to other people's opinions in order to be accepted. It's overdepending on others for our happiness and underdepending on ourselves.

Dependency should not be confused with low self-esteem, which has to do with how I value myself as an individual.

Dependency is a close cousin, but it reflects the view I have of my abilities and talents to handle life on my own. There are many talented people who secretly struggle with low self-esteem. The dependent person may accept himself, but he feels inadequate in dealing with life's situations.

The reason dependency is such a problem is that the true source of happiness is not our environment or our marriage, but our peace with God and our contentment in walking with Him. In marriage it is appropriate for us to lean and depend on our partner to some degree. That is part of intimacy and closeness. However, when two individuals constantly lean on each other, or one leans too heavily on his partner, that becomes a hindrance to the marriage relationship. One partner is drawing life from the other rather than giving to that person. Marriage is designed to be a shared partnership, and it works best when two people feel confident and capable to live on their own.

Lighting a "unity candle" in wedding ceremonies is symbolic of two individuals becoming unified in marriage. However, many people confuse marriage *oneness* with marriage *sameness.* They think that being one means thinking the same, feeling the same, and acting the same. Their goal in marriage is to be one in all areas of life.

When unity is achieved in marriage by sacrificing individuality, there is no longer a healthy marriage. For example, a husband and wife have only superficial unity if they agree with each other because they are afraid to disagree. A woman might not tell her spouse how she feels because she believes he will be offended. A steady diet of this behavior is a frustration to her and the relationship. She feels she is being dishonest, and he doesn't benefit from her input. Both lose.

Sources

In order to address the problem of dependency in a marriage, it helps to realize why we feel dependent. The major source of dependency is found in the family of origin. In some cases, children have no role models in their parents. Others have no guidelines to follow. The parents may have lacked internal peace or felt like failures in life, so their children experience embarrassment and/or a lack of security.

Dependency also develops when parents are overly critical. When a child is always told what he is doing wrong, that child doesn't gain much confidence. A child who grows up in an atmosphere of constant complaining about insignificant issues will feel inadequate. It may be reflected in poor performance in school or sports or in peer relationships. A child who does not have a place to "park himself" in the sense of feeling good about who he is and what he does feels in constant need of other people. Relying on others can be expressed in an excessive need for advice, hostility toward peers (the hostile person is simply covering up feelings of inadequacy), or avoidance of contact.

Signs of Dependency

Two statements are constant refrains among people who visit my office: "Unless he changes, there is no way I can live with him" and "I just can't live without her. I don't know what I would do." In the first statement, the person is saying that she is dependent on her partner's behavior for happiness and fulfillment. The second statement is a more obvious reflection of dependence. He is also saying that he is dependent upon her for his happiness and fulfillment. Both have the wrong focus, for genuine contentment comes only by depending on Jesus Christ.

Sometimes it is difficult to recognize when we're overdepending on our spouse. There are at least four signs that should warn us of this condition. The first is when we have difficulty accepting the differences in our spouse. He may be of a different political party, like different food, have different values with regard to money and socializing, or view child discipline from a different perspective. Our goal should not be to change our spouse, but rather to study him in order to understand him.

A second evidence of dependency is overcompensating or overprotecting a weakness or inadequacy in the spouse. Susan is a good example. She feels fairly confident and capable, and at the same time she wants to help her husband. He has trouble managing their household finances, so when a few unexpected bills come in, she knows that he will be upset and will worry about having enough money to pay those bills. So she takes care of the problem without saying anything to him.

Occasionally such action might be appropriate, but as a regular habit, this is a sign of weakness. Making him dependent on her indicates that she does not respect him. Susan is actually hindering her husband's development by not letting him learn to deal with money as a responsible adult. Also, she may begin to feel frustrated by the ongoing problem and distance herself from him emotionally.

Anger is a third evidence of dependency, especially in the Helper-Helpee (by either partner) and Active-Passive (by the active partner) marriages. This anger is the result of anxiety—the need to have things turn out a certain way in the marriage. It's reflected in loss of temper, nagging, or chronic complaining about the spouse's lack of responsibility.

Finally, a very common symptom of dependency is a feeling of being crowded or smothered. Smothering happens when the dependent person is either unwilling or afraid to make decisions on his own and is constantly asking for advice from his partner. This includes simple things like unwillingness to confirm any social engagement without checking with the partner or lack of freedom to make a 20-dollar purchase. If something goes wrong at work or at home, there is an immediate need to consult with the nondependent partner for advice and support. There are varying degrees to which the nondependent person feels smothered, but this goes on to some degree in many relationships.

Dealing with Dependency

The key to solving the dependency problem is realizing that each person is responsible for who he or she is. *That does not change after marriage.* We still have responsibility for ourselves, but now we have an additional responsibility—to support and aid the growth of our partner.

A few years ago my wife gave me a special card that emphasizes this truth: "Your heart is my heart. Your truth is my truth. Your feeling is my feeling. But the real strength of our love is that we share rather than control each other's lives."

Sharing instead of depending—that's the goal! It's two people, each with unique insights and abilities, giving to each other for their mutual benefit. Let's examine how this happens.

The first step is learning how to be content. I cannot escape the impact of Paul's statement in Philippians 4:11: "Not that I speak from want; for I have learned to be content in whatever circumstances I am." Note that Paul said he *learned* to be content, which implies that it was not automatic and that it required some time.

Contentment in this verse implies self-sufficiency. It is not self-sufficiency based solely upon self, but based upon a confidence in God and self. The reason Paul could be content in any circumstance was because his circumstances did not intimidate him—and remember that Paul was in jail when he made this statement. The reason circumstances did not intimidate him was because he was confident in himself and his relationship with Christ. He wasn't being obnoxious or presumptuous or overly confident, for over a period of years he had experienced enough successful situations involving his initiative and God's intervention so that no matter what happened it would be for his good and God's glory.

Self-sufficiency does not automatically happen for most of us. It is a learned behavior developed when we experiment with life and try to push the boundaries of what we perceive to be our personal limitations. Certainly marital upheaval is one setting where we are forced to push the boundaries.

Contentment and self-sufficiency go hand-in-hand with self-respect. If I am going to develop self-respect I must start by recognizing how God sees me as an individual. There is no doubt that you are a treasure in God's eyes. Many people feel uncomfortable with that statement, but it is true. We are highly valued by God because He has created each of us as unique expressions of Himself. It takes faith to begin to treasure ourselves as God treasures us.

One way to see why God values you, and consequently why you are important, is to identify your strengths, hobbies, wishes, and values. Some of you may not feel comfortable with these recommendations. However, if you struggle with dependency, no one else can solve that problem for you. The reason you need to identify your strengths is so that you can have an accurate assessment of the qualities and gifts that God has invested in you. Then your responsibility is to allow yourself, and God through you, to demonstrate those positive traits to other people. In this way you gain a fuller appreciation of God's work in your life, and your dignity as an important person in God's eyes increases.

For best results, take a stack of three-by-five cards and list at least 10 to 15 personal strengths—one per card. What do I mean by strengths? A strength is anything you do well in terms of vocation, habit, or hobby, and also positive personality traits, such as listening, cooperation, and tolerance. Many people have problems listing even three or four strengths. Force yourself to identify at least ten. At the beginning of each day, review your 10 to 15 strengths and select one to mentally focus on during that day.

Another helpful exercise is to compliment yourself on your strengths. You might say something like, "Charles, you really do have some capabilities and talents. You're not only a good tennis player but you also have some tremendous mathematical skills. You are a good cook, and you help your wife keep the house clean. Another strength I like is your organizational skill." The mental conversation goes on until you have completed the list of strengths.

You may feel uncomfortable doing this, but it is very important. You may think, "This is too much focus on me as an individual," but it isn't. You are recognizing your strengths and acknowledging the fact that God, in creating you as an individual, has planted within you certain capabilities and strengths. You must recognize these in order to use them, in your marriage as well as in your whole life, to bring glory to God. Another way to do this is to make your recitation a prayer: "Lord, thank You for giving me the ability to work well with children." Then review all your qualities, recognizing that they are given to you to use for His glory.

Most individuals spend too much time rehearsing their weaknesses while ignoring their strengths. They spend all their energy trying to identify what is bad without identifying and developing what is good. Often the best way to deal with weaknesses is to compensate by focusing on our strengths. The truth is that we aren't going to rid ourselves of all our weaknesses. But by using our strengths we are freed to work on our weaknesses, one at a time.

In addition to identifying your strengths, it is important for you to identify some hobbies. This addresses the question "What are you doing to enjoy life?" An important part of living life is pursuing some enjoyable activities. This helps bring necessary breathing room into our everyday pressure-filled existence.

Next, write a wish list. This list should have 20 things that you would like to do in your lifetime. They can be ridiculous or very practical. For example, you might wish to climb Mount Everest, or you might wish to buy a new car. You might desire to be a missionary, or you might want to win the ball game next week. The wish list has no limitations in terms of money, size, location, or personnel. Its purpose is to allow you to dream, to break out of your limited perspective, to gain a glimpse of what you can accomplish through God's power.

Finally, you need to list what you believe in. Write down your values. What is important to you in being a spouse? What does it mean to be a responsible worker, a responsible citizen, a responsible Christian, and a responsible parent? Most of us have these values, but often we aren't conscious of them. Identifying them allows us to know what we believe and why, so that our actions become a reflection of these values.

Identifying your strengths and focusing on them, and identifying your hobbies, wish list, and beliefs, will give you a better understanding of who you are and can lead you to personal appreciation. The more we appreciate and respect ourselves, the less dependent we are in our relationships. This allows us to move away from feeling that we *need* other people to feeling that we can *enjoy* other people.

One way to enjoy people and become less dependent is to take more initiative in social situations. Some people find it easy to avoid conversing with others, and instead to depend on people to approach them. But the person who is gaining self-respect is willing to take some risks.

The principle is similar in marriage: It is important for the dependent spouse to practice making more decisions. Before seeking the advice of a spouse, think through the situation yourself and try to reach your own conclusion. This process may be aided by recognizing your strengths, hobbies, wish list, and values.

The benefit of this process is that it allows you to stop blaming your partner for the problems in your marriage. If you want to feel victimized by your partner for the rest of your life, you can—but it will destroy you and your relationship.

Realize that feeling victimized is usually a reflection of your feelings of inadequacy and dependency. It is a mistaken belief that you are powerless to do anything about your situation. You are not powerless. As Paul learned to be content in all situations, so can we. Contentment doesn't mean accepting everything; it means feeling self-sufficient, able to deal with any circumstance. One of the best ways to deal with a struggling marriage relationship is to reduce the focus on your spouse and how he or she may have taken advantage of you. Instead, focus on your own strengths and dreams and values, seeing how you can be more completely developed as an individual created by God. This will ultimately be of great benefit to your marriage.

Dependency and Marriage Personalities

Because dependency is an individual condition, it is evident in all seven marriage personalities. The degree of dependency affects the strength and/or weakness of every marriage relationship. However, the problem of dependency is most clearly seen in Active-Passive and Helper-Helpee marriages. Because of this fact, I want to make some specific suggestions for those two marriage personalities.

In the Active-Passive marriage, it is very important that the active spouse recognize her dependency. The reason she wants him to change is not so much for his good but for hers. The more pressure she puts on the passive partner, the more he tends to withdraw, which makes her frustrated.

Instead of attacking and blaming, the active partner should confess her feelings of frustration. Here's an example: "John, I appreciate the fact that you say you will clean up the dishes while I go to the meeting. However, it really bothers me when you promise to do something and then I come home and it's not done. I'm tempted to be upset, but I think it's better to tell you how I feel and leave it at that."

If the passive partner doesn't respond, the next time she might say, "I was disappointed last time when you promised to wash the dishes and you didn't. I would like some clarification. Do you want to clean up the dishes while I'm gone at the meeting, or do you not? I'm not so concerned whether you say yes or no, but if you do say yes, I would like for it to be done, and if you say no, then I won't expect it to be done. It's really up to you." Notice that while she is honestly communicating her feelings, she is not depending on her partner to make her happy.

The passive partner must also recognize that he has a dependency problem. His natural desire is to avoid conflict, and so he depends on his spouse to carry the responsibility of the relationship. This is not a healthy way to live. It affects us physically with symptoms like high blood pressure, and it affects us emotionally, producing feelings of guilt, fear of failure, and self-doubt.

The solution is for the passive partner to take some risks and become more active. He has expected life to be easy, but it is not always that way. To gain the benefit of a happy marriage, he needs to honestly confront his partner, perhaps saying something like, "Helen, I find it very difficult to talk to you, but I'm going to risk it. I want you to hear me out before you say anything."

Another evidence of the passive person's dependency is his expectation that people accept him the way he is. To some degree that is valid, but it can be used as a manipulative ploy to not grow. It is important that you see that God's acceptance of you is complete, but an expression of that acceptance of yourself is to allow God to continue to move you beyond where you are toward maturity in Christ.

The Helper-Helpee marriage demonstrates unhealthy dependency, as we've seen earlier. In a sense, the helpee depends on the helper in much the same way as a child depends on its parents. But the helper is dependent too, for often the reason he helps is for his own benefit rather than for the good of his spouse.

The helper must recognize that when he continues to aid in the helpee's shortcomings, he actually makes his partner feel inadequate. He is really *not* helping. Suppose Denise is afraid to drive—though she has a license and is a capable driver—and doesn't like large groups. She depends on her husband, Dave, to drive her around town and to be with her at meetings. Dave, the helper, might actually help Denise by saying, "Honey, I love you, but I will not take you to your meeting tonight. You can drive to the meeting by yourself. I realize there are several people there who bother you, but you can handle it. I will support you and pray for you, but I will not do it for you. I care for you too much to let you continue to suffer like this.''

The helpee can become less dependent by putting a little distance between herself and the helper. One way to do this is to engage a close, trusted, responsible friend as an occasional adviser. This will remove some of the pressure in the marriage relationship. It is important that the helpee begin to inform the helper, and then act, instead of relying on the helper to act on her behalf.

Evidence of Progress

You know there is less dependency in a relationship when a partner feels less smothered, or when there are fewer expectations and the husband and wife are more tolerant of their differences. As a matter of fact, those differences may even become interesting and attractive. One of the most significant evidences of reduced dependency is when a couple experiences more freedom to talk with each other without complaining or withdrawing.

Dependency, in my opinion, is the most predominant problem in marriages today. It is the result of a growing deterioration of individual responsibility and sense of worth in our culture. We have become dependent upon government, neighbors, and friends to live our lives rather than depending upon our own personal character, worth, and value as individuals. If this is the case in your marriage, recognize it as God's open invitation for you to become more like the person that God intends for you to be. This will work in your relationship, for people who feel content and self-sufficient are better able to truly love their spouse.

CHAPTER 13

Healthy Self-Orientation

Self-orientation is a problem of overattention on self that is expressed in two very different ways. One extreme is commonly known as the egotist. His self-orientation is overt as he pushes for his own way, thinks he is the greatest, and aggressively expresses his superiority. The other extreme is low self-esteem. This self-orientation is covert, consisting of feelings of inferiority and of a person not getting his own way.

There must be balance between loving ourselves as God loves us and loving other people. The apostle Paul expresses that balance well: "Do nothing from selfishness or empty conceit, but with humility of mind let each of you regard one another as more important than himself; do not merely look out for your own personal interests, but also for the interests of others" (Philippians 2:3,4).

Excessive self-focus, whether expressed as egotism or low self-esteem, is a serious problem in many marriages. Let's examine each and see what steps can be taken to correct the problem.

Egotism

Egotism could best be described by the word "narcissism," which simply means an excessive interest in one's own appearance, comfort, status, skills, and character. Its roots are in the Greek legend of Narcissus, a beautiful young man who was so cocky that he refused all offers of love. As punishment for his indifference, he was made to fall in love with his own image in a mountain pool. Unable to possess his image, he wasted away until the only memory of his existence was a flower that bears his name.

Like Narcissus, egotistic people draw excessive attention to themselves. They feel compelled to put others down in order to prove their greatness. Their commitment is not to others but to themselves. They don't depend on others for survival; they can make it on their own. They do not blend well with other people, unless those individuals see life from their perspective. They insist that their point of view is always right.

Egotists have a tough time in marriage. Their interests tend to be in outside activities, such as job and hobbies, rather than in the home. This doesn't mean that they don't care about the marriage, but rather that they derive more fulfillment from their accomplishments than from their relationships.

The most obvious example of egotism is Mr. Macho in the Macho marriage. Most Active-Resistant marriages also have an egotistic partner in the resistant role. I have occasionally told egocentric partners that they are a lot like a rock in a blender. To them, anyone who does not fit in with their plans is a source of irritation.

The egotist has several fears which influence his lack of trust for people. He fears that he is not as significant as he would like to believe. He fears that he is not as independent as he would like to believe. And he greatly fears being controlled by other people. To him, being vulnerable to someone is being controlled. He is afraid that his vulnerability will be used against him, so he resists closeness even though, in many cases, he truly desires it. He cannot imagine divulging his future, feelings, thoughts, and goals to another person. Even though his fears are misguided, it is very difficult to convince him otherwise. The only person he ends up trusting is himself.

Recommendations

If you recognize that you are self-focused, one of the best things you can do is realize that it's not your nature to be warm and affectionate and caring. However, your spouse still needs your affirmation. You can compensate for your weakness by "scheduling" compliments and affirming actions such as special cards, flowers, and other forms of recognition.

Yes, this takes practice. So put a reminder on a three-by-five card at work or else at home in some place where the other spouse can't see it. Then while you're driving, or during a break in your day, identify behavior that you appreciate and rehearse an appropriate compliment to give your spouse. Then schedule when you will do it, and follow through on it. If you do this enough times, you may begin to feel like doing it, and it will become more natural.

It is also important for you to be right. Have you considered that you can sometimes be right by admitting you're not right? This means that you don't always have to know the right answer. You need to risk not always being in control. Though you do not often make mistakes, when you do it is extremely important that you take the opportunity to admit your error instead of making an excuse or blaming someone else for it. Yes, this is risky, because you believe your spouse will take advantage of you or make fun of your error. But in reality he will probably respect you more and you will have a stronger relationship.

It is important to experiment in small ways with trusting other people. For example, you might give your children some chores. After giving them your instructions, let them do the chores without any intervention from you. Then compliment them for what they did well, even if you must suggest some improvements.

The same is true for your spouse. You are afraid that she would not accept you if she knew the real you. The only way to find out is to take a risk and experiment with letting her know the real you. Jesus Christ is our model in this. First Peter 2:23 describes Christ prior to His crucifixion: "While being reviled, He did not revile in return; while suffering, He uttered no threats, but kept entrusting Himself to Him who judges righteously."

By entrusting yourself to God and to other people, you can effectively reduce some of your defensiveness and resistance to other people. Follow Christ's example when you are disappointed in your spouse, your children, or your friends. Instead of following your natural inclination to write them off, go the second mile. Give them another chance. Take some more risks. Though it's difficult, you will benefit by developing and becoming more productive as a person.

For those who live with an egotist, I have two recommendations. The first is the most difficult: Do not personalize his behavior. It is tempting to misinterpret lack of trust, distance, and pushiness as disloyalty and rejection. The self-focused person may provide things for you and perform duties to prove his love, and you will feel that this is insincere. Realize that he feels incompetent in interpersonal relationships and that this is his way of trying to compensate. If you can accept his attempts to demonstrate love, this will encourage him to do more, and in time it may become natural.

The second piece of advice may sound contradictory. The egotistic person has difficulty trusting and risking in interpersonal relationships. So instead of pushing him to be close and to share his personal thoughts and feelings, do just the opposite. If you happen to be married to a workaholic husband, encourage him to work more. The less you try to rope him in, the more he will feel a freedom to draw closer to you.

I realize you may be protesting, "I desperately need a close, affectionate relationship, but I'm not getting it with this egotist. How can I push him further? Don't I deserve a close relationship?" I agree that you should have a close relationship with your spouse, but you are much more likely to accomplish some degree of intimacy if you don't actively demand that your partner draw close to you. Pushing, arguing, complaining, and nagging will only drive him farther away. So why not try this approach, and give him some time to come to you?

Low Self-Esteem

One of the fun experiences at a carnival is the "House of Mirrors," where participants can see themselves in several different ways. One mirror may create the effect that a person is tall and skinny with a wiggle in the middle. Another mirror may show a person to be short and squatty with an oblong head. In both cases, the person's image is determined by the mirror he looks at.

In a similar way, parents are a "house of mirrors" for their children. A child's self-image is based on how he perceives others see him. The image is created by facial expressions, tone of voice, positive and negative feedback, patience or impatience, and general mannerisms.

Children are nonverbal experts and they "read" parents like a book. They desperately want and need approval from their parents, and if they subconsciously believe they are unacceptable, their self-image is distorted. They aren't mature enough to recognize that a parent can make mistakes or have a bad day. If Dad is irritable, it may be because of pressure at work or unusually heavy rush-hour traffic. But a child thinks it is his fault. If a parent doesn't explain the difference, and consistently criticizes the child and puts him down and tells him he is no good, the child is gradually programmed to believe that he is of little value. Even when he is an adult, this can have a definite negative effect on his marriage.

When I suspect this problem, I ask a person to tell me what he likes about himself. He is usually very uncomfortable; it would be much simpler if he could tell me what he does *not* like. His worth and value are not based upon internal personal worth, but on his external performance. He may actually be very successful in business or sports, but it isn't enough. He feels he has to be perfect to make up for his internally-felt shortcomings.

A woman with low self-image often approaches marriage on the basis of what she can get rather than on what she wants. She doesn't believe she can commandeer the individual who will fulfill her dreams, so she compromises. After all, if she doesn't feel good about herself, why should anyone else? If low self-esteem is acute, she may even think she doesn't deserve to be happy or successful. Then she may find it extremely uncomfortable to let other people love her because she doesn't love herself.

Recommendations

Probably the biggest challenge for people with low self-esteem is to begin to approve of themselves. The thought of liking themselves without condition seems overwhelming initially, but it can be accomplished. Also, these people need to allow others to love, approve, and affirm them—just as they are. When given a compliment, they need to learn to say "Thank you" instead of explaining away the accomplishment or the performance.

It's important to remember that valuing myself is my

responsibility. As a creation of God, I'm to be responsible to God as a good steward, and that includes viewing myself as God sees me. One of the best ways to confront low self-esteem is to literally accept all that we are, including the strengths and weaknesses. The person who rehearses only his weaknesses and denies his strengths is like a person swimming upstream in the midst of a flood. He can swim and swim and swim until he is literally dead tired, but at best he will only have stayed in the same place.

Let's examine again the example of Paul in 2 Corinthians 12:9,10: "He has said to me, 'My grace is sufficient for you, for power is perfected in weakness.' Most gladly, therefore, I will rather boast about my weaknesses, that the power of Christ may dwell in me. Therefore I am well content with weaknesses, with insults, with distresses, with persecutions, with difficulties, for Christ's sake; for when I am weak, then I am strong." Note that Paul discovered a very important secret to his success in life. He accepted his weaknesses as from God, and in the process they became the very source of his strength because they forced him to depend on Christ. The same is true for us. The person who recognizes his weaknesses is positioned to be used in a significant way by God. And that can raise your self-esteem!

The specific tools for dealing with low self-esteem are very similar to the ones recommended for dealing with dependency. I recommend that you do the exercises suggested in the previous chapter. Put your strengths on three-by-five cards and review them regularly. Identify your values and write a wish list. As you see your strengths and kindle your vision, you will begin to value yourself as a significant individual created by God.

Low self-esteem and egotism can be an issue in any marriage. However, the conditions are most evident in the Active-Resistant, Macho, and Kids' personalities. In a Kids' marriage, both partners need outside mentors to help them overcome their immaturity and low sense of worth. The other two personalities can often make improvements on their own. Let's look at them separately.

The Active-Resistant Marriage

The active partner often struggles with low self-esteem and seeks approval and affirmation from the resistant one, who responds with intimidation and hurt. The result is distancing and criticism. The more the active partner demands affirmation, the more he pushes the resistant partner away. One way to solve this problem is to observe how to catch butterflies. Often the best way is not continually chasing them, but standing still. When the butterfly feels safe, it often flies near you, and you can snatch it.

Chasing your resistant spouse sets up your own rejection, which reinforces your subconscious fear that you are not worthwhile. So stand still and leave room for the resistant one to come back into the relationship. Don't place heavy demands upon him. At the same time, get involved in your own activities. Gradually the resistant partner will begin to feel it's safe to move closer in the relationship. Admittedly, this may not seem fair or very appealing to the active partner, but it usually works.

The Macho Marriage

Mr. Macho's outward show of strength covers an internally felt weakness. His harshness, irritability, and insensitive personality push people away. Their rejection confirms that he must not be worthwhile. He often rationalizes the rejection, thinking that people reject him because he is mean, which covers up a greater subconscious fear that people reject him because he isn't worth much. That's why it is so difficult for him to be accepting, caring, and sensitive. If he adopted that behavior and people still rejected him, it would be a harsh blow to his pride. He subconsciously doesn't believe he could handle that result.

One of the best ways for Mr. Macho to correct this condition is to realize that he is going to be rejected in life, and to accept this fact. Rejection happens to everyone, deserved or not, and it's not all that bad. When Mr. Macho is put down or made fun of, but accepts it and realizes that it is not the end of the world, this reinforces his sense of self-esteem. He has confronted something that he has feared for years and dealt with it successfully.

Mr. Macho needs to stop demanding of people and instead start requesting. When he begins to *ask* for things instead of demanding them, he runs the risk of people not complying.

But he benefits in that when people do comply, they think more highly of him—which reinforces his sense of worth. In addition, it is important that he give compliments to his wife and other family members, and express gentle affection for other people with strong handshakes, pats on the back, hugs, and facial expressions that communicate approval.

How does Mrs. Macho, who also suffers from low self-esteem, deal with herself and her spouse? She has become so used to her "plight in life" that she continually reaffirms her low self-esteem. It is most important that she get on a "high-protein diet" of self-affirmation. She needs to find a responsible, caring, and insightful mentor—someone other than her husband—such as a close friend, counselor, or objective acquaintance.

Her new self-respect starts at home with her husband. When he makes a demand on her, it is important that she stand up to him in a positive manner. It can be cooperative, but on her own terms. She benefits both of them in the process, for it does not develop his self-worth when he gets away with pushing people around.

Though it may sound impossible, one of the best ways to deal with the surface anger and gruffness of Mr. Macho is through humor. Smile at him and say, "I wish you could see yourself in the mirror when you get gruff like that. You look like an old gray bear! You might try lightening up a little. You never know, you might like it!" Humor is a great method for removing tension in a relationship.

It is important to recognize that self-orientation, whether reflected in egotism or low self-esteem, is usually a reflection of childhood family experiences. So to progress in this area, it will also be necessary to come to grips with your family of origin. And that requires another chapter.

CHAPTER 14

Resolving Family-of-Origin Issues

Thanksgiving and Christmas are special times when families reunite, share life experiences, and enjoy one another. So why does my counseling load increase significantly at this time of the year? The people who come into my office are not anticipating fun and relaxation; they're dreading the tension and stress. Unresolved emotions and conflicts with parents and siblings that may lie dormant much of the year resurface before and during these gatherings.

It's important that we examine the family of origin—a person's parents, brothers, and sisters—because it has a significant effect on the health and personality of a marriage relationship. I find very few people who have not, at one time or another, had to work through feelings about their family. Often that processing of emotions does not take place until after a marriage is consummated. We cannot escape our past when we move into marriage. Our experiences affect how we view all of life—career, family relationships, and our own attitude toward God.

Marriage and family expert Dr. James L. Framo has stated that the best single prediction of how a marriage is going to turn out is based on the quality of family one comes from and the kind of marriage one's parents have. While it is not impossible to have a better marriage relationship than your parents, it is not easy.

A good marriage is not automatic, but is influenced by experiences during childhood. There are at least three ways in which the families of origin affect the stability and health of a marriage: in blending two family backgrounds; in dealing with negative emotions, traumatic events, and behavior patterns; and in postmarital involvement between a couple and their families of origin. Let's examine each one of these.

Blending Two Backgrounds

Family relationships defy understanding. Family therapists can identify communication patterns, but they do not understand how families have developed those behavior patterns and why they continue.

When two people marry, they face a challenge somewhat like climbing Mount Everest! They must begin to understand each other's family backgrounds, blend those backgrounds together, and develop their own way of relating. They must work through such areas as how to express affection, ways of expressing anger, vocational attitudes, discipline of children, vacation values, relating to extended family, spiritual understanding, work ethics, living conditions, and attitudes toward money. The challenge of blending increases in proportion to the difference in backgrounds and the strength of the personalities.

It takes a minimum of six to eighteen months for newlyweds to get through the "rumblings" of the adjusting and adapting process. Some tremors seem strong enough to register on the Richter scale. One spouse may have grown up in a family where disagreement and raised voices were virtually unknown; they either avoided conflict or dealt with it in a quiet manner. The other spouse may come from a home where complaints, criticism, and heated confrontation were common. These two people will struggle in the blending process because their negotiation styles are dramatically different.

If a couple in the first six months of marriage finds it difficult to deal with issues, they should consult a third party for help. During the first year or so of marriage, most individuals are motivated to work on their relationship because they have strong feelings of care and love. They should take advantage of those feelings and develop skills to deal with their differences, keeping in mind that their goal is not to change the other person but to make adjustments to each other.

Negative Emotions and Traumatic Events

Someone has said that life is a journey in which we are forever leaving home. One never escapes his childhood, but usually (over a period of time) is able to put those childhood experiences into perspective. However, some family experiences are so deeply ingrained in us that they negatively affect our marriage relationship. In fact most marriage dysfunction has a family-of-origin component. A person dealing with childhood family hurts is psychologically caught between his family and his spouse. The diagram demonstrates what I mean: The person is neither fully in the marriage nor fully in the family.

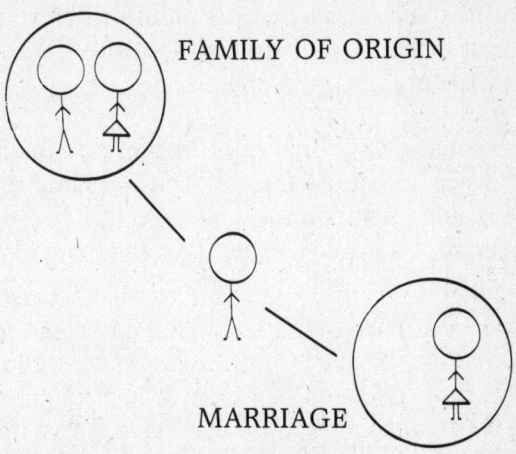

This person may seem involved in everyday marriage functioning, but mentally and emotionally he is captivated, trying to understand, resolve, and put away the past. He is unable to fully attach himself emotionally to his spouse.

Let's examine several ways in which your family of origin may negatively influence you and hinder your ability to function in marriage.

1. *Traumatic events.* In my office some patients literally fall apart when they talk about the events of their childhood. Some of their stories are horrifying: beaten with a board; forced to go on a milk route at three every morning; memories of a drunken father beating his wife. These are real-life experiences that leave deep emotional scars. For some people the trauma is not nearly as dramatic, but still very painful. They may have suffered with constant criticism or condemnation from parents or siblings. Others face a continuing mental replay of a father or mother's mean scowl of rejection.

I visited with one woman who hated her father and never wanted to see him again. Yet he had an incurable disease and she was obligated to visit him. As far as she was concerned, the sooner he died the better, for he had repeatedly beaten her and her siblings unmercifully. She was angry and bitter toward God, wondering how He could have allowed such a man to be a father. The trauma of her childhood spilled into her marriage. She could not trust anyone on an intimate level because she was deathly afraid of being hurt again. Her family had taught her that closeness was painful. Before she could begin to trust her husband, she had to resolve the bitterness toward her father.

2. *Guilt.* Some people feel guilt because of their parents' actions. It's very common for children to blame themselves for the breakup of their parents' marriage, thinking that if they had not been around, maybe their parents would have made it. This thinking is often subconscious, and of course misguided, but it's still very real.

Another source of guilt occurs when parents have regularly complained, criticized, or condemned the behavior of a child. No matter what the child does, he hears about it. Consequently he assumes a "my-fault" syndrome and finds it difficult to feel like he deserves much in life. This person finds it difficult to escape the mental tape recordings that he hears from Dad or Mom. He's "fat," "ugly," "dumb," "a klutz," or "shy." He was told such things as "You'll never amount to anything" and "The world would be a safer place if they didn't let you drive." He may go so far as to feel anxious and uncomfortable if things are going well for him. The adult who feels guilty because of constant criticism from parents during his childhood often sabotages his marriage by treating himself and/or his wife with an unending stream of criticism, just like he received from Mom and Dad.

If you were fed a continual diet of rejection, you may have established the habit of self-judging, in which you constantly evaluate and condemn your own behavior. You have faithfully adopted your parents' critical pattern, and now you treat yourself the same way they treated you. This guilt affects your marriage in two ways. First, self-criticism can so diminish your self-worth that you can't see how your spouse can love you.

Consequently, you discourage closeness and teamwork by not allowing yourself to be a full-fledged partner in the relationship. Second, a guilty person may take up this habit with the spouse, acting out his own frustration by inflicting wounds of criticism, complaint, and condemnation.

3. *Lack of acceptance*. Children desperately want approval from their parents. Some children are so anxious to be accepted that they perform in every way possible in order to earn recognition. They do what is expected and more.

Of course the compliant, performing child in most cases garners acceptance and affirmation from parents. Parents love to raise an easy child, especially one who also does well socially, academically, and athletically. However, a very subtle psychological mindset can develop in which the child gets the idea that he is worthwhile, and people will accept him, only as long as he performs.

After a while he begins to subtly and overtly resent that pressure. His resentment may grow until he reacts by breaking out of the bonds of marriage and away from what is expected of him in society. People in the community are shocked because this was a person who was always dependable and responsible—a model citizen.

Lack of acceptance can negatively affect a marriage. A person may be unable to accept genuine love from the spouse because she does not believe that she is lovable. She may even set up her partner to reject her by distancing herself as a test of the spouse's genuine love. This individual needs to learn that she is worthwhile, in and of herself, whether or not she performs. Unfortunately, this is not easy to do, and the spouse can't do a lot to help. She needs a third party, someone with whom she is not connected and for whom she does not need to perform. This person—perhaps a pastor or marriage counselor—can help her see her value and can help her work through her self-condemnation.

4. *Hurt*. Most parents, because they are so busy providing for their children and dealing with their married partner, have trouble always being sensitive to their children. Occasional hurt is a predictable part of family life. However, ongoing deep hurt

can result in shattered lives, with people seeking security and not able to find it.

Adults who have been deeply hurt as children tend to approach life apologetically instead of assertively. One young woman told me, "The only positive family memory I have is dancing around the room one Christmas with my grandfather and he said that he really liked me." The rest of her life was full of memories of family violence and being so scared at times that she would go into her closet and stand there shaking until the fights were over.

Hurt also comes from feeling ignored. One man said the only positive memory of his dad was a walk they took together one Sunday afternoon. Most of his childhood he felt like an unwanted child. This deep hurt has to be resolved or he can never truly open up to a wife. One way this man helped to resolve it was by writing a letter to his father, even though he was deceased, and expressing his feelings as well as his desire to forgive.

5. *Overprotection.* Marriages are often disrupted because the partners were overprotected while growing up. Overprotected children usually struggle with personal confidence. So much has been done for them that they don't realize what they can do for themselves. There is lurking, subconscious anxiety that undercuts their confidence in decision-making and interpersonal relationships. Overprotectionism does not allow a child to reap the consequences of his behavior, and this destroys his dignity and sense of worth.

An adult who has grown up under persistent overprotectionism may seek advice on the simplest of decisions, and even avoid decisions entirely because of fear of failure or of making the wrong decision. Such indecisiveness breeds unrest in most marriages because the partner cannot count on him. This condition often affects the Active-Passive, and the Helper-Helpee, and to some degree the Kids' marriage personalities.

6. *Closeness Anxiety.* A couple with whom I counseled both had alcoholic parents. During one interview the husband was asked to create a metaphor to describe his marriage relationship. He saw his marriage as one in which both of them were floating around in space, each encased in a plastic cylinder.

They could see each other and communicate nonverbally. However, though they were reaching out to each other, they could not touch because of their impenetrable plastic shields.

This is a powerful symbolic statement of a condition called "closeness anxiety." This occurs when someone wants to be close to the spouse but at the same time is desperately afraid of being close. This anxiety comes from two directions: A person is anxious because she is afraid she will not be close enough, and she is also anxious because she is afraid she may get too close and be hurt. This is extremely common in children of alcoholic marriages, though it is not unique to them. Closeness anxiety is almost always found in the Active-Resistant, Macho, and Pretense marriages, and sometimes in the Kids' marriage as well.

As a result of their negative family experiences, many adults carry mental burdens that weigh them down and rob them of a truly happy marriage. Resentment is one such mental burden: Bitterness imprisons and distorts healthy feelings. Some people take on a second mental burden—a vow that they will never be like the parent or parents that they hate. A vow like that inhibits their freedom to be who they are. They end up living with a negative perspective, trying not to be like someone instead of trying to reach their full potential.

A third burden is that of unanswered questions: "Why did my dad abuse me, and why did he never apologize or even acknowledge what he did to me?" Why certain things happened and why they were allowed to happen can create so much mental anguish that an individual struggles with feeling secure in a marriage.

Finally, there is the burden of carrying family secrets. You know something that no one else knows, but there is no way that the secret can be revealed because of the negative impact on other people. Therefore you continue to carry the burden alone. This is especially common among victims of incest.

These burdens can plague people for years. I know of individuals who avoid graveyards where family members are buried. Also, certain sights and smells remind them of negative events in the family. Other people suffer recurring nightmares about abuse from a sibling or parent. No one likes being imprisoned by these mental burdens, yet they persist.

Unfortunately, we cannot change our past, and it is useless to continue to fix blame because that won't change history or relieve the burdens.

Recommendations

The first thing you need to do is recognize that your parents wanted the best for you. You may react at this point and protest that I do not understand your mom or dad. That's no doubt true, yet there are very few parents who do not ultimately want the best for their children. Unfortunately, many parents who want the best also do some horrible things, and I am not trying to excuse their behavior. Instead, it is extremely important that we recognize that our parents were programmed by their parents. They were parenting the way they were taught, according to the model they had in their homes.

Also, it is important to recognize that parents are going through other life issues of which the children are often unaware. Such things as unemployment, marital discord, unpaid bills, and poor physical health can trigger abusive behavior. You can accept the strong possibility that your parents do care for you and desire the best, or you can fight it. It's your choice. However, refusing to accept that fact continues the mental suffering for you, not for them.

In order to relieve those burdens, identify some of your life difficulties that are family-related. You might review items one through six and then add any others you think of. Write them down, identifying a few specific instances from your past that illustrate your hurt. Then ask yourself, "Am I bitter or resentful toward my parents? Am I still trying to please my parents? Are there some unanswered questions that I would like to have cleared up?" List as many items as you can, as accurately as you can.

It is a clear mandate in Scripture to confess wrong attitudes. If we are bitter or resentful, we need to clear the deck of those negative emotions. Giving them over to God will not erase all the memories or all the feelings associated with these memories, but it can serve to release us from their burden so that we can go on with life. Some issues that you struggle with are not a matter of being wrong before God. You were hurt through no fault of your own. I suggest that you express your feelings of hurt and your unanswered questions to God. Better yet, write them down and read them to God. If necessary, find a caring witness to help you in this process.

The next step is to consider the possibility of confessing your negative attitudes to your parent(s). The Scripture indicates that confession of our sin to one to whom we have been embittered is necessary, according to Matthew 5:23,24. However, there are many extenuating circumstances which may complicate this for you. You simply may not be able to find it within yourself to approach your parent, no matter how convinced you are that the Scripture is correct. You can approach God and tell Him, but it hurts too much to face your parents. A second potential complication is that your parents may not be approachable. They may be in ill health, or the relationship between you may be such that they refuse to talk to you.

If you do talk to your parents, first make an appropriate confession of your wrong attitudes. Then express disappointments, hurts, and other concerns that you had as a child. This is not a "dump" session, but an updating for the purpose of improving your relationship. But be careful. If you have difficulty handling this encounter by yourself, bring a sibling, a close friend, or your spouse.

If a personal encounter is not possible or reasonable, then consider sending a letter or a cassette tape and request a response. If a parent is deceased, I often recommend that a person write a letter to the deceased parent, expressing some of his frustrations, needs, and hurts. It might also help to go to the parent's gravesite and talk to him or her there.

Sometimes memories of the family of origin are so painful that there is no way to even think about them. The mental images are like a chamber of horrors that gnash at you and try to render you emotionally immobile. Your only defense is to try to avoid them completely. But that doesn't solve your problem. You need to be free from that hurt, and this may require a professional therapist, a pastor, or a close and mature Christian friend. You need a witness who can accept the truth as you experienced it, and then declare the truth from the biblical perspective. This person can accept your pain and at the same time announce the healing of God.

As an adult it is important to recognize that you may never

get what you really want from your parents, whether it's recognition, approval, an inheritance, or even a heritage. You need to accept that fact, surrender your expectations, and accept the reality of the relationship with your parents as it is. This doesn't mean that it can never change, and certainly you should hope and pray for that. But you can't depend on the situation changing, because it may not.

Though none of us would ask for pain as a source of growth and personal development, it often serves that purpose. You might take some time to write down the advantages of your painful childhood and adolescent experiences. "What advantages?" you ask. Well, often the very negative events of our lives help mold and influence us in positive ways. For example, I know individuals who have a tremendous sensitivity to hurting children and adults because of the negative experiences of their own childhood. They are able to comfort and help these people because they understand the pain and have worked through it themselves.

Your character, life goals, values, beliefs, and motivation have been positively influenced by some of your negative experiences. Certainly there are struggles because of your family experience, but that is not all bad. If you begin to recognize the fact that those negative experiences have been used and can continue to be used for ultimate good, it helps reconnect you with life. You will benefit, and so will your marriage relationship.

Family-of-Origin Involvement

We've examined two ways that family of origin affects a marriage—in the blending of backgrounds and in the emotional pain caused by traumatic events in childhood. Our final area is the involvement of parents and in-laws in the marriage. Balance is the key word here. It is healthy neither for parents to be overinvolved in a marriage nor for there to be no active relationship with them at all.

Our family dog, Brandy, is an illustration of the balance we need. In four different pregnancies she produced 24 puppies. As soon as each pup was born, it wanted to nurse. For the first two or three weeks, our Brandy was fairly cooperative, but after awhile nursing those demanding puppies got rather old.

After six weeks she'd had enough—no more nursing. The pups whimpered, desperately searching for a warm breast full of milk. It was hard for our kids to hear the whining, but they soon forgot after watching the playful pups slurp up baby cereal. By quitting, Brandy actually helped her pups take off on their own.

The Bible says in Genesis 2:24, "For this cause a man shall leave his father and his mother, and shall cleave to his wife; and they shall become one flesh." The text clearly states that part of marriage involves leaving the family of origin so that one can cleave or bond to his marriage partner. Many marital difficulties are the result of one or both partners not leaving their family of origin. Their parents are always available when they need money, a listening ear, or a refuge in times of marital strife. Or the parents continue to impose themselves on the couple with unsolicited advice, unrealistic expectations, or excessive gifts or financial support.

It is important for both sets of parents to "cut the umbilical cord" as they watch their children marry. This is not always easy, especially if parents are overinvolved in their children's lives because of their own dysfunctional marriage. Their marriage stays alive as long as they're busy working with their children. When their children no longer allow that assistance, the parents have to face each other, and that can be disconcerting.

Sometimes parents have invested too much in the success of their children. They have dreamed for years that their child will be a college graduate, or succeed in a certain profession, or parent their grandchildren in just the right way. So Mom and Dad continue to focus on their children, even after the children are married, trying as hard as they can to position their children for success and comfort in life. In so doing, they continue to "nurse" their children instead of allowing their children to learn how to feed themselves.

A related problem is when parents are disappointed in their child's spouse, and exclude the spouse from the family, except for special occasions such as Christmas and birthdays. This kind of behavior often creates jealousy, hard feelings, and divisiveness in the marriage. When parents side with their child against the child's spouse, it's almost a sure way of driving the marriage closer to divorce court.

Recommendations

When dealing with the family of origin, there is one cardinal rule: Each person deals with his or her own parents. The daughter is going to understand her parents better than her husband, and her parents are likely to be more responsive to her. If the son-in-law attempts to run interference for his wife, it will disrupt her relationship with her parents. Another reason why this rule is important is what I call the "family understanding" that exists between children and parents. There are a few exceptions to this rule, but in most situations it works the best.

When overinvolvement with the family of origin is recognized, there needs to be some disassociation. It is important for couples to disassociate from their parents, not because they dislike them, but because it is the only way to deal with their addictive dependence on Mom and Dad. Occasionally if a child does not do this and the parents are aware of the dependency, then they must initiate action. This is not always pleasant, and it can be anxiety-producing, but it is necessary.

How do you go about the separation process? Sometimes geographic separation is required, especially if a couple and one or both parents live in the same community. When the distance between the two families is increased, there will not be the expectation to spend as much time together. There is no magic to geographic separation, but sometimes it does help.

If geographic separation can't take place, reduced social contact should be considered. This means that the couple should go beyond their parents for some of their socializing. The idea is to broaden their base. All of us learn from our social contacts, and if we limit those contacts, we limit our personal development, including our spiritual life.

It may also be necessary to approach the parents with some specific issues of concern. If parents are constantly questioning the couple's financial decisions, parenting behavior, social relationships, or domestic skills, the blood-related child should confront his or her parents with their overinvolving behavior and politely ask them to back off. For example, a wife might say something like this: "Mom and Dad, you know that I care for you and I want the very best for our relationship. However, my husband and I feel that at times you are still correcting and advising to excess. We appreciate the interest that you express in us and want that to continue. But at the same time, we need to be treated as adults. So please allow us to make our own decisions, and only give us advice when we ask for it."

Sometimes the parents may have to initiate action by telling their child that they have been presumed upon too much and that the couple needs to make it on their own.

It's not easy to deal with Mom and Dad and family-of-origin issues. Most people love their parents and don't want to hurt them. And parents don't want to hurt their children. Sometimes it's as if the children are out on the playing field of life and the parents are in the stands. The parents are clapping for their children and shouting occasional advice. However, couples must fight their own battles, and as they do they will gain self-respect and dignity, and there will be more respect between the parents and the child.

CHAPTER 15

Understanding and Preventing Affairs

Affairs are certainly not an easy subject to discuss, but a necessary one. Hardly a day goes by that I don't have to deal with this issue in counseling. The stories change but the theme remains the same—discouragement in marriage leads to affiliation with someone else.

As I approach this subject, I experience two contradictory feelings. On the one hand, I recognize the pain of so many people. Yet I also remember the restoration of so many marriages as a result of this devastating experience. As a matter of fact, I've become convinced that out of the very depth of despair marriages can be resurrected so that they are stronger than if the affair had not occurred. This is not to imply that we should encourage affairs. But if an affair has happened, we must approach it with the belief that the end result will be a better marriage.

Let's look at the story of Bob and Karen to see how an affair develops. This couple married when they were teenagers. At that time Bob was a laborer trying to keep bread on the table for his young wife and children, which eventually numbered five. He was aggressive, young, and hungry. He learned quickly, and after a few years he decided to start his own business. Hard work—six days a week and sometimes a seventh day—led to that financial security he had always desired. He bought a newer home, two cars, a microwave oven, and all the other modern conveniences a family could desire.

But Karen didn't share the joy of his success. She became more and more disheartened with the burden of raising five children with virtually no help from Bob. She was separated from her extended family and felt very alone, having little contact with the outside world besides trips to the grocery store and occasional visits with a neighbor. At times she succumbed to periods of depression and required medication to keep functioning.

It certainly was not premeditated, but one day a workman came to fix some plumbing. One conversation led to another conversation. For the first time in years she found herself talking to someone as an adult—and that someone was listening. She realized that she had not felt so peaceful in a long time. It was rewarding to think that someone was actually interested in what she had to say and listened without walking out the door in the middle of a thought to go to another job site. An affair was the natural result.

Bob came unglued when he found out. He thought he had done everything he could for his wife by providing a home and financial security, and her thanks was a kick in the face. He experienced feelings of rage, anxiety, and deep hurt. He also felt like a fool, and also guilty, realizing that he must have played some role in his wife's behavior. For days he was in shock, feeling numb and rejected. His bitterness intensified day after day until it reached almost unmanageable proportions.

At times Karen felt guilty too, yet she defended her actions. She knew it was not right, but at the same time it felt so good. She was a lonely person who needed some attention, and that attention came in the wrong way.

Affairs Defined

As you read about this marriage, you probably took sides. You may have found yourself sympathizing with Karen and her loneliness, thinking, "It serves him right for ignoring her all the time." Or you may have felt sorry for Bob because he tried to satisfy his family and was treated unfairly. But it does no good to take sides in this kind of situation, because both partners contributed to the dysfunction of the marriage. And both of them need to work through this if they want to reconcile their marriage.

Bob and Karen are now on the road to a happy marriage. Karen's affair was not the end of the world. But first they had to answer a critical question: Did they want to move on in the marriage and resolve their problems, or was this affair going to control their future? This was a decision that only the two of them could make, and they decided to move forward in their marriage, making the necessary changes.

The first step was for Bob and Karen to understand that an affair is a redefining of the marriage structure by shifting the primary loyalty away from the marriage partner. Most people think of an affair as an illicit sexual relationship. By that definition they fail to realize that Bob also had an affair. No, he did not have a relationship with another woman, but he shifted his primary loyalty away from Karen to his business. It is possible to have a primary loyalty for your children apart from your spouse. Or you can give primary loyalty to your job, church, volunteer activities, hobbies, or friends. Anytime our mental agenda and activities are devoted to a person, activity, or thing that takes priority over our spouse, then in the very strict sense of the word we are involved in an affair, for it infringes upon the exclusiveness of the marriage.

Affairs are a fact of life, whether we like it or not. The vocational marketplace in the last 20 years has escalated the contact between men and women—secretary with boss and professional-to-professional relationships. The very freedom of movement that men and women enjoy, along with unhappiness at home, are the chemistry of affairs. The attitude of our society does not help. Sexual promiscuity and extracurricular marital involvement are accepted in many circles and serve as entertainment for many people. Even those who won't actively pursue an affair can be jealous of those who do, for they can identify with their own unhappy marriage relationship and long for something more exciting.

Affairs take place because a spouse is dissatisfied with the marriage vacuum and is desperate for closeness and affirmation. When people are not receiving what they truly need and deeply want, they are tempted to look for it elsewhere. Sometimes an affair is a reaction to what the partner has or has not done, or even a payback for an affair. It can be a form of escape, such as when someone is married to a very dependent person. Many people enter an affair by sharing their problems; it feels good to be heard and understood and cared for by another person. That's what happened to Sam.

Sam had always been "Mr. Right." His dad was respected

in the community, with a successful business and involvement in many volunteer activities. Sam wanted to be like his father and consequently was very compliant with the demands and rules of his family. He went to the right school, got the right grades, performed in the right ways, and went to the right church.

When Sam married Jennifer, everyone thought she was perfect for him. They had children and became established in the community. However, eventually he realized he was not happy. Every decision he had ever made was based upon what was best for other people. He had never made a decision just for himself, and he had lost touch with who he was as a person.

This craving need to be his own person set him up for a relationship with Tanya. She listened as he talked about his life, and seemed to understand that he really cared for his wife and children, but also felt a sense of emptiness in his obligation to them. She empathized as he talked about how he both loved his father yet couldn't stand him. He felt trapped, wanting his father's approval but also wanting to live his own life and make his own decisions.

Tanya's ability to listen "hooked" Sam into the trap of an affair. She too benefited from the arrangement because she did not respect her own husband. Sam was aggressive, successful, and financially secure, the opposite of her spouse. She needed him because she wanted to move forward in life, and he needed her because he wanted to choose something to please himself without regard for other people.

Sam feels terribly guilty about his unfaithfulness. Jennifer has always supported him, and he feels obligated to her and really doesn't want to leave the security of that relationship. Yet he has strong feelings for Tanya. She seems to understand him more than anybody else, but he doesn't realize that this is mainly because he has talked more to her about his true inner feelings than he has to anyone else.

Critical First Steps

What should Sam do? Should he do what he knows is right or should he do what he wants to do? The problem with doing what is right is that he has always done what is right, and he is sick and tired of doing what other people expect of him. The problem with doing what he wants to do is that he knows it is wrong and will probably not succeed.

No one can make that decision for Sam. But I can assure him that if he chooses to do what is right, and is willing to be patient, he can gain new feelings for his wife, Jennifer.

If you have been or presently are involved in an affair, let me tell you what I told Sam and Jennifer, and Bob and Karen. First of all, the reason you were involved is due to tension in your marriage relationship. However, it is important to recognize that an affair is not on solid ground. You can't depend on an affair developing into a permanent relationship. Marriages consummated out of affairs do very poorly because the cornerstone of an affair is a dysfunctional marriage. Do not be fooled by the ecstasy of feelings and enthusiasm for this relationship. They are temporary and in most cases cannot stand the test of time. Attempts at breaking up one marriage to enter another are usually wrenching experiences that leave husband and wife decimated. Financial stress, bitterness, and problems with parents and children all assault the new marriage, destroying it as well.

Most of the time an affair is an unconscious expression of desperation by the affairing person. They are in an affair not because they want to get out of a marriage, but because they cannot live with their marriage the way it is. An affair seems the only way to motivate themselves and their spouse to get help. This is usually not a premeditated effort on the part of a person involved in an affair. But subconsciously the message being sent is, "I do not like the marriage the way it is, and I would like some improvement."

Another critical point is the necessity for the affairing person to let go of the affair. You cannot resurrect a marriage relationship with split loyalty. A choice must be made, and that choice is sometimes extremely difficult.

If you are the spouse of an affairing partner, you need to realize a few important facts. First, affairs do not break marriages; affairs come from broken marriages. The marriage was broken in the sense that it was not sufficiently meeting the needs of at least one partner. Individuals who are happy in their marriages rarely become involved with a third party.

An unhappy, unfulfilled partner is vulnerable to the affair auction block.

Realize also that affairs are rarely unilateral: They're bilateral. If your spouse has had an affair, or is having an affair, then probably you have also had or are having an affair. This may sound offensive, but stick with me for a moment. Remember our definition. Affairs are not only with *people*, but also with activities, hobbies, and other family members. The offended spouse, often unintentionally, has become too involved outside the primary loyalty to the partner. Two typical situations are a mother who becomes so focused on her children that she forgets her husband, and a husband who is so enthralled with his job that he ignores his wife. When the offended spouse appears disinterested, it gives subconscious permission for the affairing spouse to step out of the marriage. Consequently, both the offended spouse and the affairing partner bear joint responsibility for the marital breakdown. For your own good, do not allow yourself to place exclusive blame on the affairing person, because this will only further harm the marriage.

A third point is to remember that when you get beyond your hurt, there is great hope. This affair will test your commitment to marriage. Are you truly committed to your spouse for better, for worse, for richer, for poorer, in sickness, in health, till death do you part? Or are you committed only as long as it does not infringe on your comfort? There is great hope in this situation because it forces two people to focus on their relationship more than they have in years.

Remember the fire alarm going off when you were in elementary school? That fire alarm was so powerful that it motivated everyone to attention and action. An affair is a fire alarm to a marriage relationship. It motivates people to reconstruct their marriage. In the long run they may be better off than some of their friends who have drifted into a "so-so" relationship, but are not motivated to work on their marriage. This couple can be thankful, even though it has taken some deep hurt, that they are motivated to pursue a mutually fulfilling and supportive relationship.

Tips on Reconstruction

When an affair is discovered, it is usually much more

productive for the couple to solicit the aid of a third party, particularly someone who understands marriage relationships and how they function. The initial stage, from my point of view, is management. This couple needs to be "quarantined" so that the tremendous emotional strain is restricted within a circle of protection. If either or both of the partners begins to talk about this situation to a number of other people, the chances that the marriage won't survive increase significantly.

The less people know about an affair, the better. Unfortunately, when an affair becomes public knowledge, sides are taken, gossip spreads, and the couple becomes local entertainment. People feel free to give advice that the couple doesn't need. It's best to keep the problem to themselves and to trust only one or two confidential parties. This will make it easier to work through the pain and agony of this marital difficulty.

Management also recognizes that there is an initial shockwave, and that time is needed for settling. It recognizes that both parties are hurting, but in different ways. The victim feels offended and used and abused. The victimizer—the affairing person—feels trapped between obligation to a marriage and romantic attraction to another party. Both husband and wife need time to work through their hurt, and to express their feelings either individually and/or together in therapy.

It is important that the offended party not be allowed to threaten or issue ultimatums to the affairing partner. Ultimatums are an attempt by the offended party to try to reestablish a sense of security, but they rarely work. The offended party needs to learn to trust in a relationship with Christ, not in promises by the spouse.

Remember that the issue is not the third party; the issue is the couple's relationship. Constantly discussing the "whys," "hows," and "whens" of an affair only irritate the marriage; they don't improve it. If the offended partner harbors feelings of resentment, and attacks and questions the affairing partner, that sabotages the reconstructive process. Obviously the offended partner undergoes severe anxiety and questioning, but it is best to talk about it with the marriage therapist.

Management also means that the affairing spouse needs to regain confidence that the marriage relationship can work. Once he or she gains some of that confidence, there is more motivation to put energy into the marriage and to work on the relationship with some degree of comfort.

The management stage lasts anywhere from two weeks to two or three months, and sometimes longer. The next stage is the work and commitment stage. After a couple has dealt with their initial emotions, they need to start working on the areas of the relationship that led to the affair. By this point, even though there's still pain, a couple realizes that the affair is simply a symptom of their marriage difficulties. Their efforts need to be extended not in promising one another that there will never be another affair—though that is important—but in working to strengthen the relationship so that it becomes a source of fulfillment.

The problems identified in therapy will be addressed and worked through in this stage. This effort can last anywhere from two months to a year. This couple does not necessarily need counseling every week, but oversight by a caring professional during this time will be helpful, even if they only see the therapist once a month or so.

It is also important to realize that each partner needs time for healing. Two months to one year is normal, but occasionally it takes as long as two years. It is a mistake to think that only the offended spouse is experiencing pain. Both partners, in different ways, need emotional, psychological, and spiritual healing. Each experiences guilt, loss, despair, tension, and frustration. Neither has a corner on the emotional doldrums.

Trust is a major issue, and rebuilding it is a tricky task. The offended spouse has been deceived and now expects the affairing party to prove trustworthy. Bob felt he had to check on Karen, and was hesitant at times to believe her. Though understandable, this pattern doesn't work well. Bob has to learn to trust in God rather than in Karen's behavior. Though it was Karen's affair, and she needs to keep a straight course for herself and her husband, she cannot be expected to answer all his suspicions. Bob has to learn that the ointment for his emotional pain is developing a personal strength and security in Christ, then giving of himself to his wife so that trust will be rebuilt over time. Karen must also learn to trust again, giving herself to the marriage apart from the third party. She must believe that this marriage can work, and that it will not return to the ho-hum relationship of the past.

Remember that if a couple can handle this volatile situation successfully, they are establishing a relationship that is far stronger than previously. It is somewhat like a broken bone that becomes stronger than ever when it heals. The couple will have experienced some of the most difficult emotions in life and will have learned through them how to deal more successfully and honestly with each other. That becomes an important source of marital fulfillment.

I am convinced that this very difficult and heartwrenching experience can be turned to ultimate good. I have seen it happen over and over again. I would never encourage an affair, just as one would never encourage an accident, but affairs do happen and must be dealt with when they occur. Understanding why and how an affair took place can help two people handle it appropriately so that it will yield the best results. It doesn't have to be the end; it could very well be the beginning of a much more rewarding relationship.

CHAPTER 16

When Separation May Be Appropriate

In an athletic event, it's not unusual for a coach to call a time out when his team is struggling. This allows for regrouping and for evaluating what is happening on the field of play. When a coach calls a time out, he is not signaling the end of the game; he is asking for a brief intermission so his team can get their act together.

In the same way, some struggling marriages can benefit from a marital "time out." This may sound like a shocking statement from a marriage counselor. But keep in mind that my goal is stronger marriages, and sometimes the best thing possible for the long-term benefit of a relationship is a temporary separation—a time out.

The purpose of a separation is to allow each spouse to get a better handle on himself. Couples need to do this when, as much as they want the relationship, they have lost the ability to handle the relationship. They may be experiencing continued conflict, or one may feel totally numb and unable to express and cope with his deep inner hurt. The more they hurt each other, the closer they move toward dissolution.

Let me say again that the purpose of a temporary separation is to save the marriage. It's a time for couples to regain objectivity, to look in the mirror and recognize that they are participants in the conflict and need to take responsibility for their actions. It's a chance to develop themselves as individuals in order to give to each other. It's a training period, a time to "get back in shape" so they can handle the marriage relationship. This may involve evaluation of personal skills, needs, weaknesses, and failures. It allows time to read books about marriage and personal growth and to give special effort to spiritual exercise, including reactivation of a personal walk with God.

Separation is best when initiated by both parties, though usually one wants the separation more than the other. If one partner is really striving for separation, the other is wise to agree. When a separation is engineered, a third party (such as a pastor or counselor) needs to monitor the relationship. With the counselor, the couple must agree on their plan for being apart. The length of separation is usually one month to four months. However, they shouldn't try to determine the length of separation at the start.

While apart, the couple should have regular but limited contact—one or two telephone calls and one visit for a maximum of five hours per week. They should agree on how often the spouse living away from home will see the children. And they need an agenda for how they will use their time for personal growth and development. When a couple makes this kind of arrangement and fulfills it, then the separation usually has very beneficial results for the marriage.

I would encourage the spouse who may resist separation to be patient. Don't sacrifice your dignity by begging, pleading, attacking, or making suicidal threats. If your partner has left, let him go without hounding him. There is no guarantee that he will want to come back to the marriage relationship, but your chances are better when you allow him room to make his own choice for the marriage. You may feel a need to convince your spouse that you have changed. You may be tempted to use the argument, "We can't work on our marriage while we're separated." But this won't work. At this time, working on your marriage means working on yourself. If you want to guarantee the destruction of your marriage, then hound the person who has left, and he will probably make the separation permanent.

I realize that this takes great patience. But remember, you want your spouse to come back because he or she has chosen to, due to his or her own dignity and spiritual values, and not because of your pressure.

I have four suggestions for what each partner can do during the separation. First, it is important to do some reading. The reading should focus first on the Bible. Ask God to give insight and wisdom about you as an individual. Use the Scriptures not only as an instructor, but also as a source of encouragement and strength. It is also important to read some self-help books. Topics may include such areas as self-esteem, parenting tips, marriage relationship helps, and so on. Books serve as an objective input without requiring you to respond to a human being.

Second, it is important that you establish and maintain a relationship with a caring third party who is mature and objective, someone who exhibits God's wisdom as well as wisdom about life itself. Be sure that this person is not experiencing personal life difficulties at the time. It is more difficult for him to be objective if he is experiencing his own problems.

Third, involve yourself in a few projects or hobbies. This is not to keep yourself so busy that you never think or read, but to help you relax and feel good about yourself as an individual.

Finally, after you've been separated for a minimum of two weeks, it is important that you begin a process of self-evaluation. You need to ask yourself, "What kind of person am I? What have I done to contribute to this marital disarray?" You should look at your values regarding marriage and family life, and what you want for yourself as a Christian person in the long run. Hopefully, self-evaluation will help you face your strengths and weaknesses, then stimulate the process of further developing your strengths and allowing some adjustment to your weaknesses.

I am not suggesting that separation is the answer to every chronic marriage problem. It is not. I am suggesting that at times separation is the best avenue, especially when both parties desperately need a break from the action in order to recollect their thoughts and feelings. I have told many couples that a few months out of the entire length of a marriage is not that long—if used effectively for one or both partners to deal with themselves and reconnect in marriage.

CHAPTER 17

Negotiation Skills

Good communication alone does not make a marriage, but it is certainly evidence of a healthy, functioning relationship. Unfortunately, many couples are ill-equipped for effective communication, and this intensifies other marital problems. Without this necessary skill, it is much harder to keep two people together. Couples need to know how to effectively negotiate with each other. In this chapter we will examine the elements of effective communication and negotiation, and suggest some ways to accomplish this in your marriage. The first step in the process is learning to communicate who you are.

Speaking for Self

Someone has said that there are three kinds of responses in families—yes, no, and nothing. It is by far the most difficult to deal with the "nothing" response. The other person is left floating, with very little idea of what is going on in the partner's mind.

The first essential for effective communication in marriage is for each partner to be like a billboard. Billboards along busy streets and highways state a specific message: Use a certain bank, drink a particular soft drink, watch the local news program. The message is direct and clear, and it is my choice as to how I respond to it. Similarly, a couple needs to tell each other their message so they are not left guessing what the other thinks. Our job is to give our spouse messages about our beliefs, thoughts, and feelings. The purpose of this step is not to persuade, complain, or produce guilt, but to provide information. This is best accomplished by using "I" messages rather than "you" messages. "I" messages communicate my thoughts and feelings and imply responsibility for my own behavior. "You" messages communicate blame and avoid taking personal responsibility: "You always do..." "You should have..." "You never..."

In speaking for self, there are three levels of communication—what you want, how you feel, and what you think. A wife may say, "I would like to go out to dinner with you, but I feel a little afraid and embarrassed because I think it is improper to ask, since it's my birthday." Note that her declaration incorporates all three levels of communication. She could have said, "You forgot my birthday again!" or "You never take me out to eat. You even expect me to cook on my birthday!" But those statements put her husband on the defensive. By using "I" statements, she lets him know what she wants, feels, and thinks, but allows her husband to choose his response.

This form of communication shouldn't be carried to extremes. If you want the salt at the dinner table, it would be a bit ridiculous to say, "Dear, I want to tell you that I need the salt for my hamburger, but I feel embarrassed to ask you for it because it may interrupt your meal." However, on important issues, make sure you declare what you want, how you feel, and what you think. Suppose you need to discuss a situation with your spouse. You might say something like this: "Honey, there's something I need to discuss with you and I'm wondering when would be the best time to do it. It will probably take about five or ten minutes. We can do it now, if this is a good time, or later in the evening. When can we sit down and talk?" Use the same tone to tell your spouse what you think or want in specific, direct terms without trying to persuade, complain, or make him feel guilty.

It is not uncommon for someone to have little or no confidence as a communicator. I frequently hear comments like "I can't say it," "My words get all jumbled up," or "I get too upset." If you are not sure of yourself, try this kind of statement: "Honey, there is something I would like to tell you, but I really don't know how to get started or go about saying it. Would you sit down with me and let me ramble for a few minutes? You can listen to me and then tell me what you think I'm trying to say." Then don't worry about how you're communicating. Just tell your spouse what is going on inside you, and you may be surprised to find that your partner understands. If she doesn't, then let her ask some questions to try to clarify your thinking.

In our discussion of speaking for self, the partner must also be listening. That is the second important tool in communication. I like to call it "active listening."

Active Listening

Hardly anything a spouse does will communicate more love, respect, and caring to the partner than listening. One of the most important things I learned in graduate school was the significant change that takes place in a patient when a counselor actively listens, without giving advice or significant feedback. That's equally true for marriage relationships.

When I use the word "listening," I am thinking of more than just hearing another person's words. You need to be a student of your partner. That's why I call it "active listening": It's "tuning in" to another person in order to accurately hear what he is saying, both verbally and nonverbally. That's hard work! We must listen to the words but also observe inflection, tone of voice, and body language in an attempt to understand the message. Listening is often curtailed by a listener's defensiveness, lack of objectivity, or tendency to prejudge the message of the sender. It's easy to "turn off the ears" because you have "heard this before."

Here are four practical listening tips:

1) Stay within five feet of the speaker.
2) If you cannot listen, for whatever reason, agree on a time to talk about it later.
3) Do not interrupt.
4) When the speaker is finished, repeat back what you have heard and allow the speaker to agree that you understand or to explain further. If necessary, ask questions for clarification.

It really helps if the speaker knows you're listening. You can communicate by maintaining eye contact with your spouse, leaning forward, giving an occasional "uh-huh" or "please go on," and generally maintaining an open, attentive posture.

Let's see how this works with Ralph and Dottie. After dinner, Dottie approaches Ralph by saying, "Honey, I'd like to discuss our discipline of the children for a few minutes. Is now a good time, or should we set a time to talk later this evening?"

"Let's talk now," says Ralph.

Dottie sits next to Ralph, and they face each other. "Well, I've been concerned lately that the kids may be playing us against each other. I'm not sure that they know if we agree on what they can do and can't do, and when they'll be disciplined for disobeying."

"In other words, you feel we need to spend some time discussing the rules and the consequences when they break those rules?" says Ralph.

"That's right. I don't think we've done that."

"Can you give me a recent example?"

Dottie can go on to give an example from that day's activities. Once Ralph understands the problem, the two of them can discuss a solution. This kind of conversation increases a couple's confidence in their relationship because they are treating each other with respect.

Conflict

Most people consider conflict a destructive force in marriage, but it doesn't have to be. In fact, proof of your negotiation skills comes in the arena of conflict. First, recognize anger as a helpful warning that one or both individuals are offended. It's a signal that something isn't working in the relationship, and that the couple needs to discover what is prompting the anger so that correction can be made. Let me emphasize that this anger is not out of control. Violent anger—throwing objects, physical abuse, or vicious swearing—is destructive, not constructive.

Usually anger is tied to one of three basic emotions—hurt, fear, or frustration. When someone is angry, it probably means that he or she has been bruised emotionally or physically, that he is afraid, or that he feels short-circuited in accomplishing a goal. If a couple can deal with the basic emotion that spawned the anger, it is healthy for the marriage. However, extended conflict that avoids dealing with hurt, fear, or frustration damages a relationship. The Bible shares some wisdom concerning this in Ephesians 4:26: "Be angry, and yet do not sin; do not let the sun go down on your anger." In other words, don't let anger accumulate, because it tends to turn into resentment and bitterness.

What steps can you take when you are angry? First, tell your partner that you are experiencing feelings of anger. If the anger is often volatile, it is critically important that you learn some procedures to interrupt that destructive habit. One suggestion is to give each other the power to suspend an argument simply by raising your hand. The termination of the argument allows each of you to cool off, reconsider your position, and then come back together with the sincere intention of resolving the disagreement.

Second, the intensity of conflict is often neutralized by moving closer to the person with whom you are angry. This may go against your natural inclination, but if you do it anyway, you'll generally find that the decibel level drops and the intensity of anger is reduced. People who hold hands or are within three feet of each other do not shout as loudly and tend to resolve their conflicts more quickly.

Now that we've established the essentials of speaking for self, listening aggressively, and maintaining the right attitudes in conflict, let's examine one effective method of negotiation.

The Bargain Table

The Bargain Table is a structured meeting arrangement between husband and wife. It is not unusual for one marriage partner to complain, "We don't talk enough" while the other concludes, "You talk too much." The Bargain Table is one way to help satisfy both concerns. Both partners agree to meet for a preset amount of time to discuss important issues in the marriage. This way, the one who wants to talk is guaranteed at least some conversation while the resistant one knows there is a time limit—usually 10 to 15 minutes. The Bargain Table serves to help a couple nurture a relationship, plan activities, and resolve conflict. Here are seven necessary ingredients for a successful Bargain Table.

Step One—*Time*. It is important to establish a *regular* time for the two of you to meet. It doesn't matter when you meet, but it is important to keep that time commitment without too many interruptions. If you agree to meet on Monday, Wednesday, and Friday evenings from 9:45 to 10:00, then each partner has the responsibility to be there on time without coercion.

Step 2—*Place*. Pick a place in which you will not be interrupted. If you are constantly answering the telephone or responding to children's needs, this will cause problems.

Step 3—*Position*. Sit in chairs facing each other, knee-to-knee and holding hands. This helps you focus on each other and be more efficient in your discussions.

Step 4—*Length*. Allow between 10 and 15 minutes. This may not seem like much time, but you will discover that it is usually enough to talk through issues, share goals for the week, or resolve conflicts. It is important that you not go beyond the allotted time, so that both of you can be more efficient and more motivated to stay on the topic.

Step 5—*Frequency*. I suggest a minimum of twice per week, up to a maximum of six times per week. It's best to start with two times.

Step 6—*Leader*. I recommend an even number of meeting times because it is important to alternate leadership. If a couple meets twice a week, the husband should lead the discussion one time and the wife the other time. It is the leader's responsibility to determine the topic(s) and lead the discussion. It is also the leader's responsibility to make sure that the Bargain Table begins and ends on time.

Step 7—*Format*. The first item on the agenda is an appreciation statement. Each tells the other one thing that he appreciates about his partner. Then the leader introduces a topic for discussion—perhaps something to resolve, plans for the future, or just information about the day. The listener actively listens to the leader, then repeats back what he or she hears the leader say. After the listener has parroted the message back to the leader, the listener can ask questions to clarify what the leader said or give an opinion about what has been presented.

Bargain Table and Conflict Resolution

The Bargain Table is an effective method for resolving conflict. If one spouse is upset, he or she can request a ten-minute Bargain Table, which should occur within the next 24 hours. The one who is upset is leader and presents the problem.

The listener parrots what is said so that the leader is assured that the listener really understands the situation. Sometimes the matter calls for confession and forgiveness by one or both partners. Occasionally you may need to work up a new agreement in a certain area. Conflict may also originate with a third party (child, employer, relative) and may need to be discussed between the couple so that each understands and agrees about what is to be done.

When using the Bargain Table to resolve conflict, it is important to stick to a limited amount of time, such as ten minutes. This requires the two of you stay on the topic. Conversations usually deteriorate rapidly if little progress is made in the first few minutes. Progress is measured partly by the attitude that each displays. You can tell if each of you is open and receptive, so that even if the issue isn't resolved the first time, the attitude leads to productive Bargain Tables in the future.

The Bargain Table will yield one of three outcomes when used as a conflict-resolving device: capitulation, compromise, or coexistence. Capitulation is one giving in to the other because that seems easier or more appropriate. Compromise means that the two of you give in to each other and reach a solution that is palatable to both. The third possibility is peaceful coexistence, in which both of you agree to disagree.

When a couple keeps butting heads over an issue, that irritates the relationship. It's like picking at a scab every day. The best thing to do is leave it alone and let it heal. Sometimes the best thing to do with a disagreement is leave it alone for awhile. Time allows two people to settle emotionally so they can have a more productive discussion on the topic at a later time.

Most people like to try a product before they buy it. Why not try the Bargain Table for two weeks and see how it works for you? If you find that it helps improve your communication and negotiation skills, then make it a regular part of your weekly schedule.

CHAPTER 18

Marital Goal-Setting

Most couples start their marriage with great intentions, and full of mutual enthusiasm, love, and caring. But gradually, in the course of pursuing their vocations, raising children, buying a home, and establishing financial security, they can lose touch with each other. It's not intentional or premeditated, but it happens.

This last chapter could be titled "Where Do We Go from Here?" Hopefully you've identified your marriage personality and perhaps seen some detours that have taken you off the path of a healthy marriage. Now it's time to make some adjustments.

There's an advertisement on television that shows an auto mechanic standing by an engine he has just repaired. He informs us that the owner of this engine will have to pay him $450. It's really too bad that this had to happen, because all the owner had to do was use a certain oil filter that cost $4.50. The mechanic then looks directly into the camera and says, "It's up to you. You can either pay me now, or you pay me later."

Goal-setting with your spouse is an excellent marital filter. Sure, some marriages require a complete overhaul. But for most it's a case of maintaining love and working to develop relationship skills so the marriage will flourish. Of course, you can choose not to nurture your marriage. But realize that you will reap what you sow. When we water and fertilize the seeds planted in a garden, we reap a good crop. If we do not nourish the garden, we will reap a limited crop, or no crop at all. Marriage relationships are no different: They respond and produce according to the amount of nourishment they receive on an ongoing, regular, daily basis. The choice is up to you.

Purpose of Marriage

If I were to ask you, "What is the purpose of your marriage?" what would you say? Most people don't have an answer. We think about how much we love or do not love our spouse and how things are going in our marriage, but most of us have not considered that the marriage should have a clearly defined purpose. What businessman would be so presumptuous as to walk into a bank and ask for 20 million dollars without a plan to use and pay back that money? Yet many of us go through marriage without any idea of where we have been, where we are, where we want to go, and how we're going to get there.

The following is a mission statement that one couple wrote for their marriage: "Our purpose is to grow in love for each other, support each other's endeavors, and serve God by using our gifts and skills. The purpose is long-lasting, but the activities involved in fulfilling the purpose change with time." Let me suggest that you write your own mission statement. By clearly defining your overall purpose in marriage, you are much better prepared to develop and execute your plans.

Planning

Many of us spend more time planning our weekly shopping list than we do our marriage relationship. When a couple knows the purpose of their marriage, it gives their relationship a sense of meaning and destiny. A plan puts shoe leather to their purpose. It increases enthusiasm for working hard and being involved in different activities. It encourages growth and establishes a sense of security because two people know that they are working together as a team to reach a common objective. Let's examine a process that will help you establish goals as a couple.

Goal-Setting Process

1. *Evaluation*. The first step in setting goals is to find out where you are. I suggest that a couple take a day or two and

get away from their routines. If you can, leave the kids and get away to a hotel. Take a calendar, an open mind, and an honest heart.

Start with a relationship evaluation. Each of you should separately write down your observations of the following:

Our Marriage Personality is _____

1) Strengths of the marriage

2) Strengths of yourself

3) Strengths of your children

4) Weaknesses of the marriage

5) Weaknesses of yourself

6) Weaknesses of your children

7) Needs in regard to relationship with extended family

8) Financial condition

9) Personal needs

10) Personal desires

11) Children's needs

12) Spiritual condition

13) Social needs

14) Social desires

15) Needs of your living environment

16) Vocational needs

17) Vocational desires

When you complete this exercise, compare your views with each other. This evaluation process should help you "locate" your marriage, identify individual and mutual concerns, and give you information to help you set goals. If you have trouble knowing where to start, you might take the Marital Assessment Questionnaire. The questions will help spark ideas.

2. *Goals.* What do you want to do with your marriage now that you have evaluated it? No, you can't quit! You need to establish one or more specific goals in five different categories:

1) Marriage

2) Family

3) Financial

4) Personal

5) Spiritual

Try to make your goals as specific as possible. Some goals for spiritual growth may be harder to measure than a financial goal to save 3000 dollars. To help give wings to those hard-to-measure goals, identify one or more activities that contribute to the goal. For example, the goal of spiritual growth might be clarified by church attendance, a daily prayer time, a summer conference, or personal study. All of these are measurable activities that will help you know if you are making progress toward the goal.

Marriage Goals: Marital goals should take into account interpersonal skills, the sexual relationship, time together, social activities, and educational or enrichment endeavors for the marriage. Identified marital weaknesses usually prompt a few goals. If the two of you are too busy, a goal might be to have four Bargain Tables per week plus three weekends away together during the year. If the two of you want to meet new people and develop a mutual hobby, you might decide to join a ski club.

Family Goals: Each child, based upon his or her strengths and weaknesses, should be discussed as far as social, academic, and physical development. Diet, education, extracurricular activities, and chores should be identified for each child. By doing this, each of you develops sensitivity to each of your children. Children feel, even subconsciously, your individual attention and concern. So cater your goals for each child to his or her individual needs.

An important area for you to consider is how you relate to your in-laws. If there are rough spots, talk about them and develop some creative solutions. Another important area is how you approach family devotions. Details concerning individual prayer time with the children and/or Bible devotions with the entire family should be determined.

Financial Goals: Assuming that a couple is married 30 years and has an average income of 25,000 dollars per year, they will go through 750,000 dollars during their marriage! Actually many couples go through much more than that. No matter how you cut it, that's a lot of money, and it is a good idea to manage it well.

I believe that money is rarely the major cause of a marital dissolution, but in many cases it is a constant companion to problems that face a couple. It's not simply a question of who pays the bills, but an overall approach to handling money. After you have reviewed your financial condition and established your goals, it is necessary to prepare a budget. In your budget, identify planned spending, giving, retirement, and investments. A budget should be structured for monthly spending and reviewed at least every six months. There are good tools available to help couples budget, and several are identified in the Appendix.

Personal Goals: To be a viable part of a marriage relationship you need to be a healthy individual yourself. So it's important to identify areas of need and interest on an individual basis. Share your interests, educational desires, hobbies, vocational drive, and any other personal needs with each other and see how you can support each other in accomplishing those personal goals.

Spiritual Goals: I have found that two people who are individually taking responsibility to maintain their intimacy with God have an increased capacity for intimacy with each other. People develop closeness with God in different ways. What's important is that you as a couple collaborate together on what works best for each of you. Some couples study the Bible well together, but most do it best on their own. Some couples fill their spiritual needs by being in a small group Bible study. Some find it difficult to discuss spiritual issues. For them, growth is best facilitated in a large Sunday school class or a church service rather than in a one-on-one format. When establishing spiritual goals for your marriage, examine ways to exercise your spiritual muscles. Spiritual vitality comes not only from receiving but also from giving, so discuss an avenue of ministry, such as teaching a Sunday school class, singing in the choir, or helping to feed the poor.

Activities

Once you have established goals in each category, determine activities to help you fulfill your goals. If you decided to save 3000 dollars, then figure out how you will do it. Maybe you will deduct a certain amount from each paycheck. Or maybe you need to get a part-time job. Identify all the activities necessary to accomplish each goal so that you can determine if it is realistic. If you can't achieve all your goals now, prioritize them so that you can accomplish the most important ones first.

Schedule

Planning is the easy part, since you can write down goals and activities for each of the five categories but never get them done. What makes all this work is a schedule. You will need two levels of schedule. First, write down your weekly routine —when each family member gets up, school and work times, when you have dinner, when each person goes to bed, and the other predictable, regular activities of each week. It's important not only for the husband and wife, but also for the children, to have some feeling for the routine of family life.

The second schedule is a monthly calendar to record all appointments and events that are not part of the weekly routine—vacations, visits to the in-laws, doctor appointments, recitals, church events, and so on.

Even if you follow through on part of what you originally planned, I believe the exercise of getting away, looking at the purpose of your marriage, evaluating your family life, and establishing goals and activities will help your relationship. Do not expect perfection the first time you do something like this. Healthy couples constantly make adjustments as they reexamine their marital goals and the needs of their relationship. But if you have some skeletal structure, then you have an idea of where you want to go in your marriage and why.

Of course, no one is going to make you set marital goals, but remember that the people who reap the most from a relationship are those who have sown the most in it. God has planted a treasure in your marriage. If you nurture it by evaluating your relationship, establishing proper goals, and then planning and scheduling activities to fulfill those goals, then get ready to reap more fully the bounty of God's treasure!

APPENDIX

Marital Assessment Questionnaire

This questionnaire is designed to evaluate the health of your marriage. Husband and wife should fill out separate questionnaires and then compare answers.

Instructions for Use:

1. Answer each question by circling the appropriate number.
2. Respond as close to your true feelings as possible.
3. If you do not have children, omit questions 1 and 48 and answer the alternate questions instead.
4. For negatively worded questions, circle "4" if you desire a positive response. (Example: If you regularly pray with your partner, answer Question 4 by circling "4.")

Answer Key:

1	2	3	4
(Almost) Always	Frequently	Sometimes	Rarely (Never)

Circle only one response for each item.

1. Children take your energy to the degree that you have little left for one another.   1   2   3   4
   Alternate Question: The question of whether to have children is a source of conflict in your marriage.   1   2   3   4

2. Do one or both of you travel frequently away from the home because of career?   1   2   3   4

3. You have trouble enjoying your sexual relationship.   1   2   3   4

4. You do not pray for or with each other.   1   2   3   4

5. Is jealousy an issue in your marriage?   1   2   3   4

6. Do you regularly complain, whine, or think negatively?   1   2   3   4

7. Do you feel frustrated or unsatisfied after discussing or attempting to discuss an important issue with your mate?   1   2   3   4

8. Do you disagree over seemingly insignificant events or issues?   1   2   3   4

9. Do you or your spouse feel excluded by one or both sets of parents?   1   2   3   4

10. Do you have trouble making ends meet financially?   1   2   3   4

11. In your marriage, one or both of you tend to look out for "Number One" before the partner.   1   2   3   4

12. There is sickness in the immediate or extended family.   1   2   3   4

13. Are you moody?   1   2   3   4

14. As you look back on your parents' marriage, would you say they were unhappy?   1   2   3   4

15. When you go out together, it is with others, not by yourselves.   1   2   3   4

16. When you embrace your spouse, do you feel emotionally distant?   1   2   3   4

17. Do you find it easier to discuss your feelings with another member of the opposite sex than with your spouse?   1   2   3   4

18. It is difficult for you to playfully tease each other.   1   2   3   4

19. Do you question your spouse's love for you?   1   2   3   4

20. Do you question whether your mate really wants the best for you?   1   2   3   4

21. Do you experience extended periods of silence after an argument?   1   2   3   4

22. Do you doubt whether you really loved your spouse when you married?   1   2   3   4

23. Is your marriage characterized by dominance/submission?   1   2   3   4

24. You do not have clearly defined goals for your marriage.   1   2   3   4

25. Do you disagree on parenting philosophy and procedures?   1   2   3   4

26. Either one or both of you could be accused of being workaholics.   1   2   3   4

27. You disagree over the frequency and style of intercourse.   1   2   3   4

28. In your marriage you have trouble practicing forgiveness.   1   2   3   4

29. Do either or both of you have a tendency to be self-attacking or critical?   1   2   3   4

30. Do you have difficulty tolerating or dealing with your spouse's differences?   1   2   3   4

31. Do you talk to friends about your feelings and marriage more than with your mate?   1   2   3   4

32. Does the marriage experience occasions of blaming, shouting, or accusing without finalizing anything?   1   2   3   4

33. Are there unresolved hard feelings with one or both sets of parents?   1   2   3   4

34. Are you in debt?   1   2   3   4

35. One or both of you can be accused of being selfish and self-centered.   1   2   3   4

36. Substance abuse (alcohol, drugs, overmedication) is an issue.   1   2   3   4

37. Is your spouse moody?   1   2   3   4

38. In your childhood, family members rarely expressed affection.   1   2   3   4

39. Your schedules are such that you rarely see each other.   1   2   3   4

40. There is very little romantic feeling.   1   2   3   4

41. Your spouse seems irritable and has had frequent unexplained absences.   1   2   3   4

42. Laughing together is unheard of.   1   2   3   4

43. Do you question your love for your spouse?   1   2   3   4

44. Do you experience periods of silence and/or ultimatums, threats, and sarcasm?   1   2   3   4

45. When you review the circumstances that played a part in your marriage, you think of more negative reasons than positive ones.   1   2   3   4

46. Does one partner make the decisions most of the time?   1   2   3   4

47. In practice, your joint married goals usually receive less attention than your individual desires.   1   2   3   4

48. Do you lose your temper with your children?   1   2   3   4
Alternate question: Not having children is largely due to the instability of your marriage.   1   2   3   4

49. One or both of you is not satisfied sexually.   1   2   3   4

50. Your actions, in daily life, are frequently inconsistent with your spiritual beliefs.   1   2   3   4

51. Do either of you depend or lean on the other too much?   1   2   3   4

52. Do you find yourself trying to figure out, on your own, what your partner thinks or feels about things?   1   2   3   4

53. When you are together, the atmosphere is tense.   1   2   3   4

54. Are there social, financial, or vocational ties (or value differences) with one or both sets of parents which cause friction?   1   2   3   4

55. Do you disagree over your financial practices and the use of your financial resources?   1   2   3   4

56. Do you have trouble trusting other people?   1   2   3   4

57. It seems like there is one negative problem after another that faces you.   1   2   3   4

58. Have you or your spouse ever visited with a friend or professional concerning emotional difficulties?   1   2   3   4

59. It takes effort for you to stir up warm feelings for either one or both of your parents.   1   2   3   4

60. You do not get away (day, weekend) as a couple as much as you need to.   1   2   3   4

61. You feel there is a lack of motivation by one or both of you to give or to sacrifice for the other partner.   1   2   3   4

62. Do you ever fantasize about a relationship with another person?   1   2   3   4

63. Would you be afraid to pull a practical joke on your partner?   1   2   3   4

64. You imagine yourself single and free from marriage and family obligations.   1   2   3   4

65. Is either one of you stubborn and/or self-willed?   1   2   3   4

66. Your job (outside or inside the home) causes significant stress for you.   1   2   3   4

67. Sex is a battleground.   1   2   3   4

68. You have trouble agreeing on your spiritual convictions and practices.   1   2   3   4

69. Do you react negatively (defend, attack, withdraw) when your partner offends you?   1   2   3   4

70. Do you feel taken advantage of by your partner?   1   2   3   4

71. Do you or your spouse not talk about feelings, beliefs, or issues in order to avoid potential conflict?   1   2   3   4

72. Do you have difficulty resolving disagreements?   1   2   3   4

73. You cannot agree on the level of involvement you want to have with your families (parents, siblings).   1   2   3   4

74. You have trouble trusting each other financially. 1 2 3 4

75. It is a problem for you to have your own friends outside of the marriage. 1 2 3 4

76. Do you suspect that you or your spouse have unresolved emotional or psychological dif-ficulties? 1 2 3 4

77. Do you find it difficult to honestly say "I love you"? 1 2 3 4

78. Are you or your spouse more involved with outside interests (job, children, friends, hobby) than with your marriage? 1 2 3 4

79. You wish it was more fun to be at home. 1 2 3 4

80. You stay together more be-cause of external reasons (beliefs, for the kids, money, family) than because you truly love and enjoy each other. 1 2 3 4

81. Do you and your spouse com-pete for control? 1 2 3 4

82. Do you mentally rehearse, "If only he/she would, then I would..."? 1 2 3 4

83. You are on edge about how your partner is going to respond to what you say and/or do. 1 2 3 4

84. Is it difficult to consider your mate your best friend? 1 2 3 4

85. Do you keep from saying things because of previous misunderstandings, arguments, or frustrations? 1 2 3 4

Instructions for scoring and evaluation:

1. Total the numbers circled in answering the questionnaire.

2. Compare your score with the survey results by using the table below.
3. Read the description of each category following the table.

MAQ TABLE *

RANGE	CATEGORY
305-340	Optimal
275-304	Above Average
230-274	Average
200-229	Below Average
85-199	Dysfunctional

* Based on population sample results.

DESCRIPTION OF CATEGORIES:

Optimal: Couple functions exceptionally well together as individuals. They support, listen, and encourage each other and quickly resolve infrequent conflict. They deeply care for each other as they give and receive love.

Above Average: Happy with the relationship and care for each other. Negotiate well most of the time and display loyalty.

Average: Normal ups and downs. Relationship stressed occasionally and/or frequently. Struggles from outside plus misunderstandings and hurts from inside accompany pleasant, enjoyable experiences.

Below Average: Frequent difficulty. More downs than ups. Resentment, deep hurt, and extensive problems usually hound couple. Occasional times of pleasant exchange, but usually emotionally separated.

Dysfunctional: Unresolved, continuing difficulties. Abuse, despair, defeat, defensiveness and/or unhappiness. Relationship lacks skills and/or motivation to function.

Helpful Source Materials

Chapter 2

1. *National Study of Family Strengths*, by Nick Stinnet. University of Nebraska, 1981.
2. "Characteristics, Strengths of the 'Healthy' Family," by John Rosemond. *Des Moines Register*, July 22, 1984.
3. *Normal Family Processes*, by Froma Walsh. New York: The Guilford Press, 1982.
4. *Traits of a Healthy Family*, by Dolores Curran. Minneapolis: Winston Press, 1983.

Chapters 3-10

1. *Handbook of Marriage Counseling*, by Ben N. Ard, Jr., and Constance Ard. Palo Alto, CA: Science and Behavior Books, 1976.
2. *Klemer's Counseling in Marital and Sexual Problems*, by Robert F. Stahmann, Ph.D., and William J. Hiebert. Baltimore: The Williams and Wilkins Company, 1977.

Chapters 11 and 17

1. *Communication: Key to Your Marriage*, by H. Norman Wright. Glendale: Regal Books, 1974.
2. *More Communication Keys to Your Marriage*, by H. Norman Wright. Ventura: Regal Books, 1983.
3. *Alive and Aware*, by Sherod Miller, Elam W. Nunnally,

and Daniel B. Wackman. Minneapolis: Interpersonal Communication Programs, Inc., 1975.

4. *Mirages of Marriage*, by William J. Lederer and Don D. Jackson, M.D. New York: W. W. Norton & Company, 1968.

Chapter 12

1. *Telling Yourself the Truth*, by William Backus and Marie Chapian. Minneapolis: Bethany House, 1985.

Chapter 13

1. *The God-Players*, by Earl Jabay. Grand Rapids: Zondervan Publishing House, 1969.

2. *When I Say No, I Feel Guilty*, by Manuel J. Smith, Ph.D. New York: Bantam Books, 1975.

Chapter 14

1. *Healing for Damaged Emotions*, by David A. Seamands. Wheaton: Victor Books, 1984.

2. *Your Inner Child of the Past*, by W. Hugh Missildine, M.D. New York: Pocket Books, 1963.

3. *Psychotherapy and Growth*, by W. Robert Beavers, M.D. New York: Brunner/Mazel Publishers, 1977.

Chapter 18

1. *Your Money Matters*, by Malcom MacGregor. Minneapolis: Bethany House Publishers, 1977.

2. *Your Money Matters Workbook*, by Malcom MacGregor. Minneapolis: Bethany House Publishers, 1978.

BIOACTIVE CARBOHYDRATES:
In Chemistry, Biochemistry and Biology

BIOACTIVE CARBOHYDRATES:
In Chemistry, Biochemistry and Biology

JOHN F. KENNEDY, B.Sc., Ph.D., D.Sc., C.Chem., F.R.S.C., F.I.Biol.
Director of the Research Laboratory for the
Chemistry of Bioactive Carbohydrates and Proteins
Department of Chemistry, University of Birmingham, Birmingham, U.K.

and

CHARLES A. WHITE, B.Sc., Ph.D., C.Chem., M.R.S.C.
Development Manager, Vincent Kennedy Ltd.
Sutton Coldfield, West Midlands, U.K.

ELLIS HORWOOD LIMITED
Publishers · Chichester

Halsted Press: a division of
JOHN WILEY & SONS
New York · Brisbane · Chichester · Toronto

First published in 1983 by

ELLIS HORWOOD LIMITED

Market Cross House, Cooper Street, Chichester, West Sussex, PO19 1EB, England

The publisher's colophon is reproduced from James Gillison's drawing of the ancient Market Cross, Chichester.

Distributors:

Australia, New Zealand, South-east Asia:
Jacaranda-Wiley Ltd., Jacaranda Press,
JOHN WILEY & SONS INC.,
G.P.O. Box 859, Brisbane, Queensland 40001, Australia

Canada:
JOHN WILEY & SONS CANADA LIMITED
22 Worcester Road, Rexdale, Ontario, Canada.

Europe, Africa:
JOHN WILEY & SONS LIMITED
Baffins Lane, Chichester, West Sussex, England.

North and South America and the rest of the world:
Halsted Press: a division of
JOHN WILEY & SONS
605 Third Avenue, New York, N.Y. 10016, U.S.A.

© 1983 J. F. Kennedy and C. A. White/Ellis Horwood Ltd.

British Library Cataloguing in Publication Data
Kennedy, John F.
Bioactive carbohydrates in chemistry, biochemistry and biology.
1. Carbohydrates
I. Title   II. White, Charles A.
547.7'8   QD321

Library of Congress Card No. 82-9286 AACR2

ISBN 0-85312-201-6 (Ellis Horwood Ltd., Publishers — Library Edn.)
ISBN 0-85312-467-1 (Ellis Horwood Ltd., Publishers — Student Edn.)
ISBN 0-470-27527-8 (Halsted Press)

Typeset in Press Roman by Ellis Horwood Ltd.
Printed in Great Britain by R. J. Acford, Chichester.   **107939**

Table of Contents

FOREWORD 11

PREFACE 13

CHAPTER 1   INTRODUCTION
General 15
Nomenclature 16

CHAPTER 2   CLASSIFICATION
Monosaccharides 19
   Configuration 19
   Ring structures 28
   Conformation 29
   Naturally occurring monosaccharides .32
Oligosaccharides 36
Polysaccharides 42

CHAPTER 3   GENERAL CHEMISTRY
General Structures of Macromolecular Carbohydrates 46
   Primary structure 46
   Secondary structure 46
   Tertiary structure 48
   Quaternary structure 48
Effect of Structure on Solution Properties of Polysaccharides 48
General Chemical Reactions of Carbohydrates 50
   Oxidation 50
   Reduction 57
   Action of acids and bases 57
Derivatives 61
   Glycosides 61
   Ethers 63
   Esters 64
   Cyclic acetals 64

CHAPTER 4   ANALYTICAL METHODS FOR IDENTIFICATION AND DETERMINATION OF MACROMOLECULAR STRUCTURE

Isolation and Purification 66
Complete Hydrolysis 67
Methylation Analysis 68
Partial Hydrolysis 69
Periodate Oxidation 70
     Smith degradation 73
Alkaline Degradation 73
Chromatographic Techniques 76
Mass Spectrometry 78
Nuclear Magnetic Resonance Spectroscopy 78
Electrophoretic Techniques 79
Immunochemical Reactions 80
The Use of Enzymes in Structural Analysis 80
Molecular Size and Shape 82

CHAPTER 5   CHEMICAL AND BIOCHEMICAL SYNTHESES

Chemical Synthesis of Monosaccharides 88
     Ascent of series 90
     Descent of series 93
     Interconversion without changing the number of carbon atoms 95
Chemical Synthesis of Oligosaccharides 96
Chemical Synthesis of Polysaccharides and Carbohydrate-containing
     macromolecules 96
Biosynthesis 98
     Anabolism of D-glucose 101
     Biosynthesis of polysaccharides and other carbohydrate-containing
        macromolecules 108

CHAPTER 6   MONOSACCHARIDES

Acidic Sugars 116
Sugar Alcohols 117
Aminosugars 120
Deoxysugars 124
Nitrosugars 124
Halogenosugars 125
Thiosugars 126
Branched-chain Monosaccharides 127
Unsaturated Sugars 129

CHAPTER 7   OLIGOSACCHARIDES
Semi-synthetic Oligosaccharides 132
   Maltose and cellobiose 132
   Cyclomalto-oligosaccharides 133
Naturally Occurring Oligosaccharides 135
   Sucrose 135
   Lactose 136
   Trehaloses 138
   Raffinose 139
   Melezitose 140

CHAPTER 8   POLYSACCHARIDES
Plant Polysaccharides 142
   Homopolysaccharides 142
      Starch 142
      Cellulose 149
   Heteropolysaccharides 150
      Gums 150
      Mucilages 153
      Pectins 155
      Hemicelluloses 157
   Miscellaneous plant polysaccharides 161
Algal Polysaccharides 162
   Food-reserve polysaccharides 162
   Structural polysaccharides 162
   Sulphated polysaccharides 163
   Miscellaneous algal polysaccharides 164
Microbial Polysaccharides 164
   Teichoic acids 164
   Cell-wall peptidoglycans (mureins) 170
   Extracellular polysaccharides 170
   Gram-positive bacterial capsular polysaccharides 171
   Gram-negative bacterial capsular polysaccharides 172
Lipopolysaccharides 172
Fungal Polysaccharides 179
Animal Polysaccharides 179
   Glycogen 179
   Chitin 180

CHAPTER 9   GLYCOPROTEINS AND PROTEOGLYCANS
Classification 182
Animal Glycoproteins 186
   Hormonal glycoproteins 189

Serum and plasma glycoproteins. 193
Immunoglobulins 196
Blood-group substances 201
Involvement in diseases. 201
Plant and Algal Glycoproteins 206
Lectins 209
Proteoglycans and Glycosaminoglycans 211
Nomenclature. 212
Structures 215
Biological functions. 221
Involvement in diseases. 224

CHAPTER 10 GLYCOLIPIDS
Animal Glycolipids 231
Glycosylceramides (cerebrosides) 233
Gangliosides. 237
Globosides. 237
Miscellaneous animal glycolipids. 237
Involvement in disease 242
Plant and Algal Glycolipids 242
Glycosylglycerides. 243
Miscellaneous glycolipids 244
Microbial Glycolipids 245
Glycosylglycerides. 245
Phospholipids. 246
Carbohydrate esters. 247
Carbohydrate glycosides. 248

CHAPTER 11 NUCLEIC ACIDS
Primary Structure 250
Secondary Structure of DNA. 254
Secondary Structure of RNA. 256
Tertiary Structure of Nucleic Acids. 257
Function of Nucleic Acids. 259
Genetic Engineering. 263

CHAPTER 12 ANTIBIOTICS
Nucleoside Antibiotics 272
Purine derivatives 272
Pyrimidine derivatives 274
Antibiotics containing Aromatic Groups 275

Macrolide Antibiotics.....................277
  Polyene derivatives 277
  Macrocyclic-lactone derivatives (macrolides)...............277
Aminoglycoside Antibiotics.....................279
  Streptamine derivatives.....................280
  Deoxystreptamine derivatives 280
  Miscellaneous aminoglycoside antibiotics...................283
Miscellaneous Carbohydrate-containing Antibiotics 284
Biological Activity.....................284

CHAPTER 13 SYNTHETIC DERIVATIVES OF POLYSACCHARIDES
  Dye Derivatives.....................288
  Alkyl Ethers.....................289
  Cyclic Carbonates 291
  Cyclic Imidocarbonates 293
  Xanthates 294
  Applications of Synthetic Polysaccharide derivatives 295
  Chromatographic media 295
  Immobilised biologically active molecules 295
    Immobilised enzymes.....................295
    Immunoabsorbents 301
    Affinity chromatography media.....................302
    Immobilised antibiotics 303
    Immobilised polysaccharides.....................304
    Immobilised nucleic acids.....................304

CHAPTER 14 TECHNOLOGICAL ASPECTS AND APPLICATIONS
  Traditional Applications.....................305
    Construction and packaging uses 305
    Food and brewing uses.....................306
    Textile uses 306
    Pharmaceutical and cosmetic uses.....................306
    Other uses 307
  New Applications and Future Trends 307
    Oil industry 307
    Food industry.....................309
    Pharmaceutical and cosmetic industries 310
    Other uses 310
  New Production Technology 311

REFERENCES.....................312

INDEX 319

Foreword

The last 10-15 years have seen substantial progress in many areas of carbohydrate chemistry, biochemistry and biology. For example, 'the new organic chemistry' which uses understanding of stereochemistry and reaction mechanisms and aims for predictive and specific synthetic routes, has been fully developed and exploited with carbohydrates; biosynthetic pathways of glycoconjugates have now been largely elucidated: the stereochemistry of glycan chains has become much better understood and powerful physical methodologies are now available for investigations in this area: there has been much activity with new technological exploitations such as oilfield chemicals and graft copolymers; carbohydrates have been significant in the emergence of practical biotechnology, for example in enzymic routes to sweeteners and as substrates for and products of fermentation.

If progress has been made, challenges also remain. The long recognised biological functions of carbohydrates are in the storage and mobilisation of energy and in contributing to the integrity of cells and tissues through their structural and water binding properties; many proposals have recently been made however, that they could have biological importance of additional and general types, perhaps especially in intra- and inter-cellular recognition events. This has some support from newly discovered phenomena such as the influence of carbohydrate sequence on clearance of serum glycoproteins from circulation but the generality of such a function remains to be established. It might turn out to be an oversimplification to suppose that the function of a carbohydrate moiety can be dissected away from that of the larger molecule of which it may be a part. Nevertheless, the conserved nature of carbohydrate covalent structures, the substantial energy that is expended, and the considerable amount of genetic information that is stored for their synthesis would all suggest that glycoconjugates in particular have biological importance beyond our present level of understanding. Such questions will guarantee that a lively interest in carbohydrates will continue and indeed that knowledge of carbohydrates will be necessary background for diverse investigations in years to come.

Despite the considerable progress made and the importance of problems that remain, it is surprising and indeed unfortunate that no advanced and up-to-date text book of general scope has been available in this area for many years. Drs Kennedy and White are to be congratulated for deciding to write the present book to fill an important gap.

Dr. D. A. REES, D.Sc., F.R.S.
Director, National Institute for Medical Research
Medical Research Council
October 1982
Mill Hill, London, UK

Preface

The study of carbohydrates has always been of secondary importance in comparison to the study of other biological macromolecules such as proteins and nucleic acids, but the recent interest in biotechnology and renewable sources of raw materials has brought about a general upsurge of interest. For those of us who have been involved in carbohydrates for many years this second rate status has always seemed unjust and irrational and due, in part, to the lack of suitable texts which cover the whole range of interest from chemistry through biochemistry to biology of all aspects of carbohydrates from the simple building blocks (monosaccharides) through the carbohydrate polymers (oligosaccharides and polysaccharides) to carbohydrate-containing macromolecules (glycoproteins, proteoglycans, nucleic acids, lipids, antibiotics, etc.). In fact, this lack of a suitable text for students was felt personally by one of us and was the instigation of the many ideas over almost 10 years which have culminated in the production of this text.

It has been our principle aim to provide, under one cover, a full description of the chemistry, biochemistry, and biology of all groups of carbohydrates and provide an introduction to their technological aspects suitable for undergraduate use. Whilst we appreciate that the resulting text is in no way comprehensive in depth or coverage, we believe that this book will not only provide a sound basis for those reading for an Honours degree course but also provide a valuable aid to those embarking on, or involved in, carbohydrate research in all its aspects and to those academics and industrialists who are not specialists in, but require a working knowledge of, the many aspects of carbohydrates. For these reasons we have assumed no previous knowledge of carbohydrates, but a general knowledge of organic chemistry is required.

In order to teach new students, and re-educate existing specialists, we have based our nomenclature on that which is now being recommended by the International Union of Pure and Applied Chemistry and the International Union of Biochemistry and provided many illustrations and tables to allow those not familiar with the new accepted nomenclature to convert to it whilst at the same time allow new students to easily understand much of the older literature which is characterised by its use of trivial rather than systematic nomenclature. From our experiences of teaching students we have based much of our discussions on the pictorial approach to enable the reader to visualise the subtle stereochemical relationships which are the most important aspects of carbohydrate structures. For this pictorial approach we have preferred to use conformational structures rather than the traditional Haworth structures since the former provide a better understanding of the stereochemistry involved.

The authors wish to thank many friends and colleagues for their assistance in making it possible for us to write this book. Professors M. Stacey, C.B.E., F.R.S. and S. A. Barker are thanked for their help and interest in the early stages of our careers, Dr. R. S. Tipson for his valuable help in reading a substantial part of the manuscript and his advice on many aspects of nomenclature, Drs. E. Morris, R. Gigg, E. Tarelli and V. A. McKusick for their helpful suggestions and provision of copious amounts of information, the various members of the IUPAC/IUB committees who provided preprints of many documents on carbohydrate nomenclature and the large number of colleagues and students, especially Meriam H. Adam Hussain, Dr. Dave P. Atkins, A. Jane Griffiths and David L. Stevenson who have encouraged us and assisted with reading and correction of manuscripts and proofs. Finally, the authors thank our parents and friends and in particular Sandra, Helen and Elizabeth for their co-operation, understanding and encouragement during the preparation of this book.

John F. Kennedy
Charles A. White

October 1982

CHAPTER 1

Introduction

GENERAL

Carbohydrates comprise the most abundant group of natural compounds. They can be looked upon as prime biological substances, produced by the processes of photosynthesis from the atmosphere by plants for their own nutritional and physiological needs. They must not, however, be regarded solely as a phenomenon of the plant world as they are constituents of a wide range of biological systems. They are, in many cases, utilized as food by man, other animals or micro-organisms and frequently become converted into more complex compounds. They serve as sources of energy (monosaccharides) and as major devices for the storage of solar energy, and as the principle source of metabolic energy for the human body (starch and glycogen). They form the major constituents of the shells of insects, crabs, and lobsters (chitin), and the supporting tissue of plants (cellulose), and are present in the cell walls of plants and bacteria, and the soft coats of animal cells. They form compounds with proteins and lipids, and, in such combinations, are essential to many biological reactions.

Carbohydrates, so-called because they were originally believed to be hydrates of carbon having the general formula $C_n(H_2O)_n$, are multifunctional compounds containing a number of hydroxyl groups of similar or equal reactivity, and at least one asymmetric carbon atom. With accumulation of knowledge, the definition has been expanded to include polyhydroxy aldehydes, ketones, alcohols, and acids and simple derivatives thereof, but the chemistry is largely that of simple functional groups, with extensive stereochemical variations superimposed. However, the manipulation of a single, selected hydroxyl group is a difficult problem and requires complex series of reactions. The condensation reaction between two molecules of a single monosaccharide to form a dimer results in not one exclusive product, but a possibility of up to 25 different compounds, and condensation to form a trimer yields up to 176 different trisaccharides. Fortunately, nature's catalysts (enzymes) are very selective and will only produce the required disaccharide, unlike chemical synthesis which produces a mixture of products. It is this balance between simplicity and complexity that has caused some scientists to avoid a study of carbohydrates.

Most modern textbooks on chemistry or biochemistry give little mention, if any, of carbohydrates and are usually restricted to the stereochemistry of the simple monosaccharides and the structure of the simple structural materials such as starch and cellulose, often with a very historical approach. Very little mention is made of the essential roles that carbohydrates undertake. This lack of interest is by no means a recent phenomenon because as long ago as the 1930s Bell was discouraged from embarking on a study of carbohydrates "as the field had now been fully worked out". Whelan in 1957 and Rees in 1971 were also led to believe that carbohydrate chemistry and biochemistry were running down. During the past decade, however, attitudes towards carbohydrates have changed markedly.

There are many reasons for this upsurge in interest. The development of new chemical methods and chromatographic techniques has allowed achievement of syntheses that earlier carbohydrate chemists could only carry out by carefully controlled chemical transformations and crude separation techniques. Now, much more is being discovered about the structure of carbohydrates because analyses are being performed on smaller and smaller quantities of material. The advance of carbohydrate chemistry has also been helped by studies on the action of enzymes on carbohydrates and has resulted in a new understanding of enzyme action and its applications both at the large-scale industrial level and at the detailed, small-scale level, as in the biochemical processes of life. Such overall developments have given impetus to a study of the role of carbohydrates in the processes of health and disease.

The monosaccharides D-glucose (Greek γλυκυσ, meaning sweet) and D-fructose have come to the front in industrial sweetening and bulking agents and, in the form of a mixture, as a serious competitor to the conventional carbohydrate sweetener, namely cane sugar (sucrose). Such polysaccharides as xanthan gum and alginic acid are much in vogue as food additives for gelling etc., and in other industries such as oil-drilling. In combination with protein, carbohydrates are involved in the defence mechanisms of the living human cell and play a part in successful organ transplantations, etc. It is now obvious that carbohydrate chemistry and biochemistry as we know them to-day hold much in store for far-reaching discoveries of Nobel Prize-winning standard and importance. We present a balanced approach to the chemistry and biochemistry of the whole spectrum of carbohydrates from simple monosaccharides to complex polysaccharides and carbohydrate-containing macromolecules, and hope to encourage further interest in a rapidly expanding, exciting field.

NOMENCLATURE

Throughout this book, we use nomenclature that is recommended by the International Union of Pure and Applied Chemistry (IUPAC) and the International Union of Biochemistry (IUB) Joint Commission on Biochemical Nomenclature

(JCBN) and have, where possible, included those recommendations which have not yet been published. We gratefully acknowledge the assistance of members of the JCBN for the provision of the draft final documents. We have also used the internationally accepted system of chemical nomenclature in preference to the system which the Association for Science Education (ASE) proposes for teaching in British schools, since the former is that found in the original literature and used by carbohydrate chemists worldwide.

A number of abbreviations for the more common biological compounds are used throughout this book. The names of these compounds are given in Table 1.1.

In many instances a trivial name is added, in parentheses, for a sugar or sugar derivative in order to help the reader understand the older chemical literature and current biochemical and biological literature. Most of these trivial names are 'not recommended' in the nomenclature rules and recommendations and are not used in carbohydrate chemistry. However, some of these trivial names are still acceptable in biochemistry and biology, whilst the chemical and pharmaceutical industries continue to use many of the 'not recommended' and uninformative names.

Table 1.1 Abbreviations used for the common biological compounds

ADP	adenosine 5'-diphosphate
AMP	adenosine 5'-monophosphate
ATP	adenosine 5'-triphosphate
dATP	deoxyadenosine 5'-triphosphate
CDP	cytidine 5'-diphosphate
CMP	cytidine 5'-monophosphate
dCMP	deoxycytidine 5'-monophosphate
CoA	coenzyme A
CTP	cytidine 5'-triphosphate
dCTP	deoxycytidine 5'-triphosphate
DFP	diisopropyl fluorophosphate
DNA	deoxyribonucleic acid
FAD	flavin-adenine dinucleotide
FMN	flavin mononucleotide (riboflavin 5'-monophosphate)
GDP	guanosine 5'-diphosphate
dGDP	deoxyguanosine 5'-diphosphate
GMP	guanosine 5'-monophosphate
dGMP	deoxyguanosine 5'-monophosphate
GTP	guanosine 5'-triphosphate
dGTP	deoxyguanosine 5'-triphosphate
IDP	inosine 5'-diphosphate
IMP	inosine 5'-monophosphate
ITP	inosine 5'-triphosphate

Table 1.1 (*continued*)

NAD⁺	oxidized nicotinamide-adenine dinucleotide
NADH	reduced nicotinamide-adenine dinucleotide
NADP⁺	oxidized nicotinamide-adenine dinucleotide phosphate
NAD(P)⁺	indicates either NAD⁺ or NADP⁺
NADPH	reduced nicotinamide-adenine dinucleotide phosphate
NAD(P)H	indicates either NADH or NADPH
NDP	nucleoside 5′-diphosphate
NMN	nicotinamide mononucleotide
NMP	nucleoside 5′-monophosphate
dNMP	deoxynucleoside 5′-monophosphate
NTP	nucleoside 5′-triphosphate
poly(C)	synthetic polynucleotide composed of cytidylate residues
poly(G)	synthetic polynucleotide composed of guanylate residues
PPi	inorganic diphosphate
RNA	ribonucleic acid
tRNA	transfer ribonucleic acid
TDP	ribothymidine 5′-diphosphate
dTDP	thymidine 5′-diphosphate
TMP	ribothymidine 5′-monophosphate
dTMP	thymidine 5′-monophosphate
TTP	ribothymidine 5′-triphosphate
dTTP	thymidine 5′-triphosphate
UDP	uridine 5′-diphosphate
UMP	uridine 5′-monophosphate
dUMP	deoxyuridine 5′-monophosphate
UTP	uridine 5′-triphosphate
dUTP	deoxyuridine 5′-triphosphate

Classification

Carbohydrates may be classified into three groups: monosaccharides, oligo-saccharides and polysaccharides. Monosaccharides are the simple sugars which cannot be hydrolysed to smaller sugar molecules. Oligosaccharides are simple polymers of monosaccharides joined by glycosidic linkages; by definition, they contain from 2 to 10 monosaccharide units to which they can be hydrolysed. Polysaccharides are polymers of high molecular weight consisting of more than 10 units, but the division between oligosaccharides and polysaccharides is made easier since carbohydrates containing between 5 and 15 units rarely occur in nature. The majority of naturally occurring polysaccharides contain 80 to 100 units, with only a few in the range 25 to 75 units. There are some polysaccharides which contain more than 100 units, for example, native cellulose contains an average of 3000 units, or, more accurately, contains a series of polymers having a molecular weight distribution about a mean value equivalent to 3000 units. Such polysaccharides rarely exist as collections of discrete macromolecules of identical molecular weight.

MONOSACCHARIDES

Monosaccharides are classified according to the number of carbon atoms they contain. Trioses have the formula $(C_3H_6O_3)$, tetroses $(C_4H_8O_4)$, pentoses $(C_5H_{10}O_5)$ and hexoses $(C_6H_{12}O_6)$, etc.

Configuration

D-Glucose, a hexose and the most common monosaccharide, occurs in the juices of fruits and in honey and is a common hydrolysis product of polysaccharides. The structures of D-glucose and some of the other hexoses and pentoses were determined, and their stereochemical relationships proved by the work of Fischer, for which he was awarded the Nobel Prize for chemistry in 1907. Each family of monosaccharides (hexoses, pentoses, etc.) was found to comprise a collection of molecular forms (stereoisomers) which have identical structures but different three-dimensional arrangements of the atoms and functional groups. Those stereoisomers which are not mirror images of each other are referred to as diastereoisomers.

D-Glucose forms a penta-acetate (1), not a hexa-acetate, showing that there are only 5 hydroxyl groups present; since the presence of 2 hydroxyl groups on the same carbon atom is an unstable situation, there are 5 carbon atoms carrying the hydroxyl groups. The remaining carbon atom has been shown to be part of an aldehyde group (by the reaction with mild oxidizing agents to afford a mono-carboxylic acid). Reactions which destroy stereochemistry by formation of a double bond (for example, phenylosazone formation) at one carbon atom have shown that certain pairs of sugars give the same product, for example, D-glucose and D-mannose react with loss of stereochemistry at carbon atom 2 (C-2) to give the same phenylosazone (Scheme 2.1) and must therefore have the same configuration at the other carbon atoms. They are said to be epimeric at C-2. Such reactions as these, and reactions which add or remove a carbon atom have shown that the structures of monosaccharides are related as in Fig. 2.1(a) and (b), where structures are depicted in straight chain, Fischer projection formulae.

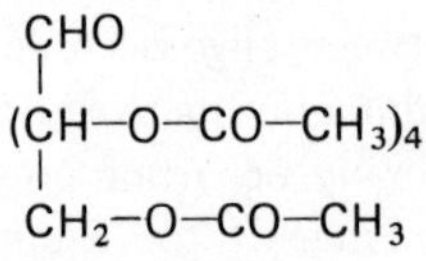

$$
\begin{array}{c}
CHO \\
|\\
(CH{-}O{-}CO{-}CH_3)_4 \\
|\\
CH_2{-}O{-}CO{-}CH_3
\end{array}
$$

An *aldehydo*-aldohexose penta-acetate

(1)

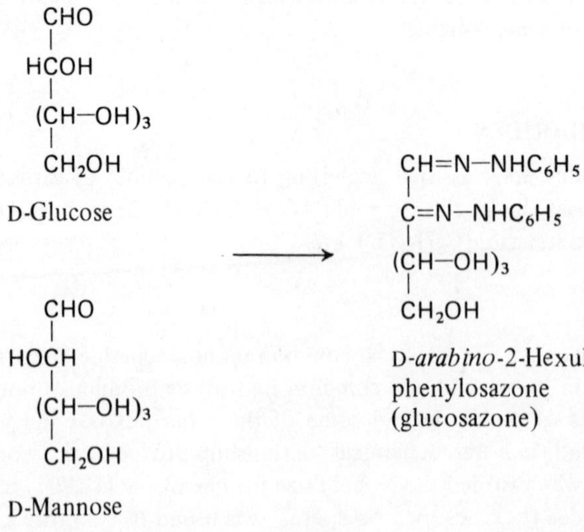

$$
\begin{array}{c}
CHO \\
|\\
HCOH \\
|\\
(CH{-}OH)_3 \\
|\\
CH_2OH
\end{array}
$$

D-Glucose

$$
\begin{array}{c}
CH{=}N{-}NHC_6H_5 \\
|\\
C{=}N{-}NHC_6H_5 \\
|\\
(CH{-}OH)_3 \\
|\\
CH_2OH
\end{array}
$$

$\longrightarrow$

$$
\begin{array}{c}
CHO \\
|\\
HOCH \\
|\\
(CH{-}OH)_3 \\
|\\
CH_2OH
\end{array}
$$

D-Mannose

D-*arabino*-2-Hexulose
phenylosazone
(glucosazone)

Scheme 2.1

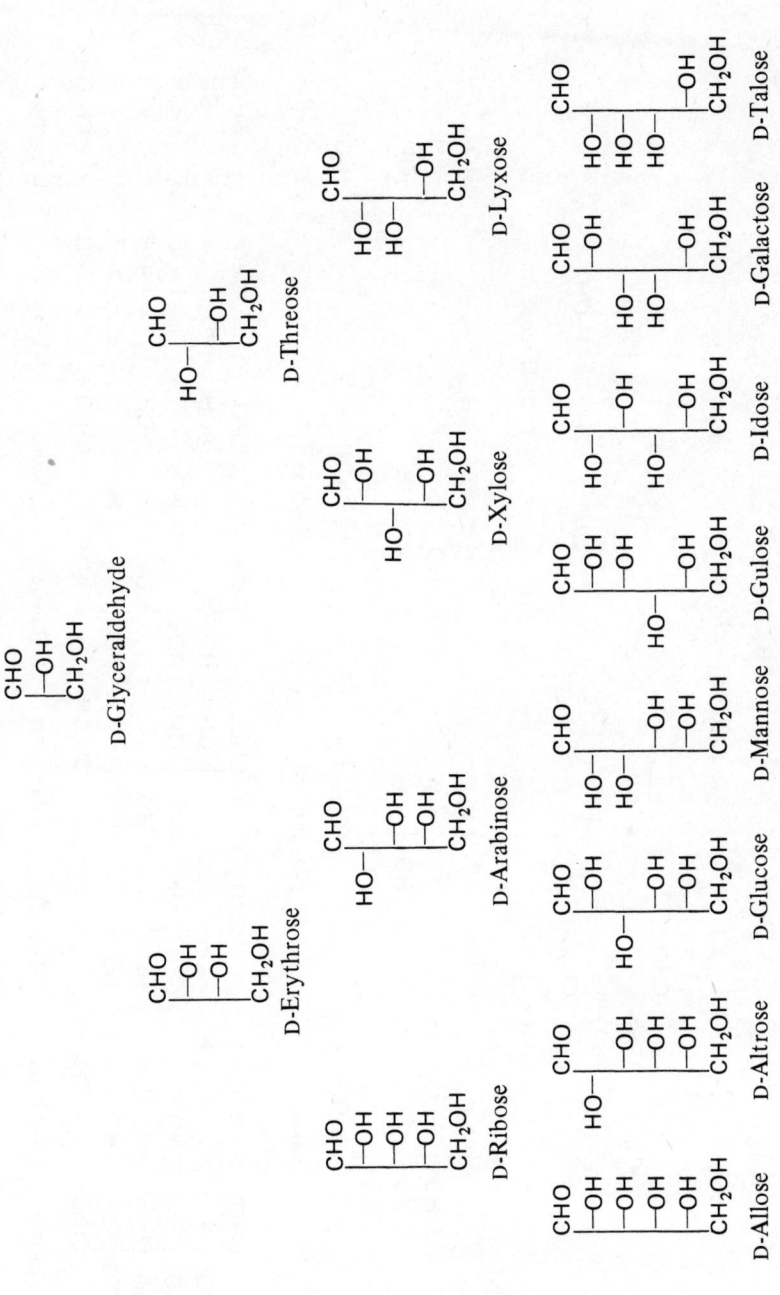

Fig. 2.1(a) – Structures of the *aldehydo*-aldoses, up to aldohexoses, of the D configuration, with hydrogen atoms omitted for clarity (for the full structure of D-Glucose see Fig. 2.2).

D-Glyceraldehyde

D-Erythrose — D-Threose

D-Ribose — D-Arabinose — D-Xylose — D-Lyxose

D-Allose — D-Altrose — D-Glucose — D-Mannose — D-Gulose — D-Idose — D-Galactose — D-Talose

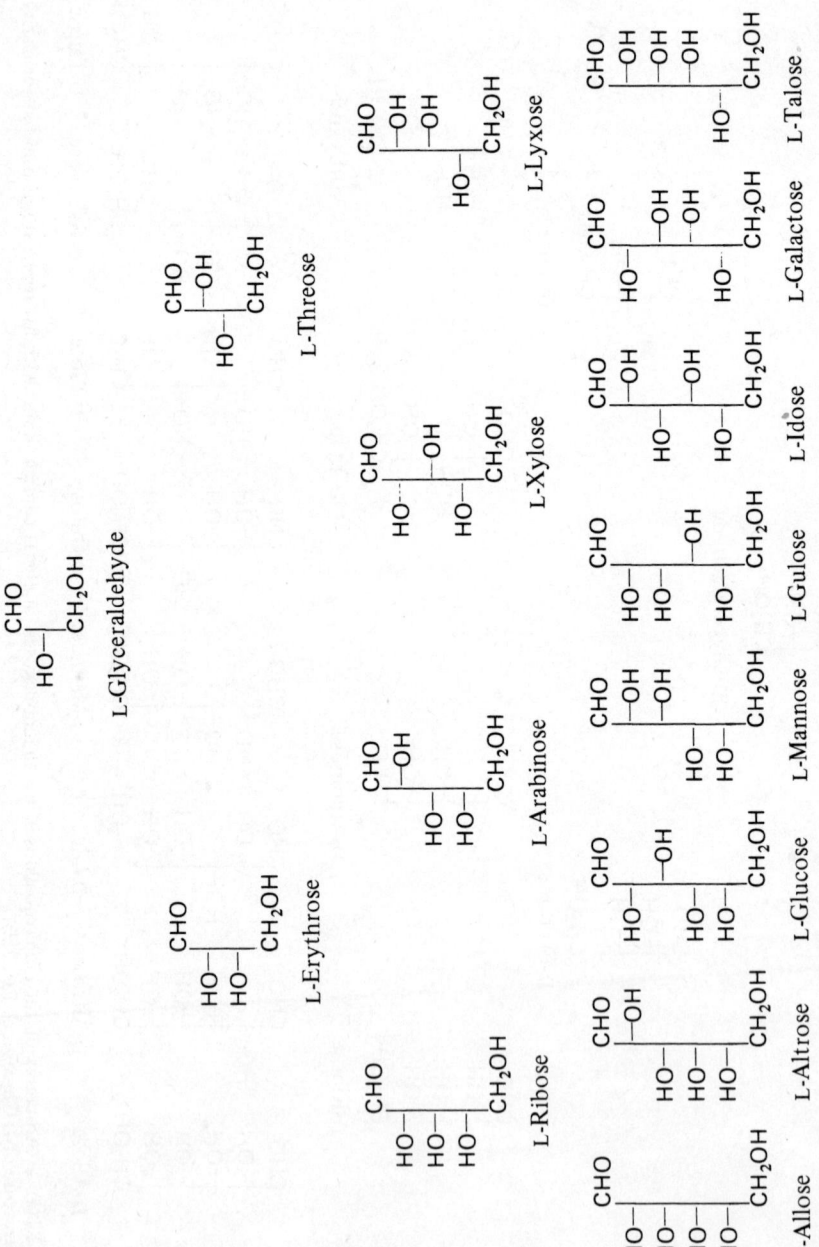

Fig. 2.1(b) – Structures of the *aldehydo*-aldoses, up to aldohexoses, of the L configuration, with hydrogen atoms omitted for clarity (for the full structure of L-Glucose see Fig. 2.2).

The stereochemistry at the penultimate carbon atom in the chain, counting the carbon atom of the aldehyde group as the first (C-1), determines the series to which the sugar belongs (that is, which enantiomeric form or absolute configuration it has). For glucose, the stereochemistry at C-5 determines whether it is D-glucose or L-glucose, D-glucose being related to D-glyceraldehyde (Fig. 2.2). To build up to D-series of D-aldopentoses, the 'initials' RAXL give the order ribose, arabinose, xylose, and lyxose which have (see Fig. 2.1(a)):

      C-4 hydroxyl groups all to the right
      C-3 hydroxyl groups first pair right, second pair left
      C-2 hydroxyl groups alternating right then left.

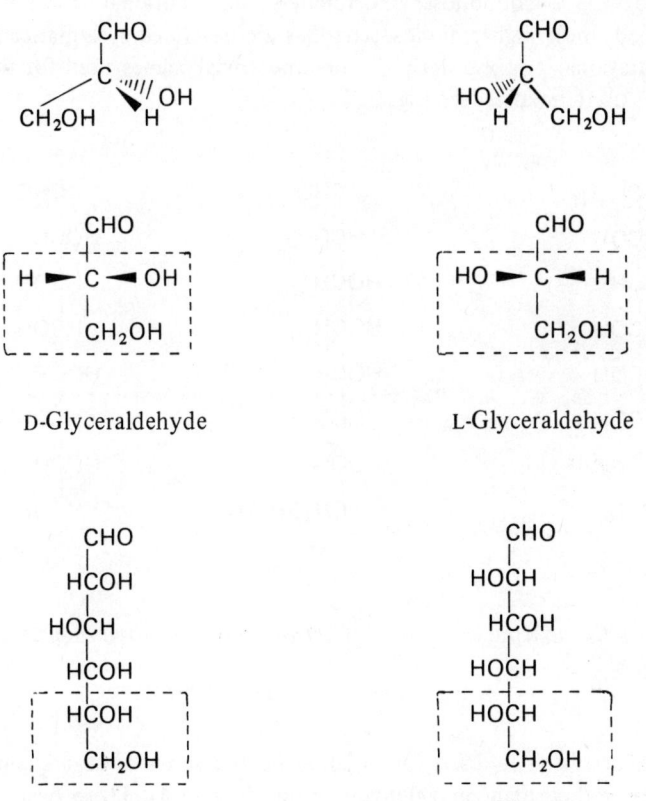

Fig. 2.2 – Relationship of the configuration at C-5 in D- and L-glucose to the configuration of D- and L-glyceraldehyde.

The mnemonic: '*All alt*ruists *gl*adly *ma*ke *gu*m *in ga*llon *t*anks' gives the correct sequences for the D-aldohexoses which can be built up as follows:

> C-5 hydroxyl groups all to the right
> C-4 hydroxyl groups, first four right, second four left
> C-3 hydroxyl groups, alternating pairs to right then left
> C-2 hydroxyl groups, alternating right then left.

. In both the above sequences it is worthwhile noting that the number of hydroxyl groups, which run first to the right and then to the left, is reduced by a half on descent of the relevant carbon atom number.

For the monosaccharides containing more than 6 carbon atoms the number of isomers doubles for every extra carbon atom. Thus, there are 16 possible isomers for the D-aldoheptoses, 32 isomers for the D-aldo-octoses, and 64 isomers for the D-aldononoses. Fortunately, no additional trivial names are used; instead, these higher monosaccharides are described systematically by use of configurational prefixes derived from the trivial names used for the monosaccharides up to hexoses (see Fig. 2.3).

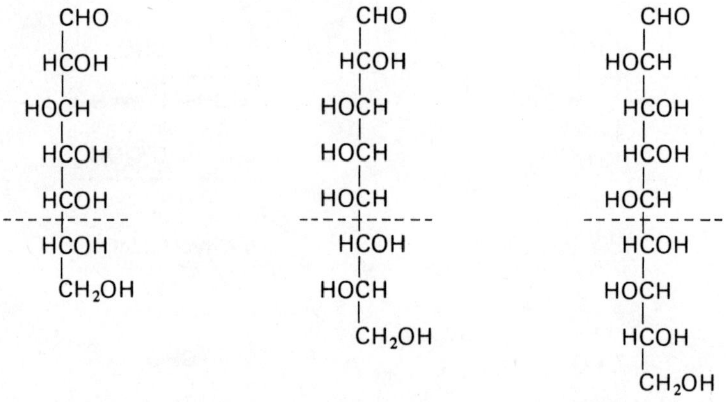

D-*glycero*-D-*gluco*-Heptose   L-*threo*-L-*altro*-Octose   D-*xylo*-L-*galacto*-Nonose

Fig. 2.3 – Naming of the higher aldoses.

A similar system is used for building up the series of sugars containing a keto group rather than an aldehydo group (Fig. 2.4). These have a ketonic carbon at C-2 and have therefore one asymmetric carbon atom less than the corresponding aldose. Higher ketoses, such as heptuloses, octuloses and nonuloses are named as derivatives of the lower ketoses, using the same system as applied to the higher aldoses (see Fig. 2.3).

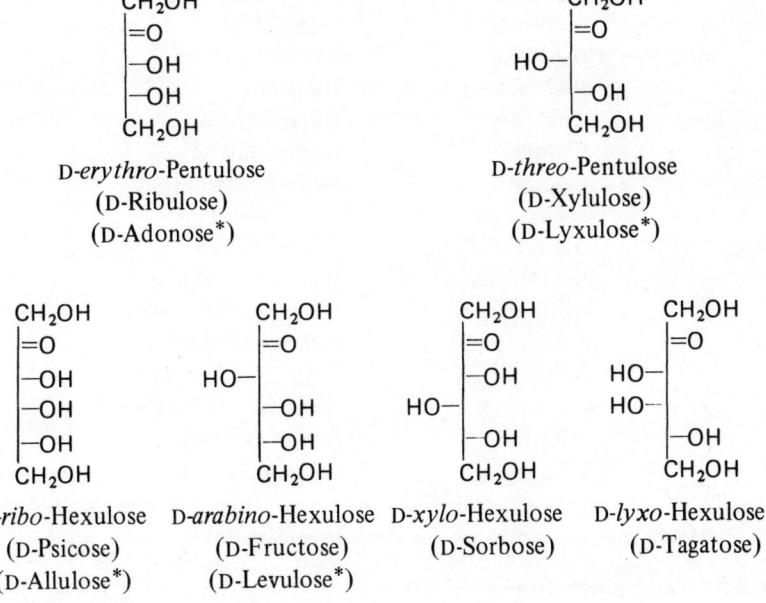

CH₂OH
=O
CH₂OH

1,3-Dihydroxy-2-propanone†
(Dihydroxyacetone)
(Glycerone)

CH₂OH
=O
—OH
CH₂OH

D-*glycero*-Tetrulose
(D-Erythrulose)
(D-Threulose*)

CH₂OH
=O
—OH
—OH
CH₂OH

D-*erythro*-Pentulose
(D-Ribulose)
(D-Adonose*)

CH₂OH
=O
HO—
—OH
CH₂OH

D-*threo*-Pentulose
(D-Xylulose)
(D-Lyxulose*)

CH₂OH
=O
—OH
—OH
—OH
CH₂OH

D-*ribo*-Hexulose
(D-Psicose)
(D-Allulose*)

CH₂OH
=O
HO—
—OH
—OH
CH₂OH

D-*arabino*-Hexulose
(D-Fructose)
(D-Levulose*)

CH₂OH
=O
—OH
HO—
—OH
CH₂OH

D-*xylo*-Hexulose
(D-Sorbose)

CH₂OH
=O
HO—
HO—
—OH
CH₂OH

D-*lyxo*-Hexulose
(D-Tagatose)

Fig. 2.4 – Structures of the ketoses, up to ketohexoses, of the D configuration (trivial names in brackets; * not recommended trivial name), with hydrogen atoms omitted for clarity.
† Not regarded as being a sugar, due to absence of asymmetric carbon atom.

The convention used for Fischer projection formulae is that the vertical bonds (carbon–carbon) lie behind the plane of the page (except the one under consideration) and the horizontal bonds (carbon–hydrogen and carbon–oxygen) project in front of the page. The aldehydo group must be placed at the top (C-1). For ketoses, the keto group is placed next to the top (C-2). Frequently, the hydrogen atoms are omitted for simplicity as in Fig. 2.1. The trivial names used in Figs. 2.1 and 2.4 are preferred for simple sugars and have corresponding systematic names (Table 2.1) which are used to describe more-complex structures.

Table 2.1 Systematic names for neutral monosaccharides

Trivial	Systematic
D-Glyceraldehyde	D-*glycero*-Triose
D-Erythrose	D-*erythro*-Tetrose
D-Threose	D-*threo*-Tetrose
D-Arabinose	D-*arabino*-Pentose
D-Lyxose	D-*lyxo*-Pentose
D-Ribose	D-*ribo*-Pentose
D Xylose	D-*xylo*-Pentose
D-Allose	D-*allo*-Hexose
D-Altrose	D-*altro*-Hexose
D-Galactose	D-*galacto*-Hexose
D-Glucose	D-*gluco*-Hexose
D-Gulose	D-*gulo*-Hexose
D-Idose	D-*ido*-Hexose
D-Mannose	D-*manno*-Hexose
D-Talose	D-*talo*-Hexose
D-Erythrulose*	D-*glycero*-2-Tetrulose
D-Ribulose*	D-*erythro*-2-Pentulose
D-Xylulose*	D-*threo*-2-Pentulose
D-Psicose	D-*ribo*-2-Hexulose
D-Fructose	D-*arabino*-2-Hexulose
D-Sorbose	D-*xylo*-2-Hexulose
D-Tagatose	D-*lyxo*-2-Hexulose

* less-preferred trivial names which are not recommended for current usage.

As may be seen from Figs. 2.1 and 2.4, the carbon atoms not at the end of the chain have four different atoms or groups attached to them and are said to be asymmetric. This characteristic gives rise to optical activity and standard solutions of different sugars have different optical rotations, not all in the same direction (Table 2.2).

Table 2.2 Optical rotations of some naturally occurring monosaccharides

Pyranose		Mutaform
D-Ribose (α)	− 23	− 24
L-Arabinose (β)	+ 191	+ 105
D-Xylose (α)	+ 94	+ 19
D-Lyxose (α)	+ 6	− 14
(β)	− 73	− 14
D-Glucose (α)	+ 113	+ 53
(β)	+ 19	+ 53
D-Galactose (α)	+ 150	+ 80
(β)	+ 53	+ 80
D-Mannose (α)	+ 29	+ 14
(β)	− 17	+ 14
L-Rhamnose	− 9	− 8
D-Quinovose	+ 73	+ 30
L-Fucose (α)	− 153	− 76
D-Fructose (β)	− 132	− 94
L-Sorbose	− 44	− 43
D-Tagatose	− 3	− 4
D-Glucuronic acid	+ 12	+ 36
D-Galacturonic acid (α)	+ 107	+ 52
(β)	+ 31	+ 52
D-Mannuronic acid (α)	+ 16	− 24
(β)	− 48	− 24
2-Amino-2-deoxy-D-glucose (α)	+ 100	+ 48
(D-Glucosamine) (β)	+ 14	+ 48
2-Amino-2-deoxy-D-glucose hydrochloride (α)	+ 100	+ 73
(D-Glucosamine hydrochloride) (β)	+ 25	+ 73
2-Acetamido-2-deoxy-D-glucose (N-Acetyl-D-glucosamine)	+ 56	+ 41
2-Amino-2-deoxy-D-galactose (α) (D-Galactosamine hydrochloride) (β)	+ 121 + 45	+ 95 + 95
2-Acetamido-2-deoxy-D-galactose (N-Acetyl-D-galactosamine)	+ 131	+ 98
5-Acetamido-3,5-dideoxy-D-*glycero*-D-*galacto*-2-nonulosonic acid (N-Acetylneuraminic acid)	− 32	− 32

Ring Structures

These projections do not completely represent the structure of monosaccharides; for example, the aldehydo group does not react as a normal aldehydo group, as it will not colour Schiff's reagent and produces a mixture of glycosides on reaction with methanolic hydrogen chloride and not a dimethyl acetal. This indicates that the aldehydo group is in some way masked. D-Glucose can cry-

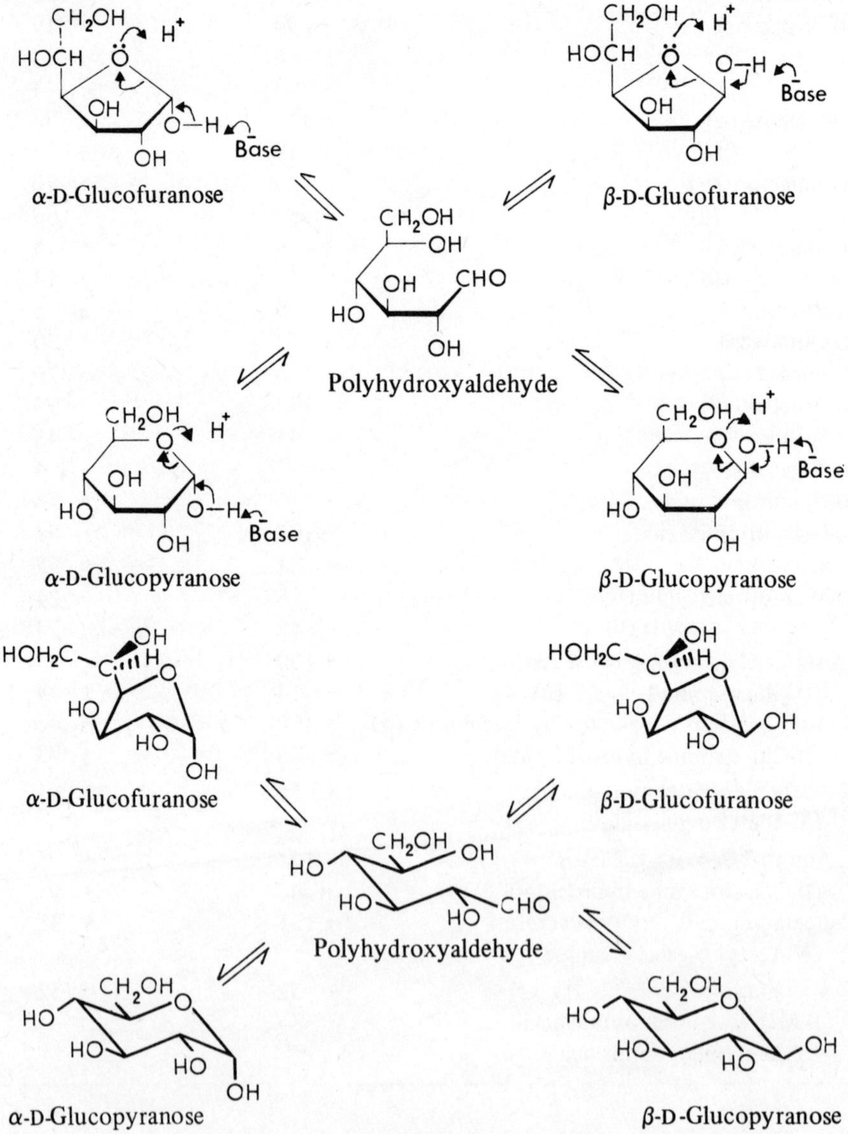

Fig. 2.5 – Mutarotation of D-glucose.

stallize, depending on conditions, in two forms that have different melting points (146° and 149°) and optical rotations (+113° and +19°) and are known as α- and β-D-pyranose forms. If these crystalline forms are dissolved in water, the optical rotations change, and both solutions reach a constant value of +53°, showing that the two forms are interconvertible — this process is called muta-rotation, and is exhibited by all mono- and most reducing di-saccharides. The different forms are known as anomers and the C-1 atom of aldoses is the ano-meric carbon. These observations were rationalized by Haworth, who devised the ring structures for monosaccharides on the basis of their existence as cyclic hemiacetals. The two forms of D-glucose are thereby shown to be due to the arrangement of the hydroxyl group at C-1 (Fig. 2.5) due to the formation of another asymmetric carbon atom (mutarotation). Haworth also established that the favoured ring size of the aldehexoses is the six-membered (pyranose) ring, which is denoted by the symbol p after the three-letter symbol for the monosaccharide (for example, Glc$p$). The five-membered (furanose) ring can and does exist in nature, and is denoted by an f (for example, Glc$f$).

Conformation

In order to visualize the six-membered ring the so-called 'Haworth formulae' are inadequate and the Haworth 'conformational structures' are used, which show puckered rings not planar rings. 'Conformation' is the word, introduced by Haworth, used to describe the arrangement in space of the atoms of a single chemical structure (configuration), the various arrangements being produced only by rotation about single bonds. There are two types of strainless pyranose rings possible, the boat (B) (2a) and the chair (C) (2b) forms, and of these, the chair is usually preferred as there are usually fewer interactions across the ring between substituents (that is, non-bonded interactions). Other strained rings exist but are only found when other constraints, such as double bonds, distort the ring. These forms include the skew (S) (3) and half-chair (H) (4) conformations.

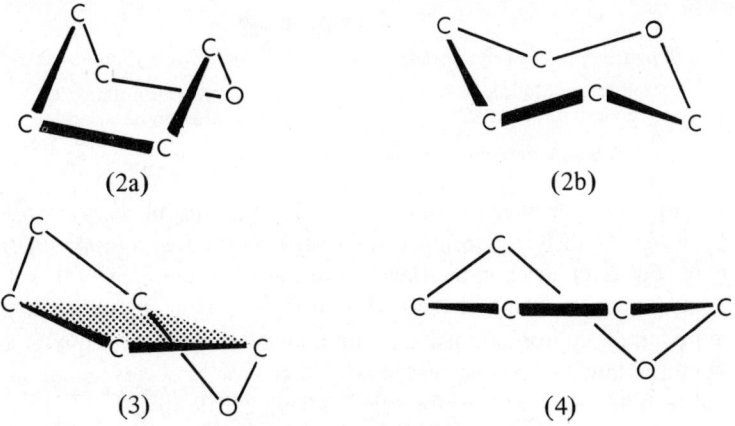

(2a)	(2b)
(3)	(4)

Reeves uses the terms *C1* and *1C* to define the ring shapes but as may be seen from Fig. 2.6, the enantiomeric (D and L) forms of a sugar in the same conformation (that is, with the same axial-equatorial arrangement) have different symbols, and must therefore always be linked to the absolute configuration of the sugar. Therefore, β-D-glucopyranose in the *C1(D)* conformation has all its substituents in equatorial positions, at the greatest distance from other sub stituents. In order to overcome these problems a revised and improved system of conformational nomenclature has been devised that is based on Reeve's system, but which defines the ring without resort to the substituents (Recommendations, 1980a). Thus, using the plane described by the oxygen atom and carbon atoms 2, 3 and 5, the rings can be defined as $^4C_1$ if C-4 is above the plane and C-1 is below it, or as $^1C_4$ for the alternative ring. (The numbering of carbon atoms appears clockwise if viewed from above.)

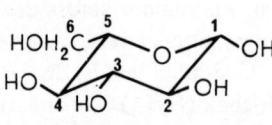

β-D-Glucopyranose

(all hydroxyl groups equatorial)	(all hydroxyl groups axial)
Reeves notation *C1*	Reeves notation *1C*
modern notation $^4C_1$	modern notation $^1C_4$

——————————————— mirror plane———————————————

β-L-Glucopyranose

(all hydroxyl groups equatorial)	(all hydroxyl groups axial)
Reeves notation *1C*	Reeves notation *C1*
modern notation $^1C_4$	modern notation $^4C_1$

Fig. 2.6 – Preferred conformations of β-D- and -L-glucopyranose.

In order to remember the orientation of the groups in the pyranose forms of hexoses in the different formula, the easiest method is to think of β-D-glucopyranose (Fig. 2.7) which in the Haworth formula has alternate hydroxyl groups above and below the plane of the ring with the C-6 atom above the ring, whilst in the preferred 'conformational' structure, all substituents are equatorial in the $^4C_1$ conformation (a possible reason why D-glucose is a very common monosaccharide in nature — it has a structure containing little strain).

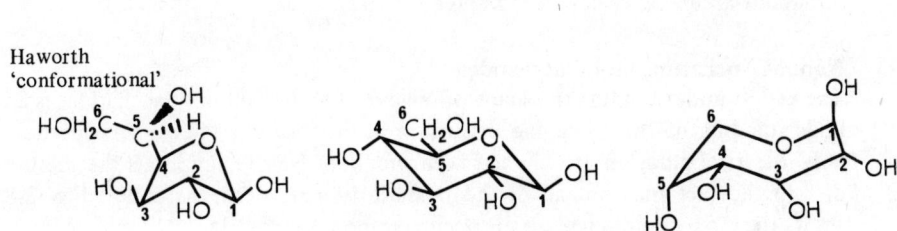

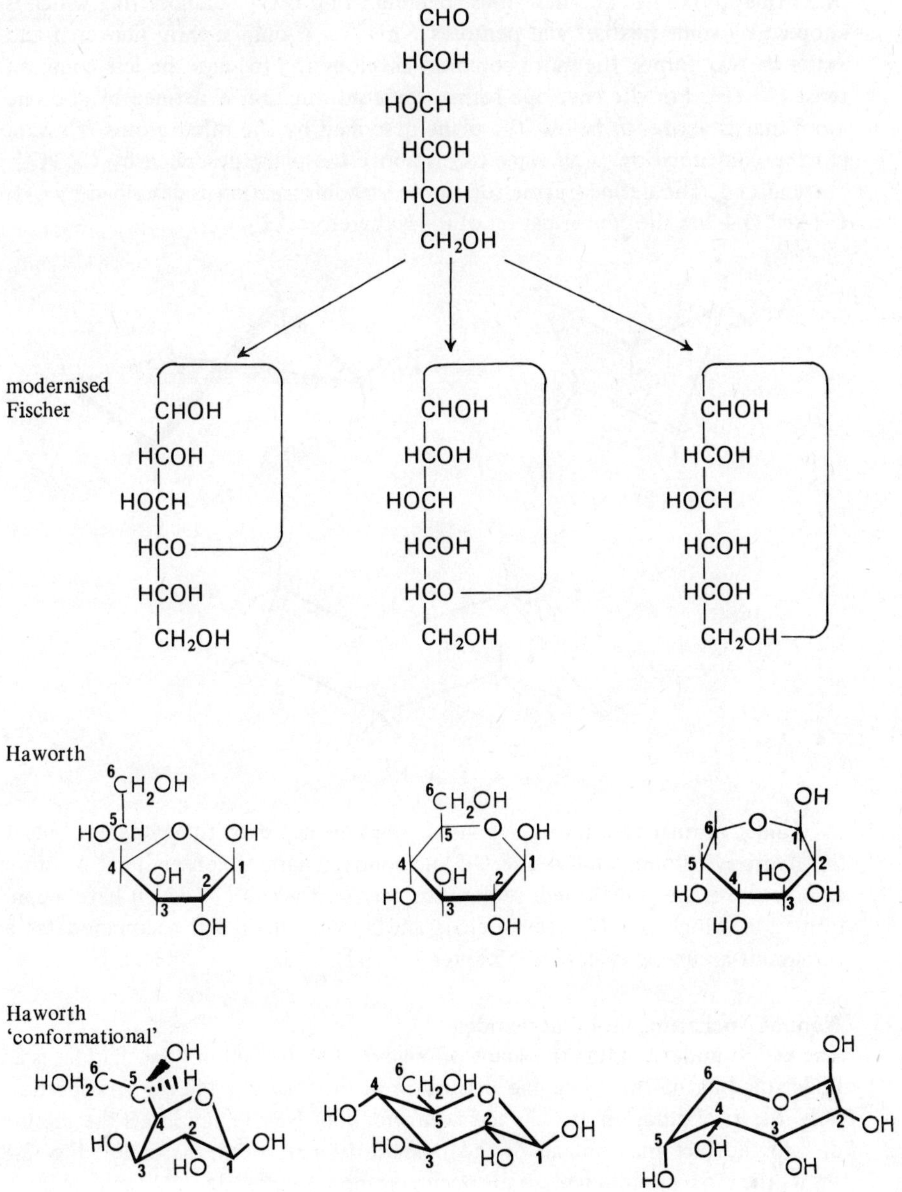

β-D-Glucofuranose-E_3 β-D-Glucopyranose $^4C_1$ β-D-Glucoseptanose

Fig. 2.7 – Conformations of β-D-glucose (hydrogen atoms omitted from Haworth structures for clarity).

As indicated earlier, hexoses can, under certain conditions, exist in rings other than pyranose. The next most common ring is the furanose ring which is adopted by some hexoses and pentoses. This ring is only slightly puckered and exists in two forms, the more common envelope (E) (5) and the less common twist (T) (6). For the envelope forms, the conformation is defined by the one atom that is above, or below, the plane described by the other atoms. Thus, in (5) the conformation is ^3E since C-3 is above the plane described by C-1, C-2, C-4 and O-4. The defined plane for the twist conformation is described by C-1, C-4 and O-4 and the conformation of (6) is therefore $^3T_2$.

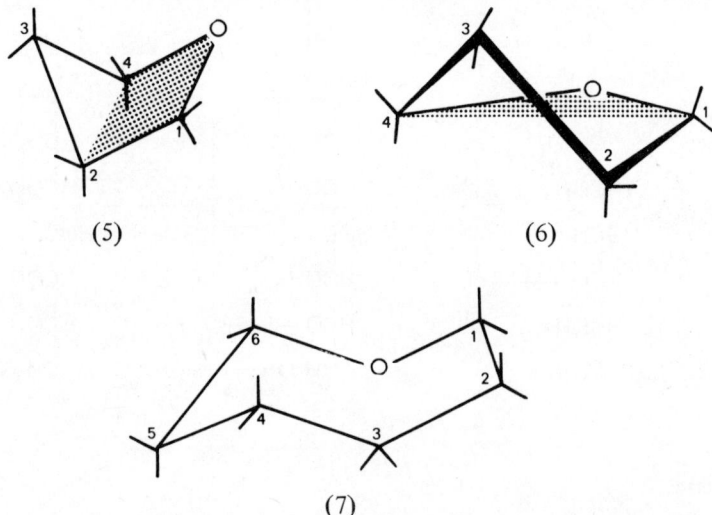

(5)   (6)

(7)

Under normal conditions, septanose rings do not exist to any extent but, if the hydroxyl groups at C-4 and C-5 of monosaccharides containing 7 or more carbon atoms are substituted, septanoses may be formed (7) which have a conformation which lies between a chair and a twist chair and accommodates a favourable anomeric effect (see Chapter 3, p. 62).

Naturally occurring monosaccharides

The key to understanding the shape of oligosaccharides and polysaccharides is an understanding of the foregoing discussion of monosaccharide isomers (particularly the configuration at C-1) and conformation. Nature simplifies the picture due to the fact that not all of the possible isomers occur naturally. Fig. 2.8 shows the most common, naturally occurring monosaccharides and such common derivatives as aminosugars and uronic acids in their preferred conformations. Structures of less common monosaccharides and other derivatives will be given in subsequent Chapters, for example, complex aminosugars in antibiotics (Chapter 12) and in microbial polysaccharides (Chapter 8).

Pentoses

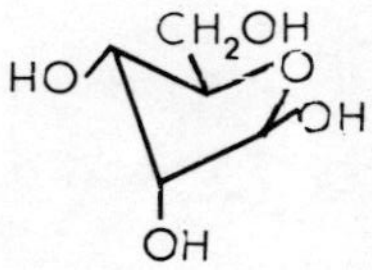

α-L-Arabinopyranose-$^4C_1$

β-D-Xylopyranose-$^4C_1$

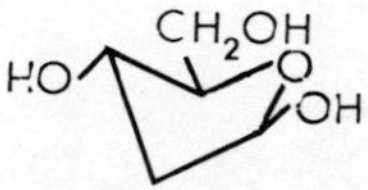

2-Deoxy-β-D-*erythro*-pentafuranose-^3E (2-Deoxy-D-ribose)

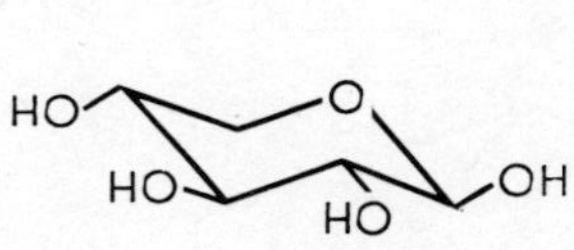

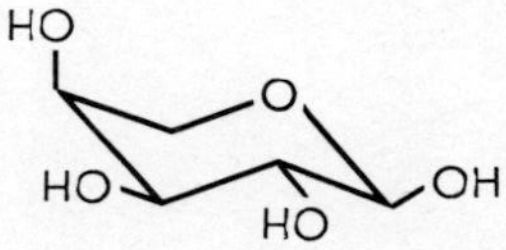

β-D-Ribofuranose-^3E

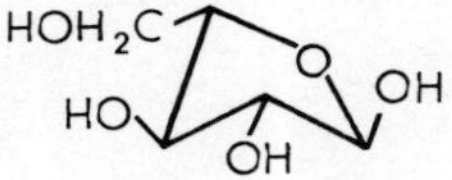

α-L-Arabinofuranose-E_3

Hexoses

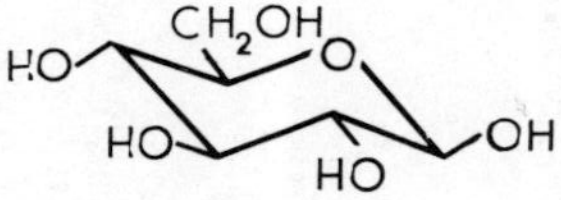

β-L-Galactopyranose-$^1C_4$

β-D-Galactopyranose-$^4C_1$

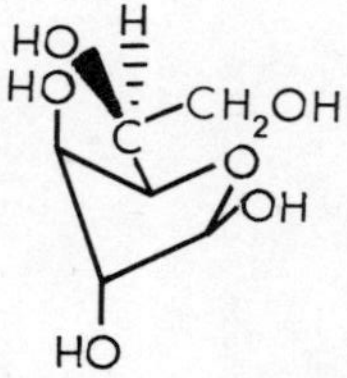

β-D-Glucofuranose-^3E

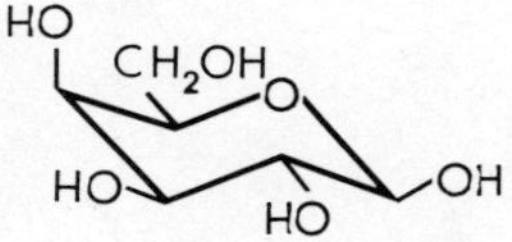

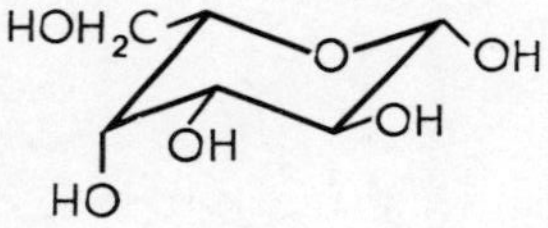

β-D-Glucopyranose-$^4C_1$

Fig. 2.8 — Structures of common monosaccharides (shown in one anomeric form only) (*continued on next page*).

Hexoses (*continued*)

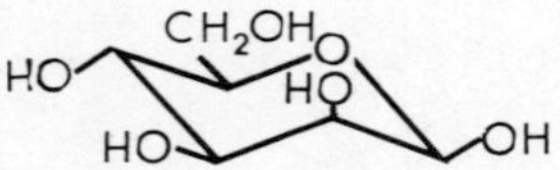

β-D-Mannopyranose-$^4C_1$

Ketohexoses

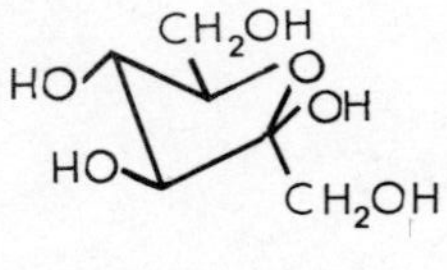

β-D-Fructofuranose-^3E

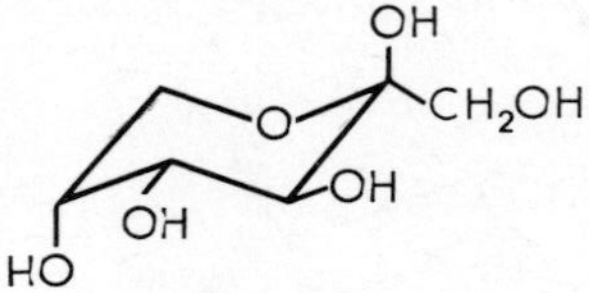

α-D-Fructopyranose-$^1C_4$

Deoxyhexoses

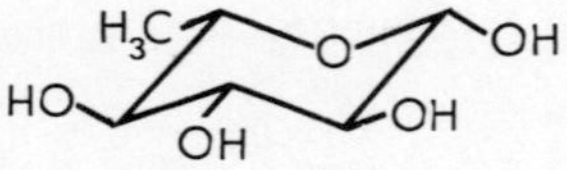

6-Deoxy-β-L-mannopyranose-$^1C_4$
(L-Rhamnopyranose)

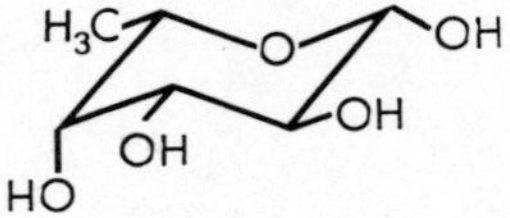

6-Deoxy-β-L-galactopyranose-$^1C_4$
(L-Fucopyranose)

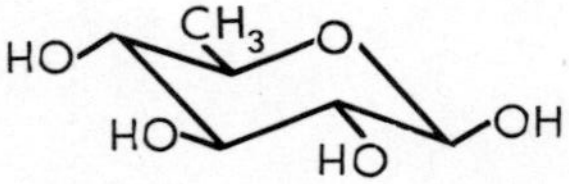

6-Deoxy-β-D-glucopyranose-$^4C_1$
(D-Quinovopyranose)

Hexuronic acids

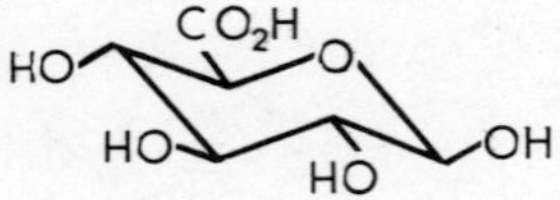

β-D-Glucopyranuronic
acid-$^4C_1$

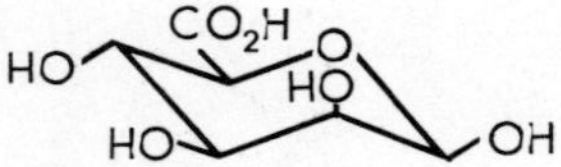

β-D-Mannopyranuronic
acid-$^4C_1$

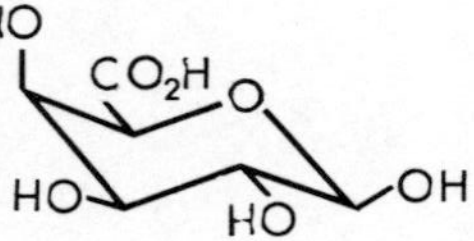

β-D-Galactopyranuronic
acid-$^4C_1$

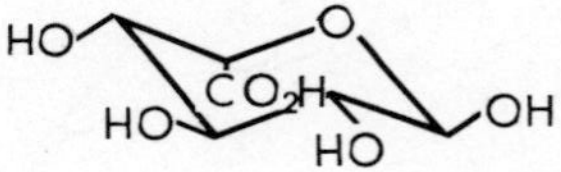

α-L-Idopyranuronic
acid-$^4C_1$

2-Amino-2-deoxyhexoses

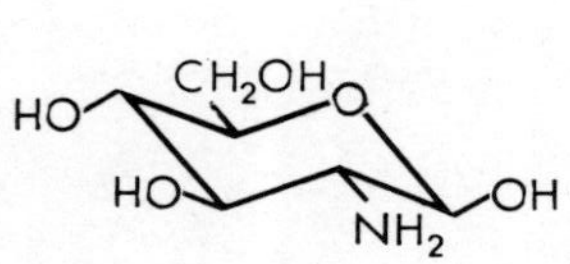

2-Amino-2-deoxy-β-D-glucopyranose-$^4C_1$ (Glucosamine)*

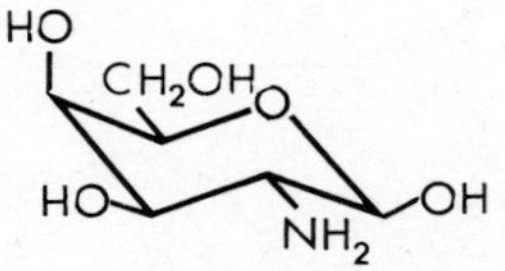

2-Amino-2-deoxy-β-D-galactopyranose-$^4C_1$ (Galactosamine)*

Neuraminic acids

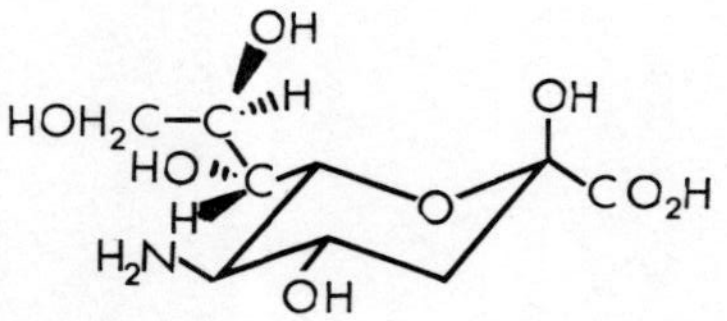

5-Amino-3,5-dideoxy-D-glycero-α-D-galacto-2-nonulopyranonic acid-$^1C_4$ (Neuraminic acid)*

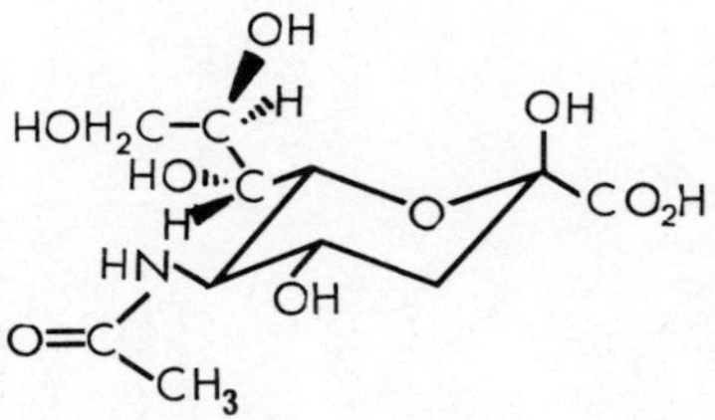

5-Acetamido-3,5 dideoxy-D-glycero-α-D-galacto-2-nonulopyranonic acid-$^1C_4$* (N-Acetylneuraminic acid)*

Fig. 2.8 — Structures of common monosaccharides (shown in one anomeric form only). See Figs. 8.9 and 12.1 for structures of less-common monosaccharides.

* These trivial names are accepted as standard biochemical and biological nomenclature but not for chemical usage.

OLIGOSACCHARIDES

When two or more monosaccharides are joined together, the bond that holds them together is known as the glycosidic bond. This is formed between the hydroxyl group on the anomeric carbon atom of one monosaccharide and any hydroxyl group on another monosaccharide through formation of an acetal (Scheme 2.2). Formation of a disaccharide by the condensation reaction (see also Chapter 5) between two identical hexopyranose ring structures can result in 11 different isomers if the identical hexopyanose residues belong to the D-series. There will of course be another series of 11 different isomers if the residues belong to the L-series and additional isomers can occur if furanose forms are also considered. The series of 11 isomers is composed of eight isomers having glycosidic linkages between C-1 of one residue, in either anomeric configuration, and C-2, C-3, C-4 or C-6 of the other pyranose residue. These are termed $(1 \rightarrow 2)$-α-D-, $(1 \rightarrow 3)$-β-D- linkages etc., where α- and β- refer to the anomeric con-

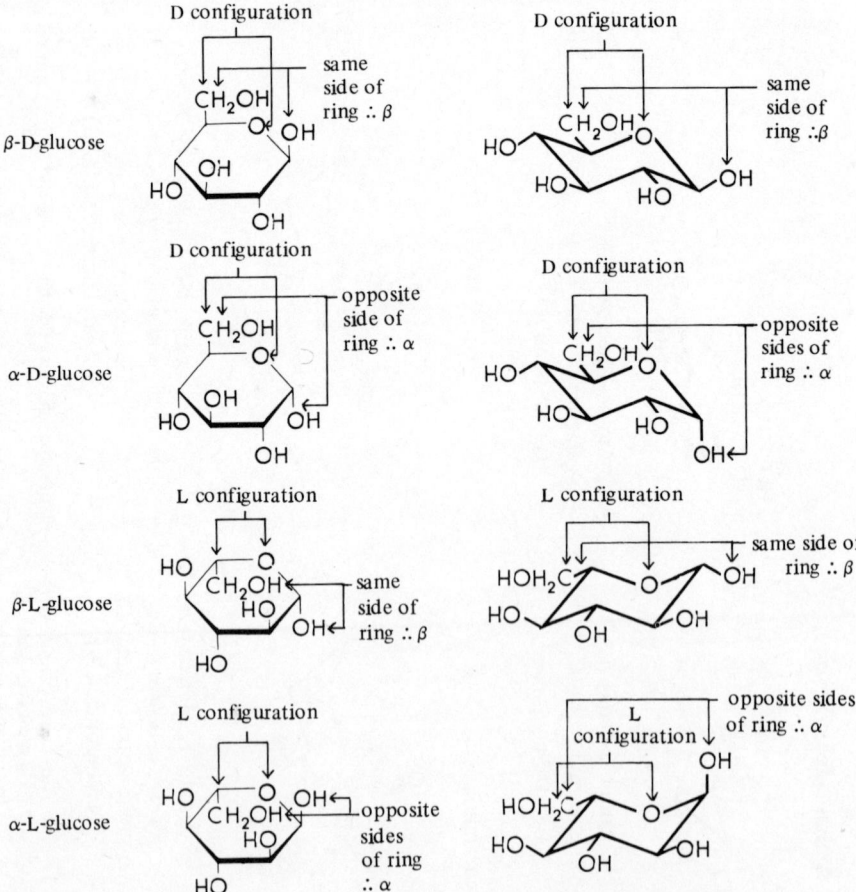

Fig. 2.9 – Definition of anomeric configuration at carbon atom 1.

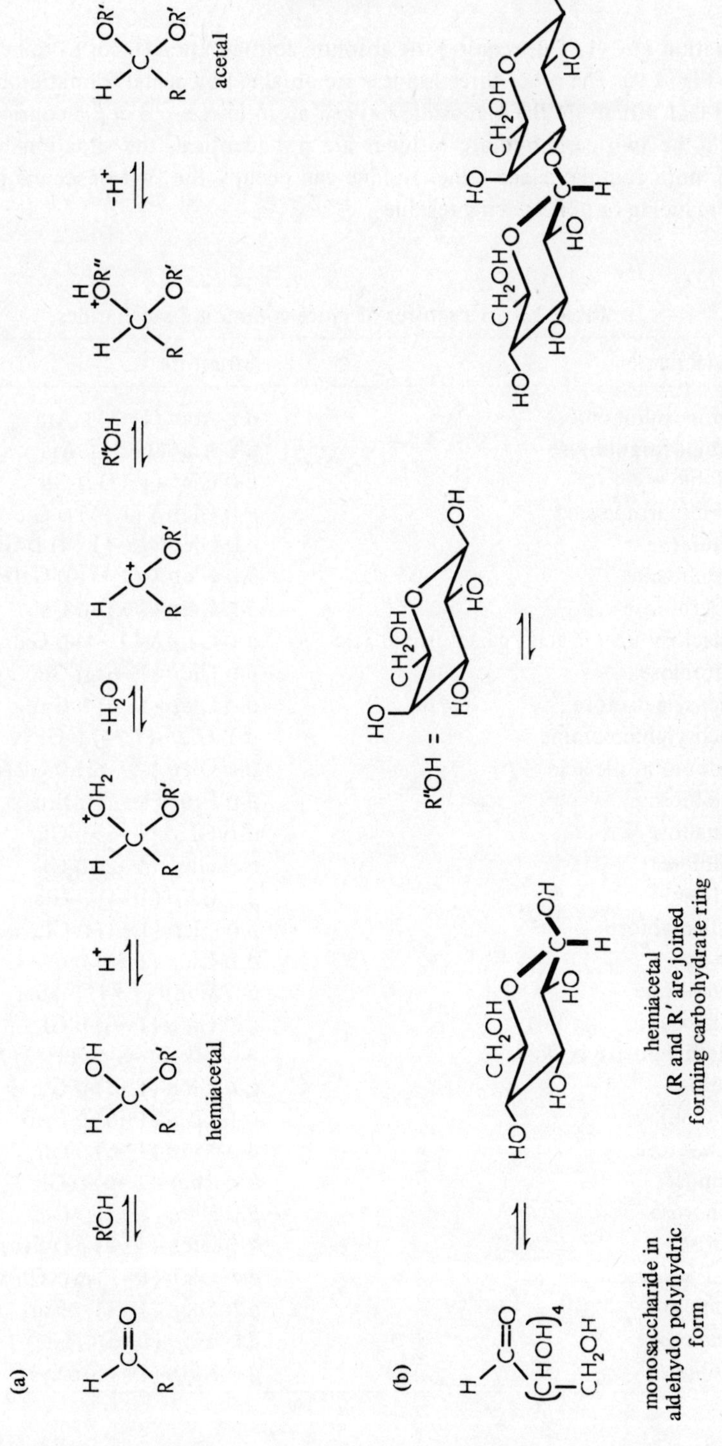
(a)
R'OH
hemiacetal
H+
-H2O
R"OH
-H+
acetal
(b)
monosaccharide in aldehydo polyhydric form
hemiacetal (R and R' are joined forming carbohydrate ring
R"OH =

Scheme 2.2

figuration at C-1. This requires the absolute configuration (D- or L- to be stated) (see Fig. 2.9). The other three isomers are obtained by acetal formation between both C-1 atoms via the glycosidic oxygen atom in α,α, α,β or β,β configuration. When the two carbohydrate residues are not identical, the situation becomes even more complex since either residue can occupy the first or second position (i.e. reducing or nonreducing residue).

Table 2.3 Structures of more-common disaccharides

Trivial name	Structure
Arabinopyranobiose	β-L-Ara$p$-(1→3)-L-Ara
Arabinofuranobiose	β-L-Ara$f$-(1→3)-L-Ara
Cellobiose	β-D-Glc$p$-(1→4)-D-Glc
Cellobiouronic acid	β-D-Glc$p$A-(1→4)-D-Glc
Chitobiose	β-D-Glc$p$NAc-(1→4)-D-GlcNAc
Chondrosine	β-D-Glc$p$A-(1→3)-D-GalN
Galactobiose	β-D-Gal$p$-(1→3)-D-Gal
(Galactosyluronic acid) galacturonic acid	α-D-Gal$p$A-(1→4)-D-GalA
Gentobiose	β-D-Glc$p$-(1→6)-D-Glc
Glucosylgalactose	β-D-Glc$p$-(1→6)-D-Gal
Glucosylglucosamine	α-D-Glc$p$-(1→4)-D-GlcN
Hyalobiouronic acid	β-D-Glc$p$A-(1→3)-D-GlcN
Inulobiose	β-D-Fru$f$-(1→1)-D-Fru
Isomaltose	α-D-Glc$p$-(1→6)-D-Glc
Kojibiose	α-D-Glc$p$-(1→2)-D-Glc
Lactose	β-D-Gal$p$-(1→4)-D-Glc
Laminarabiose	β-D-Glc$p$-(1→3)-D-Glc
Maltose	α-D-Glc$p$-(1→4)-D-Glc
Mannobiose	β-D-Man$p$-(1→4)-D-Man
Melibiose	α-D-Gal$p$-(1→6)-D-Glc
4-Methylglucosylxylose	4-O-Me-α-D-Glc$p$-(1→2)-D-Xyl
Nigerose	α-D-Glc$p$-(1→3)-D-Glc
Planteobiose	α-D-Gal$p$-(1→6)-D-Fru
Primaverose	β-D-Xyl$p$-(1→6)-D-Glc
Rutinose	β-L-Rha$p$-(1→6)-D-Glc
Sophorose	β-D-Glc$p$-(1→2)-D-Glc
Sucrose	α-D-Glc$p$-(1↔2)-β-D-Fru$f$
α,α-Trehalose	α-D-Glc$p$-(1↔1)-α-D-Glc$p$
Turanose	α-D-Glc$p$-(1→3)-D-Fru
Vicianose	β-L-Ara$p$-(1→6)-D-Glc
Xylobiose	β-D-Xyl$p$-(1→4)-D-Xyl

Table 2.4 Structures of more-common higher oligosaccharides

	Trivial name	Structure
Trisaccharides		
	Cellotriose	β-D-Glc$p$-(1→4)-β-D-Glc$p$-(1→4)-D-Glc
	Gentianose	β-D-Glc$p$-(1→6)-a-D-Glc$p$-(1↔2)-β-D-Fru$f$
	6-*O*-Glucosylmaltose	a-D-Glc$p$ 1 ↓ 6 a-D-Glc$p$-(1→4)-D-Glc
	Isokestose	β-D-Fru$f$-(2→1)-β-D-Fru$f$-(2↔1)-a-D-Glc$p$
	Isomaltotriose	a-D-Glc$p$-(1→6)-a-D-Glc$p$-(1→6)-D-Glc
	Isopanose	a-D-Glc$p$-(1→4)-a-D-Glc$p$-(1→6)-D-Glc
	Kestose	β-D-Fru$f$-(2→6)-β-D-Fru$f$-(2↔1)-a-D-Glc$p$
	Laminaratriose	β-D-Glc$p$-(1→3)-β-D-Glc$p$-(1→3)-D-Glc
	Maltotriose	a-D-Glc$p$-(1→4)-a-D-Glc$p$-(1→4)-D-Glc
	Melezitose	a-D-Glc$p$-(1→3)-β-D-Fru$f$-(2↔1)-a-D-Glc$p$
	Neokestose	β-D-Fru$f$-(2→6)-a-D-Glc$p$-(1↔2)-β-D-Fru$f$
	Neuraminolactose	NeuNAc-(2→3)-β-D-Gal$p$-(1→4)-D-Glc
	Panose	a-D-Glc$p$-(1→6)-a-D-Glc$p$-(1→4)-D-Glc
	Planteose	a-D-Gal$p$-(1→6)-β-D-Fru$f$-(2→1)-a-D-Glc
	Raffinose	a-D-Gal$p$-(1→6)-a-D-Glc$p$-(1↔2)-β-D-Fru$f$
	Umbelliferose	a-D-Gal$p$-(1→2)-a-D-Glc$p$-(1↔2)-β-D-Fru$f$
Tetrasaccharides		
	Cellotetraose	β-D-Glc$p$-(1→4)-β-D-Glc$p$-(1→4)-β-D-Glc$p$-(1→4)-D-Glc
	Maltotetraose	a-D-Glc$p$-(1→4)-a-D-Glc$p$-(1→4)-α-D-Glc$p$-(1→4)-D-Glc
	Stachyose	a-D-Gal$p$-(1→6)-a-D-Gal$p$-(1→6)-a-D-Glc$p$-(1↔2)-β-D-Fru$f$
Pentasaccharides		
	Verbascose	a-D-Gal$p$-(1→6)-a-D-Gal$p$-(1→6)-a-D-Gal$p$-(1→6)-a-D-Glc$p$-(1↔2)-β-D-Fru$f$
Cyclic oligosaccharides[*]		
	Cyclomaltohexaose	→4)-[a-D-Glc$p$]$_6$-(1
	Cyclomaltoheptaose	→4)-[a-D-Glc$p$]$_7$-(1
	Cyclomalto-octaose	→4)-[a-D-Glc$p$]$_8$-(1

[*] Previously referred to as Schardinger dextrins, cyclodextrins, cycloamyloses.

The major classification of oligosaccharides is according to the number of monosaccharide units, into di-, tri- and tetra-saccharides etc. Each classification is further subdivided into homo- or hetero-oligosaccharides (homo-oligosaccharides consist of only one type of monosaccharide); and reducing or nonreducing oligosaccharides (depending on the presence or absence of a free hemiacetal group). For example, sucrose is a nonreducing heterodisaccharide, α,α-trehalose a nonreducing homodisaccharide, and maltotriose, a reducing homotrisaccharide (see Tables 2.3 and 2.4).

Nomenclature of oligosaccharides is undergoing a process of systematisation (in common with all carbohydrate nomenclature). The original Tentative Rules (1969) stated that reducing oligosaccharides are named as glycosylglycoses, glycosylglycosylglycoses, etc., and nonreducing oligosaccharides as glycosylglycosides, etc. Further information on anomeric configuration, configuration of monosaccharides residues and positions of linkages and substitution are included. Hence, maltose is 4-*O*-α-D-glucopyranosyl-D-glucose (8), the '4' indicating that the linkage is between C-1 of one residue and C-4 of the other, the '*O*' indicating that substitution is on the oxygen atom at C-4, the 'α' indicating the anomeric configuration of the glycosidic linkages and the 'D' indicating that both monosaccharides have stereochemistry related to D-glyceraldehyde (see Fig. 2.9). Tables 2.3 and 2.4 show the structures of the more-common oligosaccharides, some of which are naturally occurring and some of which occur only as hydrolysis products of polysaccharides. Where available, trivial names have been included since these are often used for brevity, if no ambiguity is possible. Such names as agarotetraose and nigerotriose should *not* be used to describe oligomers containing two or more different monosaccharides or types of linkage, as there is no indication as to the order of monosaccharide or linkages.

(8)

Structures of oligosaccharides may be written in abbreviated form (as in Tables 2.3 and 2.4) by using a system of symbols (Recommendations 1980b) containing three letters (usually the first three letters of the trivial name) to represent both name and structure of component monosaccharides (see Table 2.5). 2-Amino-2-deoxy sugars are represented by the symbol for the parent sugar followed by the letter N, and uronic acids by A. The symbols for less common sugars can be derived from trivial names, but it is usual to give the systematic name as well. Examples include:

3,6-Dideoxy-D-*xylo*-hexose (abequose = Abe)
6-Deoxy-D-glucose (quinovose = Qui)
3-*C*-(Hydroxymethyl)-D-*glycero*-aldotetrose (D-apiose = Api)

Configuration, ring size and anomeric configuration are added by using the usual symbols (as in Tables 2.3 and 2.4). Where a branch point occurs, the branch to the main chain is added by use of a vertical arrow to the central letter of the 3-letter symbol for the parent sugar, with appropriate numbers used to denote the position of the linkage (9).

Table 2.5 Symbols used for monosaccharides

Allose	=	All
Altrose	=	Alt
Arabinose	=	Ara
Fructose	=	Fru
Fucose	=	Fuc
Galactose	=	Gal
Glucose	=	Glc
Gulose	=	Gul
Idose	=	Ido
Lyxose	=	Lyx
Mannose	=	Man
Muramic acid	=	Mur
Neuraminic acid	=	Neu
Rhamnose	=	Rha
Ribose	=	Rib
Talose	=	Tal
Xylose	=	Xyl

$$a\text{-D-Gal}p\text{-}(1\rightarrow 4)\text{-}\beta\text{-D-Glc}p\text{NAc-}(1\rightarrow 4)\text{-D-Glc}p\text{-}$$
$$\begin{array}{c} 6 \\ \uparrow \\ 1 \\ \beta\text{-D-Fru}f \end{array}$$

$$(9)$$

The linkage between the two residues, A and B, in the trisaccharide shown in Fig. 2.10 can be described as a $(1\rightarrow 6)$-linkage, which means that a glycosidic bond is formed between C-1 of residue A and C-6 of residue B. Since residue B is also linked to another residue C, by, in this case a $(1\rightarrow 3)$-linkage, residue B can be described as a 1,6-disubstituted residue.

The standard nomenclature for describing the various monosaccharide units in oligosaccharides (and polysaccharides, etc.) is based on the distinction between terminal locations of such units. In general, the appropriate terms are: 'glycosyl group', 'glycosyl residue' and 'glycose residue'. Thus, in the trisaccharide shown in Fig. 2.10, unit A is a D-glucopyranosyl group, unit B is a D-glucopyranosyl residue, and unit C is a D-galactopyranose residue.

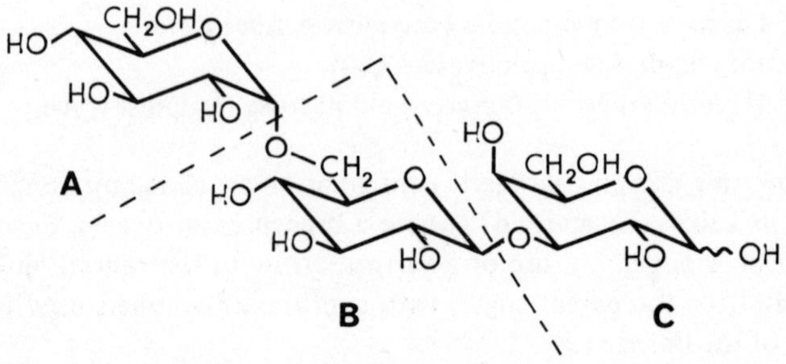

Fig. 2.10 — The trisaccharide, a-D-Glcp-(1→6)-β-D-Glcp-(1→3)-D-Galp, used as an example for the definition of oligosaccharide, etc. nomenclature (see text for details).

Oligosaccharides with branched structures are described as O-substituted oligosaccharides using a system in which a locant is used showing the position of the hydroxyl group involved in the branch point. If the branch point occurs in the glycose residue the locant alone is used whereas if the branch point occurs in a glycosyl residue or group the locant carries a superscript denoting the position of the glycosyl residue or group in the oligosaccharide, counting from the glycose residue. Thus 6-O-α-D-glucosylmaltose and panose (see Table 2.4) are both D-glucosyl derivatives of maltose with the substitution being described as 6-O-α-D-glucopyranosylmaltose and 6^2-O-α-D-glucopyranosylmaltose respectively. Although the numbering of the glycosyl residues has the inconvenience of reading from right to left in the conventional representation of oligosaccharides, it has the advantage that shortening or lengthening of chains by the usual mechanism of transglycosylation at the nonreducing end (see Chapter 5) leaves the numbering of residues in the chain unaltered. Alternative nomenclature would be α-D-glucopyranosyl-(1 → 4)-O-[α-D-glucopyranosyl-(1 → 6)-O-]-D-glucose   and α-D-glucopyranosyl-(1 → 6)-O-α-D-glucopyranosyl-(1 → 4)-O-D-glucose.

Further examples of oligosaccharides will be discussed subsequently in the chapters on oligosaccharides (Chapter 7) and antibiotics (Chapter 12).

POLYSACCHARIDES

Polysaccharides are natural macromolecules occurring in almost all living organisms, constituting one of the largest groups of natural compounds classified thus far, and function either as an energy source or as structural units in the morphology of the living material in which they are endogenous. Examples of polysaccharides possessing structural functions are: (a) cellulose, a polymer of D-glucose, that is probably the most abundant naturally occurring organic substance and is the structural material of plants, and (b) chitin, a polymer of 2-acetamido-2-deoxy-D-glucose, which is the major organic component of the exoskeleton (shells) of insects, crabs, lobsters etc.

As one of the main sources of energy for living organisms, certain polysaccharides form part of the central pathway of energy in most cells. The starches and glycogens, long-chain polymers of D-glucose, are the media for energy storage in plants and animals respectively.

Polysaccharides also perform more-specific roles such as being responsible for the type specificity of the pneumococcal polysaccharides. Other natural macromolecules, which are not composed entirely of sugar units, contain blocks of monosaccharide units as part of the molecular structure, and contribute extensively to the production and maintenance of living tissues of animals. The blood-group substances, for example, constitute a group of glycoproteins in which the arrangements of monosaccharide residues in the carbohydrate sub units contribute towards the blood-group specificity of the overall molecule.

Trivial names of the polysaccharides usually reflect their origin; examples include cellulose, the principal component of cell walls in plants, and dermatan, a polysaccharide normally occurring in its sulphated form and originally found in the dermal layer of skin (Greek, *derma*). The trivial names can also reflect some property of the isolated polymer, for example, starch, a name derived from the old English word *stercan*, meaning to stiffen.

The species origin of a polysaccharide leads to differences within a polysaccharide type. Thus, since, for example, starches from various plant sources are readily distinguished chemically, it is necessary to specify the origin in definitively naming the starch, for example, maize starch. The traditional names of long standing, such as cellulose, glycogen and amylose are still inevitably retained, but, with the increase in knowledge of the structure of these compounds, nomenclature and classification are now being made in terms of structure and, in the interests of systematisation, all new discoveries should be named systematically (Recommendations, 1980c). The term *glycan* derived from glycose, meaning a simple monosaccharide, is another word for polysaccharide, but a more specific term is obtained by using the configurational prefix of the parent sugar with the suffix 'an' to signify a polymer, for example mannan, for a polymer based on the monosaccharide mannose. Further speci ficity is achieved by inclusion of the D or L configuration, as appropriate, for example, D-glucan from D-glucose. Such nomenclature, and any classification derived therefrom, should ideally include information on chemical structure. Polysaccharides which, on hydrolysis, yield only one type of monosaccharide are called homoglycans, whereas those which can be hydrolysed to more than one type of monosaccharide are called heteroglycans, with designatory prefixes of di-, tri-, etc., for the number of monosaccharide types involved.

There is, at present, no proof of the existence of polysaccharides which contain more than about six different types of monosaccharide unit. The most common constituents are the pentose and hexose monosaccharides and monosaccharides derived from them, for example hexuronic acids, 6-deoxyhexoses, 2-amino-2-deoxyhexoses (hexosamines) and simple derivatives (including sulphates, acetates and methyl ethers), and these usually form a regular repeating-unit throughout the polymer. This repeating-unit is usually used in any chemical representation of the polysaccharide, and its structure can be written by using the same system of abbreviations and symbols used for oligosaccharides (Recommendations, 1980b). Tables 2.6 and 2.7 show the structures and sources of the common homoglycans and of some heteroglycans. These and other carbohydrate-containing compounds will be discussed more thoroughly in subsequent chapters.

Table 2.6 Structure and source of the common homopolysaccharides

Linkage	Source	Common Name
L-Arabinans		
$(1\rightarrow3)$-α-L-, $(1\rightarrow5)$-α-L- branched	Plant pectic substances	
D-Fructans		
$(2\rightarrow1)$-β-D- linear	Dandelions, dahlias, Jerusalem artichokes	Inulin
$(2\rightarrow6)$-β-D- linear	Various grasses	Levans
$(2\rightarrow6)$-β-D-, $(2\rightarrow1)$-β-D- branched	Plants and bacteria	Levans
L-Fucans		
$(1\rightarrow2)$-α-L-, $(1\rightarrow4)$-α-L- branched	Brown seaweed	Fucoidan
D-Galactans		
$(1\rightarrow3)$-β-D-, $(1\rightarrow4)$-α-D- linear	Red seaweeds	Carrageenan
$(1\rightarrow3)$-β-D-, $(1\rightarrow6)$-β-D- branched	Beef lung	
$(1\rightarrow4)$-β-D- linear	Plant pectic substances	
$(1\rightarrow5)$-β-D- linear	Penicillin mould	Galactocarolose
D-Galacturonans		
$(1\rightarrow4)$-α-D- linear	Plant pectic substances	Pectic acid
D-Glucans		
$(1\rightarrow2)$-β-D- linear	Agrobacteria	
$(1\rightarrow3)$-α-D-, $(1\rightarrow4)$-α-D- linear	*Aspergillus niger,* Iceland moss	Nigeran, elsinan isolichenan
$(1\rightarrow3)$-β-D- linear	Brown seaweeds, plants, plants, algae, fungi and yeasts	Laminaran, callose, curdlan, pachyman
$(1\rightarrow3)$-β-D-, $(1\rightarrow6)$-β-D- branched	Fungi	Scleroglucan
$(1\rightarrow3)$-β-D-, $(1\rightarrow4)$-β-D- linear	Iceland moss, cereal grains	Lichenan
$(1\rightarrow4)$-α-D- linear	Plants	Amylose
$(1\rightarrow4)$-α-D-, $(1\rightarrow6)$-α-D- linear	Fungi	Pullulan
$(1\rightarrow4)$-α-D-, $(1\rightarrow6)$-α-D- branched	Animals, plants and micro-organisms	Glycogen, amylopectin

Table 2.6 (*continued*)

Linkage	Source	Common name
(1→4)-β-D- linear	Plant cell-walls	Cellulose
(1→4)-β-D-, (1→3)-α-D- branched	Bacteria	Dextran
(1→6)-β-D- linear	Lichens	Pustulan
2-Amino-2-deoxy-D-glucans		
(1→4)-β-D- linear	Crab and lobster shells, fungi	Chitin
D-Mannans		
(1→2)-α-D-, (1→6)-α-D- branched	Yeasts	
(1→4)-β-D- linear	Seaweeds, plants	
D-Xylans		
(1→3)-β-D- linear	Green seaweed	Rhodymenan
(1→3)-β-D-, (1→4)-β-D- linear	Red seaweed	
(1→4)-β-D- linear	Plant cell-walls	

Table 2.7 Structure and source of some heteropolysaccharides

Constituent monosaccharides and chain type	Source	Common name
L-Arabinose, D-galactose, branched	Coniferous woods	
L-Arabinose, D-xylose, branched	Plant cell-walls	
DL-Galactose, linear	Red seaweeds	Agarose,
branched	Snails	porphyran
D-Galactose, 2-amino-2-deoxy-D-glucose, linear	Cornea	Keratan sulphate
D-Galactose, D-mannose, branched	Leguminous seeds, fungi	
2-Amino-2-deoxy-D-galactose, D-glucuronic acid, linear	Cornea, cartilage	Chondroitin, chondroitin sulphates
2-Amino-2-deoxy-D-galactose, L-iduronic acid, linear	Skin	Dermatan sulphate
D-Glucose, D-mannose, linear	Coniferous woods, seeds, bulbs	
2-Amino-2-deoxy-D-glucose, D-glucuronic acid, linear	Animal and mammalian tissues	Hyaluronic acid
D-Glucuronic acid, D-xylose, branched	Plant cell-walls	
L-Guluronic acid, D-mannuronic acid, linear	Bacteria, brown seaweeds	Alginic acid

CHAPTER 3

General chemistry

GENERAL STRUCTURES OF MACROMOLECULAR CARBOHYDRATES

All macromolecular carbohydrate materials have definite, three-dimensional structures, and the four aspects of these structures (primary, secondary, tertiary and quaternary structure) have essentially the same meaning for carbohydrates as for proteins and other biopolymers but the definition of each aspect is not as clear-cut as in, for example, protein chemistry. For this reason, carbohydrate structures are compared and contrasted, aspect for aspect, with protein structures.

Primary structure

For proteins. this is the sequence of aminoacid residues within the linear chain. For polysaccharides, etc. the same definition applies for linear chains, but, as discussed previously (Chapters 1 and 2), the manner in which the various mono-saccharide residues are joined is much more complex than for the corresponding combination of aminoacid residues due to the greater number of substitution positions possible in a monosaccharide molecule. A further complexity is that branched structures, occurring *via* disubstitution of a single residue, commonly exist for polysaccharides. Thus, in order to define the primary structure of a polysaccharide fully, it is essential to state the identity of all monosaccharide residues, the sequence of these residues, their position and anomeric configur-ation and the position of any other substituents. Polysaccharide primary struct-ures frequently show simple repeating sequences and these repeating sequences have been determined for many polysaccharides and other carbohydrate-con-taining macromolecules; these will be discussed in subsequent chapters.

Secondary structure

The secondary structure of proteins can be described as the spatial relationship of near neighbours which is a result of interactions such as hydrogen bonding between C=O and N—H groups, producing some degree of double-bond character and, hence, local regularities. The geometry of the individual sugar rings in a polysaccharide is essentially rigid but the relative orientations of component residues (i.e. rotation) about the glycosidic linkage determines the overall conformation of the polysaccharide. Two torsion (rotational) angles are required in order to define the glycosidic bond between two carbohydrate residues, A and B, except for $(1\rightarrow6)$-linked polysaccharides which require three angles (see Fig. 3.1). The angle ϕ is about the bond from the anomeric carbon atom to the oxygen atom that joins the two residues, the angle ψ is about the bond from the glycosylated oxygen atom of residue A to the carbon atom of residue B, and the angle ω is about the exocyclic carbon–carbon bond (see Recommendations, 1981a). The range of values obtained for the rotational angles ϕ, ψ and ω is severely restricted by steric hindrance between the adjacent rings and by non-bonding interactions between groups in adjacent residues. The restrictions are greatest for glycosidic linkages involving axial groups (as may be seen for such α-D-glucans as amylose, Fig. 3.1), and for residues containing such bulky substituents as N-acetyl in equatorial positions adjacent to the glycosidic linkage. This has the result that chains are relatively stiff with, for example, coil shapes predominating in solution. The overall secondary structure of polysaccharides is therefore heavily dependent on the primary structure.

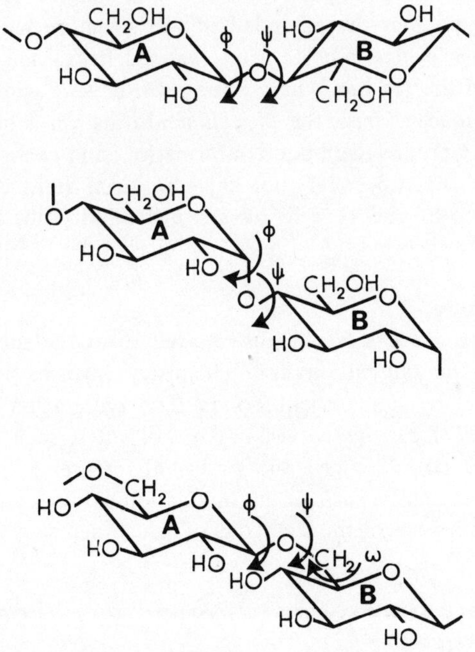

Fig. 3.1 – Rotation of individual residues about the glycosidic linkage in (i) cellulose, (ii) amylose, and (iii) dextran.

Tertiary structure

In protein structure this is the gross folding of the chain which brings together groups that are normally separated by large distances along the protein backbone, allowing such interactions as the formation of disulphide linkages, ion-pairs and hydrophobic attractions. The repeating sequences in primary structures of polysaccharides lead to regular patterns in secondary structures which lead to sterically regular gross conformations aided by favourable non-covalent interactions between hydroxyl, sulphate, amino, phosphate, carboxyl, etc. groups. Irregularities in primary and secondary structures and large branched structures inhibit tertiary structure formation whilst such external perturbations as changes in temperature and ionic concentrations can cause changes in the tertiary structure. For example, charged polysaccharides can form stable, tertiary structures by incorporation of counter-ions within the tertiary structure. A useful concept which has been used to describe the overall chain-conformation is to regard any conformation as a helix (even though it may not look like a conventional helix) and specify two parameters, namely, the number (n) of monomer residues per helix turn and this projected length (h) of each monomer residue on the helix axis. These parameters can be calculated from values of ϕ, ψ and ω (Ramachandran $et\,al.$, 1963). The allowed conformation of homopolysaccharides have values of n and h which fall into ranges which allow four distinct types to be identified (see Fig. 3.2). Type A is the extended ribbon structure with values for n of 2 to $\pm$ 4 (negative values indicate a left handed helix) and h is close to the absolute length of the residue. Where values of n cover a wider range (n = 2 to $\pm$ 10) and h approaches zero, the type B conformation is obtained (a normal helix). Type C is a crumpled ribbon conformation, and examples are characterized by many clusters between non-adjacent sugar residues in the primary structure. The fourth type, type D, has more flexibility due to the extra bond which separates the rings in (1→6)-linked polysaccharides.

Quaternary structure

This aspect of structure is frequently referred to as the subunit phenomenon and, in both protein and carbohydrate chemistry, involves the aggregation of a number of chains by noncovalent bonds. The aggregation of polysaccharide chains (Rees, 1977) can be between like molecules, such as the interaction between cellulose chains to give the structural features of plant cell-walls, or between unlike molecules, such as the interaction between xanthan helices with the unsubstituted regions of the backbone of galactomannans (see Chapter 8).

EFFECT OF STRUCTURE ON SOLUTION PROPERTIES OF POLYSACCHARIDES

Many of the simpler homopolysaccharides, for example, cellulose and starch, are insoluble in their natural, ordered states. This is because the adoption of an

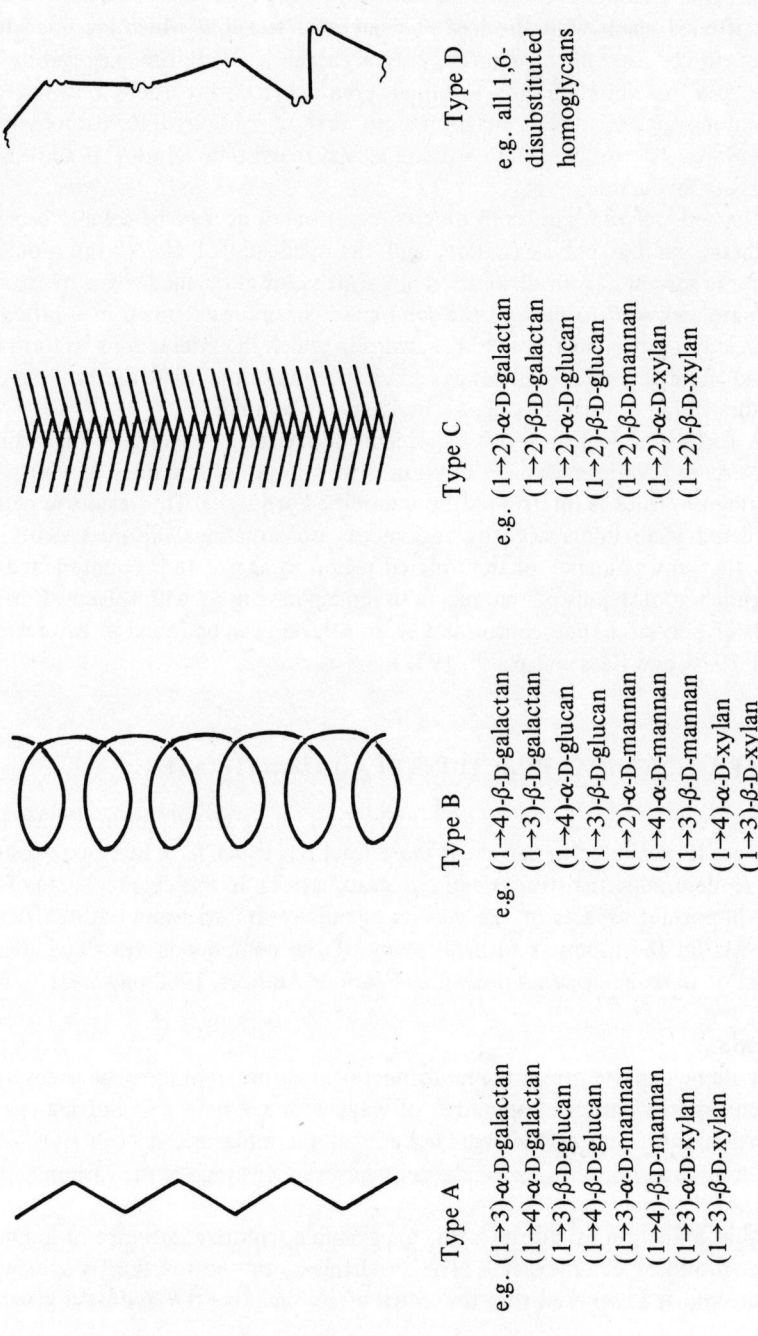

Type A

e.g. (1→3)-α-D-galactan
    (1→4)-α-D-galactan
    (1→3)-β-D-glucan
    (1→4)-β-D-glucan
    (1→3)-α-D-mannan
    (1→4)-β-D-mannan
    (1→3)-α-D-xylan
    (1→3)-β-D-xylan

Type B

e.g. (1→4)-β-D-galactan
    (1→3)-β-D-galactan
    (1→4)-α-D-glucan
    (1→3)-β-D-glucan
    (1→2)-α-D-mannan
    (1→4)-α-D-mannan
    (1→3)-β-D-mannan
    (1→4)-α-D-xylan
    (1→3)-β-D-xylan

Type C

e.g. (1→2)-α-D-galactan
    (1→2)-β-D-galactan
    (1→2)-α-D-glucan
    (1→2)-β-D-glucan
    (1→2)-β-D-mannan
    (1→2)-α-D-xylan
    (1→2)-β-D-xylan

Type D

e.g. all 1,6-
    disubstituted
    homoglycans

Fig. 3.2 — Tertiary structures found in homopolysaccharides. Type A, extended ribbon; Type B, flexible helix; Type C, crumpled ribbon, and Type D, flexible coil.

ordered conformation usually facilitates the ordered packing of chains with favourably non-bonded interactions between them. This ordered packing results in a stiffened chain with the loss of degrees of freedom which are important driving forces for dissolving the polysaccharides. Therefore aggregation of chains and precipitation are favoured even when the carbohydrate–solvent interactions are of similar magnitude to that of carbohydrate–carbohydrate interactions. The ordered-state structures may persist in solution if additional factors are favourable.

Charged polysaccharides in ordered conformations may be soluble because the charge on the polysaccharide, and the tendency of the counter-ions to disperse in solvent, favour dissolution not aggregation. Branched-chain structures, which are awkward to pack in the solid state, are more favoured in solution or in a weakly aggregated form, whilst chains in which the interactions to form the ordered state are weak will always exist in equilibrium with the random-coil structure which favours the polysaccharide being soluble.

A further biological device by which polysaccharide chains are maintained in an ordered conformation in solution is seen in polysaccharides in which the repeating sequence is interrupted by a modified sequence. This results in blocks of ordered state interspaced by regions of conformational disorder, with the result that any tendency of the ordered region to aggregate is counteracted by the tendency of the disordered region to remain in contact with solvent. Further details of polysaccharide conformations in solution can be found in two reviews (Rees, 1977, and Rees and Walsh, 1977).

GENERAL CHEMICAL REACTIONS OF CARBOHYDRATES

Some aspects of the chemistry of carbohydrates have already been discussed in the preceding chapter, in particular those reactions which have been used historically to determine the structure of monosaccharides. In this chapter some of the more important aspects of the general chemistry are discussed with particular emphasis on the products formed. Many of the compounds described are the subject of an on-going series of reviews (Various Authors, 1968 onwards).

Oxidation

As would be expected from the multifunctional nature of monosaccharides, they can undergo oxidation in a number of ways with a variety of oxidizing agents. Oxidation can occur at the reducing end of the molecule, at both ends, or at specific hydroxyl groups, or oxidation may cause cleavage of the carbon-carbon bonds.

Mild oxidation of aldoses with, for example, chlorine, bromine or iodine at pH 5, produces aldonic acids. The mechanism for the reaction is somewhat obscure but it is believed that the initial attack involves the hydroxyl group at

C-1 since β-D-glucopyranose is oxidized 250 times faster than the α-anomer. The aldose is oxidized directly to its corresponding lactone which is then slowly hydrolysed to the aldonic acid (Scheme 3.1). The free aldonic acid is difficult to isolate, due to its marked tendency to be dehydrated and revert to the lactone, but salts and such derivatives as amides and phenylhydrazones can be isolated. Alkaline oxidation with iodine (hypoiodite oxidation) similarly produces aldonic acids, and this reaction can be used as the basis for the quantitative determination of aldoses and for the determination of the reducing (terminal) residue of oligosaccharides (Ko and Somers, 1974). Ketoses are unaffected by mild oxidation with halogens.

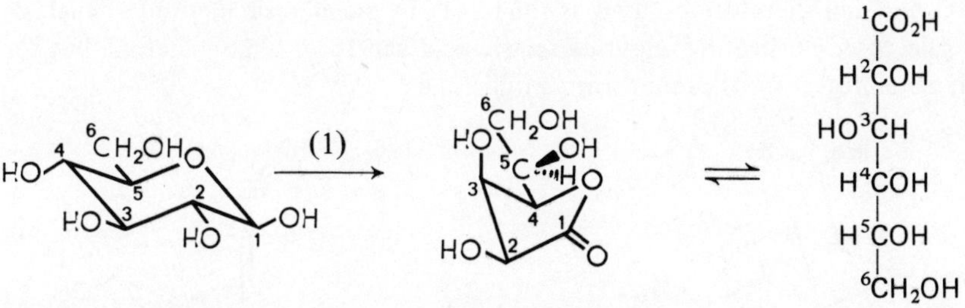

β-D-Glucopyranose   D-Glucono-1,4-lactone   D-Gluconic acid

Reagents: (1) halogens at pH 5.

Scheme 3.1

Selective oxidation of the nonreducing end of the monosaccharide (that is, C-6 of an aldohexose) with oxygen, using platinum as a catalyst, or with potassium permanganate, produces an alduronic acid. Both methods of preparation require the use of protecting groups to prevent oxidation at other positions in the molecule. Fig. 2.8 shows the structures of the naturally occurring alduronic acids. D-Glucuronic acid plays an important role in animal metabolism by aiding excretion of phenols, steroids and aromatic carboxylic acids by formation of D-glucosiduronic acids; it also occurs in heparin. D-Galacturonic acid occurs in fruit pectin; D-mannuronic acid and L-guluronic acid occur in various seaweed polysaccharides; whilst L-iduronic acid is a component of two of the glycosaminoglycans, dermatan sulphate and heparin (see Chapter 9). They are not easily isolated from their natural sources due to the drastic conditions usually required to break the glycosidic linkages. These conditions frequently result in decarboxylation and elimination reactions.

The normal form in which the alduronic acids exist is as a lactone; thus D-glucuronic acid exists as D-glucofuranurono-6,3-lactone (10), and D-galacturonic acid as D-galactopyranurono-6,3-lactone (11), because the configuration of the carboxyl and hydroxyl groups is such that a furanose ring would require a trans junction between the two rings, whereas the pyranose ring gives an unstrained structure.

Oxidation of both ends of the monosaccharide molecule leads to the formation of aldaric acids. They may be prepared by the oxidation of aldoses with nitric acid. Under the same conditions, ketoses form aldoses with one less carbon atom due to cleavage of the 1,2-bond, whereas 6-deoxyaldoses afford aldoses with one less carbon atom due to cleavage of the 5,6 bond. D-Arabinaric acid can, therefore, be formed from D-fructose, D-arabinose, D-lyxose or 6-deoxy-L-galactose (L-fucose) as shown in Scheme 3.2. D-Glucaric acid is isolated as the dilactone (12). (*meso*)-Galactaric acid (mucic acid) has very low solubility in water and can therefore be used as the basis of a gravimetric method of analysis for galactose. On heating, *meso*-galactaric acid can form a monolactone but for stereochemical reasons cannot form a dilactone.

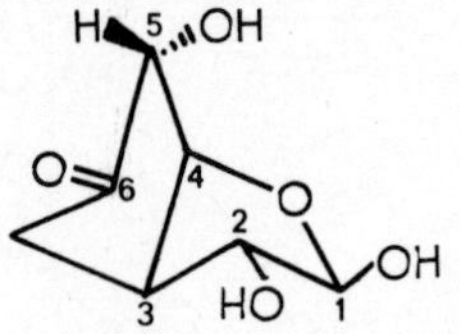

(10)

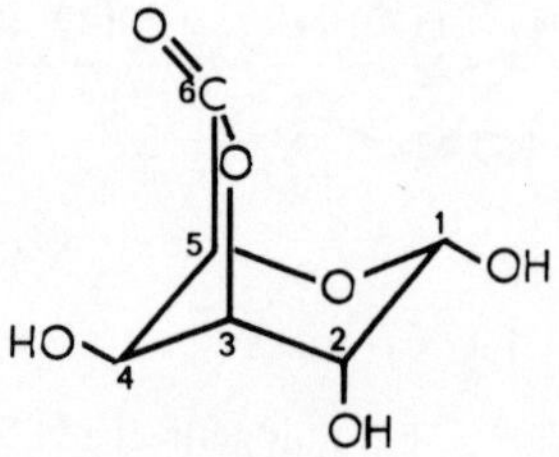

(11)

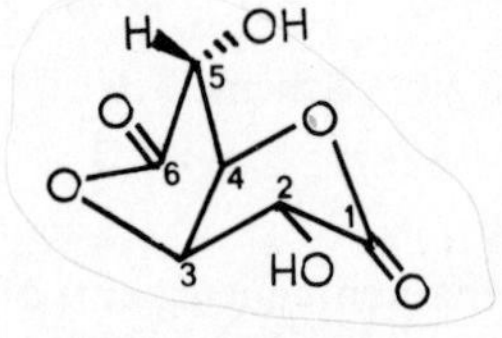

D-Glucaro-1,4;6,3-dilactone

(12)

Oxidation at the secondary hydroxyl groups is not usually accomplished directly from free sugars, but is possible using a suitably blocked derivative. Another complication is that the free aldosuloses are not usually crystalline due to the wide variety of cyclic structures which each can adopt. One possible method of preparation of aldos-2-uloses (osones) is by direct oxidation with copper(II) ions (Bayne and Fewster, 1956), aldos-3-uloses can be prepared in high yield (Angyal and James, 1970) from partially acetylated monosaccharides by using chromium(III) oxide in acetic acid (Scheme 3.3).

Cleavage of carbon-carbon bonds can be brought about by oxidation with such glycol-cleaving agents as lead(IV) acetate and periodic acid. The chemistry of these reactions is fully discussed in Chapter 4, as they are important in the structural analysis of carbohydrates.

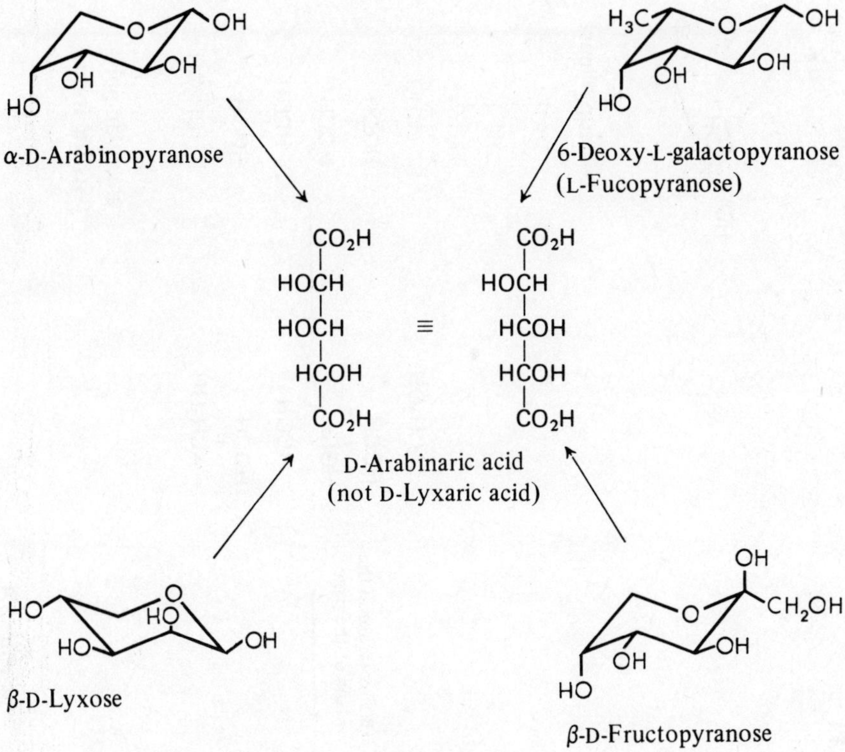

α-D-Arabinopyranose

6-Deoxy-L-galactopyranose
(L-Fucopyranose)

$$
\begin{array}{ccc}
CO_2H & & CO_2H \\
HOCH & & HOCH \\
HOCH & \equiv & HCOH \\
HCOH & & HCOH \\
CO_2H & & CO_2H \\
\end{array}
$$

D-Arabinaric acid
(not D-Lyxaric acid)

β-D-Lyxose

β-D-Fructopyranose

Scheme 3.2

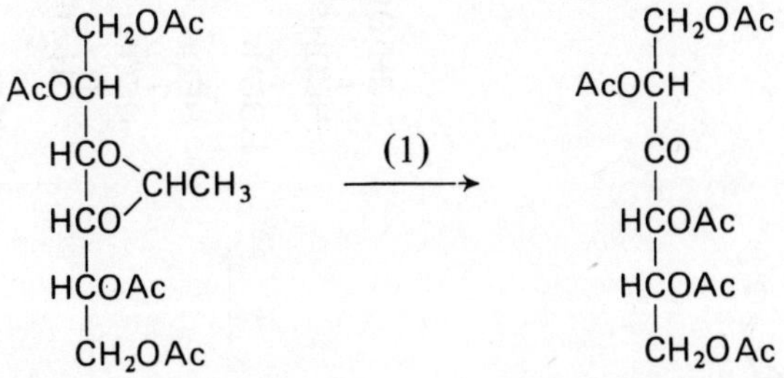

$$
\begin{array}{ccc}
CH_2OAc & & CH_2OAc \\
AcOCH & & AcOCH \\
HCO\!\!\diagdown & & CO \\
\quad\;\; CHCH_3 & \xrightarrow{(1)} & HCOAc \\
HCO\!\!\diagup & & HCOAc \\
HCOAc & & CH_2OAc \\
CH_2OAc & & \\
\end{array}
$$

1,2,5,6-Tetra-*O*-acetyl-3,4-
D-ethylidene-D-mannitol

1,2,4,5,6-Penta-*O*-acetyl-
D-*arabino*-3-hexulose

Reagents: (1) Chromium(III) oxide in acetic acid

Scheme 3.3

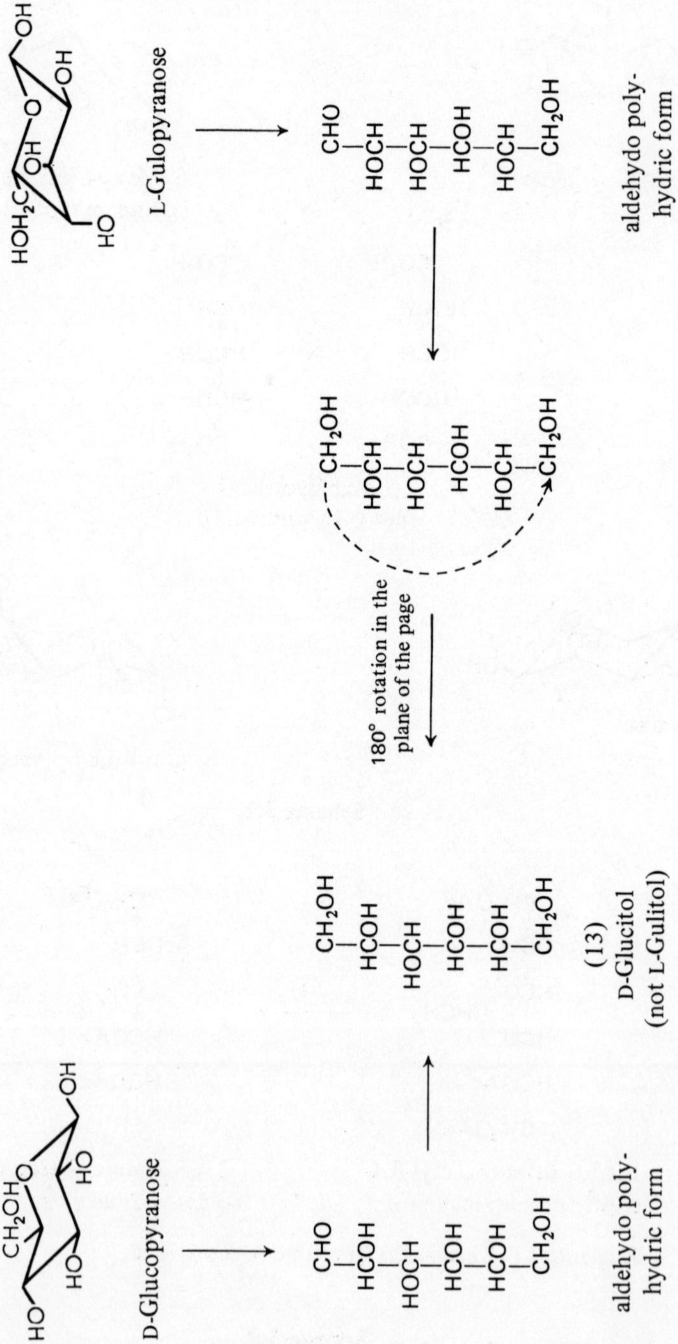

L-Gulopyranose

CHO
HOCH
HOCH
HCOH
HOCH
CH₂OH

aldehydo poly-
hydric form

CH₂OH
HOCH
HOCH
HCOH
HOCH
CH₂OH

180° rotation in the plane of the page

D-Glucopyranose

CHO
HCOH
HOCH
HCOH
HCOH
CH₂OH

aldehydo poly-
hydric form

CH₂OH
HCOH
HOCH
HCOH
HCOH
CH₂OH

(13)
D-Glucitol
(not L-Gulitol)

Scheme 3.4

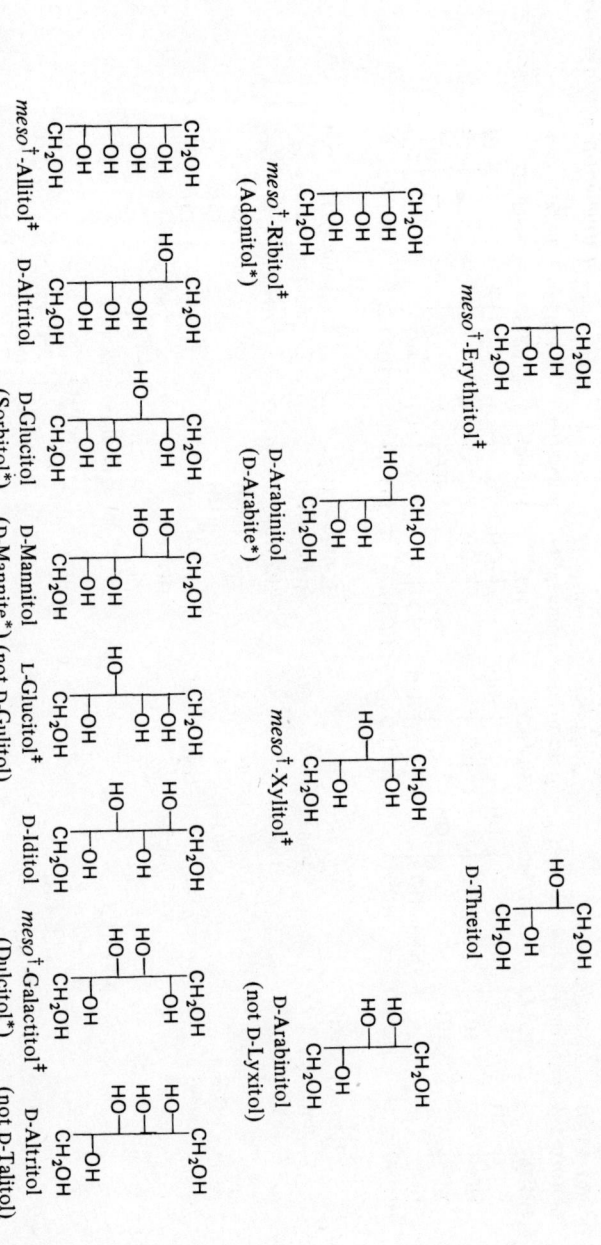

meso†-Glycerol‡

CH₂OH
OH
CH₂OH

meso†-Erythritol‡

CH₂OH
OH
OH
CH₂OH

D-Threitol

CH₂OH
HO
OH
CH₂OH

meso†-Ribitol‡
(Adonitol*)

CH₂OH
OH
OH
OH
CH₂OH

D-Arabinitol
(D-Arabite*)

CH₂OH
HO
OH
OH
CH₂OH

meso†-Xylitol‡

CH₂OH
OH
OH
OH
CH₂OH

D-Arabinitol
(not D-Lyxitol)

CH₂OH
HO
HO
OH
CH₂OH

meso†-Allitol‡

CH₂OH
OH
OH
OH
OH
CH₂OH

D-Altritol

CH₂OH
HO
OH
OH
OH
CH₂OH

D-Glucitol
(Sorbitol*)

CH₂OH
HO
OH
OH
OH
CH₂OH

D-Mannitol
(D-Mannite*)

CH₂OH
HO
HO
OH
OH
CH₂OH

L-Glucitol‡
(not D-Gulitol)

CH₂OH
HO
OH
OH
CH₂OH

D-Iditol

CH₂OH
HO
HO
OH
CH₂OH

meso†-Galactitol‡
(Dulcitol*)

CH₂OH
HO
HO
OH
OH
CH₂OH

D-Altritol
(not D-Talitol)

CH₂OH
HO
HO
HO
OH
CH₂OH

† meso- is frequently omitted.
‡ common to D- and L- series.
* trivial names not recommended for common usage.

Fig. 3.3a — Structures of the alditols, up to hexitols, of the D configuration with hydrogen atoms omitted for clarity (for the full structure of D-glucitol see Scheme 3.4). Rotations of 180° in the plane of the page gives the alternate structures, see Scheme 3.4.

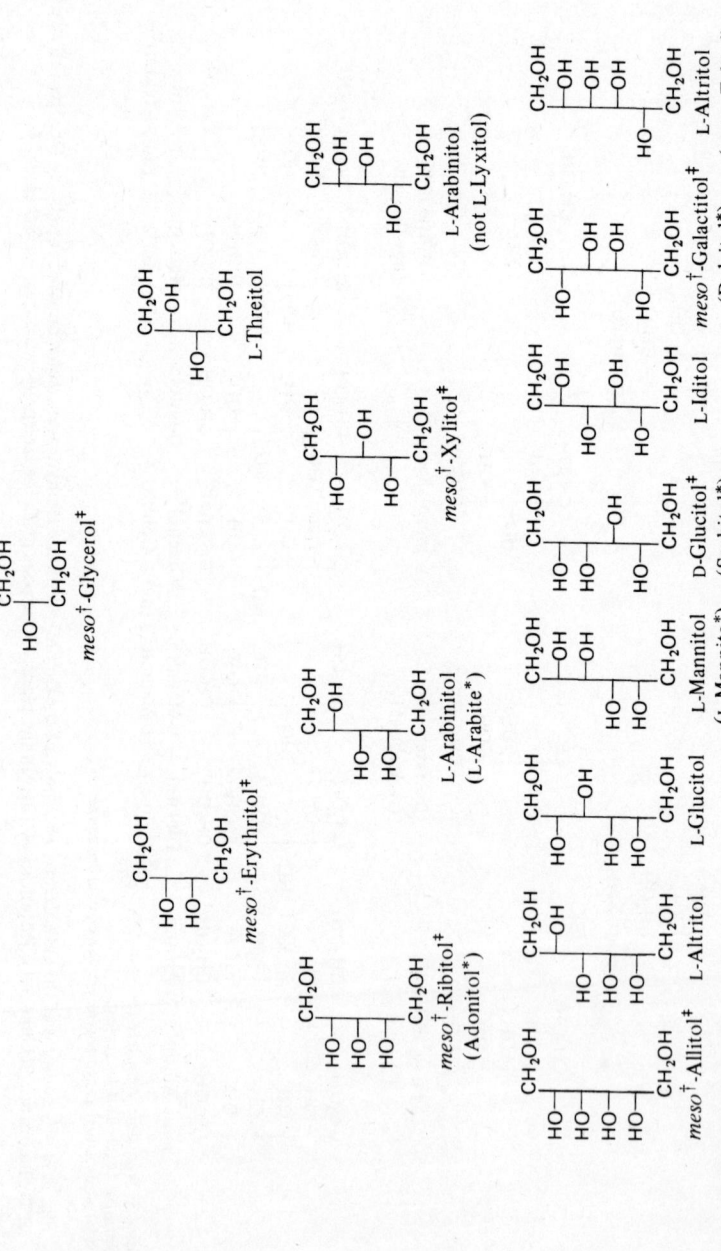

† *meso-* is frequently ommitted.
‡ common to D- and L- series.
* trivial names not recommended for common usage

Fig. 3.3b — Structures of the alditols, up to hexitols, of the L configuration with hydrogen atoms omitted for clarity (for the full structure of D-glucitol see Scheme 3.4). Rotations of 180° in the plane of the page gives the alternate structures, see Scheme 3.4.

Reduction

Reduction of the aldehyde group (potential aldehyde group if the aldose is present in a ring form) of an aldose gives a polyhydric alcohol known as an alditol and the fact that two different aldoses (for example, D-glucose and L-gulose) give the same alditol (D-glucitol (13), as shown in Scheme 3.4) was exploited by Fischer in the determination of the stereochemistry of mono-saccharides (see Chapter 2). Ketoses give a mixture of products; for example, D-fructose is reduced to a mixture of D-glucitol and D-mannitol. The structures and names of the alditols, up to hexitols are given in Figs. 3.3a and 3.3b, from which it may be seen that there are only 3 tetritols, 5 pentitols and 10 hexitols derived from the 4 tetroses, 8 pentoses and 16 hexoses respectively.

The traditional method of preparation, using sodium amalgam, has been superceded by sodium borohydride for laboratory preparations; it gives a more rapid reaction, unless the aldose is substituted at C-3 thus sterically hindering this reagent. The major drawback to the use of sodium borohydride, namely the subsequent removal of inorganic materials, has led to the development of other methods such as the use of Raney nickel in boiling ethanol (Wolfrom and Schumacher, 1955) for laboratory-scale preparations, or electrolytic reduction in alkaline media or catalytic hydrogenation for industrial usage. In the last method, extensive epimerisation of the aldose occurs prior to reduction, result-ing in a mixture of products; this has been exploited for the industrial preparation of D-mannitol from D-glucose rather than from D-mannose. A number of alditols exist in nature either free or in combined form, for example glycerol is an essential component of lipids, D-ribitol occurs in some microbial polysaccharides (see Chapter 8), and D-glucitol and D-mannitol in many fruits, plants and seaweeds.

The alditols are commonly used in the analysis of carbohydrates as precur-sors of alditol acetates, which are useful, volatile derivatives for analysis (see Chapter 4). Reduction of carbohydrates, usually monosaccharides, by reagents which produce a coloured product is used as a basis for estimation of carbo-hydrates using non-corrosive reagents (see review by White and Kennedy, 1981).

Action of acids and bases

Monosaccharides undergo isomerization and degradation with acids and bases to give a variety of products, but since alditols are remarkably stable to the action of acids and bases it may be assumed that the (potential) aldehyde or ketone group is responsible.

Aldoses are invariably more stable towards acid than towards alkali, although very little is known about their behaviour under mildly acidic conditions. Evaporation of a solution of an aldose in dilute mineral acid (for example, 1 mM) causes intermolecular-condensation reactions similar to glycoside forma-tion, to give small proportions of di-, tri- and higher oligo-saccharides. This process is called reversion. Under more drastic conditions, aldoses and ketoses undergo more-extensive dehydration reactions, to give furan derivatives (Scheme 3.5). These derivatives react with a number of phenols, aromatic amines and certain aliphatic aminoacids, in particular, L-cysteine, to give coloured products. Such reactions can be used as methods for detection and determination of carbohydrates which, in some cases, allow different types of monosaccharides to be detected in mixtures. For example, it is possible to determine pentoses in the presence of hexoses by using L-cysteine, due to the different ease of formation of the furan derivatives (pentoses react under milder conditions than those required for hexoses), and to distinguish a number of hexoses from each other due to secondary reactions taking place to differing degrees. One secondary reaction which can occur is a ring-opening reaction producing 4-oxo-pentanoic acid (laevulinic acid, 14) and formic acid. For a review of the methods used for the analysis of carbohydrates based on furan derivatives, see White and Kennedy (1981).

Aldo- or keto- hexose   ⟶ HOH_2C — O — CHO

5-(Hydroxymethyl)furan-2-aldehyde

Aldo- or keto- pentose   ⟶

Furan-2-aldehyde

6-Deoxyhexose   ⟶ H_3C — O — CHO

5-Methyl furan-2-aldehyde

Scheme 3.5

$$
\begin{array}{c}
CO_2H \\
| \\
CH_2 \\
| \\
CH_2 \\
| \\
CO \\
| \\
CH_3
\end{array}
$$

(14)

Under mildly basic conditions, such as in the presence of pyridine or aqueous calcium hydroxide, aldose ⇌ ketose isomerisation, which also results in epimerisation at C-2 (Scheme 3.6), occurs. These are known as the Lobry de Bruyn-Alberda van Eckenstein rearrangements. In conditions of 10 mM sodium hydroxide the proportions of product formed are shown in Scheme 3.6. Under more-drastic conditions, such as longer reaction times, increased temperature, or increased concentration of alkali, rearrangements take place through processes of β-elimination and benzilic acid type rearrangements (Scheme 3.7) with the formation of aldonic acid derivatives (trivial name, not accepted for current usage, saccharinic acids) (Scheme 3.8). Even more strongly basic conditions result in complex, reverse alditol reactions which give fragments containing three carbon atoms; those include 2-hydroxypropanaldehyde (15), pyruvic acid (16) and lactic acid (17).

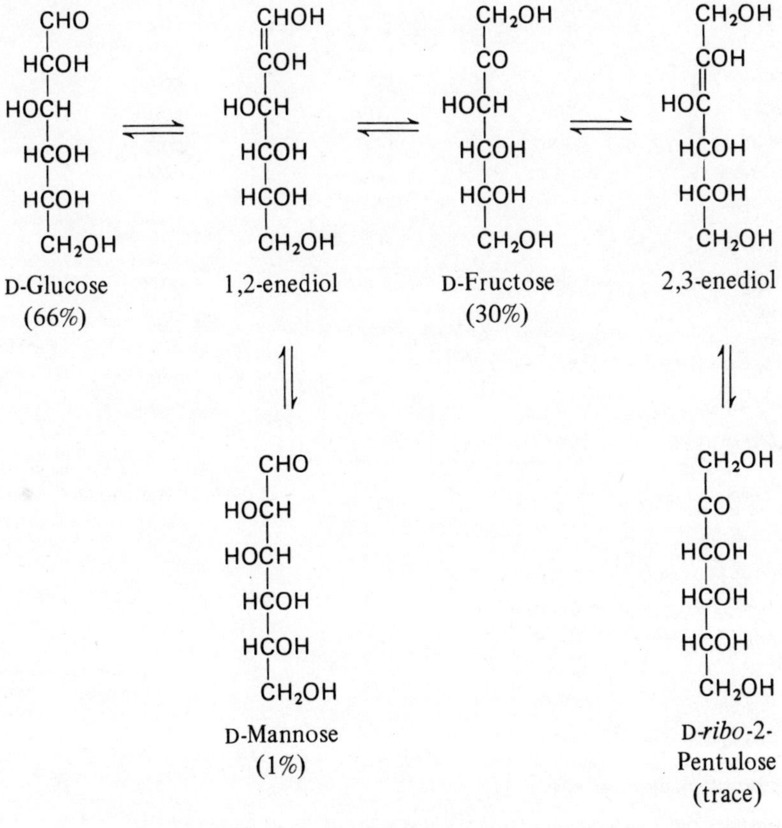

Scheme 3.6

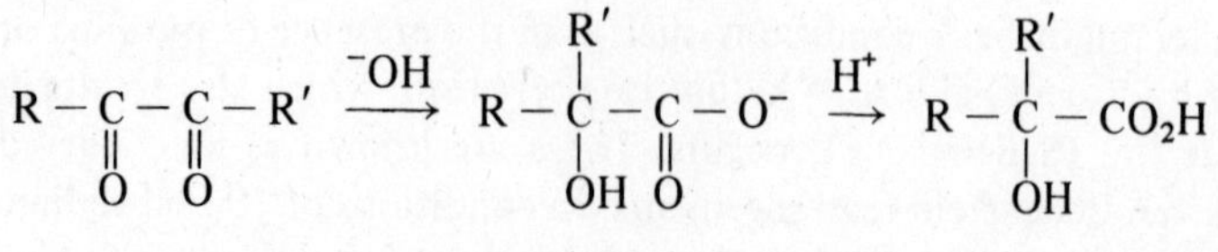

$$R - \underset{O}{\underset{\|}{C}} - \underset{O}{\underset{\|}{C}} - R' \xrightarrow{\;^-OH\;} R - \underset{OH}{\underset{|}{C}}(R') - \underset{O}{\underset{\|}{C}} - O^- \xrightarrow{\;H^+\;} R - \underset{OH}{\underset{|}{C}}(R') - CO_2H$$

Scheme 3.7

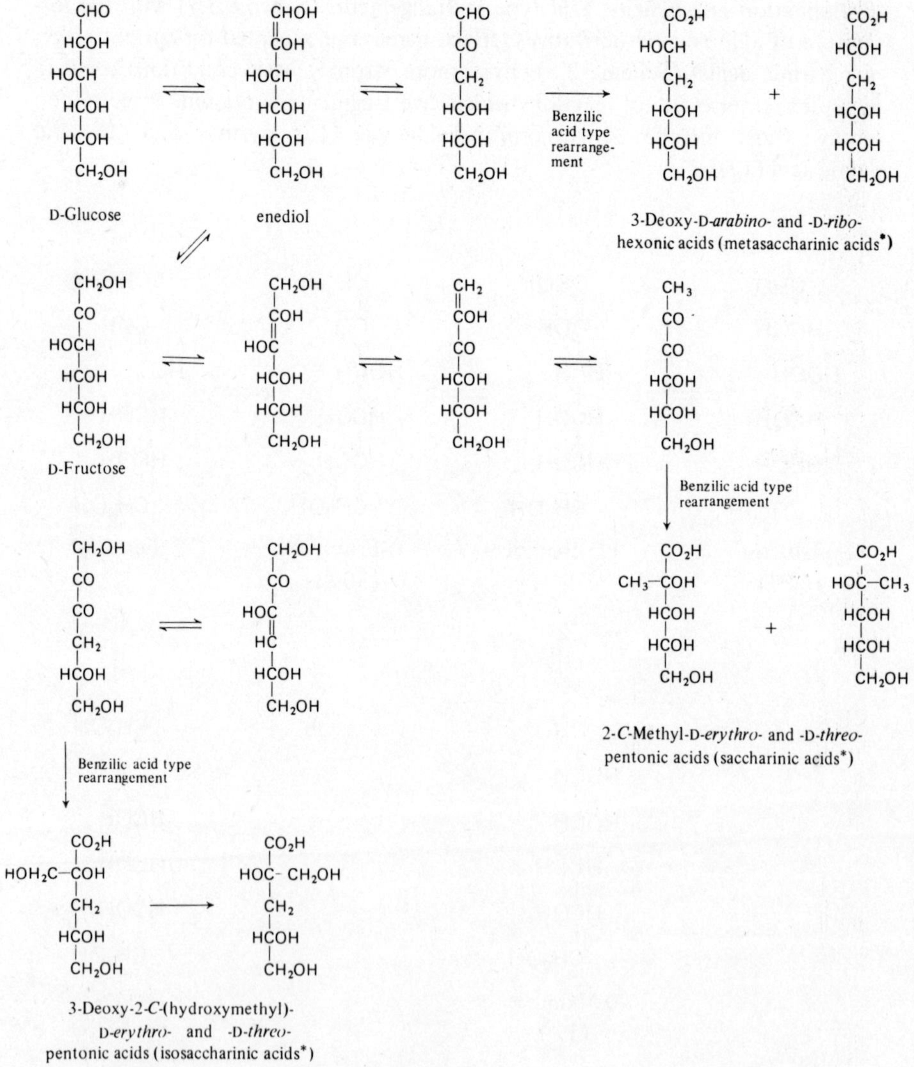

D-Glucose ⇌ enediol ⇌ (CHO / CO / CH₂ / HCOH / HCOH / CH₂OH) → Benzilic acid type rearrangement → 3-Deoxy-D-*arabino*- and -D-*ribo*-hexonic acids (metasaccharinic acids*)

D-Fructose ⇌ ⇌ ⇌ → Benzilic acid type rearrangement → 2-*C*-Methyl-D-*erythro*- and -D-*threo*-pentonic acids (saccharinic acids*)

→ Benzilic acid type rearrangement → 3-Deoxy-2-*C*-(hydroxymethyl)-D-*erythro*- and -D-*threo*-pentonic acids (isosaccharinic acids*)

* trivial names which are not accepted for current usage.

Scheme 3.8

$$CH_3 - \underset{\underset{OH}{|}}{CH} - CHO \qquad CH_3 - \underset{\underset{O}{\|}}{C} - CO_2H \qquad CH_3 - \underset{\underset{OH}{|}}{CH} - CO_2H$$

(15)   (16)   (17)

DERIVATIVES

Due to the polyfunctional nature of carbohydrates, development of the chemistry and synthesis of such compounds has depended upon the development of methods of derivatisation to react with specific hydroxyl or carbonyl groups, to protect or 'block' the groups and prevent subsequent reactions thereof. A discussion of a number of suitable derivatives will be given, but the reader is directed to reviews which deal with the subject in much greater detail (for example, Dutton, 1973 and Kennedy, 1974a) and a series which deals with the practical details of derivatisation (Whistler and Others, 1962 onwards).

It must be remembered that when monosaccharides, from pentoses upwards, are derivatised, the possibility exists that a number of isomers will be produced as a result of mutarotation. With some reactions (for example, trimethylsilylation) the rate of reaction is very much higher than that of mutarotation, with the result that essentially only one isomer is obtained from crystalline monosaccharides. On the other hand, if the monosaccharides were obtained by acid hydrolysis of polysaccharides (see Chapter 4), they will normally exist as mutarotated equilibrium mixtures and so, if the derivative is required for quantitative analysis (see Chapter 4), it is imperative that the method be standardised in order to predict exactly the ratio of isomers formed by any monosaccharide. One method used to ensure standardisation is to pre-equilibrate the monosaccharides prior to derivatisation by, for example, treating the pyridine solution with lithium perchlorate prior to addition of the silylating reagents. It is, of course, possible to study the mutarotation of carbohydrates under various conditions by trapping the isomers present in the solution using a derivatisation reaction with a reaction rate much higher than that of mutarotation.

Glycosides

As has been discussed earlier (Chapter 2), the bulk of carbohydrate found in nature exists in polysaccharides in which monosaccharides are joined together by glycosidic linkages to give full acetals (see Scheme 2.2). In a similar manner aldoses and ketoses react with simple alcohols in the presence of acid catalysts to form glycosides. Thus, the reaction of D-glucose, in the presence of anhydrous methanol containing dissolved hydrogen chloride (1–4%), produces a mixture of methyl α- and β-D-glucosides. Since this reaction (Fischer glycosidation) is thermodynamically controlled, the product obtained preferentially is the α-D-pyranoside (66%) due to the less-polar solvent having a more pronounced effect on the alignment of dipoles (see Fig. 3.4). This effect is known as the anomeric effect. If milder conditions are used (for example, less than 0.5% hydrogen chloride), this thermodynamic control is lessened and kinetic factors influence the reaction such that some of the furanosides are produced. Table 3.1 shows the products formed from D-galactose under differing conditions.

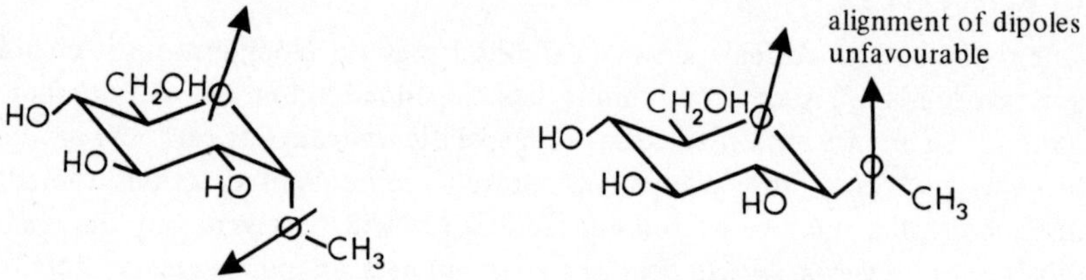

Methyl α-D-glucopyranoside   Methyl β-D-glucopyranoside

Fig 3.4 – The anomeric effect.

Table 3.1 Ratios of isomeric methyl D-galactosides produced under different conditions

Concentration of hydrogen chloride in dry methanol (%)	Temperature (°C)	Time (hours)	Furanoside		Pyranoside	
			α	β	α	β
0.5	25	6	17	33	0	50
0.5	25	940	30	7	49	14
4.0	64	3	73	4	9	14
4.0	64	20	39	5	40	16

Where the alcohol is rare, and cannot be used in large excess, an alternative method of preparation is the Koenigs-Knorr synthesis in which the appropriate glycosyl halide reacts with an alcohol in the presence of silver oxide. The preparation and reaction of the glycosyl halide is shown in Scheme 3.9.

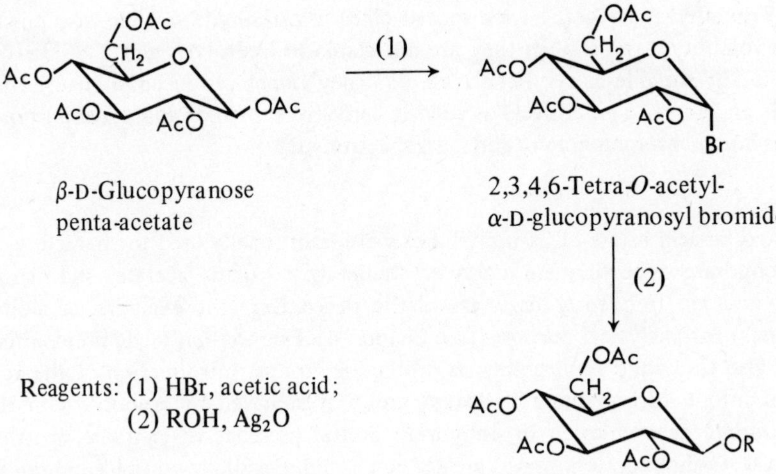

β-D-Glucopyranose
penta-acetate

2,3,4,6-Tetra-*O*-acetyl-
α-D-glucopyranosyl bromide

Reagents: (1) HBr, acetic acid;
          (2) ROH, Ag$_2$O

β-anomer (not α anomer) formed.

Scheme 3.9

Ethers

Ether derivatives of carbohydrates are stable under a variety of conditions, and are, therefore, ideal for analytical purposes, but, for synthetic purposes their stability may be a disadvantage due to the lack of reliable reactions for removal of the blocking group. Methyl ethers were (and still are) a major feature in structural analysis of many oligo- and poly-saccharides (see Chapter 4) and in determination of the ring structures of monosaccharides. They may be formed either by the Purdie (methyl iodide in the presence of silver oxide or carbonate) or the Haworth (dimethyl sulphate in aqueous alkali) procedures. Both of these procedures may require several applications before complete methylation of complex molecules is achieved and many variations thereof exist. The preferred method today is that of Hakomori (1964), which uses the dimethylsulphinyl (dimsyl) anion in dimethyl sulphoxide with subsequent treatment with methyl iodide; but there are exceptions to its successful use.

Benzyl ethers, formed by action of alkali and benzyl chloride are stable to acids and alkalis, and, because they can be removed by mild hydrogenolysis, are more widely used than methyl ethers as protecting groups. Allyl ethers, produced from allyl bromide, are also common protecting groups, since they are stable to acids, but, in the presence of a base, form vinyl ethers which are readily removed by mild acid (conditions under which isopropylidene groups are retained; see later). Certain other ethers, such as triphenylmethyl (trityl) ethers, are used due to their special properties in synthetic schemes. Triphenylmethyl ethers which, due to their size, are usually attached to the O-6 position can be removed by mild acid in the presence of ester, ether and glycosidic linkages, and, if by hydrogenolysis, also in the presence of acetals.

Trimethylsilyl ethers have a special place in carbohydrate chemistry due to their volatility, even though they are not stable to hydrolysis and are therefore not usually suitable as synthetic reagents. They can be produced in quantitative yields and are used extensively as volatile derivatives for such analytical purposes as gas-liquid chromatography and mass spectrometry.

Esters

Carboxylic acid esters of carbohydrates were traditionally used to characterise a carbohydrate since they are highly crystalline (particularly acetates and benzo-ates) and are frequently used as volatile derivatives (for example, as alditol acetates) for analytical purposes (see Chapter 4). Due to their facile preparation, they also find wide applicability as protecting groups. Introduction of the acyl group into a carbohydrate hydroxyl group is achieved by reaction with the appropriate acid chloride or anhydride in the presence of pyridine or other catalyst. Carbohydrate acetates are stable to mildly acidic conditions and can be deacetylated under basic conditions (usually using sodium methoxide), but, under mildly basic conditions, the acetate shows a tendency to migrate to free hydroxyl groups. Benzoates, are, however more stable to mildly basic conditions, showing little tendency to migrate, and they will also withstand acid conditions better. Other carboxylic acid esters used include chloroacetates and trifluoro-acetates, which are more labile and can be readily and selectively removed.

Sulphonate esters are more versatile than carboxylic acid esters due to their stability to acids and bases. They are removed by disruption of the alkyl—oxygen rather than the oxygen—sulphur bond, and are therefore very useful in the synthesis of carbohydrate derivatives (see Chapter 5). They are prepared from the sulphonic acid chloride, usually methanesulphonyl (mesyl) chloride or 4-toluenesulphonyl (tosyl) chloride, in the presence of pyridine and, usually, the carbohydrate glycoside at low temperatures. Free aldoses react rapidly with sulphonic acid chlorides, giving the sulphonylated glycosyl chloride and degrad-ation products therefrom. Sulphonate groups can be removed by nucleophilic displacement with lithium aluminium hydride.

Other esters are used for specific purposes (for example, nitrates for pro-tecting groups for methylation, phosphates for biological intermediates, and cyclic carbonates for preparation of immobilised derivatives — see Chapter 13).

Cyclic acetals

The polyhydroxylated nature of carbohydrates means that pairs of hydroxyl groups, if suitably placed, can form cyclic acetals by reaction with aldehydes or ketones in the presence of acidic catalysts (Scheme 3.10). In some cases, they react with the anomeric hydroxyl group and so fix the monosaccharide in a furanose or pyranose ring. They are stable to alkali but readily removed by acid (90% trifluoroacetic acid is recommended) or in the case of the benzylidene group, by catalytic hydrogenolysis in the presence of platinum.

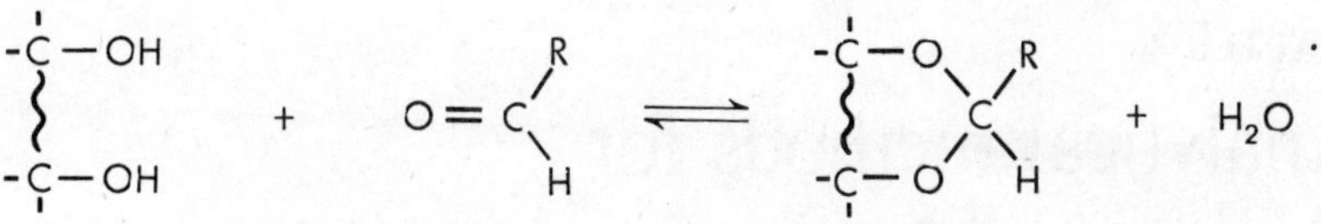

aldehyde

cyclic acetal

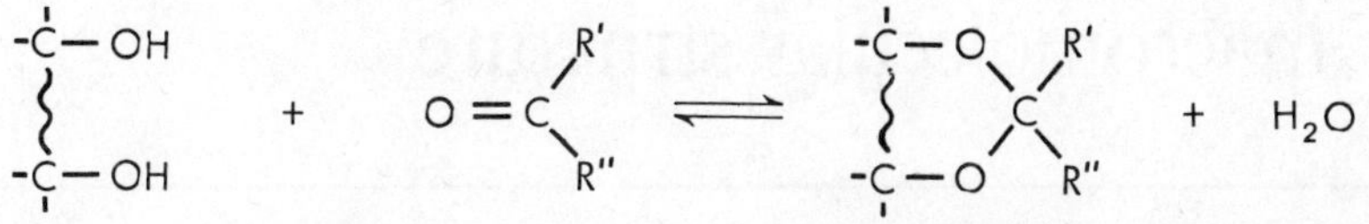

ketone

cyclic acetal (formerly cyclic ketal)

Scheme 3.10

The most commonly used carbonyl compounds are acetaldehyde, benzaldehyde and acetone but a number of others have been used. The solvent for the reaction is frequently the carbonyl compound, and the catalysts include anhydrous sulphuric acid (up to 50%), hydrogen chloride (up to 1%), and such Lewis acids as zinc chloride and boron trifluoride. In the case of isopropylidene formation from acetone anhydrous copper(II) sulphate is often used to maintain anhydrous conditions.

A naturally occurring cyclic acetal (pyruvic acid acetal) is found in certain polysaccharides (for example, xanthan gum, see Chapter 8, p. 171, which contains the S-isomer). This derivative is formed from the α-keto acid, 2-oxopropanoic acid (pyruvic acid) (16) (Scheme 3.11), and is frequently, but erroneously, referred to as a 'pyruvate', implying that it is an ester derivative.

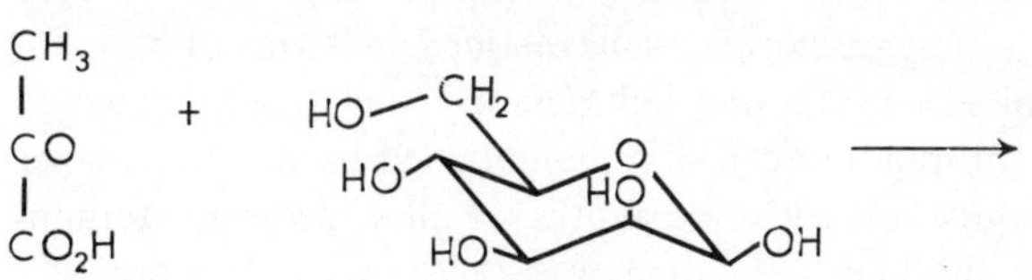

Pyruvic acid β-D-Mannose

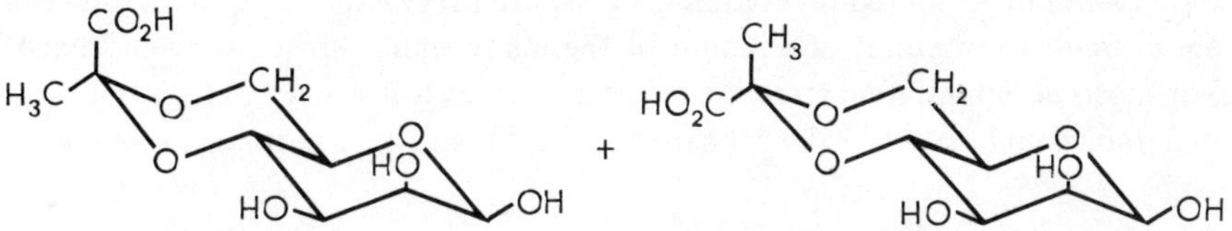

4,6-O-(S)-(1-Carboxyethylidene)-
β-D-mannopyranose

4,6-O-(R)-(1-Carboxyethylidene)-
β-D-mannopyranose

Scheme 3.11

Other derivatives are used for particular purposes, such as the formation of immobilised derivatives, and these are discussed in the relevant chapter (see later, Chapter 13).

CHAPTER 4

Analytical methods for identification and determination of macromolecular structure

In this chapter the reader is provided with an introduction to the various analytical methods available and the chemistry involved therein. The chapter discusses some of the modern physico-chemical techniques which involve sophisticated equipment but which provide more detailed aspects of overall structure. Key references have been included to give the reader a lead to practical details (see also Various Authors, 1968 onwards).

The normal sequence of events in structural analysis after identification of the macromolecule (by its biological activity for example), isolation and purification is component analysis and sequence determination (to give primary structure) using chemical and biological methods. Secondary, tertiary and quaternary structures (see Chapter 3) are obtained by physico-chemical methods which give information on the size and shape of a molecule.

No one method available for structural analysis will provide sufficient data to allow the structure of a polysaccharide to be defined in terms of its component monosaccharide units, the inter-unit linkages, and the sequence in which the units are linked. This information can only be obtained using a number of different techniques in conjunction with one another. Full structural determination is very important for a full understanding of the activity and function of a polysaccharide and its role in nature, but the necessary practical work is very time consuming, the required equipment is often very expensive, and the results are difficult to interpret on account of the many similar structures which exist. For most carbohydrate-containing macromolecules full structures have not been determined and for many the primary structure is still only partially known.

ISOLATION AND PURIFICATION

The first problem of structural analysis is one which is common to the analysis of other groups of macromolecules, and is that of isolating the material in a pure form. The definition of purity is not as clear-cut as was originally thought because microheterogeneity, the phenomenon of minor variations within a single species of compound, is now well recognized. The ensuing discussion on the separation of the carbohydrate species from various impurities, including inorganic salts and low molecular weight materials, and also macromolecular species such as proteins and lignins, is written from the general viewpoint, but it must be borne in mind that each polysaccharide will have its own peculiarities,

Wherever possible, the first stage involves solubilisation in an aqueous or an aprotic solvent such as ethylene glycol or dimethyl sulphoxide, but care must be taken to ensure that the method used and solvents chosen do not modify or degrade the structure of the macromolecule. This eliminates the use of acids, alkalis, or enzymes. The removal of low molecular weight impurities is readily performed by dialysis (distinction on basis of molecular size), ion exchange chromatography (distinction on basis of molecular charge), or gel filtration (distinction on basis of molecular size). The last two techniques are also used extensively for the separation of the desired material from contaminant macromolecules. Removal of the macromolecule from solution can be achieved by precipitation with solvents such as ethanol or acetone, or by complexation with, for example, metal ions, and, for acidic polysaccharides, quaternary ammonium salts.

Purification stages must proceed until a material of constant composition is obtained. In the past the criteria for estimation of constant composition have relied on physical and chemical measurements such as functional group analysis, specific rotation, and carbohydrate composition after hydrolysis. More recently, ultracentrifugation which gives a measure of sedimentation in a high force field, electrophoresis, which measures the mobility of the polysaccharide in an applied electric field, and the aforementioned chromatographies have all been used to investigate the purity of a preparation. The best definition of homogeneity is one based on assessment by two or more methods which rely on different criteria.

COMPLETE HYDROLYSIS

Once a pure sample of the polysaccharide has been obtained the first step in elucidating its structure is to identify and estimate the component monosaccharides. The molecule is broken down by acid hydrolysis by a mechanism which is the reverse of the Fischer reaction (see Chapter 3, p. 61) and the hydrolysate analysed by chromatographic techniques (see later this chapter). The ion-exchange chromatography of the borate complexes of neutral monosaccharides is the most common method which is used as the basis for fully automatic carbohydrate analysers.

The conditions for hydrolysis must be controlled such that complete hydrolysis is achieved with little or no degradation of the monosaccharide units — use of more than one set of hydrolysis conditions may be necessary. The ease of hydrolysis of different linkages and the stabilities of the various monosaccharides mean that the optimum conditions for each polysaccharide have to be determined. Polysaccharides containing furanose or 5-amino-3,5-dideoxy-D-*glycero*-D-*galacto*-2-nonulopyranonic acid residues, and 2-deoxy-hexoses or -pentoses, are more readily hydrolysed than those containing hexuronic acids or 2-amino-2-deoxyhexoses, with hexose-containing polysaccharides being intermediate. Conditions which have been found appropriate for hexose-containing polysaccharides are 1 M sulphuric acid at 100°C for four hours, with the use of 0.25 M sulphuric acid at 70°C for pentose-containing polysaccharides. Degradation frequently occurs in direct hydrolysis whatever conditions are used. For example, in the case of glycosaminoglycans, 4 M hydrochloric acid at 100°C for nine hours is necessary to liberate all the 2-amino-2-deoxyhexose residues, but under such conditions the majority of the hexuronic acid residues are decomposed.

Partial hydrolysis (under appropriately milder conditions) to give a small number of oligosaccharides can be useful for structural analysis, but care must be taken in interpreting the results since monosaccharides can recombine, under certain hydrolysis conditions, to give oligosaccharides linked in a manner different from that in the original polysaccharide. This process is called reversion (see Chapter 3). Certain functional groups, etc., are lost on hydrolysis and specific methods are required for their estimation. These groups include acetyl, carboxyl, carbonyl, and ether, and methods for their estimation have been reviewed (Aminoff *et al.*, 1970).

METHYLATION ANALYSIS

Once the individual monosaccharide components have been estimated, the manner in which they are linked to each other, and the sequence, has to be determined. If all the free hydroxyl groups in the polysaccharide can be reacted to form derivatives which are stable to acid hydrolysis, the hydroxyl groups produced by hydrolysis of the glycosidic linkages will indicate where linkage points were formerly located on each monosaccharide residue (see Chapter 3 for the formation of methyl ethers).

The fully methylated polysaccharide is hydrolysed to its constituent methylated monosaccharides using sulphuric acid or trifluoroacetic acid. The hydrolysis mixture can be fractionated by partition chromatography on cellulose or silica gel, by adsorption chromatography, or, best of all, by gas-liquid chromatography of volatile derivatives such as the methyl per-*O*-methyl glycosides, partially methylated alditol acetates, or partially methylated *O*-trimethylsilyl ethers. An important extension to gas-liquid chromatography for the further identification of these volatile derivatives is the use of mass spectrometry linked to gas-liquid chromatography, or more recently, the use of mass spectrometry *per se* (Rauvala *et al.*, 1981.) Reviews have been published giving the characteristic data for known, standard, partially methylated compounds (Dutton 1973 and 1974, and Bjornda *et al.*, 1970).

Methylation analysis is not without its problems, the most common being polysaccharides which contain hexuronic acid residues. These can be methylated only with considerable difficulty using the thallium salt of the hexuronic acid and reacting it with methyl iodide and thallium hydroxide. This reaction must be carefully controlled to avoid degradation and demethylation of the polysaccharide. Recently the Hakomori method has been applied to hexuronic acid-containing polysaccharides to achieve complete methylation of hydroxyl and carboxyl groups in one step. Another method by which the difficulty due to uronic acid residues can be overcome is by (indirect) reduction of the acid to an alcohol with sodium borohydride. Methylation analysis on its own will not give structural sequence data, but does identify the monosaccharide components of the polysaccharide and the position of the intermonosaccharide linkages involved (see review by Rauvala *et al.*, 1981).

PARTIAL HYDROLYSIS

If the hydrolysis of the polysaccharide is stopped before the reaction goes to completion, fragments of intermediate molecular weight can be isolated and fractionated using a number of chromatographic techniques such as gel filtration, ion-exchange chromatography, and partition chromatography. Determination of the structure of these simpler oligosaccharides is generally easier than determinations carried out on the parent polysaccharide. If the glycosidic linkages in the polysaccharide are all hydrolysed at the same rate as in, for example, the linear homopolysaccharides, the product of partial hydrolysis will consist, in the case of amylose, of a range of oligosaccharides such as maltotetraose, maltotriose, maltose and D-glucose. In heteropolysaccharides there are a number of types of glycosidic linkages and their respective rates of hydrolysis will differ, giving a degree of selectivity to the reaction. In general terms furanosides are hydrolysed at a greater rate than pyranosides by factors between 10 and 1000 which will result in removal of, for example, arabinofuranosyl residues attached to xylanopyranosyl residues in arabinoxylans. The conditions of the hydrolysis will also effect the specificity of the degradation. In mineral acids, $(1\rightarrow6)$-linkages are more stable than $(1\rightarrow4)$-linkages, but if this reaction were to be carried out in acidified acetic anhydride (containing approx. 5% sulphuric acid) the $(1\rightarrow6)$-linkages are less stable. The use of both these methods of hydrolysis will lead to different fragments which will give overlapping data to provide a better picture of the complete polysaccharide. The concentration of carbohydrate material must be kept below about 0.5% to prevent acid-catalysed polymerisation of the fragments (acid reversion), which leads to artifacts in structural analysis. Some glycoside bonds in polysaccharides can be cleaved specifically by enzymes to give oligosaccharides in a controlled manner. This method will be discussed later in this chapter.

PERIODATE OXIDATION

Oxidation of monosaccharides by glycol cleavage is a widespread method of analysis. The use of lead(IV) acetate has found little application to polysaccharide chemistry owing to the lack of suitable solvents for the carbohydrates in which the reagent does not decompose, although the use of lead(IV) acetate in pyridine has been found to oxidise rigidly-held diaxial diols which do not react readily with periodic acid. In a much more commonly employed method, periodic acid and its salts are used in aqueous solutions of pH 3–5 to avoid acid hydrolysis and the non-selective oxidations which can occur at higher pH values. The reagent reacts with vicinal hydroxyl groups to cleave the linkage between them with the consumption of one mole of periodate per diol. The products of the reaction depend on the linkages between the monosaccharide units. Oxidation of a primary hydroxyl group, adjacent to a secondary hydroxyl group, as in the case of a furanose ring structure leads to the formation of formaldehyde, whilst vicinal triol groups yield formic acid. Reaction of polysaccharides with periodic acid is followed by measurement of the amount of reagent consumed and of the formic acid and, less frequently, of the formaldehyde produced (Fig. 4.1). This allows the distinction between 1,3- and 1,6-disubstituted residues and allows a measurement of the total amount of 1,2- and 1,4-disubstituted residues.

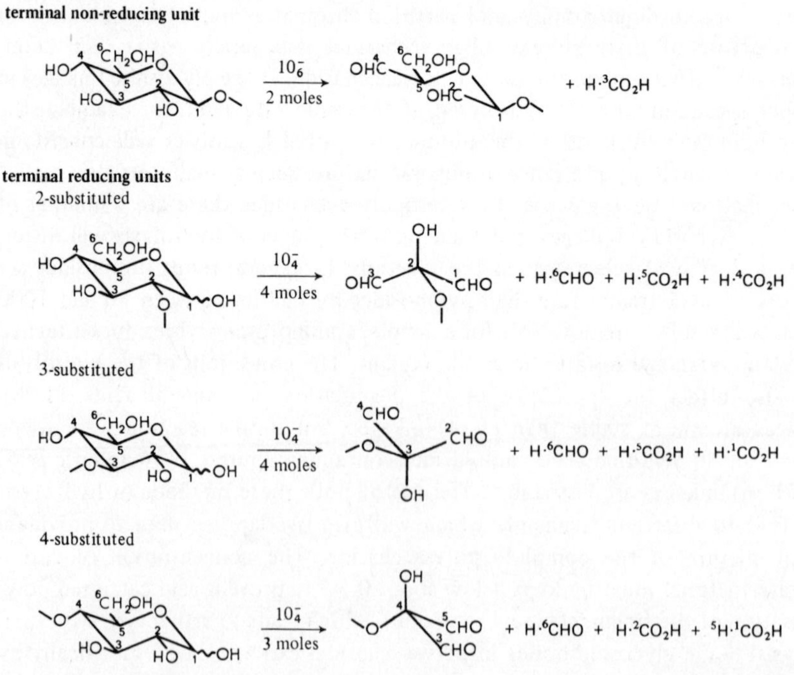

Fig. 4.1 – Periodate oxidation of substituted hexose residues (*continued on next page*).

terminal reducing units (*continued*)
6-substituted

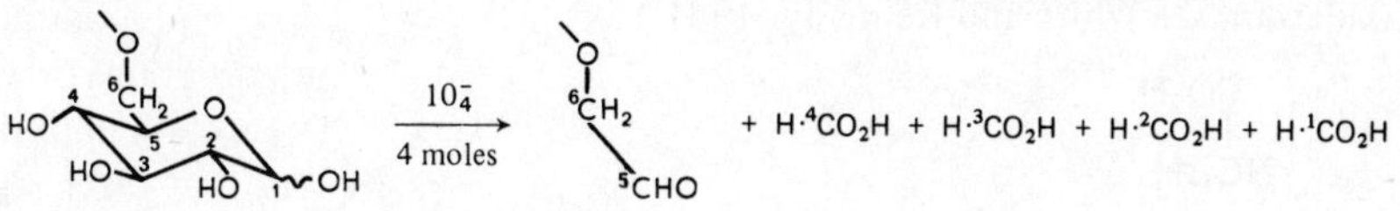

non-terminal units
1,2-disubstituted

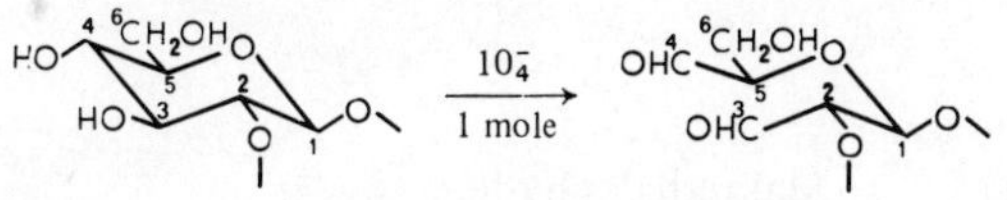

1,3-disubstituted

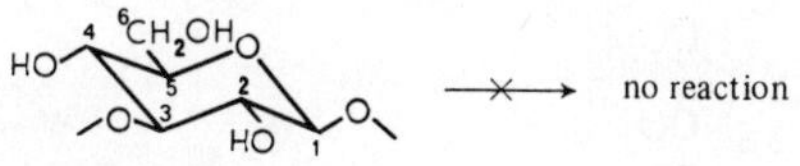

1,4-disubstituted

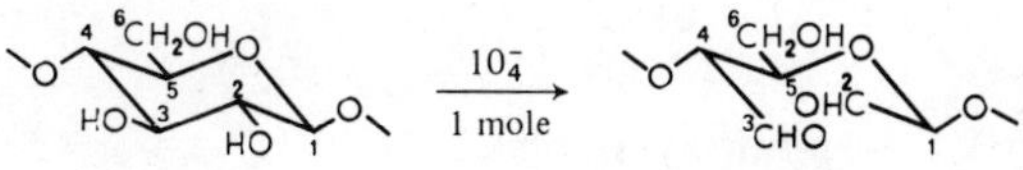

1,6-disubstituted

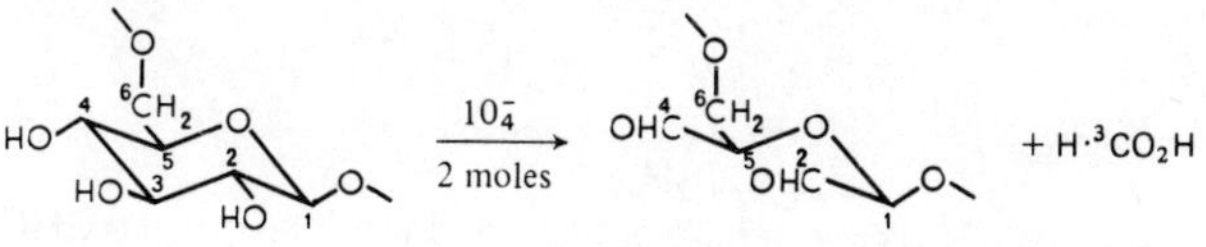

^{1}C refers to carbon atom 1 etc.

Fig. 4.1 — Periodate oxidation of substituted hexose residues.

The dialdehyde-type products of periodate oxidation are unstable in water and it is therefore desirable to reduce them, usually with sodium borohydride, to alcohols before acid hydrolysis (to split the oxidised material into the component units) is carried out. Analysis of these component products is essential because it provides a means of distinguishing between 1,2- and 1,4-disubstituted residues. The products of hydrolysis, such as glycerol, glycol aldehyde, glyceraldehyde, tetritols (such as D-erythritol), and free monosaccharides (resulting from periodate-resistant residues) are usually determined by gas-liquid chromatography as their trimethylsilyl ethers. This method again does not give complete linkage sequences, but gives information which is used in conjunction with other methods. Periodate oxidation of the products obtained by the action of alkalis on carbohydrates (see Chapter 3 and later this chapter) gives products (Fig. 4.2) which can be determined specifically by colorimetric methods. (For a review of colorimetric methods available for the analysis of the products of periodate oxidation, see White and Kennedy, 1981.)

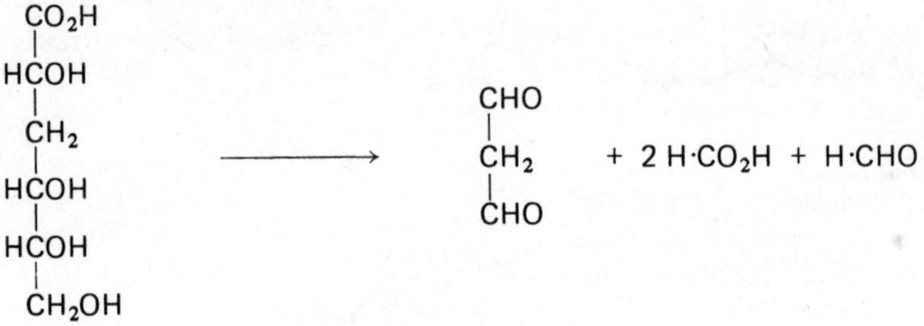

$$
\begin{array}{c}
CO_2H \\
| \\
HCOH \\
| \\
CH_2 \\
| \\
HCOH \\
| \\
HCOH \\
| \\
CH_2OH
\end{array}
\longrightarrow
\begin{array}{c}
CHO \\
| \\
CH_2 \\
| \\
CHO
\end{array}
\;+\; 2\,H{\cdot}CO_2H \;+\; H{\cdot}CHO
$$

3-Deoxy-D-*ribo*-hexonic acid   Malondialdehyde

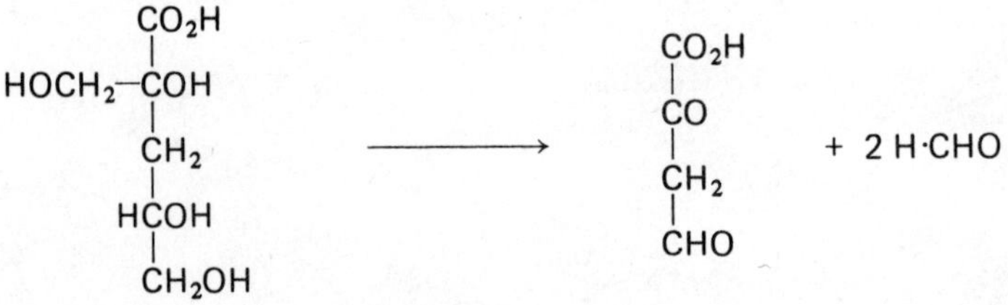

$$
\begin{array}{c}
CO_2H \\
| \\
HOCH_2{-}COH \\
| \\
CH_2 \\
| \\
HCOH \\
| \\
CH_2OH
\end{array}
\longrightarrow
\begin{array}{c}
CO_2H \\
| \\
CO \\
| \\
CH_2 \\
| \\
CHO
\end{array}
\;+\; 2\,H{\cdot}CHO
$$

3-Deoxy-2-*C*-(hydroxymethyl) β-Formyl pyruvic
-D-*erythro*-pentonic acid   acid

$$
\begin{array}{c}
CO_2H \\
| \\
HCOH \\
| \\
HCOH \\
| \\
HCOH \\
| \\
CH_2OH
\end{array}
\longrightarrow
\begin{array}{c}
CO_2H \\
| \\
CHO
\end{array}
\;+\; 2\,H{\cdot}CO_2H \;+\; H{\cdot}CHO
$$

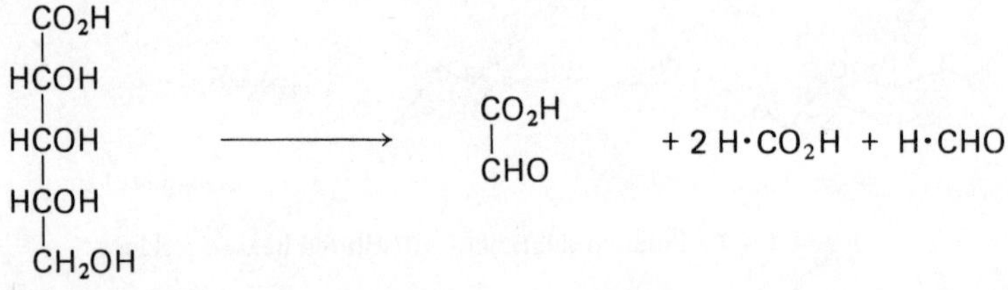

D-Ribonic acid   Glyoxylic acid

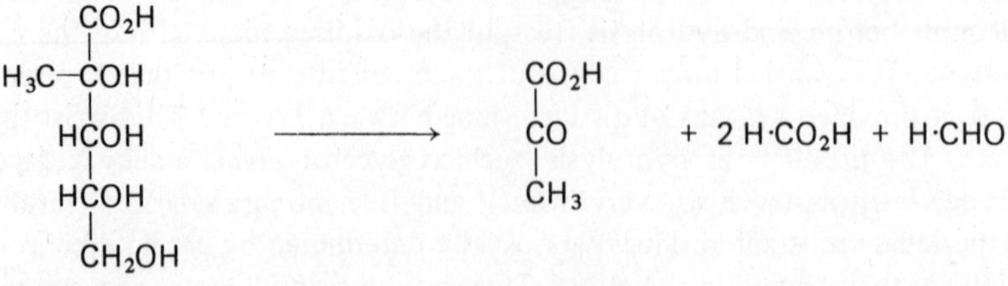

$$
\begin{array}{c}
CO_2H \\
| \\
H_3C{-}COH \\
| \\
HCOH \\
| \\
HCOH \\
| \\
CH_2OH
\end{array}
\longrightarrow
\begin{array}{c}
CO_2H \\
| \\
CO \\
| \\
CH_3
\end{array}
\;+\; 2\,H{\cdot}CO_2H \;+\; H{\cdot}CHO
$$

2-*C*-Methyl-D-*erythro*-   Pyruvic acid
pentonic acid

Fig. 4.2 – Periodate oxidation of alkali resistant residues.

Smith degradation

An important modification to the periodate oxidation, borohydride reduction and total hydrolysis sequence described above is that known as the Smith degradation, which uses mild hydrolysis of the product from borohydride reduction (usually dilute mineral acid at room temperature) to cause partial degradation with the production of specific glycosides of oligosaccharides characteristic of the original polysaccharide (Perlin, 1959). This relies on the comparative stability of the glycosidic linkage between a sugar residue (the original periodate-resistant residue) and an alditol. For example, Smith degradation of nigeran [an α-D-glucan with alternating (1→3) and (1→4) linkages, see Table 2.6] results in the production of 2-*O*-α-D-glucopyranosyl-erythritol (18, see Scheme 4.1).

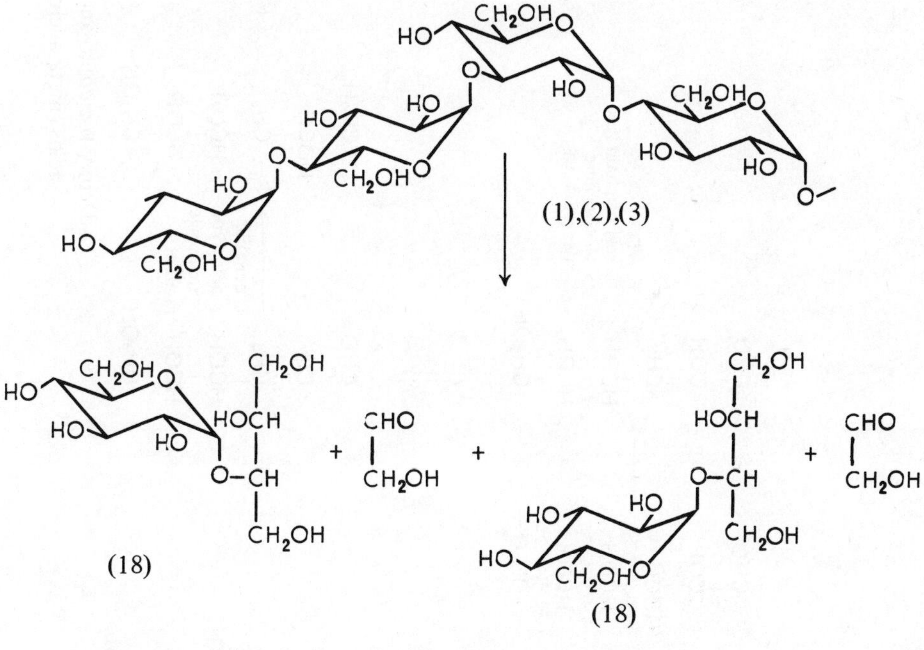

Reagents: (1) periodic acid; (2) sodium borohydride; (3) mild acid.

Scheme 4.1

ALKALINE DEGRADATION

This method of analysis of polysaccharides provides little information about the overall structure, which cannot be obtained by acid hydrolysis, but since the use is often made of alkali in the isolation of a purified sample, the type of reactions which occur should be understood (for a review see Whistler and BeMiller, 1958,

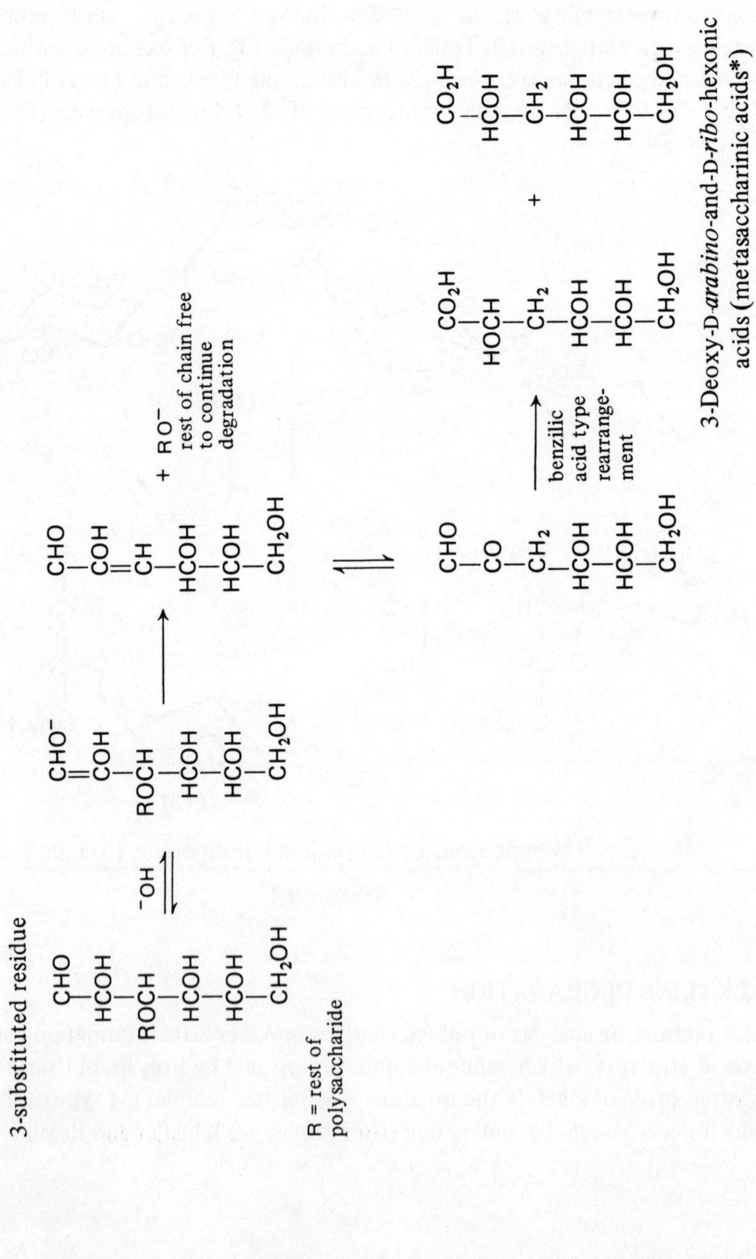

3-substituted residue

$$
\begin{array}{l}
CHO \\
HCOH \\
ROCH \\
HCOH \\
HCOH \\
CH_2OH
\end{array}
\quad \underset{\text{OH}}{\rightleftarrows} \quad
\begin{array}{l}
CHO^- \\
\parallel \\
=COH \\
ROCH \\
HCOH \\
HCOH \\
CH_2OH
\end{array}
\quad \rightarrow \quad
\begin{array}{l}
CHO \\
=COH \\
CH \\
HCOH \\
HCOH \\
CH_2OH
\end{array}
\quad + RO^-
$$

rest of chain free to continue degradation

$$
\rightleftarrows
\begin{array}{l}
CHO \\
CO \\
CH_2 \\
HCOH \\
HCOH \\
CH_2OH
\end{array}
\quad \xrightarrow{\substack{\text{benzilic} \\ \text{acid type} \\ \text{rearrange-} \\ \text{ment}}}
\begin{array}{l}
CO_2H \\
HOCH \\
CH_2 \\
HCOH \\
HCOH \\
CH_2OH
\end{array}
\quad + \quad
\begin{array}{l}
CO_2H \\
HCOH \\
CH_2 \\
HCOH \\
HCOH \\
CH_2OH
\end{array}
$$

R = rest of polysaccharide

3-Deoxy-D-*arabino*-and-D-*ribo*-hexonic acids (metasaccharinic acids*)

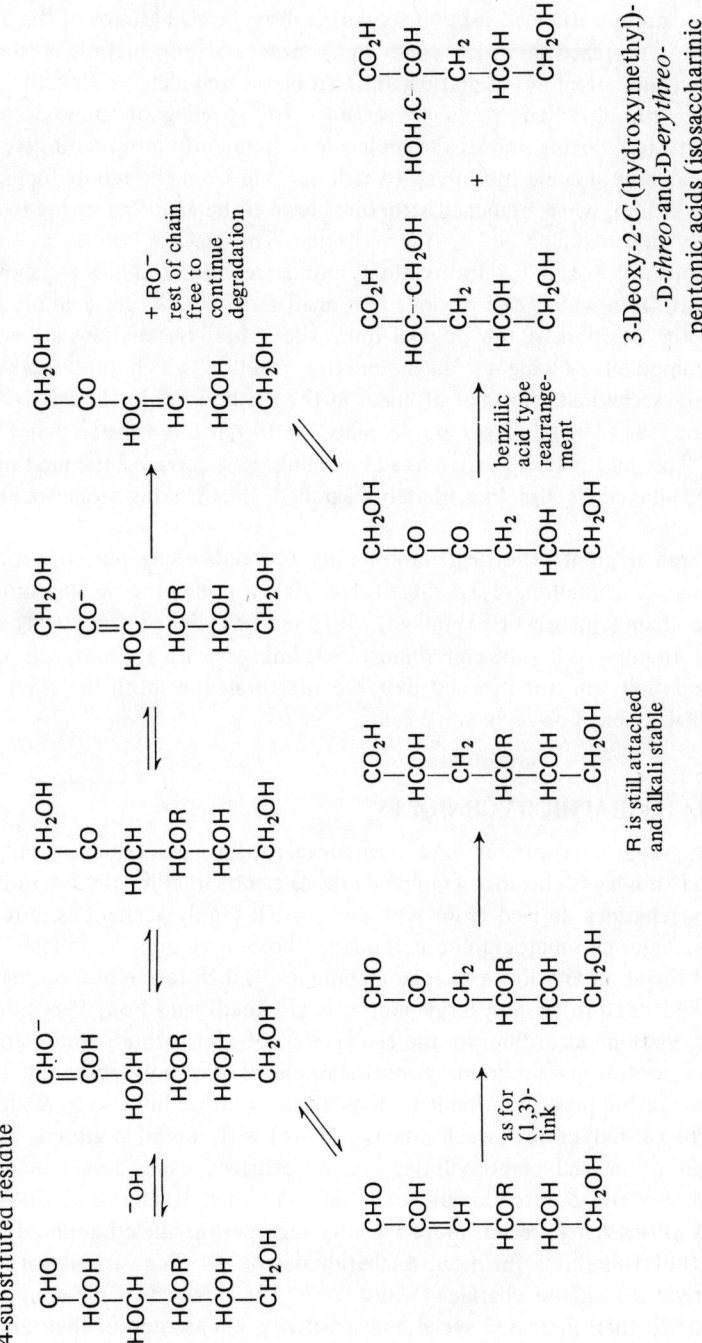

Scheme 4.2

* trivial names which are not accepted for current usage.

and Hough and Richardson, 1979). The most common reactions are the hydrolysis of ester groups attached *via* hydroxyl or carboxylic acid groups of the monosaccharide. The reaction which yields most structural information is the progressive erosion of monosaccharide units from the reducing end of the polysaccharide, the so-called 'peeling' reaction. This peeling of monosaccharide units from the reducing end of the molecule is frequently more definitive than methods such as enzyme hydrolysis (which degrade from the non-reducing end of the molecule), when branched structures have to be analysed owing to there being only one reducing end to the molecule. The reaction sequences for the degradation of 1,3- and 1,4-disubstituted monosaccharide residues are shown in Scheme 4.2 from which it is obvious that analysis of the aldonic acid produced will give the position of the original link. The 1,4-polysaccharides are not degraded completely, owing to the competing reaction which produces alkali-stable polysaccharides. Another problem in the method lies in the relative rates of reaction; the (1→3)-linkages are degraded up to ten times faster than (1→4)-linkages. This means that as soon as a (1→4)-linkage is degraded the next unit, if it is (1→3)-linked, is also immediately degraded, thus making sequence studies difficult.

At branch points the degradation only proceeds along one branch. In a polysaccharide containing 1,3,4-substituted branch points the peeling proceeds along the chain which is (1→3)-linked, with the (1→4)-linked chain being alkali-stabilised. In polysaccharides containing (1→4)-linkages with 1,4,6-branch points, the degradation will not proceed past the first branch as both the chains give rise to alkali-stable 3-deoxyhexonic acids.

CHROMATOGRAPHIC TECHNIQUES

Chromatographic techniques have been developed to aid structural analysis. Paper and thin-layer chromatographic methods can be used for the fractionation of oligosaccharides derived from partially degraded polysaccharides, but nowadays the major chromatographic methods are those based on column techniques, using gel filtration and ion exchange techniques. Gel filtration procedures using cross-linked dextran or polyacrylamide gels (Kennedy and Fox, 1980) depend on fractionation according to molecular size of the carbohydrates and are especially useful for preliminary purifications of the polysaccharide before structural techniques are applied. Ion-exchange procedures can readily be applied to carbohydrates (see Kennedy, 1974b) with ionisable groups, but the separation of neutral carbohydrates can be achieved using borate buffers to give carbohydrate–borate complexes which are then fractionated on borate forms of ion-exchange resins. More recently high performance liquid chromatographic (hplc) methods for monosaccharide derivatives (Schwarzenbach, 1979) or underivatised oligosaccharides (White *et al.*, 1980) have become more appropriate due to their increased speed and sensitivity. On account of their different criteria for separation, column techniques are often used in conjunction with each other as a means of determining the purity and any microheterogeneity of a carbohydrate sample.

From the standpoint of preparative methods, column chromatography is most useful in that large amounts of sample can often be fractionated with complete recovery of the sample in underivatised form. Nevertheless, achievement of good resolution is often only obtained with slow flow rates. For this reason, new techniques of column chromatography have also been developed for structural analysis and for the preparation of fractions for structural analysis. Affinity- or adsorption-chromatography has been used extensively for the purification of non-carbohydrate molecules and is based on selective adsorption on to an insoluble adsorbent which contains groups/molecules which interact specifically with the molecule to be purified, for example, enzyme inhibitors for enzyme purification and antibodies for antigen purification, and the technique is now being extended into the field of carbohydrate fractionation. Non-interacting impurity is removed from the bound carbohydrate, which is subsequently desorbed by disrupting the interaction in a way which does not cause degradation. The methods for desorption include changes of pH, ionic strength, or the use of an inhibitor to the interaction. The use of an immobilised form (see Chapter 13) of concanavalin A, a lectin (formerly a phytohaemagglutinin) which specifically reacts with branched-chain polysaccharides of a particular structural type, has been made for the fractionation of a number of polysaccharides and the principle has now been extended to the use of a whole series of lectins in immobilised form. Column supports coated with polyaromatic compounds have also been found to be of some use in the fractionation of polysaccharides. Recent developments in the technology of packing materials for high performance liquid chromatography mean that faster and more selective separations can be obtained and methods are reported of fractions of small oligosaccharides which take less than one hour to complete (White *et al.*, 1980).

Gas-liquid chromatography has found limited use in the structural analysis of polysaccharides, owing to the inherent requirements of the method, namely volatility and stability, under the conditions used. In practice the method has been limited to the analysis of component monosaccharides, after hydrolysis and, more importantly, to the analysis of partially methylated sugars produced in methylation analysis. Disaccharides can be made sufficiently volatile for gas-liquid chromatography. The method has the advantage of rapid analysis compared with column techniques, but the method will also, at the same time, separate the various anomers and different ring sizes of a particular monosaccharide, making the number of peaks on the chromatograms larger than the number of component monosaccharides. The need for volatile compounds for analysis has led to a number of methods of derivatisation, methyl ethers, alditol acetates, and trimethylsilyl ethers being used commonly, but other methods based on volatile products have also been employed, including the use of isopropylidene derivatives. The use of trimethylsilyl ethers of carbohydrates is preferred, owing to the ease of preparation of the derivatives at room temperature in a few minutes. This method has been extended to include derivatives of acidic monosaccharides and basic monosaccharides. More-recent developments that increase the value of gas-liquid chromatography in the structural analysis include the use of specific detectors and direct coupling of the gas liquid chromatograph to radioactive counters (gas-liquid radiochromatography) and to mass spectrometers.

MASS SPECTROMETRY

Mass spectrometry plays a large role in the structural analysis of polysaccharides, not only in the identification of compounds derived from methylation analysis, but also in the analysis of oligosaccharides directly after preparation of one of the volatile derivatives mentioned earlier (see Lönngren and Svennson, 1974). The molecular weight of small oligosaccharides can be measured and the sequence of monosaccharide units and position of glycosidic bonds have been determined, although some information on the nature of the residues present is also usually needed. The direct mass spectrometric identification of oligosaccharides containing more than four residues with the use of trimethylsilyl derivatives is difficult, but characteristic fragmentation patterns of peracetylated glycoside derivatives of pentasaccharides have been obtained and, more recently, a method has been described for the detection of D-fructose residues in permethylated oligosaccharides and which also gives information on the ratio of pyranose to furanose residues and the positions of the glycosidic linkages.

    Methods involving chemical ionisation rather than electron impact are more sensitive than conventional methods of analysis, and such methods have been used in the analysis of oligopeptides, low molecular weight fragments obtained from hydrolysis of glycoproteins. Not only was the aminoacid sequence obtained but the carbohydrate-peptide linkages could be determined by comparing the fragmentation patterns with those obtained for the various monosaccharide-aminoacid derivatives (Morris, 1980).

NUCLEAR MAGNETIC RESONANCE SPECTROSCOPY

A method which will give information on the anomeric protons in polysaccharides, provided the monosaccharide components and substitution positions are known, has been developed using nuclear magnetic resonance (n.m.r.) spectroscopy. The hydroxyl groups of the sugar residues are preferably converted to derivatives such as their methyl or trimethylsilyl ethers to eliminate from the spectrum the peak due to hydroxyl groups. The protons of the anomeric carbon atom occur at lower field than protons on the other carbon atoms, with those in the equatorial position showing larger chemical shifts than those in axial positions. Complete structural analyses of polysaccharides have been obtained with ^1H n.m.r. spectroscopy of methylated monosaccharides, and simpler polysaccharides such as glycogens.

^{13}C n.m.r., despite its fairly recent introduction as a tool in carbohydrate analysis, has already proved to be a powerful technique for the structural determination of polysaccharides, providing information on their composition, sequence and comformation. Using the Fourier transform method, it allows spectra of the polysaccharides to be obtained using only their natural abundance ^{13}C atoms; it complements ^1H n.m.r. in that it gives better signal separation owing to the wider range of chemical shifts involved. The technique can be used on relatively small amounts of material, making it particularly suited to the study of polysaccharides of biological origin, where the lack of sufficient material has, in the past, frustrated many attempts at structural elucidation (for a review of the methodology and interpretation of spectra see Jennings and Smith, 1978 and Coxon, 1980).

A recent innovation is the use of two-dimensional ^{13}C n.m.r. in which the spectrum is displayed in two dimensions, showing signal strength as a function of chemical shift in one dimension and as a function of coupling constant in the other, the net effect of which is to produce a series of peaks for each carbon resonance which is characteristic of the ^{13}C-^1H coupling constants (Hall and Morris, 1980). The sensitivity of ^{13}C n.m.r. can be increased by increasing the contents of ^{13}C atoms in the carbohydrate (see Chapter 5, p. 92).

The use of ^{19}F, and ^{31}P n.m.r. may also be useful in determination of the position of substitution of monosaccharides by another, by using derivatives of the polysaccharides such as [^{19}F] trifluoroacetates.

ELECTROPHORETIC TECHNIQUES

Electrophoresis is not a substitute for chromatography, but provides very useful complementary information because it utilizes different criteria for separation, namely molecular charge, size and shape. The use of high-voltage paper electrophoresis has been applied to the separation not only of monosaccharides but also oligosaccharides. The method is not restricted to carbohydrate derivatives which possess an electric charge of their own, such as acidic monosaccharides, basic monosaccharides, and monosaccharide sulphates and phosphates, but has been extended to include neutral compounds which can form electrically charged complexes with electrolytes such as sodium borate, arsenite, or molybdate. The relative mobilities of the carbohydrates can be varied by changing the complexing agent used, when steric factors often determine the formation of different complexes. Choice of electrolytes will often lead to identification of the carbohydrate and its structure and bonding. Separations of acidic polysaccharides have been obtained directly, using high-voltage paper electrophoresis, but separation of neutral polysaccharides requires pre-conversion to their borate derivatives.

The development of better supporting media, such as cellulose acetate strips and polyacrylamide gels in the form of rods or slabs, for electrophoretic purposes has meant that purer chromatographic materials, which are of homogenous character and possess minimal adsorption properties, are available, thus reducing tailing and resulting in quicker separations on a small scale. Methods are reported for the separation of acidic polysaccharides on cellulose acetate and polyacrylamide gels, and the application of the latter method to molecular weight determination has been discussed (Mathews, 1976).

IMMUNOCHEMICAL REACTIONS

Polysaccharides have been found to be determinants of the immunological specificites of many types of micro-organisms. The specific interaction depends on the interaction of multiple reactive groups in both the polysaccharide antigen and protein antibody, and so a method based on this type of interaction is usually specific for the structure of a polysaccharide of known structure; it can be used to indicate structural similarities in unknown polysaccharides. An example of this specificity was shown in the discovery of the heterogeneity of a beef lung D-galactan. The precipitate formed with the anti-*Pneumococcus* type XIV sera contained proportions of D-galactose and D-glucuronic acid different from those in the original separation (Heidelberger *et al.*, 1955).

THE USE OF ENZYMES IN STRUCTURAL ANALYSIS

Hydrolysis by enzymes provides an alternative method for the controlled hydrolysis of polysaccharides. The information obtained is not limited to that obtainable by analysis of the hydrolysis fragments because the specificity of enzyme action, a specificity based on type of monosaccharide and type of linkage, leads to significant data being obtained, by a process of elimination, from enzyme-resistant structures and partially hydrolysed structures. The enzymes which hydrolyse polysaccharides are, for convenience, divided into two groups, *endo*- and *exo*-polysaccharide hydrolases. *endo*-Polysaccharide hydrolases are specific for linkage and monosaccharide residue, and cause random fragmentation of homopolysaccharides to give a homologous series of oligosaccharides. Examples of this type of enzyme include α-amylase which gives a random series of D-glucose oligomers on reaction with amylose. *exo*-Polysaccharide hydrolases are specific for monosaccharide unit and stereochemistry at C-1 but do not differentiate between the residues attached glycosidically at C-1. They cleave polysaccharides by sequential removal of residues from one end of the molecule, usually the nonreducing end, which is the opposite end to that from which alkaline degradation starts. Examples of *exo*-polysaccharide hydrolases include β-amylase, which removes maltose units sequentially from amylose, producing an almost quantitative amount of maltose if the reaction goes to completion.

The first uses of enzyme analysis were in the determination of chain-length and degrees of branching in highly branched polysaccharides such as glycogen and amylopectin. Traditional methods for this analysis required the estimation of nonreducing end groups by chemical methods. The use of enzymes allows smaller quantities of material to be used and increases the speed of the determination. The method used by Lee and Whelan (1966) was based on the use of two enzymes, one of which (pullulanase) specifically hydrolyses the (1→6)-links at the 1,4,6-branch points to give linear chains of (1→4)-linked α-D-glucose units which are degraded by β-amylase to give maltose and D-glucose units, the latter arising from degradation of chains with an odd number of D-glucosyl residues. Analysis of the hydrolysis mixture for D-glucose gives a measure of the chain length because one D-glucose molecule is produced from one chain containing an odd number of D-glucosyl residues and, using the assumption that there is an equal number of odd and even chains, one D-glucose molecule is produced from two unit chains.

More recently, a number of glycoside hydrolases have been produced in sufficiently pure form to allow the development of a method of determination of monosaccharide sequences based on these enzymes. These enzymes will remove specific monosaccharide units linked by specific linkages from the nonreducing end of a polysaccharide. For example, β-D-galactosidase will remove D-galactosyl residues linked β-glycosidically to the polysaccharide. Table 4.1 gives a listing of the major polysaccharide-degrading enzymes, and reviews of the sources and methods of purification of these enzymes are available (Kennedy, 1971–1981). The method adopted can rely on the use of the enzymes sequentially or together, as in the case of enzymic degradation of keratan sulphate with β-D-galactosidase, β-D-2-acetamido-2-deoxyglucosidase, and a sulphatase, a method which showed that some D-galactosyl and 2-acetamido-2-deoxy-D-glucosyl groups at the nonreducing end of the molecule are non-sulphated. The use of sequential enzyme hydrolyses is a well-established technique particularly for the analysis of the carbohydrate residues of macromolecules (see Li and Li, 1976).

A number of glycopeptidases which will certainly prove to be of great value in the analysis of the carbohydrate moiety of glycoproteins have recently been isolated. These enzymes cleave the carbohydrate glycosidic bond adjacent to the aminoacid residue. An example of this type of enzyme is N^4-(2-acetamido-2-deoxy-β-D-glucopyranosyl) hydrogen L-asparaginate amidohydrolase [4-N-(2-β-D-glucosaminyl)-L-asparaginase, EC 3.5.1.26], which cleaves the bond between the 2-acetamido-2-deoxy-D-glucose units of glycoproteins containing the sequence D-mannose linked to N,N'-diacetylchitobiose linked in turn to an L-asparagine residue (19), that is, the glycopeptide linkage of the structure N^4-(2-acetamido-2-deoxy-β-D-glucopyranosyl) hydrogen L-asparaginate.

$$-\beta\text{-D-Man}p\text{-}(1{\to}4)\text{-}\beta\text{-D-Glc}p\text{NAc-}(1{\to}4)\text{-}\beta\text{-D-Glc}p\text{NAc-}(1{\to}4')\text{-L-Asn}$$

$$(19)$$

The hydrolysis of glycosidic linkages by enzymes involves scission of the glycosyl-oxygen bond (see Fig. 4.3), but a number of enzymes known as eliminases or lyases, usually of bacterial origin, react by a different mechanism and cause cleavage of the oxygen-aglycone bond (see Fig. 4.3) in acidic polysaccharides (such as pectins), producing unsaturated hexuronic acid units.

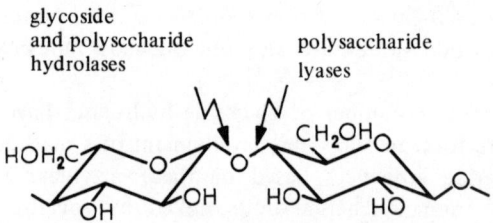

glycoside
and polysccharide
hydrolases

polysaccharide
lyases

Fig. 4.3 – Position of action of glycoside and polysaccharide hydrolases and polysaccharide lyases.

Interpretation of the results from enzyme analysis must be carried out with caution. The mode of action of the *exo*-polysaccharide hydrolases is such that it is not possible to determine from which branch(es) the terminal residue(s) have been removed: this is in contrast to the results from the alkaline degradation method. Microheterogeneity of chains within the same molecule will also make interpretation uncertain. It is essential that the enzyme used is highly purified, as other glycoside hydrolases present in the enzyme can also lead to ambiguities and incorrect assumptions. It was originally thought, for example, that all D-mannose residues in glycoproteins were α-linked, but the use of α-D-mannosidase, purified to remove all traces of β-D-mannosidase activity, disproved this.

MOLECULAR SIZE AND SHAPE

A complete description of a polysaccharide involves an estimate of its molecular size and shape. Some of the methods described above will give a measure of the size and shape as part of the analysis (for example, gel filtration, and nonreducing

Table 4.1 Enzymes which may be used for the structural analysis of carbohydrate-containing macromolecules[a]

Trivial name	Systematic name	EC number[b]
α-N-Acetyl-D-galactosaminidase	2-Acetamido-2-deoxy-α-D-galactoside acetamidodeoxygalactohydrolase	3.2.1.49
β-N-Acetyl-D-galactosaminidase	2-Acetamido-2-deoxy-β-D-galactoside acetamidodeoxygalactohydrolase	3.2.1.53
endo-α-N-Acetyl-D-galactosaminidase	D-Galactosyl-N-acetamidodeoxy-α-D-galactoside D-galactosyl-N-acetamidodeoxy-D-galactohydrolase	3.2.1.97
endo-β-N-Acetyl-D-glucosaminidase	Mannosyl-glycoprotein 1,4-N-acetamidodeoxy-β-D-glycohydrolase	3.2.1.96
α-N-Acetyl-D-glucosaminidase	2-Acetamido-2-deoxy-α-D-glucoside acetamidodeoxyglucohydrolase	3.2.1.50
β-N-Acetyl-D-glucosaminidase	2-Acetamido-2-deoxy-β-D-glucoside acetamidodeoxyglucohydrolase	3.2.1.30
β-N-Acetyl-D-hexosaminidase	2-Acetamido-2-deoxy-β-D-hexoside acetamidodeoxyhexohydrolase	3.2.1.52
exo-β-N-Acetylmuramidase	Mucopolysaccharide β-N-acetylmuramoylexohydrolase	3.2.1.92
N-Acetylmuramoyl-L-alanine amidase	Mucopeptide amidohydrolase	3.5.1.28
Agarase	Agarose 3-glycanohydrolase	3.2.1.81
Alginate lyase	Poly(1,4-β-D-mannuronide) lyase	4.2.2.3
α-Amylase	1,4-α-D-Glucan glucanohydrolase	3.2.1.1
β-Amylase	1,4-α-D-Glucan maltohydrolase	3.2.1.2
Amylo-1,6-glucosidase	Dextrin 6-α-D-glucosidase	3.2.1.33
β-L-Arabinosidase	β-L-Arabinoside arabinohydrolase	3.2.1.88
α-L-Arabinofuranosidase	α-L-Arabinofuranoside arabinofuranohydrolase	3.2.1.55
Arylsulphatase	Aryl-sulphate sulphohydrolase	3.1.6.1
exo-Cellobiohydrolase	1,4-β-D-Glucan cellobiohydrolase	3.2.1.91
Cellulase	1,4-(1,3;1,4)-β-D-Glucan 4-glucanohydrolase	3.2.1.4
Cerebroside-sulphatase	Cerebroside-3-sulphate 3-sulphohydrolase	3.1.6.8
Chitinase	Poly(1,4-β-(2-acetamido-2-deoxy-D-glucoside)) glycanohydrolase	3.2.1.14
Chondroitin ABC lyase	Chondroitin ABC lyase	4.2.2.4
Chondroitin AC lyase	Chondroitin AC lyase	4.2.2.5
Chondro-4-sulphatase	Δ4,5-β-D-Glucuronosyl-(1,4)-2-acetamido-2-deoxy-D-galactose-4-sulphate 4-sulphohydrolase	3.1.6.9

Table 4.1 (*continued*)

Trivial name	Systematic name	EC number[b]
Chondro-6-sulphatase	Δ4,5-β-D-Glucuronosyl-(1,4)-2-acetamido-2-deoxy-D-galactose-6-sulphate 6-sulphohydrolase	3.1.6.10
Cyclomaltodextrinase	Cyclomaltodextrin dextrin-hydrolase (decyclizing)	3.2.1.54
Dextranase	1,6-α-D-Glucan 6-glucanohydrolase	3.2.1.11
2,6-β-D-Fructan 6-levanbiohydrolase	2,6-β-D-Fructan 6-β-D-fructofuranosyl fructohydrolase	3.2.1.64
β-D-Fructofuranosidase	β-D-Fructofuranoside fructohydrolase	3.2.1.26
exo-β-D-Fructosidase	β-D-Fructan fructohydrolase	3.2.1.80
Fucoidanase	Poly(1,2-α-L-fucoside-4-sulphate) glycanohydrolase	3.2.1.44
α-L-Fucosidase	α-L-Fucoside fucohydrolase	3.2.1.51
β-D-Fucosidase	β-D-Fucoside fucohydrolase	3.2.1.38
α-D-Galactosidase	α-D-Galactoside galactohydrolase	3.2.1.22
β-D-Galactosidase	β-D-Galactoside galactohydrolase	3.2.1.23
Galactosylceramidase	D-Galactosyl-*N*-acylsphingosine galactohydrolase	3.2.1.46
Galactosylgalactosylglucosylceramidase	D-Galactosyl-D-galactosyl-D-glucosyl-ceramide galactohydrolase	3.2.1.47
endo-1,3-α-D-Glucanase	1,3-(1,3;1,4)-α-D-Glucan 3-glucanohydrolase	3.2.1.59
exo-1,3-α-Glucanase	1,3-α-D-Glucan 3-glucohydrolase	3.2.1.84
endo-1,3-β-D-Glucanase	1,3-β-D-Glucan glucanohydrolase	3.2.1.39
endo-1,3(4)-β-D-Glucanase	1,3-(1,3;1,4)-β-D-Glucan 3(4)-glucanohydrolase	3.2.1.6
4-*N*-(2-β-D-Glucosaminyl)-L-asparaginase	4-*N*-(2-Acetamido-2-deoxy-β-D-glucopyranosyl)-L-asparagine amidohydrolase	3.5.1.26
α-D-Glucosidase	α-D-Glucoside glucohydrolase	3.2.1.20
β-D-Glucosidase	β-D-Glucoside glucohydrolase	3.2.1 21
exo-1,4-α-D-Glucosidase	1,4-α-D-Glucan glucohydrolase	3.2.1.3
exo-1,6-α-D-Glucosidase	1,6-α-D-Glucan glucohydrolase	3.2.1.70
exo-1,3-β-D-Glucosidase	1,3-β-D-Glucan glucohydrolase	3.2.1.58
exo-1,4-β-D-Glucosidase	1,4-β-D-Glucan glucohydrolase	3.2.1.74
Glucosylceramidase	D-Glucosyl-*N*-acylsphingosine glucohydrolase	3.2.1.45
β-D-Glucuronidase	β-D-Glucuronide glucuronosohydrolase	3.2.1.31
Glycosylceramidase	Glycosyl-*N*-acylsphingosine glycohydrolase	3.2.1.62
Heparin lyase	Heparin lyase	4.2.2.7

Table 4.1 (*continued*)

Trivial name	Systematic name	EC number[b]
Heparitinsulphate lyase	Heparin-sulphate lyase	4.2.2.8
Hyaluronate lyase	Hyaluronate lyase	4.2.2.1
Hyaluronoglucosaminidase	Hyaluronate 4-glycanohydrolase	3.2.1.35
L-Iduronidase	Mucopolysaccharide α-L-iduronohydrolase	3.2.1.76
Inulinase	2,1-β-D-Fructan fructanohydrolase	3.2.1.7
Isoamylase	Glycogen 6-glucanohydrolase	3.2.1.68
exo-Isomaltohydrolase	1,6-α-D-Glucan isomaltohydrolase	3.2.1.94
exo-Isomaltotriohydrolase	1,6-α-D-Glucan isomaltotriohydrolase	3.2.1.95
Isopullulanase	Pullulan 4-glucanohydrolase	3.2.1.57
Lichenase	1,3-1,4-β-D-Glucan 4-glucanohydrolase	3.2.1.73
Lysozyme	Mucopeptide *N*-acetylmuramoylhydrolase	3.2.1.17
α-D-Mannosidase	α-D-Mannoside mannohydrolase	3.2.1.24
β-D-Mannosidase	β-D-Mannoside mannohydrolase	3.2.1.25
exo-1,2-1,3-α-D-Mannosidase	1,2-1,3-α-D-Mannan mannohydrolase	3.2.1.77
Neuraminidase	Acylneuraminyl hydrolase	3.2.1.18
Oligo-1,6-glucosidase	Dextrin 6-α-D-glucanohydrolase	3.2.1.10
Pectate lyase	Poly(1,4-α-D-galacturonide) lyase	4.2.2.2
Pectinesterase	Pectin pectylhydrolase	3.1.1.11
Pectin lyase	Poly(methoxygalacturonide) lyase	4.2.2.10
Polygalacturonase	Poly(1,4-α-D-galacturonide) glycanohydrolase	3.2.1.15
exo-Polygalacturonase	Poly(1,4-α-D-galacturonide) galacturonohydrolase	3.2.1.67
exo-Poly-α-D-galacturonosidase	Poly(1,4-α-D-galactosiduronate) digalacturonohydrolase	3.2.1.82
Pullulanase	Pullulan 6-glucanohydrolase	3.2.1.41
α-L-Rhamnosidase	α-L-Rhamnoside rhamnohydrolase	3.2.1.40
β-L-Rhamnosidase	β-L-Rhamnoside rhamnohydrolase	3.2.1.43
Sucrose α-D-glucohydrolase	Sucrose α-D-glucohydrolase	3.2.1.48
α,α-Trehalase	α,α-Trehalose glucohydrolase	3.2.1.28
endo-1,3-β-D-Xylanase	1,3-β-D-Xylan xylanohydrolase	3.2.1.32
endo-1,4-β-D-Xylanase	1,4-β-D-Xylan xylanohydrolase	3.2.1.8
D-Xylose isomerase	D-Xylose ketol isomerase	5.3.1.5
exo-1,3-β-D-Xylosidase	1,3-β-D-Xylan xylohydrolase	3.2.1.72
exo-1,4-β-D-Xylosidase	1,4-β-D-Xylan xylohydrolase	3.2.1.37

[a] The nomenclature used in this Table is identical to that used in Recommendations (1978) although that work does not necessarily comply with that recommended by IUPAC/IUB for carbohydrates.

[b] EC number stands for Enzyme Commission number, see Chapter 5, p.**98**.

end group analysis by methylation, or periodate oxidation), but specific methods are available for characterisation of the polysaccharides to give data on molecular weight, size, and distribution in any given sample.

The use of electron microscopy has been limited by the small size of the molecules which are being dealt with. They are too small to scatter electrons themselves, but the technique of casting a metal shadow on the molecules has led to single molecular patterns being obtained, but the method more frequently gives information only on molecular aggregates and conformational shape.

X-ray diffraction is another method which provides information and polysaccharides which form fibres gives satisfactory diffraction diagrams. These are usually linear molecules but the attachment of single unit side chains, if not too frequent, does not interfere with the formation of crystals and hence with the method. In highly branched polysaccharides crystallinity is only found if the high degree of substitution shows a regular pattern, but in the majority of polysaccharides crystallinity is only partial, resulting in dislocation in the crystal lattice and large areas of amorphous material, which makes the interpretation of results more difficult. This method of analysis has shown, for example, how the repeating units in glycosaminoglycans which consist of a disaccharide unit (see Chapter 9) are arranged in chains.

Colligative property measurements have been used for molecular weight determination. Below a molecular weight of 20 000 the method involving measurement on differences in vapour pressure or boiling points of pure solvent and solutions can be used, but these are limited by the sensitivity of the techniques available for measuring the small differences. Above a molecular weight of 20 000 the only method which can satisfactorily be used is the measurement of osmotic pressure. The limitation on this method is the sensitivity of measurement of the pressure differences for high molecular weight substances, the upper limit of molecular weight being of the order of 500 000. At the opposite end of the molecular weight range the nature of the semipermeable membrane dictates the limitation of the method. The newer techniques of vapour phase osmometry and dynamic osmometry have been used successfully.

Light scattering by dilute solutions of the polysaccharide provides an absolute method for the determination of molecular weights. Solutions of the polysaccharides are illuminated with monochromatic polarised or unpolarised light, and the scattered light intensity is measured as a function of the scattering angle. From these data the shape of the molecules and the molecular weight can be obtained.

Molecular weights and shapes can also be obtained from studies of sedimentation velocities of a solution of the polysaccharides under the influence of a high force field by following the changes in refractive index gradients. The rate of sedimentation obtained from these ultracentrifugation studies provides a measure of molecular weight and, on comparison with the calculated behaviour for molecular models, provides a basis for assessment of molecular shape. Fractionation by ultracentrifugal methods is now very popular, and effective separations of, for example, proteoglycans have been obtained using caesium chloride density gradients, whilst the use of neutral salt solutions at high concentrations is made for large scale preparations.

Using some, or all of the above techniques it has been possible to obtain detailed three dimensional structures for some polysaccharides and carbohydrate-containing macromolecules (for example, glycosaminoglycans). These are discussed in the relevant sections of the forthcoming chapters.

CHAPTER 5

Chemical and biochemical syntheses

This chapter describes the various reactions used to prepare monosaccharides and their polymerisation to give oligo- and poly-saccharides and discusses the reactions carried out by nature in performing synthesis of macromolecules from simple building blocks (biosynthesis).

CHEMICAL SYNTHESIS OF MONOSACCHARIDES

The total synthesis of many sugars has been achieved from non-carbohydrate materials but complex mixtures of products are obtained. In the 1860s the action of dilute alkali on formaldehyde was reported to produce a sweet syrup, which was called formose and has subsequently been shown to contain a mixture of aldoses and ketoses, including D- and L-glucose. The action of dilute alkali on acrolein dibromide does not produce the expected glyceraldehyde but a mixture of sugars named acrose. Initially a racemic mixture of D- and L-glyceraldehyde is produced some of which undergoes conversion into 1,3-dihydroxy-2-propanone (dihydroxyacetone) and then, by an aldol condensation reaction, produces a mixture of ketohexoses (Scheme 5.1). The major problem with these methods is that, at some stage of the reaction sequences, resolution of the racemic mixture (D- and L-forms) is necessary if a pure compound is to be produced. However, Fischer successfully used the second method to prepare α-acrose (a mixture of D- and L-fructose, see Scheme 5.1) from which he prepared many of the previously unknown aldohexoses using some of the reactions discussed below.

The fact that a number of monosaccharides are readily available from natural sources means that they provide suitable starting materials for the less readily available sugars. By using a naturally occurring product only one optical isomer is used, thus eliminating the need for resolution of racemic mixtures of products in most cases. A number of methods have been devised for increasing or decreasing the number of carbon atoms in the molecules (that is, ascent or descent of the homologous series) and for the interconversion of monosaccharides without changing the number of carbon atoms present. These methods have been fully reviewed (Hough and Richardson, 1972 and 1979, and Szarek, 1973) and are described here only briefly.

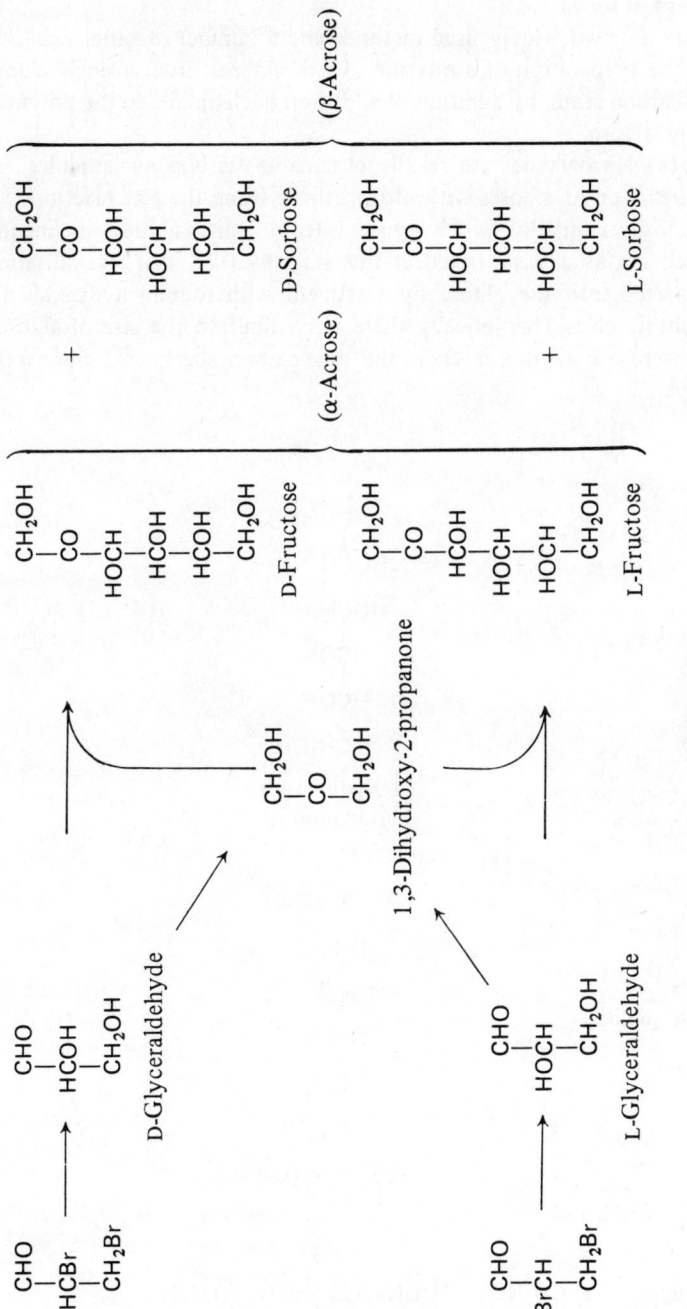

Scheme 5.1

Ascent of series

There are two widely used methods and a number of other reactions available for the preparation of a mixture of two aldoses, from a single aldose with one less carbon atom, by addition of a 'carbon nucleophile' to the potential aldehyde of the aldose.

(a) Nitroalkanes are readily obtainable 'carbon nucleophiles' prepared by the reaction of aldoses with nitromethane using the Nef reaction (Scheme 5.2) which gives initially two isomeric 1-deoxy-1-nitro-alditols in unequal amounts which are usually separated at this stage by fractional crystallisation and then converted into the aldose by treatment with sodium hydroxide followed by sulphuric acid. Theoretically there is no limit to the size of aldose which can be prepared by this method and nine-carbon sugars (aldononoses) have been prepared.

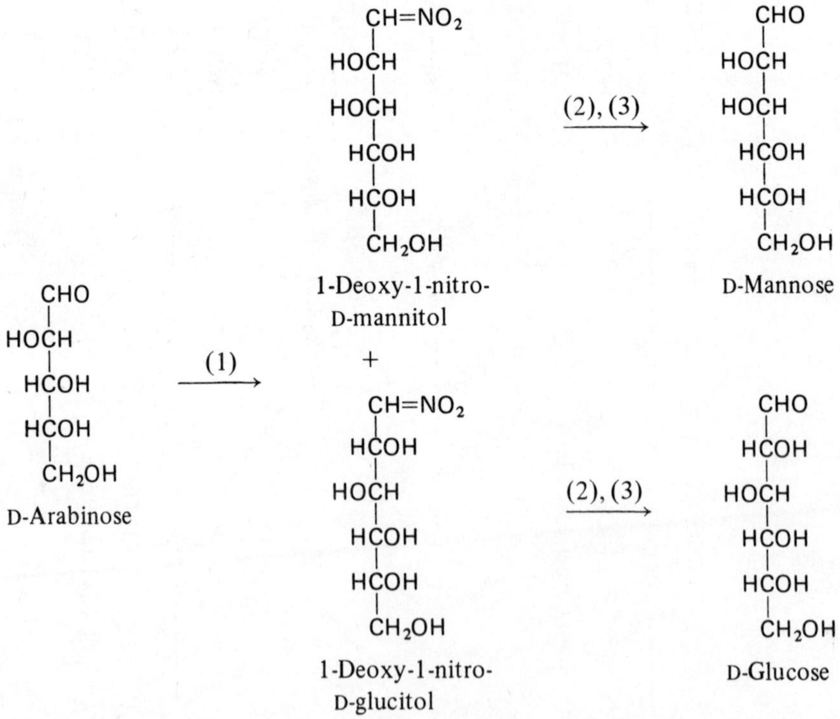

Reagents: (1) CH_3NO_2, CH_3ONa; (2) NaOH; (3) H_2SO_4

Scheme 5.2

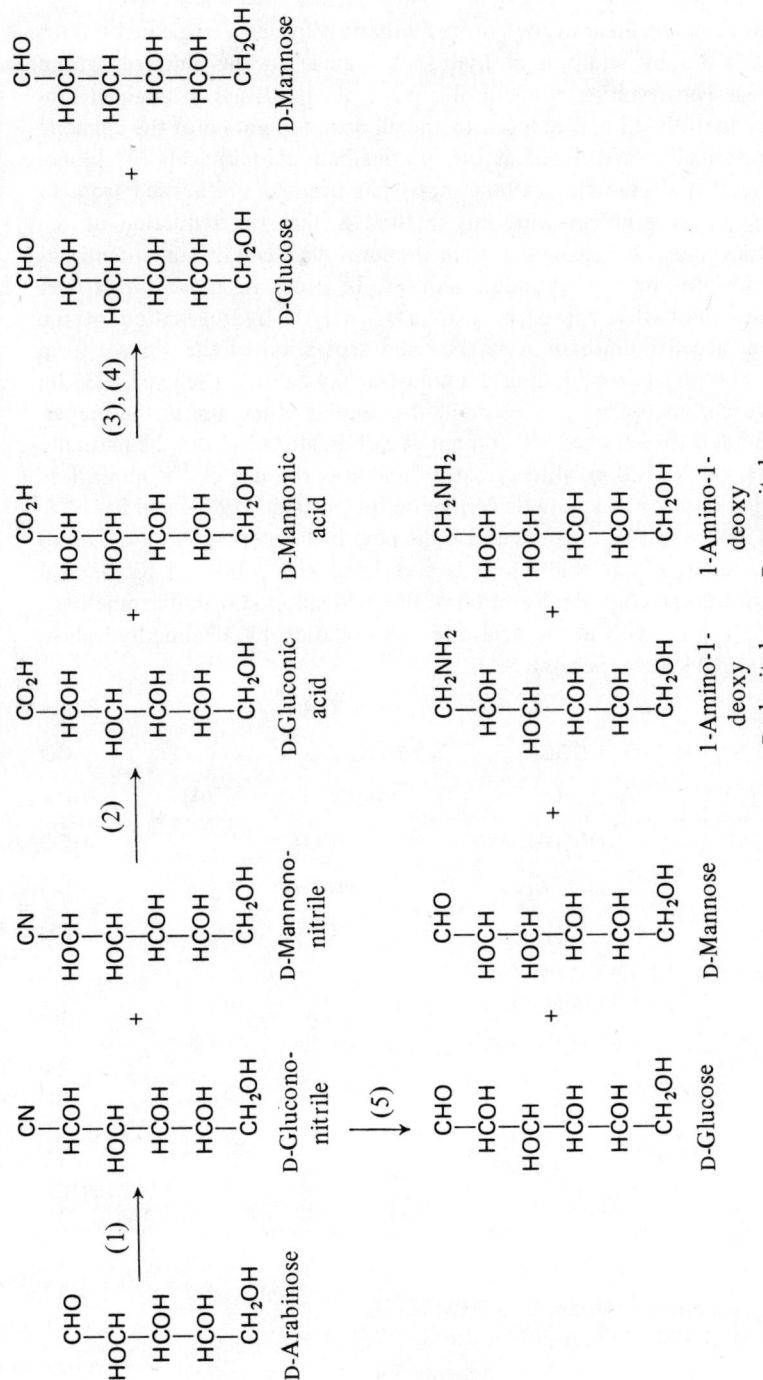

Reagents: (1) HCN or NaCN; (2) NaOH; (3) heat to form lactone; (4) Na/Hg; (5) Pd/BaSO$_4$

Scheme 5.3

(b) The Fischer-Kiliani cyanohydrin synthesis provides a single method for ascending a series by addition of hydrogen cyanide to the aldehyde group (Scheme 5.3). The resulting epimeric nitriles, again produced in unequal proportions, are hydrolysed and reduced to the aldoses. Separation of the epimeric products is normally carried out at the intermediate aldonic acids or aldonolactones stages. A decose (ten-carbon sugar) has been so synthesised from D-glucose. The major problem with this method is that the reduction of the aldonolactones must be carried out under controlled conditions to prevent over reduction to the corresponding alditols. In order to prevent this over reduction an alternative approach is to use catalytic hydrogenation of the nitriles using a palladium/barium catalyst and separation of the aldoses from each other and the corresponding 1-amino-1-deoxy-alditols (Scheme 5.3) by ion-exchange chromatography. This method is finding a new use in the preparation of aldoses with enriched ^{13}C content at carbon atom 1 (from the naturally occurring 1% to 90–100%) which greatly facilitates the use of ^{13}C n.m.r. (see Chapter 4) in the study of anomeric configuration (Serianni, 1979a and b).

(c) An aldose can be converted into the next higher ketose by oxidation to the corresponding aldonic acid which is acetylated and converted to the acid chloride with thionyl chloride. Reaction of this acid chloride with diazomethane followed by heating with acetic acid and deacetylation by alkaline hydrolysis gives the required ketose (Scheme 5.4).

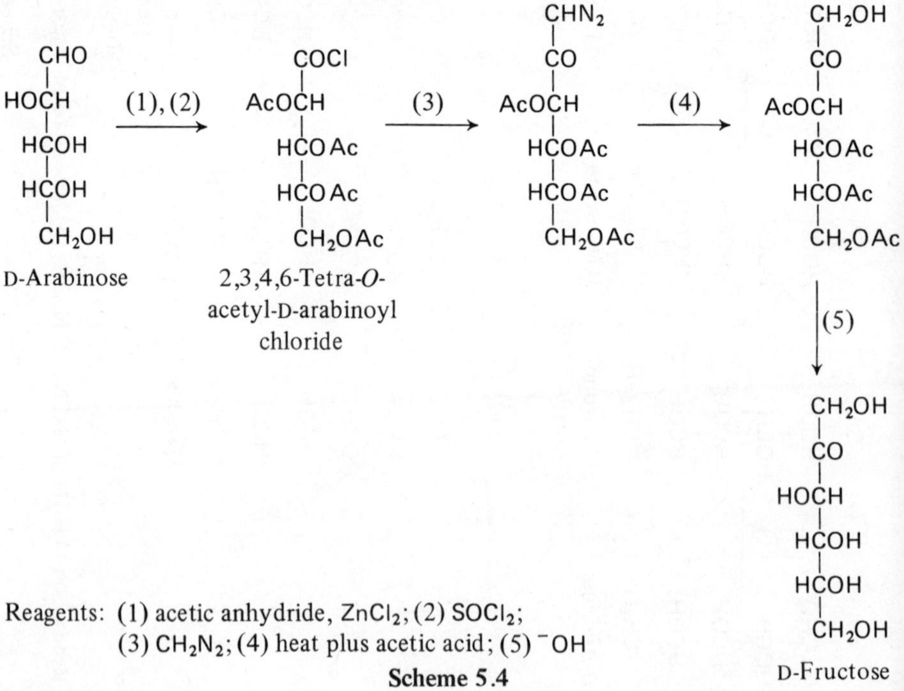

Reagents: (1) acetic anhydride, $ZnCl_2$; (2) $SOCl_2$;
(3) CH_2N_2; (4) heat plus acetic acid; (5) $^-$OH

Scheme 5.4

Other methods which have been used to ascend a series include the use of Grignard reagents, malonate esters and the Wittig reaction.

Descent of series

Removal of one of the terminal carbon atoms from an aldose to give the corresponding lower aldose can be achieved by a number of methods. The oldest laboratory method is the Wohl degradation which involves heating the aldose oxime with acetic anyhydride and zinc chloride or sodium acetate so that the oxime undergoes dehydration and acetylation to give an O-acetylated nitrile. Hydrogen cyanide is removed by an ammonia-induced reaction and the required aldose with one less carbon atom is then obtained by mild acid hydrolysis (Scheme 5.5). The yield can be increased by using sodium methoxide in chloroform rather than the traditional silver oxide/ammonia combination.

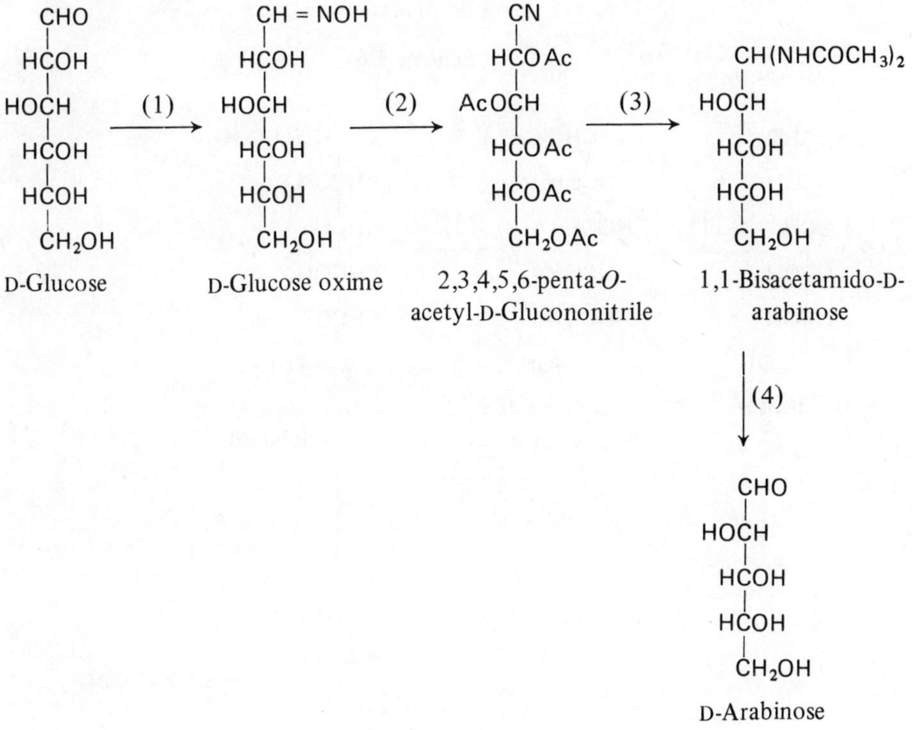

Reagents: (1) H_2NOH; (2) acetic anhydride, $ZnCl_2$; (3) NH_3; (4) H^+

Scheme 5.5

The Ruff degradation method involves the oxidation of the calcium salt of an aldonic acid with hydrogen peroxide in the presence of iron(III) ions (Fenton's reagent) to give a 2-ketoaldonic acid and, by subsequent loss of carbon dioxide, the required aldose (Scheme 5.6). Further degradation lowers the yield although the use of ion-exchange resins helps to eliminate these degradation losses.

$$
\begin{array}{ccc}
CO_2^- \cdot \tfrac{1}{2}Ca^{2+} & CO_2^- \cdot \tfrac{1}{2}Ca^{2+} & \\
| & | & CHO \\
HCOH & HCO & | \\
| & | & HOCH \\
HOCH \quad (1) & HOCH \longrightarrow & | \quad\quad + CO_2 \\
| \longrightarrow & | & HCOH \\
HCOH & HCOH & | \\
| & | & HCOH \\
HCOH & HCOH & | \\
| & | & CH_2OH \\
CH_2OH & CH_2OH & \\
\text{Calcium} & \text{Calcium} & \text{D-Arabinose} \\
\text{D-glucuronate} & \text{D-}erythro\text{-2-} & \\
& \text{pentulosonate} &
\end{array}
$$

Reagents: (1) H_2O_2, Fe^{3+} **Scheme 5.6**

$$
\begin{array}{ccc}
CHO & CH(SC_2H_5)_2 & CH(SO_2C_2H_5)_2 \\
| & | & | \\
HCOH & HCOH & HCOH \\
| & | & | \\
HOCH \quad (1) & HOCH \quad (2) & HOCH \\
| \longrightarrow & | \longrightarrow & | \\
HCOH & HCOH & HCOH \\
| & | & | \\
HCOH & HCOH & HCOH \\
| & | & | \\
CH_2OH & CH_2OH & CH_2OH \\
\text{D-Glucose} & \text{D-Glucose di-}S\text{-} & \text{D-Glucose di-(ethyl-} \\
& \text{ethyl dithioacetal} & \text{sulphone)}
\end{array}
$$

$$\downarrow (3)$$

$$
\begin{array}{c}
CHO \\
| \\
HOCH \\
| \quad\quad + \quad CH(SO_2C_2H_5)_2 \\
HCOH \\
| \\
HCOH \\
| \\
CH_2OH \\
\text{D-Arabinose}
\end{array}
$$

Reagents: (1) C_2H_5SH, HCl;
(2) $C_2H_5CO_3H$; (3) NH_3

Scheme 5.7

In the disulphone degradation method, the aldose is converted to a dithio-acetal (mercaptal) by reaction with an alkanethiol, followed by oxidation with a peracid to give the disulphone which, in dilute ammonia, undergoes cleavage of the C-1–C-2 bond to give the required product (Scheme 5.7). Due to the high yields and purity of the final products the method is to be preferred.

Other methods which can be used to descend a series include the Hofmann degradation of an acid amide with hypochlorite and the use of glycol cleavage agents to degrade a suitably blocked derivative.

Interconversion without changing the number of carbon atoms
The chemistry of conversion of aldoses into ketoses, using mildly basic conditions such as aqueous calcium hydroxide, has already been described (Chapter 3), whilst the reverse process can be carried out *via* reduction of the ketose to alditols, careful oxidation to aldonic acids and subsequent reduction to give a mixture of aldoses. The chemistry of these reactions is discussed in Chapter 3.

The preparation of some rare sugars has been achieved by inversion of con-figuration at one or more chiral centres (epimerisation) of a readily available monosaccharide. Due to the extensive rearrangements which occur with free sugars during base catalysed epimerisation these reactions are rarely carried out on unprotected monosaccharides. In order to illustrate the many methods which are, or have been, used to invert the configuration of hydroxyl groups the epi-merisation of D-glucose at C-5 to give L-idose (Scheme 5.8) is shown. The 5,6-ditosylated D-glucofuranose derivative (20) undergoes nucleophilic displacement on treatment with sodium benzoate in *N,N*-dimethylformamide to give an L-idose derivative (21). As will be seen later in this chapter, an increase in the

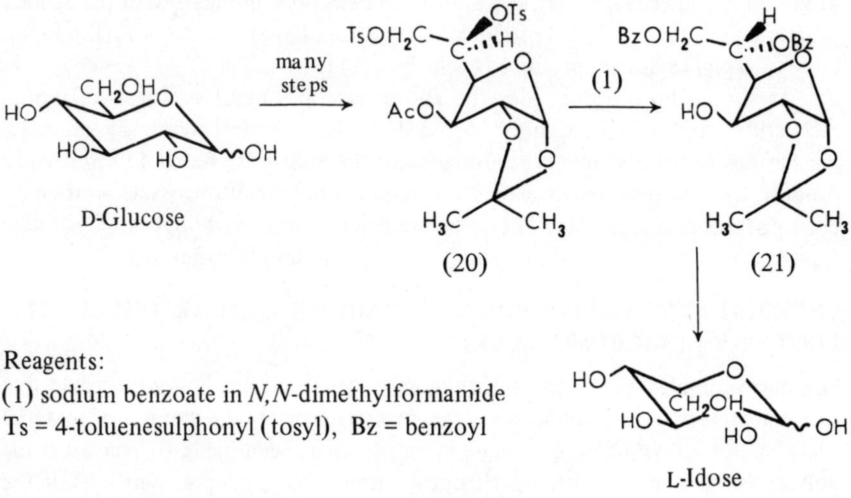

Reagents:
(1) sodium benzoate in *N,N*-dimethylformamide
Ts = 4-toluenesulphonyl (tosyl), Bz = benzoyl

Scheme 5.8

understanding of biological reactions is eliminating the need to rely on purely chemical methods since enzymes have been isolated which can perform many of these interconversions specifically (for example, epimerases EC 5.1.3. etc. and isomerases EC 5.3.1. etc.) on unprotected monosaccharides.

CHEMICAL SYNTHESIS OF OLIGOSACCHARIDES

The synthesis of oligosaccharides etc. from monosaccharides generally takes place *via* glycosidation reactions, such as Fischer glycosidation (see Chapter 3), using fully protected monosaccharides with only the positions required for bond formation free. Hence D-glucose protected at positions 2, 3 and 6 produces the expected oligo- and poly-saccharides containing (1→4)-linkages but with random arrangements of α- and β-linkages. It also contains some head to head termination products (products formed by linking C-1 of 1 residue to C-1 of another residue, as in trehaloses, Chapter 2). Separation of this mixture presents complex problems and is often impossible to achieve.

A stepwise addition of a monosaccharide (or oligosaccharide) to another monosaccharide (or oligosaccharide) can be achieved using the Koenigs-Knorr method (see Chapter 3). The carbohydrate unit which will contain the reducing end of the final product is suitably protected such that only that hydroxyl group required for bond formation remains unsubstituted (22). This is then reacted with the appropriate glycosyl halide (23) and the final product (24) is obtained with a β-D-linkage (Scheme 5.9). To synthesise an oligosaccharide with an α-D-linkage the glycosyl halide must contain a protecting group at C-2 such as nitrate which has no neighbouring group effect (25). Thus, isomaltose (26) can be prepared with only a small amount of gentiobiose (24) by-product *via* Scheme 5.10. An alternative method involves the use of 1,2-anhydro derivatives, such as Brigl's anhydride (27), which, at elevated temperatures, interacts with the acetate protecting group at C-6 (28) producing a mixture of anomers. At normal temperatures β-D-glycosides are produced (Scheme 5.11).

As should be obvious from the above descriptions of synthesis of monosaccharides and glycoside bond formation, the chemical synthesis of oligosaccharides is not a simple procedure due to the multistage reactions required to produce the properly substituted carbohydrates but small oligosaccharides have been produced successfully. The transferase activities of carbohydrate hydrolase type enzymes can also be used to build up oligosaccharide structures.

CHEMICAL SYNTHESIS OF POLYSACCHARIDES AND CARBOHYDRATE-CONTAINING MACROMOLECULES

For more-complex polysaccharides the above methods are not appropriate due to the losses, which occur at each stage, severely limiting the amount of material available for subsequent reactions. Attempts have been made to convert some polysaccharides into others by chemical means. For example, synthesis of the glycosaminoglycan heparin (see Chapter 9) has been attempted by sulphation

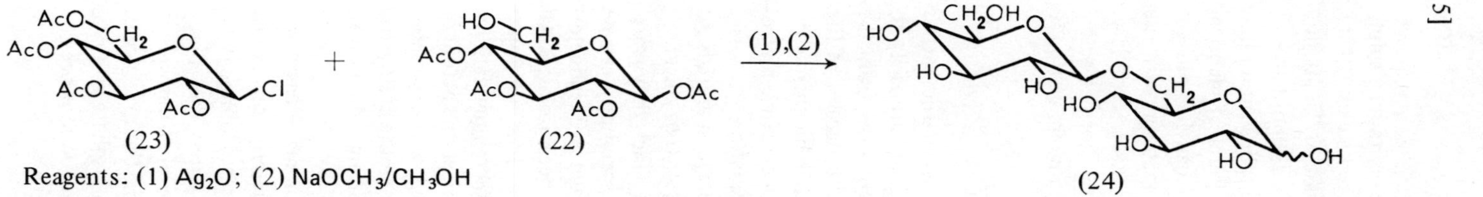

(23) + (22) →(1),(2) (24)

Reagents: (1) Ag$_2$O; (2) NaOCH$_3$/CH$_3$OH

Scheme 5.9

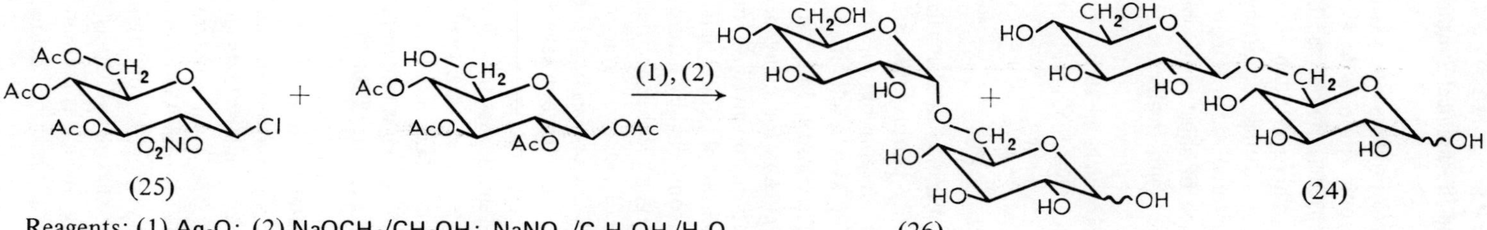

(25) + →(1), (2) (26) + (24)

Reagents: (1) Ag$_2$O; (2) NaOCH$_3$/CH$_3$OH; NaNO$_3$/C$_2$H$_5$OH /H$_2$O

Scheme 5.10

Reagents: (1)

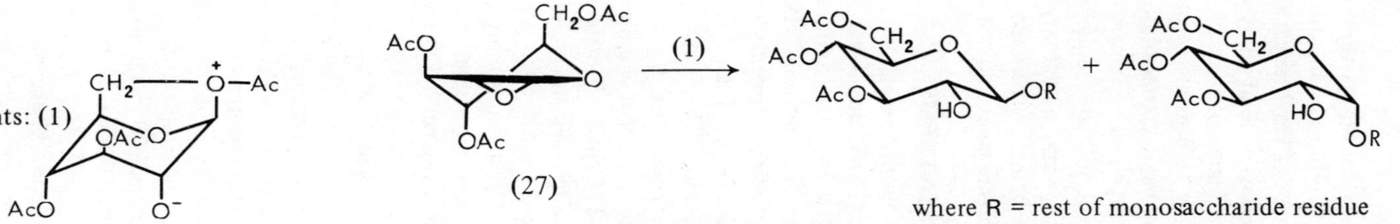

(28)   (27) →(1)

where R = rest of monosaccharide residue

Scheme 5.11

and oxidation reactions on chitin to produce a polysaccharide containing sulph-amido groups and hexopyranosyluronic acid residues (Whistler and Kosik, 1971). Starch and amylose have also been used as the polysaccharide base in the attempted conversion of a polysaccharide to heparin. Such preparations did not have the same degree of biological activity as naturally occurring heparin; this shows that it may be possible to prepare a material which satisfies the criteria of identical component composition and degree of substitution but that man has not yet developed the means to reproduce synthetically the required material with the correct primary sequence which is believed to produce the exact secondary, tertiary and quaternary structures which, in turn, result in the correct active sites being constructed to give the high biological activity found in naturally occurring macromolecules.

BIOSYNTHESIS

Carbohydrates are of central significance in the balance between the earth's 'living' and 'non-living' carbon, since photosynthesis, which leads primarily to neutral monosaccharides, is largely responsible for reversing the flow from the 'living' to the 'non-living' occurring as a result of the normal processes of life (respiration, fermentation, etc.). They also hold a central place in biochemistry, as shown by Fig. 5.1, being precursors for many naturally occurring macro-molecules. There are many reactions involved in the degradation processes (catabolism) of D-glucose to non-carbohydrate and of storage materials to simple monomeric units which are controlled by nature's catalysts (enzymes).

The main characteristic of enzymes is the specificity with which they react. Although dependent on the type of reaction catalysed, this specificity can be gauged from the fact that over 2,000 enzymes have been isolated and character-ised whilst many more are believed to exist but have not yet been isolated. All enzymes are named in terms of the reaction which they catalyse but, since 1956, enzymes have been given systematic classifications (see Recommendations, 1978) which gives an enzyme a systematic name (which describes the action of the enzyme), a commission number (EC number) based on a four-number numerical code and a common name which is more practical than the systematic name for everyday usage (see, for example, Table 5.1). For an introduction to enzymology see Palmer (1981).

This chapter will not discuss catabolic reactions; they are, in many cases, the reverse steps of the synthetic reactions (anabolism) and full descriptions can be obtained from standard biology/biochemistry texts (for example, Holum, 1978, Candy, 1980, and Stryer, 1981). The main point to note is that the energy released during catabolism is usually stored in the form of adenosine triphosphate (ATP, 29). This is stable under physiological conditions but, in the presence of a phosphoryl acceptor, the correct enzyme will transfer the phosphate group to the acceptor with release of energy which is consumed by anabolic processes. It is these anabolic processes which are described below.

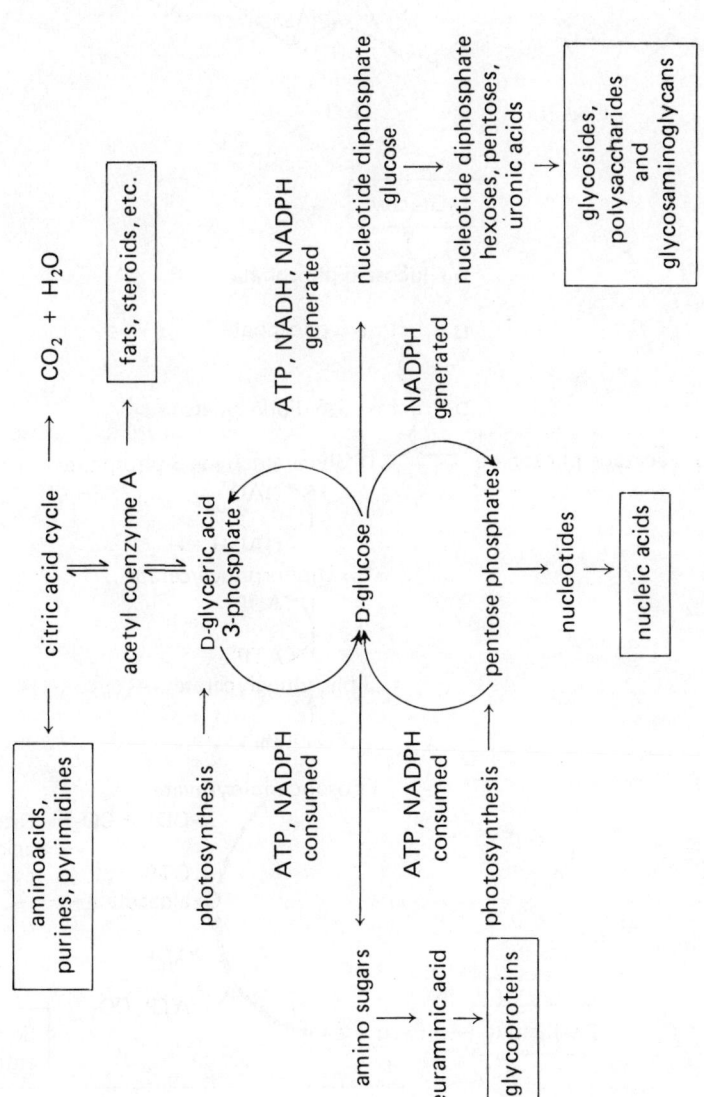

Fig. 5.1 – The central role of D-glucose in biochemistry (see Table 1.1, p. 17 for explanation of abbreviations).

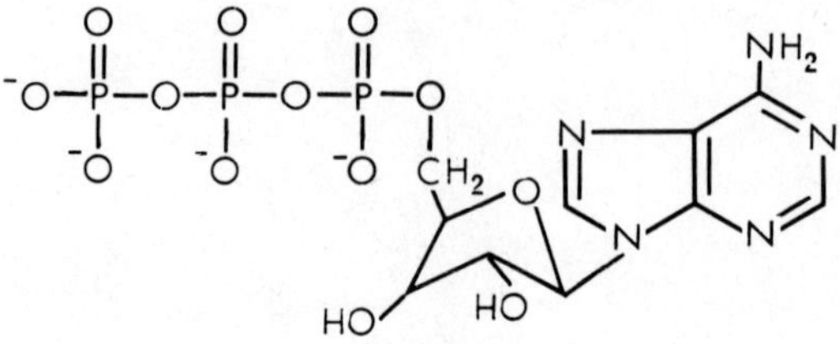

(29)

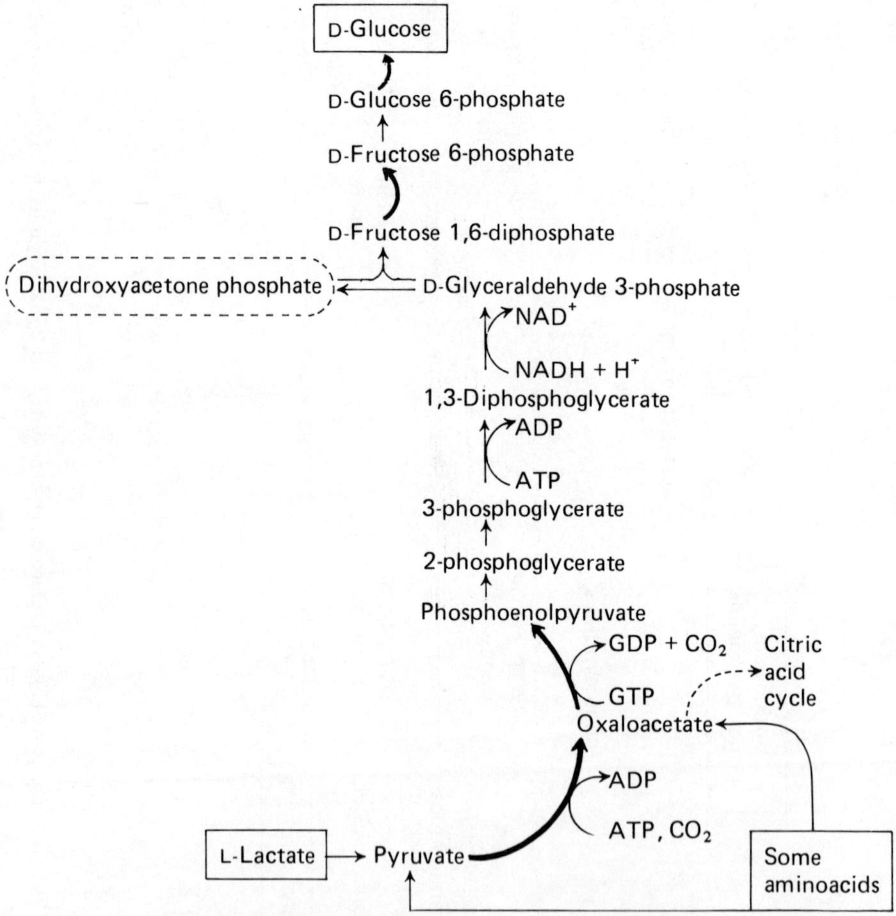

Fig. 5.2 – Gluconeogenesis. Straight arrows signify steps that are simply the reverse of corresponding steps in glycolysis. Heavy curved arrows signify steps that are unique to gluconeogenesis and are not the reverse of steps in glycolysis. Carbon skeletons from nearly all aminoacids can be used in one way or another to make D-glucose (see Table 1.1, p. 17 for explanation of abbreviations).

Anabolism of D-glucose

The biosynthesis of D-glucose from non-carbohydrate materials, known as gluconeogenesis ('glucose-new-genesis'), is outlined in Fig. 5.2. Nearly all amino-acids can be partially degraded to give a suitable precursor for gluconeogenesis but lactate, a reduction product of pyruvate, can also be used in order to maintain the body's metabolic balance. Once D-glucose has been formed, different derivatives from the phosphate esters (for example, ATP) take over the role of providing the driving force for the reactions. Through these derivatives, typified by uridine diphosphate-D-glucose (UDP-D-Glc, 30) formed from α-D-glucopyranose 1-phosphate and uridine triphosphate (UTP, 31) as shown in Scheme 5.12, the majority of interconversions and glycosylations occur. For example, D-glucose can be converted to D-galactose by epimerisation at C-4 catalysed by the enzyme UDP-D-glucose 4-epimerase (EC 5.1.3.2) or to D-glucuronic acid by oxidation catalysed by UDP-D-glucose dehydrogenase (EC 1.1.1.22). Subsequent decarboxylation of D-glucuronic acid by UDP-D-glucuronate decarboxylase (EC 4.1.1. 35) produces D-xylose. A list of the various enzymes involved in the biosynthesis of D-glucose and its subsequent conversion into other mono- and poly-saccharides is given in Table 5.1.

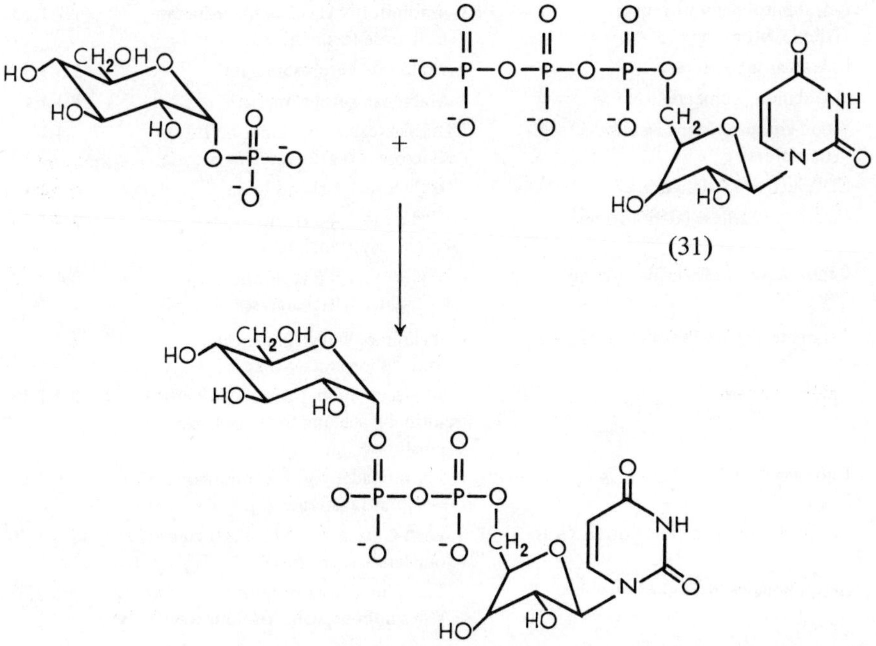

(31)

(30)

Scheme 5.12

Table 5.1 Some of the enzymes involved in the biosynthesis of monosaccharides and other carbohydrate-containing molecules[a]

Trivial name	Systematic name	EC number[b]
Acetylglucosamine phosphomutase	2-Acetamido-2-deoxy-D-glucose-1,6-bisphosphate: 2-acetamido-2-deoxy-D-glucose-1-phosphate phosphotransferase	2.7.5.2
Acylglucosamine 2-epimerase	2-Acylamido-2-deoxy-D-glucose 2-epimerase	5.1.3.8
Acylglucosamine-6-phosphate 2-epimerase	2-Acylamido-2-deoxy-D-glucose-6-phosphate 2-epimerase	5.1.3.9
Acylneuraminate cytidylyltransferase	CTP:N-acylneuraminate cytidylyltransferase	2.7.7.43
Aldonolactonase	L-Gulono-γ-lactone lactonohydrolase	3.1.1.18
Alginate synthase	GDPmannuronate:alginate D-mannuronyltransferase	2.4.1.33
Amylosucrase	Sucrose:1,4-α-D-glucan 4-α-D-glucosyltransferase	2.4.1.4
D-Arabinitol dehydrogenase	D-Arabinitol:NAD$^+$ 4-oxidoreductase	1.1.1.11
L-Arabinitol dehydrogenase	L-Arabinitol:NAD$^+$ 4-oxidoreductase (L-xylulose-forming)	1.1.1.12
L-Arabinitol dehydrogenase (ribulose-forming)	L-Arabinitol:NAD$^+$ 2-oxidoreductase (L-ribulose-forming)	1.1.1.13
D-Arabinose isomerase	D-Arabinose ketol-isomerase	5.3.1.3
L-Arabinose isomerase	L-Arabinose ketol-isomerase	5.3.1.4
Blood-group-substance α-D-galactosyltransferase	UDPgalactose:O-α-L-fucosyl-(1,2)-D-galactose α-D-galactosyltransferase	2.4.1.37
CDPglucose 4,6-dehydratase	CDPglucose 4,6-hydro-lyase	4.2.1.45
Cellulose synthase (GDP-forming)	GDPglucose:1,4-β-D-glucan 4-β-glucosyltransferase	2.4.1.29
Cellulose synthase (UDP-forming)	UDPglucose:1,4-β-D-glucan 4-β-D-glucosyltransferase	2.4.1.12
Ceramide cholinephosphotransferase	CDPcholine:N-acylsphingosine cholinephosphotransferase	2.7.8.3
Chitin synthase	UDP-2-acetamido-2-deoxy-D-glucose: chitin 4-β-acetamidodeoxy-D-glucosyltransferase	2.4.1.16
Chondroitin sulphotransferase	3'-Phosphoadenylylsulphate:chondroitin 4'-sulphotransferase	2.8.2.5
Cyclomaltodextrin glucanotransferase	1,4-α-D-Glucan 4-α-D-(1,4-α-D-glucano)-transferase (cyclizing)	2.4.1.19
Desulphoheparin sulphotransferase	3'-Phosphoadenylylsulphate: N-desulphoheparin N-sulphotransferase	2.8.2.8
Enolase	2-Phospho-D-glycerate hydro-lyase	4.2.1.11
Fructokinase	ATP:D-fructose 6-phosphotransferase	2.7.1.4

Table 5.1 (*continued*)

Trivial name	Systematic name	EC number[b]
Fructose-bisphosphatase	D-Fructose-1,6-bisphosphate 1-phosphohydrolase	3.1.3.11
Fructose-bisphosphate aldolase	D-Fructose-1,6-bisphosphate D-glyceraldehyde-3-phosphate-lyase	4.1.2.13
Galactokinase	ATP:D-galactose 1-phosphotransferase	2.7.1.6
Galactose-1-phosphate uridylyltransferase	UTP:α-D-galactose-1-phosphate uridylyltransferase	2.7.7.10
Galactosylceramide sulphotransferase	3′-Phosphoadenylylsulphate: galactosyl ceramide 3′-sulphotransferase	2.8.2.11
GDPfucose—glycoprotein fucosyltransferase	GDPfucose:glycoprotein fucosyltransferase	2.4.1.68
GDPmannose 4,6-dehydratase	GDPmannose 4,6-hydro-lyase	4.2.1.47
Glucosamine acetyltransferase	Acetyl-CoA:2-amino-2-deoxy-D-glucose N-acetyltransferase	2.3.1.3
Glucosamine-phosphate acetyltransferase	Acetyl-CoA:2-amino-2-deoxy-D-glucose-6-phosphate N-acetyltransferase	2.3.1.4
1,4-α-Glucan branching enzyme	1,4-α-D-Glucan:1,4-α-D-glucan 6-α-D-(1,4-α-D-glucano)-transferase	2.4.1.18
1,4-α-D-Glucan 6-α-D-glucosyltransferase	1,4-α-D-Glucan:1,4-α-D-glucan (D-glucose) 6-α-D-glucosyltransferase	2.4.1.24
4-α-D-Glucanotransferase	1,4-α-D-Glucan:1,4-α-D-glucan 4-α-D-glycosyltransferase	2.4.1.25
1,3-β-D-Glucan synthase	UDPglucose:1,3-β-D-glucan 3-β-D-glucosyltransferase	2.4.1.34
Glucokinase	ATP:D-glucose 6-phosphotransferase	2.7.1.2
Glucomannan 4-β-D-mannosyltransferase	GDPmannose:glucomannan 1,4-β-D-mannosyltransferase	2.4.1.32
Glucose-1-phosphate adenylyltransferase	ATP:α-D-glucose-1-phosphate adenylyltransferase	2.7.7.27
Glucose-1-phosphate guanylyltransferase	GTP:α-D-glucose-1-phosphate guanylyltransferase	2.7.7.34
Glucosephosphate isomerase	D-Glucose-6-phosphate ketol-isomerase	5.3.1.9
Glucose-1-phosphate thymidylyltransferase	dTTP:α-D-glucose-1-phosphate thymidylyltransferase	2.7.7.24
Glucose-1-phosphate uridylyltransferase	UTP:α-D-glucose-1-phosphate uridylyltransferase	2.7.7.9
Glucose-6-phosphatase	D-Glucose-6-phosphate phosphohydrolase	3.1.3.9
Glucose-6-phosphate dehydrogenase	D-Glucose-6-phosphate:NADP$^+$ 1-oxidoreductase	1.1.1.49
Glucuronate reductase	L-Gulonate:NADP$^+$ 1-oxidoreductase	1.1.1.19
L-Gulonate dehydrogenase	L-Gulonate:NAD$^+$ 3-oxidoreductase	1.1.1.45
L-Gulonolactone oxidase	L-Gulono-γ-lactone:oxygen 2-oxidoreductase	1.1.3.8
Glycerate kinase	ATP:D-glycerate 3-phosphotransferase	2.7.1.31

Table 5.1 (*continued*)

Trivial name	Systematic name	EC number[b]
Glycerol kinase	ATP:glycerol 3-phosphotransferase	2.7.1.30
Glycogen (starch) synthase	UDPglucose:glycogen 4-α-D-glucosyltransferase	2.4.1.11
Heparitin sulphotransferase	3′-Phosphoadenylylsulphate: heparitin N-sulphotransferase	2.8.2.12
Hexokinase	ATP:D-hexose 6-phosphotransferase	2.7.1.1
myo-Inositol 1-kinase	ATP:*myo*-inositol 1-phosphotransferase	2.7.1.64
myo-Inositol oxygenase	*myo*-Inositol:oxygen oxidoreductase	1.13.99.1
myo-Inositol-1-phosphate synthase	1L-*myo*-Inositol-1-phosphate lyase (isomerizing)	5.5.1.4
Ketohexokinase	ATP:D-fructose 1-phosphotransferase	2.7.1.3
Lactose synthase	UDPgalactose:D-glucose 4-β-D-galactosyltransferase	2.4.1.22
D-Lyxose ketol-isomerase	D-Lyxose ketol-isomerase	5.3.1.15
Mannose isomerase	D-Mannose ketol-isomerase	5.3.1.7
Mannose-1-phosphate guanylyltransferase	GTP:α-D-mannose-1-phosphate guanylyltransferase	2.7.7.13
1,3-β-D-Oligoglucan phosphorylase	1,3-β-D-Oligoglucan:orthophosphate glucosyltransferase	2.4.1.30
Phospho-N-acetylmuramoyl-pentapeptide-transferase	UDP-N-acetylmuramoyl-L-alanyl-D-γ-glutamyl-L-lysyl-D-alanyl-D-alanine: undecaprenoid-1-ol-phosphate phospho-N-acetylmuramoyl-pentapeptide-transferase	2.7.8.13
6-Phosphofructokinase	ATP:D-fructose-6-phosphate 1-phosphotransferase	2.7.1.11
Phosphoglucomutase	α-D-Glucose-1,6-bisphosphate:α-D-glucose-1-phosphate phosphotransferase	2.7.5.1
Phosphoglucomutase (glucose-cofactor)	D-Glucose-1-phosphate:D-glucose 6-phosphotransferase	2.7.5.5
Phosphogluconate dehydratase	6-Phospho-D-gluconate hydro-lyase	4.2.1.12
Phosphogluconate dehydrogenase (decarboxylating)	6-Phospho-D-gluconate:NADP⁺ 2-oxidoreductase (decarboxylating)	1.1.1.44
6-Phosphogluconolactonase	6-Phospho-D-gluconate-δ-lactone lactonohydrolase	3.1.1.31
Phosphoglycerate kinase	ATP:3-phospho-D-glycerate 1-phosphotransferase	2.7.2.3
Phosphoglycerate phosphomutase	D-Phosphoglycerate 2,3-phosphomutase	5.4.2.1
Phosphoglyceromutase	2,3-Bisphospho-D-glycerate:2-phospho-D-glycerate phosphotransferase	2.7.5.3
Phospho-2-keto-3-deoxy-gluconate aldolase	6-Phospho-2-keto-3-deoxy-D-gluconate D-glyceraldehyde-3-phosphate-lyase	4.1.2.14
Phosphoketolase	D-Xylulose-5-phosphate D-glyceraldehyde-3-phosphate-lyase (phosphate-acetylating)	4.1.2.9

Table 5.1 (*continued*)

Trivial name	Systematic name	EC number[b]
5'-Phosphoribosylamine synthetase	Ribose-5-phosphate:ammonia ligase (ADP-forming)	6.3.4.7
Phosphorylase	1,4-α-D-Glucan:orthophosphate α-D-glucosyltransferase	2.4.1.1
Pyruvate kinase	ATP:pyruvate 2-*O*-phosphotransferase	2.7.1.40
Ribokinase	ATP:D-ribose 5-phosphotransferase	2.7.1.15
Ribosephosphate isomerase	D-Ribose-5-phosphate ketol-isomerase	5.3.1.6
Ribosephosphate pyrophosphokinase	ATP:D-ribose-5-phosphate pyrophosphotransferase	2.7.6.1
Ribulokinase	ATP:L(or D)-ribulose 5-phosphotransferase	2.7.1.16
D-Ribulokinase	ATP:D-ribulose 5-phosphotransferase	2.7.1.47
Ribulosephosphate 3-epimerase	D-Ribulose-5-phosphate 3-epimerase	5.1.3.1
L-Ribulosephosphate 4-epimerase	L-Ribulose-5-phosphate 4-epimerase	5.1.3.4
Sphingomyelin phosphodiesterase	Sphingomyelin cholinephosphate hydrolase	3.1.4.2
Starch (bacterial glycogen) synthase	ADPglucose:1,4-α-D-glucan 4-α-D-glucosyltransferase	2.4.1.21
Sucrose-phosphatase	Sucrose-6'-phosphate phosphohydrolase	3.1.3.24
Sucrose-phosphate synthase	UDPglucose:D-fructose-6-phosphate 2-α-D-glucosyltransferase	2.4.1.14
Sucrose synthase	UDPglucose:D-fructose 2-α-D-glucosyltransferase	2.4.1.13
Sugar-phosphatase	Sugar-phosphate phosphohydrolase	3.1.3.23
Sulphate adenylyltransferase	ATP:sulphate adenylyltransferase	2.7.7.4
dTDPglucose 4,6-dehydratase	dTDPglucose 4,6-hydro-lyase	4.2.1.46
Teichoic-acid synthase	CDPribitol:teichoic-acid phosphoribitoltransferase	2.4.1.55
Transaldolase	Sedoheptulose-7-phosphate: D-glyceraldehyde-3-phosphate dihydroxyacetonetransferase	2.2.1.2
Transketolase	Sedoheptulose-7-phosphate: D-glyceraldehyde-3-phosphate glycolaldehydetransferase	2.2.1.1
Trehalose-phosphatase	Trehalose-6-phosphate phosphohydrolase	3.1.3.12
α,α-Trehalose-phosphate synthase (GDP-forming)	GDPglucose:D-glucose-6-phosphate α-D-glucosyltransferase	2.4.1.36
α,α-Trehalose-phosphate synthase (UDP-forming)	UDPglucose:D-glucose-6-phosphate 1-α-D-glucosyltransferase	2.4.1.15
Triokinase	ATP:D-glyceraldehyde 3-phosphotransferase	2.7.1.28
UDPacetylgalactosamine–protein acetylgalactosaminyltransferase	UDP-2-acetamido-2-deoxy-D-galactose: protein acetamidodeoxygalactosyl-transferase	2.4.1.41

Table 5.1 (*continued*)

Trivial name	Systematic name	EC number[b]
UDPacetylglucosamine 4-epimerase	UDP-2-acetamido-2-deoxy-D-glucose 4-epimerase	5.1.3.7
UDP-*N*-acetylglucosamine–glycoprotein *N*-acetylglucosaminyltransferase	UDP-2-acetamido-2-deoxy-D-glucose: glycoprotein 2-acetamido-2-deoxy-D-glucosyltransferase	2.4.1.51
UDPacetylglucosamine pyrophosphorylase	UTP:2-acetamido-2-deoxy-α-D-glucose-1-phosphate uridylyltransferase	2.7.7.23
UDP-*N*-acetylmuramoylalanine synthetase	UDP-*N*-acetylmuramate:L-alanine ligase (ADP-forming)	6.3.2.8
UDP-*N*-acetylmuramoyl-L-alanyl-D-glutamate synthetase	UDP-*N*-acetylmuramoyl-L-alanine:D-glutamate ligase (ADP-forming)	6.3.2.9
UDP-*N*-acetylmuramoyl-L-alanyl-D-glutamyl-L-lysyl-D-alanyl-D-alanine synthetase	UDP-*N*-acetylmuramoyl-L-alanyl-D-glutamyl-L-lysine:D-alanyl-D-alanine ligase (ADP-forming)	6.3.2.10
UDPgalactose–*N*-acylsphingosine galactosyltransferase	UDPgalactose:*N*-acylsphingosine galactosyltransferase	2.4.1.47
UDPgalactose–lipopolysaccharide galactosyltransferase	UDPgalactose:lipopolysaccharide galactosyltransferase	2.4.1.44
UDPgalactose–mucopolysaccharide galactosyltransferase	UDPgalactose:mucopolysaccharide galactosyltransferase	2.4.1.74
UDPgalactose–sphingosine β-D-galactosyltransferase	UDPgalactose:sphingosine β-D-galactosyltransferase	2.4.1.23
UDPglucose–ceramide glucosyltransferase	UDPglucose:*N*-acylsphingosine glucosyltransferase	2.4.1.80
UDPglucose dehydrogenase	UDPglucose:NAD$^+$ 6-oxidoreductase	1.1.1.22
UDPglucose 4-epimerase	UDPglucose 4-epimerase	5.1.3.2
UDPglucose–hexose-1-phosphate uridylyltransferase	UDPglucose:α-D-galactose-1-phosphate uridylyltransferase	2.7.7.12
UDPglucuronate decarboxylase	UDPglucuronate carboxy-lyase	4.1.1.35
UDPglucuronate 4′-epimerase	UDPglucuronate 4′-epimerase	5.1.3.6
UDPglucuronate 5′-epimerase	UDPglucuronate 5′-epimerase	5.1.3.12
UDPglucuronosyltransferase	UDPglucuronate β-D-glucuronosyl-transferase (acceptor-unspecific)	2.4.1.17
Xylose isomerase	D-Xylose ketol-isomerase	5.3.1.5
D-Xylulokinase	ATP:D-xylulose 5-phosphotransferase	2.7.1.17
L-Xylulokinase	ATP:L-xylulose 5-phosphotransferase	2.7.1.53
D-Xylulose reductase	Xylitol:NAD$^+$ 2-oxidoreductase (D-xylulose-forming)	1.1.1.9
L-Xylulose reductase	Xylitol:NADP$^+$ 4-oxidoreductase (L-xylulose-forming)	1.1.1.10

[a] The nomenclature used in this table is identical to that used in Recommendations (1978) although that work does not necessarily comply with that recommended by IUPAC/IUB for carbohydrates.

[b] EC number stands for Enzyme Commission number, see this chapter, p. 98.

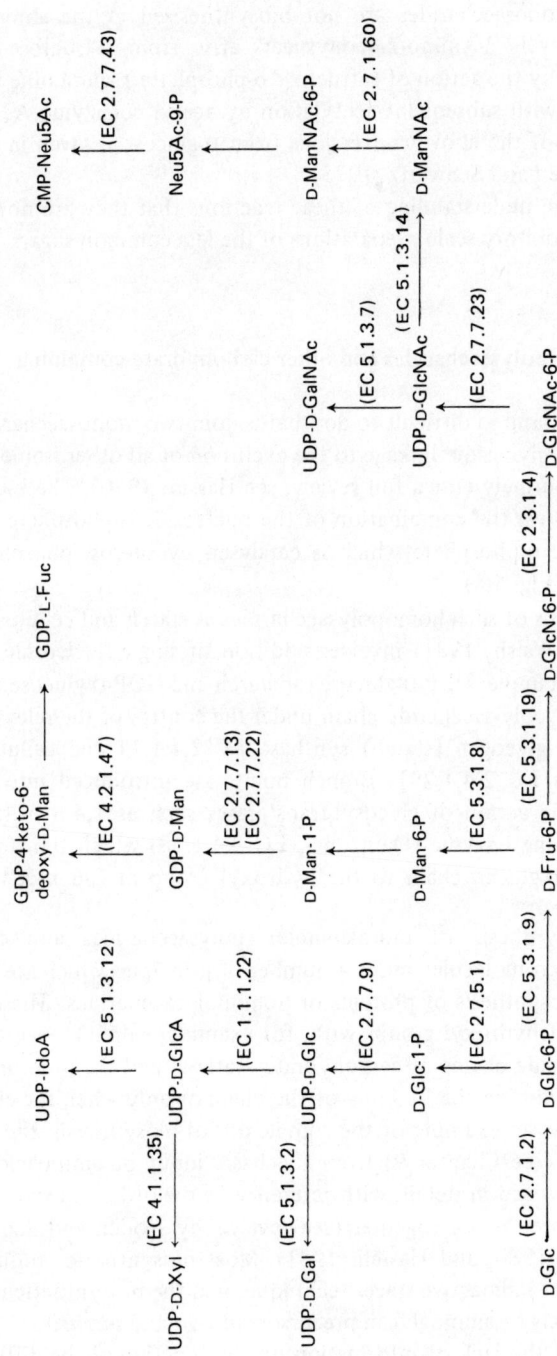

Fig. 5.3 — Biosynthetic conversion of D-glucose into some of the other biologically important monosaccharides.

Certain monosaccharides are not biosynthesised at the above nucleoside diphosphate level. 2-Amino-2-deoxysugars arise from D-fructose 6-phosphate and glutamine by the action of D-fructose 6-phosphate:L-glutamine transamidase (EC 5.3.1.19) with subsequent acetylation by acetyl coenzyme A. A schematic representation of the above conversions from D-glucose is given in Fig. 5.3 (see review by Rodén and Schwartz, 1975).

Such is the understanding of these reactions that they are now being used for *in vitro* laboratory scale preparations of the less common sugars.

Biosynthesis of polysaccharides and other carbohydrate-containing macromolecules

What man has found so difficult to do, that is, join two monosaccharides together with a specific glycosidic linkage to the exclusion of all other isomeric products, nature does routinely (for a full review, see Hassid, 1970). The biosynthesis of sucrose occurs *via* the combination of the nucleoside diphosphate of D-glucose and D-fructose 6-phosphate which is catalysed by sucrose-phosphate synthase (EC 2.4.1.14) (Fig. 5.4).

Biosynthesis of such homopolysaccharides as starch and cellulose (see review by Preiss and Walsh, 1981) involves addition of single nucleoside diphosphate residues (for example, UDP-D-glucose for starch and GDP-D-glucose for cellulose) to an oligo- or poly-saccharide chain under the control of the relevant synthases [for example, glycogen (starch) synthase EC 2.4.1.11 and cellulose synthase (GDP-forming) EC 2.4.1.29]. Branch points are introduced into the growing polymer by the action of glycosyl-transferases such as 1,4-α-D-glucan (amylopectin) branching enzyme (Q-enzyme, EC 2.4.1.18) which transfers a segment of a (1→4)-α-D-glucan chain to the hydroxyl group at C-6 in a similar glucan chain.

The biosynthesis of more-complex polysaccharides and carbohydrate-containing macromolecules raises a number of principles which are not encountered in the biosynthesis of proteins or homopolysaccharides. These include the substitution of hydroxyl groups with, for example, sulphate, acetate and phosphate etc., or side chains of carbohydrate material and the order in which these occur (that is, during the building of the chain or only when the chain has been terminated). As an example of the complexity of biosynthesis, the formation of proteoglycans (see Chapter 9) from the basic input of aminoacids and carbohydrate is discussed in detail, with reference to the order of events and how the various parts are linked together (see reviews by Rodén and Schwartz, 1975, Rodén *et al.*, 1980, and Hassell, 1981). Most biosynthetic studies have been based on use of radioactive tracer techniques and the biosynthetic incorporation of radioactive glycosaminoglycan precursors *in vivo* and *in vitro*.

In view of the lack of information on the function of the different parts of

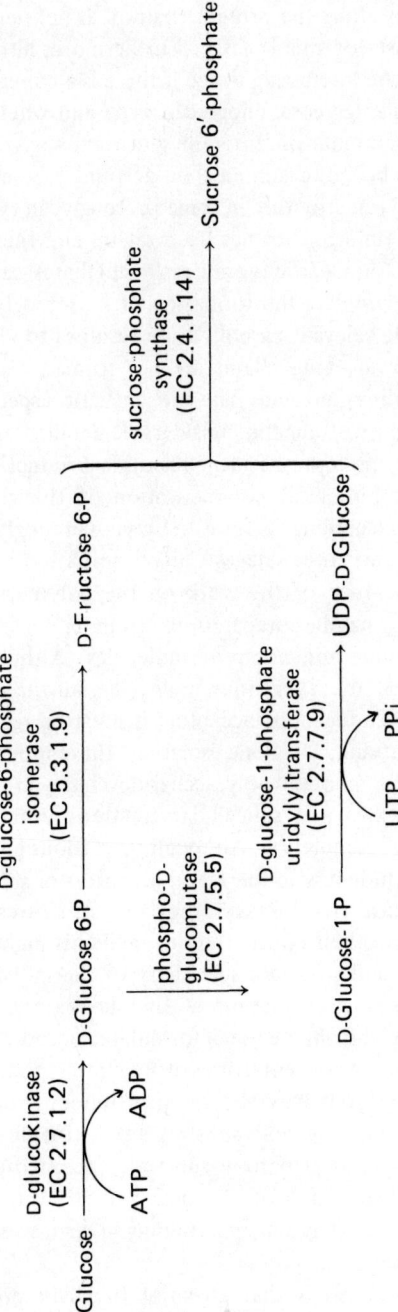

Fig. 5.4 — Biosynthesis of sucrose.

proteoglycan molecules and the importance, if any, of the spacing of the glycos-aminoglycan chains along the protein chain, it is not yet known whether a code could possibly exist for this spacing. Furthermore, although different protein chains exist, it will be interesting to see if there is a common aminoacid sequence code for a particular glycosaminoglycan type and whether there is any coding for the different amounts of different glycosaminoglycans in proteoglycans — the situation may be quite complex on account of the presence of more than one glycosaminoglycan structure in some proteoglycan types.

Once the protein sequence has been set up and the protein chain has been produced in intact form, carbohydrate residues (that is, carbohydrate block units) may be added to complete the formation of a proteoglycan molecule. Whereas the addition of the relevant carbohydrate residues to glycosaminoglycan oligo-saccharides can occur, long chains are not formed — presumably due to the absence of the primer protein. The biosynthetic aspects of the glycosamino-glycan chain have been studied in considerable detail.

Following the monosaccharide nucleotide production, which provides the basic material for biological polymerisation of the glycosaminoglycan chain (see Fig. 5.5), the reactions to form the glycosaminoglycan chains can be con-sidered to occur in three stages: chain initiation, chain propagation and chain termination. Much of the work on the polymerisation process has been carried out using enzyme preparations from endogenous material but with exogenous and donor and acceptor molecules. Although objections may be raised to the use of the exogenous molecules, on the basis that they may not represent the true endogenous acceptor, it must be realized that there is great difficulty in identifying, let alone isolating, the endogneous acceptor. Cellular biosynthetic systems contain polysaccharide chains in all stages of growth and therefore homogenates and subcellular fractions contain acceptors of various sizes and degrees of completion. Although the various glycosyl transfer reactions should ideally be studied with the actual acceptors or substances that are present *in vivo*, this does have disadvantages; the exact structures of the acceptors are, as yet, unknown as are their concentrations, and this makes determination of the kinetic parameters and substrate specificity of the individual enzymes difficult. In many instances a clear picture of the substrate specificity of the various reactions has emerged from the use of formulated acceptors of defined structures. Furthermore, when the concentrations of substrates, and/or amounts of products are known, enzyme levels may also be quantitated. However, acceptance of the results obtained using exogenous substrates is justifiable in terms of the fact that the enzymes do have very narrow substrate specificities. Once a reaction has been identified in such a way, the data and structural descriptions obtained must be applied to the situation appertaining *in vivo*, to see if the rate of enzyme action is even greater.

The biosynthetic steps that give rise to chain propagation are less well known, and the question as to how the propagation of a particular glycosamino-

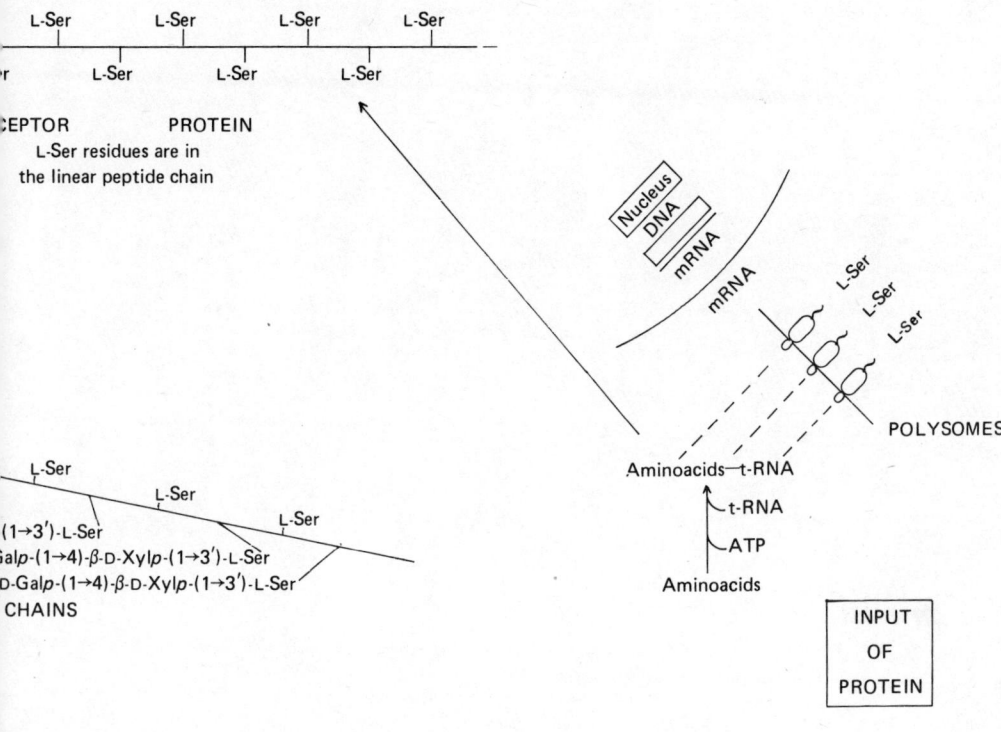

| L-Ser | L-Ser | L-Ser | L-Ser |
| L-Ser | L-Ser | L-Ser | |

CEPTOR   PROTEIN
L-Ser residues are in
the linear peptide chain

L-Ser
L-Ser
L-Ser
(1→3')-L-Ser
Galp-(1→4)-β-D-Xylp-(1→3')-L-Ser
D-Galp-(1→4)-β-D-Xylp-(1→3')-L-Ser
CHAINS

Nucleus
DNA
mRNA
mRNA

L-Ser
L-Ser
L-Ser

POLYSOMES

Aminoacids—t-RNA
t-RNA
ATP
Aminoacids

INPUT
OF
PROTEIN

KEY

a	*D-xylopyranosyltransferase*
b	*D-galactopyranosyltransferase (type 1)*
c	*D-galactopyranosyltransferase (type 2)*
d	*D-glucopyranosyluronic acid transferase (type 1)*
e	*D-glucopyranosyluronic acid transferase (type 2)*
f	*D-2-acetamido-2-deoxygalactopyranosyltransferase*
g	*O-sulphatotransferase*
AcCoA	*acetyl coenzyme A*
ADP	*adenosine 5'-diphosphate*
APS	*adenosine 5'-P-(dihydrogen phosphatosulphate)*
ATP	*adenosine 5'-triphosphate*
NAD⁺	*nicotinamide adenine dinucleotide (oxidized)*
PAPS	*adenosine 3'-phosphate-5'-P-(dihydrogen phosphatosulphate)*
PPi	*inorganic diphosphate*
UDP	*uridine 5'-pyrophosphate*
UTP	*uridine 5'-triphosphate*

glycan is selected, arising from the common glycopeptide linkage structure for a number of the glycosaminoglycans, remains unanswered. Early studies indicated the formation of a low-sulphated polysaccharide chain on incubation of a cartilagenous preparation with UDP-D-glucuronic acid and UDP-2-acetamido-2-deoxy-D-galactose, and some information came from studies on hyaluronic acid production in *Streptoccoci*. At that time the question remained as to whether the chain was propagated by addition of single monosaccharide block units or pre-produced disaccharide block units. Enzymes which incorporate radioactivity from UDP-D-[^{14}C]-glucuronic acid and UDP-2-acetamido-2-deoxy-D-[^{3}H]-galactose into growing chondroitin 4/6-sulphate chains have been recognized. It is now clear that the polymer results from the concerted action, on the glycopeptide linkage acceptor, of two glycosyltransferases: a 2-acetamido-2-deoxy-D-galactopyranosyltransferase and a D-glucopyranosyluronic acid transferase. These enzymes alternately add the two respective monosaccharide component residues of the repeating disaccharide unit directly to the chain without participation of a free disaccharide unit.

Originally it was considered that the biosynthesis of L-iduronic acid units was analogous to that of D-glucuronic acid units, but there is no evidence of either UDP-L-iduronic acid of an L-idopyranosyluronic acid transferase, and indeed such an enzyme appears to be absent. Important information on the biosynthesis of L-iduronic acid units comes from work with a microsomal fraction of a heparin-producing mastocytoma, incubation of which with UDP-D-[^{14}C]-glucuronic acid and unlabelled UDP-2-acetamido-2-deoxy-D-glucose resulted in incorporation of radioactivity into endogenous polysaccharide. When adenosine 3'-phosphate-5'-P-(dihydrogen phosphatosulphate) (a precursor of sulphate groups) was included in the incubate, the product polysaccharide contained L-[^{14}C]-idopyranosyluronic acid as well as D-[^{14}C]-glucopyranosyluronic acid residues. Pulse-chase experiments revealed that D-[^{14}C]-glucuronic acid was incorporated into the polymer during the pulse period (in the absence of adenosine 3'-phosphate-5'-P-(dihydrogen phosphatosulphate)), and in the bound form it was subsequently converted to bound L-[^{14}C]-iduronic acid during the chase period (in the presence of adenosine 3'-phosphate-5'-P-(dihydrogen phosphatosulphate)). Such experiments lead to the conclusion that, in glycosaminoglycan chains, the L-idopyranosyluronic acid residues are formed by epimerisation of D-glucopyranosyluronic acid residues at the polymer (heparin, dermatan sulphate) level by a D-glucopyranosyluronic acid 5-epimerase.

The actual mechanism of epimerisation involves loss of the hydrogen atom from C-5 of the carbohydrate ring. It must be noted that the epimerisation involves only inversion of configuration of C-5 in the D-glucopyranosyluronic acid residue — this gives an L-configuration and the C-5 epimer of D-glucuronic acid is L-iduronic acid. No alteration of the anomeric bond in the glycosidic linkage is involved — the change from β-D- to α-L- is purely one resulting from nomenclature standardisation.

The incorporation of radioactivity from [^{35}S] sulphate ion into sulphate-containing glycosaminoglycans by *in vitro* and *in vivo* systems has long been known. The fixation of radioactive sulphate depends upon a specific biosynthetic process associated with glycosaminoglycan formation, and not upon an exchange with the sulphate groups already present in the glycosaminoglycan already formed.

The sulphate groups must be transferred to the monosaccharide units at some stage after the attachment of these units to the growing proteoglycan molecule. This transfer must be affected by a sulphatotransferase and the evidence is that the transfer occurs directly from the adenosine 3'-phosphate-5'-P-(dihydrogen phosphatosulphate) to the carbohydrate.

The characteristics of the sulphatotransferase have been investigated. Evidence has been obtained from alterations in the relative amounts of chondroitin 4- and 6-sulphate- and keratan sulphate-containing proteoglycans in polysaccharide-rich tissues such as cartilage and intervertebral disc. This, together with other evidence for alterations in the rate at which [^{35}S] sulphate is incorporated into the various polysaccharides, demonstrates that different sulphatotransferases are responsible for the sulphation of the different carbon atoms.

The data available on the biosynthesis of chondroitin 4-sulphate proteoglycan have been sufficient to permit the presentation, in scheme form of many of the stages in the transformation from aminoacid right through to complete proteoglycan. This scheme has now been amplified and modified (Fig. 5.5) and it may be readily deduced from it that a large number of transferases, oxidases, deaminases, etc., are involved in the total biosynthesis of the molecule. The situation is a little more complex where more than one glycosaminoglycan chain type is attached to the protein backbone.

The biosynthesis of proteoglycans is described in detail as an example of the complexity of biosynthesis. The process is similarly very complex for other polysaccharides and carbohydrate-containing macromolecules, even if the compound appears to have a simple repeating structure.

The process of synthesising carbohydrate chains in certain glycoproteins is by preassembly of the chain on a lipid carrier with subsequent transfer of the complete chain to the protein backbone (see review by Lennarz, 1975). Monosaccharides (or monosaccharide 1-phosphates) are transferred to a polyprenol phosphate to give glycosyl phosphoryl polyprenols (for example, β-D-glucosyl dolichol phosphate (32) and β-D-glucosyl phosphoryl undecaprenol (33). These glycosyl phosphoryl polyprenols, and possibly also sugar nucleotides, transfer further carbohydrate residues to the initial glycosyl polyprenol phosphate to give linear chains. These linear chains can be transferred to other linear chains to give branched structures until chain termination occurs, when the branched chain is transferred from the lipid to a protein acceptor (Fig. 5.6).

Once man has a fuller understanding of the enzyme reactions involved and the necessary enzymes become readily available it can be anticipated that many of the chemical methods for synthesis will become redundant as *in vitro* enzyme

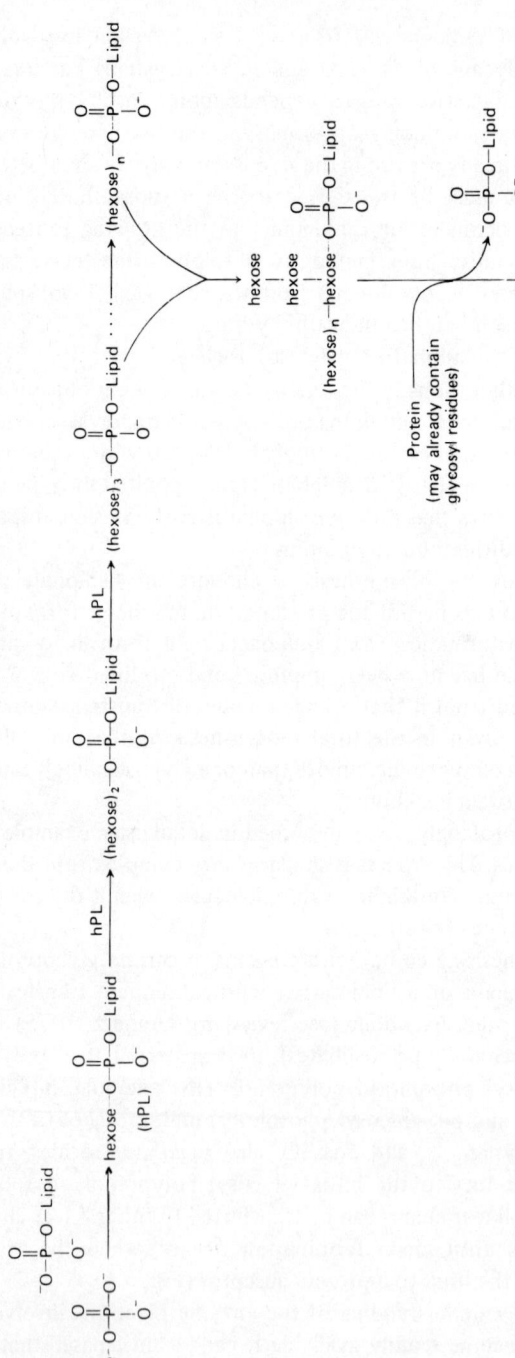

Fig. 5.6 – Schematic representation of the involvement of lipid-linked intermediates in glycoprotein biosynthesis.

controlled synthesis become commonplace. To date some tri- and tetra-saccharides have been synthesised enzymically from the activated monosaccharides (UDP-D-glucose, etc.) which had been chemically synthesised.

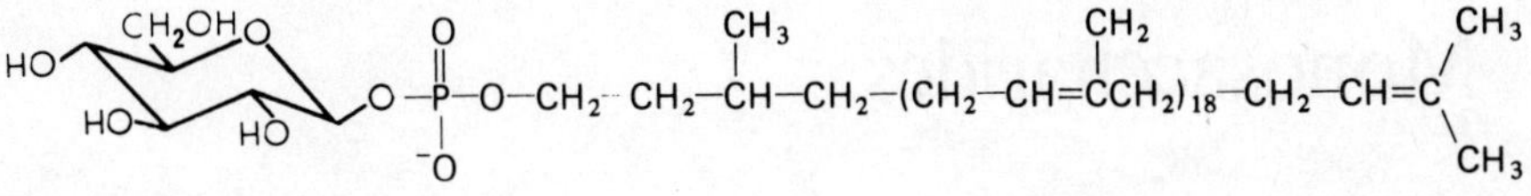

(32)

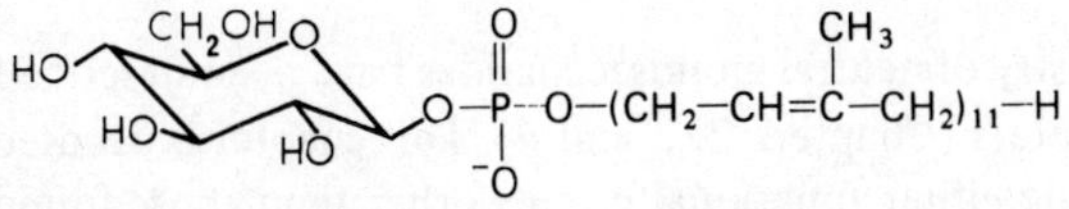

(33)

CHAPTER 6

Monosaccharides

The nomenclature and chemistry of neutral monosaccharides have been described in detail in the previous chapters (Chapters 2, 3 and 4). This chapter is devoted to monosaccharides containing either functional groups other than those found in the neutral monosaccharides (for example, carboxyl, amino, halogeno, etc.) or other (hetero) atoms within the ring structure (for example, nitrogen, carbon and sulphur). The chemistry of many of these compounds is the subject of an on-going series of reviews (Various Authors, 1968 onwards).

ACIDIC SUGARS

There are three important types of acidic sugar; these are classified according to which, otherwise neutral, terminal group has been oxidized (see Chapter 3, page 50). Hence aldonic acids are obtained by oxidation of the carbonyl group, uronic acids by oxidation of the terminal alcohol group and aldaric acids by oxidation of both the carbonyl and terminal alcohol groups. Elimination of water between the carboxyl group and a hydroxyl group leads to the formation of lactones (for example, see Chapter 3, page 51 and structures (10) and (11)). Aldaric acids have no great biological significance but aldonic acids are used in the identification and characterisation of monosaccharides (see Chapter 4, page 76). For a review of acidic sugars see Theander (1980).

By far the most important type of acidic sugars are the uronic acids, which occur almost exclusively as hexuronic acids. In biosynthetic sequences, hexuronic acids are intermediates in the conversion of hexoses into pentoses *via* a process of oxidation and decarboxylation. D-Glucuronic acid and D-galacturonic acid are found in plant gums and bacterial cell-walls, D-mannuronic acid and L-guluronic acid are found in algae (see Chapter 8) whilst D-glucuronic acid and L-iduronic acid are components of proteoglycans (see Chapter 9). The lability of the carboxyl group makes the identification of these residues in polysaccharides difficult due to decarboxylation occurring during hydrolysis, resulting in incorrect interpretation of the primary structures.

The aldonic acid from D-glucose, D-gluconic acid, in the forms of D-gluconic acid 6-phosphate and D-glucono-1,5-lactone 6-phosphate (34), is an important intermediate in carbohydrate metabolism. Another biologically important aldonic acid is vitamin C (L-ascorbic acid, the vitamin responsible for the control of scurvy), which exists as the 1,4-lactone of an unsaturated hexonic acid having an enediol structure at C-2 and C-3 represented by the Fischer structure (35) and the ring structure (36). The biosynthetic reactions of vitamin C, which include the catalysis of the final step in the transfer of hydrogen from substrate to oxygen to form water and the conversion of L-proline to L-hydroxyproline in the newly-forming collagen of tissue growth, are a consequence of the reversible redox reaction (Scheme 6.1).

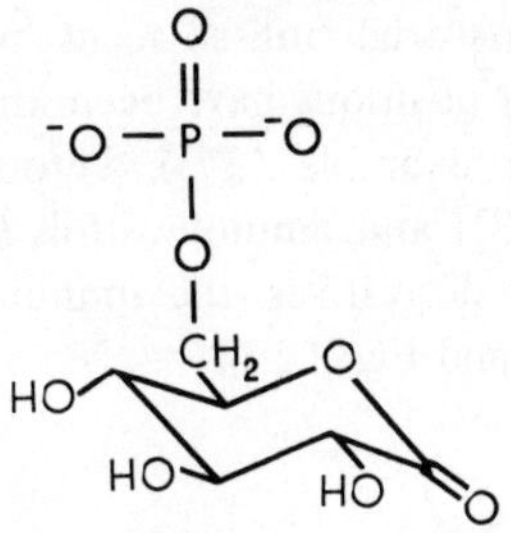

D-Glucono-1,5-lactone 6-phosphate
(34)

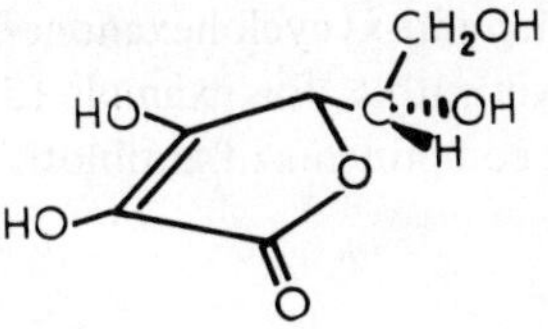

(36)

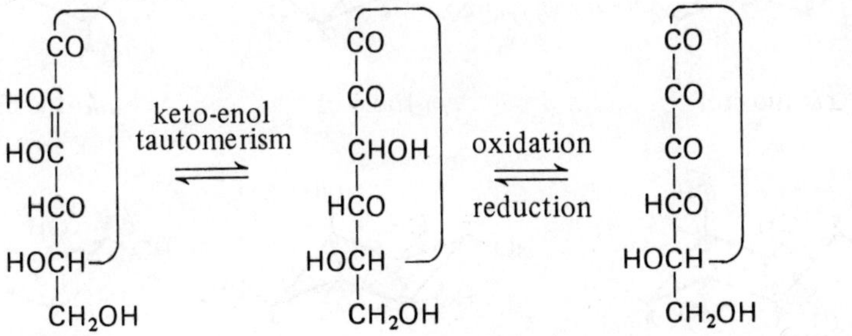

CO	keto-enol	CO	oxidation	CO
HOC	tautomerism	CO	reduction	CO
HOC	⇌	CHOH	⇌	CO
HCO		HCO		HCO
HOCH		HOCH		HOCH
CH₂OH		CH₂OH		CH₂OH

L-Ascorbic
acid
(35)

Dehydro-L-ascorbic
acid

Scheme 6.1

SUGAR ALCOHOLS

There are two groups of sugar alcohols, the first of which, the alditols, are obtained by reduction of neutral monosaccharides and have been described previously (see Chapter 3). A number of alditols occur widely in nature, particularly the hexitols D-mannitol and D-glucitol which occur particularly in seaweeds and mountain ash berries respectively. D-Glycerol and D-ribitol occur in microbial polysaccharides (see Chapter 8).

The second group of sugar alcohols are cyclic derivatives, the most common of which are derivatives of cyclohexane. These 1,2,3,4,5,6 cyclohexanehexols (cyclitols, see Recommendations, 1973), known as inositols (inosit, after the Greek ιξ, ιvoξ, meaning sinew, fibre or muscle) exist as nine stereoisomers, all but two of which are optically inactive. The structures of all the stereoisomers, which usually exist in chair forms with the greater number of hydroxyl groups in equatorial positions, are given in Fig. 6.1. Chemically, inositols undergo many of the reactions described for neutral monosaccharides and which involve hydroxyl groups. They will, for example, form isopropylidene derivatives usually involving hydroxyl groups which are both equatorial but adjacent hydroxyl groups which are both in axial (that is, diaxial) positions have been known to react. Deoxyinositols (cyclohexanepentols, for example (37)), ketoinositols (pentahydroxycyclohexanones, for example (38)) and aminoinositols (amino-deoxyinositols, for example (39)) are important derivatives, the aminoinositols being components of antibiotics (see Chapter 12 and Fig. 12.1).

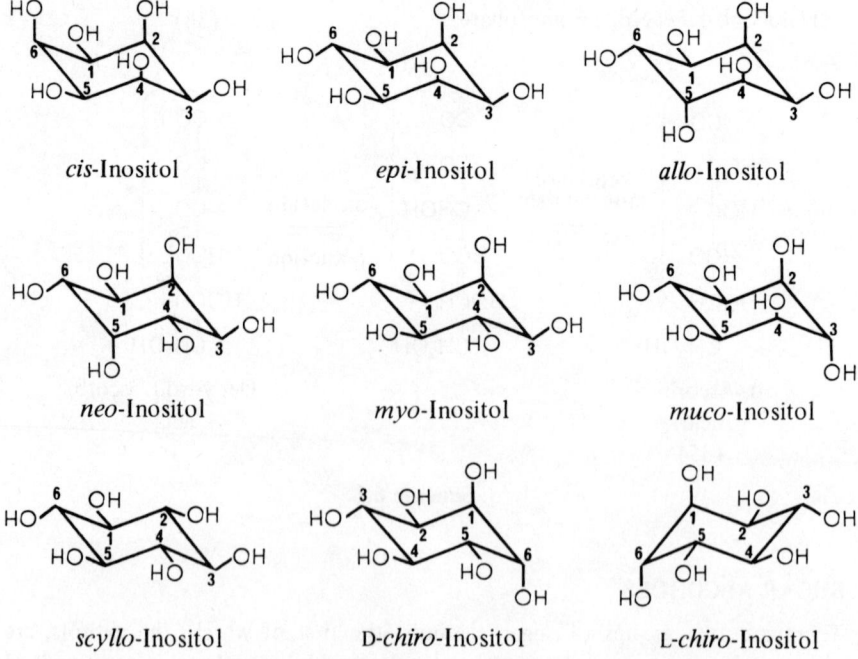

Fig. 6.1 – Structures of the nine isomeric inositols
(1,2,3,4,5,6-cyclohexanehexols, see Recommendations, 1978)

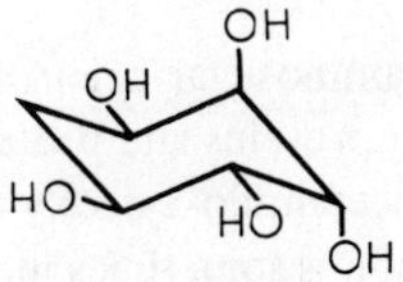

1D-1,2,4/3,5-Cyclohexanepentol
(Viburnitol)
(37)

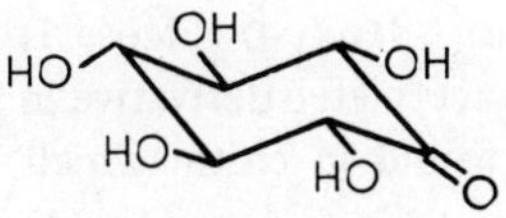

2,4,6/3,5-Pentahydroxycyclohexanone
(38)

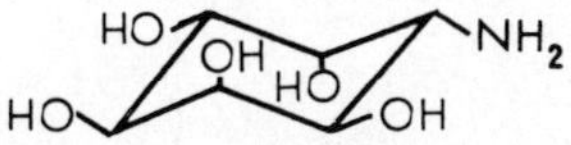

1D-1-Amino-1-deoxy-*neo*-inositol
(39)

myo-Inositol (Fig. 6.1) is the most widely distributed inositol and occurs free and combined in tissues of nearly all living species. In animals and micro-organisms it usually occurs combined as phospholipids (see Chapter 10) whilst in plants it also occurs as the hexaphosphate, phytic acid (40). The only other naturally occurring inositols are D-*chiro*- (as D-pinitol, 41), L-*chiro*- (as L-quebra-chitol, 42) and *scyllo*-inositol (Fig. 6.1). A comprehensive text on the chemistry, biochemistry and biology of cyclitols is available (Wells and Eisenberg, 1978).

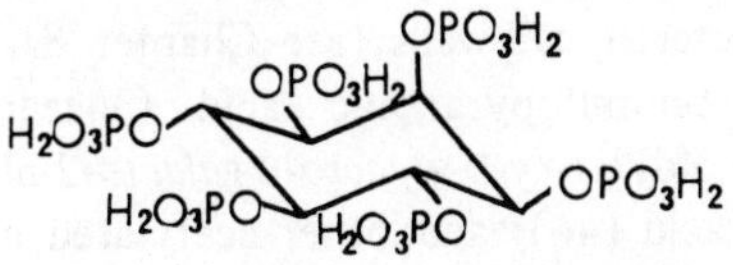

myo-Inositol 1,2,3,4,5,6-hexa-
(dihydrogen phosphate)
(Phytic acid)
(40)

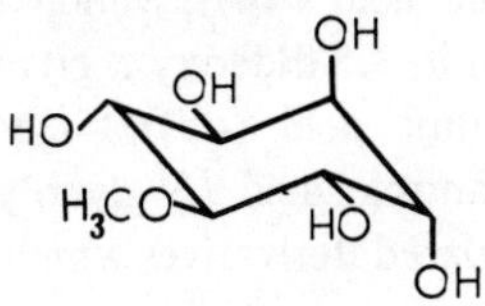

(41)

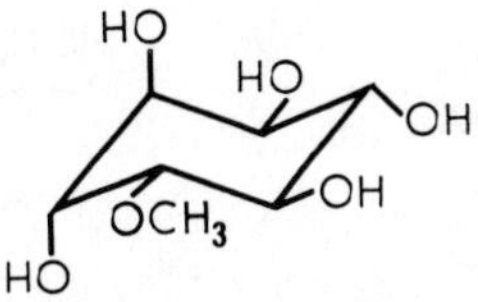

(42)

AMINOSUGARS

2-Amino-2-deoxy-D-glucose is the most abundant aminosugar occurring widely as its N-acetylated derivative in polysaccharides, glycoproteins and proteoglycans, and is found in chitin which is a $(1\rightarrow4)$-linked 2-acetamido-2-deoxy-β-D-gluco-pyranose homopolysaccharide (although N-acetylation is sometimes incomplete) analogous to cellulose and found in the exoskeletons of crustacea. 2-Acetamido-2-deoxy-D-galactose, -D-mannose and -D-talose also occur in glycoproteins but to a lesser extent. Most aminosugars rarely occur free or as simple derivatives but usually as components in oligo- and poly-saccharides. An exception to this is 5-amino-5-deoxy-D-glucopyranose (nojirimycin (43)) in which the amino group is involved in the ring giving a piperidinose ring structure.

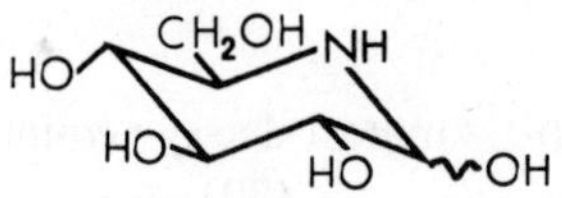

(43)

Many of the less common, naturally occurring aminosugars such as 3-amino-, 4-amino- and various diamino-sugars and aminouronic acids are found in antibiotics and microbial polysaccharides and are described in the relevant chapters (Chapters 12 and 13 respectively).

A number of higher monosaccharides exist as aminosugars and among these are 2-acetamido-3-O-(1-carboxyethyl)-2-deoxy-D-glucose (2-acetamido-2-deoxy-muramic acid (44)), which occurs in bacterial cell-walls (see Chapter 8), 5-acetamido-3,5-dideoxy-D-*glycero*-D-*galacto*-2-nonulopyranonic acid (*N*-acetyl-neuraminic acid (45)), 5-glycolylamido-3,5-dideoxy-D-*glycero*-D-*galacto*-2-non-ulopyranonic acid (*N*-glycolylneuraminic acid (46)) and other acetylated and glycolylated derivatives which occur in many glycoproteins (see Chapter 9).

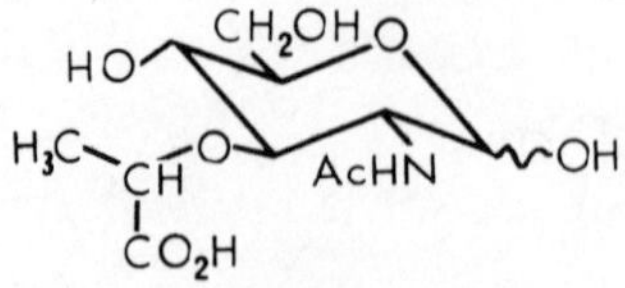

(44) 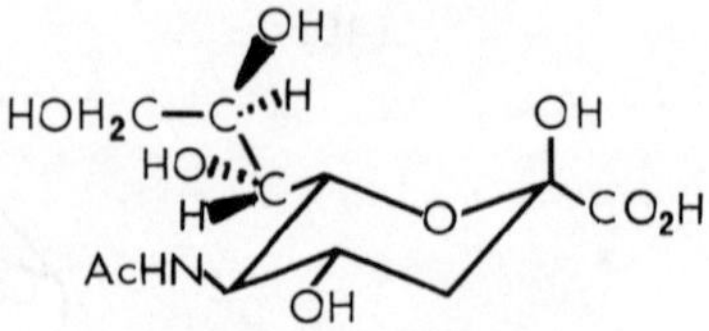   (45)

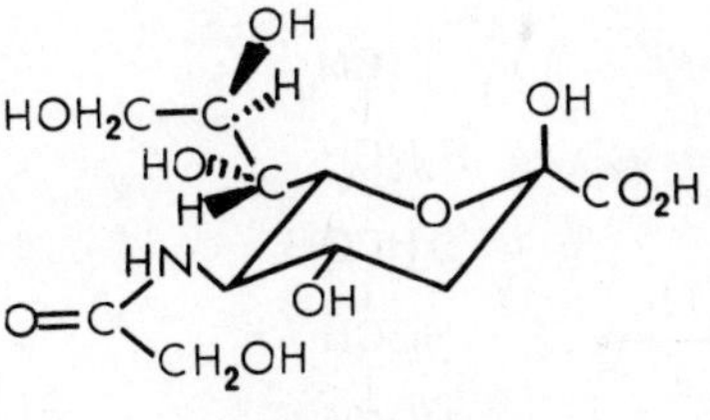

(46)

Aminosugars can be prepared from sulphonate esters (see Chapter 3) by nucleophilic displacement of the ester with ammonia, hydrazine or azide anions. The use of hydrazine is preferred to ammonia because the first-formed amine is more stable and less likely to be displaced. It can also be used to produce diaminosugars (Scheme 6.2). Alternative approaches to the preparation of aminosugars include: the addition of hydrogen cyanide to an aldose in the presence of ammonia and subsequent catalytic hydrogenation over a platinum catalyst to give an epimeric pair of 2-amino-2-deoxyaldoses containing an additional carbon atom (Scheme 6.3); the ring opening of an aldose epoxide with liquid ammonia or azide anions followed by reduction (Scheme 6.4); and the reaction of a dialdehyde with nitromethane followed by reduction (Scheme 6.5) to give a mixture of four isomers due to the formation of 3 new chiral centres with the nitro group of the intermediate product always occupying an equatorial position.

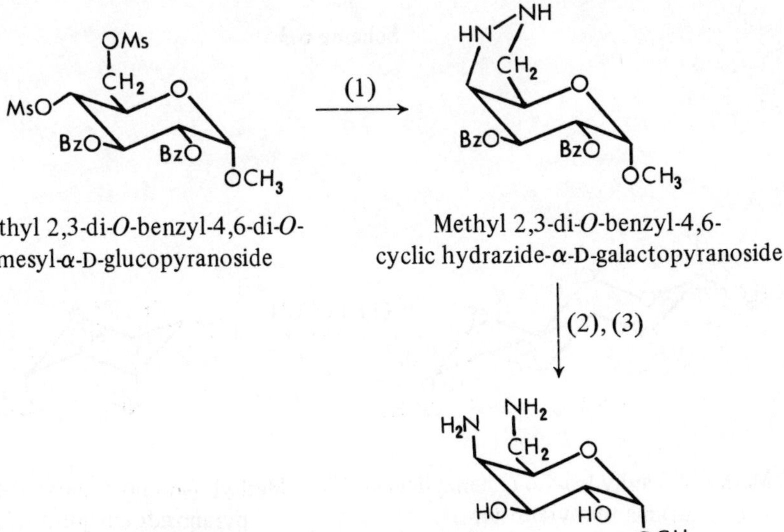

Methyl 2,3-di-*O*-benzyl-4,6-di-*O*-mesyl-α-D-glucopyranoside

(1) →

Methyl 2,3-di-*O*-benzyl-4,6-cyclic hydrazide-α-D-galactopyranoside

(2), (3)

Reagents: (1) Hydrazine; (2) NaBH$_4$; (3) debenzylation

Methyl 4,6-diamino-4,6-dideoxy-α-D-galactopyranoside

Scheme 6.2

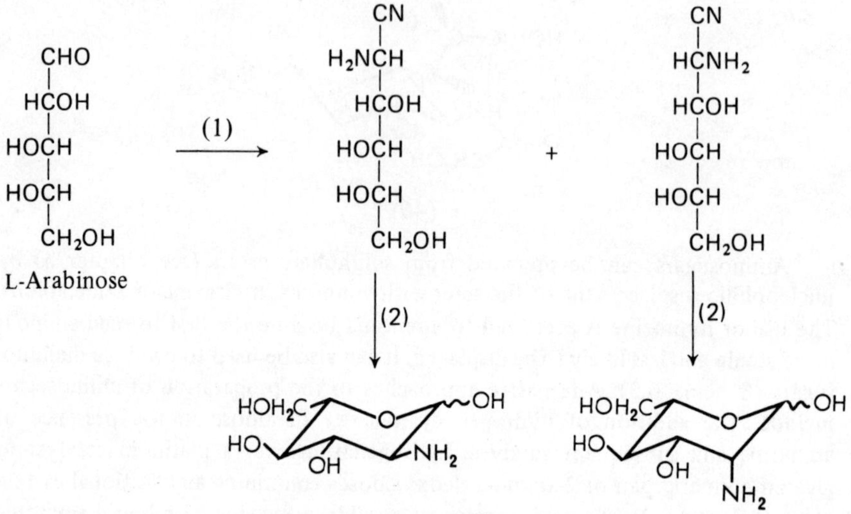

L-Arabinose $\xrightarrow{(1)}$

2-Amino-2-deoxy-L-glucose + 2-Amino-2-deoxy-L-mannose

Reagents: (1) HCN, NH$_3$, CH$_3$OH; (2) H$_2$/Pt

Scheme 6.3

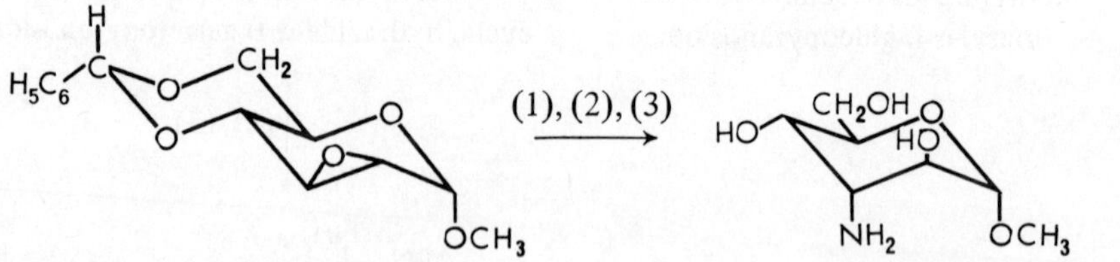

Methyl 2,3-anhydro-4,6-O-benzylidene-
α-D-mannopyranoside

$\xrightarrow{(1), (2), (3)}$

Methyl 3-amino-3-deoxy-α-D-altro-
pyranoside (major product)

Reagents: (1) NH$_3$; (2) NaBH$_4$; (3) deprotect

Scheme 6.4

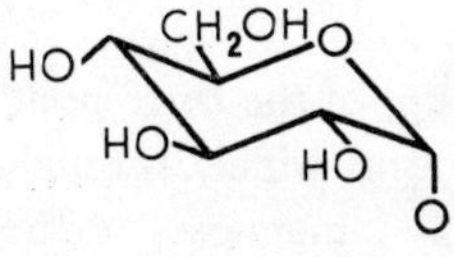

Methyl α-D-glucopyranoside

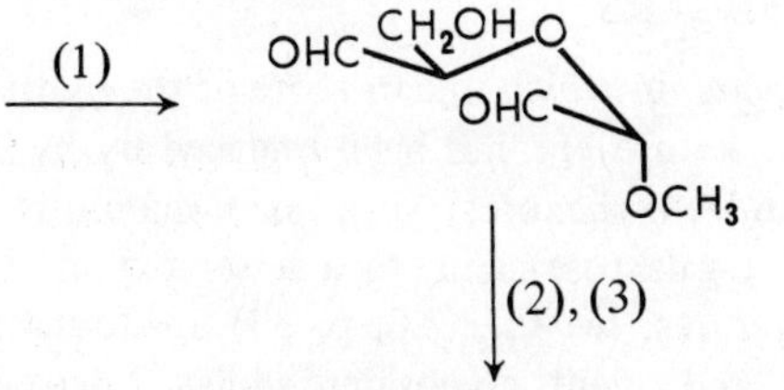

Reagents: (1) IO$_4$; (2) CH$_3$NO$_2$, CH$_3$ONa;
(3) NaBH$_4$

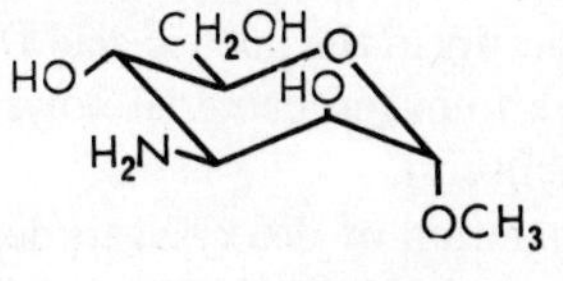

Methyl 3-amino-3-deoxy-α-D-mannopyranoside
(also gluco-, galacto- and talo-isomers)

Scheme 6.5

Interconversion of a readily available aminosugar into another aminosugar
can be achieved by reaction of the *O*-methanesulphonyl (mesyl) derivative with
sodium acetate in aqueous 2-methoxyethanol (Scheme 6.6). A recent review of
aminosugars is available (Horton and Wander, 1980).

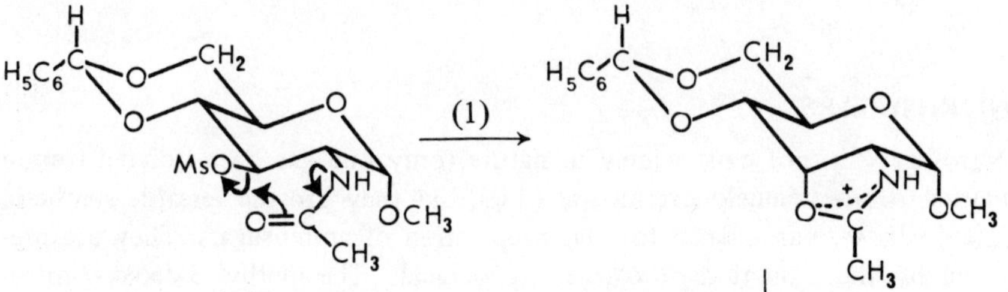

Methyl 2-acetamido-4,6-*O*-
benzylidene-2-deoxy-α-D-
glucopyranoside 3-methanesulphonate

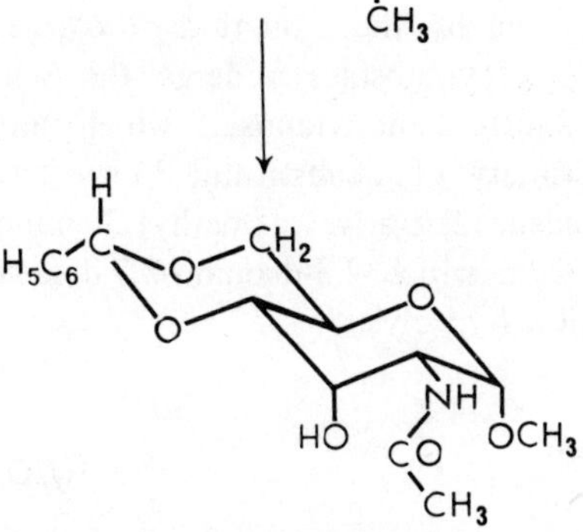

Methyl 2-acetamido-4,6-*O*-
benzylidene-2-deoxy-α-D-
allopyranoside

Reagents: (1) CH$_3$COONa

Scheme 6.6

DEOXYSUGARS

Deoxysugars, in which one or more of the hydroxyl groups of the corresponding aldose or ketose etc. has been replaced by hydrogen, occur widely throughout nature. 6-Deoxyhexoses, such as L-rhamnose (6-deoxy-L-mannose), L-fucose (6-deoxy-L-galactose) and, to a lesser extent, D-quinovose (6-deoxy-D-glucose) (for structures, see Fig. 2.8, p. 33) are found in many polysaccharides, glycoproteins and plant glycosides whilst 2-deoxy-D-*erythro*-pentose (2-deoxy-D-ribose) occurs in the nucleic acid DNA (see Chapter 11). More complex dideoxysugars are found in bacterial polysaccharides and antibiotics (see Chapters 8 and 12 respectively).

Preparation of deoxysugars depends on the availability of the corresponding halogeno derivatives which are dehalogenated under reducing conditions. Iodo- and bromo-derivatives are converted to deoxysugars by removal of the halogen atom through the action of hydrazine and Raney nickel in the presence of sodium acetate. Simple 6-deoxysugars are prepared by reduction of hexose 6-(4-toluene sulphonates) with lithium aluminium hydride. Reactions of 6-deoxysugars are similar to those for neutral monosaccharides except for those which involve the primary hydroxyl group at C-6 in neutral monosaccharides whilst other deoxysugars react as neutral monosaccharides unless the missing hydroxyl group prevents such.

NITROSUGARS

Nitrosugars do not exist widely in nature (only one has been isolated from a natural source, namely evernitrose (47)), but they provide versatile synthetic intermediates, particularly for the preparation of aminosugars. They are prepared by the oxidation of oximes by peracids. The methyl 3-deoxy-3-nitro-hexopyranosides undergo the Schmidt-Rutz reaction to give an unsaturated 3-nitro-2-enopyranoside which undergoes Michael addition reactions to give a variety of 2-substituted-3-nitrosugars (Scheme 6.7) such as the 4,6-*O*-benzylidene derivative of methyl 2-amino-2,3-dideoxy-3-nitro-D-glucopyranoside (48) from which 2,3-diamino-2,3-dideoxy-D-glucose may be obtained by reduction and hydrolysis.

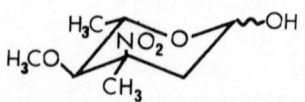

2,3,6-Trideoxy-3-*C*-methyl-4-*O*-methyl-
3-nitro-L-*ribo*-hexose (evernitrose)

(47)

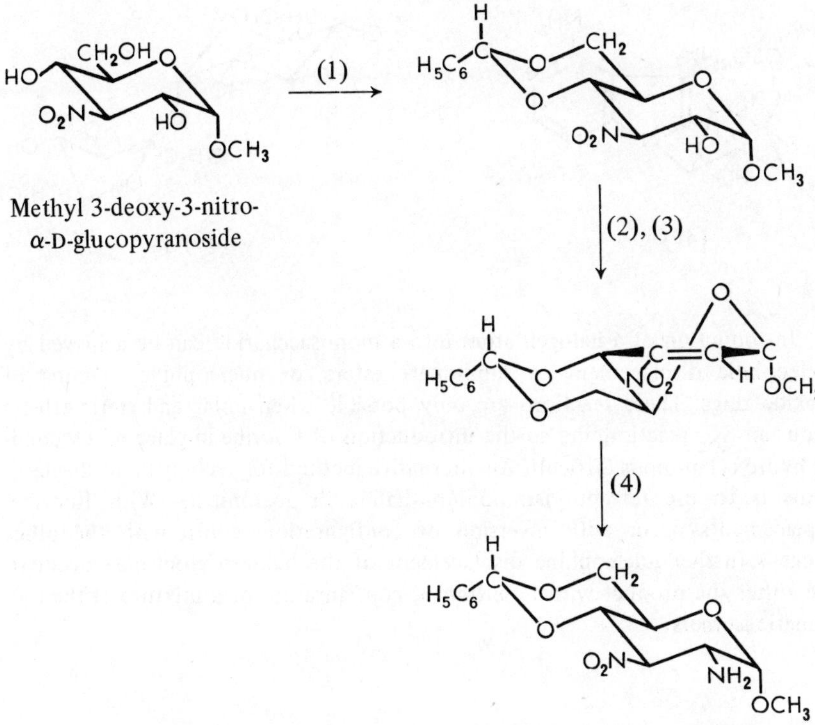

Methyl 3-deoxy-3-nitro-
α-D-glucopyranoside

Methyl 2-amino-4,6-O-
benzylidene-2,3-dideoxy-3-
nitro-α-D-glucopyranoside
(48)

Reagents: (1) C_6H_5CHO, $ZnCl_2$;
(2) Acetic anhydride, BF_3,
Et_2O; (3) $NaHCO_3$; (4) NH_3

Scheme 6.7

HALOGENOSUGARS

Only one naturally occurring halogenosugar has been isolated from natural sources, namely the antibiotic nucleocidin (49). However, much interest exists in halogenosugars because in other areas of natural products chemistry the introduction of a halogen atom has often led to the generation of compounds with interesting or different or unique biological activities. Interest in carbohydrate chemistry has, to date, centred on modified antibiotics with improved activity and on synthetic high intensity sweetening agents. A trichloro derivative of sucrose has been prepared (50) which is 2×10^3 times sweeter than sucrose itself, whilst other chlorosucroses have contraceptive properties.

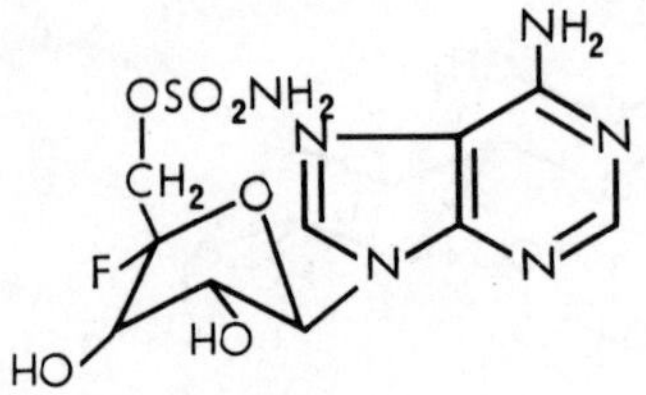

(49) 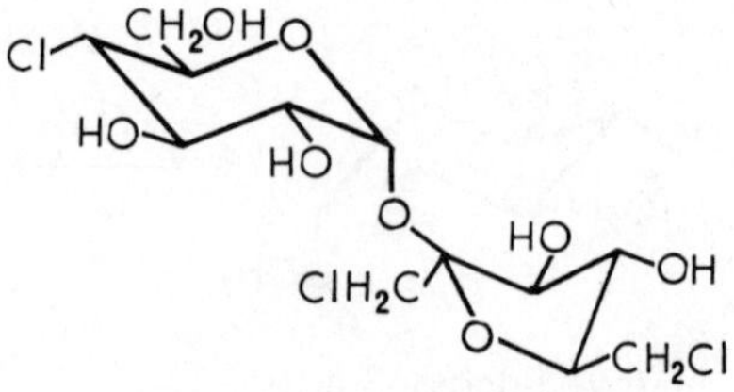   (50)

Introduction of a halogen atom into a monosaccharide can be achieved by nucleophilic displacement of sulphonate esters, or nucleophilic opening of epoxide rings. These reactions are only possible when polar and steric effects favour an S_{N_2} reaction and so the introduction of fluorine in place of a second-ary hydroxyl group is difficult. An alternative method for such difficult displacements is to use tetrabutylammonium halide in acetonitrile. With fluorine, displacements occur with inversion of configuration, whilst with the other halogens further nucleophilic displacement of the halogen atom may occur to give either the product with retention of configuration or a mixture of the two epimeric isomers.

THIOSUGARS

The replacement of an oxygen atom in a monosaccharide by sulphur gives rise to thiosugars (Horton and Wander, 1980b), of which the 1-thioglycosides are naturally occurring in the seeds of many plants, as typified by sinigrin (51), isolated from the seeds of black mustard. Over 50 such compounds are known to occur naturally and, because of their flavouring properties, are referred to as the mustard-oil glycosides.

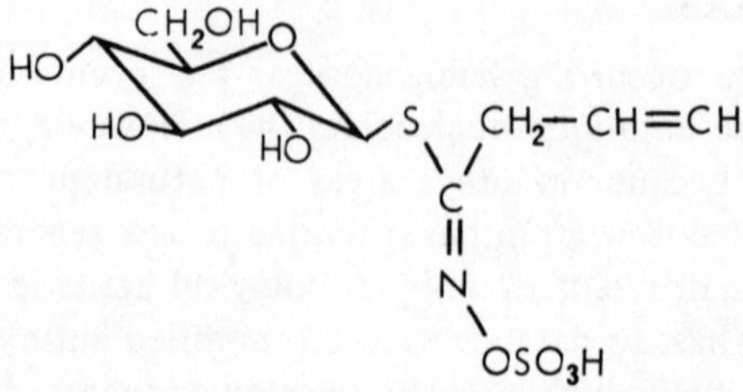

(51)

The greatly enhanced nucleophilicity of sulphur compared to oxygen allows the introduction of sulphur into monosaccharides by nucleophilic displacements of halides and sulphate esters and by ring opening of epoxides. The greater nucleophilicity of sulphur also results in the sulphur atom tending to favour its inclusion in the ring such that 4-thiohexoses, for example 4-thio-D-glucose, exist only in the furanose ring form (52) with the sulphur atom present in the ring, although 6-deoxy-4-thio-D-gulose has only been reported in the pyranose ring form (53) with the sulphur atom not in the ring. 5-Thiohexoses such as 5-thio-D-glucose (54) exist in the pyranose ring form with the sulphur atom present in the ring. Thiosugars frequently act as inhibitors to enzymes for which the corresponding non-sulphur monosaccharide is a substrate. Thus, for example, 5-thio-D-glucose 1-phosphate inhibits the isomerisation of D-glucose 1-phosphate into the 6-phosphate.

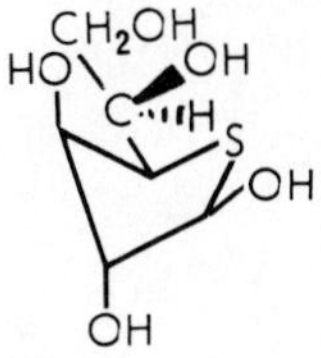

(52) 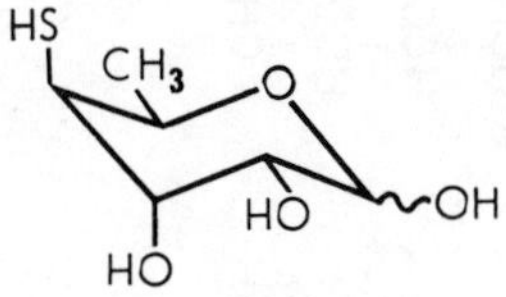 (53) 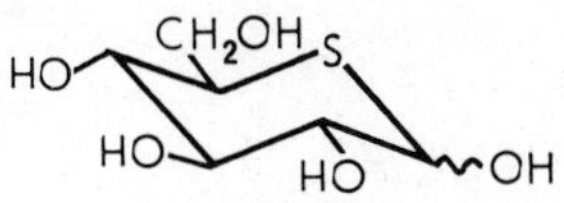 (54)

BRANCHED-CHAIN MONOSACCHARIDES

The term 'branched-chain sugar', used frequently to describe these compounds, is misleading as it can imply a branched-carbohydrate chain polysaccharide as well as a branched-carbon chain monosaccharide and the term 'branched-chain monosaccharide' is to be preferred. Naturally occurring branched-chain monosaccharides are found in antibiotics (see Chapter 12 for structures) and also in several plants including parsley (which contains apiose (55)), and witch-hazel (which contains hamamelose (56) as its digalloyl ester). Other substituents which are known to be attached to a carbon atom to give branched-chain monosaccharides include methyl, ethyl, 2-methyl-1-propenyl [$(CH_3)_2C=CH-$] and aldehydo groups (see review by Williams and Wander, 1981).

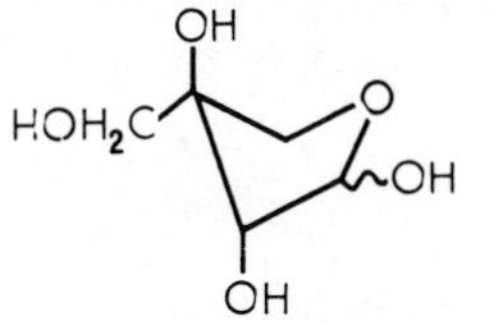

3-C-Hydroxymethyl-D-glycero-tetrose
(D-Apiose)
(55)

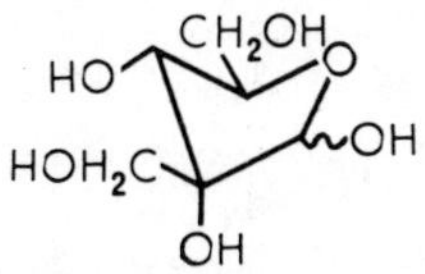

2-C-Hydroxymethyl-D-ribose
(Hamamelose)
(56)

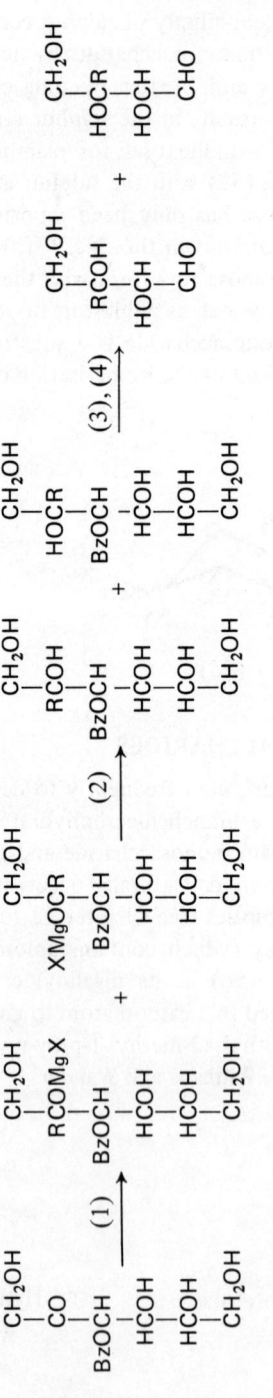

Reagents: (1) RMgX, Et₂O; (2) H⁺; (3) Pb(OAc)₄; (4) deprotect

Scheme 6.8

Synthesis of branched-chain monosaccharides is *via* the appropriate keto derivative, either by direct action of a Grignard reagent, diazomethane, nitromethane, Wittig reagents or cyanide (Scheme 6.8) or by treatment with diazomethane in a stereospecific reaction with the nucleophile approaching from an exo-position to give a spiroepoxide (57), hydrolysis of which gives a branched-chain monosaccharide containing a hydroxymethyl group (Scheme 6.9).

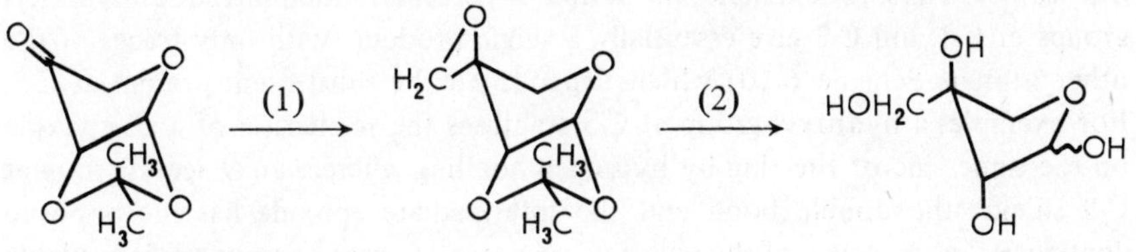

1,2-*O*-Isopropylidene-   (57)   D-Apiose
D-*glycero*-3-tetrulose

Reagents: (1) CH_3N_2; (2) H^+

Scheme 6.9

Systematic naming (Recommendations, 1980d) of branched-chain monosaccharides uses a scheme which regards the compound as being a derivative of a parent unbranched monosaccharide which contains the greatest possible number of carbon atoms, with preference for aldose rather than ketose. Thus (58) is a derivative of an octose not a 2-octulose.

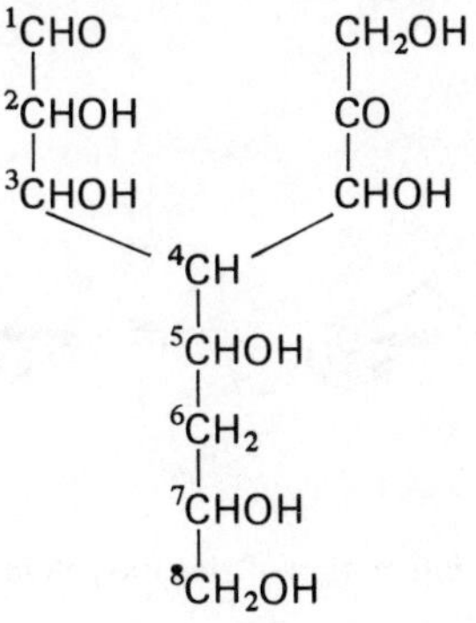

(58)

UNSATURATED SUGARS

Naturally occurring unsaturated sugars include vitamin C (36) and antibiotics which contain double bonds or vicinal dideoxy structures which are derived from unsaturated systems. Synthetic unsaturated sugars have recently become valuable intermediates for the preparation of rare sugars. For a review see Ferrier (1980).

1,5-Anhydro-2-deoxy-hex-1-enitols (see Fig. 6.2), trivially referred to as glycals (see Recommendations, 1980e for nomenclature of unsaturated monosaccharides), form useful reagents in which electrophilic attack at C-2 is favoured by the mesomeric interaction of the ring oxygen with the double bond. Whilst it is possible in theory to produce four possible isomers by such reactions, the stereoselectivity of many reagents reduces the number to two or sometimes only one isomer. Thus, for example, the action of peracids, which introduce hydroxyl groups at C-1 and C-2 give essentially a single product (with only traces of the other isomer, Scheme 6.10) which depends on the substituent present at C-3. For example, a hydroxyl group at C-3 stabilises the formation of a cis-epoxide on the same side of the ring by hydrogen bonding whereas an O-acetyl group at C-3 shields the double bond and the intermediate epoxide has the opposite configuration. A review of the addition reactions of these compounds is available (Ferrier, 1976). Pyran- and furan-2-enoses and other less-common enoses have been prepared, using the Tipson-Cohen procedure of heating the di-(4-toluene-sulphonate) ester (59) with zinc dust and sodium iodide in N,N-dimethylformamide (Scheme 6.11), but there have been few reports to date on addition reactions of these compounds.

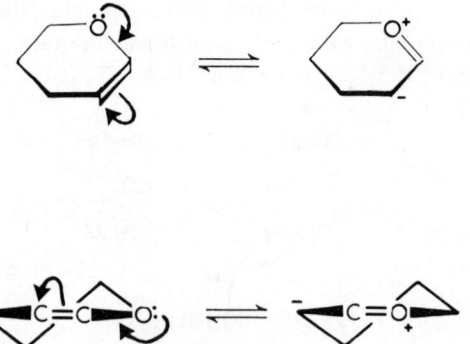

Fig. 6.2 – Mesomeric interaction of ring oxygen in 1,5-anhydro-2-deoxy-hex-1-enitols (glycals).

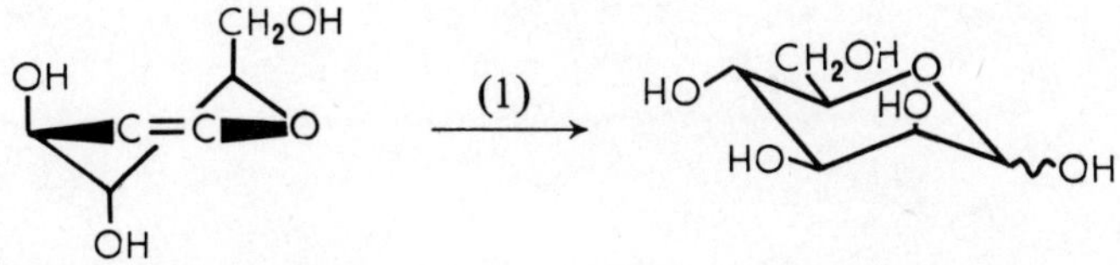

1,5-Anhydro-2-deoxy-D-*arabino*-
hex-1-enitol

D-Mannopyranose

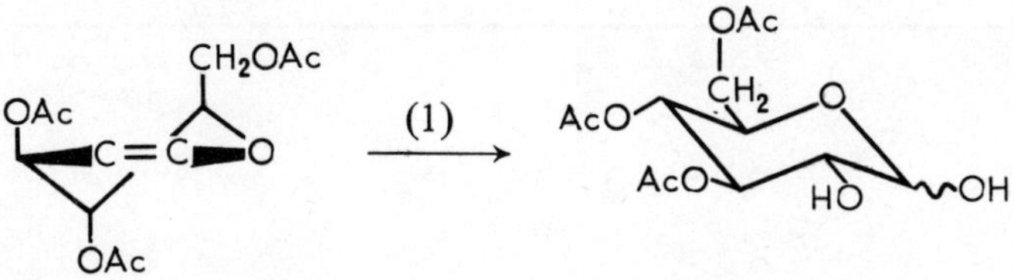

3,4,6-Tri-*O*-acetyl-1,5-anhydro-2-
deoxy-D-*arabino*-hex-1-enitol

3,4,6-Tri-*O*-acetyl-D-glucopyranose

Reagents: (1) Peracid

Scheme 6.10

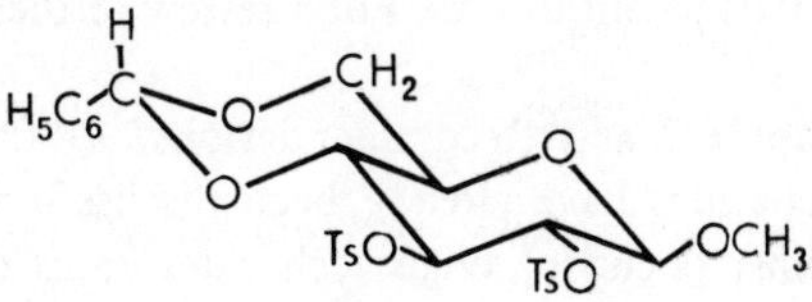

(59)

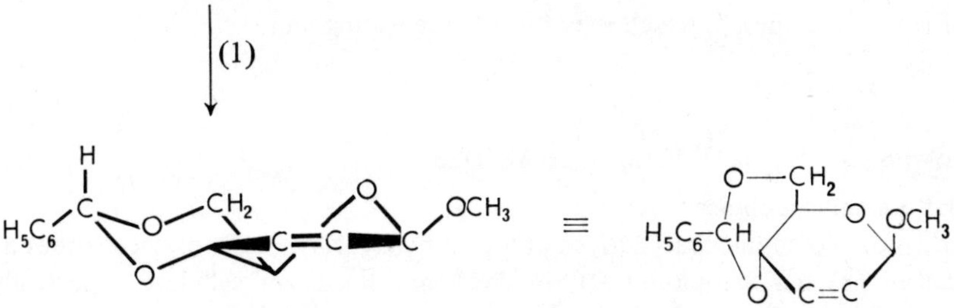

↓ (1)

Methyl 4,6-*O*-benzylidine-2,3-dideoxy-
β-D-*erythro*-hex-2-enopyranoside

Reagents: (1) NaI, Zn, DMF

Scheme 6.11

CHAPTER 7

Oligosaccharides

Naturally occurring disaccharides and trisaccharides have attracted considerable attention among scientists in the last few years. Biochemists, food scientists, nutritionists, medical scientists, physicians and consumers are greatly interested in the role of these oligosaccharides in nutrition and health. For the chemists and technologists, interest arose partly from the desire to extend their understanding of the fundamental chemistry of these compounds with the view of utilising them as chemical raw materials and industrial 'feedstocks', and partly from their presence in such active materials as antibiotics. For a review of these developments see Lee (1980).

The definition, nomenclature (Chapter 2 and Recommendations, 1980b) and synthesis (Chapter 5) of oligosaccharides have already been discussed in general terms. A number of the commonly occurring oligosaccharides, most of which are naturally occurring, are now described in more detail. Many of the compounds listed in Tables 2.3 and 2.4 are only obtainable by partial hydrolysis of polysaccharides, in which they form the repeating unit.

SEMI-SYNTHETIC OLIGOSACCHARIDES

Maltose and cellobiose

The most common disaccharides prepared by hydrolysis of polysaccharides are maltose (8) and cellobiose (60), obtained from starch and cellulose respectively. They are crystalline solids in which the free anomeric hydroxyl groups are found predominantly in the equatorial position. Thus the structure of β-maltose is 4-O-α-D-glucopyranosyl-β-D-glucopyranose whilst β-cellobiose is 4-O-β-D-glucopyranosyl-β-D-glucopyranose. They react in a manner similar to reducing monosaccharides and form most of the derivatives which monosaccharides can, having eight free hydroxyl groups.

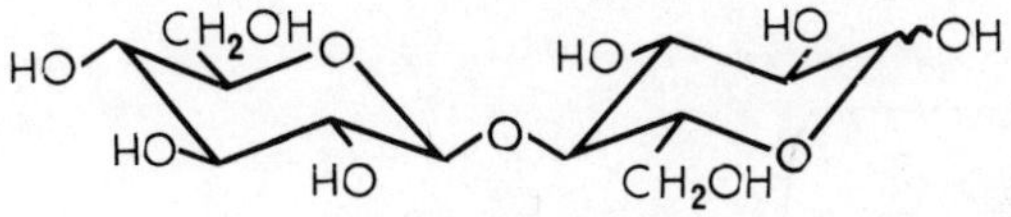

(60)

Cyclomalto-oligosaccharides

A number of cyclomalto-oligosaccharides have been prepared by the action of an enzyme from *Bacillus macerans* on starch, and include cyclomaltohexaose (61), cyclomaltoheptaose and cyclomalto-octaose (which are described in older literature as cycloamyloses, cyclodextrins or as α-, β- and γ-Schardinger dextrins respectively, after F. Schardinger, who characterised these materials as cyclic compounds). They are all crystalline solids and represent the highest molecular weight oligosaccharides which have been obtained in crystalline form. An interesting feature of the cyclic structure (61) is that all the primary hydroxyl groups (attached to C-6 of the carbohydrate residues) lie on one side of the ring whilst all the secondary hydroxyl groups (attached to C-2 and C-3) lie on the other side. These cyclic compounds serve as models for starch because each turn of the polymeric helix structure could be represented by a single closed loop containing 6, 7 or 8 monomer residues.

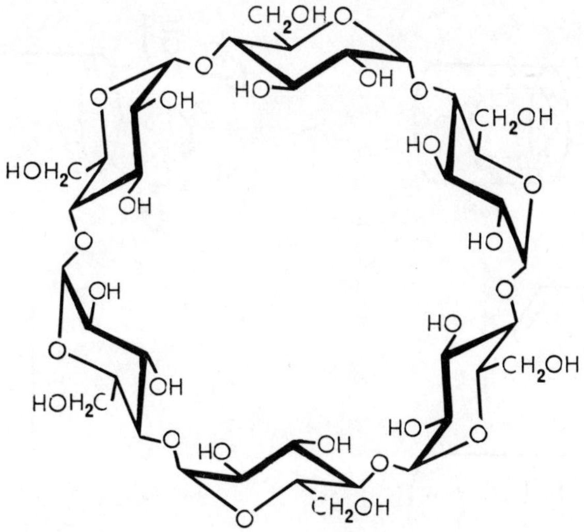

(61)

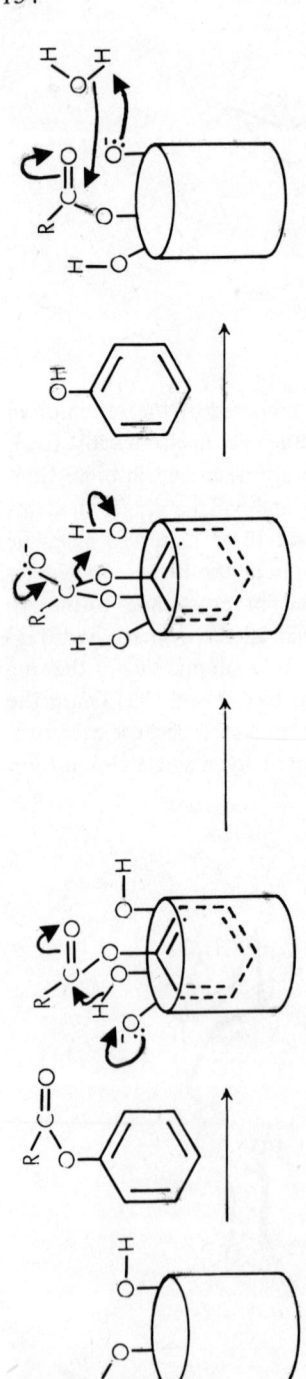

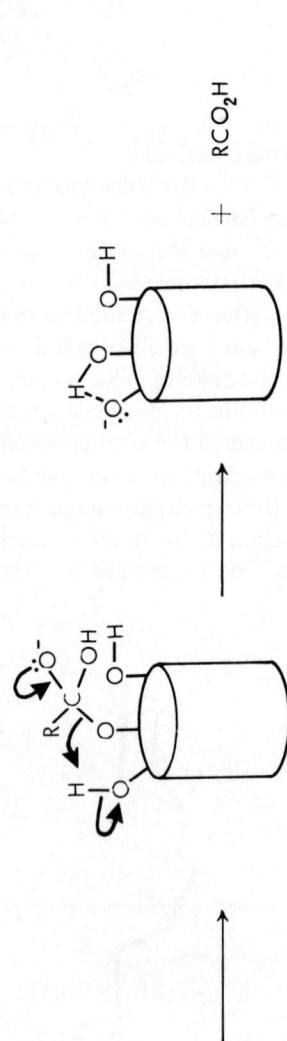

Fig. 7.1 – Schematic representation of the hydrolysis of phenyl esters catalysed by cyclomalto-oligosaccharides.

One of the more unusual properties of these compounds is their ability to bind small molecules within their cyclic structure to form so-called inclusion compounds. These crystalline solids are of interest for scientific research because they are soluble in aqueous solution and can be used to study the hydrophobic interactions which are so important in biological systems. Inclusion of a material within the cyclic structure has been shown to protect this material from the effects of light and atmosphere and to increase the water solubility of the material. Hence cyclomalto-oligosaccharides are used in the production of pharmaceuticals, pesticides, foodstuffs and toiletries as protecting agents, emulsion stabilisers and, since the dry inclusion complexes can be easily handled and stored, as bulking agents (for a review see Saenger, 1980).

The types of materials which form inclusion complexes are many, ranging from methanol and iodine to aliphatic and aromatic acids, esters and many other aromatic compounds, in which the aromatic ring lies within the cyclic structure and substituents interact with the carbohydrate hydroxyl groups at the edge of the ring *via* hydrogen bonding. An extension to this interaction is the ability of these cyclomalto-oligosaccharides to have apparent enzyme action, since they can hydrolyse a number of compounds with which they form inclusion complexes. The most studied example is the hydrolysis of phenyl esters (Fig. 7.1). This apparent enzyme action has led to these cyclomalto-oligosaccharides being used as enzyme models by substituting the free hydroxyl groups with various groups to simulate the active centre of a number of enzymes. A full account of the chemistry of cyclomalto-oligosaccharides and their use as enzyme models can be found in Bender and Komiyama (1978).

NATURALLY OCCURRING OLIGOSACCHARIDES

Sucrose

Sucrose (62) is one of the most common carbohydrates, being widely distributed throughout the plant world. It is the main soluble carbohydrate reserve and energy source and an important dietary material for humans. The principle sources for the commercial production of sucrose are sugar cane, sugar beet and the sap of maple trees.

(62)

The structure of sucrose, namely α-D-glucopyranosyl-(1↔2)-β-D-fructo-furanoside (or β-D-fructofuranosyl-(2↔1)-α-D-glucopyranoside) does not contain an aldehyde function since the glycosidic bond joins the two anomeric carbon atoms and therefore sucrose is not a reducing sugar. Hydrolysis of sucrose, by mildly acidic conditions (heating in pH 5 buffer will suffice) or enzymes, produces a mixture of equal amounts of D-glucose and D-fructose, the process being referred to as 'inversion' and the mixture as 'invert sugar' on account of the change in optical rotation from dextro to laevo due to the high laevorotation of the D-fructose. An enzyme capable of hydrolysing sucrose, β-D-fructofuranosidase and given the trivial name invertase (β-D-fructofuranoside fructohydrolase, EC 3.2.1.26) hydrolyses β-D- and not α-D-fructofuranosides whilst α-D-glucosidase (α-D-glucoside glucohydrolase EC 3.2.1.20) and not β-D-glucosidase (β-D-gluco-side glucohydrolase EC 3.2.1.21) also hydrolyses sucrose. These together prove that the configuration of the glycosidic linkages is α for the D-glucose and β for the D-fructose residues.

Lactose

Mammalian milk contains between 2.0 and 8.5% of lactose depending on the mammal either as the free disaccharide (63) or combined with other residues, such as 2-acetamido-2-deoxy-D-glucose, L-fucose, D-galactose and 5-acetamido-3,5-dideoxy-D-*glycero*-D-*galacto*-2-nonulopyranonic acid (hence an old trivial name of lactamic acid) as higher oligosaccharides (see Table 7.1). The concentration of these higher oligosaccharides is reported to be between 0.3 and 0.6%. Lactose has been reported to occur in plants but it is mainly found in milk, hence an old, trivial name 'milk-sugar'. It is not fully explained yet, but in the mammary gland part of the D-glucose present is converted to D-galactose which then combines with more D-glucose to form lactose. The infant to whom the milk is fed must immediately reconvert the D-galactose back to D-glucose during digestion. If not, there can be a number of ill-effects. Why, then, is D-glucose initially converted to D-galactose? The key may lie in an understanding of the higher oligosaccharides and their immunological reactions. It is known, for instance, that lacto-*N*-neotetraose inhibits the cross-reaction between the pneumococcal polysaccharide Type 14 antigen and its antibodies. The presence, therefore, of D-galactose may be to provide the correct structural components for the mother to transmit immunological protection to her infant.

(63)

Table 7.1 Structures of some human milk oligosaccharides

Trivial name	Structure

Disialyllacto-*N*-tetraose
α-Neup5Ac-(2→3)-β-D-Galp-(1→3)-β-D-GlcpNAc-(1→3)-β-D-Galp-(1→4)-D-Glc
6
↑
1
α-Neup5Ac

2'-Fucosyllactose
α-L-Fucp-(1→2)-β-D-Galp-(1→4)-D-Glc

3-Fucosyllactose
β-D-Galp-(1→4)-D-Glc
3
↑
1
α-L-Fucp

Galactosyllactose
[β-D-Galp-(1→3)]n-β-D-Galp-(1→4)-D-Glc   (where n = 2 − 5)

Lacto-difucosyltetraose
α-L-Fucp-(1→2)-β-D-Galp-(1→4)-D-Glc
3
↑
1
α-L-Fucp

Lacto-*N*-tetraose
β-D-Galp-(1→4)-β-D-GlcpNAc-(1→3)-β-D-Galp-(1→4)-D-Glc

Lacto-*N*-neotetraose
β-D-Galp-(1→3)-β-D-GlcpNAc-(1→3)-β-D-Galp-(1→4)-D-Glc

Lacto-*N*-fucopentaose I
α-L-Fucp-(1→2)-β-D-Galp-(1→3)-β-D-GlcpNAc-(1→3)-β-D-Galp-(1→4)-D-Glc

Lacto-*N*-fucopentaose II
β-D-Galp-(1→3)-β-D-GlcpNAc-(1→3)-β-D-Galp-(1→4)-D-Glc
4
↑
1
α-L-Fucp

Lacto-*N*-fucopentaose III
β-D-Galp-(1→4)-β-D-GlcpNAc-(1→3)-β-D-Galp-(1→4)-D-Glc
3
↑
1
α-L-Fucp

Lacto-*N*-difucohexaose I
α-L-Fucp-(1→2)-β-D-Galp-(1→3)-β-D-GlcpNAc-(1→3)-β-D-Galp-(1→4)-D-Glc
4
↑
1
α-L-Fucp

Lacto-*N*-difucohexaose II
β-D-Galp-(1→3)-β-D-GlcpNAc-(1→3)-β-D-Galp-(1→4)-D-Glc
4   3
↑   ↑
1   1
α-L-Fucp   α-L-Fucp

Lacto-*N*-hexaose
β-D-Galp-(1→4)-β-D-GlcpNAc-(1→6)-β-D-Galp-(1→4)-D-Glc
3
↑
1
β-D-Galp-(1→3)-β-D-GlcpNAc

Lacto-*N*-neohexaose
β-D-Galp-(1→4)-β-D-GlcpNAc-(1→6)-β-D-Galp-(1→4)-D-Glc
3
↑
1
β-D-Galp-(1→4)-β-D-GlcpNAc

Lactosyl-(1→2)-α-D-glucose
β-D-Galp-(1→4)-α-D-Glcp-(1→2)-D-Glc

LS tetrasaccharide a
α-Neup5Ac-(2→3)-β-D-Galp-(1→3)-β-D-GlcpNAc-(1→3)-β-D-Galp-(1→4)-D-Glc

LS tetrasaccharide b
β-D-Galp-(1→3)-β-D-GlcpNAc-(1→3)-β-D-Galp-(1→4)-D-Glc
6
↑
1
α-Neup5Ac

Table 7.1 (*continued*)

Trivial name	Structure
LS tetrasaccharide c	α-Neup5Ac-(2→6)-β-D-Galp-(1→4)-β-D-GlcpNAc-(1→3)-β-D-Galp-(1→4)-D-Glc
3'-Sialyllactose (neuraminolactose)	α-Neup5Ac-(2→3)-β-D-Galp-(1→4)-D-Glc
6'-Sialyllactose	α-Neup5Ac-(2→6)-β-D-Galp-(1→4)-D-Glc
S-5	Mixture of *N*-acetylneuraminosyl derivatives of lacto-*N*-hexaose (6 isomers) and of lacto-*N*-neohexaose (6 isomers)
S-6	Mixture of L-fucosyl derivatives of S-5 (36 isomers)
N-2	Mixture of L-fucosyl derivatives of lacto-*N*-hexaose (6 isomers) and of lacto-*N*-neohexaose (6 isomers)
N-3	Mixture of di-L-fucosyl derivatives of lacto-*N*-hexaose (15 isomers) and of lacto-*N*-neohexaose (15 isomers)

Lactose is prepared industrially from whey, a by-product of cheese manufacture. Traditionally, the process involved evaporation of the whey until the lactose crystallised from a cold solution as the monohydrate of α-lactose, or from a hot (95°) solution as the anhydrous β-lactose. However, the modern method of ultrafiltration is being applied, on an increasing scale, to purify the lactose, prior to its removal from solution, by removal of the whey proteins and fats. Lactose, as a reducing disaccharide, undergoes the reactions of normal reducing sugars and can be fermented but only by yeasts which have been adapted to lactose. With normal yeasts no fermentation occurs.

Trehaloses

Trehalose is the general name given to a family of three D-glucosyl D-glucosides, nonreducing disaccharides which form the reserve carbohydrate of insects and a number of invertebrates, and are the storage material of fungi, yeasts, algae and members of the Pteridophyta family. In mushrooms, for example, it can account for as much as 15% of the dry weight. Three linkage types are possible, namely α,α; α,β and β,β and all three anomeric configurations of the disaccharide with two pyranose rings are known but in general only α,α-trehalose (64) is the common isomer, although α,β-trehalose (65) has been isolated from honey.

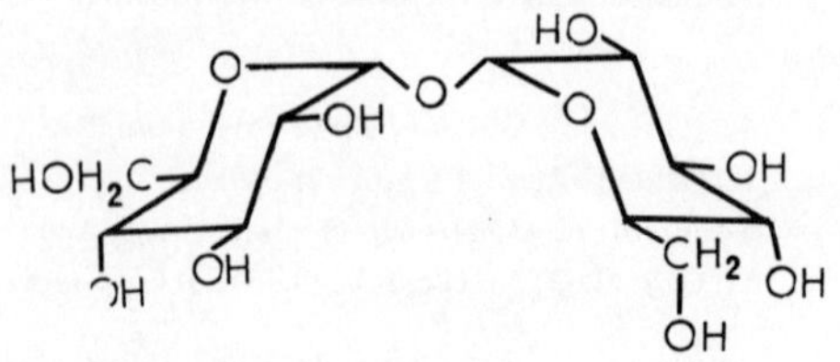

(64)

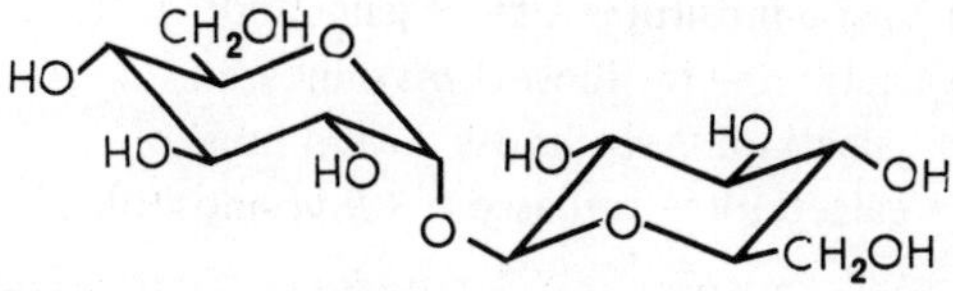

(65)

α,α-Trehalose has the structure α-D-Glc$p$-(1↔1)-α-D-Glc$p$ and derives its name from the trehala manna (from which α,α-trehalose was obtained) which forms the cocoons of a beetle of the *Larinus* family. Its trivial name of mycose or mushroom sugar reflects the other major source of the disaccharide. Its biosynthesis involves two enzymes, α,α-trehalose phosphate synthase (UDP-forming) (UDP-D-glucose:D-glucose-6-phosphate-1-α-glucosyltransferase, EC 2.4.1.15) and trehalose phosphatase (trehalose-6-phosphate phosphohydrolase, EC 3.1.3.12) which catalyse the following reactions respectively:

UDP-D-Glc + D-Glc 6-phosphate → α,α-trehalose 6-phosphate + UDP

α,α-trehalose 6-phosphate → α,α-trehalose + orthophosphate

Chemical synthesis of trehaloses tend to favour production of the α,β-isomer but heating of a mixture of 2,3,4,6-tetra-O-acetyl-D-glucose and 3,4,6-tri-O-acetyl-1,2-anhydro-D-glucose at 100°C produces a mixture of α,α- and α,β-isomers. α,α-Trehalose is relatively inert compared to many carbohydrates due to its nonreducing nature and stable glycosidic linkage (it is much more stable to mild acid than is sucrose), which is possibly why it has transport functions in some organisms. The only reactions which take place with trehaloses are those associated with the primary and secondary hydroxyl groups.

Raffinose

Raffinose is a naturally occurring plant trisaccharide which is as widely distributed as sucrose but only in low concentrations (for example, 0.05% in sugar beet and 1.9% in soybeans) and is related to sucrose as can be seen from its structure of α-D-Gal$p$-(1→6)-α-D-Glc$p$-(1↔2)-β-D-Fru$f$ (66) which can be regarded as an O-galactosylsucrose. As such, raffinose is the first member of a series of oligosaccharides in which one or more D-galactosyl residues are attached to sucrose. Other members include stachyose (a tetrasaccharide) and verbascose (a pentasaccharide) whose structures are given in Table 2.4.

These oligosaccharides are synthesised from sucrose by an unusual transfer reaction in which an α-D-galactopyranoside of *myo*-inositol, known by the trivial name galactinol (67), is the immediate D-galactosyl donor. The reaction sequences are catalysed by enzymes such as galactinol-raffinose galactosyltransferase (1-O-α-D-galactosyl-*myo*-inositol:raffinose galactosyltransferase, EC 2.4.1.67):

UDP-D-Gal + *myo*-inositol → UDP + galactinol,
Sucrose + galactinol ⇌ raffinose + *myo*-inositol,
Raffinose + galactinol ⇌ stachyose + *myo*-inositol,
Stachyose + galactinol ⇌ verbascose + *myo*-inositol.

Raffinose is prepared by isolation by direct crystallisation from the final molasses of the sucrose production from beet. It can also be prepared by extraction from cotton seed meal with subsequent precipitation of the slightly soluble raffinose with calcium or barium hydroxide.

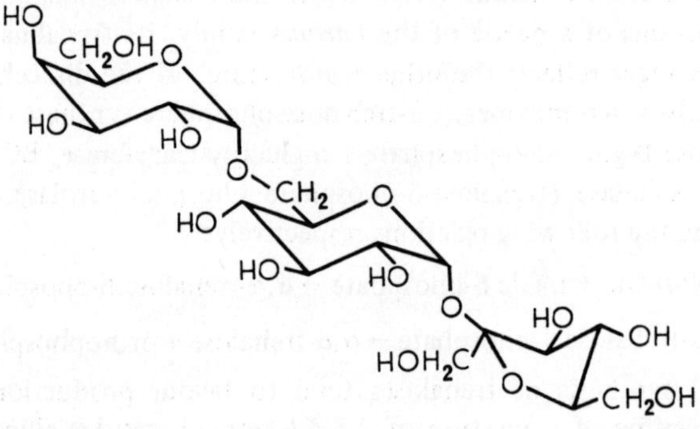

(66)

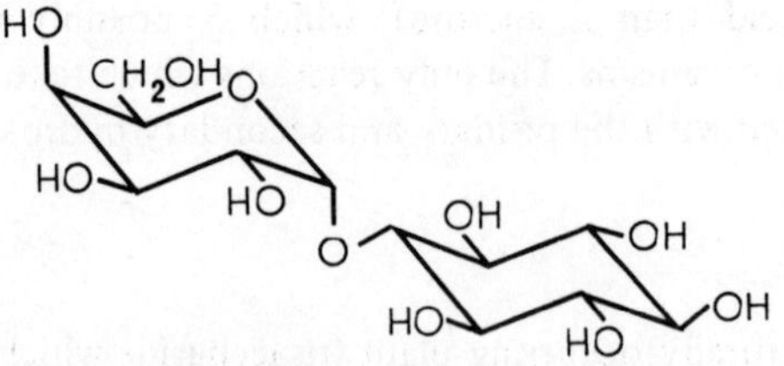

(67)

Melezitose
Melezitose, with the structure α-D-Glc*p*-(1→3)-β-D-Fru*f*-(2↔1)-α-D-Glc*p* (68), is another nonreducing trisaccharide related to sucrose, but in this case the additional monosaccharide unit is attached to the D-fructofuranosyl residue. It occurs in the exudate from insect-produced wounds of many plants including limes, poplars, Douglas fir, Virginia pine, larch (la mélèze – French meaning larch, hence the name), etc. Whether the melezitose is of plant or insect origin

is not entirely clear, particularly since the discovery of a glycosyl transferase enzyme in the bodies of the insects, which is capable of synthesising melezitose from sucrose. The presence of melezitose in honeys from the honeydew of many trees is due to interaction of enzymes from the insects with sucrose from the plant-sap and not to the bees producing the trisaccharide. These melezitose-rich honeys, in which crystallisation can occur in the honey comb, provide the best source of the compound, since the crystallised melezitose is easily separated by dilution of the honey with alcohol followed by centrifugation.

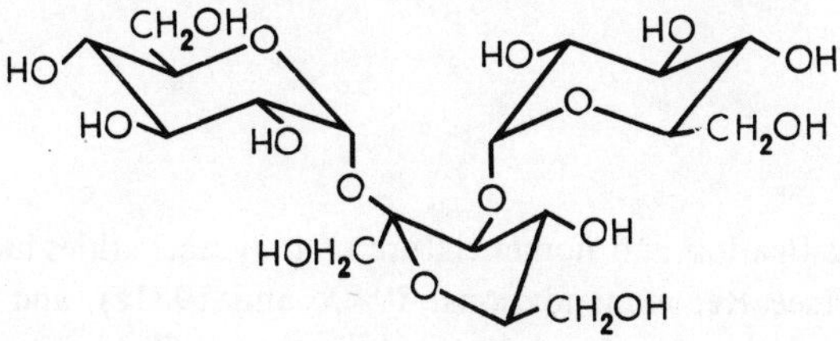

(68)

There are a number of other naturally occurring oligosaccharides containing amino-, deoxy- and other rarer monosaccharide residues which are known as oligosaccharide antibiotics. These are discussed in Chapter 12.

CHAPTER 8
Polysaccharides

The basic classification and nomenclature of polysaccharides has been discussed in Chapter 2 (see Recommendations, 1980c and 1981a), and the sources and structures of some common polysaccharides quoted (Tables 2.6 and 2.7). In the current chapter the structures of specific polysaccharides are described in detail, the polysaccharides being grouped, according to their origin, into plant, algal, microbial, fungal and animal polysaccharides. Where possible, the primary structure or simple repeating units are shown with reference to secondary and higher level structures where these are known.

PLANT POLYSACCHARIDES
Homopolysaccharides
Starch
The principle food-reserve polysaccharides in the plant kingdom are starches. They form the major source of carbohydrates in the human diet and are therefore of great economic importance, being isolated on an industrial scale from many sources (for a review of the biology of starch see Preiss and Walsh, 1981).

Starch has been found in some protozoa, bacteria and algae, but by far the major sources are plants, the carbohydrate occurring in the seeds, fruits, leaves, tubers, and bulbs in various amounts from a few percent to over 75% as in the case of cereal grains. Starch occurs in granular form, the shape of the granules being characteristic of the source of the starch. Isolation of these granules from the plant tissues can be achieved without degradation because they are insoluble in cold water, whereas many of the contaminants are soluble. The granules swell reversibly in cold water, a phenomenon used in the industrial extraction of starch to loosen the granules in the matrix, but as the temperature is raised the process becomes irreversible and eventually the granule bursts to form a starch paste. Not all starch granules in a sample burst at the same temperature, but the range of temperature of gelatinisation is characteristic of a particular starch.

The starch granule can be separated into two distinctly different components, a phenomenon first discovered in the early 1940s, although the heterogeneity of starch had been hinted at earlier. The two components, amylose and
amylopectin, vary in relative amount among the different sources from less than
2% of amylose in waxy maize to about 80% of amylose in amylomaize (both
corn starches), but the majority of starches contain between 15% and 35%
amylose. It has been proposed that the ratio of amylopectin to amylose is a
function of the ratio of starch synthetases present in the plant, one synthetase
being responsible for the production of amylose whilst the other, a complex,
branch-forming synthetase, is responsible for amylopectin production. The
determination of this characteristic amylose:amylopectin ratio for a given starch
sample is based on the binding capacity of the starch for iodine.

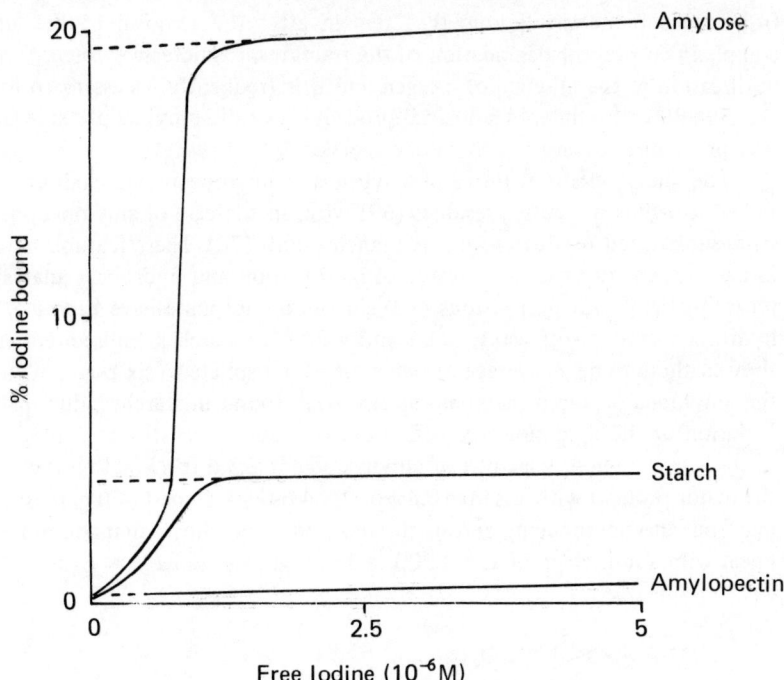

Fig. 8.1 — Absorption of iodine by a starch and its components. The amylopectin
content of this starch can be deduced from this graph.

It can be seen from Fig. 8.1 that amylose binds iodine giving a blue colouration, up to a limiting value which is determined partly by the experimental
conditions, but in the case illustrated is about 20% of iodine by weight. Amylopectin, on the other hand, binds little iodine and, in so doing, gives a red colouration whilst starch, as a mixture, is of intermediate binding ability. Extrapolation

of the linear portions of the binding curve to zero free-iodine concentration, as shown, will give the iodine binding capacity of the starch, etc. The amylose content is obtained by expressing the starch binding capacity as a percentage of the amylose binding capacity. Potentiometric measurements have traditionally been used for such determinations, but it is now being claimed that the use of spectrophotometric techniques at two wavelengths is a much more accurate method.

The most widely used method of fractionating starch into its components is to add polar organic substances to an aqueous dispersion of the starch granules which cause the amylose to form an insoluble complex. The amylose can be purified by reprecipitation usually with a different organic substance. The most suitable precipitants are found to be thymol for the initial precipitation and butan-1-ol for the subsequent purification. The amylopectin fraction is removed from the supernatant liquors that remain after the removal of the amylose complex. To prevent degradation of the fractions it is necessary to carry out the purification in the absence of oxygen and it is frequently necessary to pretreat the granule with ethanol (industrial procedure) or dimethyl sulphoxide (laboratory procedure) to ensure complete dispersion.

The characteristic features of amylose and amylopectin are chains of (1→4)-linked α-D-glucopyranosyl residues (69) with, in the case of amylopectin, 1,4,6-tri-O-substituted residues acting as branch points (70). These features have been known for many years as a result of methylation and hydrolysis analysis but, recently, significant proportions of D-glucose 6-phosphate have been isolated as hydrolysis products of waxy maize and waxy rice starches. Subsequent analysis showed there to be an average of one mole of phosphate to six D-glucose units in the amylopectin. Lipid material has also been found in starches, due mainly to inclusion of the lipid molecule within the amylose helical structure. Methylation analysis (Chapter 4, page 68) of amylose yields 2,3,6-tri-O-methyl-D-glucose as the major product with less than 0.4% of 2,3,4,6-tetra-O-methyl-D-glucose, resulting from the nonreducing end of the molecule, and shows that the molecule is linear with a unit chain of about 200 to 350 D-glucose units.

(69)

(70)

Osmotically determined molecular weights are in agreement with this chain length, but analysis of an unbranched structure is difficult. Not only is it difficult to measure the small amount of end-groups in relation to the chain-forming units, but degradation has a considerable effect; the rupture of one bond can halve the measured unit chain length. Physical methods of chain length determination, provided that independent methods for proof of homogeneity are used, have shown values for the size of the amylose molecules to be greater than values obtained by chemical methods. Light scattering and ultracentrifugation analyses show that chain lengths of up to 6000 units occur frequently. Enzyme analysis of amylose with β-amylase originally showed the molecule to be linear, producing maltose as its sole degradation product, but contamination of the enzyme with another α-amylolytic enzyme would remove any other α-D-glucosyl groups. A study of the action of pullulanase and other amylolytic enzymes on various amyloses has demonstrated that there are some 1,4,6-tri-O-substituted residues which act as branch points in the molecule. This, plus the hydrodynamic behaviour of amylose fractions, has led to the acceptance of there being a limited degree of branching in amylose.

Many of the properties of amylose can be explained in terms of its ability to adopt different molecular conformations in solution. In neutral aqueous solutions the normal conformation is that of a random coil. If there are complexing agents in the solution, amylose will form a helical structure consisting of about six D-glucosyl residues per helical turn. This is the conformation that both gives rise to the characteristic blue colouration of amylose–iodine complexes, and is responsible for the formation of complexes with fats and polar organic solvents, the complexing agent occupying a position at the centre of the helix.

The various forms of retrograded amyloses are due to variations in conformation of the amylose in solution. Retrogradation of amylose is the autodeposition of the polysaccharide in an insoluble form from solution, a phenomenon which rarely occurs with amylopectin. X-ray patterns of the retrograded amyloses has shown that the size and type of amylose and the concentration, temperature and pH of solution all contribute to the structure but two distinct X-ray patterns can be observed. The two crystalline forms of amylose are type A, which is characteristic of cereal starches and of amyloses resulting from retrogradation above 50° and type B which is characteristic of tuber starches and of retrograded amyloses at room temperature. The slow formation of these forms of amylose will allow the formation and alignment of linear chains and through the formation of hydrogen bonds eventually results in the insoluble particles. No clear picture of the conformations which exist in these forms can be given at present, but it is thought that the B-form may comprise intertwined double helices.

A third crystalline form of amylose, for which more information is available, is the so-called V-form which is obtained as a result of retrogradation in the presence of complexing agents. X-ray patterns of this form indicate a flexible helical arrangement with six or seven D-glucose units per turn, depending on the size of the complexing agent. The nature of the B-form has been related to the V-form through a mechanism involving the extension of the helices and changes in hydrogen bonding. Comparisons of X-ray diffraction patterns of the V-form have been made with those from the series of cyclomalto-oligosaccharides which are prepared by the action of an amylase from *Bacillus macerans* cyclomalto-dextrin glucanotransferase (EC 2.4.1.19) on starch (see Chapter 7). Cyclomalto-hexaose gives an X-ray pattern similar to that of the V-form and is considered to be analogous to one turn of the helix.

Amylopectin, on methylation analysis, yields 2,3,6-tri-*O*-methyl-D-glucose as its main product but the amounts of the 2,3,4,6-tetra-*O*-methyl ether of about 4% shows that the unit chain length is smaller than in amylose. Isolation of 2,3-di-*O*-methyl-D-glucose as an additional product indicates the presence of 1,4,6-linked branch points. Measurement of the unit chain length was tradition-ally carried out by estimating the formic acid liberated by periodate oxidation of the nonreducing end units, but is now more accurately determined by enzymic methods including the use of β-amylase (EC 3.2.1.2) and D-glucose oxidase (EC 1.1.3.4).

Values for the unit chain length are usually within the range 17–26 units. The arrangement of these unit chains to give a branched amylopectin could be in a variety of ways. Fig. 8.2 shows three possible arrangements, the laminated structure (a) proposed by Haworth, the herringbone or comb structure (b) proposed by Staudiner and Husemann, and the branched tree-like structure (c) proposed by Meyer and Bernfeld. There are three types of chain present in these structures; A-chains are side chains linked only through their reducing ends to the rest of the molecules, B-chains are those to which A-chains are attached, and the C-chain which carries the reducing group (there can only be one C-chain per molecule). Enzymic studies based on the degradation with β-amylase and debranching enzymes favour a multiple branched structure, the ratio of A:B chains not being consistent with the expected values for the laminated or herring-bone structures. Recent studies have led to a proposal of a modification to the Meyer tree-like structure, although much of the experimental data would satisfy the Meyer structure (Manners and Matheson, 1981). The cluster model proposed

(Fig. 8.3) satisfies the requirement that a proportion of the B chains must carry more than one A chain to account for differences in the A:B-chain ratio between the original material and partly debranched material. The various A and B chains may actually exist in double-helix conformations but are shown here as straight lines for clarity.

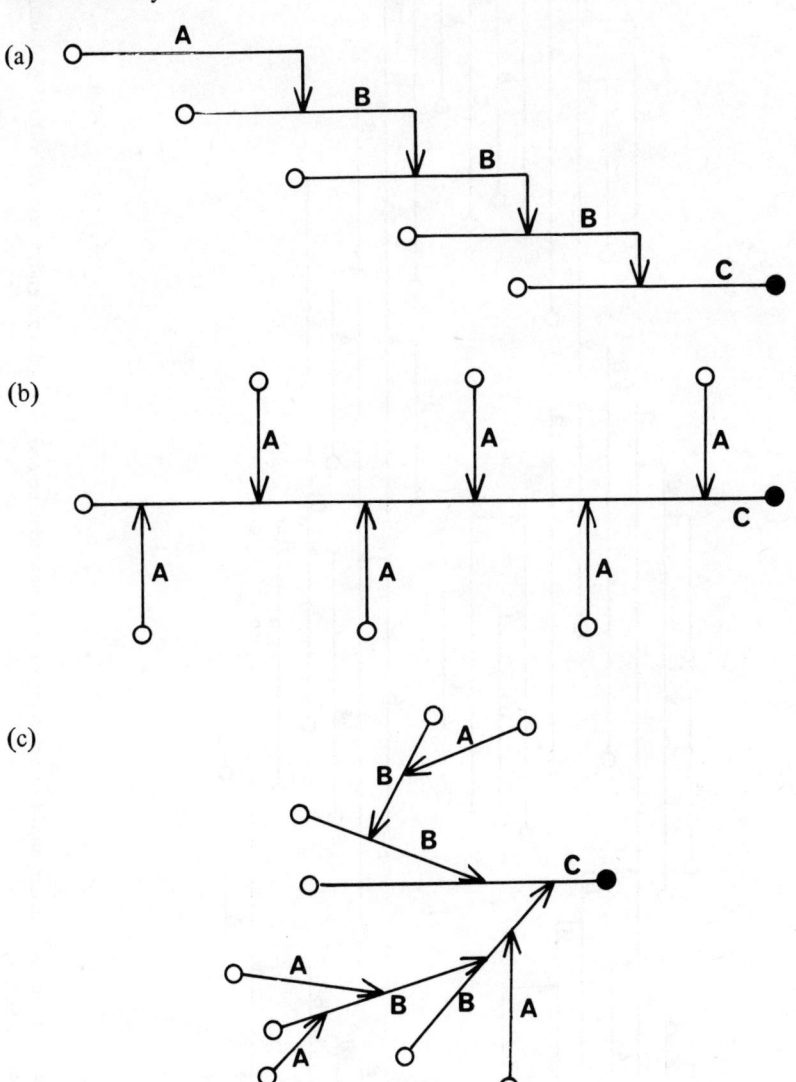

Fig. 8.2 – Standard models of amylopectin showing possible arrangements of the D-glucan chains of *ca*. 20 residues. ○ = nonreducing end, ● = reducing end, → = α-D-(1→6)-linkage, —— = [(1→4)-α-D-Glc*p*-]$_X$.

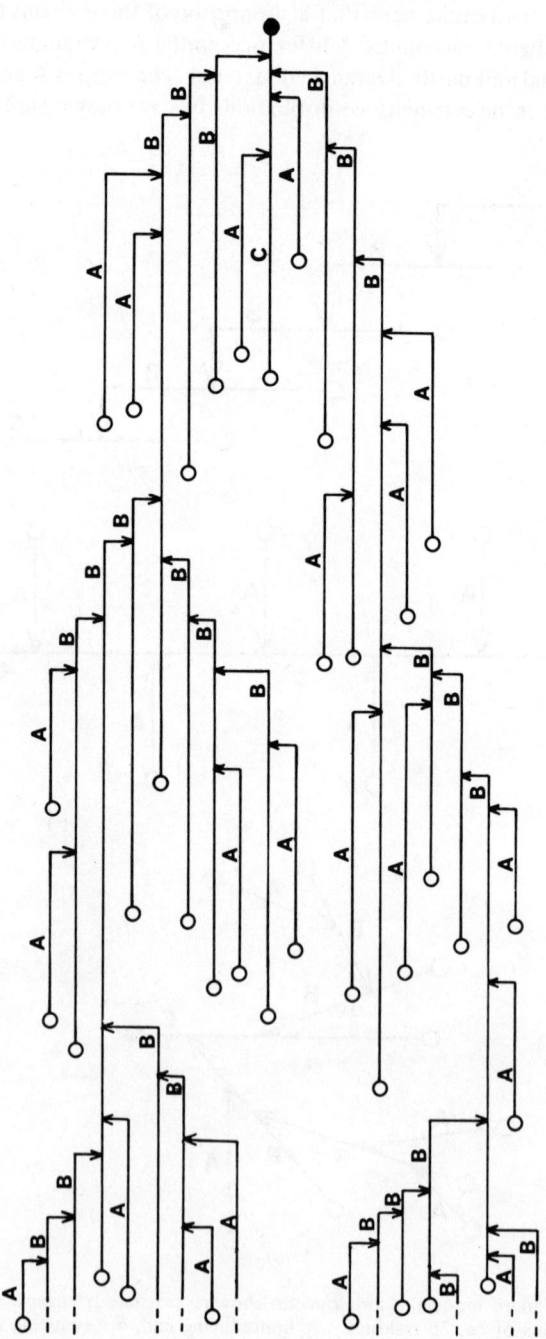

Fig. 8.3 – Proposed cluster model of amylopectin. ○ = nonreducing end, ● = reducing end, ↑ and ↓ = α-D-(1→6)-linkage, ⎯⎯ = [(1→4)-α-D-Glcp]ₓ.

The molecular size of amylopectin is almost too large to determine accurately; light scattering results indicate that there are of the order of 10^6 D-glucosyl residues per molecule making amylopectin one of the largest naturally occurring molecules. The size of the molecule has been shown to increase with increasing maturity of the parent starch in the plant.

The inability of amylopectin to bind much iodine, thereby producing the characteristic red colouration, is attributed to the large number of branch points in the molecule which disrupt any possible helix formation.

Cellulose

Cellulose is the most abundant organic substance found in nature. It forms the principal constituent of cell walls in higher plants, forming the main structural element (see review by Cabib and Shematek, 1981). It occurs in an almost pure form (98%) in cotton fibres and to a lesser extent in flax (80%), jute (60-70%) and wood (40-50%) and has also been found as a constituent of some algae and as a product of bacterial synthesis. Isolation of cellulose from most of its sources is difficult due to its insolubility in most solvents, and involves rather the solubilisation of the contaminating compounds such as hemicelluloses and lignin. The usual methods are based on alkaline pulping to remove the non-cellulosic polysaccharides, but it is difficult to remove all the contaminating monosaccharides and this has led to reports of the presence of monosaccharides other than in D-glucose in trace quantities.

The primary structure of cellulose was determined in the 1930s and little modification has subsequently had to be made to that original proposal. Methylation analysis yields over 90% of 2,3,6-tri-O-methyl-D-glucose showing that the molecule is essentially linear and, since partial hydrolysis yields cellobiose (71), it is a (1→4)-D-glucan. The β configuration of the inter D-glucosidic linkages was verified by enzymic studies. Determination of chain length by end-group analysis is inaccurate for the essentially linear molecule and has led to very low values of the order of 200 units being erroneously reported due to the occurrence of degradation during the analysis. Physical methods of chain length determination have shown that chains of up to 10,000 D-glucose units exist. Kinetic studies of the hydrolysis of cellulose have shown that over 99% of the linkages are of the same type and those which appear different do so as a result of physical effects. There has been no evidence for the presence of any other type of linkage.

(71)

The characteristic properties of cellulose are due to the tendency of the individual chains to form microfibrils through inter- and intra-molecular hydrogen bonding to give a highly ordered structure. The microfibrils associate in a similar manner to give fibres but in this case the axis of the fibres is at an angle to the axis of the microfibril whereas the individual molecules lie parallel to the microfibril axis. This regular arrangement of molecules is sufficient to allow X-ray diffraction patterns to be obtained and such indicate that cellulose from almost every natural source has an essentially similar pattern but which is different from that regenerated from derivatives or from solution. Cellulose I is the crystalline arrangement found in nature and cellulose II is that of regenerated cellulose. Variants in this classification have been noted and four other forms of cellulose have been distinguished from each other by their X-ray patterns. Cellulose III_I and cellulose IV_I have similarities in the X-ray pattern with cellulose I whilst cellulose III_{II} and cellulose IV_{II} have similarities with cellulose II. Whilst all the polymers have different molecular conformations in the unit cell, the cellulose I family (I, III_I, and IV_I) have 'bent' chain conformations and the cellulose II family (II, III_{II} and IV_{II}) have 'bent-twisted' chain conformations. The term 'bent' chain refers to the cellobiose units which correspond to the repeat distance of the fibres. The original structures proposed were based on 'straight' chain conformations which had all the D-glucopyranosyl residues in the same plane. The adoption of 'bent' chain structures with alternate D-glucopyranosyl residues in the same plane is a more satisfactory conformation because it eliminates the disadvantages of overlap of the van der Waals radii of the O-2 and C-6 atoms and of the repulsions between the H-1 and H-4 atoms and retains the intermolecular hydrogen bonding which is consistent with polarised infrared studies. Cellulose II appears to be thermodynamically more stable than cellulose I and transformation of cellulose I into cellulose II can take place in sodium hydroxide, or preferably in a mixture of sodium hydroxide and sodium sulphide.

Heteropolysaccharides

Heteropolysaccharides derived from the bark, seeds, roots and leaves of plants fall into several structural types which can be divided into two distinct groups. These are the acidic polysaccharides described as gums, mucilages and pectins, and the neutral polysaccharides known as hemicelluloses.

Gums

The plant gums or exudate gums are essentially polysaccharides containing hexuronic acid residues, in salt forms, and a number of neutral monosaccharides units, which are often esterified in highly branched structures. These gums, which may be formed spontaneously or may be induced by deliberately cutting the bark or fruit, are exuded as viscous liquids which become hard nodules on dehydration to seal the site of the injury and so provide protection from microorganisms. Many of these gums find industrial applications as thickening agents or emulsion stabilisers (see Chapter 14 and Davidson, 1980). Determination of the structure of these gums utilises the differing rates of hydrolysis of the various glycosidic linkages to produce, by selected degradation, oligosaccharides whose structures can be determined with greater ease and certainty. The most common conditions for hydrolysis include autohydrolysis (heating the acidic gum in aqueous solution) and mild hydrolysis with 0.01 M acid to cleave L-arabinofuranosyl glycosidic linkages, acid hydrolysis with 0.1–0.5 M acid or extended autohydrolysis to rupture the more labile hexopyranosyl glycosidic linkages, and strong acid hydrolysis with 0.5 M sulphuric acid to hydrolyse all but hexopyranosyluronic acid glycosidic linkages resulting in the isolation of acidic oligosaccharides, particularly of disaccharides containing one acidic residue.

Gum arabic, from various species of *Acacia*, is probably the best known example of plant gums and is typical of a number of gums which contain interior chains of (1→3)-linked β-D-galactopyranosyl residues to which chains comprised of L-arabinofuranosyl, L-rhamnopyranosyl and D-glucopyranosyluronic acid residues are attached. Autohydrolysis of arabic acid, the salt-free polysaccharide, yields L-arabinose, L-rhamnose and a D-galactosyl-L-arabinose disaccharide showing that these entities are linked to the main chains as shown in the generalised structure (72) which summarises the structural features, but does not place, uniquely, the glycosyl side chains which can be monosaccharide groups or disaccharide units attached to the outer chain. A number of other gums from *Acacia* species have been shown to have the same general D-galactan core with variations in the degree of branching and in the nature and attachment of the peripheral L-arabinosyl and L-rhamnosyl residues. Some gums, such as the gum from *A. karroo* also contain D-glucopyranosyluronic acid residues (1→4)-linked to α-D-galactopyranosyl residues. More recently an *Acacia* gum exuded by species of a subseries *Juli florae* has been shown to contain more acidic groups, to have a higher molecular weight, viscosity and methoxyl content, but a lower proportion of L-rhamnopyranosyl and L-arabinofuranosyl residues than the majority of other *Acacia* gums.

Gum ghatti from *Anogeissus latifolia* has interior chains of alternate D-glucopyranosyluronic acid and D-mannopyranosyl residues with a high proportion of L-arabinofuranosyl groups in the terminal nonreducing positions. A small proportion of L-arabinopyranosyl residues are present in the more acid stable part of the polysaccharide. The structure (73) has been formulated to show the major structural features.

Gum tragacanth has interior chains of 4-*O*-substituted α-D-galactopyranosyluronic acid residues and provides an example of a gum which is structurally related to the pectic acids. The gums from *Sterculia* and *Khaya* species also contain a D-galacturonic acid interior chain but with various amounts 2-*O*-substituted L-rhamnopyranosyl residues interspersed and a variety of constituent monosaccharides including D-glucopyranosyluronic acid groups which occur only as nonreducing end groups, unlike the D-galactopyranosyluronic acid

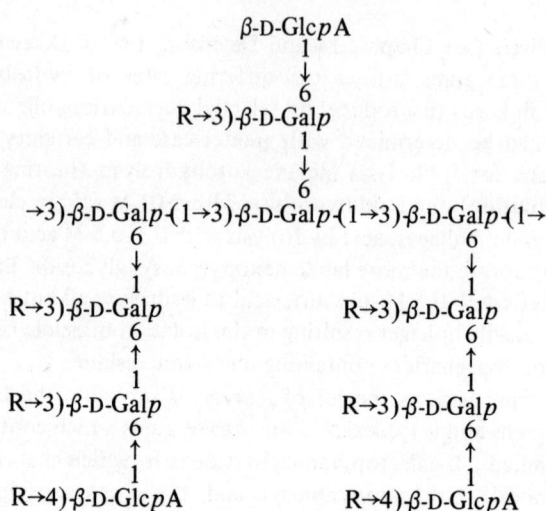

$$R = \text{L-Ara}f\text{-}(1\rightarrow, \quad \text{L-Rha}p\text{-}(1\rightarrow, \quad \alpha\text{-D-Gal}p\text{-}(1\rightarrow3)\text{-L-Ara}f\text{-}(1\rightarrow, \quad \text{or,}$$
$$\text{less frequently, } \beta\text{-L-Ara}p\text{-}(1\rightarrow3)\text{-L-Ara}f\text{-}(1\rightarrow$$

(72)

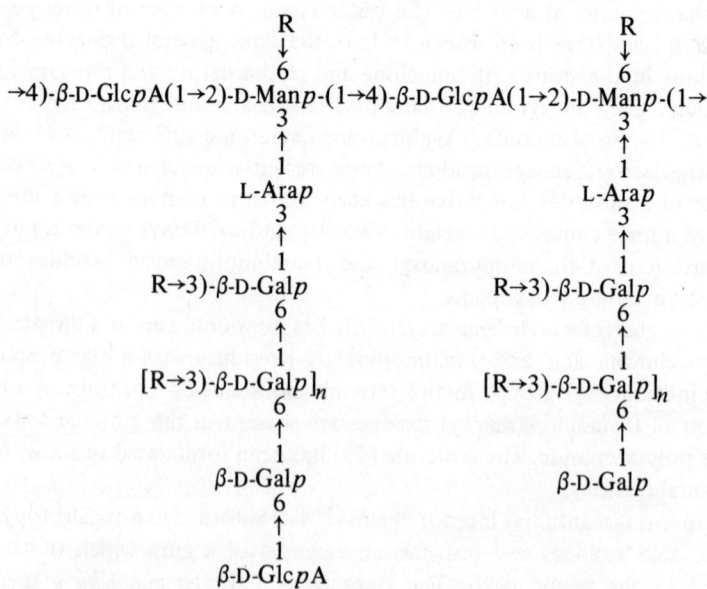

$$R = \text{L-Ara}f\text{-}(1\rightarrow, \quad \text{or less frequently L-Ara}f\text{-}(1\rightarrow2)\text{-L-Ara}f\text{-}(1\rightarrow,$$
$$\text{L-Ara}f\text{-}(1\rightarrow3)\text{-L-Ara}f\text{-}(1\rightarrow, \quad \text{or L-Ara}f\text{-}(1\rightarrow5)\text{-L-Ara}f\text{-}(1\rightarrow$$

(73)

residues which are present mainly in the inner chains. Gum tragacanth is only partially soluble in water but its major component, tragacanthic acid, has been purified and found to contain D-galacturonic acid, D-xylose, L-fucose and D-galactose with small amounts of D-glucuronic acid, L-rhamnose and L-arabinose; the important structural features are summarised in (74). A minor component of the gum has been found to be a highly branched L-arabino-D-galactan.

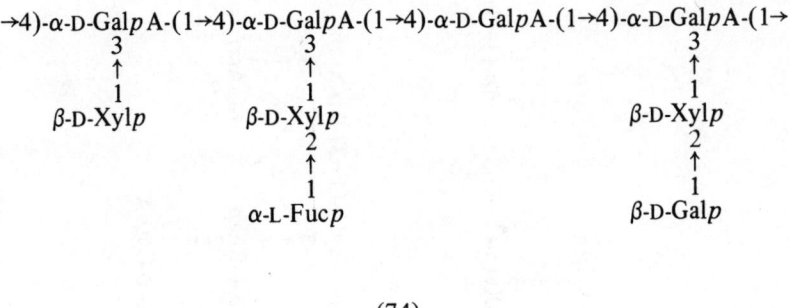

(74)

Mucilages
Mucilages have, in general, been less well characterised than many of the plant polysaccharides, but they are of a similar degree of structural complexity to the exudate gums. The presence of a particular acidic monosaccharide residue alone does not provide a basis for classification since many gums and mucilages contain both D-galactopyranosyluronic and D-glucopyranosyluronic acid residues but D-galacturonic acid is a characteristic component of many mucilages. Typical examples of mucilages include the acidic polysaccharides from slippery elm bark (75), cress seeds (76) and the husk from the seeds of *Plantago ovata* Forsk (Fig. 8.4). The role of mucilages is probably one of reservoirs for water retention to protect the seeds, etc., from desiccation. The mucilage from the seed husk of *Plantago ovata* Forsk is widely used as a prophylactic in treatment of large-bowel disorders, including diverticular disease. It is the ability of the mucilage to form a gel which retains many times its own weight of water over a wide range of concentrations that is responsible for the laxative action. Since D-xylan polymers are insoluble in water, it is proposed (Sandhu *et al.*, 1981) that the L-arabinofuranosyl and D-galactopyranosyluronic acid residues are responsible for binding water at the surface or within gels, whilst the parallel arrangement of the D-xylan chains is responsible for the gel formation.

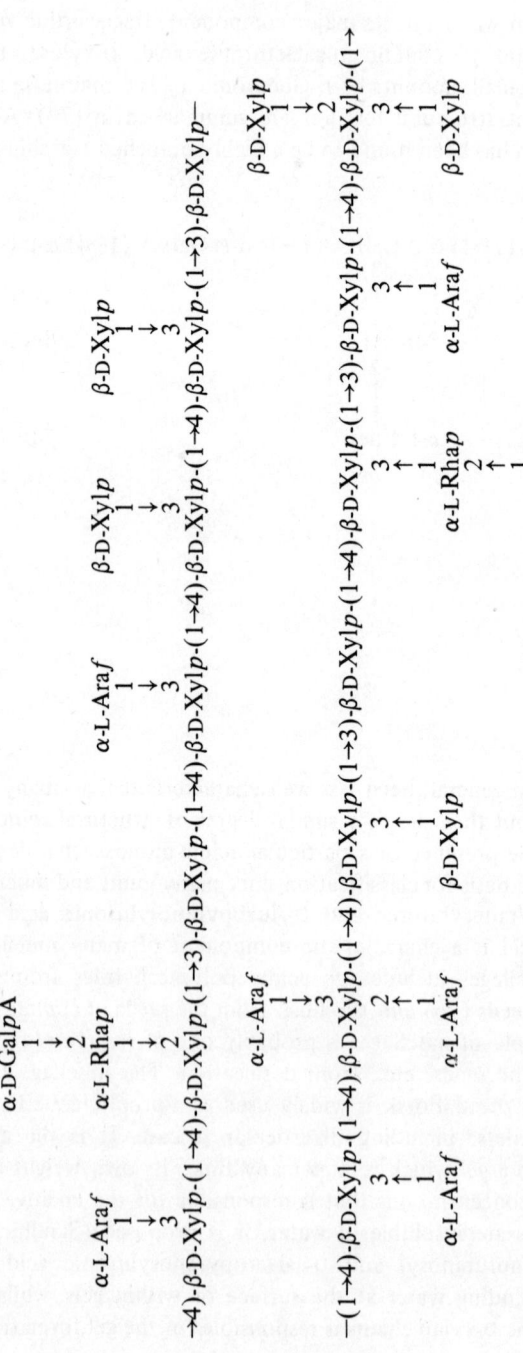

Fig. 8.4 — Representation of the main structural features of the mucilage from *Plantago ovata* Forsk.

→4)-α-D-Gal*p*A-(1→2)-L-Rha*p*-(1→4)-α-D-Gal*p*A-(1→2)-L-Rha*p*-(1→
                  3
                  ↑
                  1
               D-Gal*p*
                  4
                  ↑
                  1
             3-*O*-Me-D-Gal*p*

(75)

                    R
                    ↓
                    3
→4)-D-Gal*p*A-(1→2)-L-Rha*p*-(1→4)-D-Gal*p*A-(1→2)-L-Rha*p*-(1→
                    4   4
                    ↑   ↑
                    R   R

R = L-Rha*p*-(1→, D-Gal*p*-(1→, 4-*O*-Me-D-Glc*p*A-(1→4)-D-Gal*p*-(1→
or D-Xyl*p*-(1→4)-D-Gal*p*-(1→

(76)

Pectins

The pectins are a group of substances found in the primary cell walls and intercellular layers in land plants in which the principal constituent is D-galactopyranose. They make up 15% of the dry weight of apples and 30% of the dry weight of the rinds of citrus fruits, but occur only in small proportions in woody tissues. A group of related polysaccharides in which D-galactopyranosyluronic acid residues and not D-galactopyranosyl residues are present are termed pectic acids whilst if the uronic acid residues are present as methyl esters they are termed pectinic acids. Pectinic acids are very easily extracted with water and possess considerable gelling powers which are used commercially for gelation of fruit juices to give jellies. In contrast, the pectic acids which frequently contain the calcium salts of the hexosyluronic acid residues, are less soluble and require the use of reagents such as bis[di(carboxymethyl)amino]ethane (H$_4$ edta, ethylenediaminetetraacetic acid) or sodium hexametaphosphate for their extraction. Among the pectic substances are those types of homopolysaccharides, D-galactans, L-arabinans, and D-galacturonans but the most common pectic substances are heteropolysaccharides containing both acidic and neutral sugars.

Structural studies carried out on these homopolysaccharidic pectins established the salient features of the more complex pectins. The increased recognition of the susceptibility of pectins to acidic and basic hydrolysis indicates that these homopolysaccharides may have arisen from degradation of more-complex natural polysaccharides. D-Galactans, containing (1→4)-linked β-D-galactopyranosyl residues in linear chains, have been isolated from white lupin seeds and from red spruce compression wood; a more complex, acidic D-galactan, which has the same major structural features, has been isolated from Norwegian spruce. Highly branched L-arabinofurans, containing no other monosaccharide residues, have been isolated from mustard seeds (77), and a D-galacturonan has been isolated from sunflower heads, although this type of acidic homopolysaccharide is of infrequent occurrence, D-galactopyranosyluronic acid being more frequently found in heteropolysaccharidic pectins. The structure of this D-galacturonan has linear chains of (1→4)-linked α-D-galactopyranosyluronic acid residues.

$$\rightarrow 5)\text{-}\alpha\text{-L-Ara}f\text{-}(1\rightarrow 5)\text{-}\alpha\text{-L-Ara}f\text{-}(1\rightarrow 5)\text{-}\alpha\text{-L-Ara}f\text{-}(1\rightarrow 5)\text{-}\alpha\text{-L-Ara}f\text{-}(1\rightarrow 5)\text{-}\alpha\text{-L-Ara}f\text{-}(1\rightarrow$$

$$\begin{array}{ccccc} & 3 & & 3 & & 3 \\ & \uparrow & & \uparrow & & \uparrow \\ & 1 & & 1 & & 1 \\ \alpha\text{-L-Ara}f & & \alpha\text{-L-Ara}f & & \alpha\text{-L-Ara}f \end{array}$$

(77)

A pectin from soybean (78) is characteristic of the L-arabino-D-galactans which are the only known neutral heteropolysaccharidic pectins which have structures containing chains of (1→4)-linked β-D-galactosyl residues to which various amounts of L-arabinosyl residues are linked (1→3).

$$\rightarrow 4)\text{-}\beta\text{-D-Gal}p\text{-}(1\rightarrow 4)\text{-}\beta\text{-D-Gal}p\text{-}(1\rightarrow 4)\text{-}\beta\text{-D-Gal}p\text{-}(1\rightarrow 4)\text{-}\beta\text{-D-Gal}p\text{-}(1\rightarrow$$

$$\begin{array}{c} 3 \\ \uparrow \\ 1 \\ \text{L-Ara}f \\ 5 \\ \uparrow \\ 1 \\ \text{L-Ara}f \end{array}$$

(78)

The majority of the pectic and pectinic acids contain various proportions of neutral monosaccharides (usually between 10 and 25%) of which only L-rhamnose is found interrupting the D-galacturonic acid chains, the others being attached as side chains as shown in the generalised structure for pectic acids

(Fig. 8.5). A pectic acid isolated from soybean was the first example shown to contain D-xylopyranosyl residues which are present as mono- or di-saccharide block units (79) similar to those in tragacanthic acid.

$$\rightarrow 4)\text{-}\alpha\text{-D-Gal}p\text{A-}(1\rightarrow 2)\text{-}\beta\text{-L-Rha}p\text{-}(1\rightarrow 4)\text{-}[\alpha\text{-D-Gal}p\text{A}]_m\text{-}(1\rightarrow 4)\text{-}\alpha\text{-D-Gal}p\text{A-}(1\rightarrow$$
$$\begin{array}{ccc} 3 & & 3 \\ \uparrow & & \uparrow \\ R^1 & & R^2 \end{array}$$

$$R^1 = [\alpha\text{-D-Gal}p]_n\text{-}(1\rightarrow \quad \text{or} \quad [\alpha\text{-L-Ara}f]_n\text{-}(1\rightarrow$$
$$R^2 = \beta\text{-D-Xyl}p\text{-}(1\rightarrow, \; \alpha\text{-L-Fuc}p\text{-}(1\rightarrow 2)\text{-}\beta\text{-D-Xyl}p\text{-}(1\rightarrow,$$
$$\text{or} \; \beta\text{-D-Gal}p\text{-}(1\rightarrow 2)\text{-}\beta\text{-D-Xyl}p\text{-}(1\rightarrow$$

Fig. 8.5 – Generalised structure for pectic acids.

$$\rightarrow 4)\text{-}[\text{D-Gal}p\text{A-}(1\rightarrow 2)\text{-L-Rha}p\text{-}(1\rightarrow 4)]_n\text{-}\alpha\text{-D-Gal}p\text{A-}(1\rightarrow 4)\text{-}\alpha\text{-D-Gal}p\text{A-}(1\rightarrow 4)\text{-}\alpha\text{-D-Gal}p\text{A-}(1\rightarrow$$
$$\begin{array}{ccc} 3 & & 3 \\ \uparrow & & \uparrow \\ 1 & & 1 \\ \beta\text{-D-Xyl}p & & \beta\text{-D-Gal}p \\ & & 4 \\ & & \uparrow \\ & & 1 \end{array}$$
$$\text{L-Ara}f\text{-}(1\rightarrow 2 \text{ or } 3)\text{-}\beta\text{-D-Gal}p\text{-}(1\rightarrow 4)\text{-}\beta\text{-D-Gal}p\text{-}(1\rightarrow 4)\text{-}\beta\text{-D-Gal}p$$

(79)

Hemicelluloses
The hemicelluloses are found in close association with cellulose in plant cell walls and were originally thought to be precursors of cellulose. They have now been shown to have no part in cellulose biosynthesis but represent a chemically distinct, separate group of polysaccharides which contain residues and linkages different from those found in cellulose. It is usual to limit the term hemicellulose to cell wall polysaccharides from land plants with the exclusion of cellulose and pectins, and to classify them according to the type of monosaccharide residues present. The majority of the hemicelluloses are relatively small molecules consisting of between 50 and 200 monosaccharide residues, whilst those from hardwoods are larger molecules (150–200 residues). Some of these compounds have crystalline structures and it has been found that the backbone of the molecule of the D-xylans consists of D-xylopyranosyl residues with a rotation of $120°$ between successive residues.

D-Xylans. D-Xylans are the most common of the hemicelluloses, occurring in all parts of all land plants in proportions of between 7 and 30%. The backbone of the molecule is an essentially linear chain of (1→4)-linked β-D-xylopyranosyl residues. Homoglycans are neither common nor abundant, but a typical example is the D-xylan from Esparto grass which has been found to contain (1→4)-linked β-D-xylopyranosyl residues. As indicated by the isolation of small amounts of 2,3,4-tri-*O*-methyl-D-xylose from methylation analysis, these chains contain a single branch point located at O-3 of a D-xylopyranosyl residue. The most common hemicellulose in soft woods is an (*O*-acetyl-L-arabino)-(4-*O*-methyl-D-glucurono)-D-xylan but the most common side chain is a (1→2)-linked, or less frequently, a (1→3)-linked 4-*O*-methyl α-D-glucopyranosyluronic acid, although annual plants have been shown to contain unmethylated residues. The number of D-glucuronic acid side chains varies considerably, with the hard wood D-xylans having, on average, one acidic residue for every ten D-xylopyranosyl residues. Another common side chain in D-xylans is (1→3)-linked α-L-arabinose but these residues do not always occur as nonreducing end groups. A typical example of non-terminal L-arabinopyranosyl residues occurs in barley husk D-xylan (80).

$$→4)\text{-}\beta\text{-D-Xyl}p\text{-}(1→$$
$$3$$
$$\uparrow$$
$$1$$
$$→4)\text{-}\beta\text{-D-Xyl}p\text{-}(1→2)\text{-}\alpha\text{-L-Ara}f$$

(80)

L-Arabino-D-xylans. The L-arabino-D-xylan group of neutral polysaccharides which occur in association with acidic polysaccharides come from cereal gums. These are highly branched polysaccharides in which the β-D-xylan chains are (1→4)-linked (81) and to which are attached, in an irregular manner, single α-L-arabinofuranosyl groups *via* (1→3)-links. The polysaccharide isolated from cress seeds has been found to contain an L-arabino-D-xylan comprising chains of (1→5)-linked α-L-arabinofuranosyl residues to which are attached L-arabinofuranosyl residues and D-xylosyl groups (82).

$$→4)\text{-}\beta\text{-D-Xyl}p\text{-}(1→4)\text{-}\beta\text{-D-Xyl}p\text{-}(1→4)\text{-}\beta\text{-D-Xyl}p\text{-}(1→4)\text{-}\beta\text{-D-Xyl}p\text{-}(1→$$
$$3 \qquad\qquad\qquad\qquad\qquad\qquad\qquad\qquad 3$$
$$\uparrow \qquad\qquad\qquad\qquad\qquad\qquad\qquad\qquad \uparrow$$
$$1 \qquad\qquad\qquad\qquad\qquad\qquad\qquad\qquad 1$$
$$\alpha\text{-L-Ara}f \qquad\qquad\qquad\qquad\qquad \alpha\text{-L-Ara}f$$

(81)

$$\rightarrow 5)\text{-}\alpha\text{-}L\text{-}Ara f\text{-}(1\rightarrow 5)\text{-}\alpha\text{-}L\text{-}Ara f\text{-}(1\rightarrow 5)\text{-}\alpha\text{-}L\text{-}Ara f\text{-}(1\rightarrow$$

```
                      3                    3
                      ↑                    ↑
                      1                    1
                  α-L-Araf             α-L-Araf
                      3                    3
                      ↑                    ↑
                      1                    1
                  α-D-Xylp             α-D-Xylp
```

(82)

D-Mannans, D-galacto-D-mannans and D-gluco-D-mannans. D-Mannose is a common constituent of plant polysaccharides, occurring in homopolysaccharides, or in heteropolysaccharides in conjunction with D-galactose or D-glucose. D-Mannans occur in ivory nuts, green coffee beans and a number of other plant sources and have a common carbohydrate structure consisting of linear chains of $(1\rightarrow4)$-linked β-D-mannopyranosyl residues, which differ in chain length depending on the source; such polysaccharides are insoluble in water. The presence of traces of D-galactose in the ivory nut D-mannans may indicate that they are in fact D-galacto-D-mannans at the extreme end of the whole spectrum of D-galacto-D-mannans which occur in the seeds of leguminous plants. The structure of the polysaccharides vary, according to the source of the material, in the relative amounts of the component monosaccharide ranging from a D-galactose:D-mannose ratio of 1:1 to 1:5, but all have the same structural feature, namely chains of $(1\rightarrow4)$-linked β-D-mannopyranosyl residues to which side chains consisting of single α-D-galactopyranosyl groups attached by $(1\rightarrow6)$-linkages (83) at various intervals, for example, guaran contains a D-galactopyranosyl residue on every other D-mannopyranosyl residue. These D-galacto-D-mannans are readily soluble in water and find commercial uses as sizes and beater additives in paper making and as gelling agents in the food industry due to the highly viscous solutions they form. The position of the side chains is such that regions with and without side chains assist to give the appearance of 'hairy' and 'smooth' regions. It is the smooth regions which interact with, for example, xanthan (see also pages 48 and 171).

$$\rightarrow 4)\text{-}\beta\text{-}D\text{-}Man p\text{-}(1\rightarrow 4)\text{-}\beta\text{-}D\text{-}Man p\text{-}(1\rightarrow 4)\text{-}\beta\text{-}D\text{-}Man p\text{-}(1\rightarrow 4)\text{-}\beta\text{-}D\text{-}Man p\text{-}(1\rightarrow$$

```
           6                              6
           ↑                              ↑
           1                              1
       α-D-Galp                       α-D-Galp
```

(83)

D-Gluco-D-mannans have been isolated from hard woods in which the ratio of D-glucose to D-mannose is 1:2. Partial hydrolysis has shown the existence of disaccharides of D-glucose and D-mannose together with cellobiose, mannobiose, and mannotriose which suggests that these hemicelluloses have a random distribution of 1,4-substituted β-D-glucopyranosyl and 1,4-substituted β-D-mannopyranosyl residues in linear chains. Similar compounds have been isolated from seeds of certain iris, orchid and lily bulbs but they contain different proportions of D-glucose to D-mannose in the range 1:1 to 1:4. D-Galacto-D-gluco-D-mannans occur together with D-gluco-D-mannans in coniferous woods. Structural studies have shown that these have the same backbone as the D-gluco-D-mannans with single (1→6)-linked α-D-galactopyranosyl groups as side chains. There is also evidence that D-glucose and D-mannose occur as nonreducing end groups. These side chains are responsible for the greater solubility of these compounds compared to that of the D-gluco-D-mannans. This solubility is probably brought about by the side chains preventing the macromolecules from forming strong, intermolecular hydrogen bonds and act in the same way as the residues and groups, such as 4-O-methyl-D-glucuronic acid, L-arabinose, and O-acetylated residues, of the other hemicelluloses.

L-Arabino-D-galactans. Another group of hemicelluloses is the water-soluble L-arabino-D-galactans which are highly branched molecules with branched backbone chains of (1→3/6)-linked β-D-galactopyranosyl residues to which are attached side chains which may contain L-arabinofuranosyl, L-arabinopyranosyl, L-rhamnopyranosyl, etc., residues. Typical examples are the L-arabino-D-galactans from maritime pine (84) and from sycamore (85).

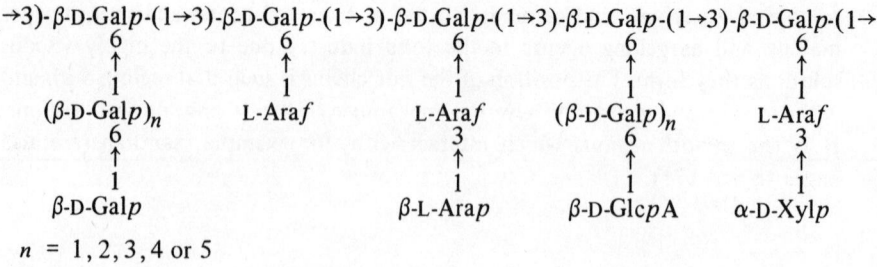

$$n = 1, 2, 3, 4 \text{ or } 5$$

(84)

$$\to 3)\text{-}\beta\text{-D-Gal}p\text{-}(1\to 3)\text{-}\beta\text{-D-Gal}p\text{-}(1\to 3)\text{-}\beta\text{-D-Gal}p\text{-}(1\to$$

6	6
↑	↑
1	1
R→3)-D-Gal$p$	R→3)-D-Gal$p$
6	6
↑	↑
1	1
R→3)-D-Gal$p$	R→3)-D-Gal$p$
6	6
↑	↑
1	1
R→3)-D-Gal$p$	R→3)-D-Gal$p$
6	6
↑	↑
R	R

R = L-Ara$f$-(1→, β-L-Ara$p$-(1→5)-L-Ara$f$-(1→, or L-Rha$p$-(1→

(85)

Miscellaneous plant polysaccharides

Lichenan is a D-glucan from Iceland moss and contains a random mixture of (1→4)- and (1→3)-linked β-D-glucopyranosyl residues in linear chains, with a higher proportion (about 70%) of (1→4) linkages. Iceland moss also contains a polysaccharide which is the α-D-analog of lichenan. This so-called isolichenan contains (1→4)- and (1→3)-linked α-D-glucopyranosyl residues with a higher proportion of the latter linkage. It also has a lower chain length of about 40–45 residues compared to 60–360 for lichenan. These polysaccharides have been important in the understanding of the mode of action of glycanases.

There are a number of glycans which occur in plants. Nigeran is an α-D-glucan with approximately equal proportions of alternating (1→3)- and (1→4)-linkages. The β-D-glucans found in plants include pustulan which contains (1→6)-linkages. Fructans also commonly occur in plants, acting as reserve carbohydrates either alone, or in conjunction with starch. They contain β-D-fructofuranosyl residues which are linked (2→1) in inulins and (2→6) in levans. Most D-fructans contain D-glucopyranosyl residues as nonreducing end groups and have relatively low molecular weights – of the order of 8,000. Grass levans have chain lengths of 20–30 units and are essentially linear.

Amyloids are a group of water soluble polysaccharides found in the seeds of a number of plants including tamarind and nasturtium and are so-called because of their staining reactions with iodine. They contain (1→4)-linked β-D-glucopyranosyl residues to which are linked single α-D-xylopyranosyl groups and 2-O-β-D-galactopyranosyl-α-D-xylopyranosyl units as side chains *via* (1→6)-linkages.

The unusual monosaccharide, L-glucose, has been reported to be among the hydrolysis products of the leaves of jute and *Grindelia* species.

ALGAL POLYSACCHARIDES

It is difficult to define algae because they encompass not only microscopic uni-
cellular organisms but also the seaweeds, the arms of which can extend to over
150 feet in length. They have no roots, stems or leaves, as have the higher land
plants, and they are most frequently found in fresh or salt water, occasionally
free floating in the water as in the case of the brown seaweeds. The polysaccharides obtained from those sources can be grouped into three classes: food-reserve,
structural, and sulphated polysaccharides. Whilst many compounds are known,
their structures still have to be determined.

Food-reserve polysaccharides

The main polysaccharides in the first class of food-reserve polysaccharides
include starch and laminaran polysaccharides. Green, red and blue-green seaweeds, and fresh water algae contain starch polysaccharides which can be fractionated into amylose and amylopectin. The absence of amylose from some
extracts can be explained in terms of its destruction during isolation with
acidic and alkaline solutions. The major differences between plant and algal
starches are the lower intrinsic viscosities and lower iodine binding powers of
the algal starches, which indicates smaller molecules. The presence of smaller
molecules is also demonstrated by X-ray diffraction studies which show that
the starch granules are less organised but still exhibit the characteristics of the
plant starches. Algal starches are more susceptible to amylolytic enzymes. The
average chain lengths vary between 10 and 19 units and small proportions of
$(1\rightarrow3)$-linked α-D-glucopyranosyl residues have been found.

Laminaran is a water soluble D-glucan which occurs as the principal reserve
polysaccharide in a number of brown algae, particularly from *Laminaria* species.
The main structural features of this polysaccharide are $(1\rightarrow3)$- and $(1\rightarrow6)$-linked
β-D-glucopyranosyl residues forming chains with some $(1\rightarrow6)$-linkages as branch
points which are terminated by reducing D-glucopyranosyl or nonreducing
D-mannitol groups. The ratio of these so-called G- and M- chains varies, but is
about 1:1 for the majority of samples. The average chain lengths vary between
7 and 11, with molecular weights corresponding to about 30 units for soluble
forms of laminaran, which indicates an average of 2–3 branch points per molecule, whilst insoluble forms contain 16–24 units with average chain lengths of
15–19 units and indicate essentially linear structures. Chains terminating in
D-mannitol have not been found in the D-glucans isolated from members of the
Chrysophycaae and Bacillariophycaae but they resemble laminaran in other
respects.

Structural polysaccharides

Brown, red, and green algae have, as a structural polysaccharide, the second class
of algal polysaccharides, a cellulose which is essentially similar to that of land

plants and comprises about 10% of the dry weight. In very close association with this cellulose are a number of hemicelluloses and similar compounds which include D-mannans, D-xylans and a lichenan type of polysaccharide consisting of linear chains of (1→4)- and (1→3)-linked β-D-glucopyranosyl residues with a lower proportion of (1→3)-linkages than is found in plant lichenan. The D-mannans isolated from red seaweed resemble the ivory nut D-mannan in that they contain essentially linear chains of about 16 (1→4)-linked β-D-mannopyranosyl residues. The D-xylans found in seaweeds differ from those in land plants by being predominantly true D-xylans containing, in the case of the red seaweed *Rhodymenia palmata*, chains of (1→3)- and (1→4)-linked β-D-xylopyranosyl residues in an irregular distribution whereas the D-xylan from green seaweed, *Caulerpa filiformis*, contains only (1→3)-linked β-D-xylopyranosyl residues.

Alginic acid is a commercially important component of brown seaweeds and is the most important mucilaginous polysaccharide which prevents desiccation of the seaweed when exposed to the air, for example, at low tide. Industrially it is important as a thickening agent and emulsion stabiliser (see Chapter 14). It has been shown that the molecule readily produces fibres which according to X-ray diffraction are essentially linear. It was originally thought to be a (1→4)-linked β-D-mannuronan but alginic acid actually consists of D-mannopyranosyluronic and L-gulopyranosyluronic acid residues. Partial hydrolysis gives degraded polysaccharides containing entirely one or the other hexuronic acid residue and a number of oligosaccharides containing both residues, and it has been suggested that alginic acid contains crystalline regions of β-D-mannuronic acid and of α-L-guluronic acid and amorphous regions containing a mixture of both residues, all (1→4)-linked.

Sulphated polysaccharides

A group of polysaccharides isolated from algae are the sulphated polysaccharides which include carrageenan and agar. Carrageenan can be fractionated into a number of polysaccharides, proportions of which vary from species to species and with the season and environment. The major structural features of this group of polysaccharides are an alternating sequence of (1→3)-linked β-D-galactopyranosyl and (1→4)-linked α-D-galactopyranosyl residues containing various degrees and sites of sulphation. κ-Carrageenan, for instance, is an insoluble D-galactan containing alternating 3-*O*-substituted β-D-galactopyranosyl 4-sulphate and 4-*O*-substituted 3,6-anhydro-α-D-galactopyranosyl residues and small proportions of (1→4)-linked D-galactopyranosyl 6-sulphate residues whereas μ-carrageenan is soluble and contains only (1→3)-linked α-D-galactopyranosyl 4-sulphate and (1→4)-linked β-D-galactopyranosyl 6-sulphate. ι-Carrageenan has a repeating structure of (1→3)-linked α-D-galactopyranose 4-sulphate and (1→4)-linked 3,6-anhydro-β-D-galactopyranosyl 2-sulphate residues with approximately 1 in 10 of these residues being replaced by (1→4)-linked β-D-galactopyranosyl 2,6-disulphate.

ζ-Carrageenan is a polymer of D-galactopyranose 2-sulphate with β-(1→4)- and α-(1→3)-linkages. λ-And χ-carrageenans are similar, each containing (1→3)-linked α-D-galactopyranosyl 2-sulphate and (1→4)-linked β-D-galactopyranosyl 2,6-disulphate and 3,6-anhydro-β-D-galactopyranosyl 2-sulphate residues; χ-carrageenan is richer in 3,6-anhydro-D-galactopyranose units compared to λ-carrageenan.

Agar is considered to consist of chains having alternating (1→3)- and (1→4)-linkages with three extremes of structure: neutral agarose which contains (1→3)-linked β-D-galactopyranosyl and (1→4)-linked 3,6-anhydro-α-L-galactopyranosyl residues, a pyruvic acid acetal-containing agarose in which the D-galactopyranosyl residues are substituted with pyruvic acid acetals, and a sulphated galactan with few, or no, 3,6-anhydro-L-galactopyranosyl or pyruvic acid acetal-containing D-galactopyranosyl residues.

Miscellaneous algal polysaccharides

There are also a number of algal mucilages which have similar properties and whose structures have not yet been determined. They usually contain L-rhamnose, D-xylose, D-glucuronic acid, D- and L-galactose and D-mannose and are typified by the mucilage from fresh water red algae, which may contain a D-galactose and D-glucuronic acid repeating sequence, together with the above neutral residues and methylated L-rhamnosyl and D-galactosyl residues; and by a mucilage from brown seaweed which contains L-fucose, D-xylose and D-galactose as nonreducing terminal residues with D-mannose and D-galactose occupying branch positions.

MICROBIAL POLYSACCHARIDES

Microbes give rise to many polysaccharides and also to macromolecules, such as glycopeptides, glycoproteins and glycolipids (see Chapter 9 and 10), to the backbones of which carbohydrate chains are attached. Many of these compounds are unique to microbes, not being found in any other general areas such as plants and animals. The polysaccharidic material can occur as an integral part of the cell-wall, as capsules surrounding the cell, or can be elaborated in culture media (extracellular polysaccharides).

Teichoic acids

The name 'teichoic acids' has been given to a group of phosphate-containing polymers, isolated from cell-walls and membranes of Gram-positive bacteria. The first known members of the group were all polymers of either glycerol phosphate or ribitol phosphate repeating units joined together *via* phosphodiester linkages. With the discovery of monosaccharide- and oligosaccharide-1-phosphate polymers in the walls of some bacteria the definition has had to be extended to include these materials.

The structure of teichoic acids can be regarded as being a combination of two chemically different parts (which are biosynthesised by different mechanisms): (a) the main polymer chain and (b) the linkage region responsible for the attachment of the teichoic acid to a peptidoglycan. Several different types of main chain have been described which contain O-ribitol, sugar and phosphate residues. These are held together in repeating units of between 10 and 50 units by the phosphate residues. 1,5-Poly(ribitol phosphate) teichoic acids (86) occur in the walls of many bacilli, lactobacilli and staphylococci and most contain D-alanine residues attached *via* O-2 of the D-ribitol residues. In *Staphylococcus aureus* 2-acetamido-2-deoxy-α- or -β-D-glucopyranosyl residues are glycosidically attached by (1→2)-linkages, whilst in strains of *Bacillus subtilis* and *Bacillus licheniformis* β-D-glucopyranosyl residues are attached by (1→2)-linkages.

1,3-Poly(glycerol phosphate) teichoic acids (87) are more widespread than ribitol phosphate teichoic acids, occurring in the walls of several species of bacteria. The hydroxyl group at C-2 of each glycerol residue is substituted by D-alanine, D-glucose and 2-acetamido-2-deoxy-D-glucose and -D-galactose. A variation in the structural pattern is observed in some bacteria which contain a 1,2-poly(glycerol phosphate) in which the 3-position is substituted by glycosyl residues such as a disaccharide of D-galactopyranose and 2-acetamido-2-deoxy-D-glucopyranose as found in the teichoic acid from *Streptomyces antibioticus* (88).

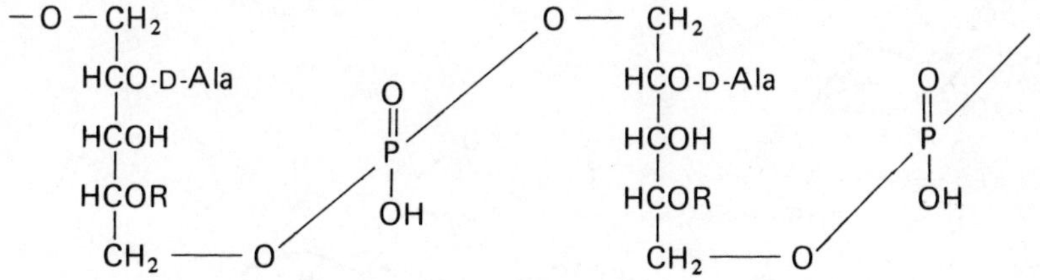

$$-O-CH_2 \quad\quad O-CH_2$$

$$HCO\text{-D-Ala} \quad\quad HCO\text{-D-Ala}$$

$$HCOH \quad\quad HCOH$$

$$HCOR \quad\quad HCOR$$

$$CH_2 - O \quad\quad CH_2 - O$$

R = α-D-GlcpNAc-(1→, β-D-GlcpNAc-(1→, or β-D-Glcp-(1→

(86)

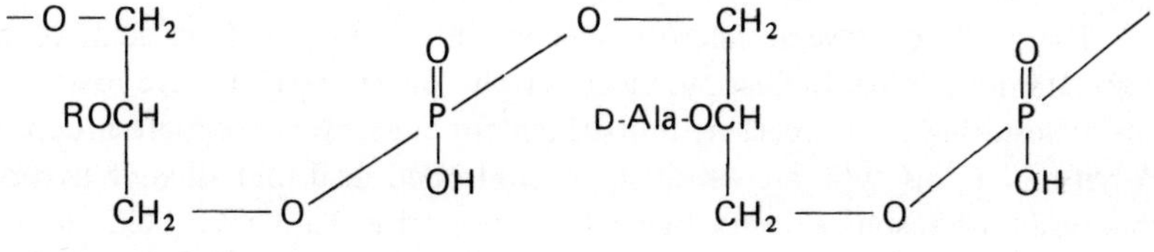

$$-O-CH_2 \quad\quad O-CH_2$$

$$ROCH \quad\quad \text{D-Ala-OCH}$$

$$CH_2 - O \quad\quad CH_2 - O$$

R = α-D-GlcpNAc-(1→, β-D-GlcpNAc-(1→, α-D-Glcp-(1→, or α-D-GalpNAc-(1→

(87)

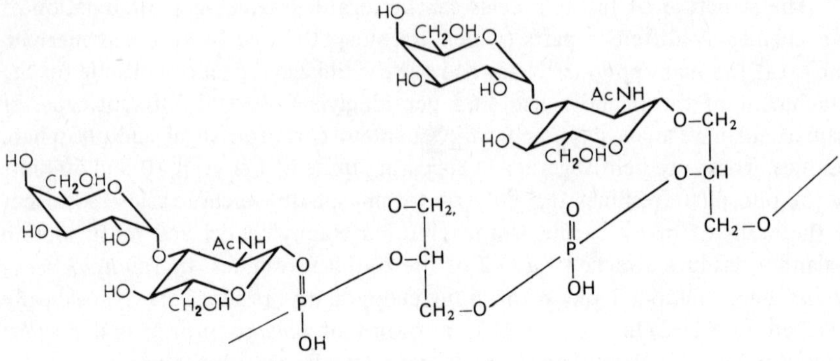

(88)

Some glycerol teichoic acids contain glycosidically-linked monosaccharides as part of the phosphodiester backbone. A poly(D-glucopyranosylglycerol phosphate) (89) has been isolated from the walls of *Bacillus stearothermophilus* whilst a strain of *Bacillus licheniformis* was found to contain more than one type of polymer chain teichoic acid, namely a mixture of poly(D-glucopyranosylglycerol phosphate), poly(D-galactopyranosylglycerol phosphate) and 1,3-poly(glycerol phosphate).

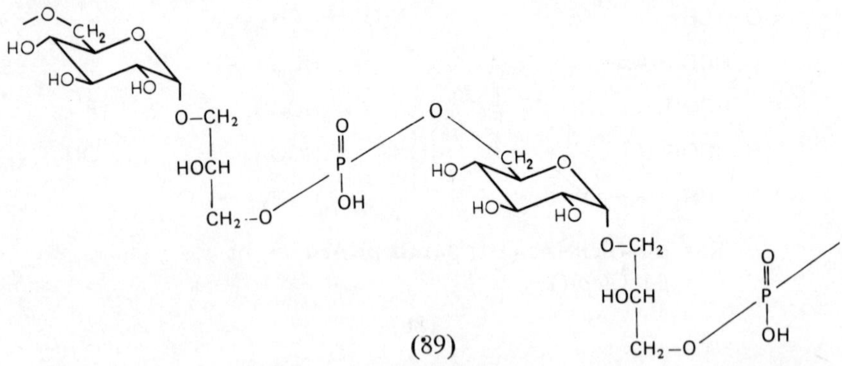

(89)

The walls of several micrococci contain glycerol teichoic acids in which 2-acetamido-2-deoxy-D-glucopyranosyl 1-phosphate residues are part of the chain, resulting in a repeating unit which contains two phosphate groups (90). Polymers of this type are sensitive to controlled acid and alkaline hydrolysis, the sugar 1-phosphate bond being hydrolysed by 0.1 M hydrochloric acid in 10 minutes at 100°C whilst the glycerol phosphate attached *via* C-4 of the carbohydrate is hydrolysed by 0.5 M sodium hydroxide in 2 hours at 20°C. This has given some insight into the structure of the linkage unit. D-Alanyl residues are frequently attached *via* O-6.

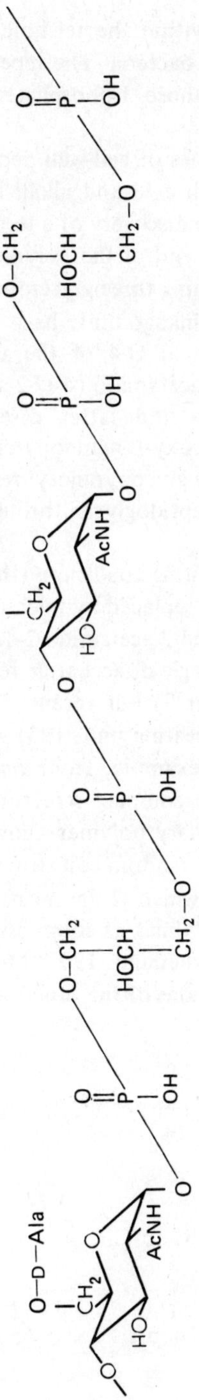

(90)

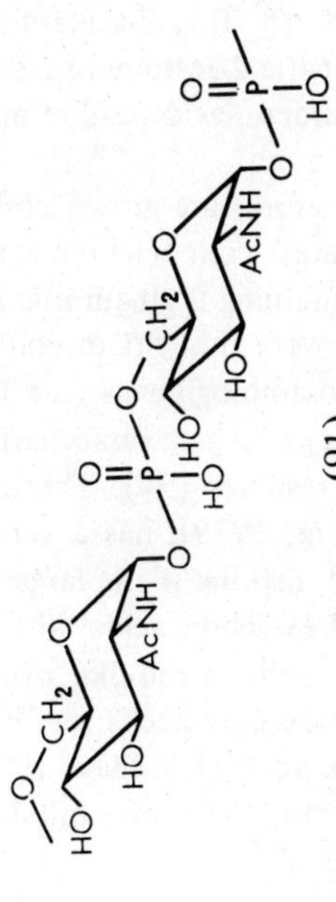

(91)

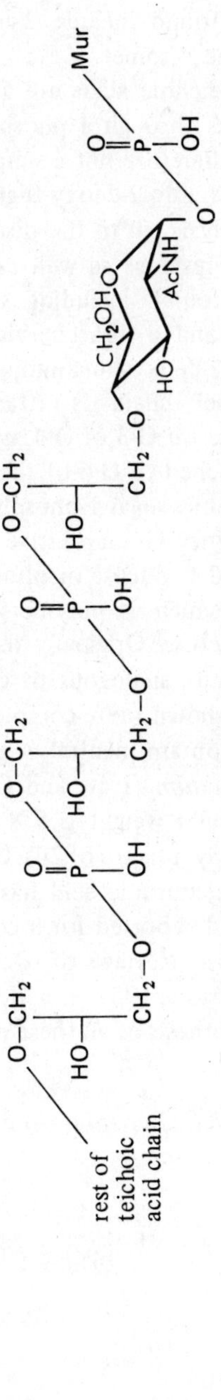

(92)

Mur = muramic acid residue of cell wall peptidoglycan

Sugar 1-phosphate polymers which are included within the teichoic acid definition have been isolated from the walls of various bacteria. The repeating units found include 2-acetamido-2-deoxy-α-D-glucopyranose 1-phosphate (91) and the β-isomer.

Teichoic acids are attached to muramic acid residues of cell-wall peptidoglycans through a phosphodiester linkage which is both acid and alkali labile (and therefore not a simple phosphodiester linkage). The discovery of a terminal 2-acetamido-2-deoxy-D-glucosyl residue at the reducing end of the polymer on hydrolysis led to the discovery of a linkage unit containing three glycerol phosphate residues as well as the aminosugar (92). Other linkage units have since been found, including substitution at O-6 rather than at O-4 of the amino sugar and a disaccharide linkage unit consisting of 2-acetamido-(4-*O*-2-acetamido-2-deoxy-D-mannopyranosyl)-2-deoxy-D-glucose. In the latter case the polymer chain is attached to the 2-acetamido-2-deoxy-D-mannopyranosyl residue *via* O-3 or O-4, whilst the 2-acetamido-2-deoxy-D-glucopyranosyl residue is attached to O-6 of the muramic acid residue in the peptidoglycan through an acid labile sugar 1-phosphate bond.

When Gram-positive organisms are grown under limiting conditions (that is, limited D-glucose or phosphate), their teichoic acids are replaced by teichuronic acids which are polymers containing D-glucuronic acid and 2-acetamido-2-deoxy-D-galactose. Originally these were thought to contain single disaccharide repeating units analogous to glycosaminoglycans (see Chapter 9) but recent studies have shown more-complex repeating tetrasaccharide repeating units (93) which can contain neutral sugar residues (94). This latter example, from *Bacillus megaterium* (Ivatt and Gilvarg, 1979), has a very large complex structure. Its molecular weight is 5×10^5, making it the largest ancillary polymer known to date (by a factor of 20). Unlike teichoic acids, which have random coil structures, this teichuronic acid has an ordered rod-like structure which is the most compressed reported for a complex polysaccharide, being 3 times as compressed as amylose. Reviews of teichoic acids (Baddiley, 1972, Sutherland, 1977, Munson and Glaser, 1981, and McArthur, 1981) give full descriptions of the function and biosynthesis of all these materials.

→4)-β-D-Glc*p*A-(1→4)-β-D-Glc*p*A-(1→3)-β-D-Gal*p*NAc-(1→6)-α-D-Gal*p*NAc-(1→

(93)

→4)-β-D-Glc*p*-(1→3)-α-L-Rha*p*-(1→3)-α-L-Rha*p*-(1→
$$3$$
$$\uparrow$$
$$1$$
β-D-Glc*p*A

(94)

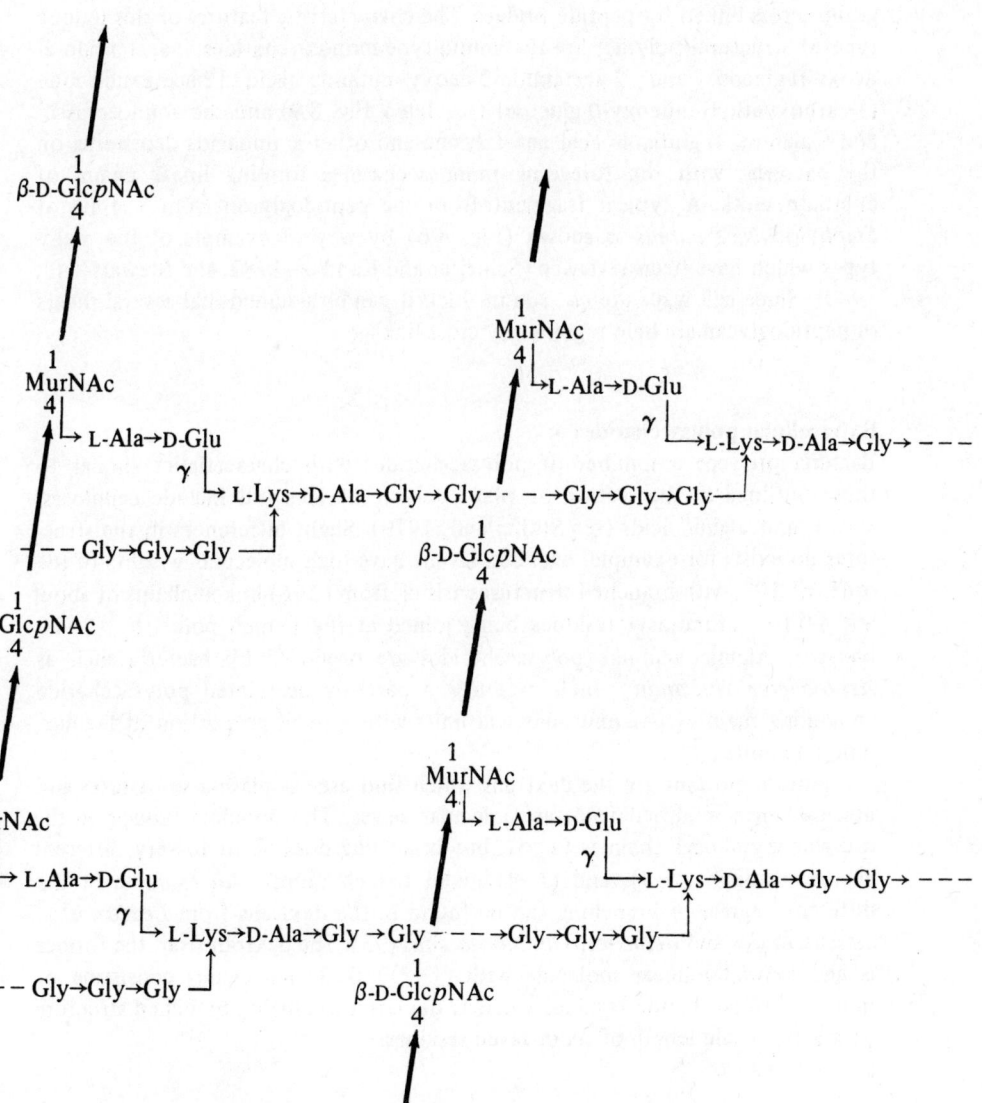

Fig. 8.6 – Schematic representation of the structure of the
peptidoglycan from a strain of *Staphylococcus aureus*.
(➜ inter carbohydrate linkage, → inter aminoacid linkages.)

Cell-wall peptidoglycans (mureins)

These highly branched, complex macromolecules occurring in bacterial cell walls consist of polysaccharide chains, in which individual residues carry an amino group, cross-linked by peptide bridges. The characteristic features of this unique type of structural polymer are the amino-type monosaccharides, 2-acetamido-2-deoxy-D-glucose and 2-acetamido-2-deoxy-muramic acid (2-acetamido-3-O-(1-carboxyethyl)-2-deoxy-D-glucose) (see later, Fig. 8.9) and the aminoacids D- and L-alanine, D-glutamic acid and L-lysine and other aminoacids depending on the bacteria, with the foregoing monosaccharides forming linear chains of alternate units. A typical fragment from the peptidoglycan from a strain of *Staphylococcus aureus* is shown (Fig. 8.6) by way of example of the many types which have been reviewed (Schleifer and Kandler, 1982, and Stewart-Tull, 1980). Since cell walls are *ca*. 20 nm thick it can be assumed that several sheets of peptidoglycan are held together by cross-linkages.

Extracellular polysaccharides

Bacteria produce a number of polysaccharides with characeristics similar to those outlined in the section on plant polysaccharides and include celluloses, levans, and alginic acids (see Sutherland, 1979). Slight differences in the structures do exist; for example, bacterial levans have high molecular weights of the order of 10^6, with branched structures arising from (2→6)-linked chains of about ten β-D-fructofuranosyl residues being joined at the branch points by (2→1)-linkages. Alginic acid-like polysaccharides are produced by bacteria such as *Azotobacter vinelandii* which produces a partially acetylated polysaccharide containing mainly D-mannuronic acid units with a small proportion of L-guluronic acid units.

More important are the dextrans which find uses as plasma substitutes and are used in a modified form as molecular sieves. The principle linkage in the α-D-glucopyranosyl chain is (1→6), but branching does occur to very different degrees through (1→3)- and (1→4)-linked branch points. An example of the different degrees of branching can be found in the dextrans from *Leuconostoc mesenteroides* and *Betacoccus arabinosaceous* (95). The dextran from the former is an essentially linear molecule with (1→3)-linked side chains consisting of mono- or di-saccharide residues whereas the latter is a highly branched structure with a unit chain length of six or seven residues.

$$\to 6)\text{-}\alpha\text{-D-Glc}p\text{-}(1\to 6)\text{-}\alpha\text{-D-Glc}p$$
$$1$$
$$\downarrow$$
$$3$$
$$\to 6)\text{-}\alpha\text{-D-Glc}p\text{-}(1\to 6)\text{-}\alpha\text{-D-Glc}p\text{-}(1\to 6)\text{-}\alpha\text{-D-Glc}p\text{-}(1\to$$

$$(95)$$

A family of related extracellular polysaccharides, many of which have not yet been fully characterised, are produced by the various strains of *Xanthomonas*, the most important for industrial purposes (see Chapter 14) being xanthan gum, which is obtained from *X. campestris*. Xanthan gum has a structure consisting of linear chains of (1→4)-linked β-D-glucosyl residues to which are attached trisaccharide side chains consisting of D-mannose and D-glucuronic acid in the molar ratio of 2:1 (see Fig. 8.7). The α-D-mannosyl residues which are linked *via* (1→3)-linkages to the D-glucan backbone are usually acetylated at C-6 whilst approximately half of the terminal α-D-mannosyl groups carry pyruvic acid acetal groups attached *via* O-4 and O-6. Variation in the amount and distribution of acetate, pyruvic acid acetal and trisaccharide side chains occurs with different strains of bacteria, Fig. 8.7 representing only an average situation rather than a specific case.

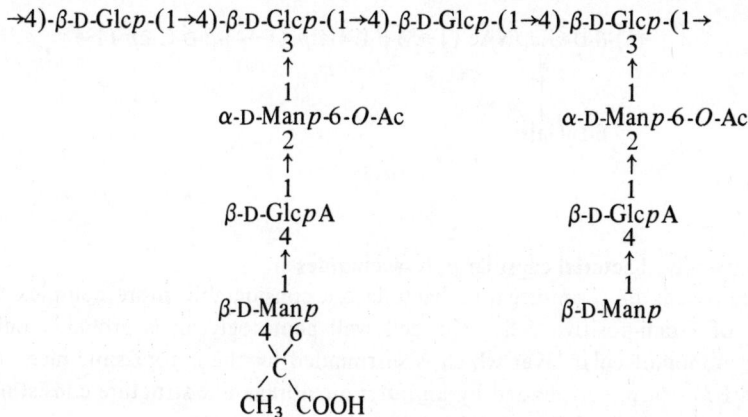

Fig. 8.7 – Repeating unit of xanthan gum shown in the acidic form. Distribution of side chains and pyruvic acid acetal reflect average values.

Gram-positive bacterial capsular polysaccharides

The Gram-positive bacteria produce polysaccharides which have complex structures and frequently contain aminosugar residues as well as neutral and acidic monosaccharides. Many of the aminosugars have been found to have rare structures (for example, diamino-trideoxysugars, etc.) which were previously regarded as 2-amino-2-deoxy-D-glucose. This was due to the inadequate specificity of the degradation method used to identify the aminosugar and the incorrect assumption that no diaminosugars etc. could exist. Mild, physicochemical methods of analysis have shown that many other aminosugars do, in fact, exist (see Fig. 8.9 and Horton and Wander, 1980a). They frequently have immunological properties which are characteristic of a particular chemical structure. The structures of a number of these polysaccharides have been found to consist of a variety of polysaccharide types.

Polysaccharides from strains of *Streptococcus pneumoniae*, which were the first non-protein materials shown to be antigenic, are produced externally to the cell wall and form capsules that cover the cells. Over 70 different types of polysaccharide have been identified and the structures of many have been established. Some, such as types 13 and 34, contain ribitol phosphate plus a number of monosaccharides and these are considered to be teichoic acids. Other polysaccharides contain simple repeating units such as type 3 which contains a disaccharide repeating unit (96) or type 14 which contains a tetrasaccharide repeating unit (97).

$$\rightarrow3)\text{-}\beta\text{-D-Glc}p\text{A-}(1\rightarrow4)\text{-}\beta\text{-D-Glc}p\text{-}(1\rightarrow$$

(96)

$$\rightarrow6)\text{-}\beta\text{-D-Glc}p\text{NAc-}(1\rightarrow3)\text{-}\beta\text{-D-Gal}p\text{-}(1\rightarrow4)\text{-}\beta\text{-D-Glc}p\text{-}(1\rightarrow$$
$$4$$
$$\uparrow$$
$$1$$
$$\beta\text{-D-Gal}p$$

(97)

Gram-negative bacterial capsular polysaccharides
The cell walls of Gram-negative bacteria are considerably more complex than those of Gram-positive cells. The cell wall peptidoglycan is probably only a single monomolecular layer which is surrounded by the cytoplasmic membrane which is, in turn, surrounded by an outer membrane-like structure consisting of protein, phospholipid, lipoprotein and lipopolysaccharides.

LIPOPOLYSACCHARIDES

The lipopolysaccharides (LPS) do not appear to be covalently linked to the peptidoglycan (unlike teichoic acids in Gram-positive bacteria), but have been shown to be located on the outer surface of the cell from which it can be removed, intact, by reagents such as phenol and propan-2-ol. These lipopolysaccharides are responsible for type specific immunological reactions. Bacteria can have more than one antigenic characteristic, many of which are sponsored by a structural feature of a/the capsular polysaccharide of the bacterium. Most of the antigenic specificity of the polysaccharides arises from the nonreducing end groups and ranges of antisera have been used in the structural analysis of such polysaccharides. The structural basis for these serological reactions can be shown by the following example. The acidic polysaccharides from *Klebsiella aerogens* and *Enterobacter 349* cross react to the extent of about 50% with the heterologous antibodies (that is, from the antiserum to the opposite polysaccharide). Structural analysis has shown that these polysaccharides both contain (1→3)-linked D-galactopyranosyl and (1→3)- and (1→4)-linked D-mannopyranosyl residues, but that the *Klebsiella aerogenes* polysaccharide contains D-manno-pyranosyluronic acid residues forming disaccharide repeating units with the D-mannopyranosyl residues, whereas the *Enterobacter* polysaccharide contains di-saccharide repeating units of D-mannopyranosyl residues attached to D-galacto-pyranosyluronic acid and to D-glucopyranosyluronic acid residues. A number of less common monosaccharides are found in the polysaccharides from Gram-negative bacteria, including 3,6-dideoxy derivatives of D-glucose, D-galactose and D-mannose and a number of aldoheptoses, the structures of which are given in Fig. 8.9.

The part of the lipopolysaccharides not responsible for antigenic activity is known as the core polysaccharide and this is attached to the lipid material (see Fig. 8.8). Compared to the complexity of the antigenic outer chains, the core polysaccharide of nearly all lipopolysaccharides consists of D-glucose, D-galactose, 2-acetamido-2-deoxy-D-glucose and a heptose which are linked to an octose. The heptose is usually L-*glycero*-D-*manno*-heptose and the octose always 3-deoxy-D-*manno*-octopyranulosonic acid (KDO). Lipid A is a common constituent of all lipopolysaccharides and has the repeating structure (98) consisting of a disaccharide of 2-acetamido-2-deoxy-D-glucopyranosyl residues to which KDO residues are attached as shown.

(98) R = long chain fatty acids (for example, lauric, myristic or palmitic acid)

A unique homopolysaccharide from Gram-negative bacteria is a polymer of 5-acetamido-3,5-dideoxy-D-*glycero*-D-*galacto*-2-nonulopyranonic acid called colominic acid which contains (2→8)-linkages and also in some samples (1→9)-internal ester linkages between adjacent residues (99).

The structures of the less common monosaccharides found in bacterial polysaccharides are given in Fig. 8.9 but their inclusion in this listing does not preclude their existence in other carbohydrate-containing macromolecules.

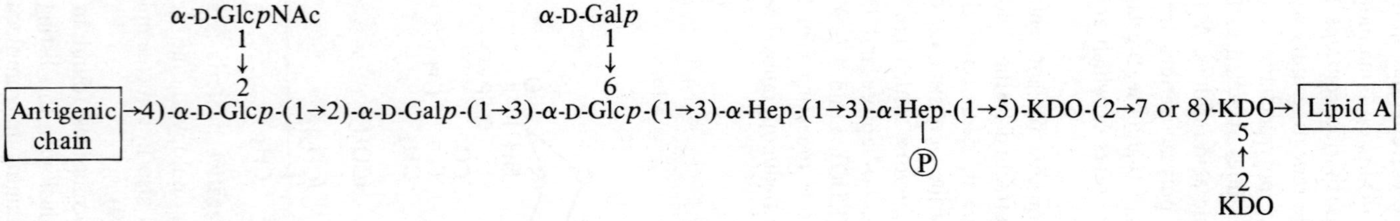

α-D-GlcpNAc
1
↓
2

α-D-Galp
1
↓
6

Antigenic chain →4)-α-D-Glcp-(1→2)-α-D-Galp-(1→3)-α-D-Glcp-(1→3)-α-D-Glcp-(1→3)-α-Hep-(1→3)-α-Hep-(1→5)-KDO-(2→7 or 8)-KDO→ Lipid A

(P)

5
↑
2
KDO

Fig. 8.8 — Structure of core polysaccharide of a lipopolysaccharide. A number of chains are crosslinked by phosphate bridges between heptose residues and by pyrophosphate bridges between the 2-amino-2-deoxy-D-glucopyranosyl residues of lipid A. (Hep = L-*glycero*-D-*manno*-heptopyranose, (P) = phosphate.)

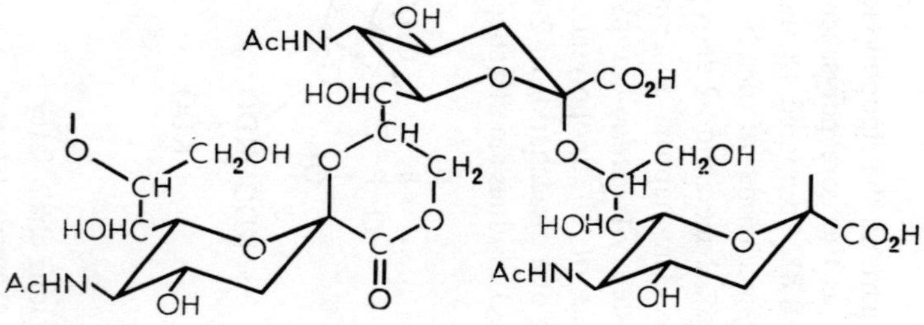

(99)

Deoxysugars

3,6-Dideoxy-β-L-galacto-
pyranose (Colitose)

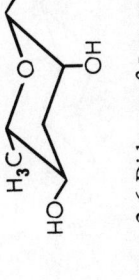

3,6-Dideoxy-β-L-manno-
pyranose (Ascarylose)

3,6-Dideoxy-β-D-galacto-
pyranose (Abequose)

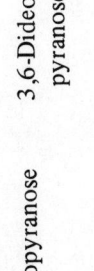

6-Deoxy-β-D-talopyranose

3,6-Dideoxy-β-D-manno-
pyranose (Tyvelose)

6-Deoxy-β-L-talopyranose

3,6-Dideoxy-β-D-gluco-
pyranose (Paratose)

Heptoses

D-glycero-β-D-gulo-
Heptopyranose

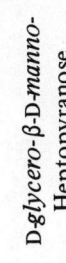

D-glycero-β-D-manno-
Heptopyranose

D-glycero-β-D-galacto-
Heptopyranose

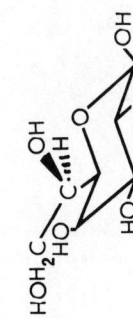

L-glycero-β-D-manno-
Heptopyranose

Fig. 8.9 – Structures of less common monosaccharides found in bacterial polysaccharides (*continued next page*)

Octose

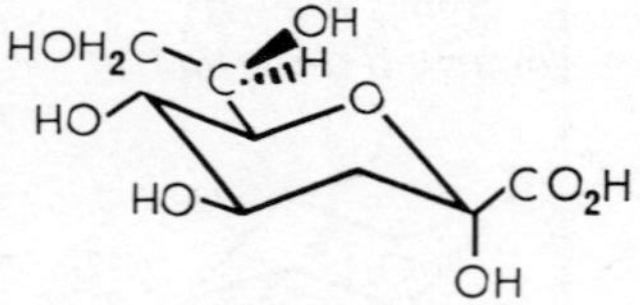

3-Deoxy-β-D-*manno*- octopyranulosonic
acid (KDO)

Uronic acids

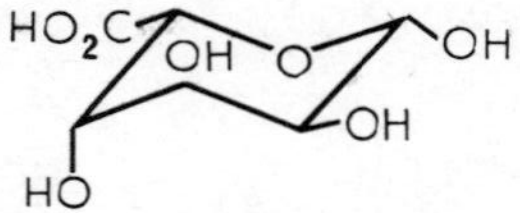

β-L-Gulopyranuronic acid

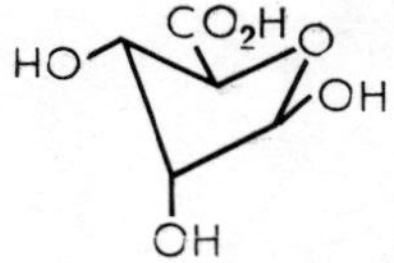

β-D-Ribofuranuronic acid

Ether derivatives

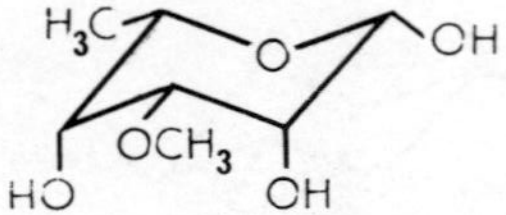

3-*O*-Methyl-6-deoxy-
β-L-talopyranose (Acovenose)

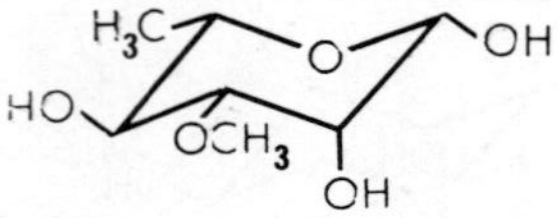

3-*O*-Methyl-β-L-rhamnopyranose
(Acofriose)

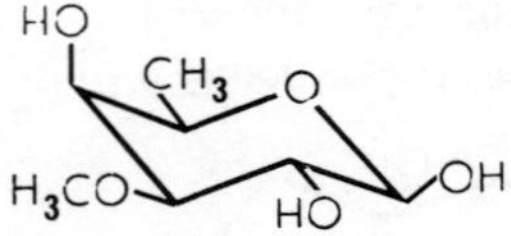

3-*O*-Methyl-β-D-fucopyranose
(Digitalose)

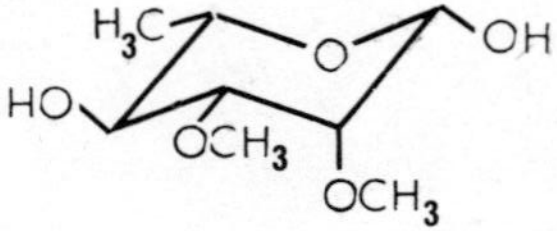

2,3-Di-*O*-methyl-β-
L-rhamnopyranose

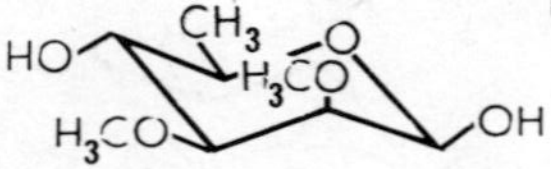

2,3-Di-*O*-methyl-β-
D-rhamnopyranose

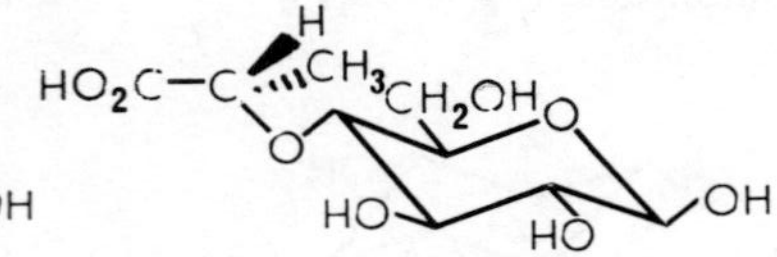

4-*O*-(1-Carboxyethyl)-
β-D-glucopyranose

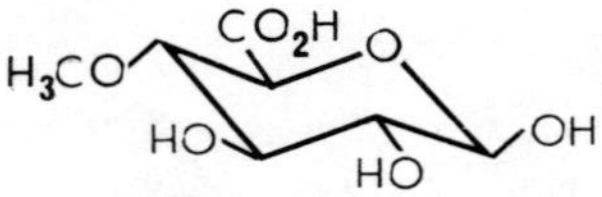

4-*O*-Methyl-β-D-
glucopyranuronic acid

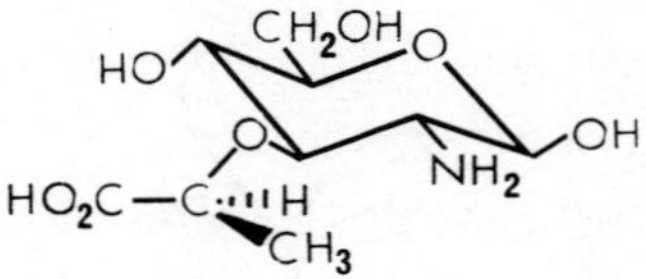

2-Amino-3-*O*-(1-carboxy-
ethyl)-2-deoxy-β-D-
glucopyranose
(Muramic acid)

Aminosugars

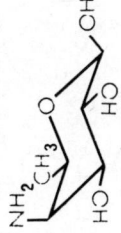

2-Amino-2-deoxy-β-
D-mannopyranose
(D-Mannosamine)

2-Amino-2-deoxy-β-
L-fucopyranose
(L-Fucosamine)

2-Amino-2-deoxy-β-
D-fucopyranose
(D-Fucosamine)

2-Amino-2,6-dideoxy-β-
L-talopyranose
(Pneumosamine)

2-Amino-2,6-dideoxy-
β-D-glucopyranose
(Quinovosamine)

2-Amino-2,6-dideoxy-
β-L-mannopyranose
(Rhamnosamine)

3-Amino-3,6-dideoxy-
β-D-galactopyranose

3-Amino-3,6-dideoxy-
β-D-glucopyranose

4-Amino-4,6-dideoxy-
β-D-glucopyranose
(Viosamine)

4-Amino-4,6-dideoxy-
β-D-galactopyranose
(Thomasamine)

2,4-Diamino-2,4,6-tri-
deoxy-β-D-glucopyranose
(Bacillosamine)

2,4-Diamino-2,4,6-tri-
deoxy-β-D-galactopyranose

Fig. 8.9 – Structures of less common monosaccharides found in bacterial polysaccharides (*continued next page*)

Aminouronic acids

2-Amino-2-deoxy-β-D-mannopyranuronic acid

2-Amino-2-deoxy-β-L-galactopyranuronic acid

2,3-Diamino-2,3-dideoxy-β-D-glucopyranuronic acid

2-Amino-2-deoxy-β-D-galactopyranuronic acid

2-Amino-2-deoxy-β-L-altropyranuronic acid

2-Amino-2-deoxy-β-D-glucopyranuronic acid

2-Amino-2-deoxy-β-L-gulopyranuronic acid

Fig. 8.9 – Structures of less common monosaccharides found in bacterial polysaccharides (shown in one anomeric form only). See Figs. 2.8 and 12.1 for other monosaccharide structures.

FUNGAL POLYSACCHARIDES

The major polysaccharides elaborated by fungi include: α-D-glucans, such as one containing only (1→3)-linked residues obtained from cell walls of *Polyporus tumulosus*; β-D-glucans, such as pachyman from *Porin cocos*, which consists of (1→3)-linked residues, and luteose which is a (1→6)-linked polymer from *Penicillium luteum*; and a number of storage products of the laminaran type which contain (1→3)-, (1→4)- and (1→6)-linked residues in linear and branched structures. The other major type of fungal polysaccharides are the D-mannans typified by the (1→6)-lined D-mannan from *Saccharomyces rouxii* and the (1→2)-linked D-mannan from *Saccharomyces cerevisiae*. The latter D-mannan has also been shown to contain phosphorylated side chains and has the structure (100), arising from the addition of (1→3)-linked D-mannopyranosyl groups to the D-mannopyranosyl phosphorylmannotriose chains. A D-galactan, galactocarolose, from *Penicillium charlesii*, is a low molecular weight polysaccharide consisting of unbranched chains of approximately ten (1→5)-linked β-D-galactofuranosyl residues.

α-D-Man*p*-(1→3)-α-D-Man*p*-(1→2)-α-D-Man*p*-(1→2)-α-D-Man*p*-(1→

α-D-Man*p*-(1→3)-α-D-Man*p*→Ⓟ

→Ⓟ = orthophosphate diester linkage

(100)

A number of heteropolysaccharides have also been isolated and characterised, including the D-galacto-D-mannan from *Cladosporium herbarum* which contains D-galactosyl residues in both pyranose and furanose forms, and a D-xylo-D-mannan from *Cryptococcus leuerentii*.

ANIMAL POLYSACCHARIDES

Glycogen

The principal reserve polysaccharide in the animal kingdom is glycogen, being found in most tissues of which the most convenient source for the purpose of extraction is liver or muscle. Human liver contains glycogen in up to 10% of its dry weight. Unlike starch, isolation and purification of glycogen is not simple. The classical method was to use strongly alkaline solutions at 100°C for about 3 hours to dissolve the tissue and then to precipitate the glycogen with ethanol, but with the development of understanding of alkaline degradation the use of milder techniques had to be sought. The use of cold dilute trichloroacetic acid for the extraction procedure results in a product the molecular size of which is some 10 times larger than that obtained with the traditional method. Methods are now available which avoid more-complete destruction during isolation so that it is possible to investigate realistically molecular weights of the isolated polysaccharide. It has been found that, for example, glycogen from the liver in cases of general glycogen storage disease has a lower molecular weight than normal. Classical analytical methods such as methylation have shown the structure of glycogen to be chains of (1→4)-linked α-D-glucopyranosyl residues with 1,4,6-trisubstituted residues as branch points.

The use of amylolytic enzymes for determination of the fine structure has indicated a tree-like structure, similar to that of amylopectin, with a unit chain length of 12 D-glucopyranosyl residues. This short chain length in a molecule which can possess a high molecular weight in the range 10^7-10^8 necessarily results in a highly branched structure, a consequence of which is the extremely limited uptake of iodine by the molecule compared even with that of amylopectin. Regions of dense branching that are resistant to the action of α-amylase are randomly distributed throughout the molecule. With the availability of paracrystalline glycogen it should be possible to use physical methods to examine the structure in greater detail.

Chitin

The most abundant of polysaccharides containing amino-type monosaccharides is chitin which occurs as a structural polysaccharide in the shells of crustacea. It also occurs in fungi and some green algae. The chemical evidence for its structure has been based on the isolation and characterisation of oligosaccharides obtained as a result of partial hydrolysis. This shows that chitin is a homopolymer of 2-acetamido-2-deoxy-β-D-glucopyranose, each residue being (1→4)-linked to form linear chains (101). The polysaccharide may be considered as an analogue of cellulose, the hydroxyl groups at C-2 positions of cellulose being replaced by acetamido groups.

(101)

Chitin rarely occurs alone in nature, it being complexed or covalently bound to protein in the shells of crabs and lobsters. This property may be attributed to the more recently discovered fact that not all the amino groups of the majority of chitins are N-acetylated. Accordingly they can operate as basic groups and thereby complex with other molecules of a suitable ionic disposition. Chitin is insoluble in water and many organic solvents, which has made its structural determination difficult, its insolubility being reflected in its low reactivity towards methylation. The majority of samples obtained as a result of treatment with mineral acid have a degree of de-*N*-acetylation and are also of lower molecular weight than chitin in its native state. X-ray diffraction studies of crystalline chitin has shown that the unit cell contains two chains with bent conformations with inter- and intra-molecular hydrogen bonding in a similar manner to cellulose.

A group of animal polysaccharides, the glycosaminoglycans, which normally exist covalently bound to protein, are discussed in the chapter on glycoproteins and proteoglycans (Chapter 9).

The occurrence, isolation, structure and chemistry of all the polysaccharides mentioned in this chapter, and of many other polysaccharides, are regularly reviewed in an ongoing series of articles (Various Authors, 1968 onwards). More detailed reviews of cell-surface carbohydrates can be found in Cook and Stoddart, 1973, Hughes, 1975, and Sutherland, 1977.

CHAPTER 9

Glycoproteins and proteoglycans

CLASSIFICATION

Many macromolecules were originally believed to consist entirely of protein and it was formerly believed that any carbohydrate found in the presence of these biological macromolecules from such sources as human red blood cells and mucous secretions was an impurity. The chemical evidence, reported in 1865, that elemental analysis of a purified mucin yielded values for carbon and nitrogen significantly lower than the values required for pure protein was inconsistent with this, but not understood at the time.

Originally the carbohydrate which was released on acidic hydrolysis was thought to be glucose. Gradually the picture emerged that a number of natural macromolecules (that is, glycoproteins) exist in which carbohydrate forms only part of the total structure. The difficulty in isolating undegraded carbohydrate moieties from the protein (except in the case of the glycosaminoglycans), and the evidence that the heterosaccharides present in a single species of glycoprotein are often not identical but show minor variations in their composition, have made the progress in structural elucidation of glycoproteins much slower, but reviews published on this subject (Gottschalk, 1972, Cook and Stoddart, 1973, Sharon, 1975, Sharon and Lis, 1979, and Various Authors, 1968 onwards) show that a vast amount of work has already been pursued. Undoubtedly improved methods of compositional analysis for carbohydrate together with the above-mentioned developments in structural analysis have led to the discovery that carbohydrate is an integral part of many molecules hitherto described as proteins. This necessary readjustment of description is one which is currently being repeated over and over again, but many authors continue to refer to some glycoproteins as proteins. Some proteins have been shown to contain no carbohydrate using the most recent methods of analysis and are therefore designated as proteins *per se*. An example of such a compound is concanavalin A, a plant lectin (see p. 209).

'Glycoproteins' is a term used (often too generally) to apply to any macromolecule which contains carbohydrate and protein, and in such loose areas of use the term really applies to molecules which if properly classified come under the headings of glycoproteins, proteoglycans and carbohydrate–protein complexes. Glycoproteins contain a protein chain which consists of about 200 or so aminoacid units which are any of the 20 naturally occurring L-α-aminoacids (Fig. 9.1). Covalently attached to this protein backbone and pendent to it is/are the carbohydrate part(s) of the molecule, consisting of hetero-oligosaccharide chains. These are usually branched (Fig. 9.2(a)) and can contain neutral monosaccharides (D-glucose, D-galactose, D-mannose or L-fucose), basic monosaccharides (2-amino-2-deoxy-D-glucose or 2-amino-2-deoxy-D-galactose) and the unique nine-carbon sugar, 5-amino-3,5-dideoxy-D-*glycero*-D-*galacto*-2-nonulopyranonic acid. The basic residues are usually *N*-acetylated and the 5-amino-3,5-dideoxy-D-*glycero*-D-*galacto*-2-nonulopyranonic acid residues may be *N*-glycolyated or *N*-acetylated, and in some cases, certain hydroxyl groups are also *O*-acetylated. Thus oligosaccharide chains are rendered mildly acidic on account of the free carboxyl group in the nine-carbon sugar.

Neutral aminoacids (one amino and one carboxyl group)

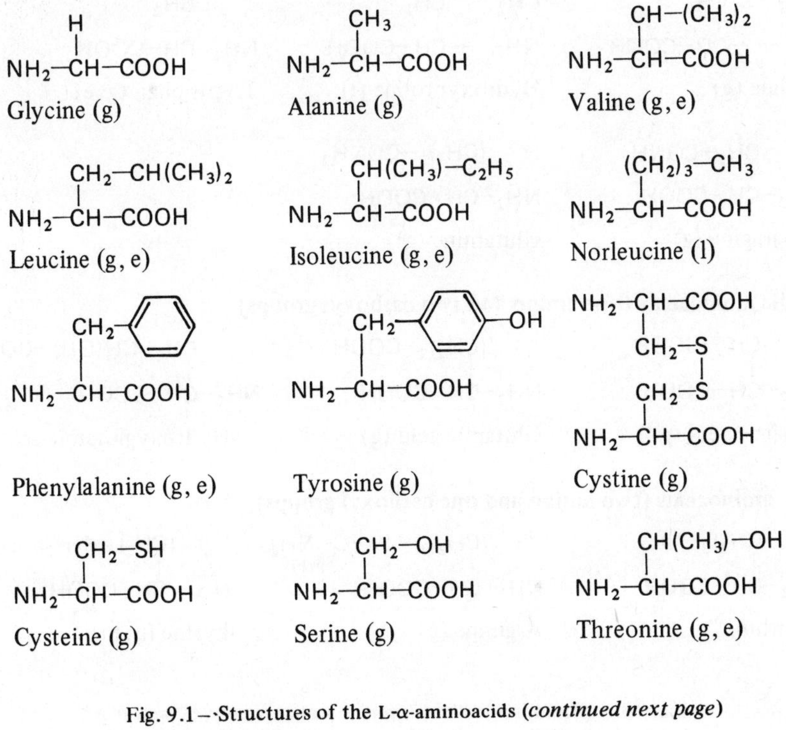

Fig. 9.1 – Structures of the L-α-aminoacids (*continued next page*)

$CH_2-CH_2-S-CH_3$
$NH_2-CH-COOH$
Methionine (g, e)

Di-iodotyrosine (l)
(Iodogoric acid)

Dibromotyrosine (l)

Thyroxine (l)
(Tetraiodothyronine, T_4)

Tri-iodothyronine (l)
(T_3)

Proline (g)

Hydroxyproline (l)

Tryptophan (g, e)

CH_2-CONH_2
$NH_2-CH-COOH$
Asparagine (g)

$(CH_2)_2-CONH_2$
$NH_2-CH-COOH$
Glutamine (g)

Acidic aminoacids (one amino and two carboxyl groups)

CH_2-COOH
$NH_2-CH-COOH$
Aspartic acid (g)

$(CH_2)_2-COOH$
$NH_2-CH-COOH$
Glutamic acid (g)

$CH_2-CH(OH)-COOH$
$NH_2-CH-COOH$
γ-Hydroxyglutamic acid[a] (l)

Basic aminoacids (two amino and one carboxyl groups)

$(CH_2)_3-NH_2$
$NH_2-CH-COOH$
Ornithine[b]

$(CH_2)_3-NH-C-NH_2$
$NH_2-CH-COOH$ $\quad$ NH
Arginine (g)

$(CH_2)_4-NH_2$
$NH_2-CH-COOH$
Lysine (g, e)

Fig. 9.1 – Structures of the L-α-aminoacids (*continued next page*)

Histidine (g)

$NH_2-CH-COOH$

$(CH_2)_2-CH(OH)-CH_2-NH_2$

$NH_2-CH-COOH$

δ-Hydroxylysine (l)

General stereochemistry for L-aminoacids

H_2N-C-H, COOH, R

a Occurrence in proteins uncertain

b Ornithine is probably not present in proteins, but is formed by the hydrolysis of arginine.

(e) Essential in man   (g) General occurrence   (l) Less common occurrence

Fig. 9.1 – Structures of the L-α-aminoacids.

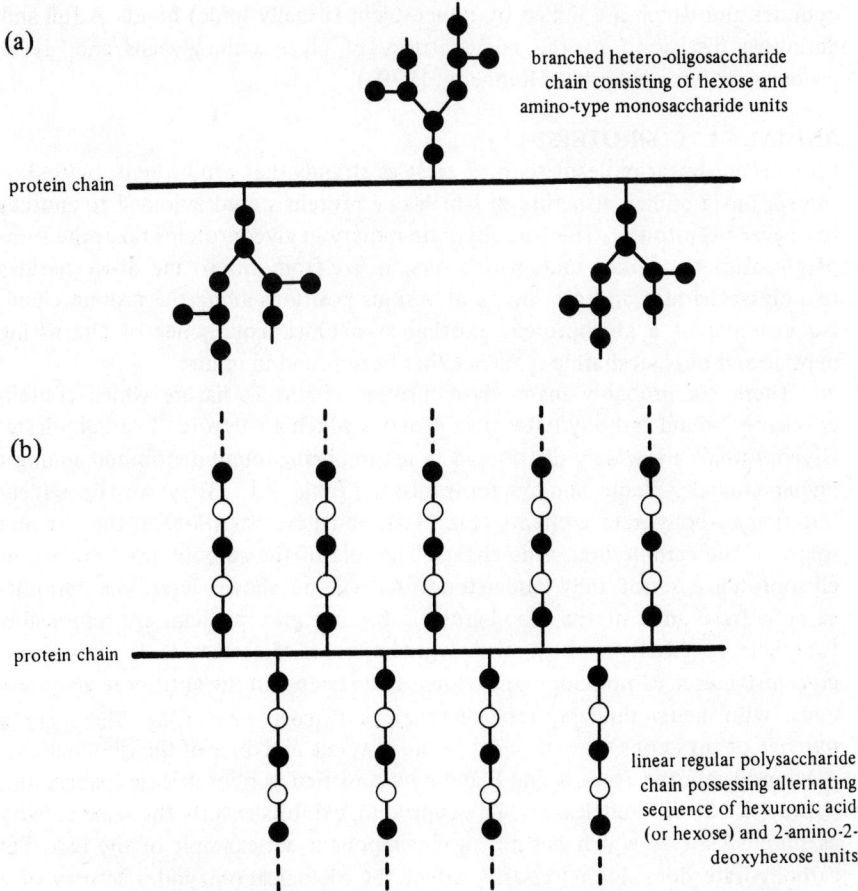

(a)

branched hetero-oligosaccharide chain consisting of hexose and amino-type monosaccharide units

protein chain

(b)

protein chain

linear regular polysaccharide chain possessing alternating sequence of hexuronic acid (or hexose) and 2-amino-2-deoxyhexose units

Fig. 9.2 – General comparative representation of (a) glycoproteins, and (b) proteoglycans

Proteoglycans also contain a backbone of protein, but the carbohydrate residue takes the form of linear chains possessing regular alternating monosaccharides (Fig. 9.2(b)) involving acidic monosaccharide (D-glucuronic acid or L-iduronic acid) and basic monosaccharide (2-amino-2-deoxy-D-galactose and 2-amino-2-deoxy-D-glucose). The basic units are usually *N*-acetylated and sometimes *N*-sulphated and the acidic units are sometimes *O*-sulphated. This results in the chains being strongly acidic, a factor recognized in their former names of 'acidic mucopolysaccharides'. The systematic name for these chains is 'glycosaminoglycans'.

A factor distinguishing glycoproteins from proteoglycans, as the names suggest, is the number of carbohydrate units per unit length (or molecular weight) of protein backbone, with protein being predominant in glycoprotein and carbohydrates predominating in proteoglycans. The term carbohydrate-protein complex is used to describe entities which contain protein and carbohydrates and which are linked by noncovalent (usually ionic) bonds. A full and definitive discussion of the nomenclature of glycosaminoglycans and glycoproteins has been published (Kennedy, 1979a).

ANIMAL GLYCOPROTEINS

Proteins are linear molecules which exist as strands that can be bent, twisted or folded, but a branch structure in which one protein strand is joined to another has never been found. The carbohydrate moiety in glycoproteins takes the form of glycosidically linked units which vary in size from mono- and di-saccharides to polysaccharides and are linked at various positions along the protein chain. No example of a glycoprotein existing as a block copolymer of alternating peptide and oligosaccharide sequences has been found in nature.

There are probably many more protein chains in nature which contain covalently bound carbohydrates than proteins which are devoid of carbohydrate. Glycoproteins are widely distributed in nature, being found distributed amongst higher animals, plants and microorganisms (Table 9.1). They contain widely differing carbohydrate contents (Fig. 9.3), and have variations in the size and shape of the carbohydrate side chains. The role of the carbohydrate moiety of glycoproteins is not fully understood. As will be shown later, the terminal carbohydrate units of the blood-group substance glycoproteins are responsible for their specificity, whilst the degradation of 5-acetamido-3,5-dideoxy-D-*glycero*-D-*galacto*-2-nonulopyranosylonic acid residues in the antifreeze glycoproteins, with neuraminidase, removes their antifreeze properties. There are a number of mysteries, one of which is the enzymic activities of the ribonucleases previously referred to as A and B and now classified as ribonuclease (pancreatic) (EC 3.1.27.5). Ribonuclease B, a glycoprotein, exhibits exactly the same activity as ribonuclease A which has no sugar component, an example of the fact that carbohydrate does not necessarily affect the biological (enzymic) activity of a molecule. A number of proposals have been put forward to explain the presence of carbohydrate, ranging from providing components for intercellular communication and handles for transportation of proteins from one part to another of a cell, to rendering proteins resistant to enzymatic degradation but allowing them to be recognized by certain receptor sites (Ryle *et al*., 1970).

Table 9.1 Distribution and function of some glycoproteins

Presumed function	Name
Enzyme	Acetyl cholinesterase
	Bromelain
	Ficin
	Porcine α-amylase
	Porcine deoxyribonuclease
	Ribonuclease (pancreatic)
	Taka-amylase (a fungal α-amylase)
	Yeast invertase (a β-D-fructofuranosidase)
Food reserve	Casein
	Endosperm glycoproteins
	Ovalbumin
	Pollen allergens
Hormone	Erythropoietin
	Follicle-stimulating hormone
	Human chorionic gonadotrophin
	Luteinizing hormone
	Thyroglobulin
Plasma and body fluids	α-, β-, and γ-Glycoproteins
Protective	Fibrinogen
	Immunoglobulin
	Interferon
	Mucins
Structural	Bacterial cell wall
	Collagen
	Extensin (plant cell wall)
Toxin	Fungal phytotoxins
	Ricin
Transport	Ceruloplasmin
	Haptoglobin
	Transferrin
Unknown	Avidin (egg white)
	Blood-group substances

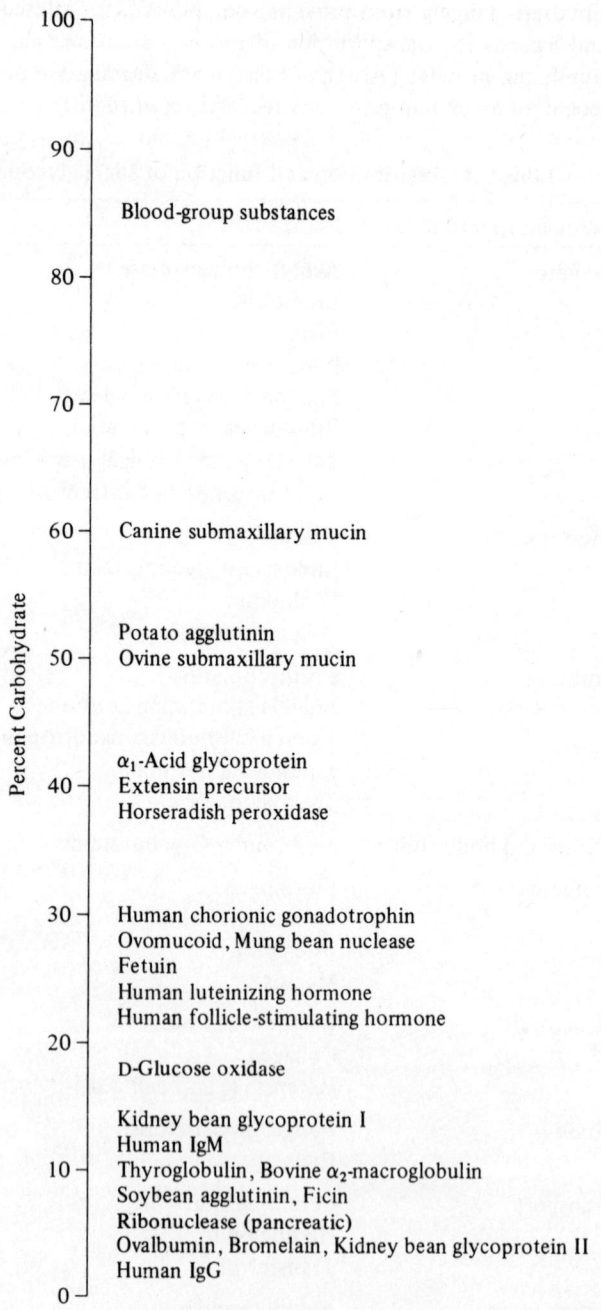

Fig. 9.3 – Carbohydrate content of some glycoproteins.

As many of the glycoproteins contain only a small proportion of carbohydrate, structural investigations are facilitated by the use of proteolytic enzymes (for example, pronase EC 3.4.24.4) to give glycopeptides which contain a small number of aminoacid residues to which are attached the intact carbohydrate chains. These glycopeptides may be analysed, not without problems, by the classical methods of periodate oxidation and methylation, or by sequential enzyme hydrolysis methods (see Chapter 4) to characterise the component monosaccharide residues and ideally give a single aminoacid residue linked to a monosaccharide unit. Only two types of linkage have been found to occur, namely *O*-glycosidic linkages to L-serine, L-threonine, hydroxy-L-proline and hydroxy-L-lysine and *N*-glycosylamide linkages to L-asparagine. Only five monosaccharide units have been shown to be involved in these linkages, L-arabinose, D-xylose, D-galactose, 2-acetamido-2-deoxy-D-glucose and 2-acetamido-2-deoxy-D-galactose. By way of example, a number of glycoproteins will be discussed to show the structure of their carbohydrate moieties since no classification can readily be made in terms of structural features.

Hormonal glycoproteins

This group of glycoproteins includes follicle-stimulating hormone (FSH), luteinizing hormone (LH), human chorionic gonadotrophin (hCG), human menopausal gonadotrophin (hMP), pregnant-mare serum gonadotrophin, and thyroid-stimulating hormone (TSH). The determination of primary structures of the carbohydrate moieties of these glycoproteins (particularly the human form) is still in its infancy due to the problems of isolating quantities of a pure hormone from closely similar (in chemical and physical nature) hormones and other macromolecules, including glycoproteins present in the media or origin of the sample. The purification of a particular hormone involves a complex series of purification stages in which advantage is taken of the properties peculiar to the hormone molecule, namely acidic and basic groups from certain aminoacid residues and acidic groups of 5-acetamido-3,5-dideoxy-D-*glycero*-D-*galacto*-nonulopyranonic acid. It is essential to monitor purification stages by determination of biological activity because no chemical (strictly abiological) method is hormone specific, and loss of a few residues can remove all biological activity; thus conditions which do not deviate markedly from the physiological have to be used. As the purification proceeds, it becomes more difficult as the remaining impurities become predominantly more and more those that are most similar to the hormone. Microheterogeneity complicates the separations relying on molecular change due to variation in, for example, the 5-amino-3,5-dideoxy-D-*glycero*-D-*galacto*-2-nonulopyranonic acid content, particularly as it now appears that some carbohydrate and aminoacid residues, particularly in certain terminal positions, are not essential for hormonal activity.

An example of a typical glycoprotein purification process is that applied to human follicle-stimulating hormone which involves a number of chromatographic separations on calcium phosphate, ion-exchange resins and gel filtration media but which has achieved a purification of 5000 fold (Butt *et al.*, 1972). Immunoadsorption methods of separation are showing great promise as the purification can theoretically take place in one stage particularly if the hormone can be isolated in very high purity initially in order to allow the specific antibody to be raised, although initial high purity is not an absolute requirement.

Immunological reactions of the hormonal glycoproteins have shown that considerable similarities exist between these hormones; for example, the antiserum to follicle-stimulating hormone cross-reacts with luteinizing hormone, human chorionic gonadotrophin and thyroid-stimulating hormone, indicating the presence of a number of common antigenic groups in these hormones as well as their specific antigenic groups. These hormones have been shown to contain subunits, which can be formed by the action of trypsin, 1 M propionic acid, 8M urea, or sodium dodecyl sulphate. According to tests carried out on human glycoproteins a pattern has emerged and it seems quite certain that the β-subunits are hormone specific whereas the α-subunits are interchangeable. Such a finding is in keeping with the similarities of the aminoacid sequences of the α-subunits but the unique characters of the β-subunits. Recombination of subunits can be effected by incubation together under physiological conditions, the resulting biological activity being greater than the sum of the biological activities of the separate subunits. It has also been found that the subunits of a particular hormone from various species are interchangeable as far as activity is concerned. More important, however, is the fact that hybrid molecules can be produced by combining subunits from different hormonal glycoproteins, the type of hormonal activity of the hybrid glycoprotein being designated by the activity in which the β-subunit used was originally involved.

The application of glycoside hydrolases to the intact human follicle-stimulating hormone for the purpose of carbohydrate sequence determination has proved disappointing due to the inhibition of release of the monosaccharide units by adjacent parts of the molecule, but it has identified the nonreducing terminal groups as 5-acetamido-3,5-dideoxy-D-*glycero*-D-*galacto*-2-nonulopyranosylonic acid which are adjacent to D-galactosyl residues. Methylation and identification of the hydrolysis products by gas-liquid chromatography amd mass spectrometry demonstrated that L-fucose groups occupy nonreducing terminal positions, D-galactosyl residues are linked in the 1- and 2-positions, the D-mannosyl residues are present as nonreducing terminal groups, 1,6-linked residues and 1,3,4-linked branch points, with the 2-acetamido-2-deoxy-D-glucosyl residues 1,6-linked, all the sugars being in the pyranose form.

The use of glycoside hydrolases and chemical methods in the analysis of human chorionic gonadotrophin has been more successful with some studies on the linkage and sequence of the carbohydrate units on the intact molecule.

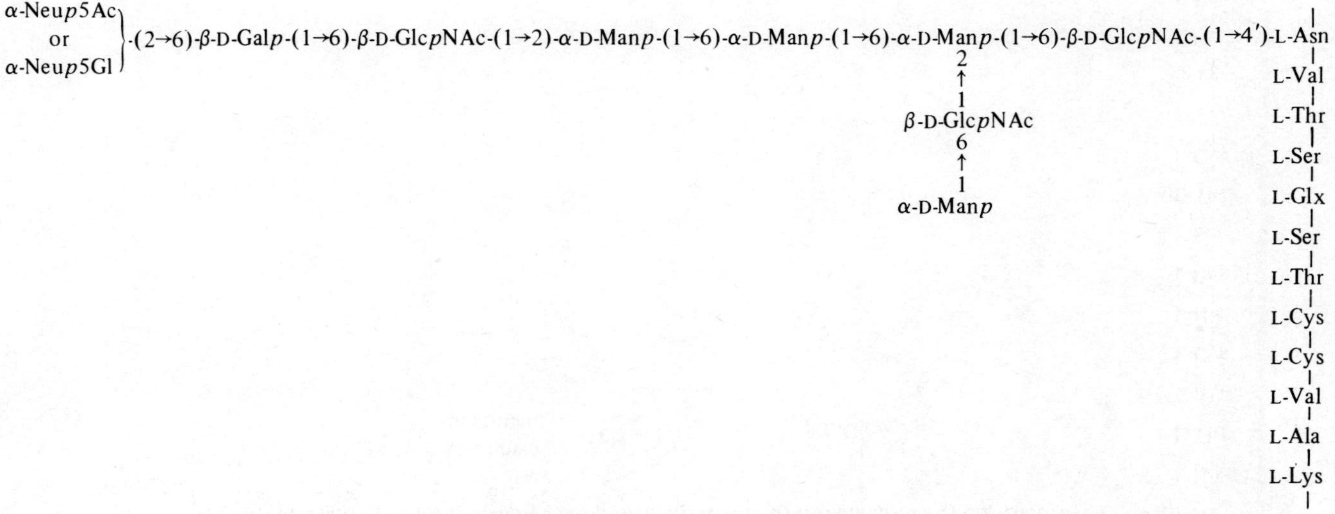

$$
\begin{array}{c}
\left.\begin{array}{c}\alpha\text{-Neu}p5\text{Ac}\\ \text{or}\\ \alpha\text{-Neu}p5\text{Gl}\end{array}\right\}\text{-}(2\rightarrow6)\text{-}\beta\text{-}D\text{-Gal}p\text{-}(1\rightarrow6)\text{-}\beta\text{-}D\text{-Glc}p\text{NAc-}(1\rightarrow2)\text{-}\alpha\text{-}D\text{-Man}p\text{-}(1\rightarrow6)\text{-}\alpha\text{-}D\text{-Man}p\text{-}(1\rightarrow6)\text{-}\alpha\text{-}D\text{-Man}p\text{-}(1\rightarrow6)\text{-}\beta\text{-}D\text{-Glc}p\text{NAc-}(1\rightarrow4')\text{-L-Asn} \\
\end{array}
$$

with branches:

$$
\beta\text{-}D\text{-Glc}p\text{NAc} \xrightarrow{\ 1\ }\!{}^{2}\qquad \alpha\text{-}D\text{-Man}p \xrightarrow{\ 1\ }\!{}^{6}
$$

Peptide chain:

—L-Val—L-Thr—L-Ser—L-Glx—L-Ser—L-Thr—L-Cys—L-Cys—L-Val—L-Ala—L-Lys—

(102)

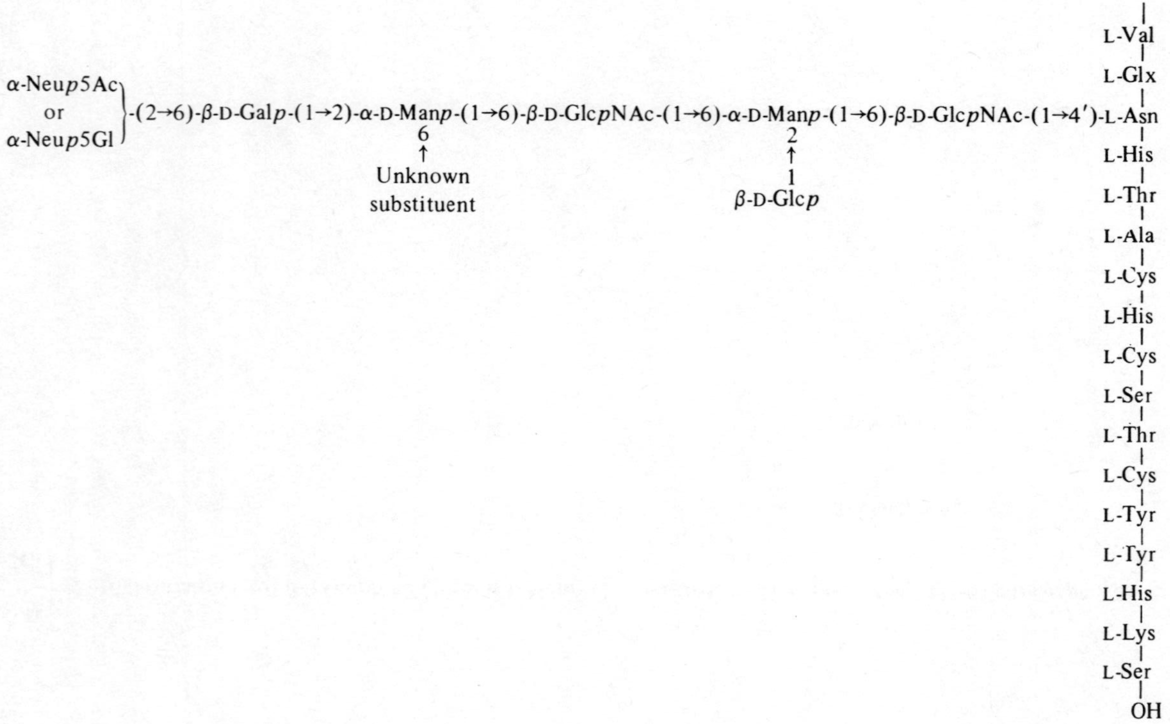

$$
\begin{array}{l}
\text{L-Val} \\
| \\
\text{L-Glx} \\
| \\
\text{L-Asn} \\
| \\
\text{L-His} \\
| \\
\text{L-Thr} \\
| \\
\text{L-Ala} \\
| \\
\text{L-Cys} \\
| \\
\text{L-His} \\
| \\
\text{L-Cys} \\
| \\
\text{L-Ser} \\
| \\
\text{L-Thr} \\
| \\
\text{L-Cys} \\
| \\
\text{L-Tyr} \\
| \\
\text{L-Tyr} \\
| \\
\text{L-His} \\
| \\
\text{L-Lys} \\
| \\
\text{L-Ser} \\
| \\
\text{OH}
\end{array}
$$

$$
\left.
\begin{array}{l}
\alpha\text{-Neu}p5\text{Ac} \\
\text{or} \\
\alpha\text{-Neu}p5\text{Gl}
\end{array}
\right\}
\text{-}(2{\to}6)\text{-}\beta\text{-D-Gal}p\text{-}(1{\to}2)\text{-}\alpha\text{-D-Man}p\text{-}(1{\to}6)\text{-}\beta\text{-D-Glc}p\text{NAc-}(1{\to}6)\text{-}\alpha\text{-D-Man}p\text{-}(1{\to}6)\text{-}\beta\text{-D-Glc}p\text{NAc-}(1{\to}4')\text{-L-Asn}
$$

Unknown substituent
6
↑
(below α-D-Manp)

β-D-Glcp
1
2
↑
(below β-D-GlcpNAc)

(103)

Studies on the pure α-subunit revealed the presence of two glycopeptide structures (102) and (103).

The structural requirements essential for the biological activity of the hormonal glycoproteins have been investigated, using a variety of techniques. Photo-oxidation has been used to modify selectively the side-chain functional groups of certain aminoacid residues, namely L-histidine, L-tryptophan and L-tyrosine, by destruction of the aromatic ring systems. Other chemical methods used to modify selectively the protein or carbohydrate residues include periodate oxidation, mild acid hydrolysis, methylation, and reaction with maleic anhydride, N-acetylimidazole, t-butyl azidoformate and formaldehyde. The use of highly purified enzymes, including trypsin, chymotrypsin, β-D-galactosidase, α-D-mannosidase, neuraminidase, etc., has also been made. It has been shown, by the application of such techniques, that terminal 5-acetamido-3,5-dideoxy-D-*glycero*-D-*galacto*-2-nonulopyranosylonic acid residues are essential for the transport, but not the biological activity of the hormones. The carbohydrate moiety, L-tryptophan residues and the guanido group of L-arginine residues have been shown to be essential for the hormonal activity of both follicle-stimulating hormone and luteinizing hormone.

Serum and plasma glycoproteins

Many of the 'proteins' in plasma and serum have now been identified as glycoproteins, only serum albumin and prealbumin having no carbohydrate moieties. The structure and functions of many of these have been reviewed, including the role of the carbohydrate in regulating the survival time of plasma glycoprotein in sera (Ashwell and Morell, 1974). Examples of these glycoproteins include α_1-acid glycoprotein (orosomucoid), transferrin, and fetuin; aspects of their carbohydrate structures are discussed by way of examples.

α_1-Acid glycoprotein is the serum glycoprotein having the highest carbohydrate content (*ca*. 40%) and much work has been carried out on its structure since variations in its content in serum occurs in some diseases. Carbohydrate analyses have shown the components to be 2-acetamido-2-deoxy-D-glucose (12.2 to 15.3%), D-mannose (4.7 to 6.5%), D-galactose (6.5 to 12.2%), L-fucose (0.7 to 1.5%) and 5-acetamido-3,5-dideoxy-D-*glycero*-D-*galacto*-2-nonulopyranonic acid (10.8 to 14.7%) in which L-fucosyl and 5-acetamido-3,5-dideoxy-D-*glycero*-D-*galacto*-2-nonulopyranosylonic acid groups are the nonreducing terminal groups linked principally to D-galactosyl residues. A number of possible structures have been postulated for the glycoprotein, after removal of the 5-acetamido-3,5-dideoxy-D-*glycero*-D-*galacto*-2-nonulopyranosylonic acid groups of which (104) is representative.

Transferrin is a glycoprotein which forms complexes with iron and is responsible for transporting iron from the storage form in tissues, especially in liver, to the metabolically functioning iron in haemoglobin. The carbohydrate chain has been characterised by periodate oxidation, methylation and glycoside hydrolase digestion to give a structure (105) for the oligosaccharide chains.

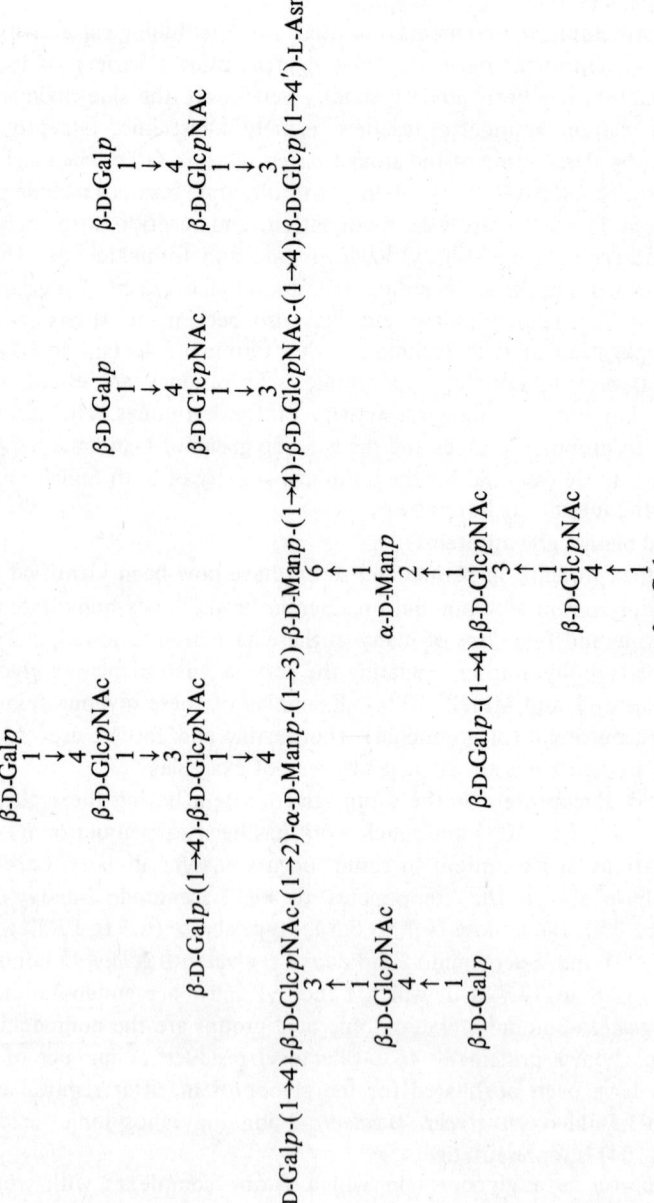

(104)

Neup5Ac-(2→6)-D-Gal-(1→3 or 4)-D-GlcNAc-(1→3)-D-Man-(1→2 or 4)-

D-Man-(1→2 or 4)-D-Man-(1→2, 4 or 6)-D-Man-(1→3 or 4)-D-GlcNAc-(1→4')-L-Asn
3
↑
1
Neup5Ac-(2→6)-D-Gal-(1→3 or 4)-D-GlcNAc-(1→3 or 4)-D-GlcNAc

(105)

```
  α-Neup5Ac           α-Neup5Ac           α-Neup5Ac
      2                   2                   2
      ↓                   ↓                   ↓
      3                   3                   3
  β-D-Galp            β-D-Galp            β-D-Galp
      1                   1                   1
      ↓                   ↓                   ↓
      4                   4                   4
  β-D-GlcpNAc         β-D-GlcpNAc         β-D-GlcpNAc
      1                   1                   1
      ↓                   ↓                   ↓
      2                  3 or 4             2, 4 or 6
```
α-D-Manp-(1→2 or 6)-α-D-Manp-(1→3)-β-D-Manp-(1→4)-β-D-GlcpNAc-(1→4)-β-D-GlcpNAc-(1→4')-L-Asn

(106)

α-Neup5Ac-(2→3)-β-D-Galp-(1→3)-α-Neup5Ac-(2→6)-α-D-GalpNAc-(1→3')-L-Ser (or L-Thr)

(107)

Fetuin is the principle glycoprotein in foetal calf serum, but becomes gradually replaced by the 'normal' glycoproteins of adult serum. Fetuin resembles α_1-acid glycoprotein in many of its properties and the structure of an oligosaccharide chain (106) has been shown to have similarities in its core structure (the carbohydrate units nearest the aminoacid unit). However, oligosaccharides have been found which are glycosidically linked to L-serine and L-threonine (107), some of which lack the internal 5-acetamido-3,5-dideoxy-D-*glycero*-D-*galacto*-2-nonulopyranosylonic acid residues (Spiro and Bhoyroo, 1974) showing the presence of a different type of oligosaccharide chain attached to the glycoprotein.

Immunoglobulins

Immunoglobulins are a group of serum glycoproteins that have antibody activity and are produced in response to stimuli by antigens. There are, at present, five classes of immunoglobulins known, which are designated IgG, IgA, IgM, IgD and IgE and those that have been examined all contain, in their monomeric form, the same fundamental structure of four polypeptides chains linked by interchain disulphide bonds. These chains are of two kinds, so-called light and heavy chains, with each monomer containing two of each (see Fig. 9.4). The light chains are of two kinds, kappa (κ) and lambda (λ), which differ in the allotypic specificity they carry. These are common to all immunoglobulin classes and an individual immunoglobulin monomer will contain two light chains, either two κ or two λ chains. The heavy chains are specific to, and determine the class of, the immunoglobulin. Each class of immunoglobulin has its own characteristic carbohydrate content which varies from about 22 monosaccharide units in IgG to about 82 units in monomeric IgM. Polymeric forms of immunoglobulin have been reported and include dimeric IgA and pentameric IgM. Macromolecular IgM is thought to contain five monomer units joined in the form of a ring from which radiate the five arms.

Normal IgG contains three glycopeptides representing two types of oligosaccharide units. Periodate oxidation analysis has shown that some of the 2-acetamido-2-deoxy-D-glucopyranosyl and D-mannopyranosyl residues are ($1\rightarrow3$)-linked and other results based on mild acid hydrolysis suggest that L-fucosyl and 5-acetamido-3,5-dideoxy-D-*glycero*-D-*galacto*-2-nonulopyranosylonic acid residues are present at nonreducing terminal positions, linked to D-galactose, with D-mannopyranosyl residues substituted at O-3 or occurring at branch points, and some 2-acetamido-2-deoxy-D-glycosyl residues, those oxidized by periodate, linked *via* O-6 or in a terminal position. These results, plus information obtained from glycoside hydrolase degradation studies, led to the proposal of structure (108) for human IgG. Similar structures have been found for human IgE and IgA, all having various amounts of nonreducing terminal 5-acetamido-3,5-dideoxy-D-*glycero*-D-*galacto*-2-nonulopyranosylonic acid and D-galactosyl residues indicating various stages of completion of the outer chains or microheterogeneity. Bovine IgG contains a glycopeptide (109) which is identical to human IgG minus the 5-acetamido-3,5-dideoxy-D-*glycero*-D-*galacto*-2-nonulopyranosylonic acid residues.

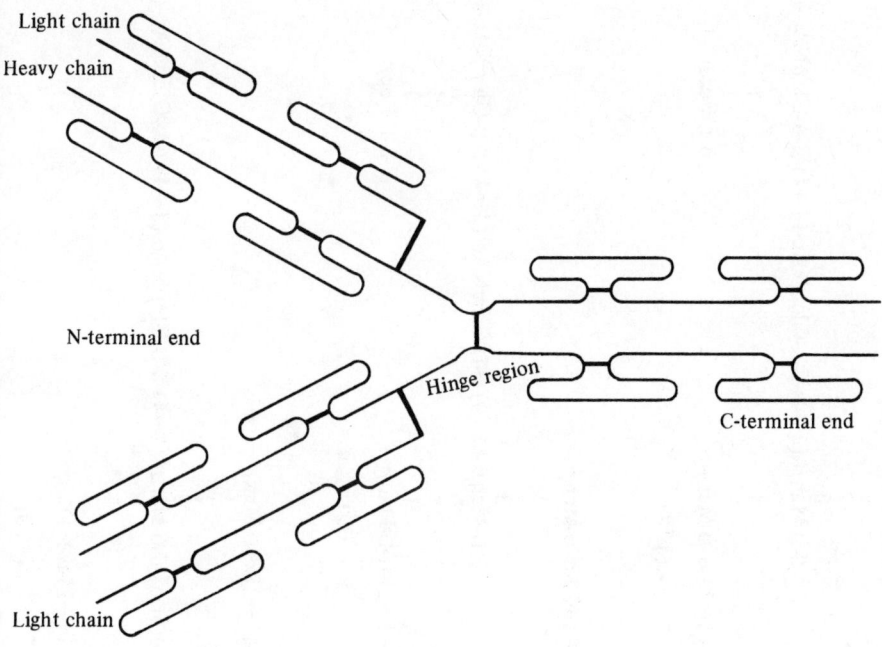

Fig. 9.4 – Schematic representation of an immunoglobin molecule.
(━ represents a disulphide bond).

Characteristically different variations in glycopeptide structures to those described above have been found in human IgA myeloma glycopeptide 11A (110), which lacks L-fucose and has an extra 2-acetamido-2-deoxy-D-glucosyl residue on the branch point D-mannosyl residue. Glycopeptide B-3 from human myeloma IgG also has a difference in the core structure (111). The high D-mannose containing glycopeptide C-1 from human IgE has a very different core structure (112) containing alternating D-mannosyl and 2-acetamido-2-deoxy-D-glucosyl residues. One of the 2-acetamido-2-deoxy-D-glucosyl residues uniquely has the α-configuration. These changes in the core structure are to be distinguished from the microheterogeneity resulting from incomplete outer chains, in that changes in the core structure can reflect genetic differences (for example, myeloma).

```
α-Neup5Ac-(2→6)-β-D-Galp-(1→4)-β-D-GlcpNAc-(1→2)-α-D-Manp
                                                      1
                                                      ↓
                                                      3
                     β-D-Manp-(1→4)-β-D-GlcpNAc-(1→4)-β-D-GlcpNAc-(1→4')-L-Asn
                     6                                 6
                     ↑                                 ↑
                     1                                 1
α-Neup5Ac-(2→6)-β-D-Galp-(1→4)-β-D-GlcpNAc-(1→2)-α-D-Manp          α-L-Fucp

                              (108)
```

```
β-D-Galp-(1→4)-β-D-GlcpNAc-(1→2)-α-D-Manp
                                     1
                                     ↓
                                     3
              β-D-Manp-(1→4)-β-D-GlcpNAc-(1→4)-β-D-GlcpNAc-(1→4')-L-Asn
              6                                 6
              ↑                                 ↑
              1                                 1
β-D-Galp-(1→4)-β-D-GlcpNAc-(1→2)-α-D-Manp          α-L-Fucp

                              (109)
```

```
α-Neup5Ac-(2→6)-β-D-Galp-(1→4)-β-D-GlcpNAc-(1→2)-α-D-Manp
                                                      1
                                                      ↓
                                                      3
β-D-GlcpNAc-((1→4 or 6)-β-D-Manp-(1→4)-β-D-GlcpNAc-(1→4)-β-D-GlcpNAc-(1→4')-L-Asn
                         6 or 4
                         ↑
                         1
β-D-Galp-(1→4)-β-D-GlcpNAc-(1→2)-α-D-Manp

                              (110)
```

α-Neu*p*5Ac-(2→6)-β-D-Gal*p*-(1→4)-β-D-Glc*p*NAc-(1→2)-α-D-Man*p*
1
↓
3
β-D-Glc*p*NAc-(1→4)-β-D-Man*p*-(1→4)-β-D-Glc*p*NAc-(1→4)-β-D-Glc*p*NAc-(1→4′)-L-Asn
6   6
↑   ↑
1   1
α-Neu*p*5Ac-(2→6)-β-D-Gal*p*-(1→4)-β-D-Glc*p*NAc-(1→2)-α-D-Man*p*   α-L-Fuc*p*

(111)

β-D-Man*p*-(1→3)-β-D-Man*p*-(1→4)-α-D-Glc*p*NAc-(1→3)-β-D-Man*p*-(1→4)-β-D-Glc*p*NAc-(1→4′)-L-Asn
6   6
↑   ↑
1   1
α-D-Man*p*   α-D-Man*p*
2
↑
1
α-D-Man*p*

(112)

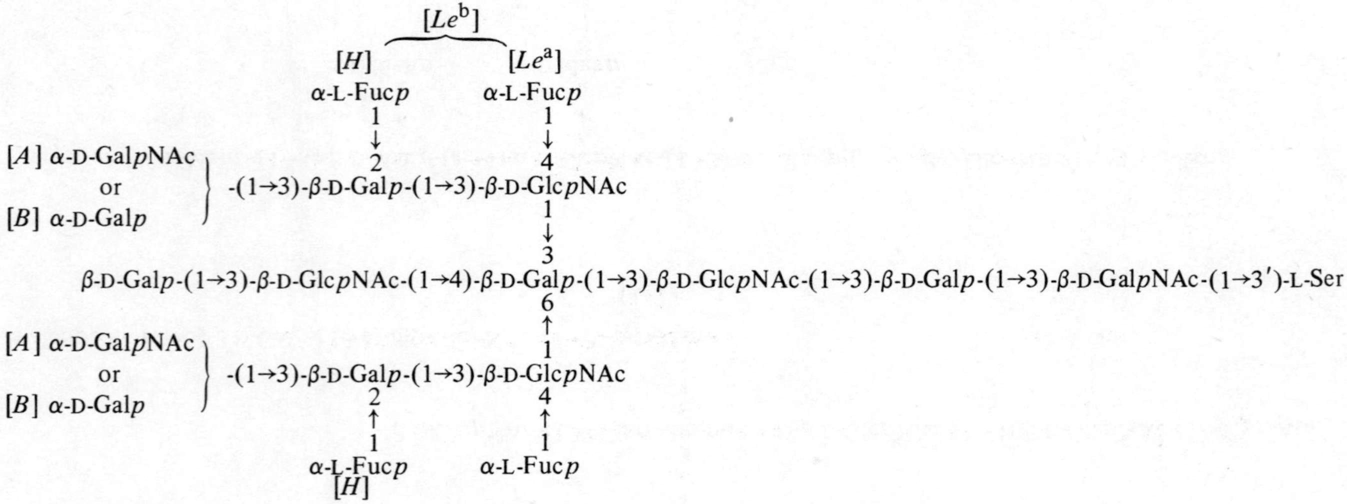

Fig. 9.5 — Composite structure of the carbohydrate chain of blood-group glycoproteins, indicating the residues which confer blood-group A, B, H(O), Le^a and Le^b specificity.

Blood-group substances

Blood-group substances are a group of structurally similar glycoproteins which occur on the surface of red blood cells and are responsible for the determination of particular blood-group types. The importance of the oligosaccharide moiety of the glycoprotein in this specificity has been demonstrated by enzymic removal of terminal 2-acetamido-2-deoxy-D-galactopyranosyl groups from type A erythrocytes or D-galactopyranosyl groups from type B erythrocytes which resulted in both being converted to type O erythrocytes. Confirmation of these results is found in the determination of specific enzymes (the relevant glycosyl-transferases involved in the blood-group substance biosynthesis) in the blood. Type A blood has an enzyme which will transfer 2-acetamido-2-deoxy-D-galactose to a core oligosaccharide whilst type B blood contains an enzyme catalysing transfer of D-galactose to the same core. Type O blood has neither enzyme.

The structure of the carbohydrate chains has been analysed using immunological methods to determine changes in serological activity on hydrolysis by acid or specific enzymes. This gives information on the specific terminal carbohydrate units responsible for the immunological specificity. Alkaline degradation has shown that linkage of the oligosaccharide chain to the protein molecule is *via* glycosidic linkages to L-serine or L-threonine. The structures of these glycoproteins with respect to their immunological properties have been reviewed (Hakomori and Kobata, 1974), and a composite structure has been proposed to indicate the residues which confer blood-group specificity for A, B, H(O), Le[a] and Le[b] (Fig. 9.5).

Involvement in diseases

Since glycoproteins are probably involved in coding and decoding of the intercellular messages required for the correct movement and assembly of cells that will eventually form the mature central nervous system, a genetic defect in their biosynthesis or regulation could account for many of the mental retardation syndromes that result from developmental impairment. However, this field remains relatively unexplored and no conclusions have yet been made.

The mechanisms by which glycoproteins are catabolised is perhaps better understood, and, with the possible exception of the removal of 5-acetamido-3,5-dideoxy-D-*glycero*-D-*galacto*-2-nonulopyranosylonic acid residues, the carbohydrate units are degraded by the sequential action of a group of lysosomal glycoside hydrolases (see Table 9.2). As will be seen later (Chapter 10), some of these enzymes are also involved in glycolipid catabolism. In some of the lipidoses impaired glycoprotein catabolism is a secondary effect but in other cases, namely fucosidosis, α-D-mannosidosis and aspartylglucosaminuria, the glycoprotein-derived storage material due to a deficiency in the required catabolic enzyme can be considered to be a major cause of the observed severe mental retardation. The structures of the storage material in many cases has been determined (see reviews

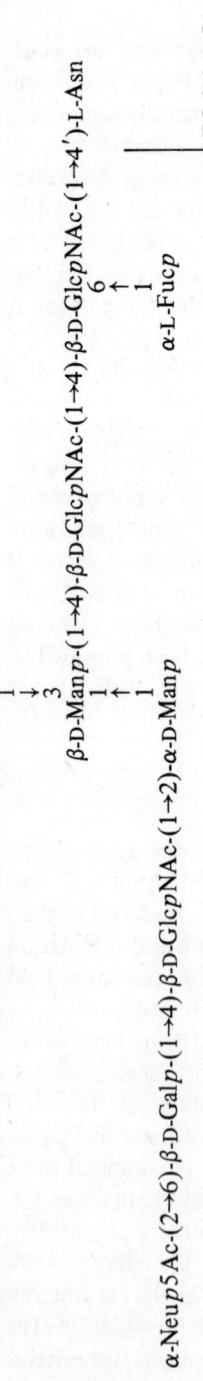

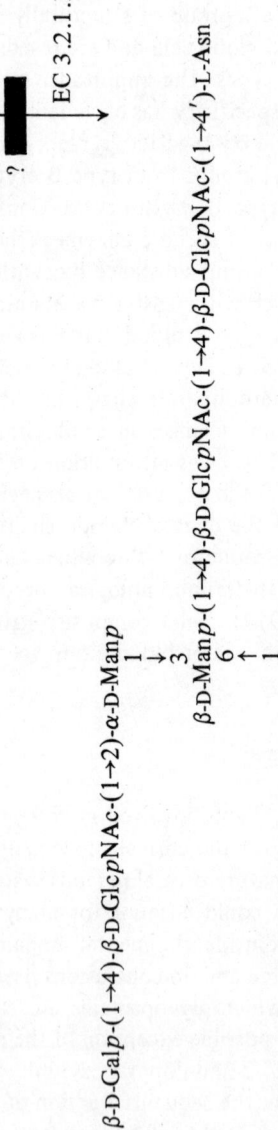

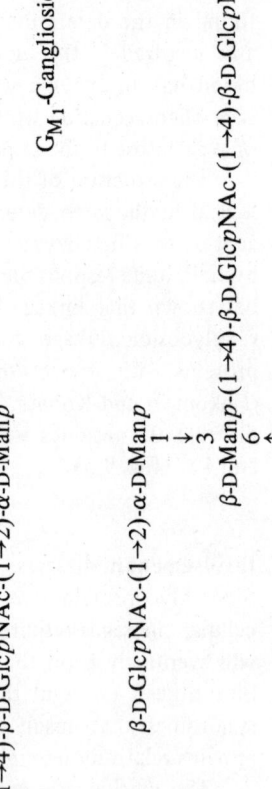

EC 3.2.1.51

EC 3.2.1.18

EC 3.2.1.23

G_{M1}-Gangliosidosis

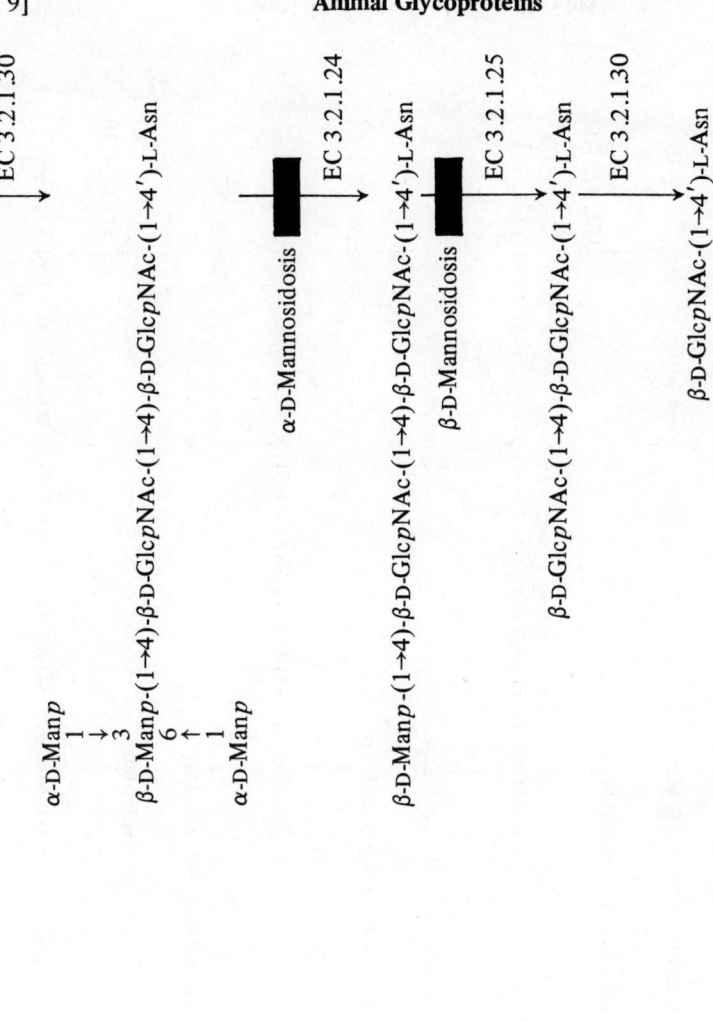

Sandoff's Disease

EC 3.2.1.30

α-D-Man*p*
1
↓ 3
β-D-Man*p*-(1→4)-β-D-Glc*p*NAc-(1→4)-β-D-Glc*p*NAc-(1→4')-L-Asn
6
↑ 1
α-D-Man*p*

α-D-Mannosidosis

EC 3.2.1.24

β-D-Man*p*-(1→4)-β-D-Glc*p*NAc-(1→4)-β-D-Glc*p*NAc-(1→4')-L-Asn

β-D-Mannosidosis

EC 3.2.1.25

β-D-Glc*p*NAc-(1→4)-β-D-Glc*p*NAc-(1→4')-L-Asn

EC 3.2.1.30

β-D-Glc*p*NAc-(1→4')-L-Asn

Aspartylglycosaminuria

EC 3.5.1.37

D-Glc*p*NAc + L-Asn

Fig. 9.6(a) – Proposed schematic catabolic pathway for immunoglobulin glycoproteins showing possible sites for blockages in known inborn errors of glycoprotein catabolism.

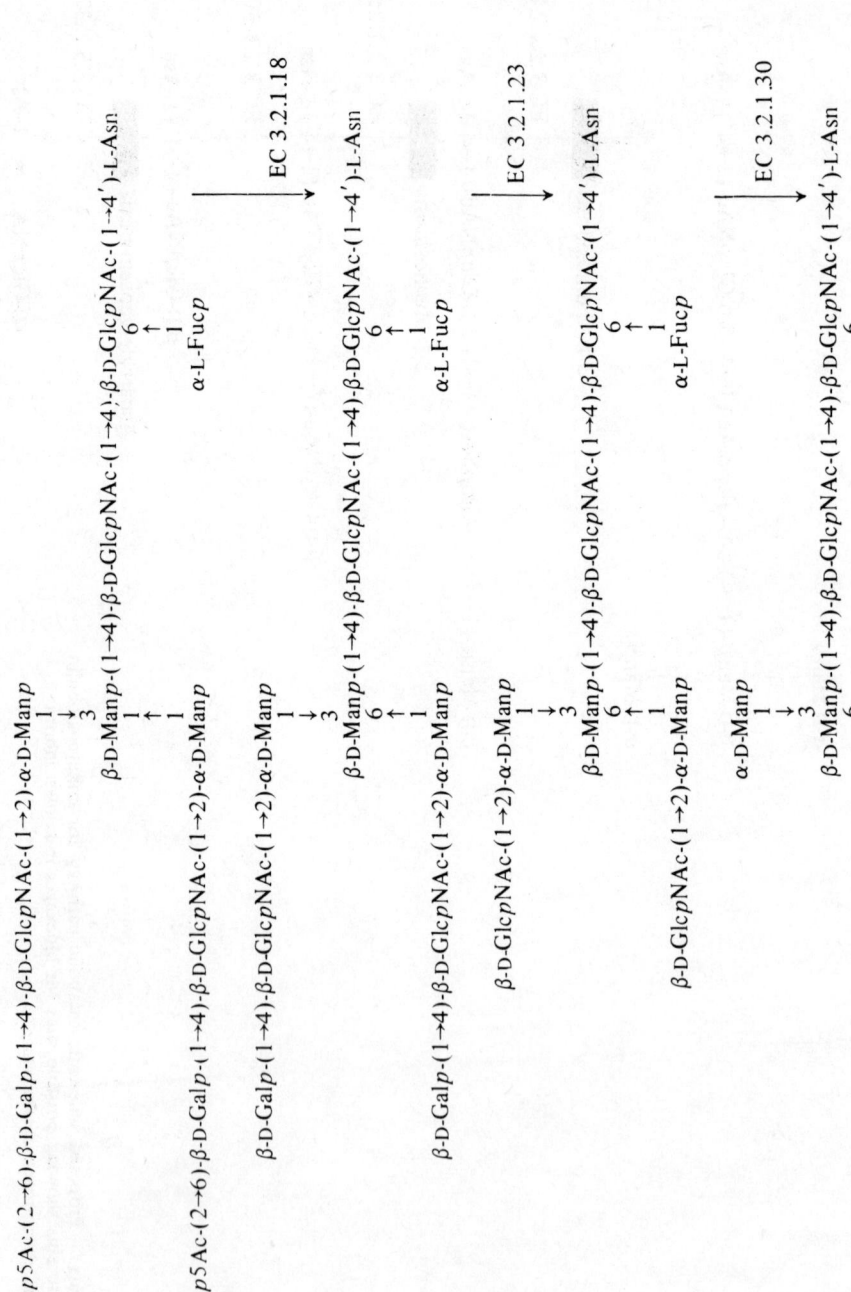

α-Neup5Ac-(2→6)-β-D-Galp-(1→4)-β-D-GlcpNAc-(1→2)-α-D-Manp
```
                                                        1
                                                        ↓
                                                        3
```
β-D-Manp-(1→4)-β-D-GlcpNAc-(1→4)-β-D-GlcpNAc-(1→4')-L-Asn
```
                                  6
                                  ↑
                                  1
                              α-L-Fucp
```
α-Neup5Ac-(2→6)-β-D-Galp-(1→4)-β-D-GlcpNAc-(1→2)-α-D-Manp

→ EC 3.2.1.18

β-D-Galp-(1→4)-β-D-GlcpNAc-(1→2)-α-D-Manp
```
                                  1
                                  ↓
                                  3
```
β-D-Manp-(1→4)-β-D-GlcpNAc-(1→4)-β-D-GlcpNAc-(1→4')-L-Asn
```
                                  6
                                  ↑
                                  1
                              α-L-Fucp
```
β-D-Galp-(1→4)-β-D-GlcpNAc-(1→2)-α-D-Manp

→ EC 3.2.1.23

β-D-GlcpNAc-(1→2)-α-D-Manp
```
                   1
                   ↓
                   3
```
β-D-Manp-(1→4)-β-D-GlcpNAc-(1→4)-β-D-GlcpNAc-(1→4')-L-Asn
```
                                  6
                                  ↑
                                  1
                              α-L-Fucp
```
β-D-GlcpNAc-(1→2)-α-D-Manp

→ EC 3.2.1.30

α-D-Manp
```
  1
  ↓
  3
```
β-D-Manp-(1→4)-β-D-GlcpNAc-(1→4)-β-D-GlcpNAc-(1→4')-L-Asn
```
                                  6
                                  ↑
                                  1
                              α-L-Fucp
```
α-D-Manp

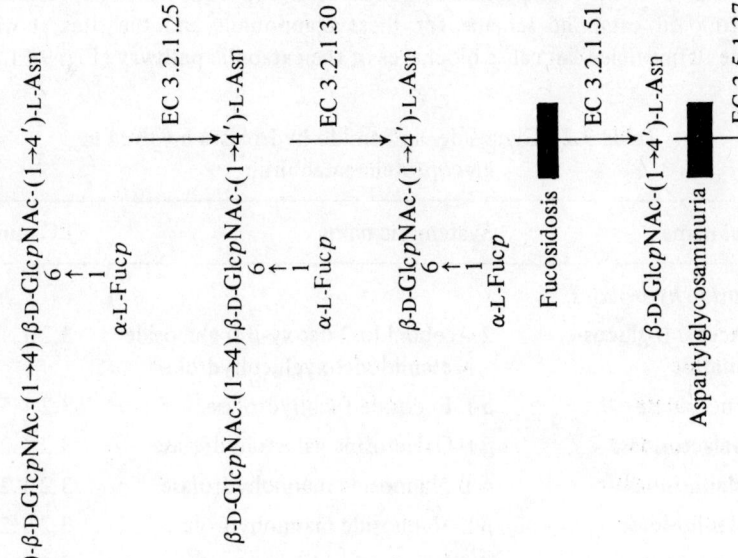

Fig. 9.6(b) — Proposed schematic catabolic pathway for immunoglobulin glycoproteins showing the site for blockage in fucosidosis, an inborn error of glycoprotein catabolism.

by Kornfeld and Kornfeld, 1976, and Dawson and Tsay, 1977), and was found to be related to the immunoglobulin structures (108–112) which has resulted in the proposed catabolic scheme for these compounds and the sites at which enzyme deficiencies can cause blockages of the catabolic pathway (Fig. 9.6).

Table 9.2 Glycoside- and amido-hydrolases involved in glycoprotein catabolism

Trivial name	Systematic name	EC number
Glycoside hydrolases		
β-*N*-Acetyl-D-glucos- aminidase	2-Acetamido-2-deoxy-β-D-glucoside acetamidodeoxyglucohydrolase	3.2.1.30
α-L-Fucosidase	α-L-Fucoside fucohydrolase	3.2.1.51
β-D-Galactosidase	β-D-Galactoside galactohydrolase	3.2.1.23
α-D-Mannosidase	α-D-Mannoside mannohydrolase	3.2.1.24
β-D-Mannosidase	β-D-Mannoside mannohydrolase	3.2.1.25
Neuraminidase	Acylneuraminyl hydrolase	3.2.1.18
Amidohydrolase		
4-*N*-(2-β-D-Glucosaminyl)- L-asparaginase	4-*N*-(2-Acetamido-2-deoxy-β-D-gluco- pyranosyl)-L-asparagine amidohydrolase	3.5.1.26

PLANT AND ALGAL GLYCOPROTEINS

It was originally believed that glycoproteins were restricted to animal origins, but the isolation of an L-asparaginyl-oligosaccharide from soya bean agglutinin (Lis *et al.*, 1964) was the first proof of their existence in plants. It is now well established that glycoproteins are widely distributed in plants and have similar functions to the animal glycoproteins and include enzymes, structural materials, etc. The carbohydrate residues in plant glycoproteins are similar to those found in animal glycoproteins with the exceptions that 5-acetamido-3,5-dideoxy-D-*glycero*-D-*galacto*-2-nonulopyranonic acid does not occur and 2-amino-2-deoxy-D-galactose has only rarely been found (in the leaf glycoproteins of *Cannabis* species) whilst D-xylose and L-arabinose, which are uncommon in animal glycoproteins, are found in many plant glycoproteins.

The number of well characterised plant glycoproteins is still very small (see Sharon and Lis, 1979) with only the glycoprotein lectins as distinct from protein lectins (see later p. 209) being investigated in sufficient detail to allow the structure of their carbohydrate moieties to be determined. However, a number of characteristic features have been discovered and these include a number of glycopeptide linkages which differ from those found in animal glycoproteins (see Fig. 9.7). Only N^4-(2-acetamido-2-deoxy-β-D-glucopyranosyl) hydrogen L-asparaginate is common to both plant and animal glycoproteins.

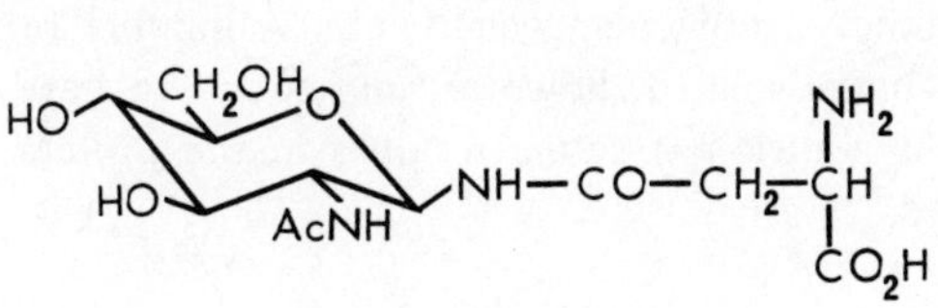

N^4-(2-Acetamido-2-deoxy-β-D-gluco-
pyranosyl) hydrogen L-asparaginate

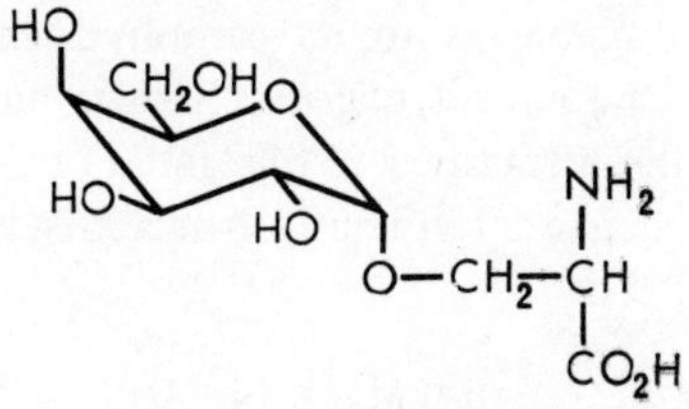

O^3-α-D-Galactopyranosyl-
L-serine

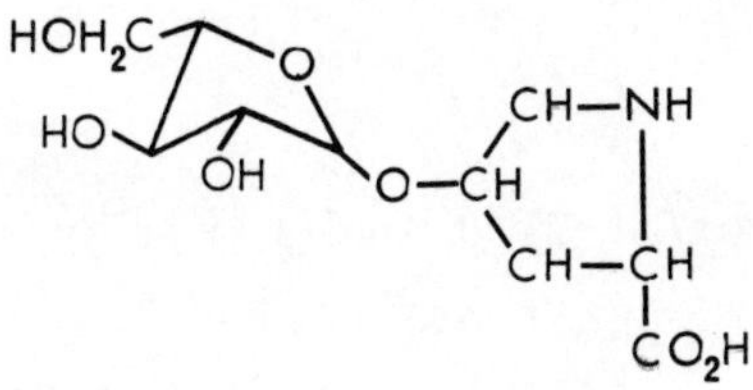

O^4-β-L-Arabinofuranosyl-
hydroxy-L-proline

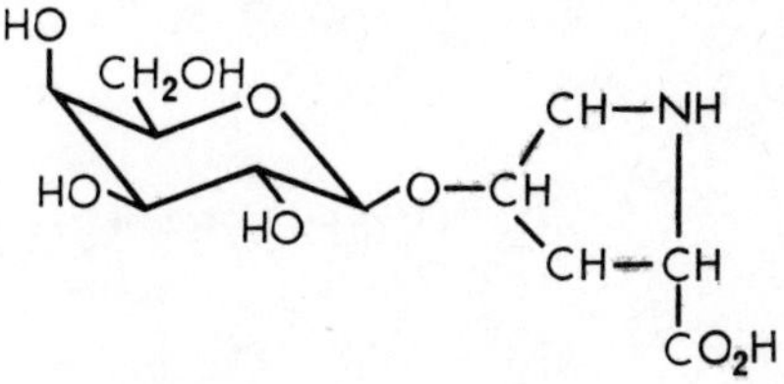

O^4-β-D-Galactopyranosyl-
hydroxy-L-proline

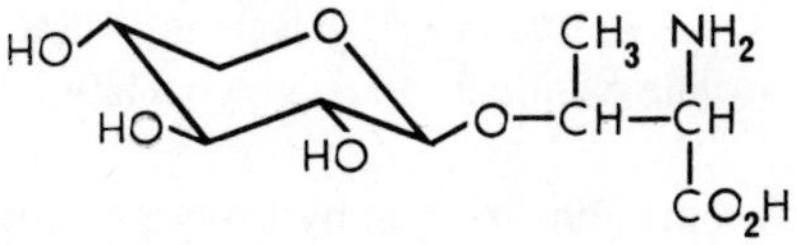

O^3-β-D-Xylopyranosyl-
L-threonine

Fig. 9.7 – Glycopeptide linkages in plant glycoproteins

Bromelain, which was identified as a glycoprotein in 1967, has, since that time, become one of the better characterised plant glycoproteins and shown to contain the core structure (113) which is common to many of the animal glycoproteins. It has been reported (Fukuda *et al.*, 1976) that the D-mannopyranosyl residue in the core region is uniquely substituted at C-2 and C-6, unlike the animal glycoproteins in which the D-mannopyranosyl residue is substituted at C-3 and C-6.

Extensin is an insoluble glycoprotein found attached to the cell walls of many plants. It is believed to have a structural function analogous to that of collagen in mammals. The insolubility of extensin, thought to be a result of covalent crosslinking to cell-wall polysaccharides, has meant that degradative techniques are used in its isolation which results in limited information being available as to its carbohydrate moiety, molecular weight, etc. A number of L-arabinosyl oligosaccharides have been isolated, however, and found to have the structures (114) and (115). In addition, L-serine residues in the protein chain are frequently D-galactosylated.

$$\beta\text{-D-Man}p\text{-}(1\rightarrow4)\text{-}\beta\text{-D-Glc}p\text{NAc-}(1\rightarrow4)\text{-}\beta\text{-D-Glc}p\text{NAc-}(1\rightarrow4')\text{-L-Asn}$$

(113)

$$\beta\text{-L-Ara}f\text{-}(1\rightarrow2)\text{-}\beta\text{-L-Ara}f\text{-}(1\rightarrow2)\text{-}\beta\text{-L-Ara}f\text{-}(1\rightarrow4')\text{-L-Hyp}$$

(114)

$$\beta\text{-L-Ara}f\text{-}(1\rightarrow3)\text{-}\beta\text{-L-Ara}f\text{-}(1\rightarrow2)\text{-}\beta\text{-L-Ara}f\text{-}(1\rightarrow2)\text{-}\beta\text{-L-Ara}f\text{-}(1\rightarrow4')\text{-L-Hyp}$$

(115)

A number of other hydroxy-L-proline-containing plant glycoproteins have been identified and isolated from other sources, including the leaves of broad beans and cannabis plants and as a component of rice bran and corn pericarp. Many of these are poorly characterised but that obtained from sandal (*Santalum album*) leaves contains 16% L-arabinose and less than 1% D-galactose. Alkaline hydrolysis showed that all hydroxy-L-proline residues were glycosylated by either L-arabinosyl di- or tri-saccharides.

A number of soluble extracellular glycoproteins, rich in hydroxy-L-proline, are found in the medium in which plant tissues are grown. These glycoproteins contain 80–95% carbohydrate which consists of D-galactose and L-arabinose in approximately equal proportions and are frequently (but incorrectly) referred to as the 'L-arabino-D-galacto-proteins'. The extracellular glycoprotein released by sycamore callus tissue contains L-arabino-D-galactan polysaccharides attached to about 50% of the hydroxy-L-proline residues. In addition, about 30% of the hydroxy-L-proline residues carry short L-arabinosyl oligosaccharides, with the trisaccharides predominating.

L-Arabino-D-galacto-glycoproteins have also been isolated from aqueous extracts of the seeds, leaves, stem and fruits of a variety of plants, a number of which exhibit lectin-like behaviour towards the β-D-glycosyl dyes (such as 1,3,5-tri-[4-*O*-β-D-glucopyranosyloxy-phenylazo]-2,4,6-trihydroxybenzene (116)) and have been designated the β-lectins (Jermyn and Yeow, 1975).

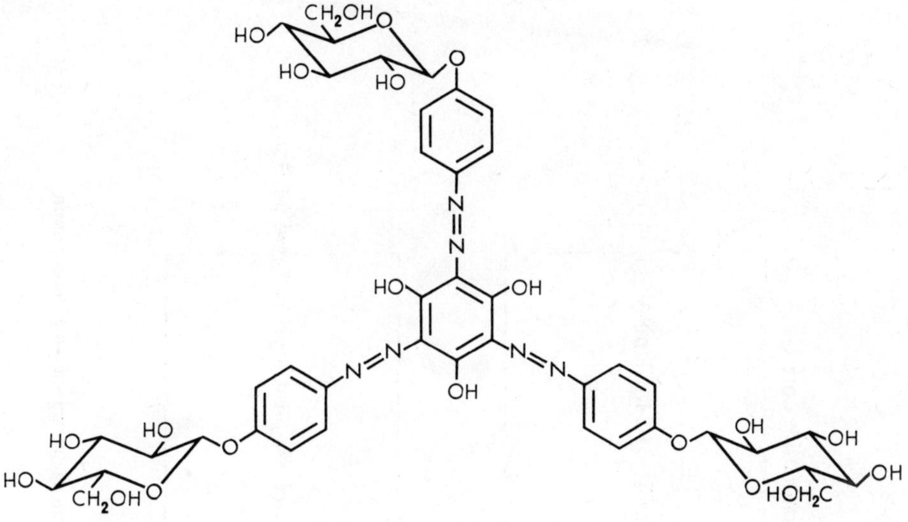

(116)

Evidence exists to indicate that many major plant polysaccharides (see Chapter 8), including starch and cellulose, contain small amounts of covalently bound protein and should be considered as glycoproteins.

Hydroxy-L-proline-rich glycoproteins have been found in green algae. These algal glycoproteins contain O^4-β-L-arabinofuranosyl-hydroxy-L-proline and O^3-α-D-galactopyranosyl-L-serine residues similar to those in extensin and, in addition, O^4-β-D-galactosyl-hydroxy-L-proline residues which are found in the L-arabino-D-galacto-glycoproteins but not in extensin.

Lectins

The large group of plant lectins (previously known as phytohaemagglutinins), which have the ability to bind carbohydrates and carbohydrate-containing macromolecules in an analogous manner to the antigen–antibody interaction, contains many glycoproteins, the structures of some of which have been elucidated (Lis and Sharon, 1977). Some plant lectins, including concanavalin A, contain no carbohydrate and are classified as protein lectins.

Soya bean agglutinin was first isolated in purified form in 1952 but was not known to be a glycoprotein until 1964. Since then much work has been expended on determination of its structure. Like most other lectins, it is now prepared by affinity chromatography (see Chapter 13, p. 302) using an immobilised form of the monosaccharide for which it possesses a specific affinity (in this case 2-amino-2-deoxy-D-galactopyranose). The carbohydrate content of soya bean agglutinin of 6% consists of D-mannose and 2-acetamido-2-deoxy-D-glucose in the ratio of 3:1. The structure of the carbohydrate unit varies due to micro-

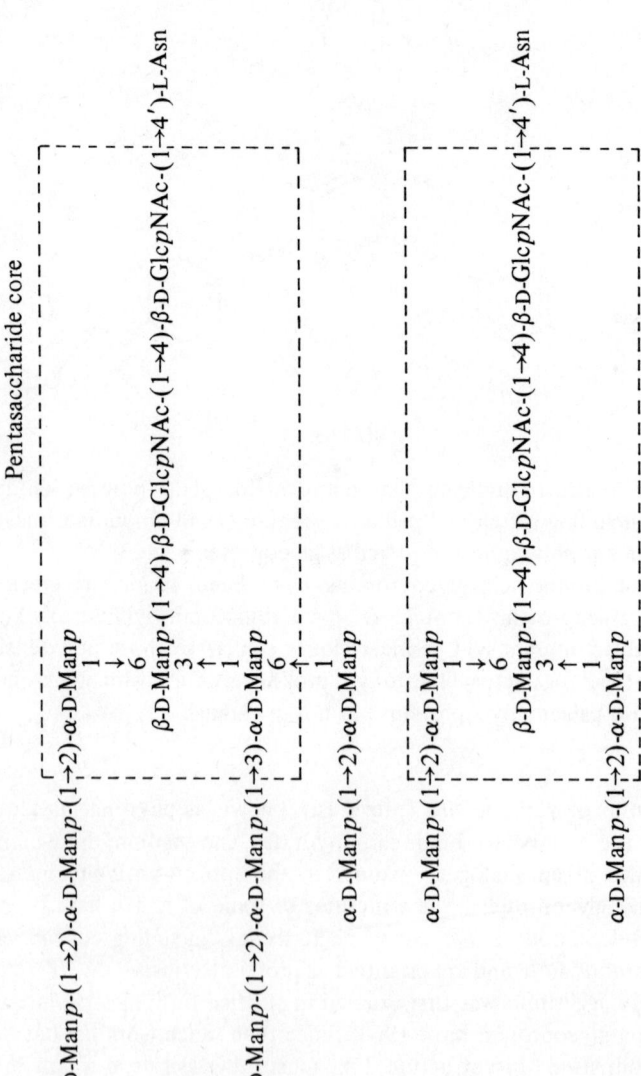

Fig. 9.8 — Structures of the carbohydrate moieties of soya bean agglutinin showing the common pentasaccharide core.

heterogeneity, but consists of a common pentasaccharide core to which addition-al D-mannosyl residues are attached, with a hepta- and undeca-saccharide having been identified (see Fig. 9.8). The structure of the pentasaccharide core region is common to that of many animal glycoproteins (for example, immunoglobulins, structures 108-110) indicating a common biosynthetic pathway for all L-asparagine-linked carbohydrate units in animals, plants and microorganisms (Sharon and Lis, 1979). Lima bean agglutinin has a similar carbohydrate com-position and structure with the exception that L-fucose is attached to one of the 2-acetamido-2-deoxy-D-glucopyranosyl residues.

Potato lectin contains 47% L-arabinose and 3% D-galactose and has a struc-ture in which some L-serine residues are substituted with a single α-D-galacto-pyranosyl group whilst all the hydroxy-L-proline residues carry L-arabinofurano-syl oligosaccharides, mainly the tri- and tetra-saccharides. The aminoacid se-quence is such that sequences of three or more hydroxy-L-proline residues are present and form a rigid, open, left-handed helix with a region (of about 163 aminoacid residues) which contains no glycosyl residues. This region which contains the carbohydrate-binding site (specific for $(1\rightarrow4)$-linked oligosaccharides of 2-acetamido-2-deoxy-β-D-glucopyranose) of the lectin contains large amounts of L-glycine and L-cysteine, the latter being present at almost every sixth amino-acid residue and all of which are cross-linked *via* disulphide bonds. This high L-glycine and disulphide linkage region is also found in wheat germ agglutinin which has the same carbohydrate specificity but which is a nonglycosylated protein and not a glycoprotein. A similar structure has been found for the glyco-protein lectin from jimson weed which contains hydroxy-L-proline (6.3%), L-cysteine (16.3%), 2-amino-2-deoxy-D-glucose (4.5%) and neutral sugars (28%, predominantly L-arabinose) and which is also specific for $(1\rightarrow4)$-linked 2-aceta-mido-2-deoxy-β-D-glucopyranosyl oligosaccharides.

The use of immobilised lectins for affinity chromatography is discussed in Chapter 13.

PROTEOGLYCANS AND GLYCOSAMINOGLYCANS

Having discussed the many varied types of glycoproteins, a more compact range of carbohydrate–protein macromolecules are now discussed. In correct nomen-clature, these are proteoglycans, and their carbohydrate components are glycos-aminoglycans. These compounds are the only source of hexuronic acids in animals and occur in nearly all parts of mammalian bodies and to lesser extents in fish and bacteria. They are amongst the essential building blocks of the macro-molecular framework of connective and other tissues. Hyaluronic acid appears to act, on account of its viscosity in solution, as a lubricant and shock absorbing gel in limb joints. The size and charged nature of the proteoglycans may allow them to operate as filtration media for the exclusion of foreign matter from the body. Heparin is unique among the glycosaminoglycans in that it possesses biological activity as a blood anticoagulant. It is therefore used therapeutically.

Nomenclature

In view of the confusion and lack of consistency in the nomenclature in this field, it is necessary to discuss a number of other relevant terms. The purpose of the introduction in 1938 of the term 'mucopolysaccharide' was to describe collectively 2-amino-2-deoxyhexose-containing polysaccharide materials of animal origin occurring either as free polysaccharides or as their protein derivatives. However, with the various subsequent discoveries of other types of carbohydrate-containing macromolecules, the term has come to be used in so many ways that it is now, in a sense, quite vague. Since the 'glycosaminoglycans' have always come within the 'mucopolysaccharide' category irrespective of the way in which that term has been used, they were described widely as 'acidic mucopolysaccharides' on account of their highly cationic nature. However, this nomenclature arose at a time when it was not realized that the glycosaminoglycans, as we call them today, are attached covalently to protein, and at a time when the polysaccharide was isolated with some aminoacids units attached. Thus, 'acidic mucopolysaccharide' means the 'glycosaminoglycan of a proteoglycan plus (sometimes) a few aminoacid units', where 'glycosaminoglycan' means purely the polysaccharide part of proteoglycan. The term 'acid mucopolysaccharide', used to a lesser extent, is synonymous with 'acidic mucopolysaccharide', whereas 'acidic polysaccharide' applies to any polysaccharide containing acidic groups. The term 'aminopolysaccharides' was also coined some time ago to describe collectively blood-group-specific substances, acidic mucopolysaccharides and chitin.

The general terms 'polysaccharide–protein' and 'mucopolysaccharide–protein complex' and the specific terms, for example, 'chondroitin sulphate–protein complex', were introduced when it was realized that the glycosaminoglycan is associated with protein, but when it (soon) became apparent that the association is stronger than that of a noncovalent complex, the general name 'protein–polysaccharide' and specific name 'chondromucoprotein' were employed to replace the three foregoing terms. These terms were all forerunners of 'proteoglycan' (general) and, for example, chondroitin 4-sulphate proteoglycan (specific).

It is unnecessary to discuss the historical aspects of the development of all these terms. It is sufficient to conclude that the terms 'acid mucopolysaccharide', 'acidic mucopolysaccharide', 'aminopolysaccharide', 'mucopolysaccharide', 'mucopolysaccharide-protein complex', 'mucoprotein', and 'protein–polysaccharide' are misleading, historical, and redundant, and that they can well be done without.

On account of the apparent regularity of the polysaccharide chains in proteoglycans and the early belief that the protein present in preparations of the polysaccharide parts represented impurity, greatest attention has been given to the glycosaminoglycan chains themselves rather than to proteoglycans as a whole. Thus the glycosaminoglycans have been named individually, but not so much according to their component monosaccharides and their simplified disaccharide repeating structures (these were often unknown at the times of original isolation), but according to trivial reasoning, for example, by naming after the source. 'Hyaluronic acid' is derived from 'hyaloid' (vitreous) plus 'uronic acid', 'chondroitin sulphate' from the Greek χονδρος (chondros — cartilage) plus 'sulphate', 'dermatan sulphate' from the root 'derm' (skin) plus 'sulphate', 'heparin' from the Greek ηπαρ (hepar — liver), 'heparan sulphate' from heparin with an altered amount of sulphate, etc., and keratan sulphate from the Greek κερας (keras — horn) after its discovery in cornea.

In all, eight glycosaminoglycans of essentially different chemical structures have been identified. Through the times, these glycosaminoglycans have been individually named in a number of ways, as shown in Table 9.3. Most of these names are used currently, and so the reader will find it useful to have this table available when consulting the primary literature. Where the term chondroitin sulphate appears in the more recent literature, this can mean chondroitin 4-sulphate or chondroitin 6-sulphate or a mixture of the two. The terms keratan sulphate I and keratan sulphate II are sometimes used to denote keratan sulphate of corneal and skeletal origin, respectively, there being some differences between the two.

However, it has been accepted by many that, pending a complete systematisation of polysaccharide nomenclature by the various nomenclature committees, only one name for each should be regarded as the one which is up-to-date. As will be seen, some of the names in being altered have been systematised to include the terminal 'an'. (The term 'chondroitin sulphate' will be used when no distinction between the 4-sulphate and 6-sulphate isomers is given.) It is recommended that only these names should be used and that use of the others, which are misleading to the uninformed, should be discontinued completely forthwith. As will be seen later, the glycosaminoglycans contain acidic (anionic) groups which are capable of forming salts. The salt type is not usually indicated when naming a particular glycosaminoglycan since it is not necessarily known which cation, of those available throughout the extraction and purification processes, was finally assimilated by the glycosaminoglycan. However, where the salt form is known this may be specified, for example, sodium hyaluronate, potassium chondroitin 4-sulphate. Also included in Table 9.3 is the extension of the semi-systematic naming system which denotes the monosaccharide units involved in the polysaccharide, but it must be recognized that in certain instances these may represent simplifications.

For the reasons of the lesser emphasis invested in, and the general irregularity of, the sequences already discussed above, the protein parts of proteoglycans have not been named, nor for that matter have they been adequately chemically identified for names to be applied to them. This is reflected in the absence of names for the proteoglycans themselves other than those which indicate the type of glycosaminoglycan(s) involved, for example, dermatan sulphate proteoglycan and chondroitin 4-sulphate–keratan sulphate proteoglycan, but such of course

Table 9.3 Nomenclature of the glycosaminoglycans

Modern name	Original name	Other names	Semi-systematic name denoting actual mono-saccharide units involved in structure[a]	Semi-systematic name denoting classes of mono-saccharide units involved in structures	General semi-systematic name
Chondroitin	Chondroitin	–	Galactosaminogluc-uronan		
Chondroitin 4-sulphate	Chondroitin sulphate A[b]	Chondroitin sulphate	Galactosaminogluc-uronan		
Chondroitin 6-sulphate	Chondroitin sulphate C[b]	Chondroitin sulphate	Galactosaminogluc-uronan		
Chondroitin 6-sulphate	Chondroitin sulphate D[c]	–	Galactosaminogluc-uronan		
Dermatan sulphate[d]	Chondroitin sulphate B[b]	Chondroitin sulphate Dermatan[e] β-Heparin	Galactosaminoiduronan	Glycosaminoglycuronan	Glycosaminoglycan
Heparin	Heparin	–	Glucosaminoglucurono-iduronan		
Heparan sulphate	Heparitin sulphate	Acetylheparan sulphate Heparan[e] Heparin monosulphate Heparin monosulphuric acid Heparin sulphate Heparitin[e]	Glucosaminoglucurono-iduronan		
Hyaluronic acid	Hyaluronic acid	–	Glucosaminoglucuronan		
Keratan sulphate	Keratosulphate	Keratan[e]	Glucosaminogalactan	Glycosaminoglycan	

a   As known so far.
b   Known originally collectively as chondroitin sulphuric acid.
c   Regarded by some as a separate glycosaminoglycan, but is really a super-sulphated chondroitin 6-sulphate and is therefore classified as such.
d   Dermatan, the non-sulphated polysaccharide equivalent to chondroitin, is only known to be produced by laboratory desulphation of dermatan sulphate.
e   Names used incorrectly irrespective of system used.

are nondescriptive of the protein. The alternative nomenclature, in the form proteochondroitin 4-sulphate, etc., has been used infrequently, but is not to be recommended. The attachment of only peptide to a glycosaminoglycan is designated by, for example, chondroitin 4-sulphate peptide.

Structures

The glycosaminoglycans can be distinguished by their compositions and primary structure, since the repeating disaccharide structures which have been discovered as general features of all of them are individually characteristic. Much of the earlier work on structure elucidation has been reviewed (Muir and Hardingham, 1975). Hyaluronic acid has the simplest of the glycosaminoglycan structures with a repeating unit composed of the monosaccharides D-glucuronic acid and 2-acetamido-2-deoxy-D-glucose linked such that there is a $(1 \rightarrow 3)$ linkage between the β-D-glucopyranosyluronic acid and the 2-acetamido-2-deoxy-D-glucopyranosyl residues, that is, the uronic acid has the β-D-anomeric configuration at C-1 from which it is linked glycosidically to position 3 of the 2-acetamido-2-deoxy-D-glucopyranosyl residue. Between the 2-acetamido-2-deoxy-D-glucopyranosyl and the β-D-glucopyranosyluronic acid residues the linkage is $(1 \rightarrow 4)$ which results in the repeating structure $[\rightarrow 4)$-O-$(\beta$-D-glucopyranosyluronic acid)-$(1 \rightarrow 3)$-O-(2-acetamido-2-deoxy-β-D-glucopyranosyl)-$(1 \rightarrow]$ (117). Chondroitin is the only other nonsulphated glycosaminoglycan which occurs naturally and is isomeric with hyaluronic acid. The repeating unit has the structure $[\rightarrow 4)$-O-$(\beta$-D-glucopyranosyluronic acid)-$(1 \rightarrow 3)$-O-(2-acetamido-2-deoxy-β-D-galactopyranosyl)-$(1 \rightarrow]$ (118). This makes the only difference between hyaluronic acid and chondroitin the orientation of one hydroxyl group on every other monosaccharide unit along the chain.

(117)

(118)

Chondroitin 4-sulphate and chondroitin 6-sulphate are varieties of chondroitin, the sulphate group being located on the 4- and 6-positions of the 2-acetamido-2-deoxy-D-galactosyl residues resulting in the repeating structures (119) and (120) respectively. Variants of chondroitin sulphate with sulphate contents greater than 1 mole per mole of disaccharide unit are known to occur but generally have no specific name. The so-called chondroitin sulphate D, obtained from shark cartilage, is, in fact, a chondroitin 6-sulphate containing, on average, more than one sulphate group per disaccharide repeating unit (sometimes referred to as 'oversulphation').

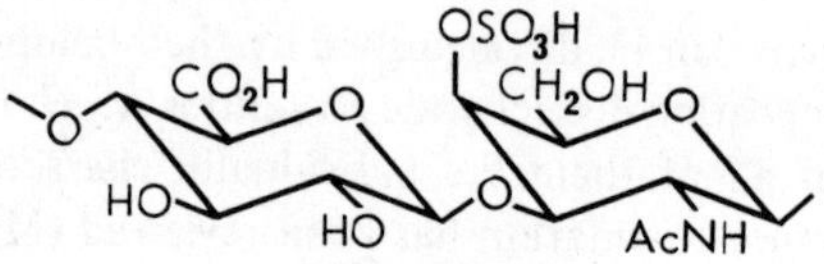

(119)

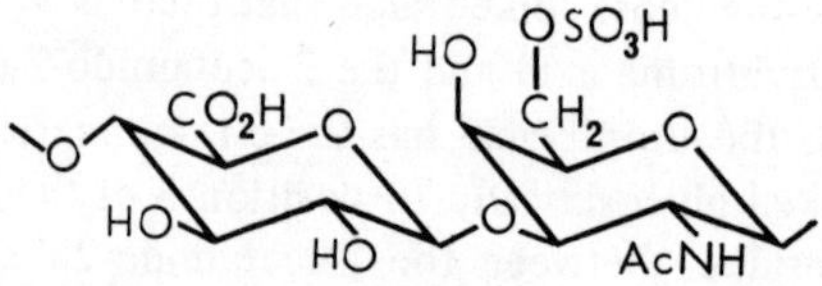

(120)

Dermatan sulphate is an isomer of chondroitin 4-sulphate with L-iduronic acid residues replacing D-glucuronic acid residues with the linkage positions and absolute orientations of the linkages remaining the same, resulting in a repeating structure (121) which differs from chondroitin 4-sulphate only in the orientation of the carboxyl group at C-5 on every other residue. Irregularities in the structure are known to exist, with one or two randomly spaced D-glucuronic acid residues replacing L-iduronic acid residues and the repeating disaccharide sometimes being di- or non-sulphated. Dermatan, the nonsulphated form of dermatan sulphate, which is isomeric with chondroitin and hyaluronic acid, and dermatan 6-sulphate, isomeric with chondroitin 6-sulphate, have not been detected in nature but this does not preclude their existence. Dermatan can be prepared by chemical desulphation of dermatan sulphate.

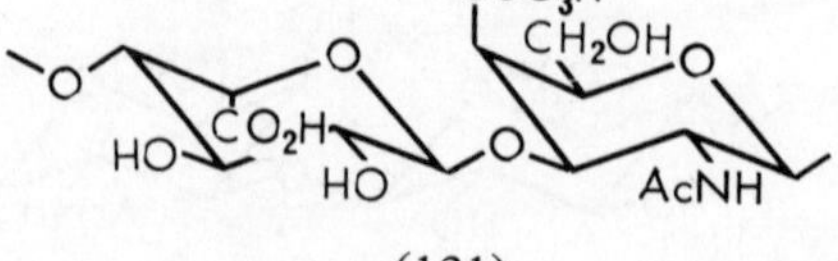

(121)

The repeating unit in heparin has been much more difficult to define and, in spite of extended efforts, it was not until the late 1960s that the location of the sulphate groups could be assigned with confidence. It was now recognized that the composition of heparin is a mixture of two disaccharide repeating units comprising L-iduronic acid 2-sulphate and 2-deoxy-2-sulphamido-D-glucose 6-sulphate (122) and D-glucuronic acid and 2-deoxy-2-sulphamido-D-glucose 6-sulphate (123). Although the monosaccharide residues are analogous to those in hyaluronic acid and dermatan sulphate, heparin is particularly different due to the anomeric configuration of the D-glucopyranosyl and 2-amido-2-deoxy-D-glucopyranosyl residues. The overall sulphate content is in the range 2–3 moles sulphate per mole disaccharide repeating unit. Heparan sulphate is not, as the name might suggest, a further sulphated version of heparin. The backbone carbohydrate structure of heparan sulphate is similar to that of heparin but the 2-amido-2-deoxy-D-glucopyranosyl residues are less frequently O-sulphated and may be N-acetylated.

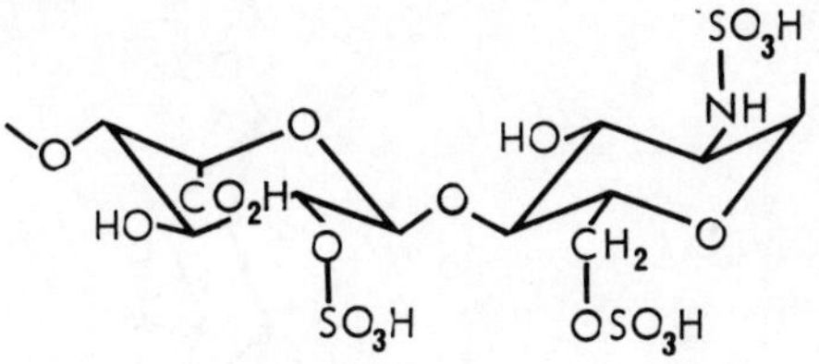

(122)

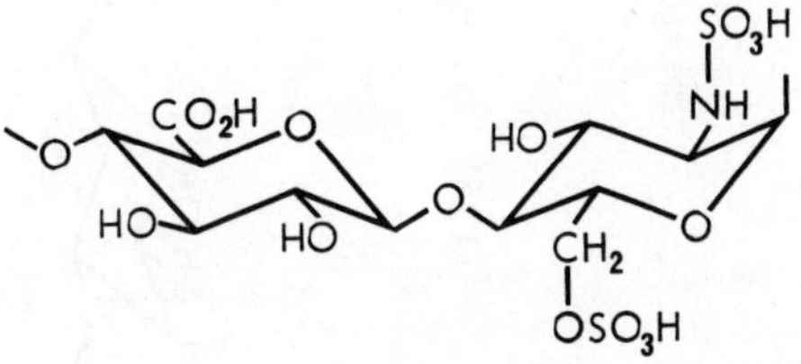

(123)

Keratan sulphate is unlike the other glycosaminoglycans in that it contains no (hex)uronic acid residues. It has a repeating disaccharide unit (124) consisting of D-galactopyranosyl and 2-acetamido-2-deoxy-D-glucopyranosyl 6-sulphate residues with the structure [→3)-O-β-D-galactopyranosyl-(1→4)-O-(2-acetamido-2-deoxy-β-D-glucopyranosyl 6-sulphate-(1→] . Variants of keratan sulphate are known in which other neutral sugars such as D-mannose, L-fucose and 5-acetamido-3,5-dideoxy-D-*glycero*-D-*galacto*-2-nonulopyranonic acid occur and in which there is more than 1 mole of sulphate per mole disaccharide repeating unit, additional sulphation occurring at C-6 of the neutral monosaccharide residues. Occasionally the neutral monosaccharides are non-sulphated.

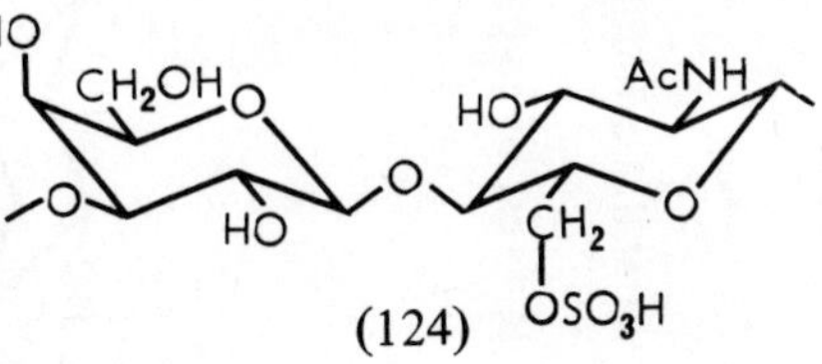

(124)

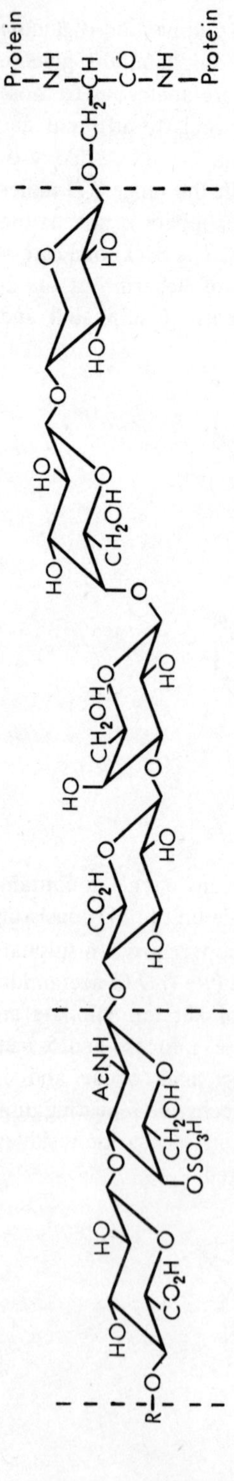

Linkage region

First disaccharide repeating unit

R = rest of glycosaminoglycan chain

(125)

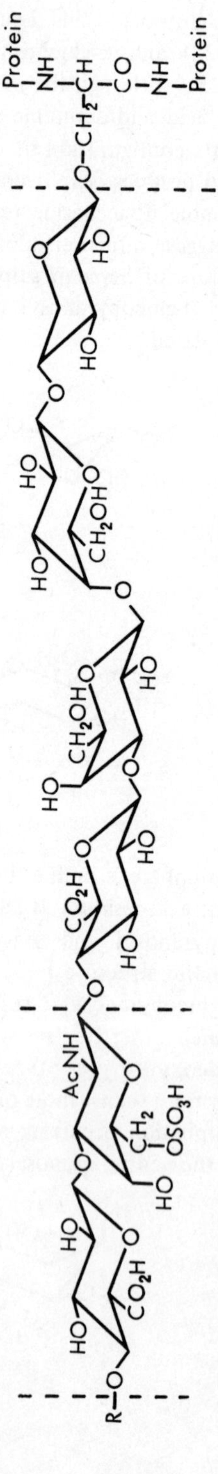

Linkage region

First disaccharide repeating unit

R = rest of glycosaminoglycan chain

(126)

Whereas the structures of the glycosaminoglycans are presented here largely as being based on repeating oligosaccharide units, it must be borne in mind that infrequent irregularities in the chains do exist, such irregularities being most apparent in the structures of heparin, heparan sulphate and keratan sulphate (for a full description see Kennedy, 1979a).

In the overall proteoglycan, the glycosaminoglycans are linked to the protein *via* a glycopeptide linkage which, in most cases, involves monosaccharide units different from those of the main polysaccharide chain. These linkage monosaccharides are glycosidically linked to one another with the reducing terminal residue being linked to a side chain of an aminoacid residue.

Chondroitin 4-sulphate-containing proteoglycan was afforded first attention in this area, and after exhaustive proteolysis, the only aminoacid remaining, in quantities large enough to account for all the glycopeptide linkages as one type, was L-serine. Partial acid hydrolysis yielded a number of oligosaccharides and glycopeptides which were fitted into an overall structure (125) in the glycopeptide linkage region and commencement of the repeating disaccharide unit. The actual linkage of chondroitin 6-sulphate to protein is identical to that for chondroitin 4-sulphate, and therefore the overall structure in the glycopeptide linkage region and commencement of the repeating disaccharide unit is structure (126).

Dermatan sulphate has also been found to conform to this general pattern in its glycopeptide linkage, including the D-glucopyranosyluronic acid residue (127). It is unclear whether heparin occurs as a proteoglycan, but all heparin samples contain aminoacids and again the glycopeptide linkage acid unit has the D-*gluco*-, not the L-*ido*-, configuration (128). The presence of D-galactose and D-xylose in preparations of heparan sulphate suggest that the glycopeptide linkage of this glycosaminoglycan may be analogous to the foregoing.

Skeletal keratan sulphate glycopeptide linkage involves 2-acetamido-2-deoxy-D-galactosyl (which does not occur in corneal keratan sulphate) residues linked to L-serine or L-threonine residues, but this may not be the only linkage type for this glycosaminoglycan.

Corneal keratan sulphate is apparently unique among the glycosaminoglycans in its glycopeptide linkage in that the glycopeptide structure somewhat represents that which occurs in many glycoproteins (129). The glycopeptide linkage has been characterised by the isolation from a partial-acid hydrolysate of N^4-(2-acetamido-2-deoxy-β-D-glucopyranosyl) hydrogen L-asparaginate, known sometimes as 2-acetamido-1-N-(L-aspart-4-oyl)-2-deoxy-β-D-glucopyranosylamine. It appears that neutral monosaccharide residues are adjacent to the 2-acetamido-2-deoxy-D-glucopyranosyl residues, and the linkage region conceivably has the structure (130).

Work on the structure of the glycopeptide linkages of chondroitin and hyaluronic acid has progressed least of all. That of chondroitin may be assumed to be identical with that for chondroitin 4-sulphate, etc., whereas that of hya-

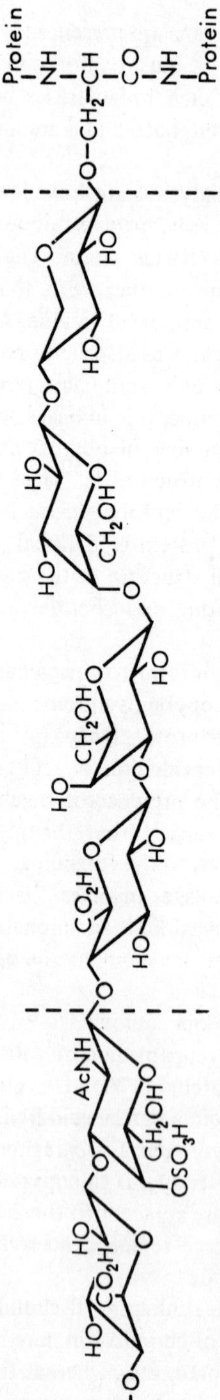

Linkage region

(127)

First disaccharide repeating unit

R = rest of glycosaminoglycan chain

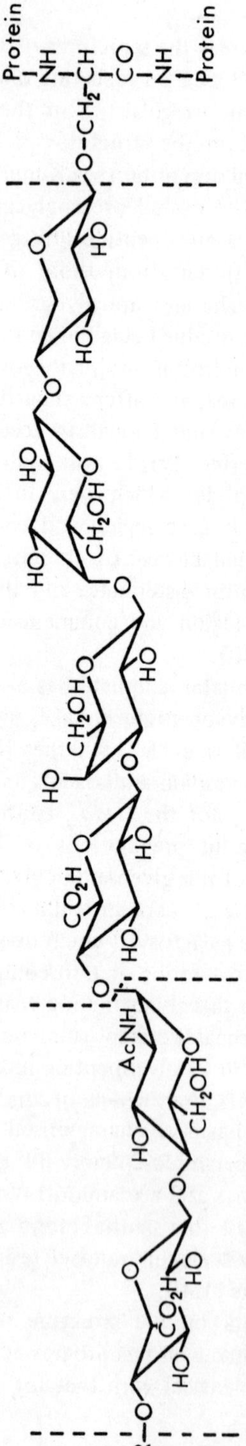

Linkage region

(128)

First disaccharide repeating unit

R = rest of glycosaminoglycan chain

luronic acid may involve D-glucose, L-arabinose, D-xylose and/or D-ribose and L-serine, but the various reports do not agree.

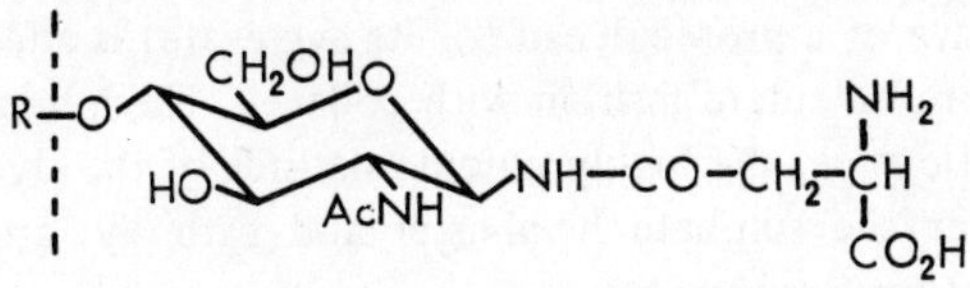

(129)

R = glycosaminoglycan chain

$$\text{D-Gal}p\text{-}(1\rightarrow?)\text{-D-Man}p\text{-}(1\rightarrow?)\text{-D-Man}p\text{-}(1\rightarrow?)\text{-D-Glc}p\text{NAc-}(1\rightarrow4')\text{-L-Asn} \begin{array}{c} \text{Protein} \\ | \\ \\ | \\ \text{Protein} \end{array}$$

(130)

Biological functions

One of the principal functions of connective tissues is to support and bind together the organs and bones — the functional parts of the body. Though the connective tissues assume different forms in different parts of the body, there is a fundamental similarity in the components. Considering the cells, the collagen fibres, cell membranes, the extracellular fibrils, the extracellular amorphous ground substance which surrounds the collagen and elastin fibres, cartilage and bone — all these very important materials contain proteoglycans, and therefore glycosaminoglycan chains, and thus these macromolecules must have a significant role. Since it is becoming increasingly apparent that connective tissues have many physiological functions in addition to being a supporting medium, they must allow transport of the many and varied 'moving' molecules. Therefore proteoglycans presumably have a profound influence on the processes of individual cells and tissues.

Considering the general location of greatest occurrence of glycosaminoglycans — connective tissue, it has been known for a long time that the tissue consists largely of collagen fibrils (see Ramachandran and Reddi, 1976, for the chemistry and biochemistry of collagen) and proteoglycans together with aqueous components. In the tissue, the protein chains of the proteoglycan chains and the collagen fibres lie side by side and the glycosaminoglycan chains of the proteoglycans interact with the collagen to give a non-covalent binding effect. The general representation of this situation (Fig. 9.9) as proposed some time ago still holds good. It must be realized, remembering the definition of a proteoglycan (many polysaccharide chains), that the size of a proteoglycan is very large; furthermore, some proteoglycans are able to form multiple aggregates of a very large size by specified interaction with a glycoprotein-like component. Thus, the overall size of a proteoglycan (or its aggregate) is adequate to permit it to interact in a multidentate fashion with collagen. The interactions are of an ionic or electrostatic type, the highly anionic natures of the glycosaminoglycan chains arising from the sulphate hemi-ester and carboxyl groups which are therefore important for this purpose.

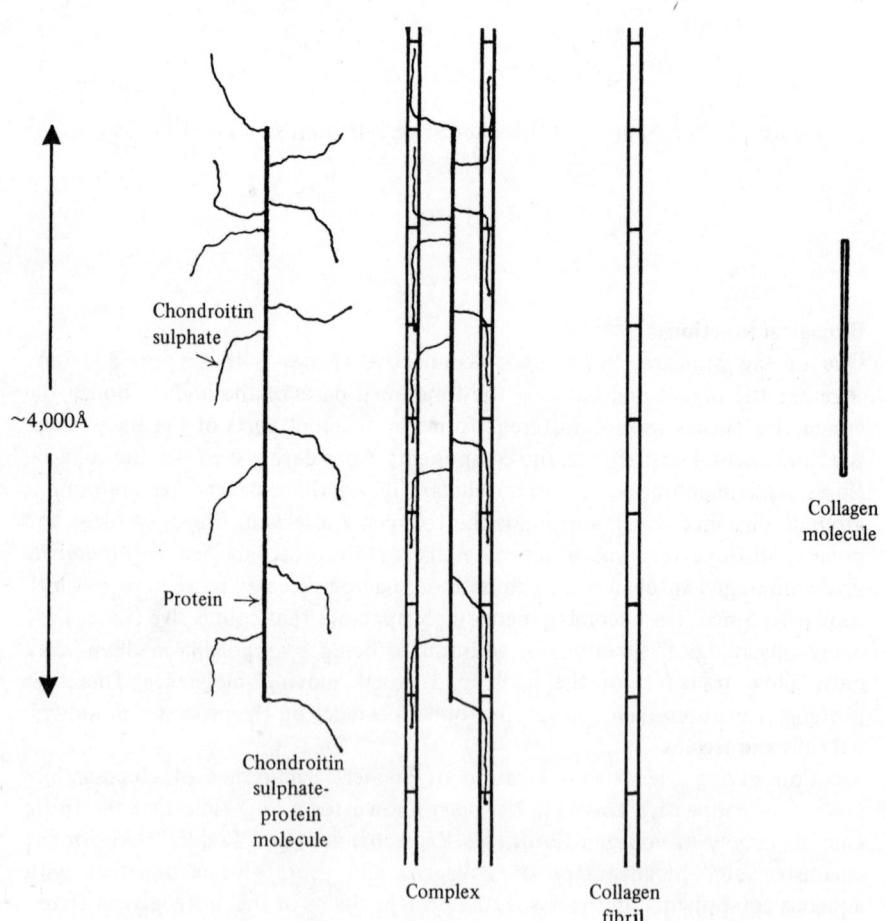

Fig. 9.9 – Schematic representation of interaction between collagen and chondroitin sulphate proteoglycan.

There are at least three binding sites for chondroitin 4-sulphate on a collagen molecule. The result of this interaction is to provide a three-dimensional network or matrix which resists disruption or separation (that is, holds the tissue together), which is suitable for the enclosure and location of an organ, which provides a buffer to external forces, but which is flexible and resilient. On account of the network, the matrix also permits the flow of important diffusable molecules and can be threaded through by arteries and veins. On this basis, it is clear that the presence of the glycosaminoglycan chains is of the utmost importance in maintaining the overall structure of tissues and the whole body and this is why they may be implicated in many of the processes of health, and, if they become faulty, in processes of disease.

In this picture of the proteoglycan and collagen fibre, it might be considered that the type of glycosaminoglycan is more important than the proteoglycan backbone, but it must be recalled that the protein dictates the spacing of the glycosaminoglycan chains and therefore is equally important. It has not yet been documented as to whether all the glycosaminoglycans are involved in this interactive way and it is unclear as to what differences there are between the function of, for example, chondroitin 4-sulphate and keratan sulphate in such a situation. Of course, the main proteoglycan chain axis to collagen fibre distance will vary since the acidic groups of the various glycosaminoglycan chains are of different strengths and exposed to different extents, not to mention any variation in the chain length of the glycosaminoglycan. Fibrillation is enhanced when connective tissue proteoglycan interacts with α-elastin, and glycosaminoglycans have been implicated in the regulation of collagen fibril diameters. Glycosaminoglycans and proteoglycans interact in fact with a whole variety of molecules *in vitro* and some of these interactions may represent functions *in vivo* (see Kennedy, 1979a).

Other justifiable suggestions for the functions of glycosaminoglycans and proteoglycans *in vivo* include wound healing, urine concentration in the kidney, storage and release of biogenic amines, maintenance of stable transport media, etc., contributions to elastogenesis, maintenance of the cornea in a transparent form, acting as cofactors in the formation of platelet clumping substance, acting as controlling agents for the hydration properties of cornea, acting as a molecular regulator to leukocyte lysosomal enzymes, maintenance of an orderly arrangement of fibrils of the corneal stroma, and metabolite control contributions to erythropoiesis.

In conclusion to the section, it is noteworthy that for the identification of the functions of carbohydrate and protein of many glycoproteins it has been possible to use their biological activity, which is frequently expressed at the nanogram or lower levels, as a sensing device. The search for specific roles of the carbohydrate and protein parts of proteoglycans is somewhat fraught with difficulty. Apart from heparin, no biological activity, in the accepted sense of the term, which can be monitored during diagnostic modification/manipulation of the macromolecule has been discovered. This of course does not mean that they do not possess such activities. Immunostudies may hold potential for sensing systems. Furthermore, there is the problem that many measurements can only be made outside of the natural environment and generally reflect only one of the multiple interactions and processes in which the macromolecule may be involved.

Involvement in diseases

Since proteoglycans occur so widely in the human body it is likely that the defects in many diseases will be related in some way to the proteoglycans. Furthermore, considering the large number of enzymes that must be involved in the biosynthesis and metabolism of the proteoglycans (see Chapter 5) and the interrelationship and control that exists between them, and between them and other tissue, etc., components, it is clear that an effect upon one of them may have far-reaching results in the reversible discontinuation of the maintenance of the production of and function of perfect tissue, etc. With this in mind, it is predictable that proteoglycan involvement is spread right across the disease types.

Whereas a considerable number of conditions has been reported to involve proteoglycan disorders in some way or other, the course of development of investigations has been greatly influenced, and dramatically limited to a narrow compass by various phenomena. First, much of the work reported is derived from studies carried out more than ten years ago when the proteoglycans were largely unrecognized as discrete intact molecules, attention therefore being focussed on the glycosaminoglycans. Secondly, attention has continued to be focussed on glycosaminoglycan rather than proteoglycan since the former is far more easily discernable in the presence of other tissue, etc., components. Thirdly, many of the clinical conditions originally examined are characterised by excessive urinary excretion of glycosaminoglycan peptides, that is, molecules from which most of the protein has been lost. Fourthly, there has been no significant systematic investigation of the involvement of the proteoglycans and/or their components — rather, discoveries of disorders have come from the recognition of an excess of material, often by histological methods. An excess may be many orders of magnitude different from the normal, whereas a decrease has a smaller maximum range and small differences go unnoticed more easily. Consequently, the diseases involving proteoglycan disorders reported to date are in fact almost exclusively characterised by an overproduction or accumulation of material. Thus the coverage of disorders by the literature relevant to this section is regrettably limited; in most instances only an end product of the disorder has been studied, usually on generally qualitative and quantitative bases without structural investigation. Since this end product has been determined as a glycosaminoglycan, it is only to be assumed that a proteoglycan disorder is involved. What is missing from an understanding of many of the disorders involving the glycosaminoglycan chain in some way is, in addition to structural information, the manner in which the whole proteoglycan is affected and at what stage(s) in the biosynthetic and degradative processes the primary disorder occurs. Of course, it may be that in some instances the proteoglycan disorder is a secondary effect. Most important, of course, is an understanding of the processes so that successful therapy can be devised.

A full review of the involvement and possible involvement of proteoglycans in various diseases is available (Kennedy, 1979a) but a brief discussion of genetic hyperglycosaminoglycanuria follows.

By far the greatest attention to the involvement of proteoglycans/glycosaminoglycans in disease has been given to a group of hereditary diseases which are characterized by the excessive urinary excretion of glycosaminoglycan material and have come to be known as the 'mucopolysaccharidoses'. The term 'mucopolysaccharidosis' is misleading, not only on account of the vague meaning of the word 'mucopolysaccharide', but also because it implies that glycosaminoglycans (acidic mucopolysaccharides) are the only storage material. This undoubtedly arises from the fact of the easily determined excessive glycosaminoglycan excretion, but it is apparent that the diseases involve complex storage disorders in which both glycosaminoglycan and other materials are affected and accumulate in tissues. It is difficult to give an expressive term to this group of diseases, but the term 'genetic hyperglycosaminoglycanuria' coined earlier (Kennedy, 1976) and selected for use here is acceptable although the urinary aspects are only some of the initial indications of far-reaching disorders. Nevertheless, there is now evidence that the primary defect in these hereditary disorders is faulty breakdown of the glycosaminoglycan(s); this therefore permits their distinction from other genetic diseases in which proteoglycan disorders and hyperglycosaminoglycanuria are secondary effects. However, it may emerge that there is also a disorder in proteoglycan protein metabolism in genetic hyperglycosaminoglycanuria since aminoacid differences as well as carbohydrate differences have been observed.

The classification (see later) of a disease as a case of genetic hyperglycosaminoglycanuria (or 'mucopolysaccharidosis') can be very arbitrary. Although some disease types are proven hereditary disorders, many diseases give rise to hyperglycosaminoglycanuria although not all of them are proven to be non-hereditary. Furthermore, there are undoubtedly many hereditary disorders which have not been investigated for (hyper)glycosaminoglycanuria. The term mucopolysaccharidosis has become something of a band wagon, with various workers seeking to add, to the classification of confirmed hereditary hyperglycosaminoglycanuria, other conditions characterised by hyperglycosaminoglycanuria but for which no genetic information is available. Variations within the classifications of individual cases has also prompted some to propose additional types. It must also be recognized that there may be several genetic disorders which exhibit a glycosaminoglycan disorder but which do not involve faulty glycosaminoglycan/proteoglycan shedding as a result of the primary enzyme defect.

In this chapter the term genetic hyperglycosaminoglycanuria is reserved for hereditary conditions where faulty proteoglycan metabolism is considered to be a primary defect. Nevertheless, whereas the meaning of this statement is immediately obvious and accepted, in so saying it is worthwhile questioning what is meant by the term primary defect. After all, whereas one may recognize that the primary defect is an enzyme deficiency (as in the case of genetic hyperglycosaminoglycanuria) or other alteration, such changes are really the result of changes in the amounts or structures of other molecules, the function of which impinges upon the molecule considered to be the primary defect. On this basis it is arguable that all primary defects can, since they involve enzymes, be traced back to protein disorders and thence back to nucleic acid sequences, etc. Furthermore, it is noticeable that anomalies are beginning to arise. For example, Sandhoff's disease is not normally considered as a case of genetic hyperglycosaminoglycanuria but it does generate a glycosaminoglycan disorder which is characterised by an accumulation of glycosaminoglycan in cultured fibroblasts and is due to a deficiency of a carbohydrate-directed enzyme.

As already indicated, the attention given to genetic hyperglycosaminoglycanuria is out of all proportion to the large range of clinical conditions known to involve proteoglycan disorders. One company has even gone to the extent of marketing urinary test papers for hyperglycosaminoglycanuria. The frequency of genetic hyperglycosaminoglycanuria is claimed to be relatively high amongst inherited diseases, although this attitude is to be questioned. The frequency of cases is of course related to the genetics; for example, the Hurler syndrome is autosomal recessive whereas Hunter syndrome is X-linked recessive, and this has a bearing on their relative frequency. The overall frequency in a Western population has been estimated at less than one per 10^5 live births. However, it is to be hoped that the consideration given these particular diseases is paving the way for successful and more rapid and direct investigation of other proteoglycan disorders, particularly with respect to identifying the primary defect. Regrettably, as yet there is little evidence of a trend to such an investigation of other diseases.

Considerable details are now known of the clinical features and the morphological, chemical and biological aspects of, and the glycosaminoglycans excreted by, the various types of genetic hyperglycosaminoglycanuria (see Table 9.4). Unfortunately, many of the conditions are manifested in childhood causing extensive deformity and mental retardation. Such characteristics of these diseases have been reviewed in detail (McKusick, 1972, and Kennedy, 1979a). The field is one in which new findings are frequently being reported.

In addition to examining the excreted end product of the disorders in genetic hyperglycosaminoglycanuria, the glycosaminoglycans, considerable attention has been given to a search for the primary defect. However, the examination of the likelihood that enzymic defects underlie the various types of genetic hyperglycosaminoglycanuria was hampered, since the enzymes in humans that normally degrade the glycosaminoglycans generally were largely, and perhaps remain, unidentified. It would seem that, in the light of certain evidence, the intracellular metabolism rather than the excretory mechanisms of the glycosaminoglycans is defective. There is now evidence for the defective degradation of glycosaminoglycans in genetic hyperglycosaminoglycanuria. Mutation, with respect to the enzymes involved in the biosynthesis and turnover of glycosaminoglycans, can result in deviation from normal control and may be responsible for these inherited disorders of connective tissue.

The six classified types of cases of genetic hyperglycosaminoglycanuria have been subclassified on the basis of clinical symptomatology, mode of genetic transmission, and nature of the glycosaminoglycan present in excess in the urine, and have been assigned type numbers (Table 9.4). Also given in the Table are relevant details of these diseases, together with details of some additional conditions which are classifiable in the same way. However, even acceptance of this somewhat arbitrary classification of types of hereditary glycosaminoglycanuria does not yield complete simplicity since hyperglycosaminoglycanuria is not always present. The best classification of these diseases would be based on the chemical aspects — the primary enzymic defect. Unfortunately, this is not yet possible since the specificities of even the enzymes which have been implicated still need to be investigated in further detail, and of course it is possible that other enzymes may be found to be involved.

Table 9.4 Classification of the better-establish

	Designation	Other names for condition	Clinical features
Type IH	Hurler syndrome	–	Early clouding of cornea grave manifestations, dea usually before age 10 yea
Type IS	Scheie syndrome	–	Stiff joints, cloudy corne aortic regurgitation, norr intelligence, ?normal life span
Type IH/S	Hurler-Scheie compound	–	Phenotype intermediate between Hurler and Sche
Type IIA	Hunter syndrome, severe	–	No clouding of cornea, milder course than in Ty IH but death usually bef age 15 years
Type IIB	Hunter syndrome, mild	–	Survival to 30s to 50s, fa intelligence
Type IIIA	Sanfilippo syndrome A	Polydystrophic oligophrenia, Heparansulphaturia	Identical phenotype: mi somatic, severe central nervous system effects
Type IIIB	Sanfilippo syndrome B		
Type IIIC	Sanfilippo syndrome C		
Type IIID	Sanfilippo syndrome D		
Type IVA	Morquio-Ullrich syndrome	Morquio syndrome, Keratansulphaturia	Severe bone changes of distinctive type, cloudy cornea, aortic regurgitation
Type IVB			Mild symptoms, cloudy cornea, short stature
Type V	Vacant[b]		
Type VIA	Maroteaux-Lamy syndrome, classic form	Polydystrophic dwarfism	Severe osseous and corne change, normal intellect
Type VIB	Maroteaux-Lamy syndrome, mild form		
Type VII	β-D-Glucuronidase deficiency (more than one allelic form)	–	Hepatosplenomegaly, dysostosis multiplex, whi cell inclusions, mental retardation

a　For details of other changes in levels of other glycosaminoglycans, see Kennedy (1979a).
b　Due to modification of earlier classifications.
c　The classification table given in McKusick (1972) records erroneously that dermatan sulphate is the principal excessive urinary glycosaminoglycan.

ypes of genetic hyperglycosaminoglycanuria

Genetics	Principal excessive urinary glycosaminoglycans[a]	Enzyme deficient
Homozygous for Hurler gene	Dermatan sulphate Heparan sulphate	α-L-Iduronidase (formerly called Hurler corrective factor)
Homozygous for Scheie gene	Dermatan sulphate Heparan sulphate	α-L-Iduronidase
Genetic compound of Hurler and Scheie genes	Dermatan sulphate Heparan sulphate	α-L-Iduronidase
Hemizygous for X-linked gene	Dermatan sulphate Heparan sulphate	L-Iduronic acid 2-sulphate sulphatase
Hemizygous for X-linked allele for mild form	Dermatan sulphate Heparan sulphate	L-Iduronic acid 2-sulphate sulphatase
Homozygous for Sanfilippo A gene	Heparan sulphate	Heparan sulphate sulphatase/ sulphamidase
Homozygous for Sanfilippo B gene (at different locus)	Heparan sulphate	α-N-Acetyl-D-glucosaminidase
	Heparan sulphate	D-Glucosamine acetyltrans- ferase
	Heparan sulphate	N-Acetyl-D-glucosamine 6-sulphate sulphatase
Homozygous for Morquio-Ullrich gene	Keratan sulphate Chondroitin 6-sulphate	N-Acetyl-D-galactosamine 6-sulphate sulphatase
	Keratan sulphate	β-D-Galactosidase
Homozygous for M-L gene	Dermatan sulphate	N-Acetyl-D-galactosamine 4-sulphate sulphatase
Homozygous for allele at M-L locus	Dermatan sulphate	
Homozygous for mutant gene at β-D-glucuronidase locus	Chondroitin 4-sulphate[c] Chondroitin 6-sulphate	β-D-Glucuronidase

CHAPTER 10
Glycolipids

Lipids, which are naturally occurring esters of long-chain fatty acids, rarely exist in a free state in an organism. They are more usually combined with protein or carbohydrate material, and as such they occur as part of the outer surface of cells. One class of lipids, known as glycolipids because of their content of a carbohydrate moiety, is a diffuse class of molecular species covering a wide range of structural types, which overlaps with other classes of lipids containing common structural features, making classification difficult and confusing. For example, some sulpholipids (sulphur-containing lipids) and phospholipids (phosphate-containing lipids) are also glycolipids, and different authors describe specific compounds in different classes, depending on the system used. For a full description of the many varied classes of lipid and the structural and biochemical properties involved the reader should refer to a general text on lipids (such as Gurr and James, 1980).

Glycolipids are widely distributed, but are usually minor components of the lipid mixture. They are associated with membrane proteinaceous material by noncovalent bonds, with the hydrophobic region buried in the outer membrane lipids and the carbohydrate region extending into the aqueous phase. The glycolipids can be removed from the membrane by use of neutral solvents, detergents, etc., in the same way as for other lipid material. Glycolipids are, therefore, a component of nearly all lipid extracts from tissue lipoproteins. The exact function of glycolipids is still the subject of much speculation. It has been suggested that glycolipids function as 'carriers' to transport carbohydrate moieties across cell membranes or as 'modifiers' which alter the physical properties of the membrane to provide the most suitable membrane for the purpose it exists. Glycolipids are known to be involved in the biosynthesis of glycoproteins and complex polysaccharides in that the lipid moiety acts as a carrier for the growing carbohydrate moiety which, on completion of its biosynthesis, is transferred to the protein (for glycoproteins) or carbohydrate (for polysaccharides) backbone (see Chapter 5). There is also good evidence to show that glycolipids exert a controlling mechanism in biosynthesis of proteoglycans (see Kennedy, 1979a) and in the inhibition of the biological activity of toxins and antiviral agents. It is known that a number of toxins, including cholera and tetanus toxins, bind to the carbohydrate moiety of glycolipids and that the specific action of such toxins can be inhibited by gangliosides, thereby providing a possible means of protection against the diseases caused by these toxins. Interferon interacts with gangliosides to provide or increase the antiviral activity of interferon. This has been demonstrated by the treatment with gangliosides of mouse cells which do not respond to interferon treatment, with the result that the cells become responsive (see Sharon, 1980).

The subsequent discussion on glycolipids uses divisions based on origin rather than chemical types. This reflects the structural complexities of glycolipids from various sources, with those from animal sources having much less diversity (mainly in the carbohydrate moiety) than those obtained from plant and microbial sources (with variations in all parts of the molecule).

For reviews of glycolipids and the background to work carried out prior to 1970 the reader should refer to McKibbin (1970), Kiss (1970), Cook and Stoddart (1973), Hakomori (1976), and Sweeley (1980), whilst up to date reviews of the occurrence, isolation, structures, chemistry and biochemistry of glycolipids from animal, plant, algal and microbial sources are available in an ongoing series of articles (see Various Authors, 1968 onwards). Nomenclature of glycolipids is governed by the IUPAC-IUB Rules for the Nomenclature of Lipids (Recommendation, 1976).

ANIMAL GLYCOLIPIDS

Most animal glycolipids are derivatives of long-chain bases related to sphingosine, the most common of which are shown in Table 10.1. Attached to these bases, *via* amide linkages, are long chain fatty acids (between 16 and 24 carbon atoms) which are usually completely or almost completely saturated (see Table 10.2). These simple sphingolipids are given the generic name ceramides (abbreviated to Cer for shorthand structural notation). Glycosphingolipids, in which carbohydrate moieties are attached *via* glycosidic linkages to the terminal hydroxyl group of the base, include neutral glycosylsphingoids (which contain no fatty acid) and glycosylceramides, acidic glycosylsphingolipids (gangliosides, which contain 5-acetamido-3,5-dideoxy-D-*glycero*-D-*galacto*-2-nonulopyranonic acid), and sulphoglycosylsphingolipids (non-recommended trivial name: sulphatides). The carbohydrate moiety usually contains between one and seven residues in a linear or branched structure, the most common components being D-glucose, D-galactose, L-fucose, 2-acetamido-2-deoxy-D-glucose and -D-galactose and 5-acetamido-3,5-dideoxy-D-*glycero*-D-*galacto*-2-nonulopyranonic acid, with D-galactose being the most common in plant glycolipids, D-glucose and D-mannose the most common in microbial glycolipids whilst 5-acetamido-3,5-dideoxy-D-*glycero*-D-*galacto*-2-nonulopyranonic acid is found mainly in gangliosides and globosides (see later in this chapter).

Table 10.1 Structure of the more common sphingoid bases[a]

Recommended name	Structure
Sphingosine (*trans*-4-sphingenine)	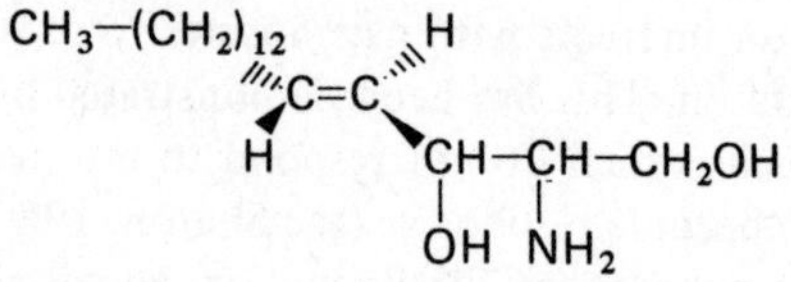 CH_3—$(CH_2)_{12}$ ... C=C ... CH—CH—CH$_2$OH, OH NH$_2$
Sphinganine (dihydrosphingosine)	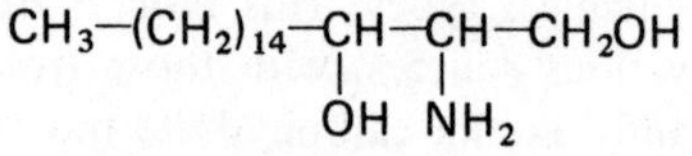 CH_3—$(CH_2)_{14}$—CH—CH—CH$_2$OH, OH NH$_2$
4D-Hydroxysphinganine (phytosphingosine)	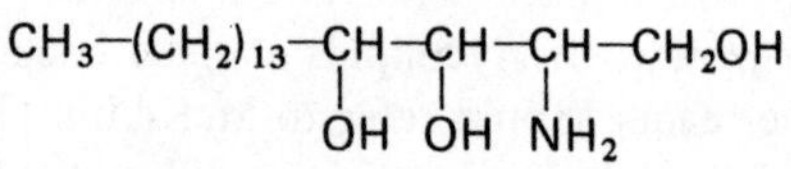 CH_3—$(CH_2)_{13}$—CH—CH—CH—CH$_2$OH, OH OH NH$_2$
4D-Hydroxy 8-sphingenine (dehydrophytosphingosine)	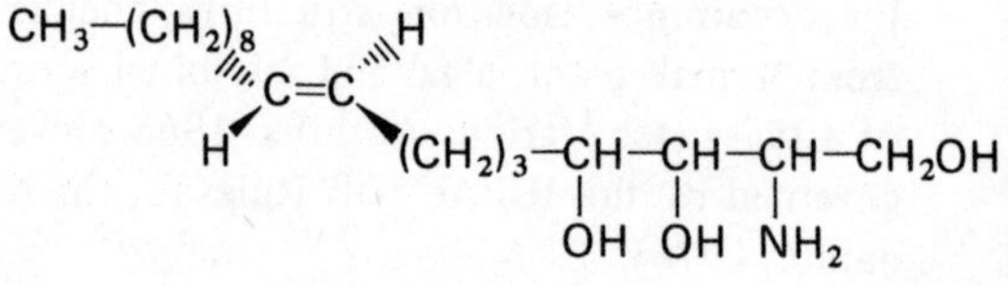 CH_3—$(CH_2)_8$ ... C=C ... $(CH_2)_3$—CH—CH—CH—CH$_2$OH, OH OH NH$_2$
Icosasphinganine[b]	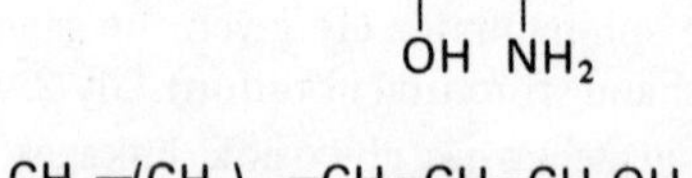 CH_3—$(CH_2)_{16}$—CH—CH—CH$_2$OH, OH NH$_2$
Icosasphingosine[c]	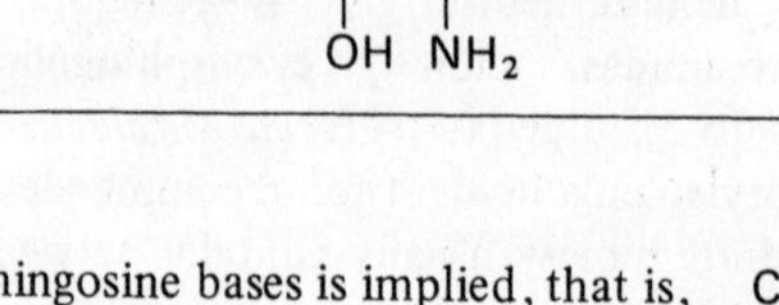 $CH_3(CH_2)_{14}$ ... C=C ... CH—CH—CH$_2$OH, OH NH$_2$
Hexadecasphinganine	CH_3—$(CH_2)_{12}$—CH—CH—CH$_2$OH, OH NH$_2$

a D-*Erythro*-configuration of sphingosine bases is implied, that is, CH_2OH / HCNH$_2$ / HCOH / R

b Formerly eicosaphinganine

c Formerly eicosaphingosine

Table 10.2 Structure of the higher fatty acids

Trivial name	Structure $CH_3-[R]-COOH$	Systematic name	Numerical[a] symbol
Capric acid [b]	$-[CH_2]_8-$	Decanoic acid	10:0
Lauric acid	$-[CH_2]_{10}-$	Dodecanoic acid	12:0
Myristic acid	$-[CH_2]_{12}-$	Tetradecanoic acid	14:0
Palmitic acid	$-[CH_2]_{14}-$	Hexadecanoic acid	16:0
Palmitoleic acid	$-[CH_2]_5-CH=CH-[CH_2]_7-$	9-Hexadecenoic acid	16:1
Stearic acid	$-[CH_2]_{16}-$	Octadecanoic acid	18:0
Oleic acid	$-[CH_2]_7-CH=CH-[CH_2]_7-$	cis-9-Octadecenoic acid	18:1(9)
Vaccenic acid	$-[CH_2]_5-CH=CH-[CH_2]_9-$	11-Octadecenoic acid	18:1(11)
Linoleic acid	$-[CH_2]_3-[CH_2-CH=CH]_2-[CH_2]_7-$	cis, cis-9,12-Octadienoic acid	18:2(9,12)
(9,12,15)-Linoleic acid	$-[CH_2-CH=CH]_3-[CH_2]_7-$	9,12,15-Octadecatrienoic acid	18:3(9,12,15)
(6,9,12)-Linoleic acid	$-[CH_2]_3-[CH_2-CH=CH]_3-[CH_2]_4-$	6,9,12-Octadecatrienoic acid	18:3(6,9,12)
Eleostearic acid	$-[CH_2]_3-[CH=CH]_3-[CH_2]_7-$	9,11,13-Octadecatrienoic acid	18:3(9,11,13)
Arachidic acid	$-[CH_2]_{18}-$	Icosanoic acid [c]	20:0
	$-[CH_2]_6-[CH_2-CH=CH]_2-[CH_2]_6-$	8,11-Icosadienoic acid [c]	20:2(8,11)
	$-[CH_2]_6-[CH_2-CH=CH]_3-[CH_2]_3-$	5,8,11-Icosatrienoic acid [c]	20:3(5,8,11)
Arachidonic acid	$-[CH_2]_3-[CH_2-CH-CH=CH]_4-[CH_2]_3-$	5,8,11,14-Icosatetraenoic acid [c]	20:4(5,8,11,14)
Behenic acid	$-[CH_2]_{20}-$	Docosanoic acid	22:0
Lignoceric acid	$-[CH_2]_{22}-$	Tetracosanoic acid	24:0
Nervonic acid	$-[CH_2]_7-CH=CH-[CH_2]_{13}-$	cis-15-Tetracosenoic acid	24:1
Cerotic acid	$-[CH_2]_{24}-$	Hexacosanoic acid	26:0
Montanic acid	$-[CH_2]_{26}-$	Octacosanoic acid	28:0

a   The notation giving the number of carbon atoms and of double bonds (separated by a colon) and the position of double bonds (in parentheses) can be used to described fatty acids, for example 16:0 for palmitic acid and 18:1(11) for 11-octadecenoic acid.

b   Not recommended because of confusion with caproic (hexanoic) and caprylic (octanoic) acids.

c   Formerly 'Eicosa-'.

Glycosylceramides (cerebrosides)

The simplest glycolipids which are found in most mammalian tissues, and particularly in high concentrations in the central nervous system, are the monoglycosylceramides or cerebrosides. Variations in the sugar, base and fatty acid components are possible, with sugar composition depending largely on the tissue source. Brain cerebrosides contain mainly D-galactosyl groups (131) whilst those from serum contain D-glucosyl groups (132), with fatty acids typically being behenic, lignoceric, nervonic or cerebronic (α-hydroxytetrasanoic) acid (see Table 10.1). A related D-galactosylsphingoid (psychosine, 133), which contains no fatty acid, and a sulphoglycosylceramide (D-galactopyranosyl 3-sulphate ceramide, 134) are as generally distributed as cerebrosides.

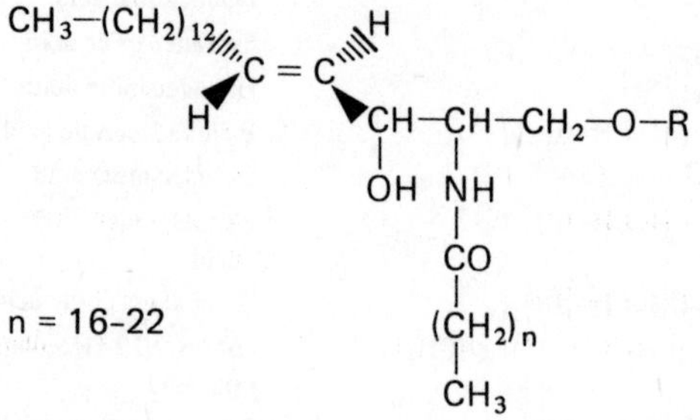

n = 16-22

(131)   −R =

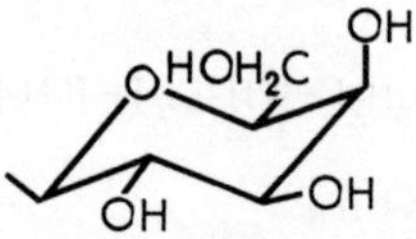

(132)   −R =

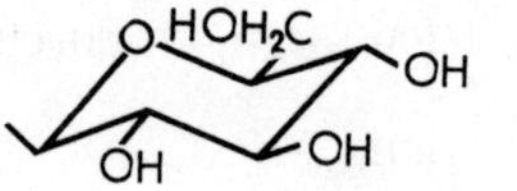

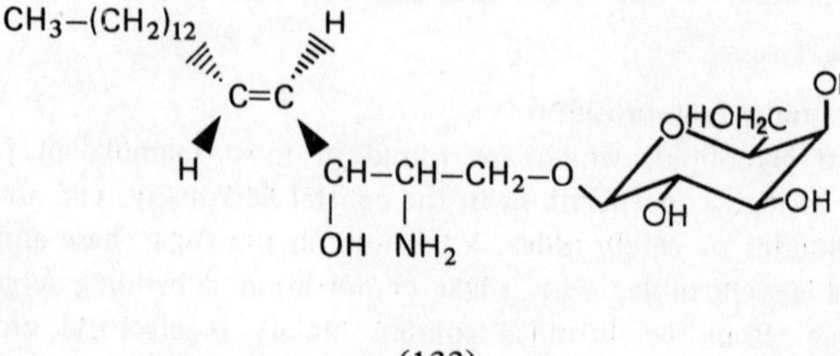

(133)

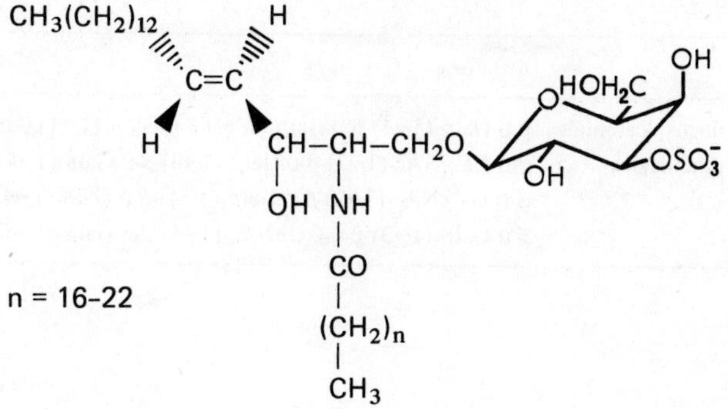

(134)

Diglycosylceramides are also widely distributed, with lactosyl ceramide (135) being the most common. It is a precursor for more-complex glycosylceramides and gangliosides. A minor diglycosylceramide found in the kidney is digalactosylceramide which contains the disaccharide 4-O-β-D-galactopyranosyl-D-galactopyranose. Higher oligosaccharides are attached to ceramide to give tri- and tetra-glycosylceramides (see Table 10.3) which occur to various degrees throughout animal tissues. The oligosaccharide components often bear a striking resemblance to those of glycoproteins produced within the same tissue, particularly in the terminal part of the chain (not the core region). Thus the monosaccharide sequences of the soluble blood-group substance glycoproteins (see Chapter 9, p. 201 and Fig. 9.5) are identical to those of the glycolipids found on the surfaces of red blood cells. Such substances exhibit identical antigenic specificities because antibodies use these external sequences for recognition.

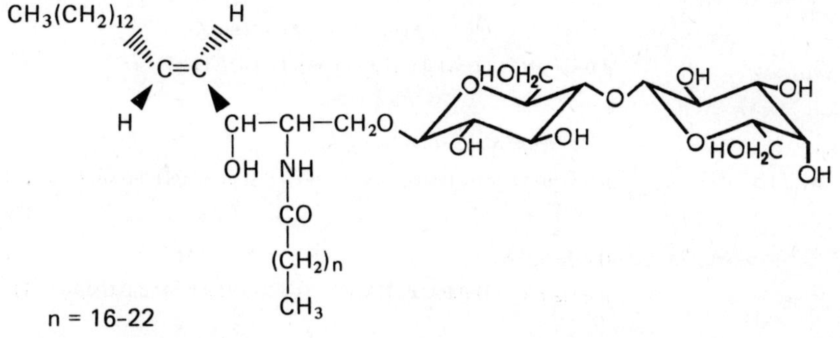

(135)

Table 10.3 Structures of some common tri- and tetra-glycosylceramides

Name	Structure
Di-D-galactosyl-D-glucosylceramide	β-D-Gal$p$-(1→4)-β-D-Gal$p$-(1→4)-β-D-Glc$p$-(1→1)-Cer
Aminoglycolipids (globosides)	β-D-Gal$p$NAc-(1→3)-β-D-Gal$p$-(1→4)-β-D-Gal$p$-(1→4)-β-D-Glc$p$-(1→1)-Cer
	α-D-Gal$p$NAc-(1→3)-β-D-Gal$p$-(1→4)-β-D-Gal$p$-(1→4)-β-D-Glc$p$-(1→1)-Cer
Ganglioside G_{A_1}	β-D-Gal$p$-(1→3)-β-D-Gal$p$NAc-(1→4)-β-D-Gal$p$-(1→4)-β-D-Glc$p$-(1→1)-Cer

Table 10.4 Structures of some gangliosides

Ganglioside	Structure
G_{M_1}	β-D-Gal$p$-(1→3)-β-D-Gal$p$NAc-(1→4)-β-D-Gal$p$-(1→4)-β-D-Glc$p$-(1→1)-Cer 3 ↑ 2 α-Neu$p$5Ac
G_{M_2}	β-D-Gal$p$NAc-(1→4)-β-D-Gal$p$-(1→4)-β-D-Glc$p$-(1→1)-Cer 3 ↑ 2 α-Neu$p$5Ac
G_{M_3}	α-Neu$p$5Ac-(2→3)-β-D-Gal$p$-(1→4)-β-D-Glc$p$-(1→1)-Cer
$G_{D_{1a}}$	β-D-Gal$p$-(1→3)-β-D-Gal$p$NAc-(1→4)-β-D-Gal$p$-(1→4)-β-D-Glc$p$-(1→1)-Cer 3 3 ↑ ↑ 2 2 α-Neu$p$Ac α-Neu$p$5Ac
$G_{D_{1b}}$	β-D-Gal$p$-(1→3)-β-D-Gal$p$NAc-(1→4)-β-D-Gal$p$-(1→4)-β-D-Glc$p$-(1→1)-Cer 3 ↑ 2 α-Neu$p$5Ac-(2→8)-α-Neu$p$5Ac
G_{D_2}	β-D-Gal$p$NAc-(1→4)-β-D-Gal$p$-(1→4)-β-D-Glc$p$-(1→1)-Cer 3 ↑ 2 α-Neu$p$5Ac-(2→8)-α-Neu$p$5Ac
$G_{T_{1a}}$	β-D-Gal$p$-(1→3)-β-D-Gal$p$NAc-(1→4)-β-D-Gal$p$-(1→4)-β-D-Glc$p$-(1→1)-Cer 3 3 ↑ ↑ 2 2 α-Neu$p$5Ac-(2→8)-α-Neu$p$5Ac α-Neu$p$5Ac
$G_{T_{1b}}$	β-D-Gal$p$-(1→3)-β-D-Gal$p$NAc-(1→4)-β-D-Gal$p$-(1→4)-β-D-Glc$p$-(1→1)-Cer 3 3 ↑ ↑ 2 2 α-Neu$p$5Ac α-Neu$p$5Ac-(2→8)-α-Neu$p$5Ac

Gangliosides

This class of glycosphingolipids contains one or more residues of 5-acetamido-3,5-dideoxy-D-*glycero*-D-*galacto*-2-nonulopyranonic acid linked to a glycosylceramide, (for example, $G_{D_{1a}}$ and $G_{D_{1b}}$ in Table 10.4) either as a single residue side chain or as a disaccharide residue side chain; these are referred to by the trivial names mono-, di-, tri-sialogangliosides, etc., depending on the number of residues of the nine carbon sugar. Because of their complex structures, and hence cumbersome chemical names, many shorthand notation systems have been employed, one of the most common being that due to Svennerholm (1963). They are all given the prefix G (for ganglioside) with subscripts A, M, D or T to denote the number of 5-acetamido-3,5-dideoxy-D-*glycero*-D-*galacto*-2-nonulopyranosylonic acid residues present; A (none), M (mono), D (di) and T (tri). To further differentiate the various gangliosides a number is assigned to each, which is usually based on the order in which the compounds separate on thin-layer chromatography. A system, devised by Weignandt (1973), is becoming more common due to its advantage that structures can be deduced from the shorthand notation once the symbols have been learnt, but, as yet, it has not superceded the Svennerholm system. The structures of some gangliosides, together with their Svennerholm notation are given in Table 10.4; the major bases present are sphingosine and icosasphingosine with some of the saturated analogues being present in minor amounts. Stearic acid is the predominant fatty acid, accounting for 85–95% of the total ganglioside fatty acid in human brain.

Gangliosides have been found in many tissues, commonly spleen, liver and kidney with the grey matter of brain being the major site of occurrence where the major gangliosides occur in the ratio $G_{M_1}:G_{D_{1a}}:G_{D_{1b}}:G_{T_{1a}}$ of 3:4:2:1. They also occur in erythrocytes, where, in common with gangliosides from spleen, the amino-group of 5-amino-3,5-dideoxy-D-*glycero*-D-*galacto*-2-nonulopyranonic acid is glycolated rather than acetylated.

Globosides

Closely related to the gangliosides are a number of glycolipids which contain an additional D-galactopyranosyl residue linked to the D-galactopyranosyl residue adjacent to the lipid moiety. These compounds, referred to by the trivial name of globosides, have very similar carbohydrate structures to the gangliosides in the regions further away from the lipid moiety (see Table 10.3).

Miscellaneous animal glycolipids

Trace quantities of glycosylglycerides (see plant glycolipids, p. 243) and phospholipids (see microbial glycolipids, p. 246) are found in the central nervous systems of several animals.

Table 10.5 Classification of the better established lipidoses

Designation	Other names	Clinical features	Principle glycolipid stored	Enzyme deficient
Fabry's disease	Angiokeratoma corporis diffusum. Hereditary dystopic lipidosis.	Pain, angiokeratoma, corneal opacities, skin lesions, renal failure.	D-Galactosyl-D-galactosyl-D-glucosyl ceramide	D-Galactosyl-D-galactosyl-D-glucosyl ceramidase
Farber's lipogranulomatosis	Ceramidase deficiency	Subcutaneous and joint swellings, dysphonia, dermatitis pyrexia, paralysis. Death by 2 years.	Ceramide	Ceramidase
Gaucher disease type I (juvenile form)	Glucosyl ceramide lipidosis (non-cerebral)	Hepatosplenomegaly, 'Gaucher' cells, variable neuropathy, encephalopathy.	D-Glucosyl ceramide	D-Glucosyl ceramidase
Gaucher disease type II (infantile form)	Glucosyl ceramide lipidosis (cerebral)	Hepatosplenomegaly, retroflexion of head, strabismus, dysphagia, choking spells, hypertonicity. Death by 1 year.	D-Glucosyl ceramide	D-Glucosyl ceramidase
Gaucher disease type III (juvenile and adult)	Glucosyl ceramide lipidosis (cerebral)	Hypersplenism, bone lesions, skin pigmentation, pingueculae occur.	D-Glucosyl ceramide	D-Glucosyl ceramidase
$G_{D_{1a}}$ Gangliosidosis		Progressive psychomotor deterioration, sensitivity to noise.	$G_{D_{1a}}$	β-D-Galactosidase
G_{M_1} Gangliosidosis type I	Neurovisceral gangliosidosis Pseudo-Hurler disease	Progressive psychomotor deterioration, hepatosplenomegaly, skeletal abnormalities, cherry-red macular spot. Death by 2 years.	G_{M_1}	β-D-Galactosidase (isoenzymes B and C)
G_{M_1} Gangliosidosis type II	Juvenile type G_{M_1}	Diffuse angiokeratoma. Onset at 2 years with survival to 10 years.	G_{M_1}	β-D-Galactosidase
G_{M_1} Gangliosidosis type III	Adult type G_{M_1}	Less severe than types I and II. Angiokeratoma, spondyloepiphyseal dysplasia.	G_{M_1}	β-D-Galactosidase
G_{M_2} Gangliosidosis type I	Tay-Sachs disease	Progressive psychomotor deterioration, dementia, blindness, cherry-red macular spot. Death by 3 years.	G_{M_2}	2-Acetamido-2-deoxy-D-galactosidase (isoenzyme A)

Disease	Clinical features	Lipid accumulated	Enzyme deficient
(infantile type) Globoside storage disease	...ation, early blindness, startle reaction, doll-like face, cherry-red macular spot. Death by 3 years.	GM_2	galactosidase (isoenzymes A and B)
Sandhoff's disease (juvenile type)	Progressive cerebellar ataxia, psychomotor retardation.	GM_2	2-Acetamido-2-deoxy-D-galactosidase (isoenzymes A and B)
GM_2 Gangliosidosis type III — Juvenile type GM_2	Ataxia, deterioration to decerebrate rigidity. Onset between 2 and 6 years with death by 5 to 15 years.	GM_2	2-Acetamido-2-deoxy-D-galactosidase (isoenzyme A)
GM_2 Gangliosidosis type IV — Adult (chronic) type GM_2	Slow progressive deterioration of gait and posture, mild ataxia, normal intelligence and vision.	GM_2	2-Acetamido-2-deoxy-D-galactosidase (isoenzyme A)
GM_3 Gangliosidosis	Poor psychomotor development, gradual hepatosplenomegaly, stubby hands and feet, large inguinal herneas, unresponsive. Early death.	GM_3	UDP-2-acetamido-2-deoxy-D-galactose : GM_3-2-acetamido-2-deoxy-D-galactosyl transferase.
Krabbe's leucodystrophy — Globoid cell leucodystrophy	Progressive psychomotor deterioration, deafness, blindness.	D-Galactosyl ceramide	β-D-Galactosyl ceramidase
Lactosyl ceramidosis	Poor psychomotor development, hypotonia, optic atrophy, hepatosplenomegaly.	GA_3	β-D-Galactosidase
Metachromatic leucodystrophy — Sulphatide lipidosis	Early onset. Psychomotor disturbances.	Sulphoglycosyl ceramides	Arylsulphatase (isoenzyme A)
Adult type	Onset after 16 years. Schizophrenia, gallbladder nonfunction.	Sulphoglycosyl ceramides	Arylsulphatase (isoenzyme A)
Late infantile type	Onset by 2 years with death by 5 years. Poor motor development, mental deterioration, hypotonia, muscle weakness.	Sulphoglycosyl ceramides	Arylsulphatase (isoenzyme A)
Juvenile type	Onset between 4 and 10 years.	Sulphoglycosyl ceramides	Arylsulphatase (isoenzyme A)
Niemann-Pick disease (types A–F) — Sphingomyelinosis (types A–F)	Variable onset and severity. Hepatosplenomegaly, variable neuropathy, jaundice, cherry-red macular spot, corneal opacity.	Sphingomyelin	Sphingomyelin phosphodiesterase

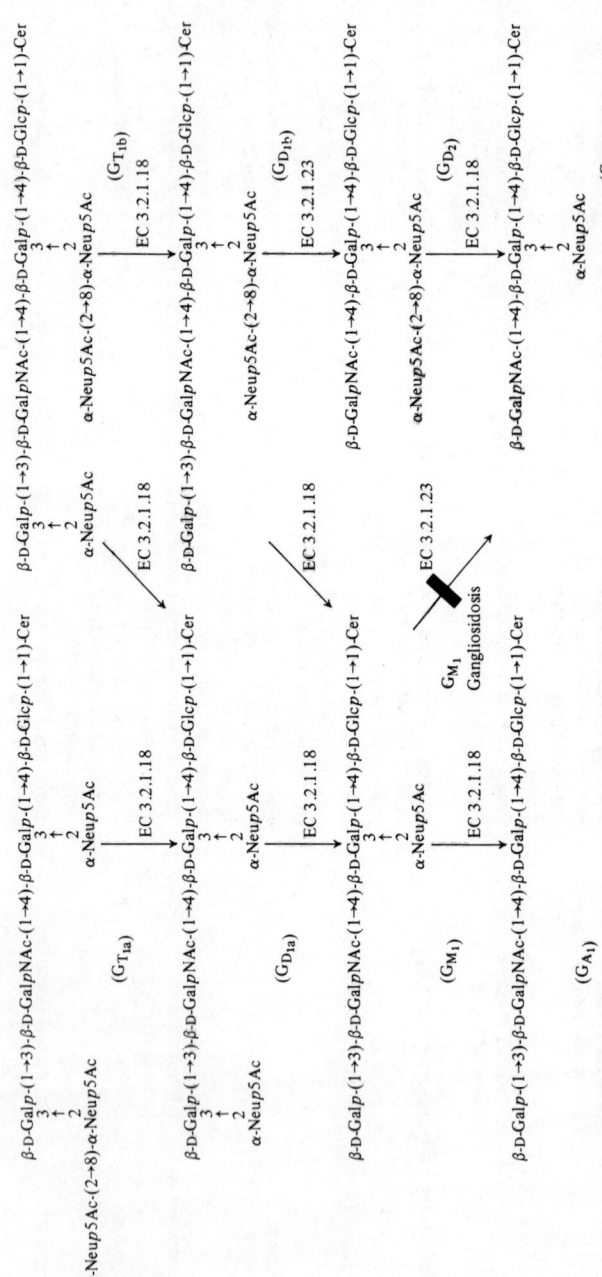

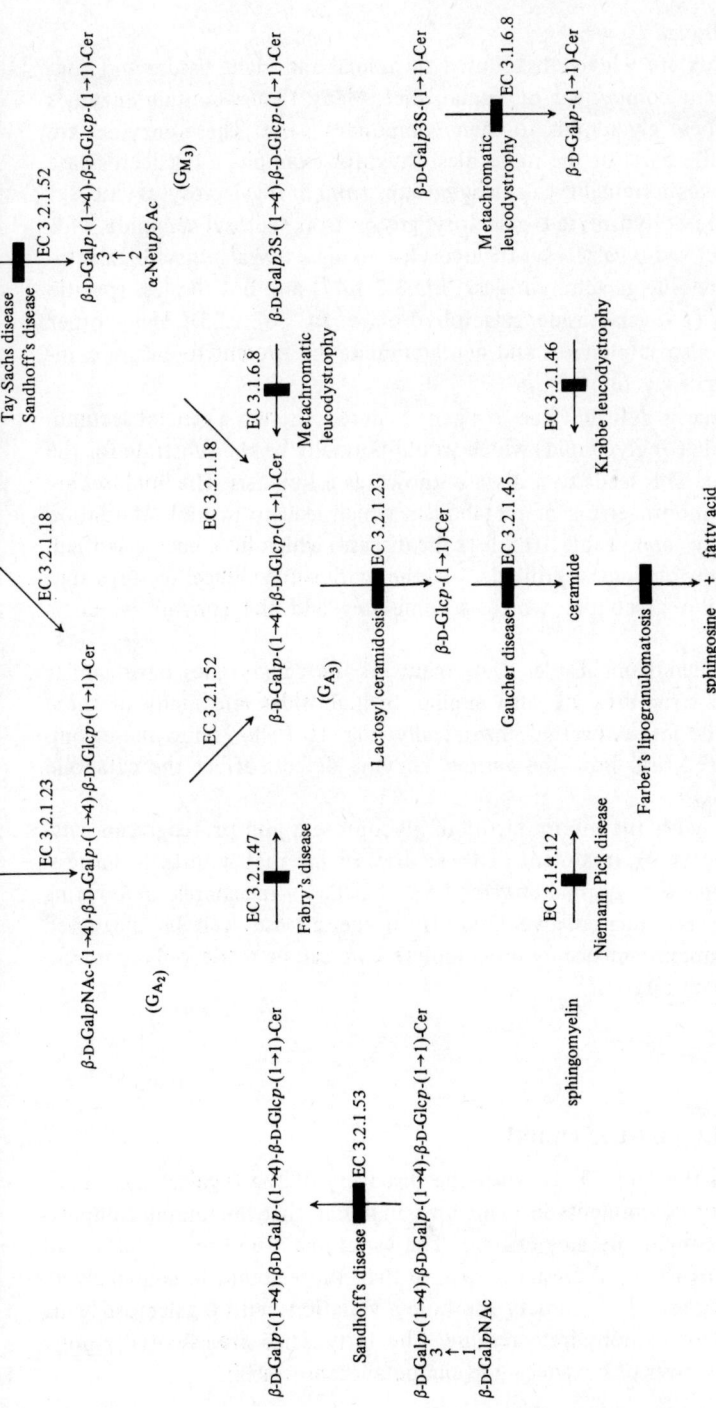

Fig. 10.1 – Glycolipid catabolic pathway showing the better established sites for blockages which give rise to the lipidoses.

Involvement in disease

Glycosphingolipids are widely distributed in animal and plant tissues and constitute a significant component of human diet. Many tissues contain enzymes which degrade these glycolipids to their component parts. These enzymes are specific for specific parts of the molecules, thus, for example, a D-galactosidase exists which cleaves terminal D-galactosyl groups from di-D-galactosyl-D-glucosyl ceramide but will not hydrolyse D-galactosyl groups from lactosyl ceramide. This enzyme is D-galactosyl-D-galactosyl-D-glucosylceramidase (D-galactosyl-D-galactosyl-D-glucosyl-ceramide galactohydrolase, EC 3.2.1.47) and not the less specific β-D-galactosidase (β-D-galactoside galactohydrolase, EC 3.2.1.23). Many other glycosidases and also sulphatases and neuraminidase are present to ensure complete degradation of glycolipids.

If any enzyme is deficient due to a genetic defect there is a general accumulation of that lipid (or glycolipid) which would normally be the substrate for the deficient enzyme. This leads to a disease known as a lipidosis. The lipidoses are a group of rare inborn errors of metabolism which lead to mental retardation and are frequently fatal. Table 10.5 lists the diseases which have been classified, on clinical and morphological grounds, together with some clinical features and, where known, the glycolipid which accumulates and the enzyme which is deficient.

As can be seen from Table 10.4, many of the gangliosides have similar structures; these structures are also similar to globosides and many of these compounds can be interconverted enzymically. Fig. 10.1 shows how these compounds are related and how the various enzyme defects affect the catabolic pathway.

In common with the inborn errors of glycoprotein and proteoglycan catabolism (see Chapter 9), treatment of these diseases has met with little success. Infusion of plasma with normal enzyme levels has had some success in lowering the amount of accumulated glycolipid. Until the diseases can be diagnosed before mental impairment occurs no complete cure can be made, only a prevention of further deterioration.

PLANT AND ALGAL GLYCOLIPIDS

It was not until the late 1950s, with the discovery of the D-galactosyl-diacyl-glycerols as major components in plant lipid material, that the unique complexity of plant glycolipids became evident. The variations found in the fatty acid and other parts of the lipid are more diverse than those found in animal glycolipids, but the carbohydrate moiety shows less variation, with D-galactose being the most abundant carbohydrate residue. The fatty acids are essentially poly-unsaturated derivatives of hexadecanoic and octadecanoic acids.

Glycosylglycerides

The major glycerolipids of chloroplasts are mono-D-galactosyl diacylglycerol (136) and the sulpholipid, sulphoquinovosyl diacylglycerol (137) which contains a carbon–sulphur bond at C-6. The accepted lipid nomenclature for these compounds are 1,2-diacyl-[β-D-galactopyranosyl (1'→3)]-*sn*-glycerol and 1,2-diacyl-[6-sulpho-α-D-quinovopyranosyl-(1'→3)]-*sn*-glycerol but in carbohydrate-accepted nomenclature these compounds are β-D-galactopyranosyl-(1→1')-2',3'-diacyl-D-glycerol and 6-deoxy-α-D-glucopyranosyl 6-*C*-sulphate-(1→1')-2',3'-diacyl-D-glycerol respectively, (D-quinovose ≡ 6-deoxy-D-glucose). The mono-D-galactosyl diacyl glycerols from *Chlorella vulgaris* mainly contains the fatty acids octadecenoic acid and octadecadienoic acid when grown in the dark but up to 20% octadecatrienoic acid when grown in the light, whilst those from spinach chloroplast have 25% hexadecatrienoic and 75% octadecatrienoic acids and from *Euglena gracilis* contain hexadecatetrenoic acid. Sulphoquinovosyl diacylglycerols contain more of the saturated fatty acids (mainly palmitic acid) than are found in D-galactolipids, with that from spinach leaf containing 27% palmitic, 39% octadecadienoic and 28% octadecatrienoic acids.

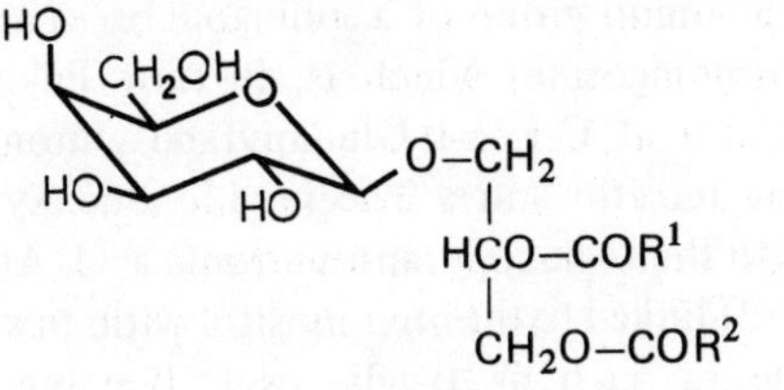

(136)

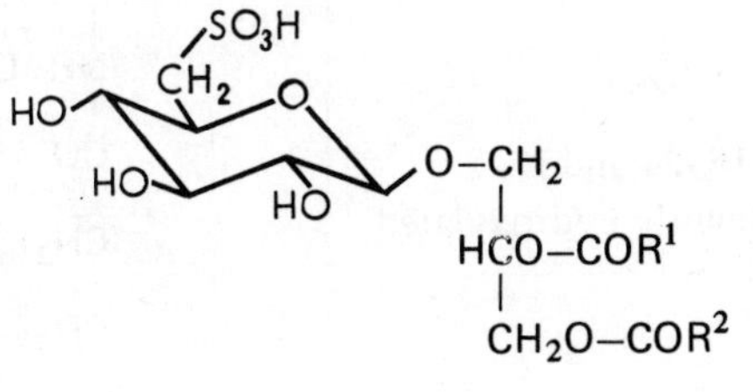

(137)

Another common glycosylglyceride found in higher plants and algae is digalactosyl diacylglycerol (138) which contains the same high proportions of polyunsaturated fatty acids (mainly octadecatrienoic acid) as the mono-D-galactosyl derivative.

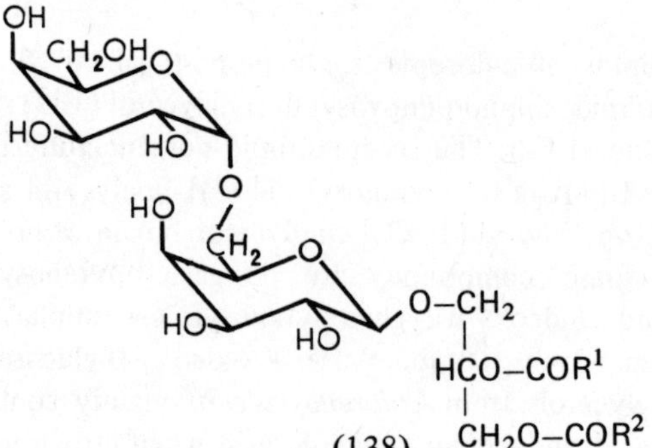

(138)

Miscellaneous glycolipids

A number of glycolipids occur as minor components in plants. These include D-glucocerebrosides (see animal glycolipids, p. 233), phospholipids (see microbial glycolipids, p. 246), phytoglycolipids, and sterol glycosides. In the group of phosphosphingolipids, isolated from corn, soya bean, wheatgerm, flax, cotton and sunflower seeds, known as phytoglycolipids (139), the fatty acid residue is linked to the amino group of a sphingoid base (usually phytosphingosine or dehydrophytosphingosine) which is, in turn, linked *via* phosphate to a residue of *myo*-inositol at C-1. α-D-Glucopyranosyluronic acid residues are attached at C-6 of the inositol and a 2-acetamido-2-deoxy-α-D-glucopyranosyl group is (1→4)-linked to the D-glucopyranosyluronic acid. An α-D-mannopyranosyl group is usually (1→2)-linked to the *myo*-inositol with, in some cases, additional carbohydrate moieties such as D-galactosyl, D-arabinosyl, and L-fucosyl residues and groups attached to the 2-acetamido-2-deoxy-D-glucosyl group.

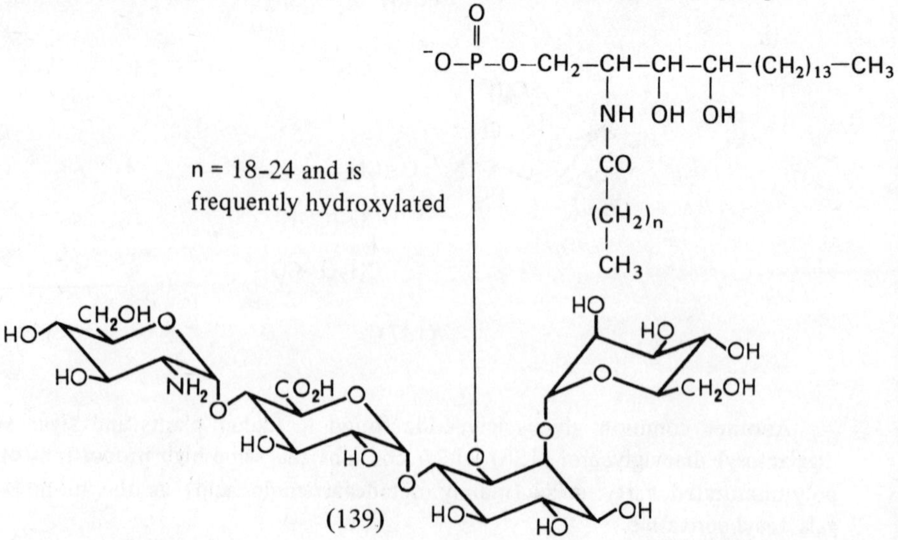

n = 18–24 and is frequently hydroxylated

(139)

A number of sterol and acylsterol glycosides (140) have been isolated in trace amounts from plants. In these glycolipids the sterol is usually β-sitosterol but cholesterol has now been identified in many higher plants and algae (particularly red algae). The carbohydrate is, in some cases, acylated at C-6 with fatty acids (particularly hexadecanoic and octadecanoic acids and their unsaturated derivatives), as shown in (140).

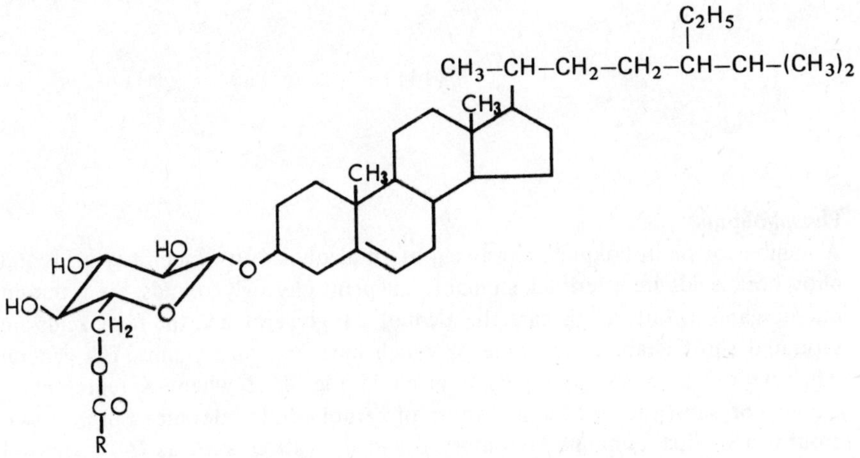

(140)

MICROBIAL GLYCOLIPIDS

The majority of bacterial carbohydrate–lipid materials are essentially high molecular weight polymers, known as lipopolysaccharides, distinguishable from glycolipids on account of their water solubility. The structures of these materials have been discussed in Chapter 8. The occurrence of sphingolipids and cerebrosides is rare, with the major component being glycosylglycerides, esters of carbohydrates and glycosides of hydroxy fatty acids and hydroxylated hydrocarbons containing terminal phenolic groups.

Glycosylglycerides

The glycosylglycerides found in bacteria, particularly the micrococci, are similar to those found in plants with the exceptions that D-mannose and D-glucose are more predominant than D-galactose and a large proportion of the fatty acids have branched chains. A di-D-mannosyl diacylglycerol (141) is most abundant although a mono-D-mannosyl derivative occurs. Glycosylglycerides isolated from *Pneumococci* consist of, *inter alia*, D-galactosyl-D-glucosyl-diacylglycerols whilst those from *Streptococci* and *Mycoplasma* contain mono- and di-D-glucosyl diacylglycerols.

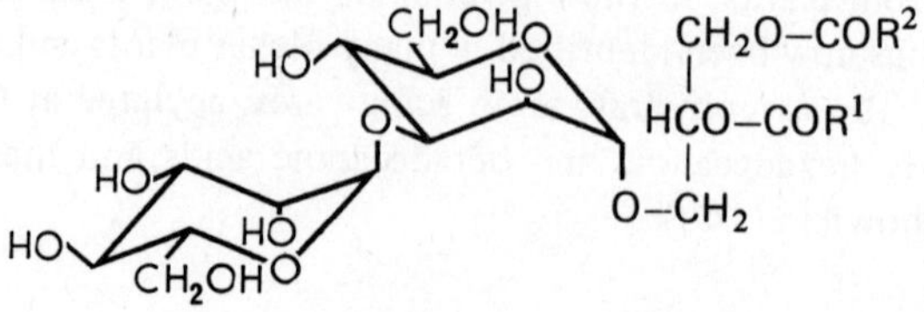

(141)

Phospholipids

A number of phospholipids, consisting of an alcohol with which fatty acids and phosphoric acids are esterified, similar to the plant phytoglycolipids, are found in microorganisms but in this case the alcohol is D-glycerol, and the fatty acids are saturated short chain acids, some of which have branched chains. The general structure of these phospholipids is given in Fig. 10.2 where X represents a number of substituents of which those of carbohydrate relevance fall into two groups. The first contains *myo*-inositol and derivatives such as O-D-mannosyl inositols. Thus structures such as (142), the so-called phosphatidyl inositol mannosides from *Micrococcus phlei* and *M. tuberculosis*, are obtained.

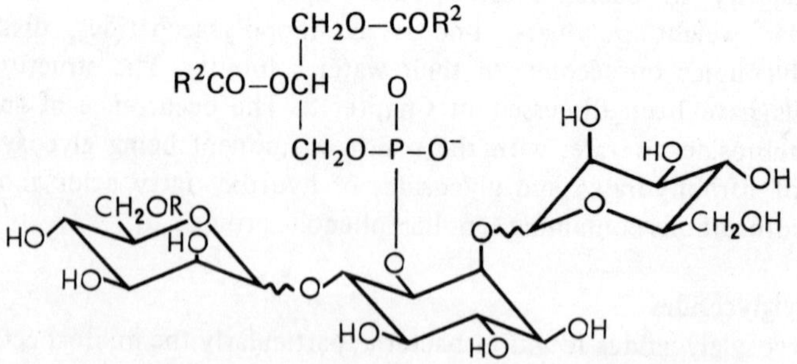

$$R = \begin{cases} \text{D-mannosyl, D-mannosyl disaccharide,} \\ \text{D-mannosyl trisaccharide,} \\ \text{D-galactosyl,} \\ \text{D-arabinosyl, or} \\ \text{L-fucosyl} \end{cases}$$

(142)

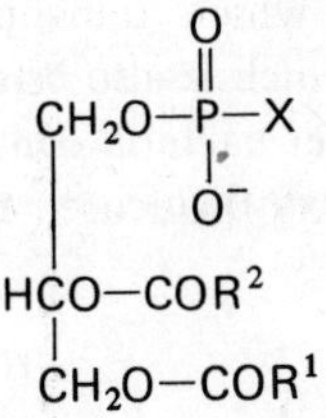

Fig. 10.2 – General representation of the glycerolphospholipids. X = organic bases, aminoacids, alcohols, carbohydrates, etc.

The second group of phospholipids, which are related to the above, have glycerol in place of inositol, and some of this group have 2-acetamido-2-deoxy-D-glucosyl residues linked to C-2 or C-3 of free glycerol residues (143).

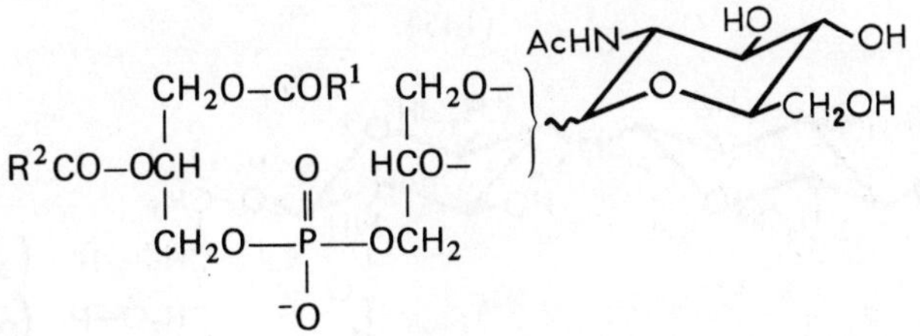

(143)

Carbohydrate esters

These constitute a whole family of complex glycolipids which are mainly confined to the *Mycobacteria*. Cord factor, so-called because it is found in the waxy capsular material of virulent strains of tubercule bacilli where it causes the bacteria to string together in a long cord or chain, is an ester of α,α-trehalose, it being esterified with two molecules of the mycolic acid fatty acids, such as the 60 carbon atom acid as found in cord factor from *Mycobacterium smegmatis* shown in (144).

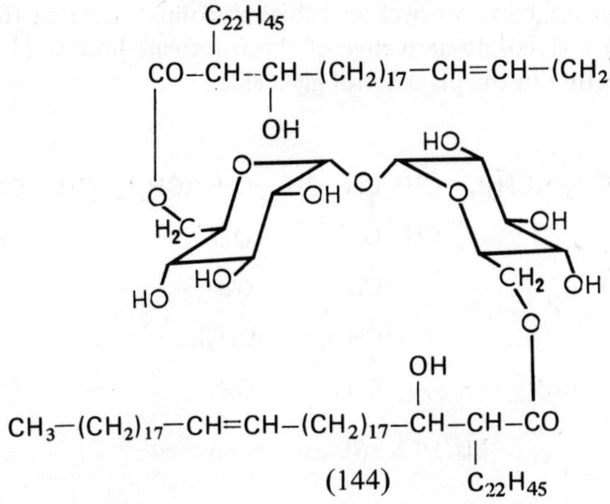

(144)

Esters of *myo*-inositol in which D-mannosyl residues are glycosidically linked to C-2 of *myo*-inositol which is also esterified at both C-1 and C-6 (145) are found in *Mycobacteria*. Other bacteria contain esters of D-glucose and other sugars including 2-amino-2-deoxy-D-glucose, as in the glycolipid (146) from *Bacillus acidocaldarius*.

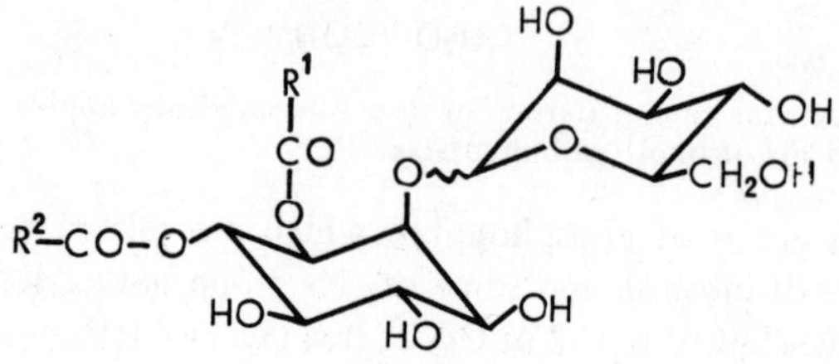

(145)

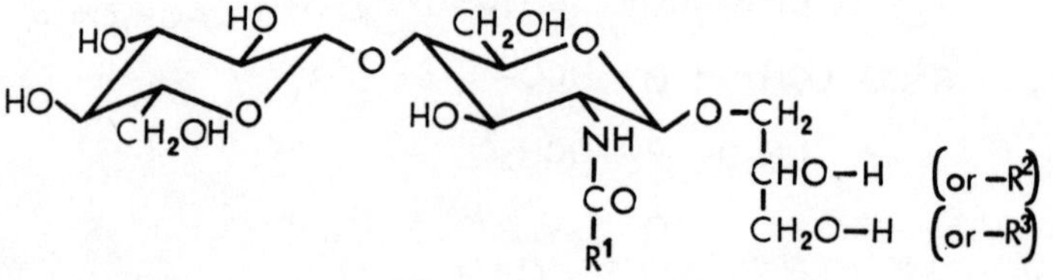

(146)

Carbohydrate glycosides

The major glycosides are the mycosides from *Mycobacteria* which contain a long chain, highly branched, hydroxylated hydrocarbon terminated by a phenol group to which the carbohydrate moiety is glycosidically linked (see Fig. 10.3). The carbohydrate is usually a di- or tri-saccharide and frequently contains 6-deoxy-L-talosyl, 3-*O*-methyl-6-deoxy-L-talosyl (which may also be acetylated at C-2 and C-4), 2-*O*-methyl-L-fucosyl, 2-*O*-methyl-L-rhamnosyl or 2,4-di-*O*-methyl rhamnosyl residues. A novel microbial glycolipid, isolated from *Bacillus acidocaldarius*, is a glycoside derivative of the triterpene hopane (147) and has an analogous structure to the plant sterol glycosides.

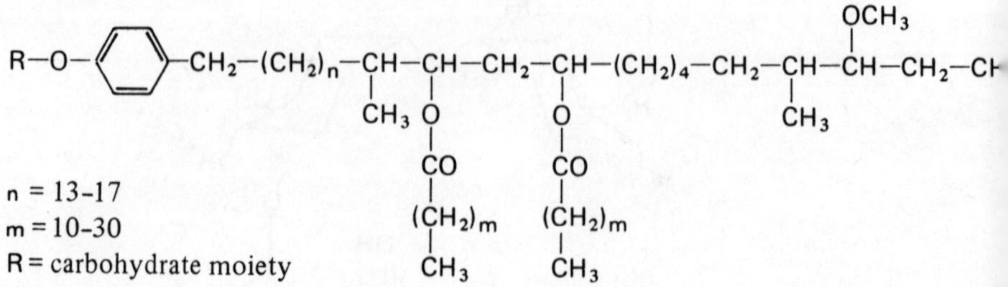

n = 13–17
m = 10–30
R = carbohydrate moiety

Fig. 10.3 – Structure of mycosides.

(147)

CHAPTER 11

Nucleic acids

Nucleic acids are high molecular weight polymers, containing carbohydrate, phosphate and heterocyclic bases, which occur in every living cell. Deoxyribonucleic acid (DNA), which contains 2-deoxy-D-ribose as the sole carbohydrate, is the molecule of heredity which stores genetic information in the nucleus of the cell, whereas ribonucleic acid (RNA), which contains D-ribose as the sole carbohydrate, is the molecule responsible for the transfer of genetic information into protein structure and is found in the cytoplasm outside the cell nucleus. Viruses contain either DNA or RNA but not both nucleic acids.

The component parts of nucleic acids, namely nucleosides and nucleotides, also occur as part of the biosynthetic process. Nucleosides consist of carbohydrate (D-ribose or 2-deoxy-D-ribose) linked *via* β-D-glycosidic bonds to the heterocyclic bases (see later, Fig. 11.2) which are either purines (linked *via* position 3 of the base), or pyrimidines (linked *via* position 1 of the base). Nucleotides are nucleoside phosphates with the phosphate linked to the carbohydrate at positions C-5 and C-3 (and C-2 in D-ribose). The nomenclature, conformational descriptions, abbreviations and symbols for nucleic acids and their constituents are described in Recommendations (1970 and 1981b).

PRIMARY STRUCTURE

DNA consists of a backbone of 2-deoxy-D-ribofuranosyl residues linked by phosphodiester bonds at positions C-3 and C-5 (see Fig. 11.1). To this backbone are linked, in an apparently random order, the bases adenine, guanine, cytosine and thymine (see Fig. 11.2) together with small or trace amounts of 5-methyl cytosine, 5-hydroxymethyl cytosine and a number of N-methyl purines. The molecular weight of DNA is difficult to determine due to degradation, which can be brought about even by simply pouring a solution from one vessel to another, but values up to 10^9 have been reported. The variable part of DNA is its sequence of bases which is the key to the biological role of DNA (see p. 259); however the bases are present as complementary base pairs in which the ratio of adenine:thymine and guanine:cytosine equal 1:1 but the amounts of adenine and guanine are not normally equal.

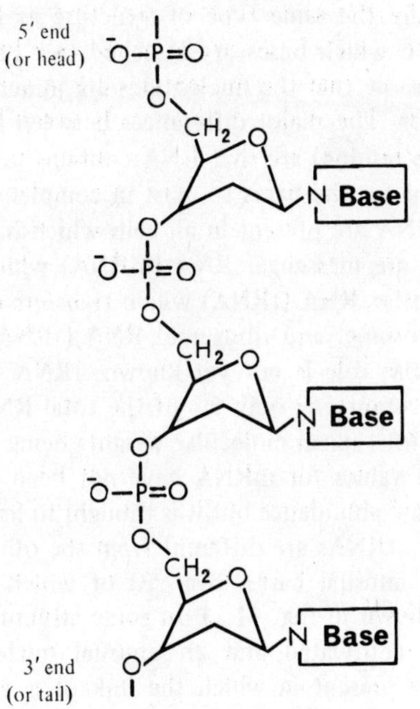

Fig. 11.1 – Repeating structures of DNA chains.

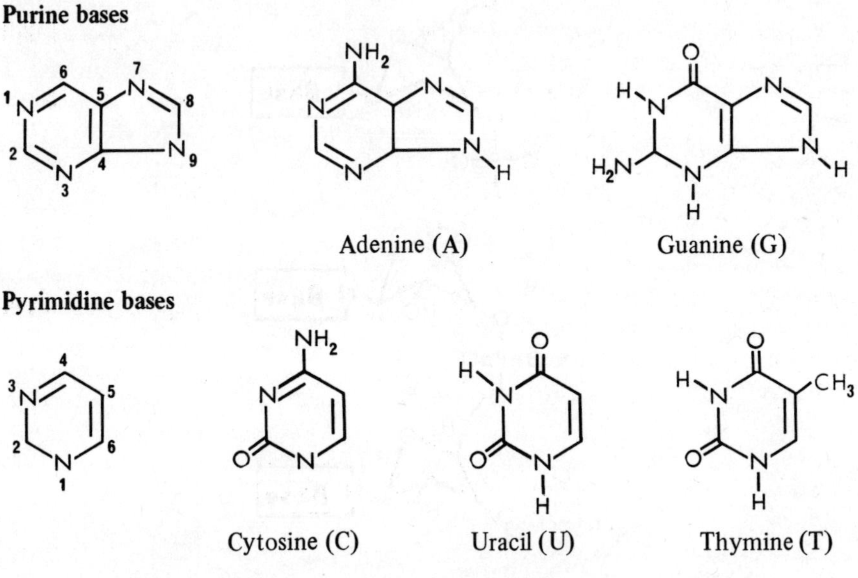

Purine bases

Adenine (A) Guanine (G)

Pyrimidine bases

Cytosine (C) Uracil (U) Thymine (T)

Fig. 11.2 – Common heterocyclic bases present in nucleic acids.

RNA has essentially the same type of structure as DNA, namely a sugar-phosphate backbone to which bases are attached (see Fig. 11.3). No evidence has been obtained to show that the nucleotides are joined by other than $3' \to 5'$ phosphodiester linkages. The major differences between DNA and RNA (apart from the carbohydrate residue) are that RNA contains uracil, not thymine and there is no requirement for the bases to exist in complementary base ratios. At least three kinds of RNA are present in all cells which have nuclei and/or synthesise protein. These are messenger RNA (mRNA) which is the template for protein synthesis, transfer RNA (tRNA) which transfers aminoacids in an activated form to the ribosome, and ribosomal RNA (rRNA) which is present in ribosomes but its precise role is not yet known. rRNA is the most abundant and mRNA the least, comprising only 5% of the total RNA. The sizes of these RNAs are different, with typical molecular weights being $\approx 10^6$ for rRNA, and $\approx 10^4$ for tRNA. The values for mRNA have not been determined due to its transient nature and low abundance but it is thought to have a molecular weight in the region of $\approx 10^5$. tRNAs are different from the other RNAs in that they contain a number of unusual bases, over 50 of which have been identified (some of which are shown in Fig. 11.1). In some structures C-2 of the D-ribofuranosyl residues is methylated and an unusual nucleoside, pseudouridine (Ψ, 148), can also be present in which the linkage is *via* the 5 and not the 1 position of uracil.

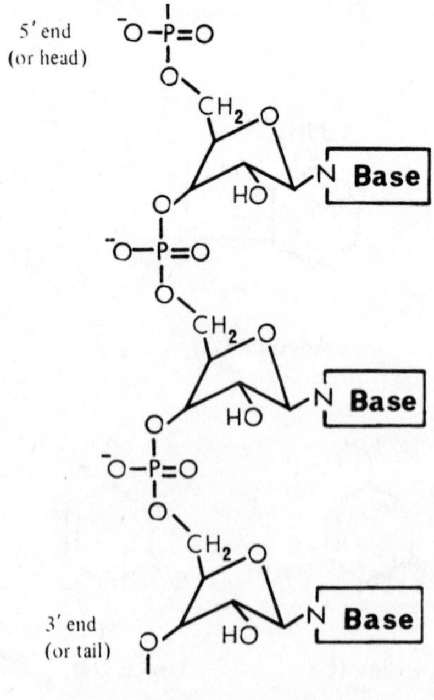

Fig. 11.3 – Repeating structures of RNA chains.

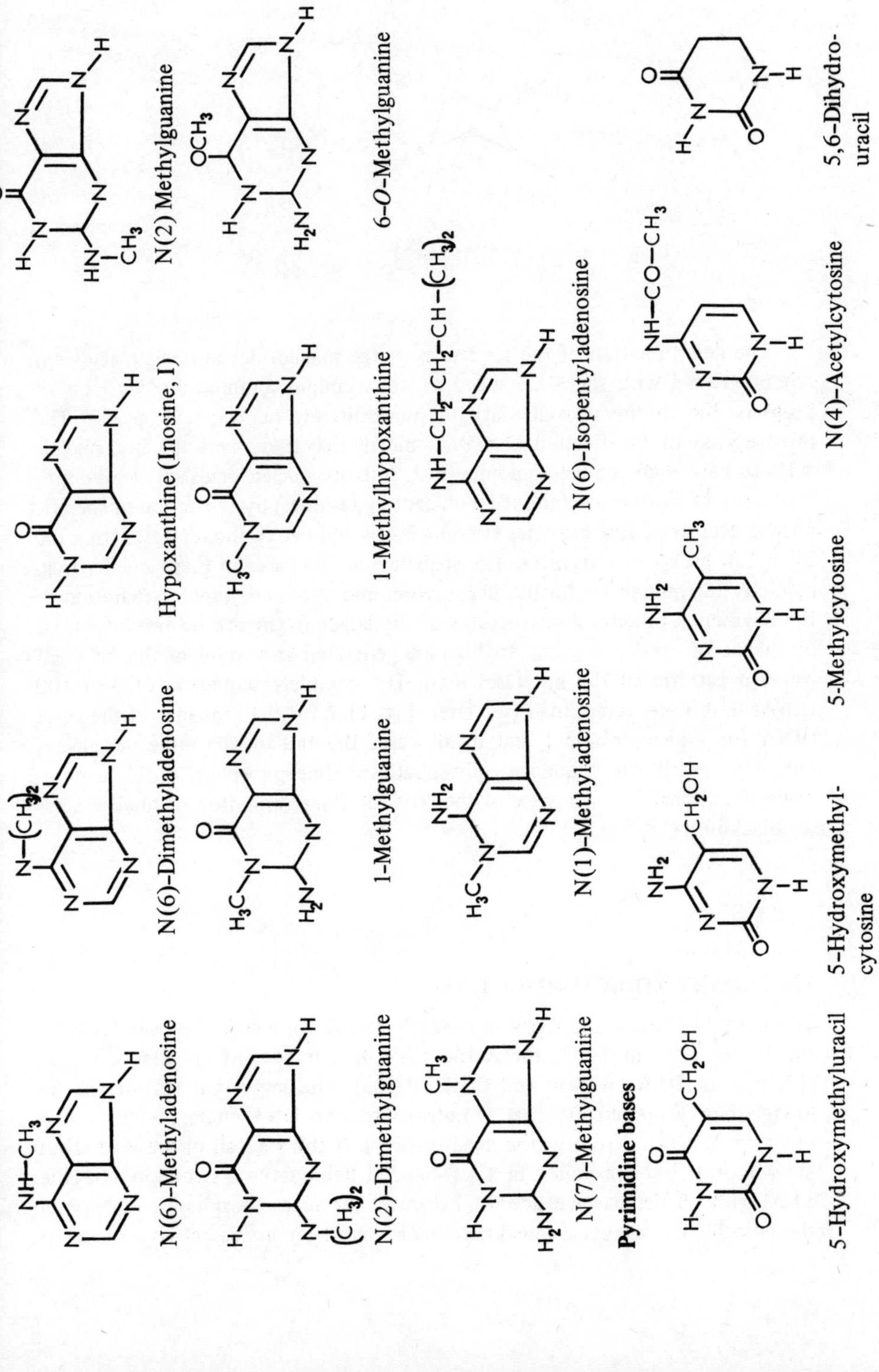

Fig. 11.4 – Some unusual bases found in tRNA.

N(2) Methylguanine

6-*O*-Methylguanine

5,6-Dihydrouracil

Hypoxanthine (Inosine, I)

1-Methylhypoxanthine

N(6)-Isopentyladenosine

N(4)-Acetylcytosine

N(6)-Dimethyladenosine

1-Methylguanine

N(1)-Methyladenosine

5-Methylcytosine

5-Hydroxymethylcytosine

N(6)-Methyladenosine

N(2)-Dimethylguanine

N(7)-Methylguanine

Pyrimidine bases

5-Hydroxymethyluracil

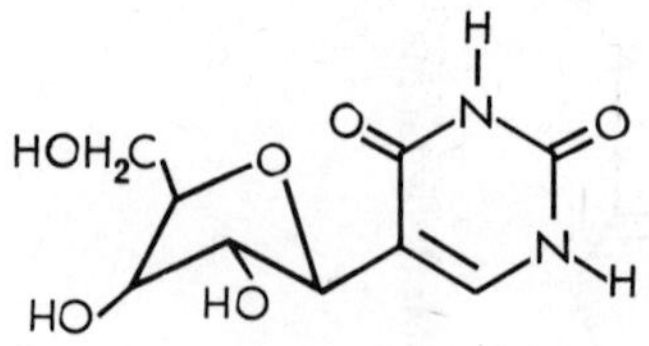

(148)

The determination of the sequences of the nucleotides in nucleic acids has not progressed with the same speed as, for example, aminoacid sequencing of proteins due to the unavailability of pure, discrete nucleic acid species. The relative ease of purification of tRNAs meant that these were the first nucleic acids to have their sequences determined. Initially nucleic acids are cleaved into fragments of modest size (about 50 nucleotide residues) by the action of specific nucleic acid degrading enzymes (ribonucleases and deoxyribonucleases from the EC 3.1.4. group of enzymes). The sequence of the bases in these smaller fragments is determined by further degradation and chromatographic separation of the fragments. Finally, the structures of the larger fragments are put into order by means of overlap sequences which are generated as a result of the different cleavage patterns of the nucleases used. The complete sequences of over 100 tRNAs have been determined (see later, Fig. 11.7 for the sequence of the yeast tRNA for L-phenylalanine) and in all cases the tail of the molecule always terminates with the sequence –phosphate–cytidine–phosphate–cytidine–phosphate–adenosine. For a review of the structural determination of nucleic acids see Blackburn (1979a).

SECONDARY STRUCTURE OF DNA

The work of Watson and Crick in the early 1950s, for which they were awarded the Nobel Prize in 1962, forms the basis of our present knowledge on the structure of DNA (Watson and Crick, 1953a). The important features of the model they proposed are that it consists of two DNA chains, which run in opposite directions (that is, the head of one coil and the tail of the second coil are adjacent) but are coiled in a left-handed helix about a common axis (Fig. 11.5) with all the bases inside the helix and the sugar-phosphate backbone on the outside. The chains are held together by hydrogen bonds between the bases,

with adenine always paired with thymine and guanine always paired with cytosine (Fig. 11.6) which explains the requirement for complementary base pair
ratios. There are ten residues per complete turn of the helix. There has been
much refinement of the original double-helix model and various modifications
have been proposed including a side-by-side model in which the coils turn into
a right-handed double helix for 1.7 nm and then revert back to a left-handed
double helix for a further 1.7 nm. For a review of the history of the development of models for the structure of DNA and the recent modifications, see
Blackburn, 1979b.

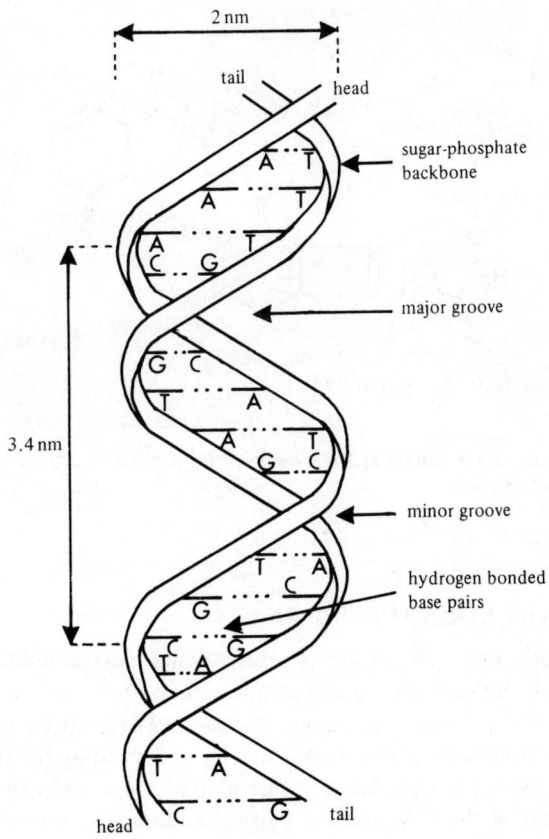

Fig. 11.5 – Double helical DNA showing hydrogen bonds between base pairs
(A = adenine, C = cytosine, G = guanine, and T = thymine).

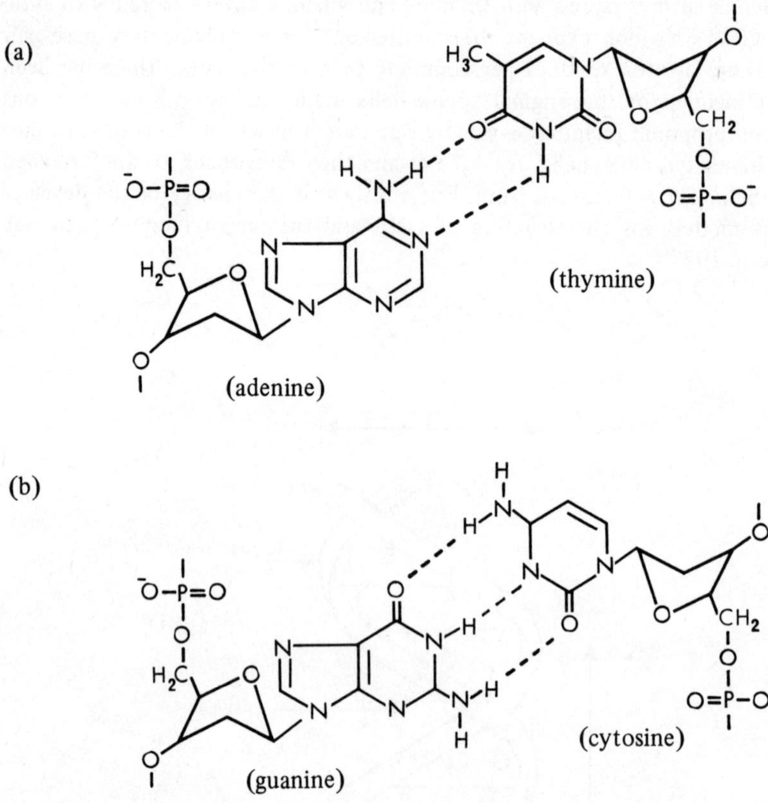

(a)

(b)

Fig. 11.6 – Base pairing in DNA between (a) adenine and thymine, and (b) guanine and cytosine.

SECONDARY STRUCTURE OF RNA

Apart from a small proportion of viruses which possess double stranded helical RNA, in which the bases occur in complementary base pair ratios, most naturally occurring RNA species are single stranded. These single strands do contain regions of double-helical structure which are produced by the formation of loops. In the helical regions the bases in one part of the strand can pair with bases in another part of the helix but the pairing is frequently imperfect. Adenine pairs with uridine whilst guanine pairs with cytosine and, less efficiently, with uridine. Where one or more bases along a strand are not complementary with the other part of the strand then they may be looped out to facilitate pairing of the other bases. This results in about 50% of the bases present being paired and a common conformation of the nucleic acids has been shown to have a cloverleaf structure as typified by the yeast L-phenylalanine tRNA (Fig. 11.7). It is conventional to show this structure as a flat leaf but it must be remembered that each loop is in fact a helix. Further examples of the secondary structure of RNA are contained in the review by Blackburn (1979b).

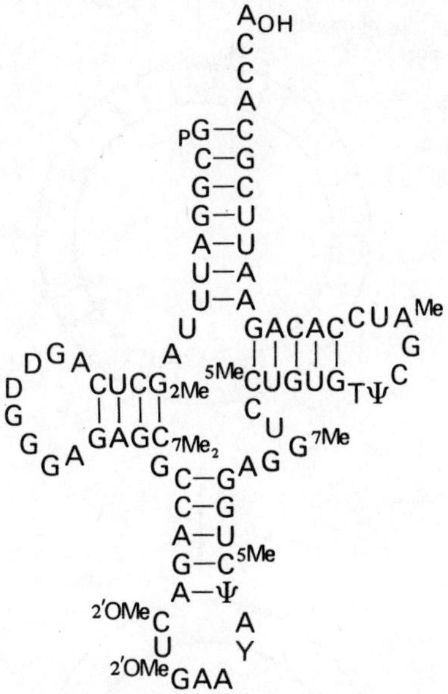

Fig. 11.7 — The cloverleaf structure of yeast phenylalanine transfer ribonucleic acid (tRNAPhe).

TERTIARY STRUCTURE OF NUCLEIC ACIDS

The image of DNA as a double helix requires considerable development to bring it closer to that of DNA in a living cell. For example, the *Escherichia coli* bacterium is 2 μm long but the DNA chromosome extracted from it is 1.1 mm long and some DNA from bacteriophage particles expand in aqueous solution to occupy a volume 15 times the size of the head cavity of the phage. Thus the tertiary structure of DNA is obviously a very important aspect of its structure.

Electron microscopy has shown that some intact DNA molecules are circular. This structure is brought about by the helix having unequal length strands at each end such that, for example, both heads are longer than both tails by between four and ten bases, which have a complementary structure (see Fig. 11.8). These ends are held together by the complementary bases and the breaks in the strands converted into normal nucleotide linkages by a 'repair' enzyme (a ligase) to give a closed loop. This circular DNA can itself be twisted to give a more compact structure known as supertwisted DNA.

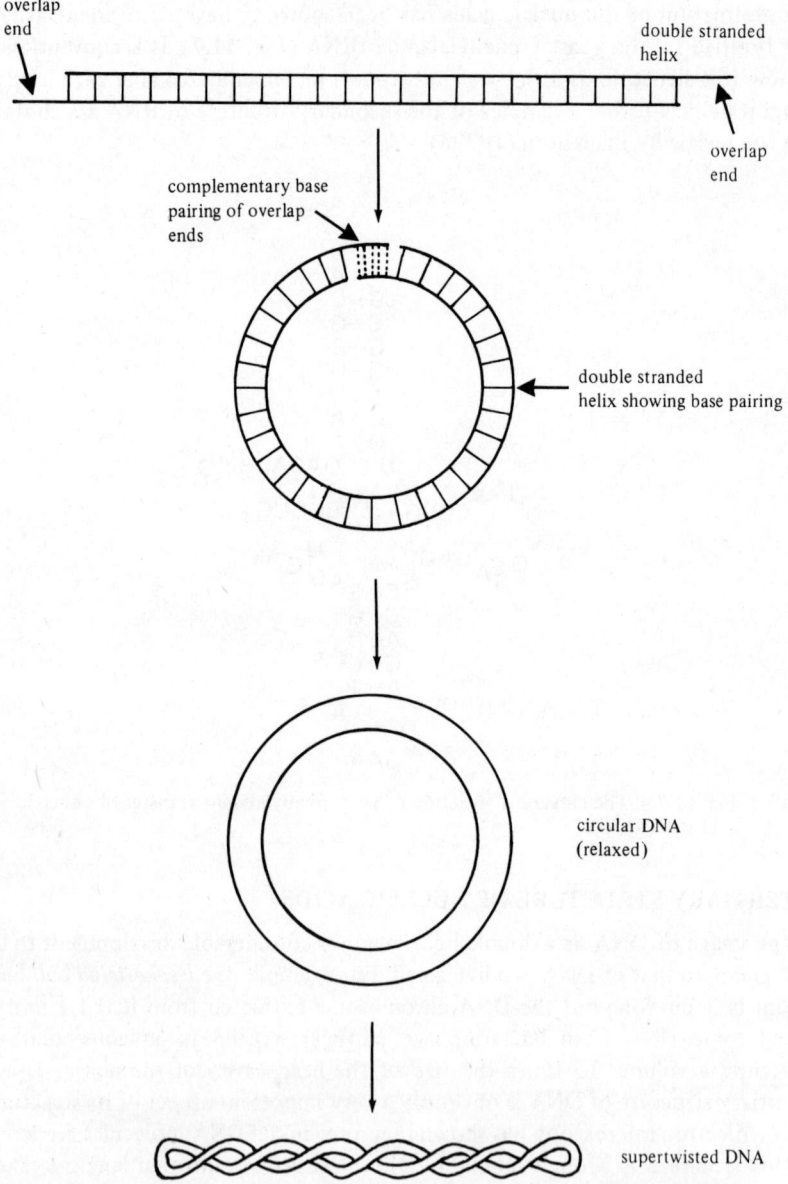

Fig. 11.8 – Schematic representation of the formation of tertiary structures of DNA.

Electron microscopy has also shown that RNA molecules have compact tertiary structures which are held together by hydrogen bonding between bases. These hydrogen bonds are not the same as those between the usual base pairs which hold the helices of the secondary structure together, with extensive use being made of the C-2 hydroxyl group of the D-ribofuranosyl residues as donors or acceptors of hydrogen bonds. The cloverleaf structure of tRNA is folded such that an 'L'-shaped conformation is obtained with the exclusion of water molecules with the anticodon region at one extremity and the tail of the molecule at the other. A more extensive discussion of the tertiary structure of nucleic acids can be found in Blackburn (1979b).

FUNCTION OF NUCLEIC ACIDS

The double helical model of DNA was used by Watson and Crick (1953b) to explain the mechanism for the replication of DNA. Each strand of a 'parent' DNA molecule acts as a template for a 'daughter' molecule which itself acts as a template for its other companion strands (Fig. 11.9), all of which contain an exact copy of the original due to the specific pairing of the bases. The unwinding of the DNA molecules, at the replicating forks, is promoted by binding numerous protein molecules to the parental DNA molecules. It has been proposed that complementary RNA (cRNA) is involved in this replication (see review by Blackburn, 1979c).

The base sequences in DNA hold the heredity data and control the sequence of aminoacids in protein synthesis. Two separate stages take place in this control. Firstly, the information is transcribed, in the cell nucleus from the DNA to mRNA by the DNA acting as a template for the formation of the mRNA, with biosynthesis taking place in a $5' \rightarrow 3'$ direction (Fig. 11.10). Only one strand of the DNA is used unless the DNA is damaged or if the strands are separated, when both strands act as templates. Secondly, the translation of the mRNA information into protein sequence takes place in the cytoplasm.

For successful translation of the information in the mRNA into protein sequence, the genetic code, a sequence of three bases (or codons) in the mRNA which codes for a given aminoacid, is followed, in the ribosome by specific tRNA–aminoacid complexes which have the complementary three bases in the anticodon region (see Fig. 11.7). The ribosome moves along the mRNA molecule binding an aminoacid from the correct tRNA–aminoacids, which have bound to the mRNA, to the forming protein chain through the action of the various ribosomal enzymes (see Fig. 11.11). *N*-Formylmethionine always acts as the first residue since this represents the starting code (AUG or GUG) for transmission whilst the codons UAA, UGA and UAG terminate the protein synthesis. Table 11.1 shows the possible codons and the aminoacids for which they code. After synthesis the protein can be modified by removal of a terminal residue or terminal sequence, formation of disulphide bonds or conversion of residues to others by, for example, hydroxylation. For a fuller explanation of protein synthesis and the genetic code the reader should consult Stryer (1981).

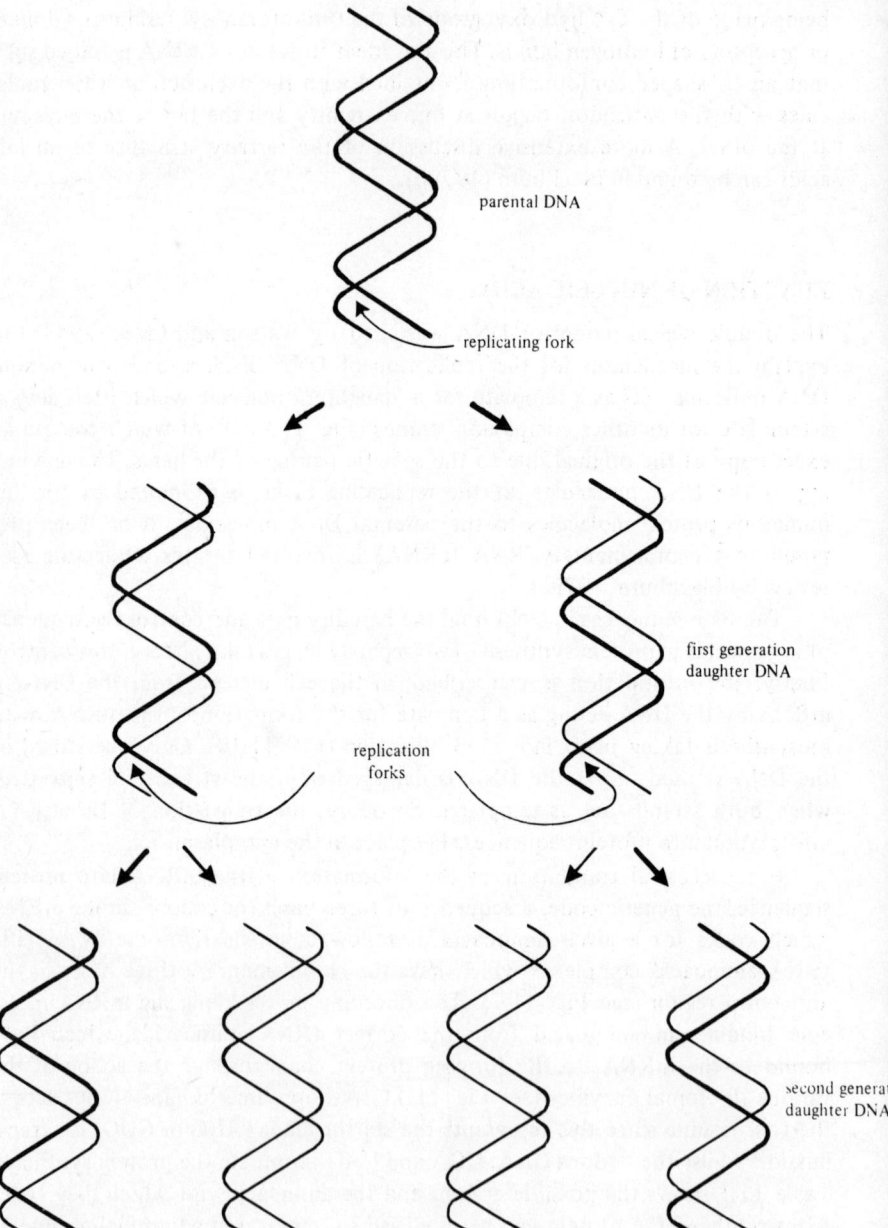

parental DNA

replicating fork

first generation
daughter DNA

replication
forks

second generation
daughter DNA

Fig. 11.9 – Replication of DNA (parental DNA strands shown in heavier print).

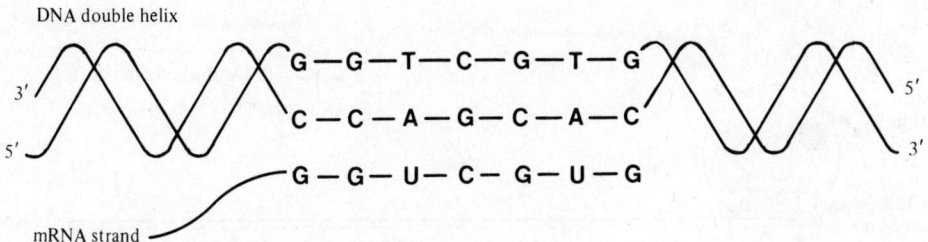

Fig. 11.10 – Biosynthesis of mRNA.

Table 11.1 The genetic code

First position (5'-end)	Second position				Third position (3'-end)
	U	C	A	G	
U	Phe[a]	Ser	Tyr	Cys	U
	Phe	Ser	Tyr	Cys	C
	Leu	Ser	Stop[b]	Stop[b]	A
	Leu	Ser	Stop[b]	Trp	G
C	Leu	Pro	His	Arg	U
	Leu	Pro	His	Arg	C
	Leu	Pro	Gln	Arg	A
	Leu	Pro	Gln	Arg	G
A	Ile	Thr	Asn	Ser	U
	Ile	Thr	Asn	Ser	C
	Ile	Thr	Lys	Arg	A
	Met	Thr	Lys	Arg	G
G	Val	Ala	Asp	Gly	U
	Val	Ala	Asp	Gly	C
	Val	Ala	Glu	Gly	A
	Val	Ala	Glu	Gly	G

a   All L-aminoacids except glycine

b   Termination signal, does not code for any aminoacid

a) initiation

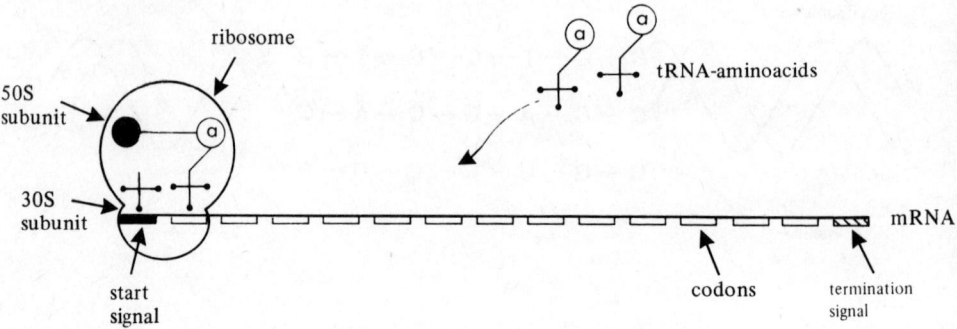

b) elongation

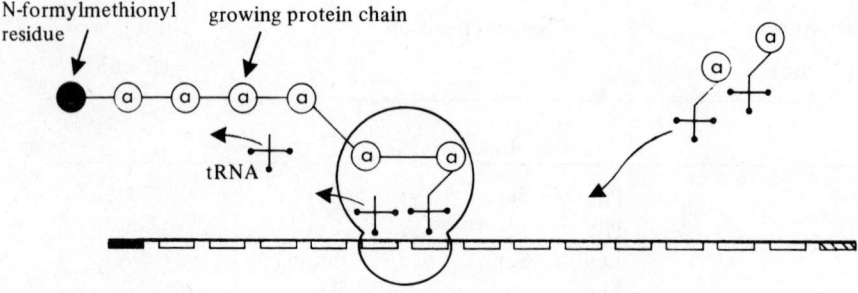

c) termination

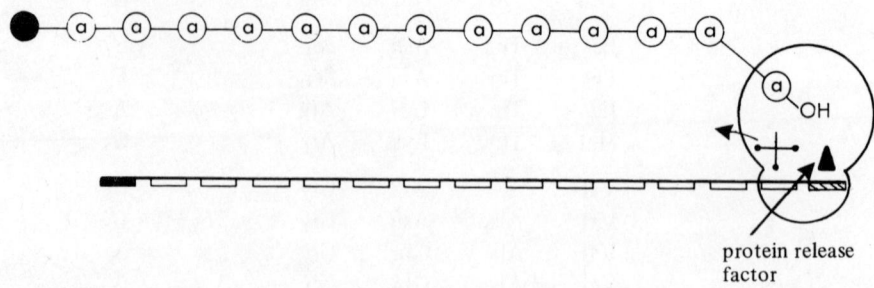

Fig. 11.11 – Transmission of the nucleic acid sequence in mRNA into protein sequence *via* the action of ribosomes and various tRNA aminoacids.

GENETIC ENGINEERING

Two of the fundamental objectives of genetic engineering are the correction of genetic defects and the augmentation of sound genes by others to improve the biosynthetic processes. To date, much work has been carried out in preparing synthetic genes to carry out a nonnatural but important process. This requires the insertion of the required genetic information into the DNA molecule of a chosen species (normally plasmids of *Escherichia coli* which are small, circular chromosomal elements found in the bacterial cytoplasm and which replicate with the bacterium).

A major success in this field is the synthesis of human insulin by *E. coli*. The first stage of the process is to prepare a complementary DNA (cDNA) to the mRNA for the synthesis of proinsulin (a precursor of active insulin). This is then inserted into the plasmid by cutting the plasmid with a specific DNA ligase and joining the DNA molecule to it to reform the circular shape in a manner similar to the formation of circular DNA discussed earlier (p. 257), using base pairing of unequal ends to hold the parts of the molecule together and 'repairing' the cut with another DNA ligase. The closed, circular nucleic acid containing the insulin gene is then incubated to increase the number of plasmids containing the insulin gene and allowed to react in a medium from which human insulin can ultimately be extracted.

Other examples in which genetic engineering of DNA molecules has led to the production of biologically important materials, which cannot be prepared with the required activity or purity by normal chemical methods, by bacterial fermentation include the production of peptide hormones (for example, somatostatin) and proteins (for example, interferon, the antiviral agent). One particularly important aspect is that a useful function from a pathological organism can be transferred into a nonpathological organism, thereby avoiding the use of a pathological organism. For further examples and discussion of the more practical aspects of genetic engineering including the application to industrial processes, see the reviews by Atherton *et al.* (1979), Wu (1979), Zadrazil and Sponar (1980), Gilbert and Villa-Komaroff (1980), and Setlow and Hollaender (1979 and 1980).

CHAPTER 12
Antibiotics

An antibiotic is a compound, usually elaborated by microorganisms, which inhibits the growth of other microorganisms and animal and plant tumours. Synthetic antibiotics, having structures similar to the naturally occurring materials, are produced by biosynthetic reactions, arising from natural organisms, or by chemical reactions (see Rinehart and Suami, 1980). Those elaborated by *Streptomyces* species are frequently given names ending in 'mycin' whilst those from other sources use the ending 'micin'. The mechanism of action often involves interference with DNA, RNA or protein synthesis. There are many varied types of compound which possess antibiotic properties (see Sammes, 1977 onwards) and as early as 1944, when streptomycin, an aminoglycoside antibiotic, which is used in the treatment of tuberculosis, was isolated, it was discovered that naturally-occurring antibiotics contained carbohydrate moieties. In the last 20 years the number of known carbohydrate-containing antibiotics has increased rapidly and the discovery of many unusual and unique amino-, deoxy- and branched-chain monosaccharides (see Fig. 12.1) has stimulated increased interest in the distribution of these unusual carbohydrates in nature. The number of known naturally occurring aminosugars reflects this interest with four being known in 1950, 20 in 1960, 50 in 1970 and to date over 80 are known.

The carbohydrate-containing antibiotics can be grouped into several broad classes, in some of which the compounds are largely or completely carbohydrate whilst in others the carbohydrate is only a small part of the molecule. For extensive coverage of the structures and action of carbohydrate-containing antibiotics the reader is referred to the numerous reviews and books which are available. Reviews of the earlier work on carbohydrate-containing antibiotics are available (for example, Henessian and Haskell, 1970, Umezawa, 1976, Reden and Dürckheimer, 1979, and Horton and Wander, 1980a), whilst the structure, isolation, properties and mode of action are reviewed in two ongoing series (Various Authors, 1968 onwards, and Sammes, 1977 onwards). In this chapter carbohydrates are referred to by their trivial names where their systematic name is given in Fig. 12.1.

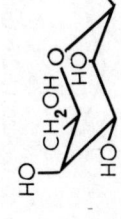

Aldoses

3-Deoxy-D-*glycero*-β-D-*glycero*-pentafuranose

2,6-Di-*O*-methyl-β-D-mannopyranose (Curamicose)

β-D-Psicofuranose

β-D-Talopyranose

4-*C*-Fluoro-5-sulphamido-β-D-ribofuranose

6-Deoxy-β-D-*arabino*-5-hexulofuranose (Hygromycin A)

6-Deoxy-2,4-di-*O*-methyl-β-D-galactopyranose (Labilose)

6-Deoxy-4-*O*-methyl-β-D-galactopyranose (Curacose)

Deoxysugars

6-Deoxy-2,3-di-*O*-methyl-β-D-allopyranose (Mycinose)

Fig. 12.1 – Structures of some of the less common monosaccharides found in antibiotics (*continued next page*)

2,6-Dideoxy-β-D-xylo-hexopyranose (Boivinose)

2,6-Dideoxy-4-O-methyl-β-D-lyxo-hexopyranose (Olivomose)

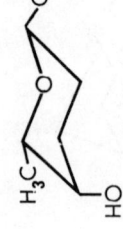

2,3,6-Trideoxy-β-L-threo-hexopyranose (Rhodinose)

2,6-Dideoxy-β-D-ribo-hexopyranose (Digitoxose)

2,6-Dideoxy-3-O-methyl-β-D-ribo-hexopyranose (Cymarose, Variose)

2,3,6-Trideoxy-β-D-erythro-hexopyranose (Amicetose)

2,6-Dideoxy-β-L-lyxo-hexopyranose (L-Oliose)

2,6-Dideoxy-3-O-methyl-β-L-arabino-hexopyranose (L-Oleandrose)

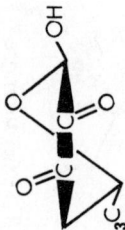

4,6-Dideoxy-2,3-hexodiulopyranose (Actinospectose)

Deoxysugars (*continued*)

2,6-Dideoxy-β-D-arabino-hexopyranose (Olivose)

6-Deoxy-β-D-erythro-2,5-hexodiulofuranose

3-O-Acetyl-2,6-dideoxy-β-D-lyxo-hexopyranose (Acetyl-D-oliose)

Aminosugars

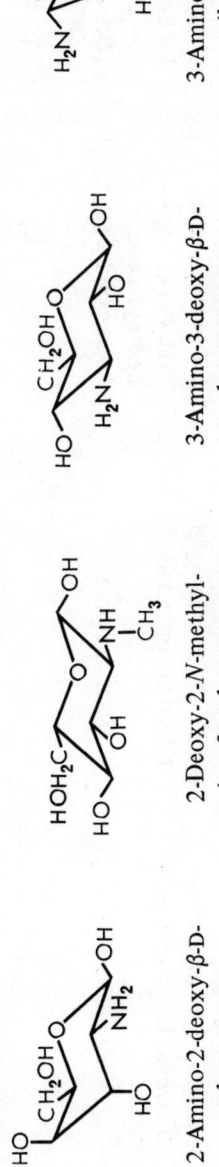
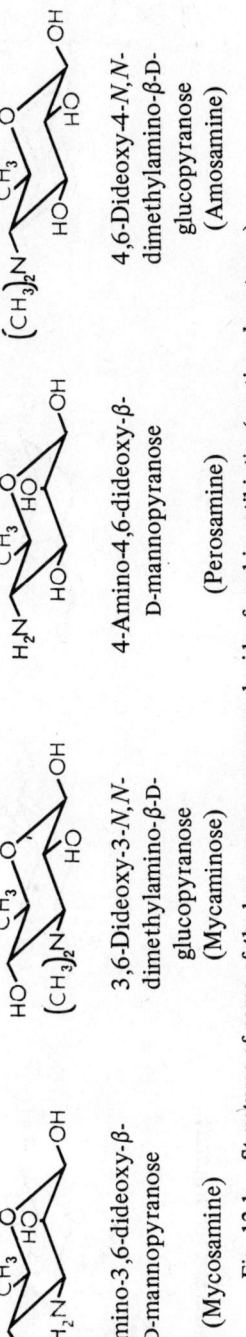

2-Amino-2-deoxy-β-D-gulopyranose

2-Deoxy-2-N-methyl-amino-β-L-glucopyranose

3-Amino-3-deoxy-β-D-glucopyranose (Kanosamine)

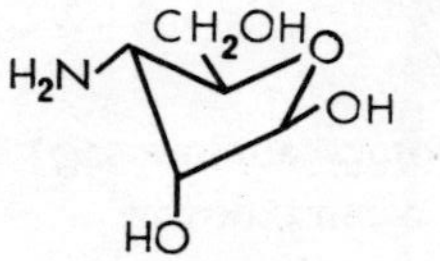

3-Amino-3-deoxy-β-D-ribofuranose

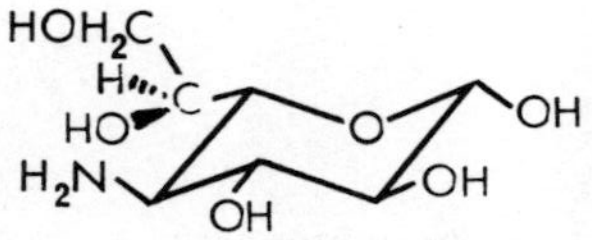

4-Amino-4-deoxy-β-L-*glycero*-L-*gluco*-heptopyranose

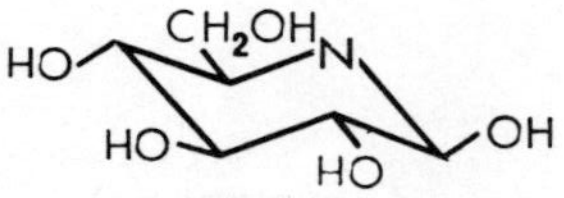

5-Amino-5-deoxy-β-D-glucopyranose (Nojirimycin)

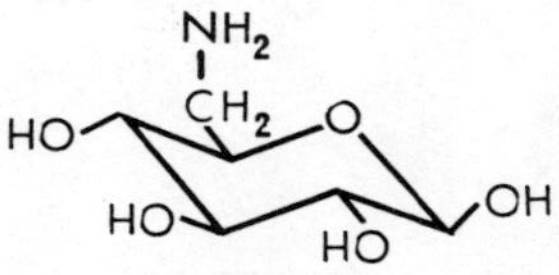

6-Amino-6-deoxy-β-D-glucopyranose

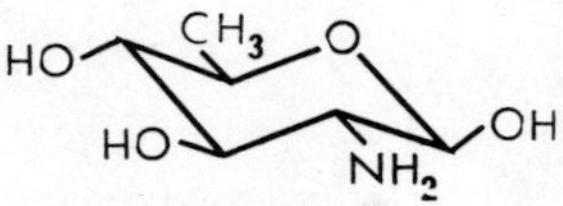

2-Amino-2,6-dideoxy-β-D-glucopyranose (Quinovosamine)

3-Amino-3,6-dideoxy-β-D-mannopyranose (Mycosamine)

3,6-Dideoxy-3-N,N-dimethylamino-β-D-glucopyranose (Mycaminose)

4-Amino-4,6-dideoxy-β-D-mannopyranose (Perosamine)

4,6-Dideoxy-4-N,N-dimethylamino-β-D-glucopyranose (Amosamine)

Fig. 12.1 – Structures of some of the less common monosaccharides found in antibiotics (*continued next page*)

Aminosugars (*continued*)

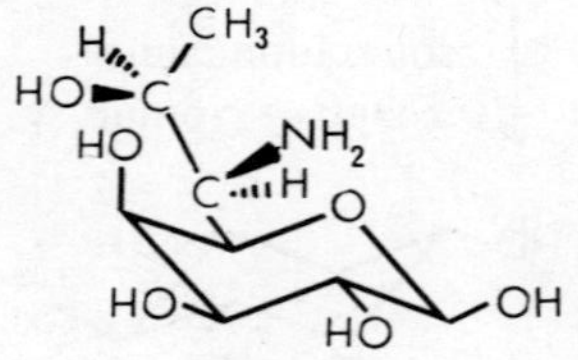

6-Amino-6,8-dideoxy-β-
D-*erythro*-D-*galacto*-
octopyranose
(Lincosamine)

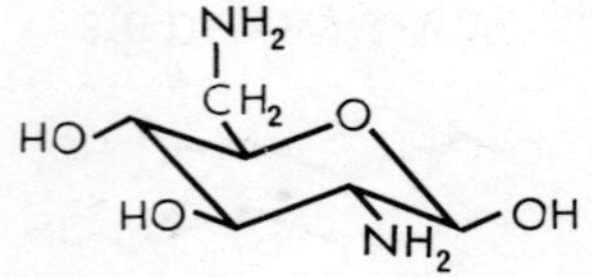

2,6-Diamino-2,6-dideoxy-
β-D-glucopyranose

(Neosamine C)

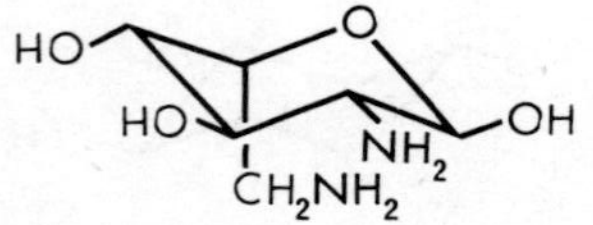

2,6-Diamino-2,6-dideoxy-
α-L-idopyranose

(Paromose)

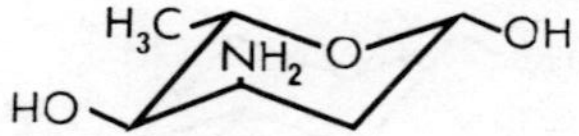

3-Amino-2,3,6-trideoxy-β-
L-*ribo*-hexopyranose

(Ristosamine)

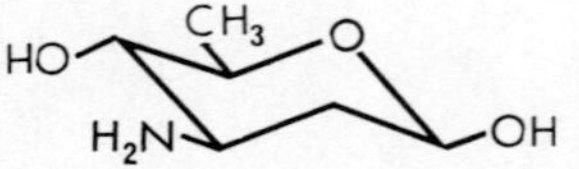

3-Amino-2,3,6-trideoxy-α-
D-*arabino*-hexopyranose

(Acosamine)

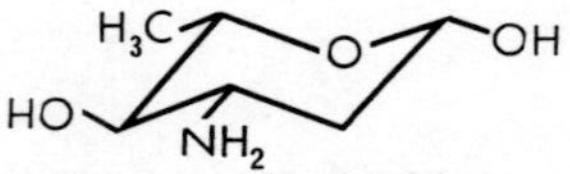

3-Amino-2,3,6-trideoxy-β-
L-*lyxo*-hexopyranose

(Daunosamine)

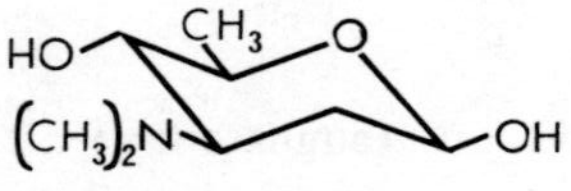

3-*N*,*N*-Dimethylamino-
2,3,6-trideoxy-β-D-*xylo*-
hexopyranose
(Angolosamine)

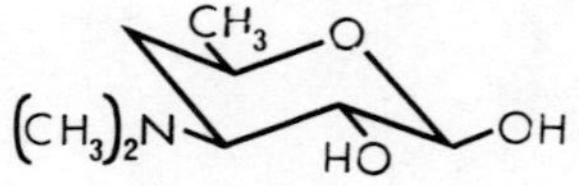

3-*N*,*N*-Dimethylamino-
3,4,6-trideoxy-β-D-*xylo*-
hexopyranose
(Desosamine, Picrocin)

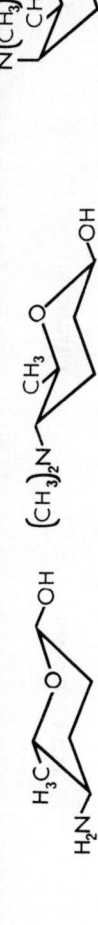
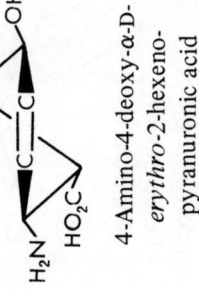
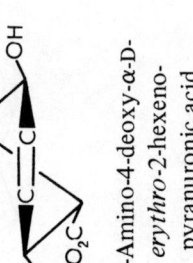
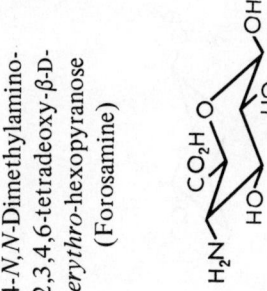
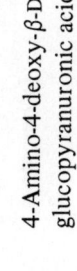
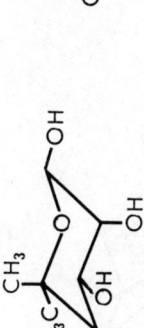
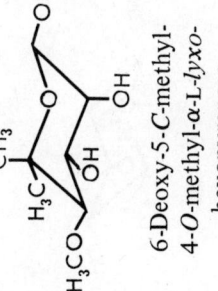
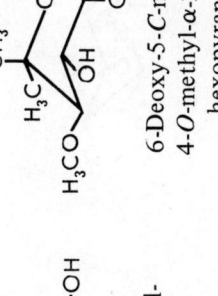
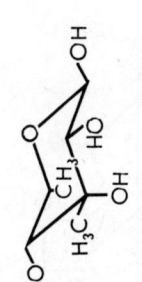
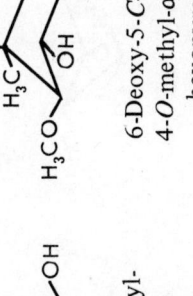
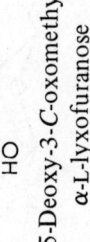
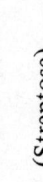

3-*N,N*-Dimethylamino-2,3,6-trideoxy-β-L-*lyxo*-hexopyranose (Rhodosamine)

4-Amino-2,3,4,6-tetra-deoxy-β-L-*erythro*-hexopyranose (Tolyposamine)

4-*N,N*-Dimethylamino-2,3,4,6-tetradeoxy-β-D-*erythro*-hexopyranose (Forosamine)

4-*N,N*-Dimethylamino-2,3,4,6-tetradeoxy-β-D-*threo*-hexopyranose (Ossamine)

2,4-Diamino-2,3,4,6-tetra-deoxy-β-D-*arabino*-hexopyranose (Kasugamine)

Aminouronic acids

4-Amino-4-deoxy-α-D-*erythro*-2-hexeno-pyranuronic acid

4-Amino-4-deoxy-β-D-glucopyranuronic acid

5-Amino-5-deoxy-β-D-allofuranuronic acid

Branched-chain monosaccharides

6-Deoxy-3-*C*-methyl-β-D-mannopyranose (Evalose)

6-Deoxy-3-*C*-methyl-α-L-talopyranose (Vinelose)

6-Deoxy-5-*C*-methyl-4-*O*-methyl-α-L-*lyxo*-hexopyranose (Noviose)

5-Deoxy-3-*C*-oxomethyl-α-L-lyxofuranose (Streptose)

Fig. 12.1 – Structures of some of the less common monosaccharides found in antibiotics (*continued next page*)

Branched-chain monosaccharides (*continued*)

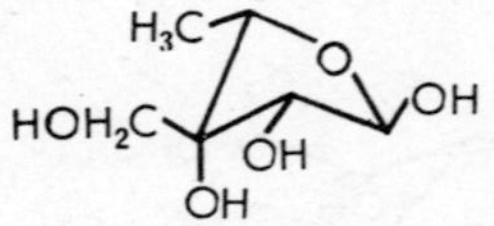

5-Deoxy-3-*C*-hydroxy-
methyl-α-L-lyxofuranose

(Dihydrostreptose)

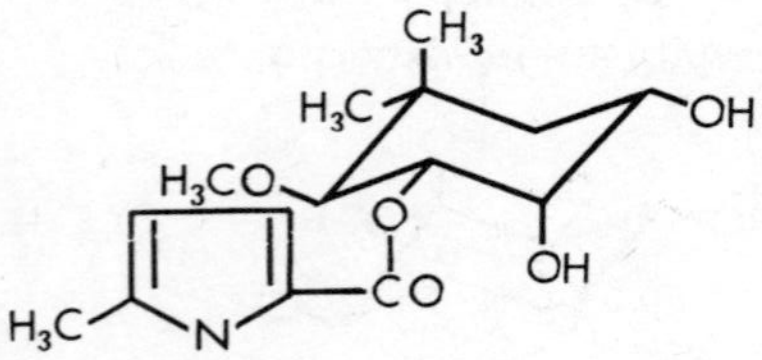

6-Deoxy-5-*C*-methyl-4-*O*-
methyl-3-*O*-(5-methyl-2-
pyrrolyl)-β-L-*lyxo*-
hexopyranose
(Coumerose)

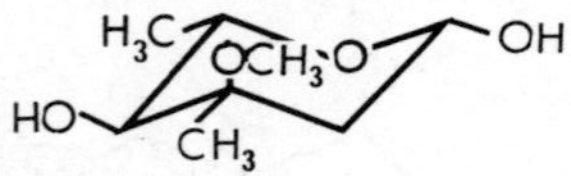

2,6-Dideoxy-3-*C*-methyl-
3-*O*-methyl-β-L-*ribo*-
hexopyranose

(Cladinose)

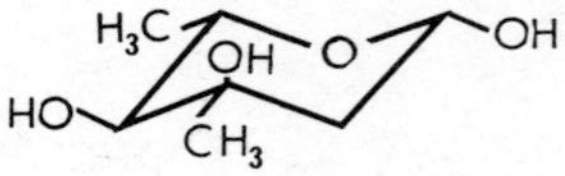

2,6-Dideoxy-3-*C*-methyl-
β-L-*ribo*-hexopyranose

(L-Mycarose)

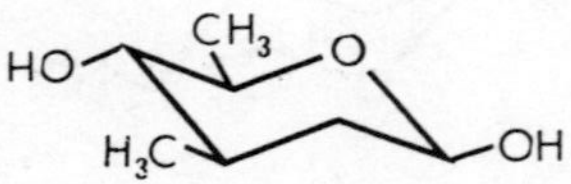

2,6-Dideoxy-3-*C*-methyl-
β-D-*arabino*-hexopyranose

(Evermicose)

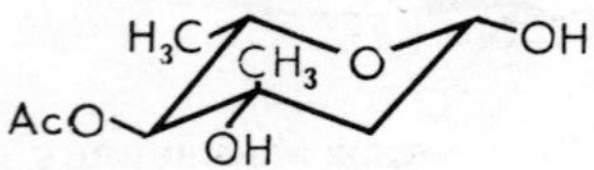

4-*O*-Acetyl-2,6-dideoxy-
3-*C*-methyl-β-L-*arabino*-
hexopyranose

(Olivomycose)

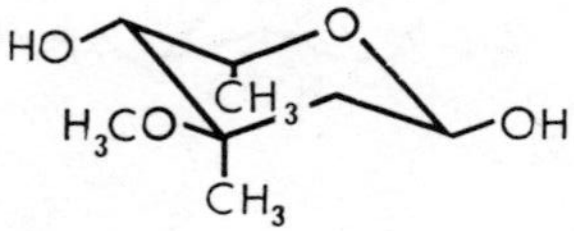

2,6-Dideoxy-3-*C*-methyl-
3-*O*-methyl-α-L-
xylo-hexopyranose

(Arcanose)

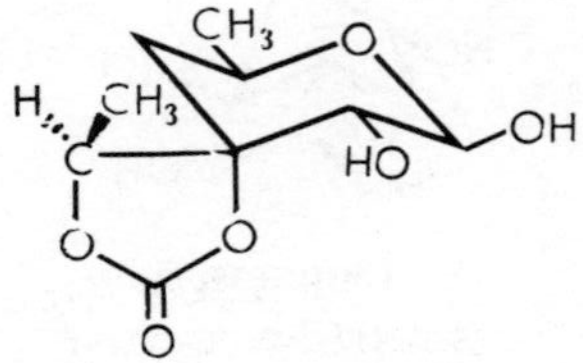

4,6-Dideoxy-3-*C*-[(S)-1-
hydroxyethyl] -β-D-*ribo*-
hexopyranose 3,3′-cyclic
carbonate
(Aldgarose)

4-*C*-(1-Hydroxyethyl)-2,6-dideoxy-β-L-*lyxo*-hexopyranose

3-Amino-2,3,6-trideoxy-3-*C*-methyl-β-L-*lyxo*-hexopyranose (Vancosamine)

4-*O*-Methyl-3-*C*-methyl-3-nitro-2,3,6-trideoxy-β-L-*arabino*-hexopyranose (Evernitrose)

2,3,6-Trideoxy-4-*C*-(1-oxo-2-hydroxyethyl)-β-L-*threo*-hexopyranose (L-Pillarose)

Cyclitol derivatives

1-Deoxy-3-*O*-carbomoyl-1-guanidino-*scyllo*-inositol

(Bluensidine)

1,3-Dideoxy-1,3-diguanidino-*scyllo*-inositol

(Streptidine)

1,3-Di-(*N*-methylamino)-*myo*-inositol

(Actinamine)

1D-(1,3,5/4,6)-1,3-Diamino-1,2,3-trideoxy-4,5,6-cyclohexanetriol

(2-Deoxystreptamine)

1D-(1,3,5/4,6)-1-Amino-1,2,3-trideoxy-3-*N*-methylamino-4,5,6-cyclohexanetriol (Hyosamine)

1D-1-Amino-1-deoxy-*neo*-inositol

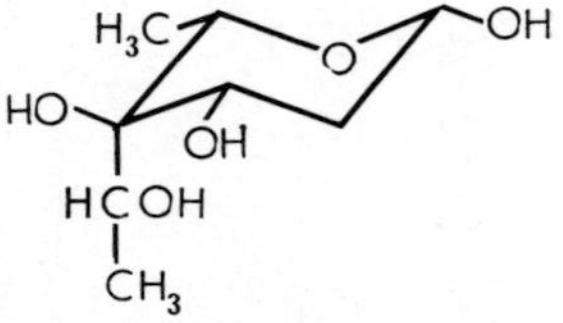

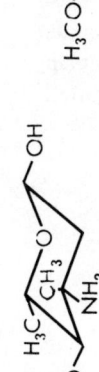

Fig. 12.1 – Structures of some of the less common monosacchardies found in antibiotics (shown in one anomeric form only). See Figs. 2.8 and 8.9 for other monosaccharide structures.

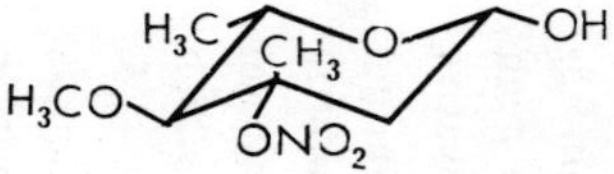

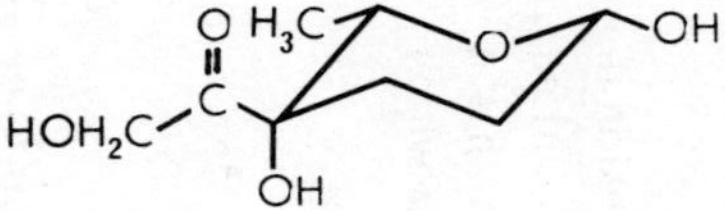

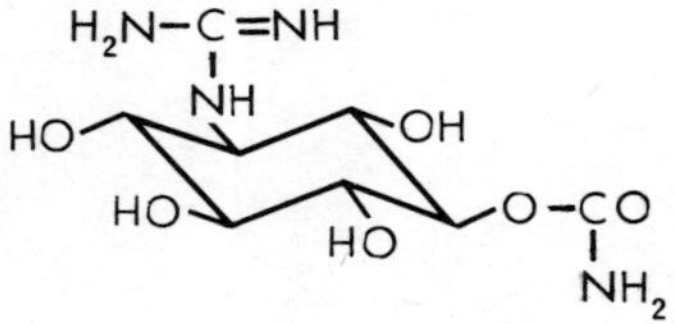

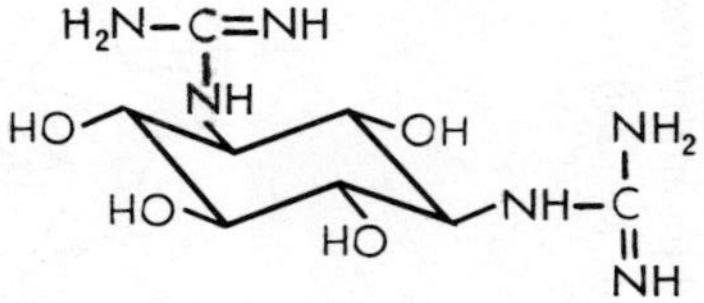

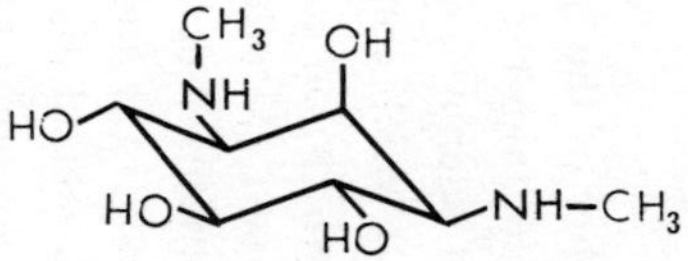

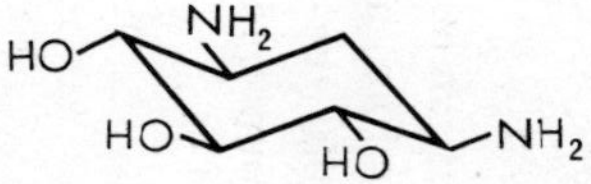

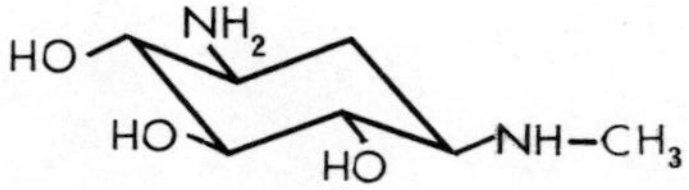

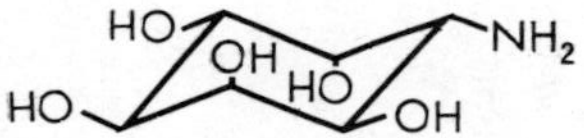

NUCLEOSIDE ANTIBIOTICS

Only a limited number of nucleosides can be accepted by nature for inclusion in the biosynthetic processes, and therefore, most nucleoside antibiotics contain either a 'normal' sugar or base whilst the corresponding base or sugar has a structure which is not normally encountered in the common nucleosides which make up DNA or RNA (see Chapter 11).

Purine derivatives

Puromycin (149) was the first member of the nucleoside antibiotic group to be discovered – in the early 1950s. It contains the unusual aminosugar, 3-amino-3-deoxy-D-ribose. A family of related adenine-containing nucleosides have been isolated and include nucleocidin (49) which contains a sulphuric acid derivative of a fluorosugar, septacidin (150) which, on acid hydrolysis, gives the unusual aminosugar 4-amino-4-deoxy-L-*glycero*-L-*gluco*-heptose, glycine and isopalmitic acid, cordycepin (151), which contains 3-deoxy-D-*glycero*-D-*glycero*-pentose, and the angustmycins A (decoyinine, 152) and C (psicofuranine, 153) which contain the ketosugar psicose or the related diketosugar 6-deoxy-D-*erythro*-2,5-hexodiulose. Examples of antibiotics containing 'non-natural' bases include formycin (154) and tubercidin and its analogues toyocamycin and sangivamycin (155) in which the nitrogen atom at position 7 is replaced by a substituted carbon atom.

(149)

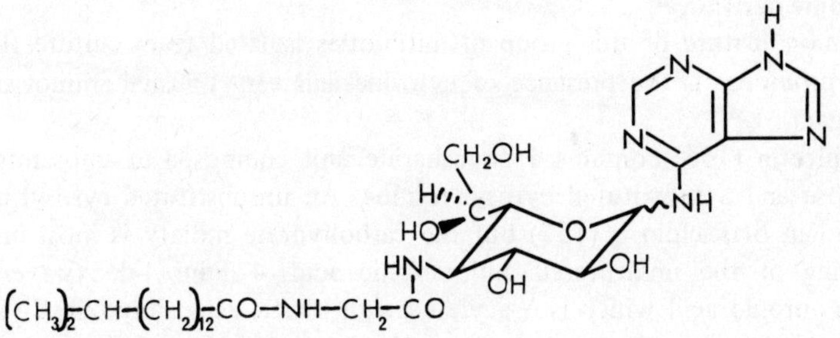

(150)

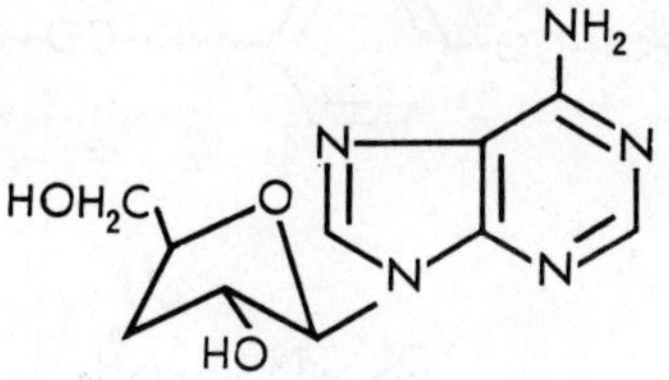

(151)

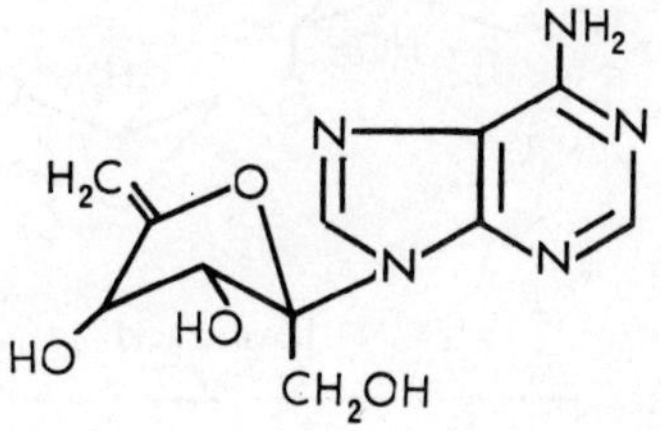

(152)

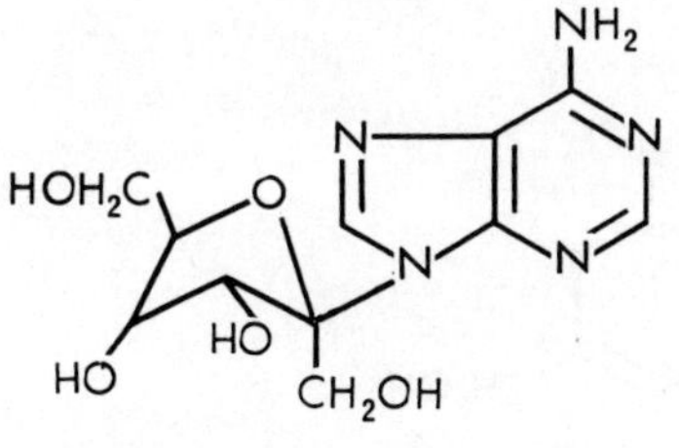

(153)

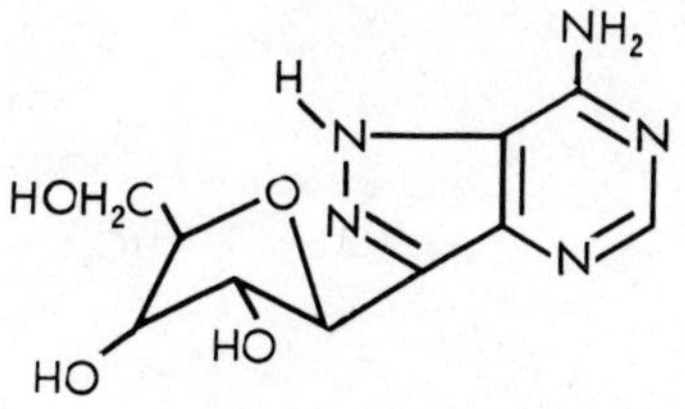

(154)

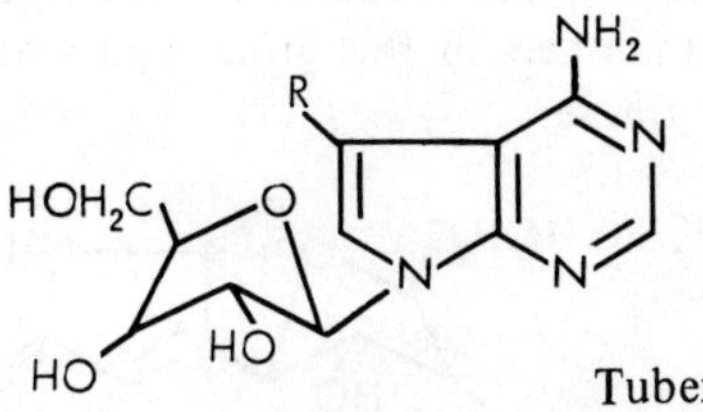

(155)

Tubercidin: R = H
Toyocamycin: R = CN
Sangivamycin: R = CONH$_2$

Pyrimidine derivatives

A common feature of this group of antibiotics isolated from culture filtrates of *Streptomyces* is the presence of cytosine and very unusual amino- and deoxy-sugars.

Amicetin (156) contains a disaccharide unit composed of amosamine and amicetose and a substituted cytosyl residue. An unsubstituted cytosyl residue is found in blasticidin S (157) but the carbohydrate moiety is most unusual, consisting of the unsaturated aminouronic acid, 4-amino-4-deoxy-D-*erythro*-2-hexenouronic acid which is *N*-acylated with blastic acid. Polyoxin C (158) is an example of an antibiotic containing 5-hydroxymethyluracil. It also contains 5-amino-5-deoxy-D-allofuranuronic acid.

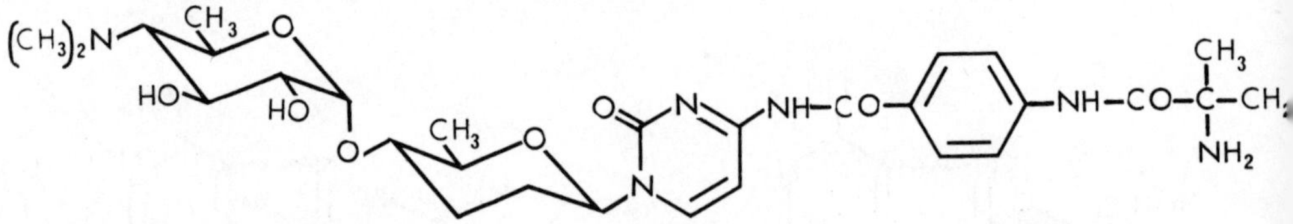

(156)

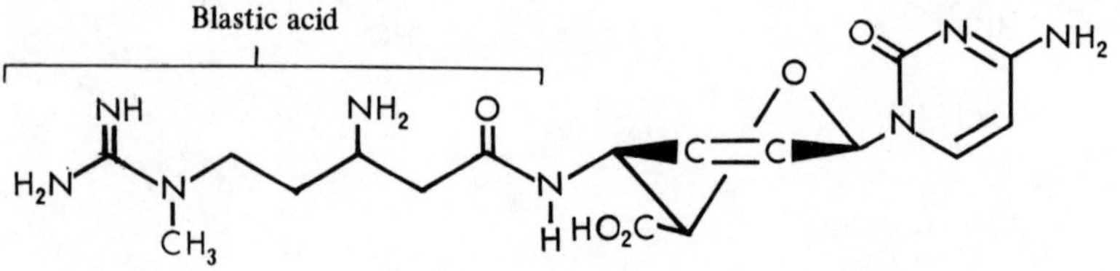

(157)

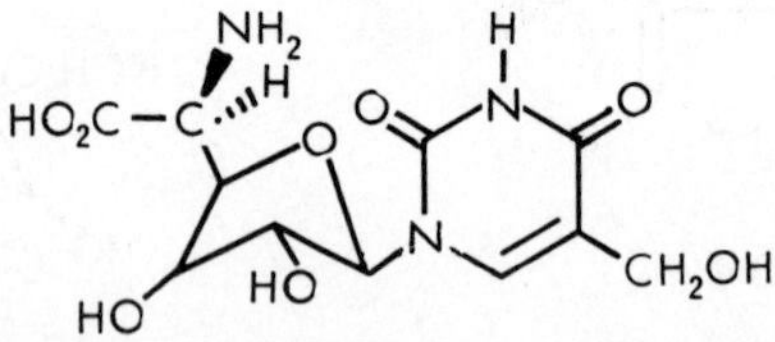

(158)

A number of nucleosides, which contain non-natural pyrimidine bases, have been identified. Typical of this group is showdomycin (159), a *C*-glycoside which, in common with others in this group and with the non-natural purine nucleosides, contains D-ribose.

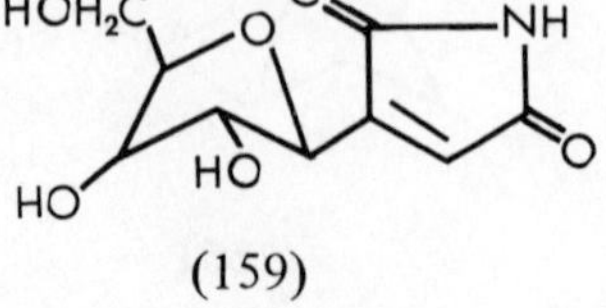

(159)

ANTIBIOTICS CONTAINING AROMATIC GROUPS

This group of antibiotics have characteristic aromatic systems to which one to three carbohydrate residues are attached, either singly or as oligosaccharide units. Typical examples of this group include those frequently referred to as the anthracycline antibiotics because of the tetracyclic aromatic system, such as daunomycin (160) which contains daunosamine, and the cinerubins, pyrromycins and rhodomycins, a family of red coloured antibiotics which contain *inter alia* the *N,N*-dimethyl analogue of daunosamine, rhodosamine (see Fig. 12.1). Pyrromycin has the structure (161) whilst other members of the rhodomycins contain the tetracyclic structure (162) and one or two carbohydrate residues in addition to rhodosamine. Rhodomycin II contains 2,6-dideoxy-L-*lyxo*-hexose, whilst rhodomycin III contains, in addition, the trideoxysugar rhodinose.

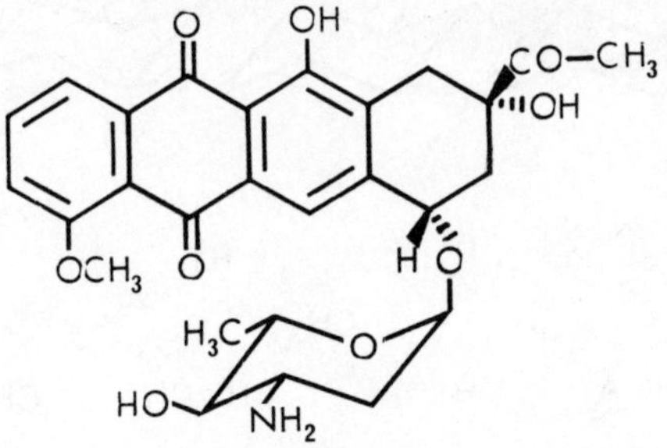

(160)

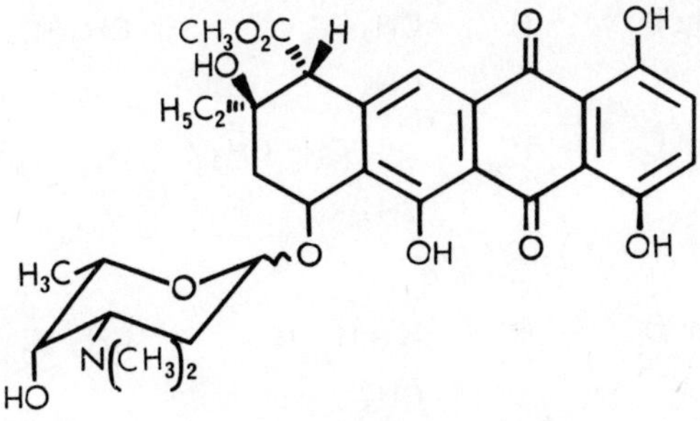

(161)

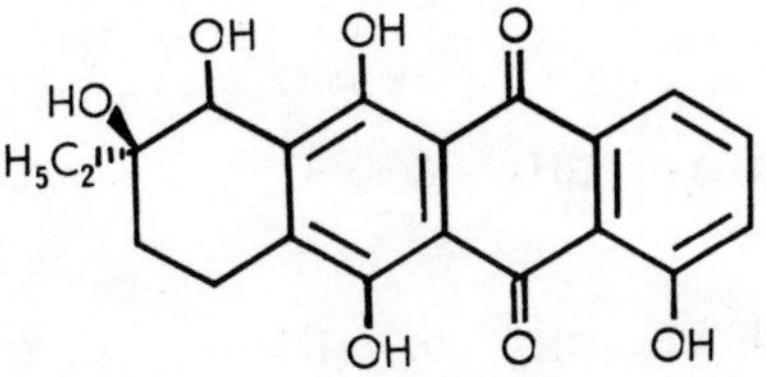

(162)

Another family of antibiotics in this group which contains a characteristic aromatic system is that of the chromomycin antibiotics which include both olivomycins and chromomycins, the general structures and relationships being shown in Fig. 12.2.

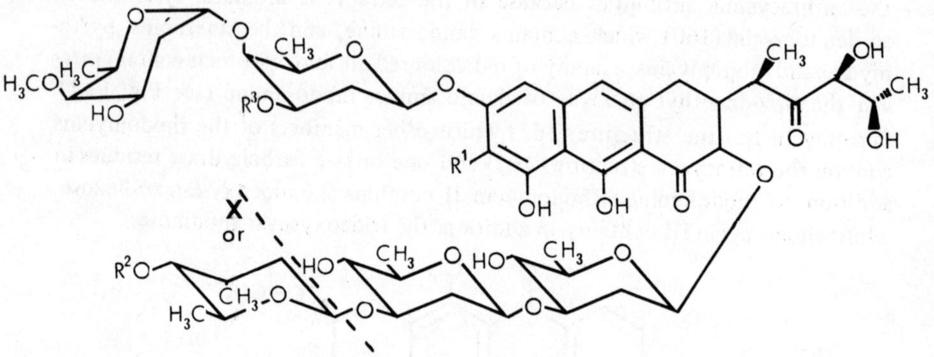

		R^1	R^2	R^3
Olivomycin A	H	$\begin{array}{c}CH_3\\\backslash\\CH-CH_2\\/\\CH_3\end{array}$	$CH_3{-}\overset{O}{\overset{\|}{C}}$
Olivomycin B	H	$CH_3{-}\overset{O}{\overset{\|}{C}}$	$CH_3{-}\overset{O}{\overset{\|}{C}}$
Olivomycin C	H	$\begin{array}{c}CH_3\\\backslash\\CH-CH_2\\/\\CH_3\end{array}$	H
Olivomycin D	H	X = H	$CH_3{-}\overset{O}{\overset{\|}{C}}$
Chromomycin A_2	CH_3	$\begin{array}{c}CH_3\\\backslash\\CH-CH_2\\/\\CH_3\end{array}$	$CH_3{-}\overset{O}{\overset{\|}{C}}$
Chromomycin A_3	CH_3	$CH_3{-}\overset{O}{\overset{\|}{C}}$	$CH_3{-}\overset{O}{\overset{\|}{C}}$
Chromomycin A_4	CH_3	X = H	$CH_3{-}\overset{O}{\overset{\|}{C}}$

Fig. 12.2 – The structural relationships between olivomycins and chromomycins.

MACROLIDE ANTIBIOTICS

The sugar moiety of macrolide antibiotics forms only a small but important part of the molecule, the main component being a large lactone ring. This ring can contain a conjugated polyene system or a polyfunctional, almost macrocyclic ring.

Polyene derivatives

These substances, which are elaborated by *Actinomyces* and usually have pronounced activity in inhibiting the growth of fungi, exhibit complex ultraviolet spectra on account of the conjugated polyene system. The carbohydrate-containing macrolide antibiotics in this group belong to two general types, those with conjugated tetraene and those with conjugated heptaene systems. Typical of the first type, in which all the double bonds have the *trans* arrangement, is rimocidin (163) which contains a single residue of mycosamine, a common feature of many other polyene macrolides. The conjugated heptaenes, which have stronger antifungal activities than the tetraenes, do not always have the all-*trans* arrangement found in the tetraenes, but their general insolubility and instability have impeded complete characterisation. Antibiotic 67-121-C is the first example, reported in 1977, of a disaccharide component in a heptaene antibiotic; it contains 4-O-β-D-mannopyranosylmycosamine.

(163)

Macrocyclic-lactone derivatives (macrolides)

This extensive group of antibiotics which is active against Gram-positive organisms contain a characteristic large lactone ring which has a large number of substituents on it. The differences in biological action are a result of subtle changes in the size of the macrolide ring, the number and type of functional groups present and the nature and position of attachment of the carbohydrate moiety. There are essentially two types of macrocyclic-lactone antibiotics, those which contain aminosugars and those which contain deoxysugars.

Picromycin (164) was the first macrolide antibiotic to be discovered, and, together with the related narbomycin and the pair of antibiotics, methylmycin and neomethylmycin (165), contains the aminosugar desosamine, but the member of this group most widely used medicinally is erythromycin (166). This antibiotic contains the branched-chain monosaccharide cladinose, in addition to desosamine.

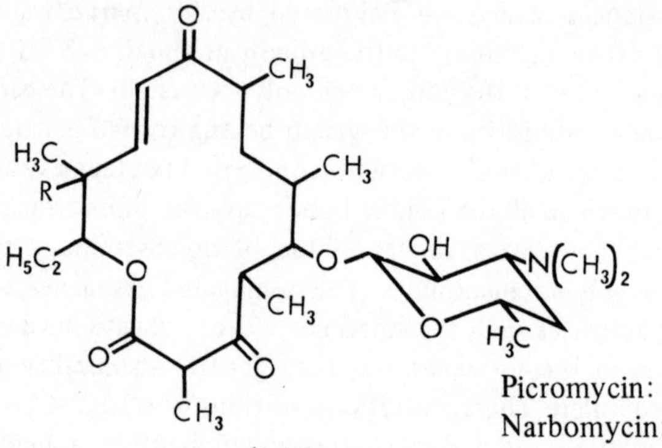

Picromycin: R = OH
Narbomycin: R = H

(164)

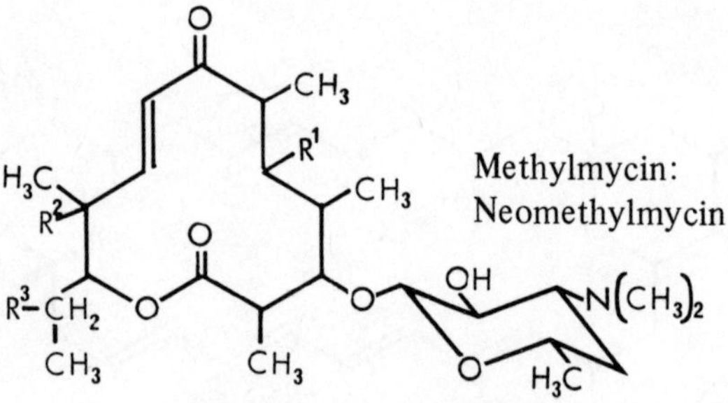

Methylmycin: $R^1 = R^3 = H; R^2 = OH$
Neomethylmycin: $R^1 = R^2 = H; R^3 = OH$

(165)

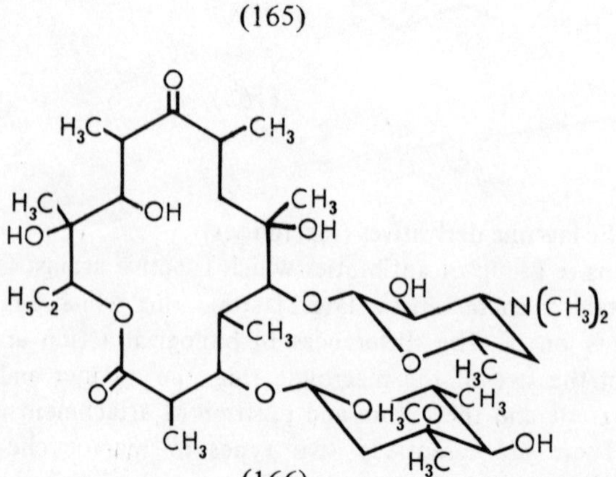

(166)

The spiramycin complex (foromacidins) which contains three components (167) consists of a single forosaminyl residue and a disaccharide unit of mycarose and mycaminose.

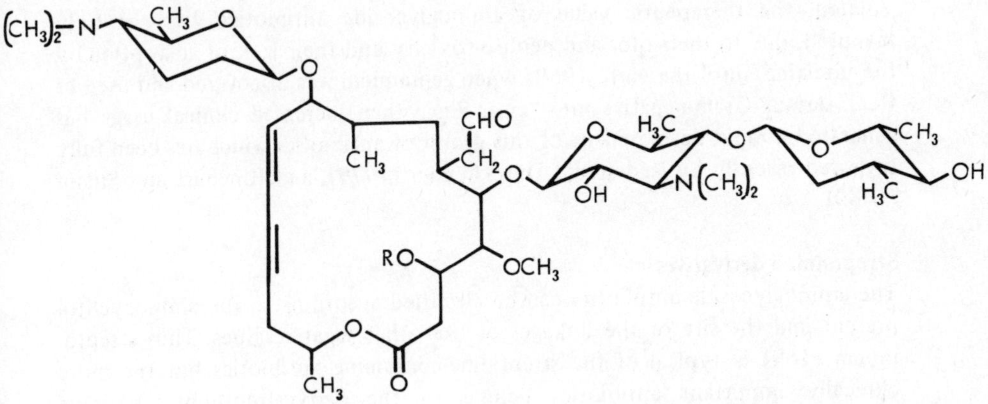

(167)

An example of those macrocyclic-lactone antibiotics which only contain deoxysugars as the carbohydrate moiety is provided by lankamycin (168) which contains the deoxysugars, chalcose (4,6-dideoxy-3-*O*-methyl-D-*xylo*-hexose) and the branched-chain monosaccharide, arcanose.

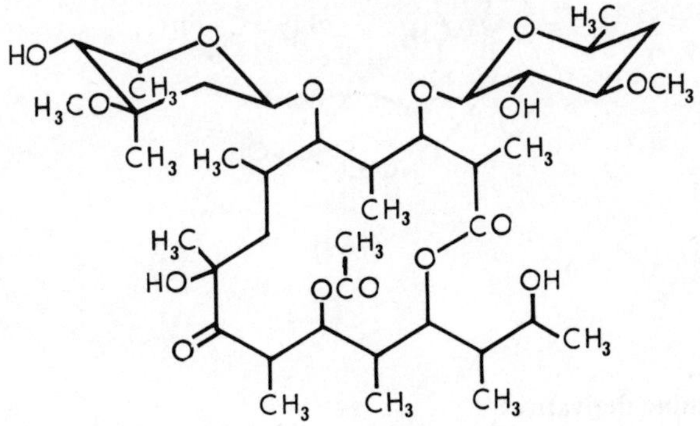

(168)

AMINOGLYCOSIDE ANTIBIOTICS

This class of antibiotics, referred to by some authors as aminocyclitol antibiotics, is perhaps the most interesting to carbohydrate chemists and biochemists in that these antibiotics consist completely of carbohydrate material. The fundamental structural feature of this group is an aminocyclitol residue (hence the alternative name) to which is attached one or more aminosugars and occasionally other carbohydrate residues. They are stable, colourless, basic compounds which are readily soluble in water but only slightly soluble or insoluble in organic solvents. Although streptomycin was the first carbohydrate-containing antibiotic to be isolated, the therapeutic value of aminoglycoside antibiotics was not fully favoured, due to their oto- and nephro-toxicity and their lack of adsorption by the intestine, until the early 1960s when gentamicin was discovered and used to treat serious Gram-negative infections. Since then increased clinical usage has generated a rapid development of this group of antibiotics which has been fully reviewed recently by Reden and Dürckheimer (1979), and Rinehart and Suami (1980).

Streptamine derivatives

The aminoglycoside antibiotics can be classified according to the aminocyclitol present and the site of the linkages of the other sugar residues. Thus streptomycin (169) is typical of the streptidine-containing antibiotics but the more clinically important antibiotics belong to the deoxystreptidine-containing antibiotics which can be subdivided into three groups.

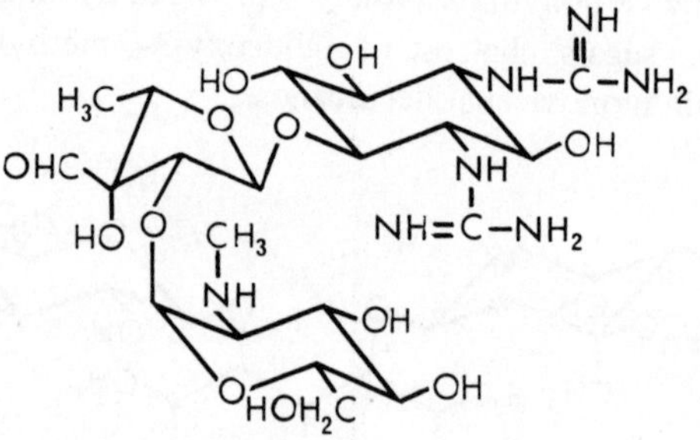

(169)

Deoxystreptamine derivatives

The 4-substituted deoxystreptamine antibiotics, which have no real clinical importance, include neamine (neomycin A, 170). Neomycins B and C (see Fig. 12.3) are 4,5-disubstituted deoxystreptamine antibiotics and therefore contain additional carbohydrate residues attached to the 5 position of the deoxystreptamine residue of neamine. Another related group of 4,5-disubstitued deoxystreptamine antibiotics is the paromomycins (see Fig. 12.3) which contain 2-amino-2-deoxy-D-glucose rather than 2,6-diamino-2,6-dideoxy-D-glucose which is found in neomycins.

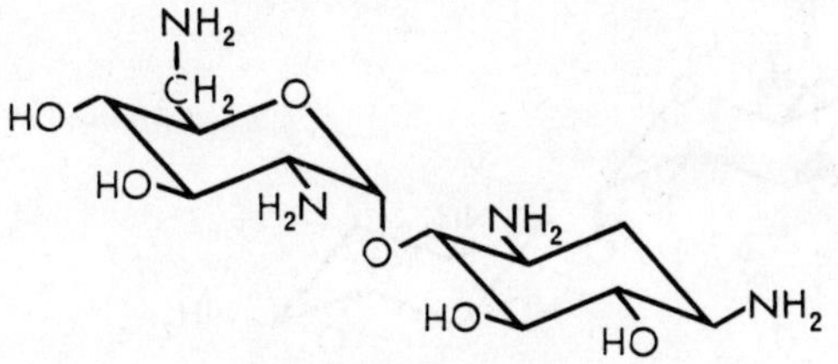

(170)

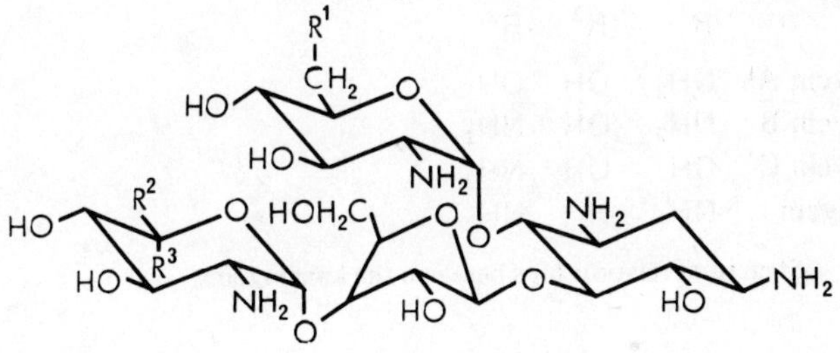

	R^1	R^2	R^3
Neomycin B	NH_2	H	CH_2NH_2
Neomycin C	NH_2	CH_2NH_2	H
Paromomycin I	OH	H	CH_2NH_2
Paromomycin II	OH	CH_2NH_2	H

Fig. 12.3 – The structural relationships between neomycins and paromomycins.

The third group of deoxystreptamine antibiotics is the 4,6-disubstituted deoxystreptamine derivatives, which can be readily distinguished from the 4,5-disubstituted derivatives on account of their larger optical rotations ($[\alpha]_D =$ 120-160° compared to 4-80°). These are probably the most important of the three groups, consisting of the kanamycins and the gentamicins. These related antibiotic types differ from each other in the residue attached to the 6-position of deoxystreptamine, the kanamycins containing kanosamine (see Fig. 12.4), whilst the gentamicins contain 3-deoxy-3-N-methylaminopentoses, some of which contain 4-C-methyl groups. Fig. 12.5 lists only five gentamicins of the many which are naturally occurring; others contain different substituents (usually hydroxyl, amino or methyl groups or hydrogen atoms) at the eight positions indicated. Sisomicin (171) is related to the gentamicins but contains an unsaturated aminosugar attached to the 4-position of deoxystreptamine.

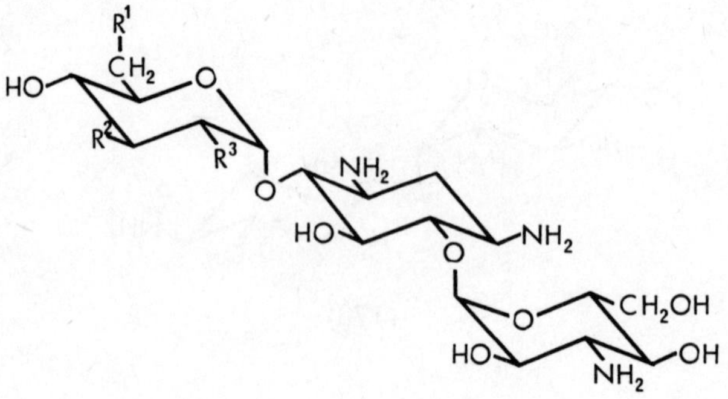

	R^1	R^2	R^3
Kanamycin A	NH_2	OH	OH
Kanamycin B	NH_2	OH	NH_2
Kanamycin C	OH	OH	NH_2
Tobramycin	NH_2	H	NH_2

Fig. 12.4 – Structural relationships between the kanamycins.

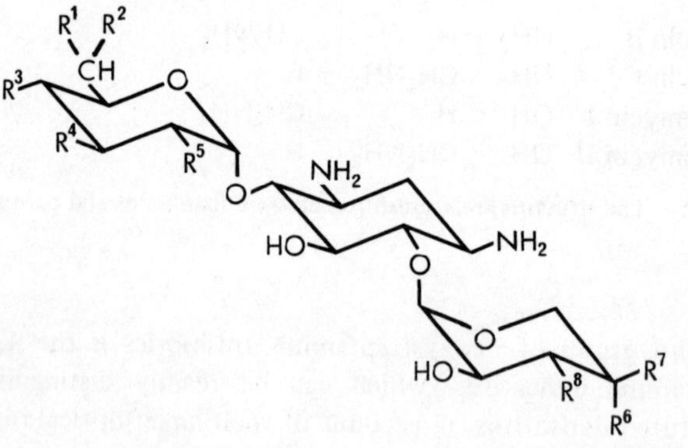

	R^1	R^2	R^3	R^4	R^5	R^6	R^7	R^8
Gentamicin C_1	CH_3	$NHCH_3$	H	H	NH_2	OH	CH_3	$NHCH_3$
Gentamicin C_2	CH_3	NH_2	H	H	NH_2	OH	CH_3	$NHCH_3$
Gentamicin C_{1a}	H	NH_2	H	H	NH_2	OH	CH_3	$NHCH_3$
Gentamicin B	H	NH_2	OH	OH	OH	OH	CH_3	$NHCH_3$
Gentamicin A	H	OH	OH	OH	NH_2	H	OH	$NHCH_3$

Fig. 12.5 – Structural relationships between the gentamicins.

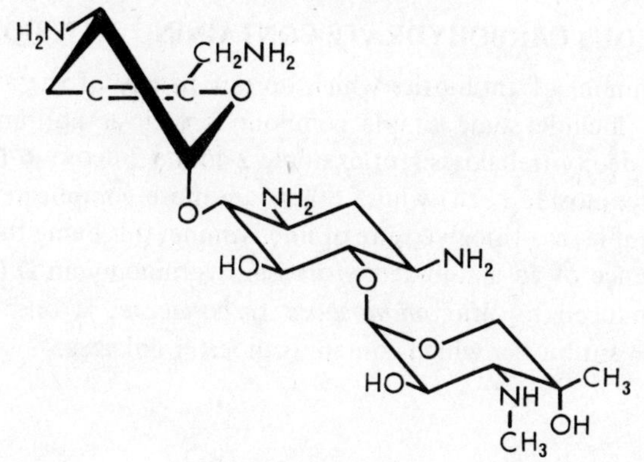

(171)

Miscellaneous aminoglycoside antibiotics

There are a number of aminoglycoside antibiotics which do not contain either of the above cyclitol derivatives. These include the simple 1D-*chiro*-inositol derivative kasugamycin (172), which contains kasugamine as its amidine derivative, and apramycin (173) which contains an octadiose that exists as a rigid bicyclic system.

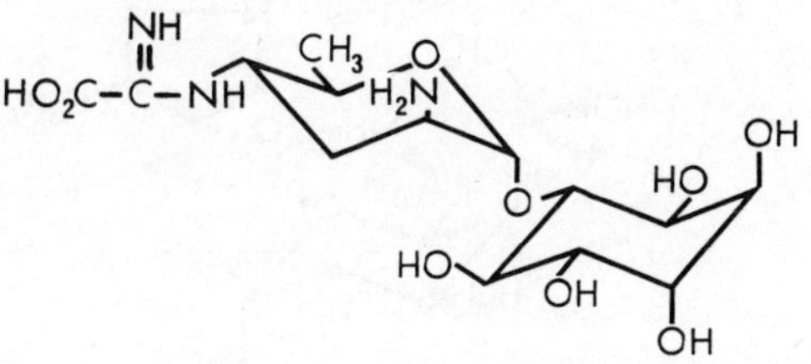

(172)

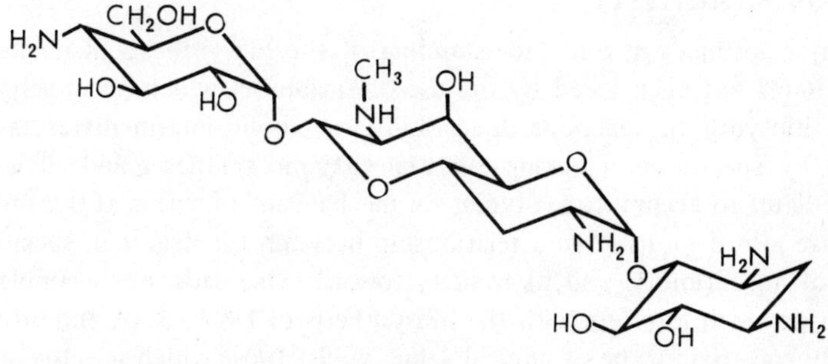

(173)

MISCELLANEOUS CARBOHYDRATE-CONTAINING ANTIBIOTICS

There are a number of antibiotics which do not fit any of the above classes or groups. These include some simple compounds such as nojirimycin (43) and 2/4-amino-2/4-deoxy-trehaloses (for example 2-amino-2-deoxy-α-D-glucopyranosyl-α-D-glucopyranoside (174) whilst others are more complicated. Lincomycin (175), for example, is a thioglycoside of lincosamine, this being the first example of the occurrence of an amino-deoxy-octose. Everninomycin D (176), an octasaccharide produced by *Micromonospora carbonaceae*, is one of a group of oligosaccharide antibiotics which contain orthoester linkages.

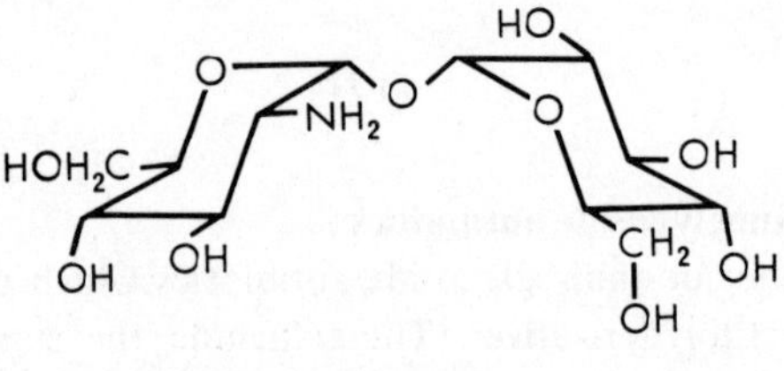

(174)

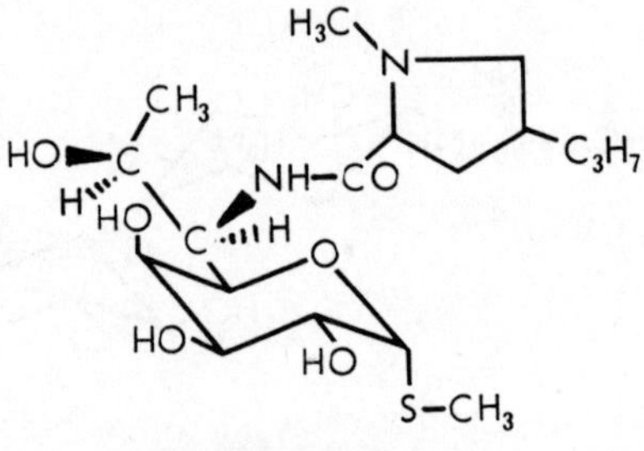

(175)

BIOLOGICAL ACTIVITY

The major advances in our understanding of the biosynthesis of nucleic acids and proteins has been aided by the use of antibiotics which selectively inhibit specific biosynthetic reactions. Inaccessible metabolic intermediates have been studied by specifically blocking essential enzymic syntheses and allowing the intermediates to accumulate. Studies on mechanisms of action at this molecular level have also demonstrated a relationship between the degree of specificity of action of an antibiotic and its toxicity toward living cells. For example, those antibiotics which interfere with the biosynthesis of DNA, RNA and protein are normally too toxic to be of clinical value, whilst those which selectively inhibit protein synthesis are frequently nontoxic and clinically useful.

(176)

The nucleoside antibiotics interfere with the synthesis of DNA and RNA by virtue of their close structural similarity to normal nucleosides. They are therefore highly toxic to living cells. Cordycepin (151) is incorporated into RNA by the normal synthetic processes, but since the 3'-hydroxyl group is lacking, no further nucleotides can be added and chain termination occurs. Puromycin (149) bears close structural resemblance to the aminoacid-bearing end of tRNA and inhibits protein synthesis by competing with aminoacyl tRNA in the ribosome for the activated carboxyl group on the growing peptide chain.

The antibiotics containing aromatic groups have different modes of action. The anthracycline antibiotics such as daunomycin (160) bind strongly to DNA and inhibit the synthesis of RNA through steric interference with the RNA polymerase. Daunomycin binds to both strands of DNA by formation of hydrogen bonds with both the amino groups of daunosamine and hydroxyl groups of the aromatic ring system. The aromatic moiety of the antibiotic fits in between the base pairs whilst the carbohydrate moiety projects into the minor grooves of DNA (see Fig. 11.5) and thereby inhibits the RNA polymerase. The chromomycin antibiotics (Fig. 12.2) also bind to DNA but do not intercalate with the base pairs. They inhibit DNA replication.

The exact mode of action of the macrolide antibiotics has not been elucidated fully but they are thought to render cell membranes permeable to small metabolites, with the result that subsequent metabolic processes are hindered by the loss of these metabolites. Erythromycin (166) is known to inhibit cell-free protein synthesis by interacting with the 50S ribosomal subunit (see Fig. 11.11), thereby inhibiting the synthesis of proteins induced by mRNA.

The aminoglycoside antibiotics appear to have modes of action similar to those of the macrolide antibiotics since they inhibit protein synthesis whilst allowing uninhibited synthesis of DNA or RNA. Streptomycin (169) binds irreversibly to the 30S ribosomal subunit when no mRNA is bound and thereby alters the function but not the formation of the mRNA, tRNA and ribosome complex. In altering the function of the ternary complex, streptomycin inhibits the incorporation of L-phenylalanine, stimulated by polyuridine, into protein, but stimulates the incorporation of other aminoacids (L-isoleucine, L-serine and L-leucine) for which polyuridine does not normally act as the code. The neomycins (Fig. 12.3), kanamycins (Fig. 12.4) and gentamicins (Fig. 12.5) also disturb the fidelity of reading polynucleotides, supposedly by alteration of the triplet code and configuration of the 30S ribosome subunit. From studies on the many structural variations, which have been isolated or synthesised, it has become evident that the number and position of the amino groups are of importance for the efficacy of these antibiotics.

Lincomycin (175), classified under the miscellaneous group of antibiotics, interferes with the protein synthesis in Gram-positive organisms by inhibiting the binding of aminoacyl tRNA to the 50S ribosomal subunit.

Much of the interest in the area of carbohydrate-containing antibiotics is in the production, either by biosynthesis or chemical methods (or a combination of the two), of novel derivatives of antibiotics to alter specific properties of the compound (such as solubility, stability, toxicity or specificity). The reviews by Reden and Dürckheimer (1979) and Rinehart and Suami (1980) and the ongoing series of reviews (Various Authors, 1968 onwards, and Sammes, 1977 onwards) provide up to date descriptions of the work which has been carried out in this area.

CHAPTER 13

Synthetic derivatives of polysaccharides

This chapter describes a number of derivatives of carbohydrates, which are more frequently prepared from polysaccharides than from monosaccharides, etc., and applications of such derivatives. Derivatives of carbohydrates which can be prepared from all types of carbohydrates, such as ethers, esters, etc., have already been described (see Chapter 3) and therefore compounds such as cellulose acetate and rayon are not described in this chapter. The applications of a number of industrially important derivatives is discussed in Chapter 14.

DYE DERIVATIVES

The dyeing of polysaccharides has been studied as an art for centuries for the production of coloured cotton fabrics which are cellulose-based. Traditional methods of dyeing cotton depended on the formation of insoluble dye molecules on the fibres, or of hydrogen bonds between the dye molecules and the fibres, but in the strict sense these cannot be considered as dye derivatives. However, two classes of dyes react with polysaccharides to produce covalently bound derivatives.

The di- and tri-azine dyes are formed by the attachment of chromogenic groups to, for example, 2,4,6-trichloro-*sym*-triazine. The triazinyl group then reacts with primary hydroxyl groups (although secondary hydroxyl groups are not inert) in the polysaccharide to give a dyed polysaccharide (177). Dyes in this group include the Procion® dyes (dichloro-*sym*-triazinyl) and Cibacron® Blue 3G-A (a monochloro-*sym*-triazinyl) and a number of dyed polysaccharides are commercially available including Amylochrome® (Roche) and Blue Dextran® 2000 (Pharmacia). A related group of dyes, the Reactone® dyes which contain trichloropyrimidinyl groups, react in an analogous way to the trichloro-*sym*-triazinyl dyes, but the extent of their subsequent reaction is somewhat less.

The Remazol® type of reactive dyes combine with polysaccharide hydroxyl groups (preferentially the primary hydroxyl groups), by way of unsubstituted intermediates, to give polysaccharide ethers (178).

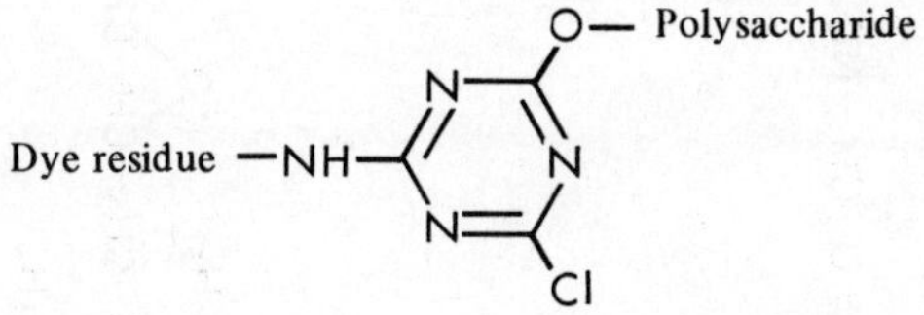

(177)

Dye residue—NH—SO₂—CH₂—CH₂—O—Polysaccharide

(178)

ALKYL ETHERS

The reaction of monochlorocarboxylic acids with polysaccharides produce a range of carboxyalkyl ethers, essentially with the secondary hydroxyl groups, the most common being carboxymethyl ethers (179) which are produced by the action of monochloroacetic acid (Scheme 13.1). Derivatives of carboxyalkyl ethers which are important synthetically include the hydrazide (180) which, for carboxymethyl cellulose, is commercially available, the azide (181) and the isocyanate (182), which can be prepared from the parent carboxyalkyl derivative as shown in Scheme 13.1.

Reaction of polysaccharide with an aminoalkyl chloride, such as 2-diethylaminoethyl chloride (Scheme 13.2), produces an ether of which O-(2-diethylaminoethyl)-polysaccharides (183) are the most common and are commercially available as derivatives of dextran (DEAE-Sephadex®) and agarose. However, other aminoalkyl and alkylaminoalkyl groups may be introduced by using the appropriate activated amine to give 2-aminoethyl, 2-ethylaminoethyl and 2-triethylammoniumethyl derivatives and other derivatives containing different alkyl substituents. The amino or substituted amino group can be further derivatised using, for example, epichlorohydrin, to give di- (184) or mono- (185) chlorohydrins from 2-aminoethyl or 2-ethylaminoethyl derivatives. With 2-diethylaminoethyl derivatives the epichlorohydrin acts as an alkyl halide to produce a quaternary ammonium salt containing an epoxy group (Scheme 13.2).

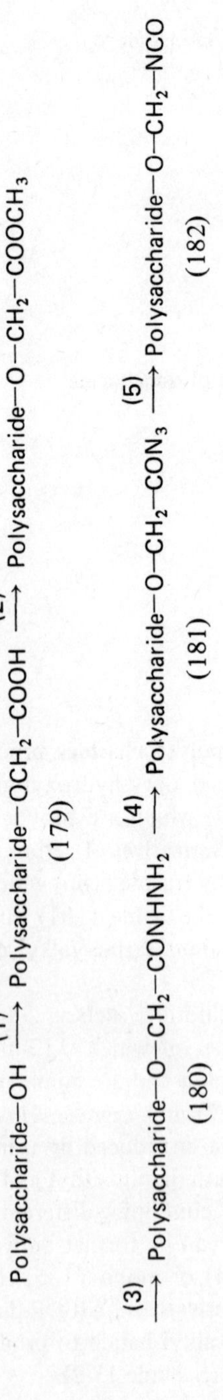

Polysaccharide—OH $\xrightarrow{(1)}$ Polysaccharide—OCH$_2$—COOH $\xrightarrow{(2)}$ Polysaccharide—O—CH$_2$—COOCH$_3$

(179)

$\xrightarrow{(3)}$ Polysaccharide—O—CH$_2$—CONHNH$_2$ $\xrightarrow{(4)}$ Polysaccharide—O—CH$_2$—CON$_3$ $\xrightarrow{(5)}$ Polysaccharide—O—CH$_2$—NCO

(180)   (181)   (182)

Reagents: (1) ClCH$_2$COOH, $^-$OH; (2) CH$_3$OH, H$^+$; (3) NH$_2$NH$_2$; (4) NaNO$_2$, H$^+$; (5) H$^+$

Scheme 13.1

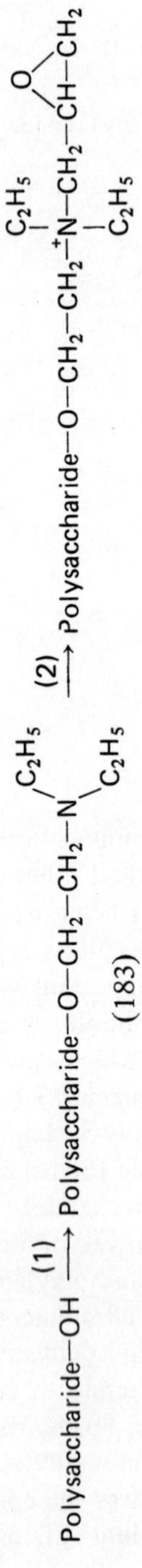

Polysaccharide—OH $\xrightarrow{(1)}$ Polysaccharide—O—CH$_2$—CH$_2$—N$\begin{smallmatrix}C_2H_5\\\\C_2H_5\end{smallmatrix}$ $\xrightarrow{(2)}$ Polysaccharide—O—CH$_2$—CH$_2$—$\overset{+}{N}\begin{smallmatrix}C_2H_5\\\\C_2H_5\end{smallmatrix}$—CH$_2$—CH—CH$_2$

(183)

Reagents: (1) (C$_2$H$_5$)$_2$NCH$_2$CH$_2$Cl, $^-$OH; (2) CH$_2$—CH—CH$_2$—Cl, H$^+$

Scheme 13.2

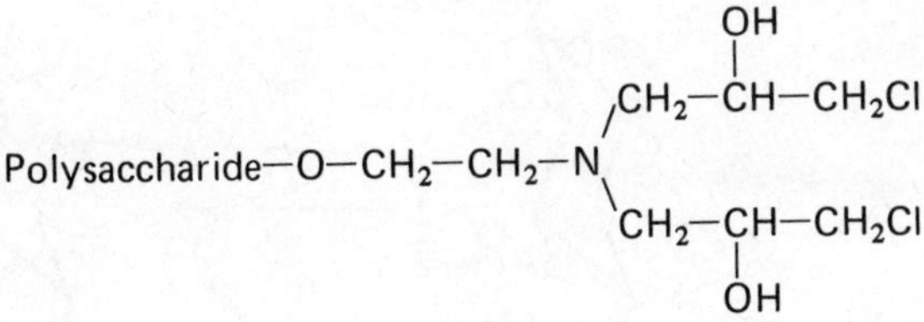

$$\text{Polysaccharide}-O-CH_2-CH_2-N\begin{cases} CH_2-\underset{\underset{OH}{|}}{CH}-CH_2Cl \\ CH_2-\underset{\underset{OH}{|}}{CH}-CH_2Cl \end{cases}$$

(184)

$$\text{Polysaccharide}-O-CH_2CH_2-N\begin{cases} C_2H_5 \\ CH_2-\underset{\underset{OH}{|}}{CH}-CH_2Cl \end{cases}$$

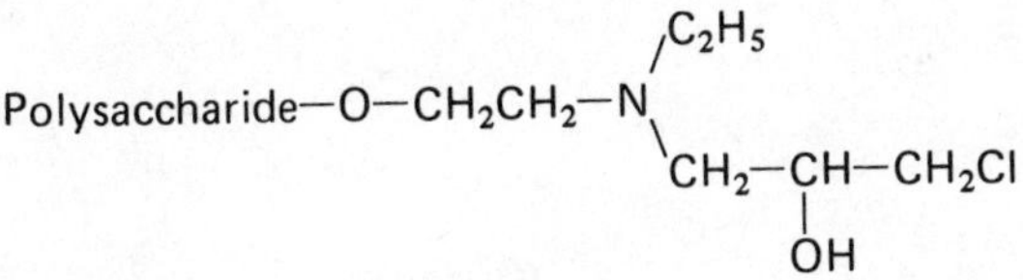

(185)

CYCLIC CARBONATES

Although cyclic and acylic carbonates of monosaccharides have been known for some time, little interest was shown in such derivatives of polysaccharides until the early 1970s, when the conditions for the production of cyclic derivatives, with minimum acylic substitution, were developed. The reaction of ethylchloroformate in anhydrous organic solvents produces cyclic carbonate derivatives (186) of a number of polysaccharides, including cellulose, nigeran, xylan, inulin and cyclomalto-oligosaccharides. In inulin strained *trans*-4,6- (187) and -1,3-carbonate (188) groups can be formed with the D-fructofuranosyl residues. Simple compounds, such as aminoacids, have been shown to react with these derivatives through nucleophilic attacks (Scheme 13.3). A stable covalent bond is produced *via* opening of the carbonate ring in either of two ways to give two possible products (189 or 190).

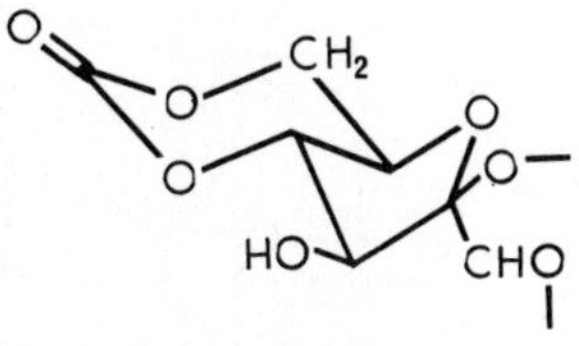

(187) 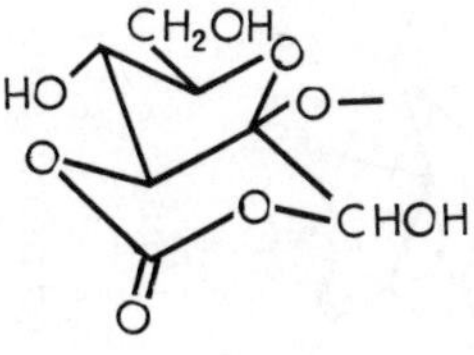　　　　　　　(188)

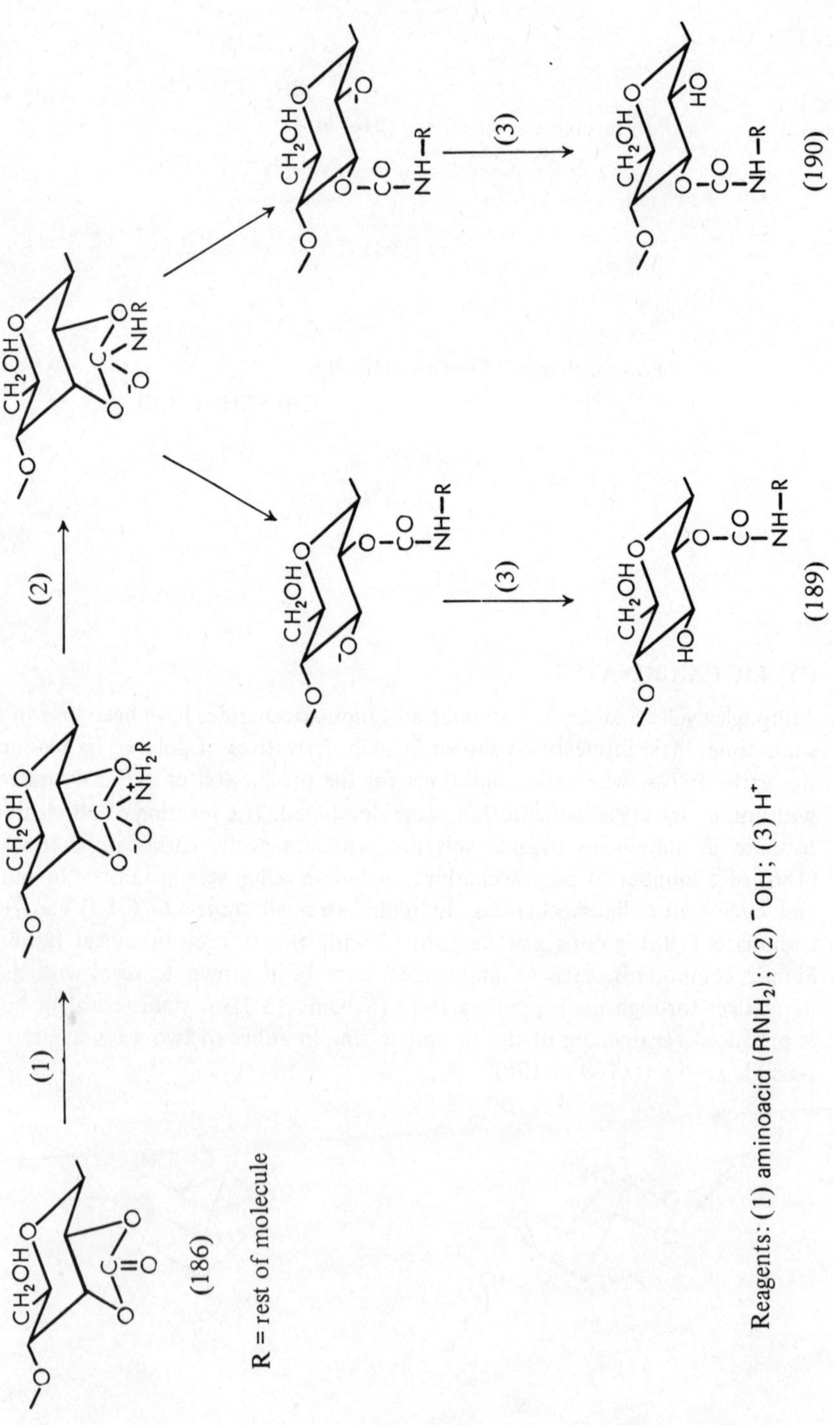
(186)
R = rest of molecule
(1)
(2)
(3)
(3)
(189)
(190)
Reagents: (1) aminoacid (RNH_2); (2) ^-OH; (3) H^+

Scheme 13.3

CYCLIC IMIDOCARBONATES

These compounds, which are closely related to cyclic carbonates, are traditionally called cyclic imidocarbonates although there is some evidence which indicates that the real situation is not as simple as originally thought. The action of cyanogen bromide on dextrans or cellulose produces a *trans*-2,3-imidocarbonate (191) whilst with agarose, the absence of vicinal hydroxyl groups prevents the formation of an energetically favourable imidocarbonate and the reaction has been shown, by the use of ^{13}C n.m.r. and specific chemical tests (Kohn and Wilchek, 1982), to involve cyanate esters (192). The cyclic imidocarbonates react in a similar manner to the cyclic carbonates with single molecules such as aminoacids (Scheme 13.4), whilst the cyanate esters react *via* the mechanism shown in Scheme 13.5 which gives an isourea derivative.

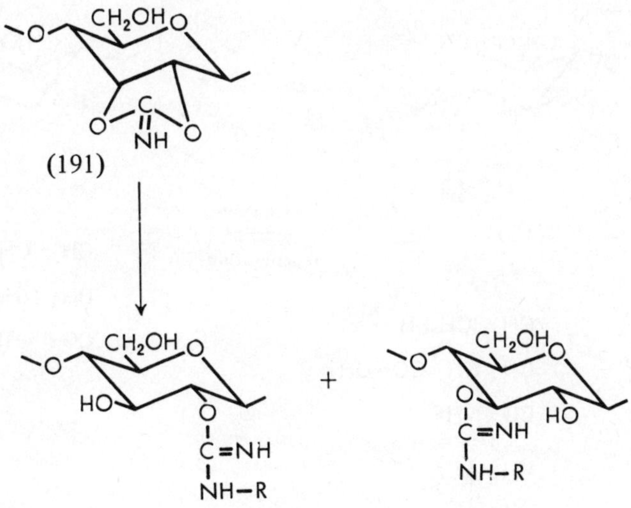

Scheme 13.4

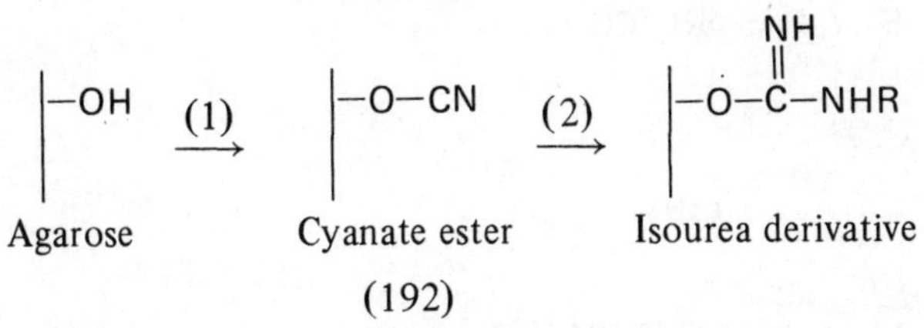

Reagents: (1) CNBr; (2) aminoacid etc. (RNH₂)

Scheme 13.5

XANTHATES

Xanthates are produced by the action of alkaline carbon disulphide on a polysaccharide, the most common derivative being cellulose xanthate (193). Xanthates do not react directly with amines and aminoacids but activation of these with N-acetylhomocysteine thiolactone (194) allows their reaction through the formation of disulphide linkages (Scheme 13.6). This process can be reversed by treatment with a thiol compound (usually L-cysteine) which regenerates the xanthate.

A number of other less common derivatives of polysaccharides have been reviewed, together with those mentioned herein (Kennedy, 1974a).

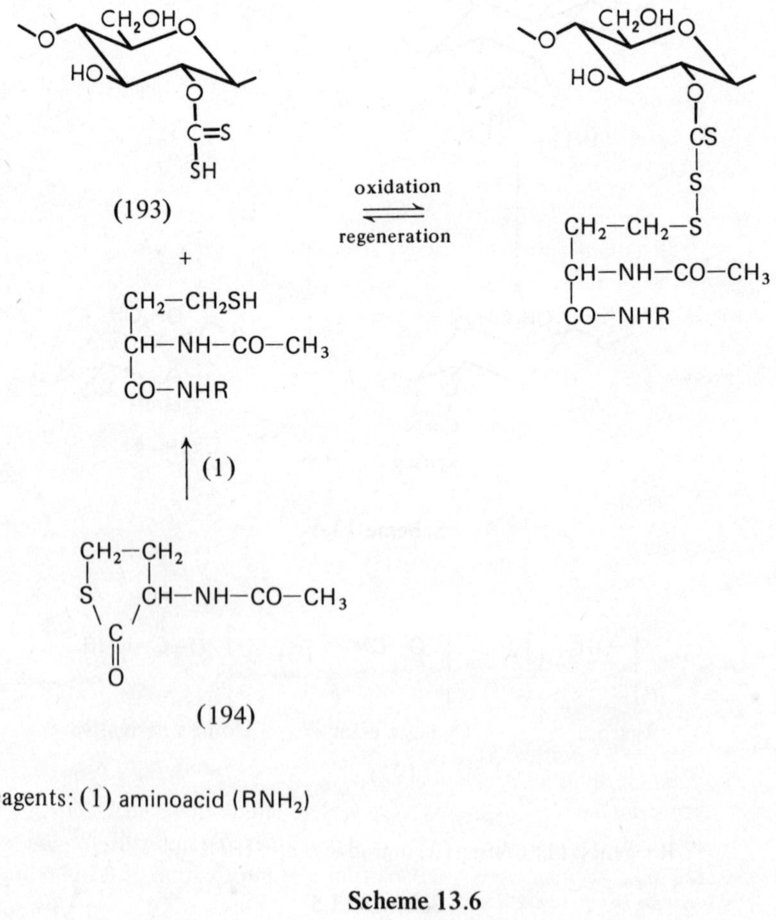

Reagents: (1) aminoacid (RNH_2)

Scheme 13.6

APPLICATIONS OF SYNTHETIC POLYSACCHARIDE DERIVATIVES

Chromatographic media

Cross-linking of soluble polysaccharide molecules gives an insoluble three-dimensional structure that swells in liquids, particularly in water, to give a gel. The most common method of cross-linking polysaccharides comes from their reaction with epichlorohydrin, and cross-linked dextrans, commercially available as the Sephadex® G series (Pharmacia), are well known. The degree of cross-linking is controlled in order to control the size of the pores of the gel; the more cross-linking, the smaller the pore size. Gels with larger pore sizes can be prepared by cross-linking agarose with 1,3-bis-(2,3-epoxypropoxy)-butane and again these are commercially available under the trade names of Bio-Gel® A series (Bio-Rad) and Sepharose® (Pharmacia). As such, these gels are used for the separation of molecules using the size/shape of the molecule as a basis for separation (gel filtration chromatography).

When these cross-linked polysaccharides are used in derivatisation reactions, the resulting insoluble derivatives are used for a variety of chromatographic methods. Carboxymethyl (CM) derivatives of cellulose or dextran are used as cation exchange supports whilst a range of anion exchange supports can be obtained by the formation of alkylaminoalkyl derivatives, with strongly basic anion exchange supports being quaternary ammonium derivatives (such as diethyl-(2-hydroxypropyl)-aminoethyl derivatives (195) and weakly basic anion exchange supports being primary, secondary or tertiary amino derivatives (most commonly diethylaminoethyl (DEAE) derivatives are used). Other derivatives of cross-linked polysaccharides are prepared, as a means of activating the cross-linked polysaccharide, to allow other molecules to be attached in order to produce, for example, affinity chromatographic supports (see later, p. 302).

$$\text{Polysaccharide}-O-CH_2-CH_2-\overset{+}{N}-CH_2-CH-CH_3$$

with C_2H_5 groups on the nitrogen and OH on the carbon

(195)

Immobilised biologically active molecules

Immobilised enzymes

Enzymes have been used by man for hundreds of years in the preparation of food, drink and clothing, but it was not until the beginning of the century, when the first individual enzyme (an amylase) was isolated, that full use could be made of the highly specific nature of most enzymes. Despite the tremendous advances that have been made in the isolation and purification of enzymes over the last few decades, the complex nature of the mixtures in which enzymes exist *in vivo* still makes purification of enzymes a lengthy and usually very expensive procedure. Re-isolation of enzymes, after use, is generally impractical because of the low concentrations usually employed, and consequently enzymes have not been used widely for industrial purposes.

In recent years, biotechnology has moved beyond the whole-cell phase, and the use of enzymes, immobilised on inert supports to aid stability and ease of recovery, has developed to an extent when it is no longer simply an aspect of microbiology; it has become a discipline in its own right, brought about by interactions between enzymologists, microbiologists and engineers. However, one must not be led by all the extensive literature which has now been published on the chemical production of such compounds to think that the principle of immobilisation is something new. The overall principle of attachment of a biologically active molecule to an insoluble matrix is simple and simulates the natural mode of action and environment of enzymes, antibodies, antigens, etc., which are carried on the surfaces or in the interiors of cells, or which are embedded in biological membranes and tissues. Indeed, as is often discovered, 'Nature was there first' and the greater proportion of the biologically active molecules in the human body exist at some time in an immobilised form. Although a precise biological activity has been identified for some of the molecules present in the body, many if not all of the others can be regarded as insoluble biological reactors of some description, for example, the proteoglycans in their tissue matrix-forming role. However, perhaps less attention has been given to the immobilised forms, rather than the soluble forms of such molecules since most chemical techniques, analyses, and manipulations are designed to be carried out in solution, and the chemistry of activity in the solid phase is less well developed.

In natural systems, the immobilisation of biologically active macromolecules such as enzymes and glycoprotein hormones may well be a reversible process, according to whether the macromolecule is originally synthesised in the solid or liquid phase. However, it is quite certain that immobilised forms of such active macromolecules easily become converted into soluble forms to be transported to a new site at which they perform their function – and by virtue of performing that function, they may once again become immobilised. In this respect the natural immobilised molecules differ markedly from those prepared in the laboratory. This is because synthetically-immobilised biologically active molecules are usually required to perform their biological function without being released into the surrounding solution and thereby contaminating it.

There are many applications of immobilised, biologically active molecules. Immobilised enzymes are principally used to effect the reaction catalysed by the free enzyme, but in a simplified form since the enzyme (insoluble) can be very easily and simply removed from the substrate and products (soluble) by filtration or centrifugation, whereas use of the soluble enzyme in the conventional fashion requires subsequent laborious separation of the enzyme from the products by, for example, gel filtration and ion-exchange chromatography. Further advantages of immobilised enzymes are that: the enzyme becomes stabilised to decomposition in storage and to heat on immobilisation, the reaction of the enzyme may be rapidly terminated without the addition of foreign substances, the enzyme may be packed into a column and used for continuous conversion processes, the products of the enzymic action are not contaminated with any unwanted biologically active material, and the immobilised enzymes can be easily re-used. Also, changes in stability and kinetic properties are sometimes found upon immobilisation, and these may be put to good use. Uses include: simplification of reactors, industrial processes and clinical analyses, employment in analytical chemistry and bio-chemistry — that is, enzyme electrodes, etc. (see Carr and Bowers, 1980), sequence analysis and synthesis, separation techniques, isolation of compounds related to enzymes, and use in membrane and chromatographic column forms.

A number of methods of immobilisation of biological molecules exist (Fig. 13.1), and no one method is perfect for all molecules or purposes. When attaching a biologically active molecule to an insoluble support, it is important to avoid a mode of attachment that reacts with or disturbs the active site(s) of the molecule, as otherwise a loss of activity will result on binding. It is also important to avoid overloading the matrix when binding molecules, since overloading leads to overcrowding and hence reduced activity, by reason of steric hindrance of approach of the substrate etc. molecules to the active sites of the bound molecules. However, it does not follow that limited loading of the enzyme molecules on the matrix surface will be successful, since hydrogen bonding and hydrophobic forces may occur between immobilised enzyme and 'free' molecules, thus causing the latter to block up the spaces between the immobilised molecules. Attention to the way in which the macromolecule can be immobilised and the choice of matrix is also a matter of importance. A number of matrix types and techniques have been used in the field of immobilisation, and it can be concluded that there is no ideal or universal support matrix or immobilisation technique. For specific applications many of the support matrices available can be discounted because of their characteristics. In a medical application, for example, where an immobilised enzyme is in contact with blood or tissue a material which evokes an immune response (wool support) or clotting reaction (glass support) should not be chosen, a support based on methacrylate or silicone rubber, which are inert in these aspects, being preferable. On the other hand, for continuous-flow reactors, materials with poor dimensional stability (such as cellulose, starch gels and dextrans) should be avoided with preference being given to, for example, controlled-pore glass or ceramic material.

The choice of support matrix is also influenced by its effect on the characteristics of the enzyme and its substrate. Comparison of the activity of an enzyme bound to a matrix with the activity of a freely dissolved enzyme at various pH levels has shown that if the enzyme is attached to a negatively charged matrix,

(a) Adsorption

(b) Ion Exchange

(c) Entrapment*

(d) Microencapsulation*

(e) Cross-linking

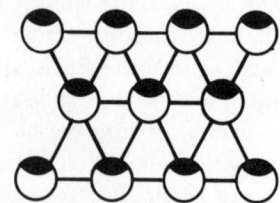

(f) Copolymerisation*

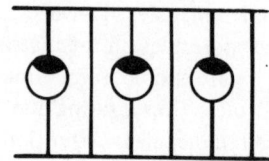

(g) Entrapment and Cross-linking*

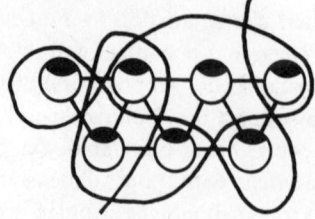

(h) Covalent attachment

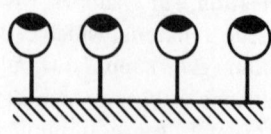

Fig. 13.1 – Diagramatic methods of enzyme immobilisation.
◒Enzyme molecule, * Diffusion controlled.

for example DEAE-cellulose, the pH optimum is shifted towards the alkaline side: the immobilised enzyme reaches maximum activity at apparently higher alkalinity. This effect is due to the negatively charged groups of the matrix attracting a thin 'film' of positive hydrogen ions, thereby creating a microenvironment for the bound enzyme that has a higher hydrogen ion concentration (lower pH) than the concentration in the surrounding solution where the pH is actually measured. Similarly, for a positively charged matrix, for example CM-cellulose, the apparent shift in optimum pH is to the acid side (Fig. 13.2). The characteristics of the support matrix can be such that the substrate for the enzyme is attracted to the matrix, whilst the products of enzyme action may be unaffected. It is also possible to prepare support matrices which will allow easy removal of the immobilised enzyme from the reaction medium. Examples which have already been used are magnetic supports and film-forming materials, both methods allowing the recovery of the immobilised enzyme from reaction media containing other insoluble matter which makes separation by filtration impossible. The ideal support for a given application is one which would increase substrate binding, decrease product inhibition, shift the apparent pH optimum to the desired value, discourage microbial growth and could be readily recovered for reuse.

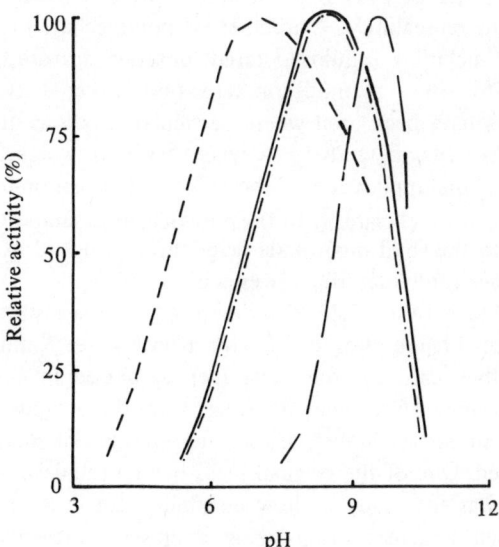

Fig. 13.2 – The effect of microenvironment of the pH-activity profile of an immobilsed enzyme. ———— soluble enzyme; — — — — immobilised enzyme, cationic support; — · — · — immobilised enzyme, neutral support; — — — — immobilised enzyme, anionic support.

Full discussions of all the methods available and their suitability to particular applications can be found in the many books and reviews on the subject, (for example, Zaborsky, 1972; Wiseman, 1975; Trevan, 1980, and Kennedy and Cabral, 1982a) and in an ongoing series of literature surveys (Sturgeon and Kennedy, 1979 onwards). A review of a number of materials, including non-carbohydrate materials suitable for solid supports is also available (White and Kennedy, 1980).

The use of polymeric carbohydrate derivatives for enzyme immobilisation has received more emphasis than hydrophobic supports, since the latter may lead to the destabilisation of the enzyme. The major advantage of the use of polysaccharidic material is that the solid state residual hydroxyl groups provide a protective hydrophobic environment for the attached macromolecule. Immobilisation within the pores of macroporous polysaccharides gives added protection from exposure to destabilising influences whilst overcoming the disadvantage of poor diffusion of higher molecular weight substrates associated with microcrystalline polysaccharides.

In order to attach the enzyme chemically to a polysaccharide, the latter must first be activated in such a way that the enzyme can subsequently be attached under conditions which will not cause its inactivation. The most common method, for laboratory scale use, is the use of the so-called cyclic *trans*-2,3-imidocarbonate (see p. 293), whilst for large scale industrial uses cellulose xanthate (see p. 294) is particularly attractive on account of its ease of production and reuseability. A number of polysaccharides have been used as solid supports including cellulose, starch, dextran, agarose, alginic acid and carrageenans. Many other methods of activation, using derivatives described above, and others have been used where particular reactions must or must not be used to preserve enzyme activity. A recent method, which uses particularly mild conditions, is the application of the ability of transition-metal oxides and hydrous oxides to form chelates with the polysaccharide support (Fig. 13.3). The enzyme couples to the (hydrous) oxide layer through ligand exchange mechanisms which have been fully described (Kennedy, 1979b).

A novel approach to the field of immobilised enzymes is the immobilisation of microbial cells with retention of life (for a review, see Kennedy and Cabral, 1982b) so that they can reproduce and thereby act as an automatically self-renewing form of immobilised enzyme. Apart from the obvious advantage which this type of system has for industrial use, the potential of such systems has yet to be fully realised. One of the original ideas behind the development of immobilised enzymes was the study of how enzymes react in their natural environment, immobilised enzymes often being a closer representation of natural systems than soluble enzymes. The immobilisation of whole cells means that enzymes can be readily studied in situations which resemble their natural environment. With the development of more immobilised-cell systems it may become possible to apply this technology to the investigation of enzyme deficiency disorders by studying comparatively the action of particular enzymes in affected cells and in normal cells. A development of this could lead to more-accurate diagnosis and ultimate treatment (by implantation of immobilised whole normal cells into the affected areas) of enzyme deficiency disorders.

There are two major disadvantages in the use of polysaccharides for support materials, namely their nonspecific adsorption properties and their susceptibility to microbial attack. Nonspecific adsorption of protein can be avoided or overcome on a laboratory scale by washing the final product with a high ionic strength buffer, but this process can inactivate an enzyme and, for an industrial process, is frequently too expensive. The second disadvantage could possibly be overcome by immobilisation of antibiotics (see below, p. 303) but has not, as yet, been attempted successfully.

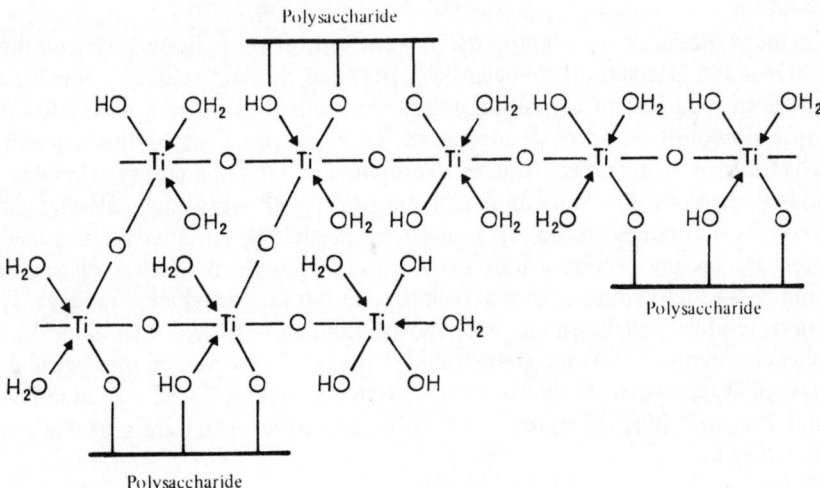

Fig. 13.3 – Schematic representation of polysaccharides chelated with hydrous titanium(IV) oxide.

Immunoadsorbents
Immobilised antibodies are principally useful for the purification of homologous antigens, usually by a type of column chromatography (immunoadsorption) in which the solution of impure antigen is passed through a bed of immobilised antibody: the specific antigen is adsorbed by the antibody whilst impurities are washed through the column. Subsequently, the antigen may be desorbed from the column in pure form. Thus the lengthy conventional techniques of various types of column, etc., chromatography are short-circuited. Immunoadsorption can of course also be applied in the reverse sense, using insolubilised antigen to purify an antibody. Immunoadsorption is a very versatile technique since many

macromolecules are antigenic and therefore antibodies can be raised to them; but an important prerequisite is, of course, that the antigen which is to be immobilised can be obtained in pure form or that the antibody to be insolubilised can be obtained in pure and/or highly specific form. Immobilised antigens and antibodies are also of use in radioimmunoassay techniques.

Carbohydrate polymers, particularly Sepharose® *trans*-2,3-imidocarbonate, have been used extensively to prepare immunoadsorbents.

Affinity chromatography media

Affinity chromatography is a technique in which substances are separated on the basis of the differing strengths of their interactions with the support material which has been modified to contain groups with specific interactions. The interactions used can be divided into chemical and biological interactions.

Chemical interactions. Many proteins have hydrophobic sites exposed on their surfaces and interactions between these sites and chromatographic media which has been modified to contain hydrophobic residues provides a means for the separation/purification of such proteins. This type of affinity chromatography, which has the alternative name of hydrophobic interaction chromatography, is widely used for the extraction and purification of many materials including enzymes, hormones, nucleic acids and whole cells. The chromatographic media used are usually polysaccharide derivatives (frequently derivatives of agarose) containing such groups as ω-aminoalkyl, ω-carboxyalkyl and alkyl residues. The latter residues can be simple aliphatic or aromatic residues, such as hexyl or phenyl residues, or more complicated, such as derivatives formed with dye molecules, examples of which include Acridine Yellow, Cibacron® Blue 3G-A and Procion® Blue. Many of these chromatographic media are available commercially.

Biological interactions. In this type of affinity chromatography the residue attached to the chromatographic support is usually one of low molecular weight but one for which the macromolecule to be purified has a specific affinity. Thus for the purification of carbohydrate-directed enzymes, an immobilised carbohydrate, for which the enzyme is active, is used. Many such products are available under the trade name Selectins® (Pierce). Carbohydrates, either in the form of polysaccharides or as carbohydrate-containing macromolecules such as glycoproteins, etc., can be purified by immobilisation of lectins (see Table 13.1 and Chapter 9, p. 209) to retain the selected carbohydrate macromolecule until the elution conditions are altered to disrupt the lectin–carbohydrate affinity. A number of lectins, etc., are commercially available bound to carbohydrate supports, including agarose (for example, ConA-Sepharose®, immobilised concanavalin A from Pharmacia; and Glycosylex® A and Glycaminosylex®, immobilised concanavalin A and wheat germ agglutinin, respectively, from Miles).

Table 13.1 Carbohydrate specificity of some lectins

Lectin	Carbohydrate residue specificity
Concanavalin A	α-D-glucosyl α-D-mannosyl
Dolichos biflorus agglutinin	terminal 2-acetamido-2-deoxy-α-D-galactosyl group
Helix pomatia lectin	2-acetamido-2-deoxy-D-galactosyl
Jimson weed lectin	2-acetamido-2-deoxy-β-D-glucosyl
Kidney bean agglutinin	2-acetamido-2-deoxy-D-galactosyl
Lens culinaris lectin	α-D-mannosyl
Lentil lectin	α-D-glucosyl α-D-mannosyl
Lima bean agglutinin	2-acetamido-2-deoxy-D-galactosyl
Limus polyphenus lectin	5-acetamido-3,5-dideoxy-D-*glycero*-D-*galacto*-2-nonulopyranosylonic acid
Lotus tetragonolubus agglutinin	α-L-fucosyl
Pea tree agglutinin	2-acetamido-2-deoxy-D-galactosyl D-galactosyl
Potato lectin	2-acetamido-2-deoxy-D-glucosyl
Ricinus communis lectin	2-acetamido-2-deoxy-D-galactosyl D-galactosyl
Soya bean agglutinin	D-galactosyl
Ulex europeus agglutinin (form I) (form II)	 α-L-fucosyl 2-acetamido-4-*O*-(2-acetamido-2-deoxy-β-D-glucopyranosyl)-2-deoxy-D-glucosyl
Vicia graminea lectin	5-acetamido-3,5-dideoxy-D-*glycero*-D-*galacto*-2-nonulopyranosylonic acid
Wheat germ agglutinin	2-acetamido-2-deoxy-D-glucosyl

Immobilised antibiotics

The most recent innovation in the field of immobilisation has been the preparation of immobilised antibiotics. Where an anti-bacterial surface is required (for example, water storage tanks, industrial membranes, chromatographic columns), such surfaces could be realised by using cellulose-based paints, membranes, etc., and insolubilisation of the antibiotic by covalent attachment. In such cases, loss of the antibiotic would be minimal. Other applications, which have come to light, include provision of selective protection against microbial attack of paper and legal documents, of canvas and chromatographic media based on cellulosic materials, and of cellulose-based packings of cooling towers. The techniques also provide a novel form of sterility for sheets and other cotton-based fabrics and gauze, and for treating infected root canals in teeth before root filling. Also, where it is required to have a slow continual release of antibiotics but a higher initial release (for example, bandages and surgeons' thread), immobilised antibiotics can be expected to be of use. Since cellulose and other polysaccharides and their derivatives are used extensively in a number of forms as accessories to life, active immobilised antibiotics could well be of great use in a number of other areas (for example, food packaging materials).

Immobilised polysaccharides

A number of polysaccharides and carbohydrate-containing macromolecules have been immobilised by reaction with imidocarbonate derivatives of polysaccharides. These derivatives have been used to study the interactions between carbohydrate-containing macromolecules and other macromolecules. Examples include the interaction of glycosaminoglycans with lipoproteins and the interaction of carbohydrates with carbohydrate-directed enzymes. The latter example has been used as a method of purifying such enzymes (by affinity chromatography).

Insoluble derivatives of carbohydrates such as the dye-derivatives and immobilised glycosaminoglycans have been used as solid phase substrates for enzymes including α-amylase (EC 3.2.1.1), β-amylase (EC 3.2.1.2) and hyaluronidases (hyaluronate 3- and 4-glycanohydrolase, EC 3.2.1.36 and 3.2.1.35).

Immobilised nucleic acids

Polysaccharides, particularly cellulose, have been used almost exclusively for the immobilisation of nucleic acids and polynucleotides. These solvent-insoluble derivatives are used for the fractionation and purification of other nucleic acids, nucleotides, etc., isolation of single stranded nucleic acids by base pairing, analysis of base-sequences, affinity supports for nucleic acid-directed enzymes and nucleic acid-binding proteins.

CHAPTER 14

Technological aspects and applications

TRADITIONAL APPLICATIONS

Currently, the industrial uses of polysaccharides and carbohydrate-containing macromolecules are dominated by the plant polysaccharides, starch and cellulose, which are used and have been used in some cases for hundreds of years, in the polymeric or depolymerised and derivatised forms in a number of industries. The traditional uses of carbohydrates have been reviewed (Stacey, 1973).

Construction and packaging uses

Wood, the major source of cellulose, in which the polysaccharide exists in association with lignin, oils, resins, minerals and pigments, etc., is one of the most useful and versatile structural and building materials in use. Technology has advanced its usefulness from both the production and usage points of view. The improvement of wood by the introduction of preservatives, plastic fillers, fire retardants, etc., to give plywoods, fibreboards, blockboards and veneers, although now commonplace, has been quite remarkable. A major use for softwoods lies in pulp for the paper industry for newsprint, books, packaging and boardmaking, etc., the demand for which increases at an evergrowing rate with the demand from the newer industries of computing, copying and convenience goods adding the needs for specialist products to those for the more traditional papers, etc.

Other forms of cellulose include cotton (the purest form in which cellulose occurs naturally), flax, jute, sisal, hemp and various straws and grasses, all of which are used in the construction and packaging industries to produce papers, (cotton, straws and grasses) and rope (sisal and hemp).

Derivatives of cellulose, particularly esters and ethers, have for a long time held a special place in the packaging industry for the production of transparent wrappings and films. Cellulose acetate film can be laminated to itself, to foil or the plastic films (particularly polythene films which produce a tough heat seal barrier film useful for packing meat and cheese).

Starch and its derivatives find many uses in the paper industry as sizes, stiffeners and adhesives. The more common derivatives include esters, ethers, phosphates, oxidized starches, hydroxyalkyl starches and cationic starches.

Food and brewing uses

Starch (and its components) is the major food polysaccharide with the main sources being maize, wheat, rice, potato, tapioca and sago. These various starches are used for a variety of foodstuffs which depend on the nature of the starch granule and their associated constituent waxes and oils. Maize is used whole for animal feedstuffs, wheat for bread, and barley for the brewing industry. The various polysaccharides used in the food industry are the subject of a recent book (Blanshard and Mitchell, 1979).

Sucrose, the household commodity, obtained from sugar cane and sugar beet, is used in the food industry in large quantities as a sweetening agent and preservative and as a raw material for the fermentation industry where it is used in forms which are by-products of sugar refining such as molasses, treacles and syrups.

A number of other oligosaccharides are used in the food industry, but to a much lesser extent than sucrose, and these include maltose and cellobiose (degradation products of starch and cellulose) and lactose (which is obtained as a by-product from milk after removal of the curd in cheese production). Lactose can be used in fermentation processes, but it required the development of yeasts which had been modified to lactose fermentation since normal yeasts have no action on lactose. Uses of these oligosaccharides have been reviewed (Lee, 1980).

Textile uses

Cellulose has been used for many years as a material for the production of textiles with cotton being one of the world's major fibres. With the introduction of man-made fibres, the position of cotton has declined but the developments of cellulose based man-made fibres (for example, rayon and triacetate) have ensured that carbohydrate-based textiles will retain their position for some time yet, especially for use and wear in hot climates. The dyeing of cellulose fabrics has been discussed in Chapter 13 (p. 288).

Pharmaceutical and cosmetic uses

Many carbohydrates are used in the pharmaceutical and cosmetic industry to bind preparations or to act as 'inert' bulking agents for small quantities of active ingredients. Among those used are D-glucose, sucrose, mannitol and α,α-trehalose with starch (and its derivatives) being used for its adhesive properties. Starch is also used as a talc substitute. Dextran and lower molecular weight fractions are used as plasma substitutes, which restore blood volume in patients who have lost considerable amounts of blood or are in a state of shock. Other fractions improve blood flow in capillaries and, as the sulphate derivatives, have anticoagulant, antilipemic and anti-ulcer activity.

Other uses
Derivatives of cellulose (mainly the acetate-butyrate, propionate and acetate-phthalate) are used in the plastics industry to make sheets, films, coatings and backing materials whilst fatty acid, alkyl or alkoxy esters and ethers of non-reducing disaccharides, including sucrose, α,α-trehalose and maltitol, form a group of surface active agents (surfactants) with an extraordinary range of applications, extending from industrial detergents and surface coatings to food emulsifiers and antimicrobial agents (see Lee, 1980, for a review).

NEW APPLICATIONS AND FUTURE TRENDS

With the development of microbial technology, that is, the multidisciplinary science of microbiology applied to production of industrially important materials, the value of producing polysaccharides has increased. The production and isolation of microbial (bacterial) polysaccharides has the advantages, compared to production by and from growing plants, of assured production and quality which is unaffected by marine pollution, tides, weather, war, famine, drought, etc., which affect the production of plant polysaccharides, whilst production can be geared to market trends and located such that convenient, cheap substrates can be utilised.

The uses to which microbial polysaccharides are put arise from the natural biological functions of polysaccharides, including thickening agents in joint fluids, protectants from desiccation and lubricants. Whilst the time taken between the initial reporting of xanthan gum to its pilot scale production was of the order of twelve years, our present understanding of how structural features affect the properties of polysaccharides and our ability to modify bacteria through genetic engineering (see Chapter 11, p. 263) has resulted in greater investment in time (and money) for this area of biotechnology with a number of polysaccharides (see Table 14.1) being developed more rapidly as possible industrially important materials (see reviews by Berkely *et al.*, 1979, Bull *et al.*, 1979, Sandford, 1979, and Davidson, 1980).

Oil industry
Perhaps the greatest single potential market for microbial polysaccharides is that provided by the oil industry for enhanced oil recovery and drilling muds. Enhanced oil recovery requires polymers which improve water flooding techniques by increasing efficiency of contact with, and displacement of, oil. Alternatively, the polymer must reduce the flow capacity of the solution in the rock system, either by increasing viscosity of the solution or by decreasing the permeability of the system. A prerequisite for the polymer is that it must be unaffected by the salt concentrations and temperatures found in oil wells. Drilling muds are aqueous suspensions, containing clays and colloidal materials, which lubricate drill heads and counterbalance the upward pressure of oil. As a pre-

requisite of these uses, the polymers used in drilling muds must have high viscosities to maintain the colloidal properties of the mud. This viscosity must again be relatively insensitive to temperature but pseudoplastic properties are essential. Xanthan and scleroglucan have been compared favourably with the petroleum based polymers traditionally used because of their greater insensitivity to temperatures, etc., but the prices are, at present, a major drawback.

Table 14.1　Polysaccharides, with (potential) commercial importance, from microbial and fungal origins

Polysaccharide	Organism	Trade name
Alginate	*Azotobacter vinelandii, Pseudomonas aeruginosa*	
—[a]	*Arthrobacter viscosus*	PS B-1797, PS B-1973
PS-7	*Azotobacter indicus*	PS-7
Baker's yeast glycan	*Saccharomyces cerevisiae*	BYG
—[a]	*Bacillus polymyxa*	
—[a]	*Chromobacterium violaceum*	
—[a]	*Cryptococcus laurentii* variant *flavescens*	
Curdlan (succino-glucan)	*Alcaligens faecalis* variant *myxogenes*	
Dextran	*Leuconostoc, Acetobacter* and *Klebsiella* species	Various
Elsinan	*Elsinoe leucospila*	
Erwinia polysaccharides	*Erwinia* species	Zanflo
—[a]	*Hansenula* species	
—[a]	*Pseudomonas* species	
Pullulan	*Aureobasidium pullulans*	
—[a]	*Rhinocladiella elatior*	
—[a]	*Rhinocladiella mansonii*	
Scleroglucan	*Sclerotium* species	Actigum CS Polytran F.S.
—[a]	*Tremella mesenterica*	
Xanthan	*Xanthomonas campestris*	Keltrol, Kelzan, Rhodigel 23

[a] No specific name is used for the polysaccharide.

Food industry

Polysaccharides are included into foods to function, among other purposes, as suspending agents, thickeners, gelling agents and ice crystal formation controllers. Plant polysaccharides such as starch, alginate, guar gum and locust bean gum have been used in various amounts, but the increase in demand for instant and processed foods has led to the use of microbial polysaccharides for many processes (see Table 14.2). New uses are continually being developed, with proposals to include these polysaccharides in bread to improve the texture and water retention properties. The inclusion of microbial polysaccharides into new food formulations is probably easier than replacing plant polysaccharides in existing formulations, due to the multifunctional nature of these new polysaccharides, since it is difficult to adjust the balance of wetting agents, thickening agents and stabilisers to that of the accepted product.

Table 14.2 Functions and potential food uses of microbial polysaccharides

Function	Polysaccharide	Potential use
Stabiliser of low pH gels	Xanthan	Milk shakes
Gelling agent	Curdlan, xanthan, scleroglucan, alginate	Jellies, custards, gravies, sauces, instant dry desserts, pie fillings
Colloidal stabiliser	Xanthan, alginate, scleroglucan	Ice cream, milk shakes
Non-caloric materials	Curdlan, pullulan	Additives for diabetic and dietetic foods (desserts, dressings, etc.)
Film and fibre former	Curdlan, pullulan	Edible films and fibres
Water-retention agent	Curdlan, pullulan	Sausages, ham, starchy jellies
Binding agent	Curdlan	Meat products (e.g. burgers), pastas, jellies
Pseudoplastic thickeners/stabilisers	Curdlan, xanthan, alginate	Sauces, dressings, gravies spreads, bakery fillings
Deodorant	Curdlan	Boiled rice
Coating agent	Xanthan, scleroglucan	Sauces and gravies for pasta and meat products
Crystallisation inhibitor	Xanthan, alginate	Ice cream, sugar syrups
Foam stabiliser	Alginate	Whipped toppings

The major drawback to development of these polysaccharides for food uses is the cost of the materials, and their approval for food use, but some of this can be offset by using existing, approved gels in mixtures which have properties different to the materials in isolation. The use of polysaccharide mixtures as new gelling agents has been reviewed (Dea, 1979).

A related area of carbohydrate uses in the food industry which has resulted from the biotechnological advances of recent years is the production of single cell protein (SCP) and other fermentation products from carbohydrate feedstocks which are often waste products from other food manufacturing processes (alcohol can be produced from waste whey which contains lactose, see p. 136).

Pharmaceutical and cosmetic industries

The pharmaceutical and cosmetic industries use a number of polysaccharides, such as those used in the food industry to form gels, colloids, thixotropic solutions, extrudable pastes and creams, etc., and to form films to bind tablets and produce protective creams. There are also a number of specific uses of carbohydrates in the pharmaceutical industry which have come about as a result of developments in genetic engineering and microbial technology.

Production of carbohydrate-containing antibodies on a commercial scale has revolutionised the treatment of infections, etc., and genetic manipulation and engineering is producing new or modified antibodies or increasing the yields obtained for existing ones. Similar production of enzymes, antigens, glycoprotein hormones, and other biologically active carbohydrate macromolecules can be expected to bring about similar revolutions in clinical treatment. Recently purified polysaccharides of bacterial origins have been prepared for use as antigenic vaccines against meningococcal and pneumococcal infections and, due to the ability of certain of these polysaccharides to cross react with other antisera, they may also provide immunity against other infections. The advantages of using purified polysaccharide vaccines is the low risk of adverse reactions compared to vaccines containing whole cells (either living or dead) and such vaccines can give immunity to infection caused by antibiotic-resistant bacteria.

Reviews of the developments in this field can be found in the ongoing series of biennial conference reports (Various Editors, 1974 onwards) and the series by Wiseman (1977 onwards).

Other uses

Production of carbohydrates by biotechnological processes has resulted in quantities of materials being available as raw materials for other industries, which have traditionally been made from oil, but with the ever-decreasing supply of oil, renewable carbohydrate sources may hold the key to the economic future of the industrialised countries. One advantage which carbohydrates have over many oil-based chemicals is that the correct stereochemical arrangements of the product can be present in the carbohydrate which makes them suitable starting products for the chemical synthesis of other natural products which require the correct stereochemical arrangement for their natural function (Harman, 1979).

NEW PRODUCTION TECHNOLOGY

The major drawback to the use of fermentation technology for the industrial production of, or utilisation of, carbohydrate materials is the cost of production. At present batch culture techniques are used, in which the fermenter is charged and the reaction allowed to proceed for a given time, after which the contents are removed in order to harvest the product. The down-time inherent in this method (caused by harvesting, sterilisation and recharging) could be reduced, and almost eliminated, if continuous culture methods were to be adopted. This, together with the ease of control, greater uniformity, reduced reactor volumes, etc., which are associated with continuous operation, would increase production and lower the final cost of the product. Things are not quite as simple as they appear and the problems of strain stability, low product concentration, and contamination problems have so far thwarted many attempts to improve the efficiency of production.

The future holds many opportunities for engineers, geneticists, micro-biologists and biochemists in the rapidly expanding science of biotechnology to develop and improve production until economically viable products can be obtained. This gives mankind a future which is not locked into the ever-dwindling supplies of oil and oil-based products.

References

Aminoff, D., Binkley, W. W., Schafer, R. and Mowry, R. W. (1970), in *The Carbohydrates, Chemistry and Biochemistry*, W. Pigman and D. Horton (eds.), Academic Press, New York, 2nd edn., **IIB**, Chap 45.

Angyal, S. J. and James, K. (1970), *Chem. Comm.*, **320**.

Ashwell, G. and Morell, A. G. (1974), *Advances Enzymol.* **41**, 99.

Atherton, K. T., Byrom, D. and Dart, E. C. (1979), in *Microbial Technology: Current State, Future Prospects*, A. T. Bull, D. C. Ellwood and C. Ratledge (eds.), Cambridge University Press, Cambridge, p. 379.

Baddiley, J. (1972), *Essays Biochem.* **8**, 35.

Bayne, S. and Fewster, J. A. (1956), *Advances Carbohydr. Chem.* **11**, 43.

Bender, M. L. and Komiyama, M. (1978), *Cyclodextrin Chemistry*, Springer, Berlin.

Berkeley, R. C. W., Gooday, G. W. and Ellwood, D. C. (eds.) (1979), *Microbial Polysaccharides and Polysaccharases*, Academic Press, London.

Björndahl, H., Hellerqvist, C. G., Lindberg, B. and Svensson, S. (1970), *Angew. Chem. Internat. Edn.* **9**, 610.

Blackburn, G. M. (1979a), in *Comprehensive Organic Chemistry*, E. Haslam (ed.), Pergamon Press, Oxford, **5**, Chap 22. 4.

Blackburn, G. M. (1979b), in *Comprehensive Organic Chemistry*, E. Haslam (ed.), Pergamon Press, Oxford, **5**, Chap 22. 1.

Blackburn, G. M. (1979c), in *Comprehensive Organic Chemistry*, E. Haslam (ed.), Pergamon Press, Oxford, **5**, Chap 22. 5.

Blanshard, J. M. V. and Mitchell, J. R. (1979), *Polysaccharides in Food*, Butterworths, London.

Bull, A. T., Ellwood, D. C. and Ratledge, C. (eds.) (1979), *Microbial Technology: Current State, Future Prospects*, Cambridge University Press, Cambridge.

Butt, W. R., Lynch, S. S. and Kennedy, J. F. (1972), in *Structure-Activity Relationships of Protein and Polypeptide Hormones*, M. Margoulies and F. C. Greenwood (eds.), Internat. Cong. Ser. 241, Exerpta Medica, Amsterdam, Part 2, p. 355.

Cabib, E. and Shematek, E. M. (1981), in *Biology of Carbohydrates*, V. Ginsburg and P. Robbins (eds.), Wiley, New York, 1, p. 51.

Candy, D. J. (1980), *Biological Functions of Carbohydrates*, Blackie, Glasgow.

Carr, P. W. and Bowers, L. D. (1980), *Immobilized Enzymes in Analytical and Clinical Chemistry*, Wiley, New York.

Cook, G. M. W. and Stoddart, R. W. (1973), *Surface Carbohydrates of the Eukaryotic Cell*, Academic Press, London.

Coxon, B. (1980), in *Developments in Food Carbohydrates–2*, C. K. Lee (ed.), Applied Science, London, p. 351.

Davidson, R. L. (ed.) (1980), *Handbook of Water-Soluble Gums and Resins*, McGraw Hill, New York.

Dawson, G. and Tsay, G. C. (1977), in *Research to Practice in Mental Retardation*, P. Mittler (ed.), University Park Press, Baltimore, III, p. 157.

Dea, I. C. M. (1979), in *Polysaccharides in Food*, J. M. Blanshard and J. R. Mitchell (eds.), Butterworths, London, p. 229.

Dutton, G. G. S. (1973), *Advances in Carbohydr. Chem. Biochem.* 28, 11.

Dutton, G. G. S. (1974), *Advances in Carbohydr. Chem. Biochem.* 30, 9.

Ferrier, R. J. (1976), in *Carbohydrates*, G. O. Aspinall (ed.), M.T.P. Internat. Rev. Sci. Organic Chem., Ser. 2, Butterworths, London, 7, Chap 2.

Ferrier, R. J. (1980), in *The Carbohydrates, Chemistry and Biochemistry*, W. Pigman and D. Horton (eds.), Academic Press, New York, 2nd edn., IB, Chap 19.

Fukuda, M., Kondo, T. and Osawa, T. (1976), *J. Biochem. (Tokyo)* 80, 1223.

Gilbert, W. and Villa-Komaroff, L. (1980), *Scientific American* 242(4), 68.

Gottschalk, A. (ed.) (1972), *Glycoproteins*, Elsevier, Amsterdam, 2nd edn.

Gurr, M. I. and James, A. T. (1980), *Lipid Biochemistry: An Introduction*, Chapman and Hall, London, 3rd edn.

Hakomori, S.-I. (1964), *J. Biochem. (Tokyo)* 55, 205.

Hakomori, S.-I. (1976), in *Carbohydrates*, G. O. Aspinall (ed.), M.T.P. Internat. Rev. Sci. Organic Chem., Ser. 2, Butterworths, London, 7, Chap 7.

Hakomori, S.-I. and Kobata, A. (1974), in *The Antigens*, M. Sela (ed.), Academic Press, New York, 2, p. 80.

Hall, L. D. and Morris, G. A. (1980), *Carbohydr. Res.* 82, 175.

Hanessian, S. and Haskell, T. H. (1970), in *The Carbohydrates, Chemistry and Biochemistry*, W. Pigman and D. Horton (eds.), Academic Press, New York, 2nd edn., IIA, Chap 31.

Harmon, R. E. (ed.) (1979), *Asymmetry in Carbohydrates*, Dekker, New York.

Hascall, V. C. (1981), in *Biology of Carbohydrates*, V. Ginsburgh and P. Robbins (eds.), Wiley, New York, 1, p. 1.

Hassid, W. Z. (1970), in *The Carbohydrates, Chemistry and Biochemistry*, W. Pigman and D. Horton (eds.), Academic Press, New York, 2nd edn., IIA, Chap 34.

Heidelberger, M., Dische, Z., Neeley, W. B. and Wolfrom, M. L. (1955), *J. Amer.*

Chem. Soc. **77**, 3511.

Holum, J. R. (1978), *Organic and Biological Chemistry*, Wiley, New York.

Horton, D. and Wander, J. D. (1980a), in *The Carbohydrates, Chemistry and Biochemistry*, W. Pigman and D. Horton (eds.), Academic Press, New York, 2nd edn., **1B**, Chap 16.

Horton, D. and Wander, J. D. (1980b), in *The Carbohydrates, Chemistry and Biochemistry*, W. Pigman and D. Horton (eds.), Academic Press, New York, 2nd edn., **1B**, Chap 18.

Hough, L. and Richardson, A. C. (1972), in *The Carbohydrates, Chemistry and Biochemistry*, W. Pigman and D. Horton (eds.), Academic Press, New York, 2nd edn., **IA**, Chap 3.

Hough, L. and Richardson, A. C. (1979), in *Comprehensive Organic Chemistry*, E. Haslam (ed.), Pergamon Press, Oxford, **5**, Chap 26. 1.

Ivatt, R. J. and Gilvarg, C. (1979), *J. Biol. Chem.* **254**, 2759.

Jennings, H. J. and Smith, I. C. P. (1978), in *Methods in Enzymology*, G. Ginsburg (ed.), Academic Press, New York, **50**, p. 39.

Jermyn, M. A. and Yeow, Y. M. (1975), *Aust. J. Plant Physiol.* **2**, 501.

Kennedy, J. F. (1971-1981), in *Carbohydrates Chemistry – Specialist Periodical Reports*, J. S. Brimacombe (ed.), The Chemical Society, London, **4-12**, part II.

Kennedy, J. F. (1974a), *Advances in Carbohydr. Chem. Biochem.* **29**, 305.

Kennedy, J. F. (1974b), *Biochem. Soc. Trans.* **2**, 54.

Kennedy, J. F. (1976), *Advances Clin. Chem.* **18**, 1.

Kennedy, J. F. (1979a), *Proteoglycans – Biological and Chemical Aspects in Human Life*, Elsevier, Amsterdam.

Kennedy, J. F. (1979b), *Chem. Soc. Rev.* **8**, 221.

Kennedy, J. F. and Cabral, J. M. S. (1982a), in *Solid Phase Biochemistry: Analytical and Synthetic Aspects*, W. H. Scouten (ed.), Wiley, New York, (in press).

Kennedy, J. F. and Cabral, J. M. S. (1982b), in *Applied Biochemistry and Bioengineering*, L. B. Wingard and I. Chibata (eds.), Academic Press, New York, **4**, (in press).

Kennedy, J. F. and Fox, J. E. (1980), in *Methods in Carbohydrate Chemistry*, R. L. Whistler and J. N. BeMiller (eds.), Academic Press, New York, **8**, p. 13.

Kiss, J. (1970), *Advances Carbohydr. Chem.* **24**, 382.

Ko, A. M. Y. and Somers, P. J. (1974), *Carbohydr. Res.* **34**, 57.

Kohn, J. and Wilchek, M. (1982), *Enzyme Microb. Technol.* **4**, 161.

Kornfeld, R. and Kornfeld, S. (1976), *Ann. Rev. Biochem.* **45**, 217.

Lee, C. K. (ed.) (1980), *Developments in Food Carbohydrate–2*, Applied Science, London.

Lee, E. Y. C. and Whelan, W. J. (1966), *Arch. Biochem. Biophys.* **116**, 162.

Lennarz, W. J. (1975), *Science* **188**, 986.

Li, Y. T. and Li, S.-C. (1976), in *Methods in Carbohydrate Chemistry*, R. L.

Whistler and J. N. BeMiller (eds.), Academic Press, New York, **7**, p. 221.

Lis, H. and Sharon, N. (1977), in *The Antigens*, M. Sela (ed.), Academic Press, New York, **4**, p. 429.

Lis, H., Sharon, N. and Katchalski, E. (1964), *Biochim. Biophys. Acta* **83**, 376.

Lonngren, J. and Svensson, S. (1974), *Advances Carbohydr. Chem. Biochem.* **29**, 41.

Manners, D. J. and Matheson, N. K. (1980), *Carbohydr. Res.* **90**, 99.

Mathews, M. B. (1976), in *Methods in Carbohydrate Chemistry*, R. L. Whistler and J. N. BeMiller (eds.), Academic Press, New York, **7**, p. 116.

McArthur, H. A. I. (1981), *British Polymer J.* **13**, 111.

McKibbin, J. M. (1970), in *The Carbohydrates, Chemistry and Biochemistry*, W. Pigman and D. Horton (eds.), Academic Press, New York, 2nd edn., **IIB**, Chap 44.

McKusick, V. A. (1972), *Heritable Disorders of Connective Tissue*, C. V. Mosby, St. Louis, 4th edn.

Morris, H. R. (1980), *Nature* **286**, 447.

Muir, H. and Hardingham, T. E. (1975), in *Biochemistry of Carbohydrates*, W. J. Whelan (ed.), M.T.P. Internat. Rev. Sci. Biochem., Ser. 1, Butterworths, London, **5**, Chap 4.

Munson, R. S. and Glaser, L. (1981), in *Biology of Carbohydrates*, V. Ginsburg and P. Robbins (eds.), Wiley, New York, **1**, p. 91.

Palmer, T. (1981), *Understanding Enzymes*, Ellis Horwood, Chichester.

Perlin, A. S. (1959), *Advances Carbohydr. Chem.* **14**, 9.

Preiss, J. and Walsh, D. A. (1981), in *Biology of Carbohydrates*, V. Ginsburg and P. Robbins (eds.), Wiley, New York, **1**, p. 199.

Ramachandran, G. N., Ramakrishman, C. and Sasisekharan, V. (1963), in *Aspects of Protein Structure*, G. N. Ramachandran (ed.), Academic Press, New York, p. 121.

Ramachandran, G. N. and Reddi, A. H. (eds.) (1976), *Biochemistry of Collagen*, Plenum, New York.

Rauvala, H., Finne, J., Krusius, T., Kärkkäinen, J. and Järnefelt, J. (1981), *Advances Carbohydr. Chem. Biochem.* **38**, 389.

Recommendations (1970), Abbreviations and Symbols for Nucleic Acids, Polynucleotides and their Constituents (1970), *Eur. J. Biochem.* **15**, 203; and (1972), *Eur. J. Biochem.* **25**, 1.

Recommendations (1973), Nomenclature of Cyclitols (1975), *Eur. J. Biochem.* **57**, 1.

Recommendations (1976), Nomenclature of Lipids (1977), *Eur. J. Biochem.* **79**, 11.

Recommendations (1978), Enzyme Nomenclature (1979), Academic Press, New York; Supplement 1 (1980), *Eur. J. Biochem.* **104**, 1; Supplement 2 (1981), *Eur. J. Biochem.* **116**, 423; and Supplement 3 (1982), *Eur. J. Biochem.* **125**, 1.

Recommendations (1980a), Conformational Nomenclature for Five and Six-

Membered Ring Forms of Monosaccharides and their Derivatives (1980), *Eur. J. Biochem.* **111**, 295.

Recommendations (1980b), Abbreviated Terminology of Oligosaccharide Chains, *J. Biol. Chem.* **257**, 3347.

Recommendations (1980c), Polysaccharide Nomenclature, *J. Biol. Chem.* **257**, 3352.

Recommendations (1980d), Nomenclature of Branched-Chain Monosaccharides (1981), *Eur. J. Biochem.* **119**, 5.

Recommendations (1980e), Nomenclature of Unsaturated Monosaccharides (1981), *Eur. J. Biochem.* **119**, 1.

Recommendations (1981a), Symbols for Specifying the Conformation of Polysaccharides, *Eur. J. Biochem.* (in press).

Recommendations (1981b), Abbreviations and Symbols for the Description of Polynucleotide Chains, *Eur. J. Biochem.* (in press).

Reden, J. and Dürckheimer, W. (1979), *Topics in Current Chemistry* **83**, 105.

Rees, D. A. (1977), *Polysaccharide Shapes*, Chapman and Hall, London.

Rees, D. A. and Welsh, E. J. (1977), *Angew. Chem. Internat. Edn.* **16**, 214.

Rinehart, K. L., Jnr. and Suami, T. (eds.) (1980), *Aminocyclitol Antibiotics*, A.C.S. Symp. Ser. 125, Amer. Chem. Soc., Washington.

Rodén, L. and Schwartz, N. B. (1975), in *Biochemistry of Carbohydrates*, W. J. Whelan (ed.), M.T.P. Internat. Rev. Sci. Biochem., Ser. 1, Butterworths, London, **5**, Chap 3.

Rodén, L., Forsee, T. W., Jensen, J., Feingold, D. S., Prihar, H., Bäckström, M., Höök, M., Jacobsson, I., Lindahl, U., Riesenfeld, J. and Malmström, A. (1980), in *Mechanism of Saccharide Polymerisation and Depolymerisation*, J. J. Marshall (ed.), Academic Press, New York, p. 395.

Ryle, M., Chaplin, M. F., Gray, C. J. and Kennedy, J. F. (1970), in *Gonadotrophins and Ovarian Development*, W. R. Butt, A. C. Crooke and M. Ryle (eds.), Livingstone, Edinburgh, p. 98.

Saenger, W. (1980), *Angew. Chem. Internat. Edn.* **19**, 344.

Sammes, P. G. (ed.) (1977 onwards), *Topics in Antibiotic Chemistry*, Ellis Horwood, Chichester, **1-5**.

Sandford, P. A. (1979), *Advances Carbohydr. Chem. Biochem.* **36**, 265.

Sandhu, J. S., Hudson, G. J. and Kennedy, J. F. (1981), *Carbohydr. Res.* **93**, 247.

Schleifer, K. H. and Kandler, O. (1972), *Bacteriol. Rev.* **36**, 407.

Schwarzenbach, R. (1979), in *Biological and Biomedical Applications of Liquid Chromatography* 2, G. L. Hawk (ed.), Chromatographic Science Ser. 12, Dekker, New York, p. 193.

Serianni, A. S., Nunez, H. A. and Barker, R. (1979a), *Carbohydr. Res.* **72**, 71.

Serianni, A. S., Clark, E. L. and Barker, R. (1979b), *Carbohydr. Res.* **72**, 79.

Setlow, J. K. and Hollaender, A. (eds.) (1979), *Genetic Engineering, Principles and Methods*, Plenum, New York, **1**.

Setlow, J. K. and Hollaender, A. (eds.) (1980), *Genetic Engineering, Principles and Methods*, Plenum, New York, 2.

Sharon, N. (1975), *Complex Carbohydrates, Their Chemistry, Biosynthesis and Functions*, Addison-Wesley, Massachusetts.

Sharon, N. (1980), *Scientific American* **243(5)**, 80.

Sharon, N. and Lis, H. (1979), *Biochem. Soc. Trans.* **7**, 783.

Spiro, R. G. and Bhoyroo, V. D. (1974), *J. Biol. Chem.* **249**, 5704.

Stacey, M. (1973), *Chem. and Ind.*, **222**.

Stewart-Tull, D. E. S. (1980), *Ann. Rev. Microbiol.* **34**, 311.

Sturgeon, C. M. and Kennedy, J. F. (1979 onwards), *Enzyme Microb. Technol.* **1**, 53, 129, 210 and 290; **2**, 66, 155, 244 and 318; **3**, 76, 160, 260 and 367; and **4**, 50, 118, 198, 276 and 356.

Stryer, L. (1981), *Biochemistry*, W. H. Freeman, San Francisco, 2nd edn.

Sutherland, I. W. (ed.) (1977), *Surface Carbohydrates of the Prokaryotic Cell*, Academic Press, London.

Sutherland, I. W. (1979), *Trends Biochem. Sci.* **4**, 55.

Svennerholm, L. (1963), *J. Neurochem.* **10**, 613.

Sweeley, C. C. (ed.) (1980), *Cell Surface Glycolipids*, A.C.S. Symp. Ser. 128, Amer. Chem. Soc., Washington.

Szarek, W. A. (1973), in *Carbohydrates*, G. O. Aspinall (ed.), M.T.P. Internat. Rev. Sci., Organic Chem., Ser. 1, Butterworths, London, **7**, Chap 3.

Tentative Rules (1969), Carbohydrate Nomenclature, Part 1 (1971), *Eur. J. Biochem.* **21**, 455; and (1972), *Eur. J. Biochem.* **25**, 4.

Theander, O. (1980), in *The Carbohydrates, Chemistry and Biochemistry*, W. Pigman and D. Horton (eds.), Academic Press, New York, 2nd edn., **IB**, Chap 23.

Trevan, M. D. (1980), *Immobilized Enzymes, An Introduction and Applications in Biotechnology*, Wiley, London.

Umezawa, S. (1976), in *Carbohydrates*, G. O. Aspinall (ed.), M.T.P. Internat. Rev. Sci., Organic Chem., Ser. 2, Butterworths, London, **7**, Chap 5.

Various Authors (1968 onwards), in *Carbohydrate Chemistry – Specialist Periodical Reports*, The Chemical Society, London.

Various Editors (1974 onwards), *Enzyme Engineering*, Plenum, New York; **2**, (1974) E. K. Pye and L. B. Wingard Jnr. (eds.), **3** (1978) E. K. Pye and H. H. Weetall (eds.), **4** (1978) G. B. Broun, G. Manecke and L. B. Wingard Jnr. (eds.), and **5** (1980) H. H. Weetall and G. P. Royer (eds.).

Watson, J. D. and Crick, F. H. C. (1953a), *Nature* **171**, 737.

Watson, J. D. and Crick, F. H. C. (1953b), *Nature* **171**, 964.

Wells, W. W. and Eisenberg, F. Jnr. (eds.) (1978), *Cyclitols and Phosphoinositides*, Academic Press, New York.

Weigandt, H. (1973), *Hoppe-Seylers Z. Physiol. Chem.* **354**, 1049.

Whistler, R. L. and BeMiller, J. B. (1958), *Advances Carbohydr. Chem.* **13**, 289.

Whistler, R. L. and Kosik, M. (1971), *Arch. Biochem. Biophys.* **142**, 106.

Whistler, R. L. and Others (eds.) (1962 onwards), *Methods in Carbohydrate Chemistry*, Academic Press, New York, **1** (1962), **2** (1963), **3** (1963), **4** (1964), **5** (1965), **6** (1972), **7** (1976) and **8** (1980).

White, C. A. and Kennedy, J. F. (1980), *Enzyme Microb. Technol.* **2**, 82.

White, C. A. and Kennedy, J. F. (1981), *Techniques Carbohydr. Metabolism*, **B312**, 1.

White, C. A., Corran, P. H. and Kennedy, J. F. (1980), *Carbohydr. Res.* **87**, 165.

Williams, N. R. and Wander, J. D. (1980), in *The Carbohydrates, Chemistry and Biochemistry*, W. Pigman and D. Horton (eds.), Academic Press, New York, 2nd edn., **IB**, Chap 17.

Wiseman, A. (ed.) (1975), *Handbook of Enzyme Biotechnology*, Ellis Horwood, Chichester.

Wiseman, A. (ed.) (1977 onwards), *Topics in Enzyme and Fermentation Biotechnology*, Ellis Horwood, Chichester, **1-5**.

Wolfrom, M. L. and Schumacher, J. N. (1955), *J. Amer. Chem. Soc.* **77**, 3318.

Wu, R. (ed.) (1979), *Methods in Enzymology*, Academic Press, New York, **68**.

Zaborsky, O. R. (1973), *Immobilized Enzymes*, C.R.C. Press, Cleveland.

Zadrazil, S. and Sponar, J. (eds.) (1980), *DNA — Recombination, Interactions and Repair*, Pergamon, Oxford.

Index

A

abbreviations 17, 40, 41, 44
abequose 175
absolute configuration 23
Acacia gums 151
acetal formation 36, 61
2-acetamido-3-*O*-(1-carboxyethyl)-2-deoxy-D-glucose 120, 170
2-acetamido-2-deoxy-D-galactose 120, 165, 168, 189, 215, 219, 231
2-acetamido-2-deoxy-α-D-glucopyranose 197
N^4-(2-acetamido-2-deoxy-β-D-glucopyranosyl) hydrogen-L-asparaginate 207, 219
2-acetamido-2-deoxy-D-glucose 120, 136, 165, 168, 170, 173, 180, 189, 190, 193, 196, 215, 231, 244, 247
2-acetamido-2-deoxy-D-glucosyl 6-sulphate 217
2-acetamido-2-deoxy-D-mannose 120, 168
2-acetamido-2-deoxy-D-talose 120
5-acetamido-3,5-dideoxy-D-*glycero*-α-D-*galacto*-2-nonulopyranonic acid 35, 120, 136, 173, 183, 186, 189, 190, 193, 196, 217, 231
acetates 64, 171
3-*O*-acetyl-2,6-dideoxy-β-D-*lyxo*-hexopyranose 266
4-*O*-acetyl-2,6-dideoxy-3-*C*-methyl-β-L-*arabino*-hexopyranose 270
N-acetylneuraminic acid 35, 120
acetyl-D-oliose 266
α_1-acid glycoprotein 193
acidic mucopolysaccharide 212
acid mucopolysaccharide 212
acofriose 176
acosamine 268
acovenose 176
acrose 88
actinamine 271
actinospectose 266

acylsterol glycosides 245
adenosine triphosphate 98
adonitol 55, 56
D-adonose 25
adsorption chromatography 68, 77
affinity chromatography 77, 209, 295, 302, 304
agar 163, 164
agarose 45, 164, 289, 293, 300
aggregation 48, 50
aldaric acids 52, 116
aldgarose 270
alditol acetates 68, 77
alditols 55, 56, 117
aldol condensation 88
aldonic acids 50, 116
aldonic acid lactones 51, 92
aldoses 21, 22, 265
aldosuloses 52
alduronic acids 51
alduronic acid lactones 51
algae 162
alginate 163, 308, 309
alginic acid 45, 163, 170, 300, 308, 309
alkaline degradation 73, 179, 201
alkali-resistant residues 72
allitol 55, 56
allose 21, 22
D-allulose 25
allyl ethers 63
altritol 55, 56
altrose 21, 22
amicetin 274
amicetose 266, 274
amidohydrolases 206
aminoacids 101, 108, 170, 183–185, 207, 218–221, 259, 291
aminoacid sequence 78, 211, 213, 259
2-amino-3-*O*-(1-carboxyethyl)-2-deoxy-β-D-glucopyranose 176

5-amino-5-deoxy-D-allofuranuronic acid 269, 274

2-amino-2-deoxy-β-L-altropyranuronic acid 178

4-amino-4-deoxy-D-*erythro*-2-hexenopyranuronic acid 269, 274

2-amino-2-deoxy-β-D-fucopyranose 177

2-amino-2-deoxy-β-L-fucopyranose 177

2-amino-2-deoxy-β-D-galactopyranose 35, 183, 186, 209

2-amino-2-deoxy-β-D-galactopyranuronic acid 178

2-amino-2-deoxy-β-L-galactopyranuronic acid 178

2-amino-2-deoxy-D-glucopyranose 35, 120, 183, 186, 209, 211, 248, 280

3-amino-3-deoxy-β-D-glucopyranose 267

5-amino-5-deoxy-D-glucopyranose 120, 267

6-amino-6-deoxy-β-D-glucopyranose 267

2-amino-2-deoxy-β-D-glucopyranuronic acid 178

4-amino-4-deoxy-β-D-glucopyranuronic acid 269

2-amino-2-deoxy-β-D-gulopyranose 267

2-amino-2-deoxy-β-L-gulopyranuronic acid 178

4-amino-4-deoxy-L-*glycero*-L-*gluco*-heptopyranose 267, 272

2-amino-2-deoxyhexoses 35, 68, 108, 120

aminodeoxyinositols 118

2-amino-2-deoxy-β-D-mannopyranose 177

2-amino-2-deoxy-β-D-mannopyranuronic acid 178

1D-1-amino-1-deoxy-*neo*-inositol 119, 271

aminodeoxyoctoses 284

3-amino-3-deoxy-D-ribofuranose 267, 272

6-amino-6,8-dideoxy-β-D-*erythro*-D-*galacto*-octopyranose 268

3-amino-3,6-dideoxy-β-D-galactopyranose 177

4-amino-4,6-dideoxy-β-D-galactopyranose 177

2-amino-2,6-dideoxy-β-D-glucopyranose 177, 267

3-amino-3,6-dideoxy-β-D-glucopyranose 177

4-amino-4,6-dideoxy-β-D-glucopyranose 177

5-amino-3,5-dideoxy-D-*glycero*-α-D-*galacto*-2-nonulopyranonic acid 35, 68, 183

2-amino-2,6-dideoxy-β-L-mannopyranose 177

3-amino-3,6-dideoxy-β-D-mannopyranose 267

4-amino-4,6-dideoxy-β-D-mannopyranose 267

2-amino-2,6-dideoxy-β-L-talopyranose 177

aminoinositols 118, 279

aminopolysaccharide 212

aminosugars 120, 171, 177, 264, 267–269

4-amino-2,3,4,6-tetradeoxy-β-L-*erythro*-hexopyranose 269

aminotrehaloses 284

3-amino-2,3,6-trideoxy-α-D-*arabino*-hexopyranose 268

3-amino-2,3,6-trideoxy-β-L-*lyxo*-hexopyranose 268

1D-(1,3,5/4,6)-1-amino-1,2,3-trideoxy-3-*N*-methylamino-4,5,6-cyclohexanetriol 271

3-amino-2,3,6-trideoxy-3-*C*-methyl-β-L-*lyxo*-hexopyranose 271

3-amino-2,3,6-trideoxy-β-L-*ribo*-hexopyranose 268

aminouronic acids 120, 178, 269

amosamine 267, 274

α-amylase 80, 180, 304

β-amylase 81, 145, 146, 304

amyloids 161

amylopectin 44, 108, 143, 146, 180

amylose 44, 47, 98, 143

1,5-anhydro-2-deoxy-hex-1-enitols 130

anomeric configuration 36, 92

anomeric effect 61, 62

antibiotics
    aminocyclitol 279–280
    anthracycline 275
    classification 264
    deoxystreptadine 250
    effect on protein synthesis 284
    heptaene 277
    immobilised 304
    mode of action 264, 284–287
    streptidine 280
    tetraene 277

anticodon 259

antifreeze glycoprotein 186

apiose 127

apramycin 283

arabic acid 151

L-arabinans 155, 156

D-arabinaric acid 52, 53

arabinitol 55, 56

arabite 55, 56

arabinofuranobiose 38

L-arabinose 151, 153, 158, 206, 221

α-L-arabinofuranose 33

O^4-β-L-arabinofuranosyl-hydroxy-L-proline 207

L-arabino-D-galactans 153, 160

L-arabino-D-galacto-glycoproteins 208

L-arabino-D-galacto-proteins 208

D-*arabino*-hexulose 25

arabinopyranobiose 38

α-L-arabinopyranose 33
arabinose 21, 22, 189, 208, 211, 244
L-arabino-D-xylans 158
arcanose 270, 279
ascarylose 175
L-ascorbic acid 117, 129
aspartylglycosaminuria 203
asymmetric carbon atom 25, 26, 29
augustamycins 272
autohydrolysis 151
automatic analysis 67

B

bacillosamine 177
bacterial cell walls 164, 170, 172
barley husk D-xylan 158
base pairing 255, 256
benzilic acid type rearrangement 59, 60, 74
benzoates 64
benzyl ethers 63
benzylidene group 64
Betacoccus arabinosaceous dextran 170
biotechnology 296, 307, 310
blastic acid 274
blasticidin S 274
blood-group type specificity 201, 235
bluensidine 271
boat conformation 29
boivinose 266
borate complexes 67, 76
branched-chain monosaccharides 127, 264, 269–271
branched-chain sugar 127
Brigl's anhydride 96
bromelain 207

C

callose 44
carbohydrate-peptide linkage 78, 81
carbohydrate-protein complex 186
carboxymethyl cellulose 289, 295
carboxymethyl ethers 289, 295, 299
4-*O*-(1-carboxymethyl)-β-D-glucopyranose 176
carrageenans 44, 163, 300
Caulerpa filiformis D-xylan 163
cDNA 263
cellobiose 38, 132, 149, 160, 306
cellobiouronic acid 38
cellotetraose 39
cellotriose 39
cellulose 42, 45, 47, 108, 149, 162, 170, 180, 209, 288, 291, 293, 295, 297, 300, 304, 305
cellulose acetate 305, 307
cellulose acetate electrophoresis 80
cellulose xanthate 294, 300

ceramides 231
cereal gums 158
cerebrosides 233
chair conformation 29
chalcose 279
chitin 42, 45, 98, 120, 180
chitobiose 38
chloracetates 64
chlorosucroses 125
cholesterol 245
chondroitin 45, 214, 215, 219
chondroitin sulphate 45, 112, 213, 221–223
chondroitin 4-sulphate 111, 113, 213, 214, 215, 219, 229
chondroitin 6-sulphate 213, 214, 215, 219, 229
chondroitin sulphate D 216
chondroitin 4-sulphate peptide 215
chondroitin sulphate-protein complex 212
chondroitin 4-sulphate proteoglycan 212
chondrosine 38
chromomycins 276, 286
cinerubins 275
cladinose 270, 278
cloverleaf structure 257
CM-cellulose 295, 299
codon 259
colitose 175
collagen 221–223
colligative properties 86
colominic acid 173
colorimetric analysis 58, 72
complementary base pairs 250, 252, 255, 256
complexation 67
concanavalin A 77, 182, 209, 303
configuration 19, 23
conformation 29
connective tissue 221
cord factor 247
cordycepin 272, 286
core structure 196, 197, 207, 210, 211
coumerose 270
cress seed mucilage 153
cRNA 259
cross-linked agarose 295
cross-linked dextran 295
crumpled ribbon 48
curacose 265
curamicose 265
curdlan 44, 308, 309
cyanate esters 293
cyanohydrin synthesis 92
cyclic acetals 64
cyclic carbonates 64, 291
cyclitols 118, 271
cycloamyloses 39

cyclodextrins 39
1D-1,2,4/3,5-cyclohexanepentol 119
cyclohexanehexols 118
cyclohexanepentols 118
cyclomaltoheptaose 39, 133
cyclomaltohexaose 39, 133
cyclomalto-octaose 39, 133
cyclomalto-oligosaccharides 39, 133, 146, 291
cymarose 266

D

daunomycin 275, 286
daunosamine 268, 275, 286
DEAE-dextran 289
deaminases 113
decarboxylation 51, 101, 116
decoyinine 272
3-deoxy-D-*arabino*-hexonic acid 60, 74
6-deoxy-β-D-*arabino*-5-hexulofuranose 265
1-deoxy-3-*O*-carbamosyl-1-guanidino-*scyllo*-inositol 271
6-deoxy-2,3-di-*O*-methyl-β-D-allopyranose 265
6-deoxy-2,4-di-*O*-methyl-β-D-galactopyranose 265
6-deoxy-D-*erythro*-2,5-hexodiulofuranose 266, 272
2-deoxy-β-D-*erythro*-pentafuranose 33, 124
6-deoxy-β-L-galactopyranose 34, 124
6-deoxy-β-D-glucopyranose 34, 124
6-deoxy-α-D-glucopyranose 6-*C*-sulphate 243
3-deoxy-D-*glycero*-D-*glycero*-pentafuranose 265, 272
deoxyhexoses 34, 68, 124
3-deoxy-2-*C*-(hydroxymethyl)-D-*erythro*-pentonic acid 60, 72, 75
5-deoxy-3-*C*-hydroxymethyl-α-L-lyxofuranose 270
3-deoxy-2-*C*-(hydroxymethyl)-D-*threo*-pentonic acid 60, 75
deoxyinositols 118
3-deoxy-D-*manno*-octopyranulosonic acid 173, 176
6-deoxy-β-L-mannopyranose 34, 124
3-deoxy-3-*N*-methylaminopentoses 281
6-deoxy-4-*O*-methyl-β-D-galactopyranose 265
2-deoxy-2-*N*-methylamino-β-L-glucopyranose 267
6-deoxy-3-*C*-methyl-β-D-mannopyranose 269
6-deoxy-5-*C*-methyl-4-*O*-methyl-α-L-*lyxo*-hexopyranose 269

6-deoxy-5-*C*-methyl-4-*O*-methyl-3-*O*-(5-methyl-2-pyrrolyl)-α-L-*lyxo*-hexopyranose 270
6-deoxy-3-*C*-methyl-α-L-talopyranose 269
1-deoxy-1-nitro-alditols 90
5-deoxy-3-*C*-oxomethyl-α-L-lyxofuranose 269
deoxypentoses 33, 68
3-deoxy-D-*ribo*-hexonic acid 60, 72, 74
deoxyribonucleases 254
deoxyribonucleic acids
   circular DNA 257, 263
   classification 250
   complementary DNA 263
   function 250, 259–262, 284–287
   immobilised 304
   nomenclature 250
   primary structure 250
   replication 259, 264
   secondary structure 254
   supertwisted DNA 257
   tertiary structure 257
2-deoxy-D-ribose 33, 124, 250
2-deoxystreptamine 271, 280
deoxysugars 124, 175, 264, 265, 266
2-deoxy-2-sulphamido-D-glucose 6-sulphate 217
6-deoxy-D-talopyranose 175
6-deoxy-L-talopyranose 175, 248
6-deoxy-4-thio-D-gulose 127
dermatan 43, 216
dermatan sulphate 45, 213, 214, 216, 219, 229
dermatan 6-sulphate 216
desosamine 268, 278
dextran 45, 47, 170, 289, 293, 295, 297, 300, 306, 308
diacylglycerol 245
dialysis 67
2,6-diamino-2,6-dideoxy-D-glucopyranose 268, 280
2,3-diamino-2,3-dideoxy-β-D-glucopyranuronic acid 178
2,6-diamino-2,6-dideoxy-α-L-idopyranose 268
diaminosugars 120, 121, 171
2,4-diamino-2,3,4,6-tetradeoxy-β-D-*arabino*-hexopyranose 269
1D-(1,3,5/4,6)-1,3-diamino-1,2,3-trideoxy-4,5,6-cyclohexanetriol 271
2,4-diamino-2,4,6-trideoxy-β-D-galacto-pyranose 177
2,4-diamino-2,4,6-trideoxy-β-D-glucopyranose 177
diastereoisomers 20
diazine dyes 288
diazomethane 127

2,6-dideoxy-β-D-*arabino*-hexopyranose 266
1,3-dideoxy-1,3-diguanidino-*scyllo*-inositol 271
3,6-dideoxy-3-*N,N*-dimethylamino-β-D-glucopyranose 267
4,6-dideoxy-4-*N,N*-dimethylamino-β-D-glucopyranose 267
3,6-dideoxy-β-D-galactopyranose 175
3,6-dideoxy-β-L-galactopyranose 175
3,6-dideoxy-β-D-glucopyranose 175
4,6-dideoxy-2,3-hexodiulopyranose 266
4,6-dideoxy-3-*C*-[(S)-1-hydroxyethyl]-β-D-*ribo*-hexopyranose 3,3'-cyclic carbonate 270
2,6-dideoxy-L-*lyxo*-hexopyranose 266, 275
3,6-dideoxy-β-D-mannopyranose 175
3,6-dideoxy-β-L-mannopyranose 175
2,6-dideoxy-3-*C*-methyl-β-D-*arabino*-hexopyranose 270
2,6-dideoxy-3-*O*-methyl-β-L-*arabino*-hexopyranose 266
2,6-dideoxy-4-*O*-methyl-β-D-*lyxo*-hexopyranose 266
2,6-dideoxy-3-*C*-methyl-3-*O*-methyl-β-L-*ribo*-hexopyranose 270
2,6-dideoxy-3-*C*-methyl-3-*O*-methyl-α-L-*xylo*-hexopyranose 270
2,6-dideoxy-3-*O*-methyl-β-D-*ribo*-hexopyranose 266
2,6-dideoxy-3-*C*-methyl-β-L-*ribo*-hexopyranose 270
2,6-dideoxy-β-D-*ribo*-hexopyranose 266
dideoxysugars 124, 173
2,6-dideoxy-β-D-*xylo*-hexopyranose 266
diethylaminoethyl dextran 289
diethylaminoethyl ethers 289, 295, 299
digalactosylceramide 235
digalactosyl diacylglycerol 243
digitalose 176
digitoxose 266
dihydrostreptose 270
dihydroxyacetone 25, 88
1,3-dihydroxy-2-propanone 25, 88
1,3-di-(*N*-methylamino)-*myo*-inositol 271
4-*N,N*-dimethylamino-2,3,4,6-tetradeoxy-β-D-*erythro*-hexopyranose 269
4-*N,N*-dimethylamino-2,3,4,6-tetradeoxy-β-D-*threo*-hexopyranose 269
3-*N,N*-dimethylamino-2,3,6-trideoxy-β-L-*lyxo*-hexopyranose 269
3-*N,N*-dimethylamino-2,3,6-trideoxy-β-D-*xylo*-hexopyranose 268
3-*N,N*-dimethylamino-3,4,6-trideoxy-β-D-*xylo*-hexopyranose 268
2,6-di-*O*-methyl-β-D-mannopyranose 265
2,3-di-*O*-methyl-β-D-rhamnopyranose 176
2,3-di-*O*-methyl-β-L-rhamnopyranose 176

2,4-di-*O*-methyl rhamnose 248
disaccharides 36, 38, 132
disialyllacto-*N*-tetraose 137
disolution 67
disulphone degradation 95
DNA 124, 250
Dolichos biflorus agglutinin 303
double-helix 255–256
dulcitol 55, 56
dyeing 288

E

electron microscopy 86, 257, 258
β-elimination 59
elsinan 44, 308
emulsion stabiliser 163
enantiomers 23
end-group analysis 145, 149
endo-polysaccharide hydrolases 80
envelope conformation 32
enzyme commission number 83, 98, 102, 206
enzymes 80, 83, 98, 102, 187, 206, 295, 296
epimerases 96, 101, 112
epimerisation 57, 59, 95, 101, 112
epimers 20
erythritol 55, 56
erythromycin 278, 286
D-*erythro*-pentulose 25
erythrose 21, 22
D-erythrulose 25
Esparto grass D-xylan 158
ethers 63, 176
evalose 269
evermicose 270
everninomycins 284
evernitrose 124, 271
extended ribbon 48
exo-polysaccharide hydrolases 80
extensin 208, 209
exudate gums 150

F

Fabry's disease 238, 241
Farber's lipogranulomatosis 238, 241
fatty acids 173, 230, 233
fermentation 306, 310, 311
Fenton's reagent 94
fetuin 193, 196
film-forming materials 299
Fischer formulae, modernised 31
Fischer formulae, projection 20, 21, 26
Fischer glycosidation 36, 61, 67, 96
Fischer-Kiliani reaction 92

4-C-fluoro-5-sulphamido-β-D-ribofuranose 265
follicle-stimulating hormone 188–190, 193
food uses 306, 309
formycin 272
β-formyl pyruvic acid 72
foromacidins 279
forosamine 269, 279
D-fructans 161
β-D-fructofuranose 34, 170
α-D-fructopyranose 34
D-fructose 25, 161
FSH 189
fucoidan 44
β-L-fucopyranose 34
D-fucosamine 177
L-fucosamine 177
L-fucose 124, 136, 153, 163, 183, 190, 193, 196, 217, 231, 244
fucosidosis 205
fucosyllactose 137
furan-2-aldehyde 58
furan derivatives 58
furanose ring 29, 68

G

G_{A_1} 236
D-galactans 155, 156, 163, 179
galactaric acid 52
galactinol 139
galactitol 55, 56
galactobiose 38
galactocarolose 44, 179
β-D-galactofuranose 179
D-galacto-D-mannans 159, 179
β-D-galactopyranose 33
β-L-galactopyranose 33
O^4-β-D-galactopyranosyl-hydroxy-L-proline 207, 209
O^3-α-D-galactopyranosyl-L-serine 207, 209
β-D-galactopyranuronic acid 34
D-galactopyranurono-6,3-lactone 52
galactosamine 35
D-galactose 21, 33, 136, 153, 159, 164, 173, 179, 183, 189, 190, 193, 196, 208, 211, 217, 219, 231, 233, 244
L-galactose 22, 33, 164
D-galactosyl-L-arabinose 151
D-galactosyl diacylglycerol 243
D-galactosylglycerol phosphate 166
galactosyllactose 136
D-galactosylsphingoids 234
D-galactosyl 3-sulphate ceramide 234
(galactosyluronic acid)-galacturonic acid 38
D-galacturonans 155
D-galacturonic acid 116, 151, 153, 155, 156
gangliosides 231, 236, 237, 242

ganglioside nomenclature 237
Gaucher disease 238, 241
gangliosidosis 202, 238–242
gas-liquid chromatography 64, 68, 71, 77, 190
G_{D_1} 236
$G_{D_{1a}}$ gangliosidosis 238
G_{D_2} 236
gel filtration chromatography 67, 69, 76, 86, 190, 297
gel formation 153, 155, 159, 309
genetic code 259–262
genetic engineering 263, 307
genetic hyperglycosaminoglycanuria 215
gentamicins 280, 281, 286
gentianose 39
gentobiose 38, 96
globosides 236, 237, 242
D-glucans 161, 171, 179
D-glucaro-1,4;6,3-dilactone 52
glucitol 55, 56, 118
D-glucocerebrosides 233, 244
α-D-glucofuranose 28
β-D-glucofuranose 28, 31, 33
D-glucofuranurono-6,3-lactone 51
D-gluco-D-mannans 159, 160
gluconeogenesis 101
D-gluconic acid 51, 117
D-glucono-1,4-lactone 51
D-glucono-1,5-lactone 6-phosphate 117
α-D-glucopyranose 28
β-D-glucopyranose 28, 30, 31, 33
β-L-glucopyranose 30
D-glucopyranuronic acid 151
β-D-glucopyranuronic acid 34
glucosamine 35
glucose 20, 21, 22
D-glucose 21, 23, 99, 160, 161, 163, 171, 173, 183, 221, 231, 233, 306
L-glucose 22, 23, 161
D-glucose oxidase 146
β-D-glucoseptanose 31
glucosylgalactose 38
glucosylglucosamine 38
D-glucosylglycerol phosphates 166
6-O-glucosylmaltose 39, 42
D-glucuronic acid 116, 153, 158, 164, 168, 171, 186, 215, 216, 217, 244
β-D-glucuronidase deficiency 228
glycals 130
glycan 43
glyceraldehyde 21, 22, 23
D-glyceraldehyde 21, 23
L-glyceraldehyde 22, 23
D-glycero-D-galacto-heptose 175
D-glycero-D-gulo-heptose 175
glycerol 55, 56, 118, 246

glycerol phosphate 164, 168
D-*glycero*-D-*manno*-heptose 175
L-*glycero*-D-*manno*-heptose 173, 175
glycerone 25
D-*glycero*-tetrulose 25
glycogen 43, 44, 179–180
glycolipids
    catabolism 201, 241
    classification 230
    extraction 230
    fatty acid structures 233
    function 230
    -glycoprotein similarities 235
    in biosynthesis 113, 114, 230
    involvement in diseases 238–242
    nomenclature 231
    sphingoid base structures 232
5-glycolylamido-3,5-dideoxy-D-*glycero*-D-*galacto*-2-nonulopyranonic acid 120, 183, 237
N-glycolylneuraminic acid 120
glycopeptide linkages 78, 81, 112, 196, 201, 207, 218–221
glycopeptides 189, 193, 196, 197
glycoproteins
    carbohydrate content 188, 189, 193, 208, 209
    catabolism 201–206
    classification 182–186
    function 187, 193, 201
    -glycolipid similarities 235
    hormones 189–193, 296
    immobilised 296
    involvement in diseases 201–206
    purification 190
    role of carbohydrate chain 186, 193
    synthesis 113
glycosaminoglycans
    function 221–224
    immobilised 304
    involvement in diseases 224–229
    linkage region 218–222
    nomenclature 186, 213, 214
    repeating unit 213, 215–219
    repeating unit irregularities 219
    structures 215–217
    synthesis 96, 108
glycose residue 41
glycoside hydrolases 81, 190, 193, 196, 206
glycosides 61
glycosidic linkage 36, 61, 82, 108, 189, 201
glycosphingolipids 231
glycosylamide linkage 189
glycosylceramides 231, 233, 236
glycosylglycerides 237, 243, 245
glycosyl group 41
glycosyl residue 41

glycosylsphingoids 231
glycosylsphingolipids 231
glycosyltransferases 112, 201
glycoxylic acid 72
G_{M_1} 236
G_{M_1} gangliosidosis 202, 238, 240
G_{M_2} 236
G_{M_2} gangliosidosis 238
G_{M_3} 236
G_{M_3} gangliosidosis 239
Gram-negative bacteria 172, 280
Gram-positive bacteria 164, 168, 171, 277, 286
green coffee bean D-mannan 159
Grignard reagents 93, 129
G_{T_1} 236
guar gum 309
gulitol 55, 56
gulose 21, 22
L-guluronic acid 116, 163, 170, 176
gum arabic 151
gum ghatti 151
gum tragacanth 151

H

Hakomori methylation 63, 69
half-chair conformation 29
hamamelose 127
Haworth conformational structures 29, 30, 31
Haworth formulae 29, 30, 31
Haworth methylation 63
hCG 189
helix 48, 145, 254
Helix pomatia lectin 303
hemicelluloses 157–160, 163
heparan sulphate 213, 217, 219, 229
heparin 96, 211, 213, 214, 216, 219
heptoses 24, 173, 175
heptuloses 24
heterocyclic bases 251, 253
heteroglycan 43
hetero-oligosaccharides 40, 183
hexoses 26, 33
hexuloses 25, 26
hexuronic acids 34, 68, 211
higher aldoses 24
higher ketoses 24
high performance liquid chromatography 76
high-voltage electrophoresis 79
Hofmann degradation 95
hMP 189
homoglycan 43
homo-oligosaccharides 40
hormonal activity 189
hormones 187, 189
hormone subunits 190

human chorionic gonadotrophin 188, 189, 190–193
human menopausal gonadotrophin 189
Hunter syndrome 226, 228
Hurler syndrome 226, 228
hyalobiouronic acid 38
hyaluronic acid 45, 211, 213, 214, 215, 219
hydrolysis 67, 69, 82, 189
4-*C*-(1-hydroxyethyl)-2,6-dideoxy-β-L-*lyxo*-hexopyranose 271
5-(hydroxymethyl)furan-2-aldehyde 58
2-hydroxypropanaldehyde 59
hygromycin A 265
hyosamine 271

I

iditol 55, 56
α-L-idopyranuronic acid 34, 112
idose 21, 22
L-iduronic acid 116, 186, 216
L-iduronic acid 2-sulphate 217
IgA 196, 197
IgD 196
IgE 196, 197
IgG 196, 197
IgM 196
imidocarbonates 293, 300, 302
immobilised
    antibiotics 303–304
    antibodies 301–302
    enzymes 295–301
    enzymes, methods 297–299
    enzymes, reactors 297
    glycoprotein hormones 296
    glycosaminoglycans 304
    lectins 203–303
    microbial cells 300
    nucleic acids 304
    polysaccharides 304
    proteoglycans 296
immunoadsorption 190, 301–302
immunoglobulins 196, 197, 206
immunological specificity 80, 171, 172, 190
inclusion compounds 135
industrial processes 297, 305–311
inositol 118, 139, 244, 246
interconversion 123
inulin 44, 161, 291
inulobiose 38
inversion of configuration 95
invertase 136
invert sugar 136
iodine-binding 143, 145, 149, 161, 162
ion exchange chromatography 67, 69, 76, 190, 295, 297
isokestose 39
isolation 66

isolichenan 44, 161
isomaltose 38, 96
isomaltotriose 39
isomerases 96
isomerization 57
isopanose 39
isopropylidene derivatives 65, 78, 118
isosaccharinic acids 60, 75
ivory nut D-mannan 159, 163

J

jimson weed lectin 211, 303
jute 161

K

kamamycins 281, 286
kanosamine 267, 281
kasugamine 269, 283
kasugamycin 283
KDO 173, 176
keratan sulphate 45, 81, 213, 214, 217, 219, 229
keratan sulphate I 213
keratan sulphate II 213
kestose 39
ketohexoses 34
ketoinositols 118
ketoses 25
Khaya gum 151
Kidney bean agglutinin 303
Koenigs – Knorr synthesis 62, 96
kojibiose 38
Krabbe's leucodystrophy 239, 241

L

labilose 265
lactic acid 59
lacto-*N*-difucohexaose 137
lacto-difucosyltetraose 137
lacto-*N*-fucopentaose 137
lacto-*N*-hexaose 137
lacto-*N*-neohexaose 137
lacto-*N*-neotetraose 137
lactose 38, 136, 306, 310
lactosyl ceramide 235
lactosyl ceramidosis 239, 241
lactosyl-(1→2)-α-D-glucose 137
lacto-*N*-tetraose 137
laevulinic acid 58
laminarabiose 38
laminaran 44, 162, 179
laminaratriose 39
lankamycin 279
lectins 77, 206, 209–211
β-lectins 208
Lens culinaris lectin 303
lentil lectin 303

Leuconostoc mesenteroides dextran 170
levan 44, 161, 170
D-levulose 25
LH 189
lichenan 44, 161, 163
ligand exchange mechanisms 300
light scattering 86, 145, 149
lima bean agglutinin 211, 303
Limus polyphenus lectin 303
lincomycin 284, 286
lincosamine 268, 284
lipid A 173
lipid carrier 113, 230
lipid-linked intermediates 114, 230
lipidosis 242
lipopolysaccharides 172–174
Lobry de Bruyn-Alberda van Eckenstein
    rearrangement 59
locust bean gum 309
Lotus tetragonolubus agglutinin 303
LPS 172
luteinizing hormone 188, 189, 193
LS tetrasaccharides 137
luteose 179
lyxitol 55, 56
D-*lyxo*-hexulose 25
lyxose 21, 22
D-lyxulose 25

M
macroporous polysaccharides 300
magnetic supports 299
malondialdehyde 72
maltitol 307
maltose 38, 40, 132, 306
maltotetraose 39
maltotriose 39, 40
D-mannans 159, 163, 179
mannite 55, 56
mannitol 55, 56, 118, 306
mannobiose 38, 160
β-D-mannopyranose 34
4-*O*-β-D-mannopyranosylmycosamine 277
β-D-mannopyranuronic acid 34
D-mannosamine 177
D-mannose 20, 21, 151, 159, 160, 171, 173,
    183, 190, 193, 196, 207, 209, 211,
    217, 244
L-mannose 22
α-D-mannosidase 82
β-D-mannosidase 82
mannosidosis 203
mannotriose 160
D-mannuronic acid 163, 170

maritime pine L-arabino-D-galactan 160
Maroteaux-Lamy syndrome 228
mass spectrometry 64, 68, 78, 190
melezitose 39, 140
melibiose 38
mesyl esters 64
metabolic disorders 201–206, 224–229,
    238–242, 301
metachromatic leucodystrophy 239, 241
metasaccharinic acids 60, 74
methanesulphonates 64
methylation 63, 64, 68, 86, 144, 149, 158,
    180, 181, 189, 190, 193
3-*O*-methyl-6-deoxy-L-talopyranose 176,
    248
2-*C*-methyl-D-*erythro*-pentonic acid 60, 72
methyl esters 155
methyl ethers 63, 77
3-*O*-methyl-β-D-fucopyranose 176
2-*O*-methyl-L-fucose 248
5-methylfuran-2-aldehyde 58
methylmycin 278
4-*O*-methyl-3-*C*-methyl-3-nitro-2,3,6-tri-
    deoxy-β-L-*arabino*-hexopyranose 271
2-*C*-methyl-D-*threo*-pentonic acid 60
4-*O*-methyl-β-D-glucopyranuronic acid 176
4-methylglucosylxylose 38
3-*O*-methyl-β-L-rhamnopyranose 176
2-*O*-methyl-L-rhamnose 248
microfibrils 150
microheterogeneity 66, 77, 82, 189, 197,
    211
milk oligosaccharides 137
molasses 140
molecular size 86, 145, 149, 179
monosaccharide
    biologically important 107
    branched-chain 127
    classification 19
    immobilised 302
    nomenclature 24, 26, 116
    1-phosphates 164
Morquio-Ullrich syndrome 228
mRNA 252
mucic acid 52
mucilages 153, 163, 164
mucopolysaccharide 212
mucopolysaccharide-protein complex 212
mucopolysaccharidosis 225
muramic acid 120, 167, 168, 170, 176
mureins 170
mutarotation 29, 61
mycaminose 267, 279
L-mycarose 270, 279
mycinose 265
mycosamine 267, 277
mycose 139

N

narbomycin 278
nasturtium seed D-glucan 161
neamine 280
Nef reaction 90
neokestose 39
neomethylmycin 278
neomycins 280, 286
neosamine C 268
neuraminic acid 35
neuraminidase 186
neuraminolactose 39, 138
Niemann-Pick disease 239, 241
nigeran 44, 161, 291
nigerose 38
nitrates 64
nitromethane 129
nojirimycin 120, 167, 284
nomenclature
    branched-chain monosaccharides 129
    gangliosides 237
    general 16
    glycolipids 231
    glycosaminoglycans 186, 212
    monosaccharides 24, 26
    nucleic acids 250
    oligosaccharides 40
    polysaccharides 43, 47
    proteoglycans 186, 212
    unsaturated monosaccharides 130
nonoses 24, 90
nonuloses 24
Norwegian spruce D-galactan 156
noviose 269
nuclear magnetic resonance 78, 92
nucleocidin 125, 272
nucleosides 250, 272
nucleotides 250
nucleotide sequence 254

O

octoses 24, 173, 176
octuloses 24
oil recovery 307
L-oleoandrose 266
oligosaccharide
    classification 19, 40
    components in lipids 235
    formation 36
    nomenclature 40, 41, 42
    nonreducing 40
    1-phosphate 164
    reducing 40
    structures 39, 40, 132–141
    synthesis 96, 108
    uses 306
L-oliose 266

olivomose 266
olivomycins 276
olivomycose 270
olivose 266
optical rotation 26, 27, 136, 281
orosomucoid 193
osmotic pressure 86, 145
osones 52
ossamine 269
oxidases 113
oxidation
    alkaline 51
    halogen 50
    hypoiodite 51
    lead(IV) acetate 52, 70
    periodic acid 52, 70–73, 86, 189, 193
    secondary hydroxyl groups 52
    selective 51
4-oxo-pentanoic acid 58

P

pachyman 44, 179
panose 39, 42
paper chromatography 76
paratose 175
paromomycins 280
paromose 268
partition chromatography 68, 69
pea tree agglutinin 303
pectic acid 44, 151, 155
pectin 82, 155
pectinic acids 155
peeling reaction 76
pentahydroxycyclohexanones 118
2,4,6/3,5-pentahydroxycyclohexanone
    119
pentasaccharides 39
pentoses 26, 33
pentuloses 25, 26
peptidoglycans 165, 167, 168, 170, 172
periodate-resistant residues 71
perosamine 267
phenylosazone formation 20
phosphates 64
phosphatidyl inositol mannosides 246
phospholipids 230, 244, 246
physicochemical methods 86, 171
phytic acid 119
phytoglycolipids 244
phytohaemagglutinin 77, 209
picrocin 268
picromycin 278
L-pillarose 271
D-pinitol 119

Plantago ovata Forsk mucilage 153
plant cell walls 155, 157, 208
plant gums 150
planteobiose 38
planteose 39
plasma glycoproteins 187
pneumococcal polysaccharides 43, 80, 172
pneumosamine 177
polyacrylamide electrophoresis 80
polyoxin C 274
polyprenol phosphates 113
polysaccharide
    branched chain 50, 127
    classification 19
    derivatives, uses 300
    dyed 288
    ethers 288
    hydrolases 80
    immobilised 304
    nomenclature 43
    -protein complex 212
    purified vaccines 310
    synthesis 96, 108
porphyran 45
potato lectin 211, 303
precipitation 67, 144, 179
preferred conformation 29, 30
pregnant-mare serum gonadotrophin 189
primaverose 38
protecting groups 61
protein-polysaccharide 212
proteoglycans
    classification 186, 211
    -collagen interaction 221–223
    function 211, 221–224
    insoluble forms 296
    involvement in diseases 224–229
    linkage region 218–221
    nomenclature 186, 211
    synthesis 110
psicofuranine 272
D-psicose 25, 265, 272
psychosine 234
pullulan 44, 308, 309
pullulanase 81, 145
Purdie methylation 63
purification 66, 190
purines 250, 251, 253
purity, definition of 66
puromycin 272, 286
pustulan 45, 161
pyranose ring 29
pyrimidines 250, 251, 253
pyrromycins 275
pyruvate 65
pyruvic acid 59, 65, 72
pyruvic acid acetal 65, 164, 171

Q

L-quebrachitol 119
β-D-quinovopyranose 34
quinovosamine 177, 267
D-quinovose 124, 243

R

racemic mixtures 88
raffinose 39, 139
random coil 48, 145, 168
reduction
    catalytic hydrogenation 57
    electrolytic 57
    Raney nickel 57
    sodium borohydride 57
regenerated cellulose 150
retrogradation 145
Reeves notation 30
repeating unit 44, 142
reversion 57, 68, 69
β-L-rhamnopyranose 34
rhamnosamine 177
L-rhamnose 124, 151, 153, 156, 164
rhodinose 266, 275
rhodomycins 275
rhodosamine 269, 275
rhodymenan 45, 163
Rhodymenia palmata D-xylan 163
ribitol 55, 56, 118
ribitol phosphate 164, 172
β-D-ribofuranose 33
β-D-ribofuranuronic acid 176
D-*ribo*-hexulose 25
D-ribonic acid 72
ribonucleases 186, 254
ribonucleic acids
    classification 250
    complementary RNA 259
    function 259–262, 284
    immobilised 304
    messenger RNA 252
    nomenclature 250
    primary structure 252
    replication 261, 264, 284–287
    ribosomal RNA 252
    secondary structure 256
    tertiary structure 258
    transfer RNA 252, 257
    transfer RNA-aminoacids 259
D-ribose 21, 221, 250, 274
D-ribulose 25
Ricinus communis lectin 303
rimocidin 277
ring structures 28
ristosamine 268
RNA 250
rod-like structure 168

rotational angle 47
rRNA 252
Ruff degradation 94
rutinose 38

S

saccharinic acids 59, 60
Sandhoff's disease 203, 226, 239, 241
Sanfilippo syndrome 228
sangivamycin 272
Schardinger dextrins 39, 133
Scheie syndrome 228
Schmidt-Rutz reaction 124
scleroglucan 44, 308, 309
seaweed 162
septacidin 272
septanose ring 32
serum glycoproteins 187
showdomycin 274
sialyllactose 138
single cell protein 310
sinigrin 126
sisomicin 281
β-sitosterol 245
skew conformation 29
slippery elm bark mucilage 153
Smith degradation 73
sophorose 38
sorbitol 55, 56
D-sorbose 25
soya bean agglutinin 209, 303
soybean pectins 156, 157
sphingoid bases 232, 244
sphingolipids 231
sphingosine 231
spiramycins 279
stachyose 39
starch 43, 98, 108, 142, 162, 209, 297, 300,
    305, 306, 309
starch granules 142, 162
Sterculia gum 151
stereoisomers 19
sterol glycosides 244
streptidine 271, 280
streptomycin 280, 286
streptose 269
structure
    primary 46, 98, 116, 142, 149, 189, 215,
        250, 252
    quaternary 48, 98, 142, 190, 196
    secondary 46, 98, 142, 254, 256
    tertiary 48, 98, 142, 150, 256, 257
sucrose 38, 40, 108, 135, 306, 307
sulphates 215–217
sulphatides 231
sulphoglycosylceramides 234
sulphoglycosylsphingolipids 231

sulpholipids 230
sulphonates 64
sulphoquinovosyl diacylglycerol 243
sulphotransferases 113
surface active agents 307
sycamore L-arabino-D-galactan 160
systematic names 24, 26, 43, 83, 98, 102,
    186, 206, 264

T

D-tagatose 25
talitol 55, 56
β-D-talopyranose 265
talose 21, 22
tamarind seed D-glucan 161
Tay-Sachs disease 238, 241
teichuronic acids 168
teichoic acids 164–168, 172
tetrasaccharides 39
tetroses 26
tetruloses 25, 26
thickening agents 150, 163, 307, 309
thin-layer chromatography 76
4-thio-D-glucose 127
5-thio-D-glucose 127
threitol 55, 56
D-*threo*-pentulose 25
threose 21, 22
D-threulose 25
thyroid-stimulating hormone 189
Tipson-Cohen procedure 130
4-toluenesulphonates 64, 124
tolyposamine 269
torsion angle 46
tosyl esters 64
toyocamycin 272
tragacanthic acid 153, 157
transferases 113
transferrin 193
transition-metal hydroxides 300
transition-metal oxides 300
α,α-trehalose 38, 40, 138, 247, 284, 306,
    307
α,β-trehalose 138
triazine dyes 288
2,3,6-trideoxy-β-D-*erythro*-hexopyranose
    266
2,3,6-trideoxy-4-*C*-(1-oxo-2-hydroxyethyl)-
    β-L-*threo*-hexopyranose 271
2,3,6-trideoxy-β-L-*threo*-hexopyranose 266
trifluoroacetates 64
trimethylsilyl ethers 61, 64, 68, 77
trioses 26
triphenylmethyl ethers 63
trisaccharides 39, 132
trityl ethers 63

trivial names 17, 24, 38, 39, 40, 43, 83, 98,
102, 206, 213, 264
tRNA 252
TSH 189
tubercidin 272
turanose 38
twist conformation 32
tyvelose 175

U

Ulex europeus agglutinin 303
ultracentrifugation 67, 87, 145
ultrafiltration 138
umbelliferose 39
uronic acids 51, 116, 176

V

vancosamine 271
variose 266
verbascose 39
viburnitol 119
Vicia graminea lectin 303
vicianose 38
vinelose 269
viosamine 177
vitamin C 117, 129

W

wetting agents 309
wheat germ agglutinin 211, 303
whey 138, 306, 310
Wittig reaction 93, 129
Wohl degradation 93

X

xanthan gum 65, 159, 171, 307, 308, 309
xanthates 294
X-ray diffraction 86, 145, 146, 150, 162,
163, 181
D-xylans 153, 157, 163, 291
xylitol 55, 56
xylobiose 38
D-*xylo*-hexulose 25
D-xylo-D-mannans 179
β-D-xylopyranose 33
O^3-β-D-xylopyranosyl-L-threonine 207
xylose 21, 22, 153, 158, 164, 189, 206, 219,
221
D-xylulose 25